HUMAN RIGHTS WATCH

WORLD REPORT
2002

EVENTS OF 2001

November 2000–November 2001

HUMAN RIGHTS WATCH

New York   •   Washington   •   London   •   Brussels

Copyright © 2002 by Human Rights Watch.
All rights reserved.
Printed in the United States of America

ISBN:1–56432–267–x
Library of Congress Control Number: 2001098759

Cover photograph: In a camp for internally displaced people, Afghans dig graves for family members who have died. Afghanistan, November 2001. © 2001 Zalmai Ahad

Cover design by Rafael Jiménez
Text design and composition by Jenny Dossin

Addresses for Human Rights Watch

350 Fifth Avenue, 34th Floor, New York, NY 10118-3299
Tel: (212) 290-4700, Fax: (212) 736-1300, E-mail: hrwnyc@hrw.org

1630 Connecticut Avenue, N.W., Suite 500, Washington, DC 20009
Tel: (202) 612-4321, Fax: (202) 612-4333, E-mail: hrwdc@hrw.org

33 Islington High Street, N1 9LH London, UK
Tel: (44 20) 7713 1995, Fax: (44 20) 7713 1800, E-mail: hrwuk@hrw.org

15 Rue Van Campenhout, 1000 Brussels, Belgium
Tel: (32 2) 732-2009, Fax: (32 2) 732-0471, E-mail: hrwbe@hrw.org

Web Site Address: http://www.hrw.org
Listserv address: Listserv address: To subscribe to the list, send an e-mail message to hrw-news-subscribe@igc.topica.com with "subscribe hrw-news" in the body of the message (leave the subject line blank).

Human Rights Watch is dedicated to protecting the human rights of people around the world.

We stand with victims and activists to prevent discrimination, to uphold political freedom, to protect people from inhumane conduct in wartime, and to bring offenders to justice.

We investigate and expose human rights violations and hold abusers accountable.

We challenge governments and those who hold power to end abusive practices and respect international human rights law.

We enlist the public and the international community to support the cause of human rights for all.

HUMAN RIGHTS WATCH

Human Rights Watch conducts regular, systematic investigations of human rights abuses in some seventy countries around the world. Our reputation for timely, reliable disclosures has made us an essential source of information for those concerned with human rights. We address the human rights practices of governments of all political stripes, of all geopolitical alignments, and of all ethnic and religious persuasions. Human Rights Watch defends freedom of thought and expression, due process and equal protection of the law, and a vigorous civil society; we document and denounce murders, "disappearances," torture, arbitrary imprisonment, discrimination, and other abuses of internationally recognized human rights. Our goal is to hold governments accountable if they transgress the rights of their people.

Human Rights Watch began in 1978 with the founding of its Europe and Central Asia division (then known as Helsinki Watch). Today, it also includes divisions covering Africa, the Americas, Asia, and the Middle East. In addition, it includes three thematic divisions on arms, children's rights, and women's rights. It maintains offices in New York, Washington, Los Angeles, London, Brussels, Moscow, Dushanbe, and Bangkok. Human Rights Watch is an independent, nongovernmental organization, supported by contributions from private individuals and foundations worldwide. It accepts no government funds, directly or indirectly.

The staff includes Kenneth Roth, executive director; Michele Alexander, development director; Reed Brody, advocacy director; Carroll Bogert, communications director; John T. Green, operations director, Barbara Guglielmo, finance director; Lotte Leicht, Brussels office director; Michael McClintock, deputy program director; Patrick Minges, publications director; Maria Pignataro Nielsen, human resources director; Malcolm Smart, program director; Wilder Tayler, legal and policy director and Joanna Weschler, United Nations representative. Jonathan Fanton is the chair of the board. Robert L. Bernstein is the founding chair.

The regional directors of Human Rights Watch are Peter Takirambudde, Africa; José Miguel Vivanco, Americas; Sidney Jones, Asia; Elizabeth Andersen, Europe and Central Asia; and Hanny Megally, Middle East and North Africa. The thematic division directors are Joost R. Hiltermann, arms; Lois Whitman, children's rights; and LaShawn R. Jefferson, women's rights.

The members of the board of directors are Jonathan Fanton, chair; Robert L. Bernstein, founding chair; Lisa Anderson, David M. Brown, William Carmichael, Dorothy Cullman, Gina Despres, Irene Diamond, Fiona Druckenmiller, Edith

.   .   .

Human Rights Watch mourned the passing this year of one of our colleagues, Ruth Clarke. Ruth, who died suddenly on November 3, 2001, had served as the database manager of our development and outreach department. We are deeply saddened by her death.

ACKNOWLEDGMENTS

A compilation of this magnitude requires contributions from a large number of people, including most of the Human Rights Watch staff. The contributors were:

Fred Abrahams, Juliette Abu-Iyun, ACCEPT (Bucharest Acceptance Group), Sahr Muhammed Ally, Elizabeth Andersen, Alexander Anderson, John Anderson, Pinar Araz, Jacqueline Asiimwe, Jonathan Balcom, Suliman Ali Baldo, Jo Becker, Liuda Belova, Clary Bencomo, Olivier Bercault, Rachel Bien, Johanna Bjorken, Mike Bochenek, Matilda Bogner, Farhat Bokhari, Sebastian Brett, Reed Brody, A. Widney Brown, Bruni Burres, Whitney Bryant, Maria Burnett, Annel Cabrera, Center for Justice and International Law (CEJIL), Center for Legal and Social Studies (Centro de Estudios Legales y Sociales, CELS), Mustafa Cero, Julie Chadbourne, Ritu Chattree, Jana Chrzova, Allyson Collins, Sara Colm, Marijke Conklin, Zama Coursen-Neff, Joanne Csete, James Darrow, Rachel Denber, Alison Des Forges, Puja Dhawan, Richard Dicker, Srdjan Dizdarevic, Corinne Dufka, Maura Dundon, Elizabeth Eagen, the European Roma Rights Centre, Jamie Fellner, Chloe Fevre, Janet Fleischman, Loubna Freih, Anne Fuller, Jessica Galeria, Arvind Ganesan, Tasha Gill, Giorgi Gogia, Eric Goldstein, Steve Goose, Patti Gossman, Jeannine Guthrie, Dalia Haj-Omar, Julia Hall, Jason Halperin, Joel Harding, Helsinki Committee for Human Rights in Bosnia and Herzegovina, Joost R. Hiltermann, Mark Hiznay, Jonathan Horowitz, Alison Hughes, the Humanitarian Law Center, Bogdan Ivanisevic, Anne James, LaShawn R. Jefferson, Mike Jendrzejczyk, Tejal Jesrani, Sidney Jones, Pascal Kambale, Natasa Kandic, Kamini Karlekar, Juliane Kippenberg, Robin Kirk, Andrea Lari, Lotte Leicht, Michael Lerner, Diederik Lohman, Chirumbidzo "Rumbi" Mabuwa, Bronwen Manby, Anne Manuel, Joanne Mariner, Ani Mason, Veronica Matushaj, Michael McClintock, Hanny Megally, Memorial, Darlene Miller, Rebecca Milligan, Patrick Minges, Hania Mufti, Cesar Munoz, Smita Narula, Hannah Novak, Binaifer Nowrojee, Isis Nusair, Pat Nyhan, Vikram Parekh, Alison Parker, Darian Pavli, Leon Peijnenburg, Alexander Petrov, Carol Pier, Maria Pignataro Nielsen, Vitalii Ponomarev, Lutz Prager, Maria Pulzetti, Natalie Rainer, Sara Rakita, Regan Ralph, Nandini Ramnath, Casey Reckman, Rachael Reilly, Gary Risser, Camilla Roberson, Romanian Helsinki Committee, Jemera Rone, Michael Roney, Indira Rosenthal, Kenneth Roth, Shalu Rozario, Arsen Sakalov, Joe Saunders, Jeff Scott, Elahe Sharifpour-Hicks, Virginia Sherry, Acacia Shields, John Sifton, Miranda Sissons, Malcolm Smart, Leah Snyder, Dana Sommers, William Sothern, Mickey Spiegel, Joe Stork, Marie Struthers, Jonathan Sugden, Brigitte

Suhr, Judith Sunderland, Peter Takirambudde, Tony Tate, Carina Tertsakian, Martina Vandenberg, Smita Varia, Alex Vines, José Miguel Vivanco, Ben Ward, Mary Wareham, Liz Weiss, Joanna Weschler, Lois Whitman, Daniel Wilkinson, Anna Wuerth, Charli Wyatt, Wen-Hua Yang, and Saman Zia-Zarifi.

Michael McClintock and Malcolm Smart edited the report, with layout and production assistance by Jonathan Horowitz , Jenny Dossin, and Patrick Minges. Various sections were reviewed by Reed Brody, Lotte Leicht, Rachael Reilly, and Joanna Weschler. Andrew Ayers, Michael Bochenek, Marijke Conklin, James Darrow, Maura Dundon, John T. Green, Jonathan Horowitz, Patrick Minges, Minky Worden, and James Ross proofread the report.

CONTENTS

EUROPE AND CENTRAL ASIA   267

MIDDLE EAST AND NORTH AFRICA   389

INTRODUCTION

In the wake of the September 11 attacks on New York and Washington, the United States government articulated a single overriding goal—defeating terrorism—and sought to build a global alliance committed to that end. Yet determined as this campaign has been, it remains to be seen whether it is merely a fight against a particular set of criminals or also an effort to defeat the logic of terrorism. Is it a struggle only against Osama bin Laden, his al-Qaeda network, and a few like-minded groups? Or is it also an effort to undermine the view that anything goes in the name of a cause, the belief that even a deadly attack on skyscrapers filled with civilians is an acceptable political act?

The September 11 attacks were antithetical to the values of human rights. Indeed, it is the body of international human rights and humanitarian law—the limits placed on permissible conduct—that explains why these attacks were not legitimate acts of war or politics. If the human rights cause stands for anything, it stands for the principle that civilians should never be deliberately slaughtered, regardless of the cause. Whether in time of peace or war, whether the actor is a government or an armed group, certain means are never justified, no matter what the ends.

As many of the world's governments join the fight against al-Qaeda, they face a fundamental choice. They must decide whether this battle provides an opportunity to reaffirm human rights principles or a new reason to ignore them. They must determine whether this is a moment to embrace values governing means as well as ends or an excuse to subordinate means to ends. Their choice will not determine whether any particular perpetrator is captured or killed. But over the long term it will affect the strength of the ends-justify-the-means ideology that led a group of men deliberately to crash civilian passenger planes into the World Trade Center and the Pentagon. Unless the global anti-terror coalition firmly rejects this amorality, unless the rules of international human rights and humanitarian law clearly govern all anti-terror actions, the battle against particular terrorists is likely to end up reaffirming the warped instrumentalism of terrorism.

Unfortunately, the coalition's conduct so far has not been auspicious. As this introduction describes, its leading members have violated human rights principles at home and overlooked human rights transgressions among their partners. They have substituted expediency for the firm commitment to human rights that alone can defeat the rationale of terrorism. Whatever its success in pursuing particular terrorists, the coalition risks reinforcing the logic of terrorism unless human rights are given a far more central role.

THIS REPORT

This report is Human Rights Watch's twelfth annual review of human rights practices around the globe. It addresses developments in sixty-six countries, covering the period from November 2000 through November 2001. Most chapters examine significant human rights developments in a particular country; the response of global actors, such as the European Union, Japan, the United States, the United Nations, and various regional organizations; and the freedom of local human rights defenders to conduct their work. Other chapters address important thematic concerns.

Highlights of 2001 include, on the positive side, several strikes against the impunity that so often underwrites severe abuses, including the surrender of former Yugoslav President Slobodan Milosevic for trial before the International Criminal Tribunal for the former Yugoslavia; the indictment in Chile of former President Augusto Pinochet (although the prosecution was then ended on medical grounds); an Argentine judicial decision declaring the country's amnesty laws unconstitutional; and rapid progress toward the establishment of the International Criminal Court, with forty-seven of the needed sixty countries having ratified its treaty by early December. Other milestones include the entry into force of the protocol outlawing the use of child soldiers; the highlighting at the World Conference Against Racism of caste-based discrimination as an issue of global concern; the international community's speed and resolve (for the first time in a decade of Balkan atrocities) in defusing the armed ethnic conflict in Macedonia; and the U.N. Commission on Human Rights' condemnation of ongoing Russian atrocities in Chechnya and the government's persistent failure to hold abusers accountable. On the negative side, the World Trade Organization agreed to launch a new round of talks on reducing barriers to trade without giving the protection of labor rights a significant place on the agenda; efforts to create internationally sponsored tribunals were stalled in the case of Cambodia and proceeding painfully slowly in the case of Sierra Leone, while the principal architects of atrocities in East Timor in 1999 continued to walk free in Indonesia; and abusive wars and political violence continued to claim large numbers of civilian victims in Algeria, Angola, Burundi, Colombia, the Democratic Republic of Congo, Indonesia, and Sudan.

This report reflects extensive investigative work undertaken in 2001 by the Human Rights Watch research staff, usually in close partnership with human rights activists in the country in question. It also reflects the work of the Human Rights Watch advocacy team, which monitors the policies of governments and international institutions that have influence to curb human rights abuses. Human Rights Watch publications, issued throughout the year, contain more elaborate accounts of the brief summaries collected in this volume. They can be found on the Human Rights Watch website, www.hrw.org.

As in past years, this report does not include a chapter on every country where Human Rights Watch works, nor does it discuss every issue of importance. The failure to include a particular country or issue often reflects no more than staffing limitations and should not be taken as commentary on the significance of the problem.

There are many serious human rights violations that Human Rights Watch simply lacks the capacity to address.

The factors we considered in determining the focus of our work in 2001 (and hence the content of this volume) included the severity of abuses, access to the country and the availability of information about it, the susceptibility of abusive forces to influence, and the importance of addressing certain thematic concerns and of reinforcing the work of local rights organizations.

HUMAN RIGHTS VALUES AS AN ANTIDOTE TO TERRORISM

Any fight against terrorism is only in part a matter of security. It is also a matter of values. Police, intelligence units, even armies all have a role to play in meeting particular terrorist threats. But terrorism emanates as well from the realm of public morality. Terrorism is less likely when the public embraces the view that civilians should never be targeted—that is, when the public is firmly committed to basic human rights principles.

It is beyond the scope of Human Rights Watch's work to address the political grievances, let alone the pathology, that might lead a group of men to attack thousands of civilians. Our concern is with the mores that would countenance such mass murder as a legitimate political tool. Sympathy for such crimes is the breeding ground for terrorism; sympathizers are the potential recruits. Building a stronger human rights culture—a culture in which any disregard for civilian life is condemned rather than condoned—is essential in the long run for defeating terrorism.

Many of the policies of the major powers, both before and after September 11, have undermined efforts to build a global culture of human rights. These governments often embraced human rights only in theory while subverting them in practice. Reversing these policies is essential to building the strong human rights culture needed to reject terrorism.

The importance of such a policy reappraisal is especially acute in the Middle East and North Africa, where al-Qaeda seems to have attracted many of its adherents. But it is also needed more broadly—in evaluating the policies guiding the new global coalition against terrorism and in assessing the conduct of many of the leading members of that coalition.

THE MIDDLE EAST AND NORTH AFRICA

The Middle East and North Africa do not have a monopoly on producing practitioners of terrorism. Armed groups have resorted to attacking civilians and sowing terror in Colombia, India, Spain, Sri Lanka, Spain, the United Kingdom, and many other places. The rationale of various groups may have differed, but the amorality of their methods was comparable.

Yet today the focus of global attention is on al-Qaeda, both because of the target of its alleged actions—the world's superpower—and because of the magnitude of its presumed and projected crimes. Thus the Middle East and North Africa is one of the regions where it is essential to affirm a culture of human rights as an antidote to terrorism.

Many in the region see Western tolerance for human rights abuse reflected in the failure to rein in Israeli abuse of Palestinians or to restructure sanctions against Iraq to minimize the suffering of the Iraqi people. Such policies—both closely followed in the region—suggest that the West's commitment to human rights is one of convenience, to be forsaken when abuses are committed by an ally or in the name of containing a foe. That grievance has become all the more acute since September 2000 as the death toll mounts from Israeli-Palestinian violence and as Iraqi sanctions drag on with no indication that Saddam Hussein will acquiesce to U.N. demands.

But a feeble commitment to human rights can also be found in the West's attitude toward the region as a whole. Saudi Arabia and Egypt provide good examples. Saudi Arabia, the home of Osama bin Laden as well as fifteen of the nineteen presumed hijackers of September 11, imposes strict limits on civil society, severely discriminates against women, and systematically suppresses dissent. But Western governments to date have contented themselves with purchasing Saudi oil and soliciting Saudi contracts while maintaining a shameful silence toward Saudi abuses. Egypt, home of the accused September 11 ringleader as well as other key al-Qaeda leaders, features a narrowly circumscribed political realm and a government that does all it can to suffocate peaceful political opposition. Yet as a "partner" for Middle East peace, Egypt has secured from the U.S. government massive aid and tacit acceptance of its human rights violations.

In societies where basic freedoms flourish, citizens could have pressed their government to respond to grievances, on threat of being publicly scorned and voted out of power. But in Egypt, Saudi Arabia, and many of the other countries where Osama bin Laden strikes a chord of resentment, governments restrict debate about how to address society's ills. They close off avenues for peaceful political change. They leave people with the desperate choice of tolerating the status quo, exile, or violence. Frequently, as political options are closed off, the voices of non-violent dissent are upstaged by a politics of radical opposition.

The West has quietly accepted this pattern of repression because, in the short term, it seems to promise stability, and because the democratic alternative is feared. Indeed, the brilliance of the strategy from the perspective of these repressive governments is that they have created a political landscape in which the only available alternative to supporting their authoritarian rule is risking their overthrow by radical opponents. In an environment in which the political center has been systematically silenced, these governments can credibly portray themselves as the only bulwark against extremism.

The challenge for global proponents of human rights—and for any successful campaign to defeat the logic of terrorism—is to recognize the role that governmental repression plays in constructing this dilemma. The more the government closes off legitimate avenues of dissent, the more the government's portrayal of itself as the only alternative to repressive radicalism becomes a self-fulfilling prophecy.

The conduct of the Saudi government is illustrative. As corruption flourishes among the ruling family and the country's vast but finite oil wealth proves inadequate to provide a promising economic future for a rapidly growing population, the Saudi government's position is increasingly precarious. But just when the need for openness is greatest, so are the dangers. With peaceful political opposition firmly repressed, the voices of violence and intolerance have grown in volume. Riyadh can thus claim that it alone stands before the abyss, that human rights must be suppressed for their own protection, that democratization would lead to its own demise. The stark choice today, it is posited, has now been reduced to blocking any political liberalization, as occurred in Algeria in 1992 when the country's military chiefs intervened to head off an imminent electoral victory by an Islamist party, or witnessing a repetition of the Iran scenario of 1979, in which the West's backing away from the authoritarian Shah led to a repressive theocratic state.

Only from an ahistorical vantage point are the choices so stark and unappealing. An immediate democratic transition may not be possible in such a warped political environment, but steps can and should be taken to begin to provide a meaningful array of electoral choices. Of course, in a democracy there is no guarantee of any particular political result. But if pressure is put on authoritarian governments to allow a spectrum of political options, the likelihood increases that democracy will lead to governments that respect human rights.

Several Middle Eastern and North African governments have begun the process of liberalization without empowering extremists. In recent years, Morocco and Jordan have become more open societies, while Qatar and Bahrain have begun to loosen political restraints and have promised to hold elections. Kuwait already has an elected parliament, although its powers are limited and all women and many other native-born residents continue to be denied the vote. Even in Iran, a gradual and partial political opening has corresponded with the emergence of a movement demanding respect for civil liberties. Although the correlation is not always neat, these experiences suggest that the appeal of violent and intolerant movements diminishes as people are given the chance to participate meaningfully in politics and to select from a range of political parties and perspectives. Promoting the full respect for human rights needed to produce this range of political options thus should be a central part of any anti-terrorism strategy for the region. But if the West continues to accept repression as the best defense against radical politics, it will undermine the human rights culture that is needed in the long run to defeat terrorism.

THE GLOBAL COALITION

In the days following September 11, various governments tried to take advantage of the tragedy by touting their own internal struggles as battles against terrorism. For example, President Vladimir Putin of Russia embraced this rhetoric to defend his government's brutal campaign in Chechnya. China's foreign minister

Tang Jiaxuan did the same to defend his government's response to political agitation in Xinjiang province. Egyptian Prime Minister Atef Abeid, brushing off criticism of torture and summary military trials, rejected "call[s] on us to give these terrorists their 'human rights'" and suggested that Western countries should "think of Egypt's own fight against terror as their new model." Israeli Prime Minister Ariel Sharon repeatedly referred to Palestinian Authority President Yasir Arafat as "our bin Laden." Alluding to September 11, Malaysian Deputy Prime Minister Abdullah Ahman Badawi defended administrative detention under his country's long-abused Internal Security Act as "an initial preventive measure before things get beyond control." A spokesman for Zimbabwean President Robert Mugabe justified a crackdown on independent journalists reporting on abuses by his government as an attack on the "supporters" of terrorism.

Particularly in the case of Russia, this cynical strategy seemed to work. In the days following September 11, German Chancellor Gerhard Schroeder and Italian Prime Minister Silvio Berlusconi said that Russia's actions in Chechnya must be reassessed. The U.S. government, which in April had supported the U.N. resolution condemning atrocities in Chechnya, began to play down its human rights concerns and play up alleged links between Chechen rebels and the Qaeda network. In general remarks at the Asia Pacific Economic Cooperation summit in Shanghai in October, in the presence of Putin but without reference to any particular country, U.S. President George W. Bush did publicly warn that "the war on terrorism must not be a war on minorities" and that countries need to "distinguish between those who pursue legitimate political aspirations and terrorists." But during a bilateral summit with Putin in November, Bush spoke at length of Russian progress toward respect for human rights and democratic principles while mentioning Chechnya only to praise "President Putin's commitment to a political dialogue." Nothing was said publicly about Russian atrocities and the continuing impunity of those who commit them.

Uzbekistan further illustrates the selectivity of concern with attacks on civilians. With the possible exception of Turkmenistan, Uzbekistan has done the most among the post-Soviet states to perpetuate the ruthless repression of the Soviet era. There are no political parties, no independent media, no civil society of any sort. Efforts by Muslims to pray outside the state-controlled mosque are met harshly, with torture and long prison sentences frequent. As a state bordering Afghanistan, Uzbekistan was an obvious potential military ally of the United States, particularly since it faces its own al-Qaeda-linked rebel movement, the Islamic Movement of Uzbekistan. But it remains unclear whether the U.S. government will prevent its new military alliance with Uzbekistan from becoming an endorsement of the repressive policies of Uzbek President Islam Karimov. President Bush repeatedly insisted that the U.S. campaign against terrorism was not directed against Islam, yet the U.S. government made no visible effort to curb Uzbekistan's severe repression of Muslims who wanted only to practice their faith peacefully outside state control. The biggest opportunity lost was when, as required by legislation, the U.S. State Department in October named "countries of particular concern" for their repression of religious freedom. Uzbekistan, an obvious candidate under any objective standard, was not on the list. (Nor, for that matter, was Saudi Arabia, despite the

State Department spokesman's admission that there is "no religious freedom" there.)

This inconsistent attention to violent abuse against civilians could be found elsewhere as well. Washington (though not the European Union) put effective pressure on Belgrade to surrender former Yugoslav President Slobodan Milosevic for trial in The Hague for the depredations he allegedly sponsored in Bosnia, Kosovo, and Croatia. But throughout the year NATO troops in Bosnia failed to arrest former Bosnian Serb political leader Radovan Karadzic from his sanctuary in Bosnia, and the international community did little to pressure Belgrade to surrender former Bosnian Serb military leader Ratko Mladic, both of whom stand accused of comparable crimes. Closer to home, the U.S. government continues to shelter Emmanuel "Toto" Constant, the ruthless former Haitian paramilitary leader, from Haiti's efforts to secure him for trial. During the military dictatorship of 1991-94, Constant oversaw the killing and tortured of many Haitian civilians who were perceived as opponents of military rule.

In some parts of the world, particularly Africa, violent abuse against civilians was virtually ignored by the U.S. government, except insofar as a link might be found with al-Qaeda. Atrocities were routine in conflicts in Angola, Burundi, the Democratic Republic of Congo, and Sierra Leone, yet the U.S. government's attention seemed to focus almost exclusively on Sudan, Somalia, and other countries in the Horn of Africa where the Qaeda network was said to operate. Typical was the November visit to Washington of Nigerian President Olusegun Obasanjo; no mention was made of soldiers' recent massacre of civilians in central Nigeria, but President Obasanjo was praised for his support of the fight against terrorism.

The message sent by this inconsistency was that, as seen from Washington, violence becomes intolerable based not on *whether* civilians are attacked but on *whose* civilians are attacked and who is doing the attacking. Attacks against civilians on U.S. soil are to be vigorously opposed, but attacks against other civilians often are not. Rebel or insurgent attacks on civilians are condemned, but government attacks on civilians—especially attacks by key government allies—are ignored. Such a message hardly helps to build broad public support for human rights.

The annual meeting next March in Geneva of the U.N. Commission on Human Rights will test the West's willingness to condemn violence against innocent civilians wherever it occurs. For the last two years, with reluctant but eventual support by the U.S. government and the European Union, the commission has condemned Russia for its atrocities in Chechnya and its failure to prosecute those responsible. Now is no time to abandon that effort, as Russian forces continue to be responsible for summary executions, torture, and arbitrary arrests, and no progress has been made in bringing the authors of past massacres to justice. Western governments will also be judged by whether they finally mount a serious effort at the commission (for the first time without U.S. membership) to condemn China's persistent repression. In the case of Washington, it will be judged by whether it applies laws designed to sanction religious repression in Uzbekistan and Saudi Arabia. Finally, the question remains whether the West will overcome its traditional downplaying of atrocities in sub-Saharan Africa. To squander such opportunities to condemn and curb political violence will suggest that violent attacks on civilians warrant serious action only when they strike close to home. It will not take long for the world to see through this selectivity.

THE IMPORTANCE OF
ENFORCEABLE HUMAN RIGHTS STANDARDS

If the battle against terrorism is to be understood as a fight for human rights, the most ardent combatants have often been the least willing to be bound by its principles. Washington stands out because its resistance to enforceable human rights standards has been most fundamental. That is not to say that the United States ignores human rights; most U.S. citizens enjoy a wide range of rights protections. But Washington has never been willing to subject itself to binding international human rights scrutiny. September 11 offered an opportunity to rethink this unwillingness. Washington immediately realized that to fight a global terrorist network, it needed global cooperation—for gathering intelligence, blocking finances, making arrests, and defending the legitimacy of its military efforts. The U.S. government's appeal for help was widely answered, but that did not alter Washington's resistance to international human rights law.

Often the U.S. government simply refuses to ratify leading human rights treaties, such as those on women's rights, children's rights, and economic, social and cultural rights. Most significantly in time of war, the U.S. government still has not ratified the First Additional Protocol of 1977 to the Geneva Conventions of 1949—the leading standards on the use of air power, Washington's primary warfare tool.

Moreover, when periodically the U.S. government ratifies a human rights treaty, whether under a Republican or Democratic administration, it always does so in a way to ensure that there will be no right of enforcement, so that ratification imposes no practical constraint on official action. The formal embrace of a treaty thus becomes an act for external consumption—an empty declaration that the United States is part of the international human rights system—not an act to grant or even solidify rights in the United States.

Perhaps the greatest disappointment is that the Bush administration actually intensified U.S. opposition to the International Criminal Court—a potential forum for prosecuting future crimes against humanity such as the attacks of September 11. With the number of countries that have ratified the ICC treaty growing rapidly, the treaty's entry into force in 2002 is a virtual certainty. But Washington has opposed the court because it theoretically could be used to scrutinize the conduct of U.S. armed forces. Just two weeks before it launched its bombing campaign in Afghanistan, the Bush administration endorsed legislation that would authorize sanctions against governments that ratify the ICC treaty (other than NATO and certain other key allies)—legislation that, in modified form, was working its way through Congress in early December. The administration's endorsement was part of a tactical bargain that allowed overdue U.N. dues to be paid and was supposed to give the president the power to waive sanctions. Yet even in this light, the Bush administration's willingness to endorse an attack on the ICC at a time when it was appealing for international cooperation in the fight against terrorism smacked of hypocrisy. It seemed that the Bush administration was willing to seek protection for its own citizens, but determined to undermine an institution that many governments see as essential for the protection of others.

This resistance to accountability—which was replicated in international negotiations on climate change, nuclear weapons, biological weapons, small arms, and racism—gave the U.S. government the latitude, for example, to continue using cluster bombs in Afghanistan, even though these imprecise weapons with their history of littering the landscape with deadly and highly volatile bomblets had caused a quarter of the bombing-related civilian deaths in Yugoslavia. More fundamentally, this resistance to accountability heightened global unease about the U.S. use of force, especially in light of repeated incidents of civilian casualties. The U.S. government seems to assume that if its policy is to respect international humanitarian law, its conduct should be beyond reproach. But much of the rest of the world understandably condemns the United States for refusing to countenance any independent enforcement, or even formal scrutiny, of the standards it claims to uphold. Accountability is a key missing component of the legitimacy that Washington seeks but so often fails to achieve.

THE FUTURE OF AFGHANISTAN

Human rights will also be put to the test as the international community works to construct a post-Taliban Afghanistan. The Taliban had an abysmal human rights record, most notably its systematic discrimination against women, its ready use of violence against those who failed to abide by its harsh vision of Islam, and its periodic resort to massacres of perceived sympathizers with its military adversaries. The demise of this regime creates an opportunity for positive change in Afghanistan. But many of the forces vying to replace the Taliban, including elements of the Northern Alliance, also have horrendous human rights records, ranging from their own massacres in recent years to their part in the destruction of vast swathes of Kabul while they shared power in 1992-96.

The test of the anti-terror coalition's commitment to human rights will come in the pressure it exerts on the Afghan parties to break definitively with the atrocities of the past. The international community should not simply replace the Taliban with whichever set of forces gains de facto control of the country, joins a broad-based coalition, and promises to cooperate in the fight against international terrorism. That would risk replacing a regime that helped to sponsor international attacks on civilians with one that simply directs its violence against civilians inward. It would also severely handicap Afghanistan as it struggles to rebuild and to meet dire humanitarian needs. In the short term, even if abusive commanders must be accepted as the de facto powers in certain parts of Afghanistan, intense pressure should be put on them to avoid reprisals against civilians or captured or surrendering combatants. In the longer term, those responsible for the worst atrocities should be precluded from any role in a future Afghan government or in any Afghan security forces.

Meanwhile, the international community should actively collect evidence of abuses by all Afghan factions, make that evidence available to either a newly established international tribunal or a reinforced national court, and ensure that no amnesty is given to those responsible for serious crimes. The U.N.-sponsored accord on Afghanistan, agreed to in Bonn in December, was a useful step in this direction. The international community should also work to end discrimination against women so they are given a full opportunity to participate in a new government, and to ensure that civil society as a whole, including women, is given a meaningful voice in determining priorities for reconstruction and economic development. These are among the steps that will allow Afghans to break from a long line of persecutors, rather than simply substitute one set of persecutors for another.

HUMAN RIGHTS IN THE WEST

In the West, the danger of an inappropriate balance between security and human rights was particularly acute after September 11 because of the focused nature of the anti-terrorism efforts. If the entire population had faced scrutiny under new security measures, popular pressure might have gone a long way toward avoiding unreasonable restraints on rights. But because the anti-terrorism effort was aimed largely at young men from the Middle East and North Africa, most residents of Western countries believed that they would not be personally targeted by new law enforcement powers. In these circumstances, political leadership is required to ensure that rights are not unnecessarily sacrificed in the rush to enhance security. Such leadership was largely lacking.

For example, emergency legislation rushed through the US Congress, the so-called USA Patriot Act, permits the indefinite detention of nondeportable non-citizens once the attorney general "certifies" that he has "reasonable grounds to believe" that the individual is engaged in terrorist activities or endangers national security. These broad and vague criteria could allow the attorney general to certify and detain any alien in the United States who had any connection, however tenuous or distant in time, with a group that had once unlawfully used a weapon to endanger a person.

Still more flagrant in its affront to international fair-trial standards was President Bush's order establishing "military commissions" to prosecute non-U.S. citizens. To begin with, the order was notably vague about the crimes that could give rise to the commission's jurisdiction. The commission could be used to try people accused of membership in al-Qaeda, involvement in the undefined crime of "international terrorism," or harboring anyone charged with these offenses. It thus extended far beyond any traditional use of military tribunals—to address offenses by combatants in war—to include people who might be charged with acts far removed from Afghanistan or any other armed conflict.

Moreover, the virtual lack of procedural protections in the order raised the prospect of suspects being tried, convicted, and even executed with no appearance before an independent judicial tribunal, no right to appeal, no right to a public trial, no presumption of innocence, no right to confront evidence or testimony against them, and no requirement that proof be established beyond a reasonable doubt. Some of these due-process transgressions may still be remedied through the adoption of additional regulations—none had been issued through early December—but the Bush order itself displayed a disturbing indifference to international fair trial standards and long-expressed U.S. values. While promising "a full and fair trial," the order explicitly rejected scrutiny of military commission proceedings by any other court, domestic or international, and ignored the Uniform Code of Military Justice—the procedural code used for regular courts-martial—which would have ensured most basic fair trial rights.

Such indifference to human rights standards will undermine the important value, as people accused of violent abuse are punished, of ensuring that justice is done and can be seen to be done. By precluding public confidence that the rule of law is being applied fairly, secret, summary trials of accused terrorists undermine the principles of human rights that stand in the way of terrorism. A Spanish judge's refusal to extradite alleged al-Qaeda members to the United States without assurances that they would avoid trial before such commissions illustrates at a practical level the obstacle that such fair-trial shortcuts pose to cooperative efforts to bring accused criminals to justice.

The Bush order, even if later modified by the fine print of regulations, also threatens to silence the U.S. voice in support of human rights. Washington had routinely objected when similar military tribunals were used against alleged "terrorists" in Peru, Nigeria, Russia, and elsewhere. By suddenly proposing to sponsor similar travesties of justice in the face of its own security threats, the U.S. government compromises its capacity to defend human rights abroad. Indeed, tomorrow's military dictators need do nothing more than photocopy the Bush order to secure a repressive mechanism that promises to be highly effective in warding off U.S. criticism. Finally, the proposed military commissions, as the other conduct outlined above, send the profoundly damaging message that human rights are mere standards of convenience, to be applied when other countries face security threats, but not when the United States is at risk. Such *a la carte* principles, of course, are no principles at all.

Similar human rights compromises could be found in other aspects of the global response to terrorism. Australian Prime Minister John Howard, stoking post-September 11 fears of foreigners, built his candidacy for reelection in November around his summary expulsion, in blatant violation of international refugee law, of asylum-seekers who had reached outlying Australian territory. Proposed European Union-wide security measures included a broad definition of terrorism that threatens freedom of association and the right to dissent; a European arrest warrant to facilitate transfer of terrorist suspects without fair-trial safeguards; and a "re-evaluation" of the right to seek asylum in Western Europe in light of new security considerations. Proposals by the British government would permit the prolonged arbitrary detention of foreigners suspected of terrorist activity and severely curtail the right to seek asylum. The Indian government used the new focus on terrorism to push for sweeping new police powers of arrest and detention—powers last used to crack down on political opponents, social activists, and human rights defenders. The U.S. government detained over 1,000 suspects following the September 11 attacks, but threw a shroud of secrecy over the cases that made it impossible to determine whether criminal justice powers were being appropriately applied.

At the United Nations, Western governments are rushing to push through an anti-terrorism treaty that, according to the draft of early December, threatened to codify an overly broad definition of terrorism without adequate guarantees that the fight against terrorism would be circumscribed by human rights guarantees. Ironically, the major obstacle to adopting the treaty was not states defending human rights but states arguing that terrorist means should be tolerated if used as part of a war for "national liberation." The result threatens to be an anti-terrorism treaty that reinforces the ends-justify-the-means rationale of terrorism.

HYPOCRISY MATTERS

This hypocrisy matters because it is profoundly more difficult to promote the values of human rights if some of the most visible and powerful proponents seek to exempt themselves from these same standards. This exceptionalism remains strong after September 11, as governments seek to justify extraordinary constraints on rights in the name of combating extraordinary threats. Yet in the long term, this trend is counterproductive. If the logic of terrorism, not just immediate terrorist threats, is ultimately to be defeated, governments must redouble their commitment to international standards, not indulge a new round of excuses to ignore them.

HUMAN RIGHTS DEFENDERS

August 2001 marked the first anniversary of the U.N. secretary-general's special representative for human rights defenders. Hina Jilani was the first to carry out the post's mandate, which called for her to press for the implementation of the 1998 Declaration on Human Rights Defenders and intervene in cases of threats to and harassment of human rights defenders worldwide. Since October 2000, Jilani had sent urgent appeals and communications to, among others, the governments of Colombia, Guatemala, Indonesia, Iran, Malaysia, Tunisia, and the United Kingdom voicing her concerns over the targeting of human rights defenders in those countries. Jilani worked closely with other U.N. thematic mechanisms, such as the special rapporteurs on torture, on extrajudicial, summary or arbitrary executions, and on violence against women, and the chairman-rapporteur of the Working Group on Arbitrary Detention. Since her appointment, Jilani had focused on countries where immediate attention to the safety of human rights defenders was needed. She visited Kyrgyzstan in August, where she stated her concerns that basic civil rights were not being systematically observed; Kyrgyz authorities refused to allow her to meet with Topchubek Turgunaliev, a political activist who was in a prison hospital at the time.

Colombia continued to be extremely dangerous for human rights defenders. On December 13, 2000, Fernando Cruz Peña, from the city of Cali, Valle, was forcibly disappeared. Cruz represented Colombians accused of support for guerrilla groups. On December 24, 2000, Fernando Rafael Castro Escobar, from Sabanas de Angel, Magdalena, was killed. Castro served as the personero of Sabanas de Angel, and collected local reports of rights violations. On February 12, 2001, Iván Villamizar Luciani, a former public advocate, was shot and killed by ten gunmen outside the Free University in Cúcuta, Norte de Santander, where he was serving as president. On February 17, Carmenza Trujillo Bernal, a member of the Caldas Human Rights Committee, was killed in Chinchiná, Caldas. On May 5, Gonzalo Zárate Triana, a founding member of the Meta Civic Committee for Human Rights, was killed in Villavicencio. On May 12, Dario Suárez Meneses, the leader of a local displaced group, was killed, in the city of Neiva, Huila. On May 19, José Jorge Navarro G. was killed near San Antonio, Tolima. He was the director of a local chapter of the Colombian Red Cross. Kimy Pernia Domicó, a leader of the indigenous Emberá-Katío, was forcibly "disappeared" on June 2, in Tierralta, Córdoba, and was presumed dead. On September 2, former Apartadó, Antioquia, town council member José de Jesús Geman was killed in a Bogotá hotel. Geman was preparing to deliver material to the attorney general's office as part of the continuing case against retired general Rito Alejo del Río, who was being investigated for supporting paramilitary groups. Alma Rosa Jaramillo Lafourie's, a lawyer who worked with the Middle Magdalena Development and Peace Program (Programa de Desarrollo y Paz del Magdalena Medio, PDPMM), was found dead on July 1 near the city of Barrancabermeja, Santander, after she had been kidnapped by paramilitaries who had been engaged in a deadly campaign against rights workers in the region. On July 18, Eduardo Estrada, also with PDPMM, was murdered in the town of San Pablo, Bolívar. On September 19, armed men shot and killed Roman Catholic nun and human rights defender Yolanda Cerón Delgado in front of a church in Tumaco, Nariño. On September 20, Juan Manuel Corzo, the director of the attorney general's investigative unit in the city of Cúcuta, Norte de Santander, was shot and killed as he drove with his mother. At the time, Corzo was investigating several killings of colleagues. On October 17, Julian Rodríguez Benítez, a member of CREDHOS, a human rights group, was killed in Barrancabermeja, Santander. Also in 2001, Miguel Ignacio Lora, Yolanda Paternina, Carlos Arturo Pinto, María del Rosario, and Maria del Rosario Rojas Silva were killed. All had investigated paramilitary or guerilla activities.

In October 2001, human rights lawyer Digna Ochoa was found shot to death in her Mexico City office. A note left by her side warned members of the Miguel Agustín Pro Juarez Human Rights Center, where Ochoa had worked for several years, that the same could happen to them.

Aceh province experienced the loss of at least seven human rights defenders over the past year. On December 6, 2000, four workers for the Rehabilitation Action for Torture Victims of Aceh (RATA) were stopped outside Lhokseumawe, North Aceh, and abducted by a group of armed soldiers and civilians. Three of them were extrajudicially executed. On February 28, Muhamad Efendi Malikon, the secretary of the human rights organization Care Forum for Human Rights (Forum Peduli HAM-Aceh Timur) was killed in Peukan Langsa village, East Aceh. On March 29, Suprin Sulaiman, a lawyer with Koalist-HAM in South Aceh was killed after accompanying his client to a police interrogation session. On September 8, Yusuf Usman, also a member of Forum Peduli HAM-Aceh Timur, was killed. On October 3, the body of an Indonesian Red Cross (PMI) volunteer, Jafar Syehdo, known as Dabra, from Bireun, Aceh was discovered shot in North Aceh. The PMI was the lead agency responsible for removing the bodies of those killed in the conflict and helping return them to their families.

In India, in November 2000, T. Puroshottam, the joint secretary of the Andhra Pradesh Civil Liberties Committee (APCLC) was stabbed to death by a group of unidentified men. In February 2001, Azam Ali, the district secretary of the Nalgonda branch of APCLC was killed by two sword-wielding youths.

In Uzbekistan, Shovruk Ruzimuradov, an activist in the Human Rights Society of Uzbekistan, died in custody, apparently tortured to death by police. Officers arrested forty-four-year-old Ruzimuradov on June 15 in southwestern Uzbekistan and held him incommunicado for some twenty-two days before returning his corpse to his family on July 7. In June, Viktor Popkov, a Russian human rights defender, died of wounds inflicted when his car was shot at in Chechnya.

HUMAN RIGHTS WATCH WORLD REPORT 2002

AFRICA

Women inside a mosque that had just been attacked by the gendarmes in Côte d'Ivoire.

AFRICA OVERVIEW

MAJOR POLITICAL DEVELOPMENTS

Longstanding wars continued to plague several countries in sub-Saharan African countries; in others, political leaders and parties engaged in elections, some of them more satisfactory than others. Everywhere, human rights defenders continued the struggle to improve respect for basic human rights. The year 2001 saw new international attention to Africa, mainly focused on combating the scourge of diseases related to HIV (human immunodeficiency virus) and on efforts to counter impoverishment aggravated by the globalization of the world economy. But African human rights issues, from those related to public health crises and the economy to the stark immediacy of repression, lost visibility as the international community turned to combating terrorism in the wake of the September attacks in the U.S.

THE SEPTEMBER 11 ATTACKS: COLLATERAL DAMAGE IN AFRICA

Just how big an impact would the September 11 attacks in the United States have on Africa? It was a question which was on the minds of state and non-state actors alike across the continent as the year closed. Though everything remained fluid, the devastation wrought by the attacks could mean:

Political Fallout in a Number of Countries

Pre-existing political tensions between Muslim and Christian populations in a number of African countries threatened to become more inflamed, and increasingly violent. Côte d'Ivoire, Ethiopia, Kenya, Nigeria, South Africa, and Tanzania all faced the possibility of worsening communal tensions. Bloody riots between Muslims and Christians in Kano, northern Nigeria, following demonstrations against the U.S. bombing of Afghanistan, had already left a high death toll. A pro-Taliban demonstration was also reported in Kenya's predominantly Muslim coastal city, Mombasa.

Restrictions on Political and Civil Rights

Governments in the region might manipulate and redefine terrorism to justify crackdowns on legitimate dissension. The U.S. "with us or against us" mantra could set a trend in Africa with African leaders labeling their opponents as terrorists and justifying restrictions on civil liberties that would previously have seemed unacceptable. In the aftermath of the attacks, President Abdoulaye Wade of Senegal proposed the adoption of an African pact against terrorism. He said the move would help the continent "to team up with the world coalition against this evil" and commit each African state "not to accept on its territory individuals or groups with terrorist intentions." Responding to President Wade's call, more than ten heads of state and delegates from twenty other African countries attended a one-day summit on October 18 in Senegal to discuss terrorism-related issues and closed the meeting with a declaration against terrorism. In particular, there were growing concerns that these steps would detrimentally affect refugee populations, particularly Muslim refugees, and encourage growing xenophobia and anti-refugee sentiment.

Subordination of Human Rights Concerns to Diplomacy's Antiterrorism Priorities

The Horn/East Africa region, where a number of al-Qaeda cells were suspected, was seen as a likely focus of U.S. interest. Sudan enthusiastically announced its cooperation in the fight against terror, leveraging its intelligence resources regarding al-Qaeda to reshape its bilateral relations. Kenya, Ethiopia, and Eritrea appeared ready to use the opportunity to marginalize reformist elements. African governments in a position to contribute to the global fight against terrorism by providing access to intelligence, airfields, and military bases might take advantage of a willingness on the part of more powerful nations like the U.S. to overlook abuses which might previously have come under greater scrutiny. For example, an October massacre by the Nigerian army of at least two hundred people in Benue State went all but unremarked during President Obasanjo's visit to the United States just a few weeks later to discuss the antiterrorism campaign.

Declining Economic Activity

Falling consumer demand in Western economies as a recession took hold might send commodity prices, already depressed, into a slump, and export-oriented countries into a nosedive; investment inflows would be dampened because of the combined effect of heightened perceptions of risk and the fall in prices for Africa's exports. Almost every sector would be affected: travel and tourism, a mainstay of a number of countries, would be badly disrupted, and recession and unemployment among African immigrants in the diaspora would decrease remittances sent to support their relatives at home.

Reduced Humanitarian and Development Assistance

The expected global downturn and a ratcheting up of security and defense expenditures in the west, could translate into major cuts in both development and humanitarian aid. President Thabo Mbeki of South Africa warned on October 3 that: "We have to ensure that there is no possibility of these attacks creating negative consequences, whereby the development issues that we have been grappling with for decades are sidelined to the margins of the global agenda. The countries of the world must simultaneously deal decisively with terrorism and effectively address and defeat poverty and underdevelopment."

HIV/AIDS STRAIGHT TALK: AFRICA TAKES STEPS TO CHANGE

To many Africans, the continent's key challenge was the response to HIV/AIDS. Of the estimated twenty-two million people to have died of AIDS-related illness worldwide by the end of 2000, seventeen million were Africans. The most severely affected region was southern Africa, including Botswana, with the highest known prevalence of HIV/AIDS in the world, and South Africa, with the largest number of people living with AIDS in any country in the world. There were around twenty-five million Africans living with AIDS, 3.8 million of whom were infected in 2000 alone.

In the past year, AIDS in Africa gained an unprecedented level of media coverage. With it came some public and political will to fight the worst epidemic in the history of mankind, as well as growing scrutiny of the pandemic's root causes. Nearly every government from tiny Gabon to repressed Mauritania engaged in high-level discussions about the problem, and the failure or success of their programs. At a special summit of the Organization of African Unity (OAU) in Abuja, Nigeria, in April 2001, OAU member states pledged to use 15 percent of their annual budgets to fight AIDS, tuberculosis, and other infectious diseases. Whether this would happen, particularly in countries with notoriously opaque budgets, was yet to be seen. Even with the Abuja Declaration, the current cost of the recommended drug treatments remained unfeasible in much of Africa.

There was global pressure on the pharmaceutical industry to remedy this situation, through lowered prices, donations, and relaxation of patent laws. In April, following a sustained campaign against them, pharmaceutical companies dropped a court challenge to a South African law enacted in 1997, but not yet promulgated, that would allow the production and importation of generic AIDS drugs. It was a major victory for the treatment lobby both in South Africa and internationally, with potentially important benefits for health and human rights. A similar law was passed in Kenya in March, and was pending in other countries, but the flow of cheap drugs was yet to be seen. Drug firms in Uganda also appealed to the government to allow them to produce anti-retroviral drugs locally.

Botswana, a relatively rich country, announced that, hopefully by 2002, all such drugs would be free for its 350,000 infected citizens. In the first week of September, Nigeria announced that it would be the first country in Africa to launch trials with generic drugs, which, in initial phases, would treat 15,000 Nigerians, for around U.S. $350 a year per person. Several countries moved first to provide the cheap, effective, and easy to provide drug nevirapine to women before giving birth in order to prevent mother-to-child transmission. But South Africa, despite its economic resources and success in facing down the drug industry, was held back by the embarrassing performance of President Thabo Mbeki, who persisted in questioning the link between HIV and AIDS. An NGO, the Treatment Action Campaign, went to court to force the government to provide drug treatment that, it argued, would even save the government money.

SOUTH AFRICA AND NIGERIA— THE ANCHOR COUNTRIES?

Since the extraordinary political and constitutional transition of 1994, South Africa had established a reputation for openness, transparency, and rational leadership on a turbulent continent. But in 2001, President Thabo Mbeki's government seemed to prefer to invest political capital in fighting public relations skirmishes rather than addressing the economic and social challenges that confronted the country. In February, there were extraordinary allegations by Steve Tshwete, the minister for police, of a conspiracy by three politicians-turned-businessmen to oust Mbeki from office. Observers were alarmed by the willingness to use the tools of state security to tackle what seemed to be an internal party issue. The government was plagued by corruption scandals in connection with a multi-million rand arms deal. African National Congress Chief Whip Tony Yengeni, former chair of parliament's committee on defense, was charged with corruption, perjury, and fraud; other arrests were anticipated. President Mbeki's refusal to confront his country's catastrophic AIDS epidemic risked undermining all other achievements.

Although the president's reputation and standing had been damaged, most observers thought the situation was retrievable. By general consensus, the transformation of South Africa's political landscape over the previous seven years had been so profound that it was irreversible. South Africa could still count on one of the most progressive constitutions in the world, guarded by an impeccable Constitutional Court; vigorous independent news media, unions, and academia; ample provision for a constitutional opposition; and government policies that—despite ongoing controversies on their direction—generally managed to negotiate reconciliation of the demands for radical redistribution of wealth with the needs of economic growth.

South Africa's continued regional leadership was demonstrated late in the year, as the first of about seven hundred South African peacekeeping troops arrived in Burundi. Their task was to form a protection force for politicians returning from exile to join a power-sharing transitional government that was sworn in on November 1.

In Nigeria, the continent's most populous country, it seemed as though time might be running out for President Olusegun Obasanjo. In May 1999, sixteen years of military rule had ended. Though many Nigerians were skeptical, they had nonetheless hoped that the new civilian government would take the difficult steps to restore accountable government and the rule of law, as well as Nigeria's standing in the world. More than two years later, the country was a land of rising discontent, and questions multiplied about the president's leadership capabilities.

In the past year, Nigeria saw a surge of religious and ethnic conflicts at the cost of thousands of lives. Riots, the ravaging of churches and mosques, violent demonstrations, military and police abuses, and a general lawlessness continued to tear at the daily lives of Nigerians. In October, the Nigerian army was responsible for massacring at least two hundred unarmed civilians in central Benue State, in an area torn by ongoing ethnic conflict. Corruption remained rampant, despite the adoption of anti-corruption legislation in 2000, distorting economic management, corrupting law enforcement, and starving desperately needed public services. In his Independence Day speech on October 1, the president conceded that his administration had failed to lift most Nigerians out of poverty, end violence, and solve other huge obstacles that the country confronted. Yet he offered little hope that these issues would be addressed in the remainder of his term.

Nigeria still enjoyed a comparatively greater degree of freedom in contrast to the dark days of military rule, and a commission set up in 1999 to investigate human rights abuses committed under previous governments had somewhat dented the historical wall of impunity. But the country desperately needed a democratically enacted constitution, accountable politicians and civil servants, and restored respect for the rule of law. With government revenue coming almost exclusively from a single source, Nigeria's substantial oil and gas deposits, it would remain extremely difficult to create a functioning democracy.

BUCKING THE TREND?

A few countries registered success in strengthening or maintaining democratic institutions. Botswana and Mauritius headed the table, and South Africa remained an example in many ways, but Mali, Mozambique, Ghana, and Senegal were also strong contenders for Africa's first division status. Botswana had the highest credit rating in Africa from the international ratings agency Moody's—four notches above that of South Africa—and ranked alongside central European countries. Mauritius was ranked second (behind Tunisia and ahead of Botswana) out of twenty-four countries surveyed in the World Economic Forum's Africa Competitiveness Report.

The connection between economic prosperity and stable political institutions was underlined by the September 13, 2000 elections in Mauritius. An opposition alliance, of the Mouvement Socialiste Mauricien (MSM) and Mouvement Militant Mauricien (MMM), swept into power in a landslide victory with high turnout. Outgoing Prime Minister Navinchandra Ramgoolam gracefully accepted defeat. In terms of the electoral pact, the MSM leader Sir Anerood Jugnauth would be prime minister for the next three years and then hand over the reins to the MMM leader, Paul Berenger, for the final two years. In the meantime, they would introduce a constitutional amendment to give the president, a ceremonial figure, more power; Sir Anerood would become president. Berenger would be the first non-Hindu to occupy the premiership since Mauritius won independence in 1968.

Ghana saw a peaceful transfer of power when, on January 7, President Jerry Rawlings, who came to power in two coups and retained power through two subsequent elections, stepped down from his nineteen year presidency and surrendered power to John Kufuor. Like Mali and Senegal, Ghana looked set to become one of the "democratic dominos" in West Africa. Once in power, the new president promised sweeping human rights improvements. In July, Ghana's parliament voted unanimously to repeal the criminal libel law first introduced by the British colonial administration. At this writing, debate was underway regarding legislation to establish a mechanism for truth telling and reconciliation in relation to past abuses. Kufuor also agreed to exhume for positive identification and proper reburial the bodies of eight generals who had been executed in 1979 on charges of corruption and treason. This was the first official step towards confronting and resolving various extrajudicial executions which took place both before and during Rawlings' reign.

Mozambique remained another African success story, though it faced some serious threats during the year. The country's post-conflict stability continued to be reinforced by the generally human rights-friendly leadership of President Joachim Chissano, and by robust economic growth. The economy grew by nearly 15 percent in the first half of the year, recovering strongly from the devastating 2000 floods. But the government's reputation was tarnished by attacks against journalists. In November 2000, unknown attackers gunned down journalist Carlos Cardoso, editor of the independent *Metical* who had been sharply critical of hard line elements in both the ruling party and the opposition in the wake of political clashes that left forty-one people dead. In a separate attack later the same day, a gang stopped Radio Mozambique journalist Custodio Rafael on his way home from work. The attackers reportedly told him, "You talk a lot," before beating him and cutting his tongue with a knife. In January, a Mozambican parliamentary commission visited northern Cabo Delgado province to investigate the suffocation-deaths of more than one hundred imprisoned opposition demonstrators in the town of Montepuez. The commission had joint government and opposition membership. A Mozambican human rights group that carried out its own inquiry blamed the tragedy on both police negligence and retaliation for the killing of six police officers during the protests.

ELECTIONS, BUT NOT NECESSARILY DEMOCRACY

A number of other African countries held presidential or parliamentary elections during the year. However, all were characterized by intimidation of the media and opposition, killings, and gross and widespread vote rigging. Leaders in Guinea, Malawi, Namibia, Zambia, and elsewhere attempted or were reported to be considering constitutional amendments to overcome term limits and remain in power.

Political and social unrest continued to plague Côte d'Ivoire during 2001, following presidential and parliamentary elections in late 2000. Laurent Gbagbo, leader of the Front Populaire Ivorien (FPI), was installed as president despite very serious concerns surrounding the legitimacy of the October presidential elections—over the widespread violence and the exclusion of principal opposition leader Alassane Ouattara from the contest. Gbagbo then used the same methods as his predecessor during the December parliamentary elections, including incitement of religious and ethnic hatred. Ouattara was once again not allowed to run. In both October and December security forces arrested, tortured, and killed perceived opposition supporters, including foreigners and members of northern ethnic groups. After assuming office, Gbagbo failed to acknowledge the flawed manner in which he had become head of state, to promise new elections, to seek accountability for the violence, or to take adequate steps to ensure that, under his leadership, Côte d'Ivoire would be characterized by the rule of law, not by ethno-religious tension and military impunity.

In Benin, presidential elections in late March 2001 saw the reelection of President Mathieu Kerekou. Kerekou failed in the first round to gain a majority, so a runoff with the runner-up, Nicephore Soglo, was called. Soglo, citing widespread fraud, dropped out before the final round, and encouraged his supporters to boycott as well. The runoff was further delayed by the resignation of several members of the electoral commission in protest at the way the vote was organized. The third place contender also pulled out, leaving only the fourth-place primary finisher, Bruno Amoussou. This dubious run-off slate gave Kerekou the presidency, with 84 percent of the votes. Earlier in the year, on January 19, police beat up two journalists working for private media and violently broke up a demonstration they were covering in the capital, Cotonou.

The election campaign in Chad was marred by intimidation and violence, but on May 27 Idriss Deby was re-elected president with more than 67 percent of the vote. Opposition candidates alleged fraud and called for the result to be annulled, appealing to the constitutional court. A quarter of the members of the electoral commission resigned in protest in advance of the announcement of Deby's victory. On May 28, Brahim Selguet, an opposition activist, was shot and killed by the police as they violently broke up an opposition meeting. Six opposition presidential candidates were briefly detained at the meeting, and were again arrested in the morning of May 30 with some thirty other opposition activists and trade unionists. They were all released without charge the same day, but two of the opposition leaders, Ngarledjy Yorongar and Abderhamane Djesnebaye, were reportedly tortured, including being beaten with iron bars, during their detention.

Uganda's March presidential election and May parliamentary elections were both marred by manipulation and human rights abuses. As political parties are not allowed to operate freely in Uganda, opposition presidential candidates had to mobilize support and resources as individuals. Incumbent president Yoweri Museveni, however, relied on the administrative and political officials of the ruling "movement system" to bring in the vote. Harassment of journalists and editors, self-censorship, and inequality in media access intensified as the date for the poll neared. Supporters of opposition candidates were also threatened and harassed when campaigning for their candidates. In January, unidentified gunmen killed a member of President Museveni's campaign task force, and, in a separate incident, two supporters of opposition presidential candidate Dr. Kizza Besigye. At least one person was killed when members of the Presidential Protection Unit opened fire on opposition demonstrators on March 3. Both international observers and Ugandan human rights groups expressed concern at the role played by the Ugandan army in the election and that elections took place on a far from level playing field. Museveni was declared the winner. At least seven people were shot dead on June 27, in violence surrounding parliamentary elections. On July 6, the Foundation for Human Rights Initiative, a national NGO, criticized the government's treatment of Besigye and strongly condemned what it called the authorities' "persistent, consistent and violent intolerance and disrespect for divergent views."

Gambia's tense presidential election was held on October 18. After pressure from the international community, President Yahya Jammeh had lifted a ban on opposition parties in July, inviting former politicians who had sought political asylum in other countries to return. On August 27, President Jammeh expelled Deputy British High Commissioner Bharat Joshi for attending an open press conference, which Jammeh alleged was an opposition party rally. The day before the election, security forces opened fire on a crowd of opposition supporters, killing at least one. In the days following the election, private radio station Citizen FM was shut down and state security agents reportedly detained its owner for four hours.

On November 28, 2000, Mauritania's 40th anniversary of independence, President Ould Taya promised democratic reform, and on December 4, the government held consultations with political parties. It was announced that proportional representation in the legislature would be introduced in the 2001 elections, and that the government would fund political parties, based on their performance in municipal polls. Not a week later, Union of Democratic Forces leader Ould Daddah was arrested upon his return to Mauritania, and charged with "contact with terrorist groups." He was released on December 13. On June 14, 2001, three members of the opposition Front Populaire Mauritanien were jailed, accused of conspiring with Libya to foment the violent overthrow of the government. Their lawyers alleged numerous serious irregularities in the proceedings and initially withdrew in protest; they later agreed to represent the three men, while making clear their concern at government interference and other fair trial concerns.

In Guinea-Conakry opposition parties criticized as a "constitutional coup d'état" and a "masquerade" a referendum held on November 11, 2001, in which 98 percent of those who voted supposedly supported changes to key constitutional provisions. The proposed changes would increase presidential terms from five to seven years and allow presidents to remain in office indefinitely, giving incumbent president Lansana Conte the option of a third term. An 87 percent turnout was reported, though observers estimated that only 20 percent of the population could have voted. In Malawi too, controversy surrounded the issue of whether President Bakili Muluzi should be allowed a third term in office when his current term expires in 2004, something that would entail alteration of the constitution. Malawi's two largest churches issued separate letters warning President Muluzi against standing for reelection, prompting a government statement in May denying that either the cabinet or the ruling party had discussed a constitutional amendment. But in August, a debate on whether the president should extend his rule into a third term resurfaced. "Muluzi will stand again in 2004 because people want him. We will change the constitution so Muluzi can stand," said a key supporter.

In two other countries whose leaders were mooted to be set to join "third term" campaigns requiring constitutional change, external and internal pressure provided a check on ambitions in that direction. But though President Daniel arap Moi of Kenya hinted at an exit at the end of his second and constitutionally-last term, he invested heavily in a careful succession plan and efforts to hinder a full constitutional review. In Zambia, which had appeared to be losing any claims to democracy, President Chiluba, with his party in revolt and facing massive public pressure and predictions of large-scale violence, on May 3 abandoned his efforts to change the constitution's two-term limit and announced that he would step down when his second term ended at the end of the year. The news sparked celebrations in the country.

SILENCING THE CRITICS

In too many countries, effective mechanisms for querying, much less contesting or contributing to, government policy and operations were lacking. In the absence of autonomous electoral authorities, independent judiciaries, and the provision of equal access for competing political factions to government controlled media, opposition voices could only rely on getting their message across through the much-harassed independent media and the grassroots influence of trade unions or civil society organizations. Burkina Faso, Cameroon, Equatorial Guinea, Gabon, Kenya, Mauritania, Swaziland, Tanzania, Zimbabwe, and numerous other countries remained reluctant to commit themselves to the imperatives of democracy and respect for human rights.

In Equatorial Guinea, the government continued to use military courts, repressive laws, and arbitrary arrests and prosecutions to restrict political freedoms. In November 2000, hundreds of copies of the latest issue of independent weekly *La Opinion* were seized by the authorities in Mongome, a town in the east of Equatorial Guinea. The newspapers were confiscated on the order of the government's representative in the district. According to the government, the paper was too close to the opposition. In February 2001, the mayor of Malabo closed the offices of the Equatorial Guinea press association.

On April 1, 2001, President Blaise Compaore of Burkina Faso publicly apologized for the torture and "all other crimes" committed by his government in a blanket act of state contrition. However, the 1998 killing of journalist Norbert Zongo remained a source of both national and international outrage. To commemorate the two-year anniversary of Zongo's death, human rights advocates and opposition parties along with members of the international press attempted to gather in Ouagadougou in December 2000 to demand that the perpetrators be found and prosecuted. Many journalists were prevented from entering the country by security forces and riot police thwarted commemoration activities.

In Cameroon, police in Yaounde dispersed supporters of the opposition Social Democratic Front as they marched on November 27, 2000, to demand the creation of an independent electoral commission. Five opposition parties walked out of parliament on December 7, 2000, as the house passed a bill creating an election-monitoring body known as the Observatoire National des Elections, its members to be appointed single-handedly by President Paul Biya. In July 2001, police raided the offices of independent newspaper *Mutations*, seized copies of the paper, and summoned the publisher, Haman Mana, to a hearing, accusing him of having published confidential state documents. Mana refused to reveal his source, citing Cameroonian law; he was released on August 3. On October 3, 2001, police summoned Jean-Marc Soboth, editor-in-chief of the independent *La Nouvelle Expression* and demanded that he reveal his sources for a story about security measures in the country's English-speaking provinces. The authorities maintained that the newspaper revealed a "defense secret." The journalist refused to do so, again citing privilege, and was released the same day.

Togolese police used tear gas on August 14, 2001, to break up a demonstration by opposition parties and human rights activists demanding the release of opposition leader Yawovi Agboyibor, sentenced to six months imprisonment for defamation. He had reportedly said in 1998 that the prime minister, Messan Kodjo, was associated with a militia whose members killed supporters of his party, the Comité Action pour le Renouveau.

Guinea Bissau saw new problems following an alleged coup plot in November 2000. General Ansumane Mané, the former leader of the disbanded military junta, was killed in early December 2000 in mysterious circumstances after challenging the president over military promotions. Despite national and international appeals, there was no independent investigation of his death. Ten opposition leaders, including several parliamentarians, who had also criticized the government handling of the promotions, were arrested without warrant between November 24 and 26, 2000. They were not freed until March. Journalists were also under threat. In March, the deputy procurator-general threatened to bomb a radio station, Radio Bombolom, in order to interrupt a radio debate about the alleged coup attempt. In mid-September the attorney general reportedly went to Radio Pidjiquiti and threatened its workers after they refused to give him the tapes of a program on which journalists had commented on his appointment.

Gabon's President Bongo promoted a constitutional amendment to give former heads of state immunity from legal prosecution. Several privately owned radio stations and television channels were regularly threatened with withdrawal of their broadcasting licenses by the authorities. But some news from Gabon was good. The satirical weekly *La Griffe*, banned two years before, was authorized in late July by the National Communication Council to begin publishing again. Two of its publishers, who had been sentenced to eight years in prison, received a presidential pardon on October 29th, 2000. Another satirical publication, *La Cigale Enchantée*, closed down at the same time for accusing the minister in charge of infrastructure of corruption, remained banned.

In the Horn of Africa, political liberties faced serious threats. Eritrea's strongman President Isaias Aferwerki cracked down harshly on those who dared to speak out. In February, the president removed the minister of local government after he questioned the country's leadership. In May, fifteen members of the seventy-five strong central committee of the ruling party published an open letter demanding reforms. Among the signatories were several former ministers and ambassadors, and three generals. On September 18 and 19, the government arrested without charge eleven signatories of the "G-15" letter—three others were abroad and one had previously retracted his signature of the letter. In July, the government arrested student leader Semere Kesete for strongly protesting the government's management of the university's mandatory summer work program. On September 19, the government withdrew the licenses of all eight independent newspapers in the country, claiming they had violated media law and undermined national unity. The minister of information (previously the security chief) announced that he would review each newspaper to determine whether it could reopen. At this writing, none had reopened. The government-controlled media were left as the only source of information for Eritrea's citizens.

In neighboring Ethiopia, there was a marked erosion of civil liberties during 2001. The government jailed civil rights advocates, political rivals, students, and journalists without formal charges, and police used excessive force against unarmed civilians. In March, key members of the Tigrayan People's Liberation Front, the lead party in the government coalition, issued a twelve-point critique of the prime minister's policies. The dissenters, joined by members of other government parties, complained that the government had concluded a premature and unfavorable peace agreement with Eritrea. They also accused the prime minister, Meles Zenawi, of corruption.

In Rwanda, the government continued to disregard the constitution's guarantee of the right to form political parties. The ruling Rwandan Patriotic Front (RPF) maintained a ban on the activities of all other parties, while the RPF itself recruited new members and campaigned in district elections. The government barred former president Pasteur Bizimungu from organizing a new political party and harassed party members and journalists reporting the story.

Tanzania's image was badly tarnished by serious abuses in the semi-autonomous islands of Zanzibar during late January and early February. Police blocked a demonstration by opposition supporters against the much-criticized 2000 elections, marred by serious violence and described by the Commonwealth as a "shambles." A climate of harassment and repression of political activity continued for the better part of the year. On October 9, 2001, a deal was signed by the Zanzibar authorities and the opposition agreeing on tension-reducing measures including electoral reform, provision of equal access to all parties on state media, and the holding of by-elections for seats that remained vacant after the disputed 2000 elections.

Zimbabwean President Robert Mugabe's indifference to legal norms and encouragement of political violence persisted—threatening the entire southern African subregion with instability. Against the backdrop of a worsening economic crisis precipitated in part by the violent seizure of white-owned commercial land, the government continued its hard line attitude towards the political opposition, media, and judiciary. Widespread violence was visited on opposition supporters, especially in rural areas, and on the owners and residents of white-owned commercial farms by veterans of the liberation war and supporters of the ruling party. The police did little or nothing to intervene to protect those who were the victims of this violence; human rights organizations noted increasing politicization of the criminal justice system. The year saw the forced resignation of the chief justice, Anthony Gubbay, on the grounds that the government, which had itself scorned court orders, could no longer guarantee his personal safety. Leading opposition leaders were also subjected to arrests on controversial charges of inciting violence and harassment of supporters of the Movement for Democratic Change (MDC) had worsened severely by the end of the year. In November, more than twenty MDC activists were arrested in Bulawayo, on charges of involvement in the murder of a war veteran leader; the MDC suggested that the veteran had been killed by the security forces to silence him. Zimbabwe faced increasing diplomatic isolation, including the first public criticism from its neighbors in the Southern African Development Community (SADC).

Also in the south the year was a difficult one for King Mswati of Swaziland. Under pressure to implement governmental reforms, faced with increased HIV infection in his population, a worsening economy, and an outspoken media, King Mswati attempted to maintain iron-fisted control. For its part, the opposition demanded an end to the twenty-seven-year ban on political parties and the state of emergency, and called for the creation of an interim government. In January, leaders of this movement were arrested and charged with "misconduct." Royal Decree No.2, promulgated on June 24, gave the king the power to ban any book, magazine or newspaper, prohibited anyone from impersonating or ridiculing the king, prevented legal challenges to any of the monarch's executive decisions, and eliminated bail for a range of crimes, including holding illegal public demonstrations. The decree also gave the justice minister the power to appoint and fire judges at will, and prohibited newspapers from challenging publishing bans. But one month later, the king bowed to international pressure and revoked the decree. After a four-month court battle the *Guardian*, an independent weekly, had a banning order against it overturned on September 3. In November, amid a crackdown on the opposition, President Joachim Chissano of Mozambique, speaking on behalf of SADC, expressed concern that the situation in Swaziland threatened the stability of the subregion.

Namibia, which had boasted one of the most liberal constitutions at the time of its independence in 1990, saw serious threats to its liberties during 2001. President Sam Nujoma's outspoken attacks on gays, lesbians, foreigners, and white Namibians, as well as his dismissal of several judges, created a troubling environment for human rights during the year. In March, the government imposed an advertising boycott on the independent *Namibian*, claiming the paper was too critical of its policies.

There was some good news on a different front. The internet became an ever more useful tool for the dissemination of information on the continent—despite the efforts of governments such as Zimbabwe's, where the pending Post and Communications Act would give the government unfettered powers to intercept postal and electronic communications. At this writing, however, eleven African countries had no private sector involvement in providing Internet service. In those countries, such as Ethiopia and Niger, costs remained exorbitant for local users, and government monitoring of communication easy. Lines could be cut off with no explanation, access to websites blocked, and owners of cyber cafés forced to supply government intelligence officials with copies of e-mails sent or received by them. Even in Mauritania, where the private sector was not barred, the two private Internet service providers had very close ties to the president.

SMOLDERING FIRES

Wars continued to smolder and flare across the continent, most seriously in Angola, Burundi, Democratic Republic of Congo (DRC), Liberia, and Sierra Leone. Despite repeated commitments to peaceful resolution of conflict, the warring parties remained heavily engaged in armed operations. In the Great Lakes area, the warring factions' forced recruitment of civilians, including children, appreciably escalated.

The war in the DRC continued to be characterized by shocking brutality. Talks meant to forward implementation of the Lusaka agreements to end hostilities resumed following Joseph Kabila's assumption of the presidency in January. International pressure on Uganda and Rwanda to withdraw their troops from Congo increased. A preliminary inter-Congolese dialogue took place in Gaborone in mid-August, with follow up "national dialogue" convened on October 15 in Addis Ababa. But incessant disagreements between Congolese rebels and the government and a shortfall in funding prevented much progress being made at the talks. Relations between Rwanda and Uganda worsened, owing to a combination of personal animosities between the top leadership and colliding interests in the DRC war, and further undermined progress towards a solid cease-fire and a political solution to the conflict.

Burundi endured its eighth year of civil war—intertwined with conflicts in neighboring DRC and Rwanda—with both governmental and rebel forces guilty of killing, raping, and assaulting civilians and destroying their property. Civilian casualties, however, were fewer than in previous years, and there were fewer large-scale massacres. Late in the year the government and opposition political parties hobbled towards implementing the Arusha Accord signed in August 2000. Following installation of a transitional government on November 1, rebel movements stepped up combat; one of them abducted hundreds of schoolboys, apparently to force them to become child soldiers.

In West Africa, the countries of the Mano River Union—Liberia, Sierra Leone, and Guinea—were caught up in an ongoing subregional conflict which spilled across borders. From late 2000 to April 2001 fierce fighting occurred between Sierra Leonean rebels and their Liberian government allies in a series of border clashes with the armed forces of neighboring Guinea. Thousands of Liberian and Sierra Leonean refugees in Guinea were trapped in the border attacks. For their part, the Guinean authorities allowed Liberian rebels to operate from their territory, and seemed at minimum to have provided logistical support and sponsored cross-border incursions into Liberia. The rebel incursion into northern Liberia continued to make gains, with serious abuses against civilians by both rebel and Liberian government forces. Thanks in large part to the deployment of British forces in 2000 and their continued presence, together with some 17,000 U.N. peacekeepers' move into former rebel strongholds in Sierra Leone, and the disarming of over 20,000 Sierra Leonean rebel and government troops, there was at year's end some hope of a lasting peace in Sierra Leone. However, there appeared to be no end to the renewed civil war in Liberia, and the continued instability in the subregion.

There also seemed no end to conflict in Angola, as attacks by the rebel National

Union for the Total Independence of Angola (UNITA) led by Jonas Savimbi, and to a much lesser extent government troops, resulted in yet more civilian casualties. The continuing violence formed a grim backdrop to hints of a political deal to break the deadlock between the warring parties. In August, President José Eduardo dos Santos' announcement that he would not run in the country's next elections was greeted with surprise and skepticism. Many were aware of the reality that the refusal by the government to re-enter negotiations for a political solution would leave the country stuck in a military standoff.

In Sudan, war raged on, with President al-Bashir continuing his practice of dropping bombs on civilians in the south and preventing humanitarian aid from getting to them. Oil money, which first began to flow into the government's coffers in late 1999, continued to fuel intensified fighting in the south, with predictable results for human rights.

Just over a year after a U.N. peacekeeping force had been fully wound down in February 2000, the Central African Republic was plunged into an ongoing political and human rights crisis when former President Andre Kolingba spearheaded his third coup attempt in five years on May 28. Reports said fifty people were killed in the fighting to regain government control after rebels took over the airport, radio station, and other parts of Bangui's infrastructure. Although the coup was swiftly put down by the forces of President Ange-Félix Patassé, with the assistance of Libyan troops (not to mention Chadian troops and rebel troops from DRC), unrest continued in the months following as unarmed civilians, particularly members of the Yakoma ethnic group to which Kolingba belongs, were targeted for arbitrary detention and arrest. The government reportedly tortured and killed numerous civilians and members of the security forces.

The Republic of Congo (Brazzaville) continued to limp back to normalcy after the ferocious civil wars of 1993, 1997, and 1998. The past year was officially one of "national reconciliation," and a "non-exclusive dialogue" which was scheduled to end in April. A reconciliation convention was held, but no election date had been set at this writing.

FLEEING WARS, ONLY TO FIND MORE WOES

War continued to swell the tide of refugees and internally displaced persons, spawning bleak, overcrowded camps, where responsible authorities were barely able to provide the necessities of life and violence often seemed uncontrolled. As of January 2001, there were at least 3,346,000 refugees in Africa out of a total 14,544,000 worldwide. The numbers of internally displaced people also remained high, with Angola, Sierra Leone, Eritrea, and Sudan having the largest populations. In many conflicts more people were internally displaced than crossed international borders: about 4.4 million Sudanese were internally displaced and 420,000 were refugees in neighboring countries. Yet international law and structures for protecting the internally displaced remained weaker than those for refugees.

The major refugee crisis of the year occurred in Guinea, which experienced enormous upheaval while serving as host to some 400,000 refugees from Sierra

Leone and Liberia. Several months of fierce cross-border fighting between Guinean government forces and Sierra Leonean rebels acting together with Liberian government troops drove refugees and local residents alike from their homes in border regions. At the same time, the Guinean government closed its border to new Liberian refugees who were trying to escape the civil war. As refugees moved inland to escape the border violence, they remained vulnerable to beatings, strip searches, extortion, sexual assault, arbitrary arrest and detention, and widespread intimidation at the hands of the Guinean authorities. Sierra Leonean refugees who fled the dire conditions in Guinea by walking home through Revolutionary United Front (RUF) territory were raped, killed, and abducted for fighting or forced labor by the RUF rebels as they attempted to reach Sierra Leonean government-held towns. The Office of the U.N. High Commissioner for Refugees (UNHCR) and the Guinean government finally agreed to move the camps further inland and to provide facilitated return by boat from Conakry to Sierra Leonean refugees who wanted to return home. The situation in Guinea remained difficult for both refugees and NGO workers through April 2001. By May 2001, an organized relocation program had moved some 60,000 refugees inland. Some 35,000 refugees were returned to Sierra Leone. By mid-2001, the situation seemed significantly calmer.

HUMAN RIGHTS DEFENDERS: RESILIENT IN A RISKY ENVIRONMENT

The human rights community remained one of the most dynamic segments of civil society in Africa. But while human rights organizations were able to operate without hindrance from state agencies in countries such as Botswana, Ghana, Mauritius, Nigeria, Senegal, and South Africa, security forces in numerous other countries closely scrutinized their activities. Activists were arrested, beaten and detained in Angola, Burundi, Cameroon, Chad, Côte d'Ivoire, Guinea-Bissau, Liberia, Zimbabwe, and elsewhere. In Sierra Leone and DRC, among other places, an active human rights community challenged abuses despite a hostile environment.

In Guinea-Bissau, soldiers and state security police arrested Fernando Gomes, former president of the Liga Guineense dos Direitos Humanos (LGDH), at his home on November 25, 2000. He was severely beaten in the presence of his family and neighbors and, although seriously ill as a result of the beating, was denied medical treatment while in detention. After his release on November 30, 2000, he was refused permission to travel abroad for treatment until January 2001.

In Angola, Rafael Marques, a leading critic of the government and representative of the Open Society Foundation, faced harassment by government officials twice during the year. In December 2000, Marques was prevented from leaving the country. In July 2001, Marques was assaulted and arrested by police for taking pictures of tents in the Viana resettlement camp. A week prior to Marques' arrest, government demolition of houses in the Boa Vista section of Luanda, in order to force residents to Viana, had resulted in two deaths. Yet the Angolan government did allow greater discussion of concerns about the ongoing war.

Four members of Cameroon's Collectif contre l'Impunité were arrested in April and detained at the central police station in Douala. The authorities alleged they had held an illegal demonstration, though it appeared that their detention was in fact related to an investigation of the January "disappearance" of nine youths. The U.N. Human Rights Committee in June ruled that the government of Cameroon pay U.S. $137,000 to Cameroonian human rights activist Albert Mukong, in compensation for abuses committed against him by Cameroonian authorities in 1988 and 1990, when his book *Prisoner Without a Crime* was banned and he was detained incommunicado.

In Chad, the period following the May election saw a violent crackdown on human rights defenders. The government banned gatherings of more than twenty people. On June 11, tear gas canisters and what was believed to be a grenade were hurled into a crowd of peaceful demonstrators gathered in front of the French embassy in the capital N'Djamena. Among those injured was leading activist Jacquy Moudeina. Numerous pieces of shrapnel lodged in her leg and she was hospitalized. Several human rights defenders fled Liberia and applied for political asylum. The Liberian Bar Association conducted a boycott of the courts in October to protest the harassment of colleagues who were detained for calling for due process protections in the courts. Despite intensifying state harassment, a few brave activists continued to work undaunted.

The head of Amnesty International in Gambia, Mohammed Lamin Sillah, was detained incommunicado for four days in late October after he had been picked up by state security agents for "questioning." Sillah's arrest was one among a reported score of arrests in the wake of the presidential poll.

There were efforts to tighten regulatory regimes on NGOs in a number of countries including Eritrea, Ethiopia, Mauritania, Rwanda, and Uganda. In Uganda, NGOs operated generally quite freely and became more outspoken during 2001 in their critique of the human rights practices of their government. But a draft law, the Nongovernmental Organizations Registration (Amendment) Bill, would require that NGOs obtain a special permit from the registration board before they could operate. It would also increase the registration board's powers to reject or revoke an NGO's registration; and it would stiffen the penalties for operating without official sanction, potentially criminalizing legitimate NGO activities.

In Rwanda, a restrictive NGO law came into force in April, giving the government wide-ranging powers to interfere with the work of NGOs, and to suspend or dissolve associations. The Rwandan government was also preparing a decree to increase the government's control over the day-to-day work of NGOs. The government stepped up harassment of the leading human rights NGO LIPRODHOR after the organization published a statement critical of prison conditions.

In neighboring Burundi, local authorities threatened a human rights observer from Ligue Iteka, one of the main human rights NGOs in the country, who was leading an investigation into the government's arming of civilians.

Conditions for human rights defenders worsened in the Horn. The Eritrean government tolerated the operation of only one human rights organization, Citizens for Peace in Eritrea, but only so long as it limited advocacy to the rights of war victims. In Ethiopia, police arrested two leading activists, Professor Mesfin Woldemariam and Dr. Berhanu Nega, in early May and held them in custody until June. The government leveled spurious charges against both that they had "incited students to riot." Mesfin was the founding president of the Ethiopian Human Rights Council (EHRCO). On the day of the arrests, the government raided and sealed the EHRCO offices, although the closure was lifted after ten days.

Two of the main human rights organizations in Mauritania, SOS-Esclaves and the Association Mauritanienne des Droits de l'Homme (AMDH) continued to be denied registration by the government and were therefore restricted in their activities.

African activists Kodjo Djissenou and Ndungi Githuku, of Togo and Kenya respectively, were two of the four winners of the Reebok Human Rights Award for activists under age thirty. Kodjo Djissenou, a youth activist, had been working to protect human rights in Togo since the age of twelve. Ndungi Githuku, who had used his talents as a playwright, graphic artist, and performer since the age of nineteen to raise awareness of police torture, political corruption, and democratic principles, became the first artist to win the award. In October, D. Zacarias Camuenho, president of the Bishops' Conference of Angola and Sao Tome, won the Sakharov peace prize—indicating the growing role of the churches as a possible mediator between the two parties in the Angolan conflict.

REGIONAL INTERGOVERNMENTAL BODIES

African Union:
Making Over the Organization of African Unity

The year marked what was touted as the beginning of a new era for African cooperation. At the July summit of the Organization of African Unity (OAU) in Lusaka, members agreed to set up a new organization, the African Union (A.U.); its first summit would be held in 2002, in Pretoria, South Africa. Ivorian diplomat Amara Essy was elected secretary-general after an all-night round of voting. The A.U., like the OAU, would be based in Addis Ababa.

The treaty establishing the A.U. had important new provisions strengthening the (theoretical) commitment of its member states to human rights. The A.U. would also be looking into a common currency, a continental parliament, and a court of justice. The summit decided to incorporate the OAU mechanism for conflict prevention, management, and resolution as one of the organs of the A.U. It conspicuously failed to do the same for the African Commission on Human and People's Rights, also an OAU body—this was said to be an oversight that could be corrected.

The launching of the African Union coincided with the introduction of the New African Initiative (NAI), intended to address Africa's chronic failure to address its economic and political problems. The plan was announced by the outgoing chair, President Frederick Chiluba of Zambia, and was later formally launched on October 23 at a ceremony in Abuja, Nigeria, attended by presidents Olusegun Obasanjo of Nigeria, Thabo Mbeki of South Africa, Abdoulaye Wade of Senegal, and Abdelaziz Bouteflika of Algeria. The NAI was a merger of the Millennium Partnership for the African Recovery Programme (MAP) proposed by the governments of South Africa, Nigeria, and Algeria and the OMEGA plan proposed by President Abdoulaye Wade of Senegal. In October, the NAI was renamed the New Partnership for Africa's Development (NEPAD).

At first glance, the concept of the African Union looked promising. But, apart from words, it was far from clear that it represented any real progress. The core ideal continued to be that continental cooperation should be a means to facilitate and consolidate respect for democracy and human dignity across the continent. But the obstacles that had prevented the OAU from achieving these aims remained. The African Union would need to overcome the same ingrained clash of cultures and egos that perennially split the Anglophone, Francophone, and Arab constituencies of the organization. The refusal of member states to surrender their veto power had ensured that the OAU had served merely as a clearinghouse for discussions that could be ignored at will. Moreover, the OAU had failed to insist that its members respect democratic and human rights norms. The much stronger human rights language of the African Union might prove no less difficult to enforce. At the World Conference Against Racism, held in Durban, South Africa, just a few weeks after the last OAU summit, African countries largely refused to see racism and other forms of intolerance as a problem that affected them internally—except with regard to black-white relations especially in southern African countries—and focused instead on the demand for reparations for the Atlantic slave trade.

Clear leadership from South Africa and Nigeria in particular would help to address these issues. President Olusegun Obasanjo expressed a strong determination to make the new initiatives succeed. In his words: "Within and outside Africa we must put the Afro-pessimists and other cynics to shame by coming together to work for the success of NAI." Most probably President Obasanjo meant well. But it would take more than presidential assurances to deliver a system that could be relied on to fight effectively for peace, good governance, human rights, and economic development.

Southern African Development Community

The Southern African Development Community (SADC), which had struggled to find common ground and speak with a unified voice in 2000, hit its stride in mid-2001 and made significant progress toward increasing its ability to engage in conflict resolution in the region. SADC tended toward greater cohesion in the past year, attending the G8 conference in Genoa as a block instead of as individual states, and in its efforts to resolve the Zimbabwean crisis—seen as a threat to the entire subregion. Considered the most significant step taken by SADC in its twenty-year history, but with unclear consequences for human rights, was the creation of a southern Africa free trade zone, which came into effect on September 1, 2000.

At a meeting in Windhoek in March, through a Protocol on Politics, Defense and Security Cooperation, SADC turned the chairmanship of its security organ into a one-year rotating position with clear reporting lines to the heads of state. President Robert Mugabe had held this position since 1999; he was replaced by President Joachim Chissano of Mozambique. This summit committed the community's fourteen members to resolving conflicts in the region and for the first time adopted operational principles and rules for the security organ. Nevertheless, going into the August summit in Blantyre, Malawi, all sources pointed to a continuation of low key "quiet diplomacy" towards Zimbabwe. But the final communiqué of the Blantyre summit for the first time publicly "expressed concern on the effects of the Zimbabwe economic situation on the region," and in the months following, SADC took a more active role in trying to find a solution. When an initially promising deal brokered in August by the Commonwealth in Abuja, Nigeria, started to break down, SADC leaders convened a further meeting in Harare in September. There they were reported to have pressed President Mugabe to settle the crisis, and some appeared ready to break ranks with him, a big change from "quiet diplomacy." The meeting ended with a recommitment by Harare to end land seizures in exchange for funding by Britain of its land reform program; once again, the commitment seemed to have little effect. Meanwhile on September 20, SADC agreed to create a special ministerial task force on land issues in the region, the Food, Agriculture and Natural Resources Directorate.

Economic Community of West African States (ECOWAS)

Like its southern African counterpart, ECOWAS added force to its Protocol relating to the Mechanism for Conflict Prevention, Management, Resolution, Peace-keeping and Security, signed in Lomé, Togo in December 1999. However, human rights considerations remained low on the various diplomatic agendas pursued, and ECOWAS member states demonstrated a general unwillingness to criticize each other's human rights records.

ECOWAS took the lead in rejuvenating the troubled Sierra Leonean peace process by facilitating a ceasefire agreement between the government of Sierra Leone and the rebel Revolutionary United Front (RUF), signed on November 10, 2000 in Abuja, Nigeria. In December 2000, the heads of state of the fifteen-member organization directed the deployment of a force along the borders of Guinea, Liberia, and Sierra Leone. But the entire plan was abandoned after it ran into major hurdles. Guinea argued that force's mandate was too weak; neither Guinea nor Liberia signed the status of forces agreement; and ECOWAS insisted upon U.N. Security Council involvement and funding.

In May 2001, the ECOWAS Mediation and Security Council, the United Nations, the Government of Sierra Leone, and the RUF met in Abuja to review the implementation of the peace deal. The review meeting stressed the need for the Sierra Leonean government to facilitate the restoration of authority to areas previously under RUF control where UNAMSIL, the U.N. peacekeeping force, had been deploying. During the meeting, a six-member RUF delegation agreed to withdraw its combatants from Kambia district, a point of departure for infiltration into neighboring Guinea. The withdrawal would enable the deployment of troops from the Sierra Leone Army to ensure the cessation of armed incursions into the two countries.

Some progress was also recorded towards the implementation of the Plan of Action of the April, 2000 Accra Declaration on War-Affected Children in West

Africa. In March, ECOWAS and Canada signed an agreement for the establishment of a Child Protection Unit within the ECOWAS Secretariat.

THE INTERNATIONAL RESPONSE

Human Rights on Hold?

The events of September 11, 2001, seemed destined to reduce yet further the chances of serious diplomatic attention to human rights issues in Africa by the wider international community. With the spotlight on efforts to build and maintain a global anti-terrorism coalition, there was likely to be more tolerance towards countries that had previously been castigated as human rights abusers. At this writing, it was already evident that talk about human rights, good governance, and accountability was markedly reduced, and abuses more easily tolerated, as the U.S. in particular became more preoccupied with short-term considerations such as access to intelligence, airfields, and military bases.

But the more the international community uncritically aligned itself with autocratic regimes in exchange for their support, facilities, and cooperation, the more it risked unwittingly creating long-term instability, perfect conditions for further terrorist support. A more prudent policy would seek to prevent security issues from disproportionately influencing dealings with Africa. First, it would be essential to continue to support movement toward democracy and respect for human rights on the basis of explicit benchmarks. Second, as supplements to human rights protection, economic and social uplift would be key. Third, external pressure—rather than silence and condemnation—would be a prerequisite for meaningful political and economic development.

United Nations

The U.N. was engaged in a wide variety of African crises, including those in Angola, DRC, Eritrea, Ethiopia, Liberia, and Sierra Leone, and showed a greater sense of urgency and commitment than in the previous year.

There was a renewed focus on demobilization, the peace process, political dialogue, and economic rehabilitation in the DRC. Two groundbreaking reports, in which the U.N. showed an increased willingness to "name and shame" individuals involved in the illicit arms-for-diamonds trade, examined the link between the exploitation of natural resources and the fueling of conflict. On Liberia/Sierra Leone, U.N. efforts centered on deploying targeted sanctions to stem the flow of illicit diamonds and arms flows; in May 2001, the purchase of diamonds exported from Liberia (believed to originate mainly from rebel-held territory in Sierra Leone) was banned; and in December 2000 and November 2001 the committee monitoring these sanctions followed the example of the Angola committee in issuing hard-hitting reports. There was also some forward movement toward the setting up of a special court for Sierra Leone and enhancing the capability of the U.N. peacekeeping force to protect the civilian population there—though the human rights agenda was still often trumped by political considerations. With respect to Angola, the main activity concentrated on monitoring and verification by the sanctions panel on arms and illicit diamonds and on improving the response of government and U.N. agencies to the needs of internally displaced persons.

The U.N. began to engage with the issues surrounding HIV/AIDS, so key for Africa. The Security Council discussed AIDS three times over eighteen months, including a meeting in the summer of 2000 in which, for the first time, the pandemic was characterized as a security concern. In late June 2001, the first ever General Assembly session about a disease was held. Secretary-General Kofi Annan officially declared the creation of a Global Fund to fight AIDS, tuberculosis, and malaria, hoping to raise U.S. $7-10 billion for the purpose. However, nothing like this sum had been pledged by November, while NGOs criticized a lack of transparency in administering the fund and an implicit refusal to use the money for treatment as well as prevention. Annan also met with the executives of the seven major drug firms to investigate ways of lowering the price of HIV/AIDS drugs. Both the World Health Organization (WHO) and UNAIDS welcomed the offers by Indian pharmaceuticals manufacturer Cipla to provide drugs at low prices. The WHO advocated "differential pricing" of drugs on the basis of a country's economic strength to the World Trade Organization; though this was partly a concession to drug company resistance to a global reduction in prices. The International Labor Organization put out guidelines on AIDS in the workplace and joined UNAIDS. The World Food Programme launched several special feeding projects for people living with HIV/AIDS, including one in Congo. Though criticized as tokenistic, they were at least a recognition of the need.

European Union

Though the lack of coherence in European Union (E.U.) policy towards Africa endured, there were attempts to remedy the problem through improved coordination. France and the United Kingdom, the dominant players, continued to state a commitment to ending their tradition of competitive foreign policies toward Africa, though the practice did not always live up to the rhetoric. Clear policy differences among key European players remained, and were evident in policy conflicts among E.U. member states, especially the U.K. and France, regarding Côte d'Ivoire, the Mano River Countries, the Great Lakes, and Zimbabwe. While Britain spoke out strongly against President Robert Mugabe of Zimbabwe, for example, France's President Jacques Chirac received the president in Paris after a special OAU summit in Libya focusing on the African Union. The British foreign office was quoted as being shocked by the French decision.

Under the Swedish presidency, the E.U. appointed Hans Dahlgren, the state secretary of the Swedish Ministry of Foreign Affairs, as its special envoy to Guinea, Liberia, and Sierra Leone, responsible for framing a coordinated E.U. policy on the three countries and promoting cooperation with the U.N. and the Economic Community of West African States. Dahlgren affirmed the E.U.'s support for sanctions against Liberia. An E.U. delegation led by Dahlgren visited Mali, Guinea, Sierra Leone, and Liberia between May 29 and June 1. Talks focused on the serious humanitarian and political crisis in the region. The visit included meetings with the presidents of the four states and representatives of relief organizations and civil society. The E.U.'s special envoy to Ethiopia and Eritrea, Sen. Rino Serri, appointed in December 1999, played an important role in ensuring that human rights issues were highlighted in Europe's response to the conflict between and developments within the two countries.

The E.U. invoked article 96 of the Cotonou Agreement, the human rights clause of the document regulating its relations with members of the African-Caribbean-Pacific (ACP) group of countries, in relation to Côte d'Ivoire, Liberia, and Zimbabwe in 2001, calling for consultations on worsening respect for human rights, democratic principles, and rule of law. The E.U. also acted in unison in protest at the crackdown by the Eritrea government on dissenters. All member states recalled their ambassadors for consultations after Eritrea expelled the Italian ambassador following his critical comments about the government's human rights record. At a meeting in October with the heads of state of Algeria, Nigeria, Senegal, South Africa, and the representative of Egypt's head of state, E.U. officials committed the union to supporting the NAI.

However, the same coordinated approach was absent in policy regarding the Great Lakes, where the E.U. seemed to defer to Belgian and French leadership. The United Kingdom continued its support for Rwanda and Uganda, while other member states, especially France and Belgium, leaned more toward Kinshasa. On June 30, Belgian Prime Minister Guy Verhofstad signaled the resumption of bilateral cooperation with the DRC by signing a new aid package, dedicated to health, education, and infrastructure. He also pledged to use Belgium's six-month presidency of the E.U. to lobby other member states to reengage with the DRC. The E.U.'s special envoy for the Great Lakes, Aldo Ajello, continued to be active on the diplomatic front for the E.U. The region was also visited by several high-level European delegations, including the Belgian prime minister and foreign minister, and E.U. commissioner Poul Nielson. For his part, French Foreign Minister Hubert Vedrine visited the region in August.

The ACP-E.U. Joint Parliamentary Assembly sent a delegation on a fact-finding mission to Sudan from June 26 to July 2, 2001. In a September report, the delegation urged the Sudanese government to improve its record in human rights and also noted that the record of rebel groups on human rights "is also very far from being acceptable." By resolution of November 1, 2001, the ACP-E.U. Joint Parliamentary Assembly stated that it believes the SPLM/A should not seek formal control over any E.U. funding, which would then allow for resumption of E.U. humanitarian assistance to SPLA areas. It also called on the government of Sudan to take more effective action against torture, discrimination against Christians, and abductions (which particularly affect women and children).

United Kingdom

Prime Minister Tony Blair of the United Kingdom pledged to make Africa a priority of the Labor Party's second term. In July 2001, during the G-8 Summit in Genoa, the prime minister announced plans to build on the launch of the U.S. $1.5

billion U.N. global health fund with a five-point "modernization plan" for Africa linking trade, aid, investment, conflict resolution, and the fight against AIDS to combat poverty in the world's poorest continent. Britain would provide $200 million to the U.N. fund. While debt campaigners criticized the fund as "inadequate" and "a gimmick," it did at least represent a commitment to the continent rare among Western leaders. Britain was one of the few wealthy countries that actually increased aid to Africa during the year, though from a low base. Government officials linked the commitment to a government white paper of December 2000 entitled "Eliminating World Poverty: Making Globalization Work for the Poor." Like other European countries, however, Britain refused to accede to the demand made at the World Conference Against Racism that the historical slave trade be acknowledged as a crime against humanity for which reparations were due.

The United Kingdom backed the "New African Initiative," under which poor countries would receive financial help and better access to rich Western markets in return for cleaning up their governments and economic reform. The prime minister renewed his pledge in September at a meeting with six "reforming" African presidents—of Botswana, Ghana, Mozambique, Nigeria, Senegal, and Tanzania—focused on trade, good governance, and conflict resolution. The only public statement from the meeting, however, was a response to the September 11 attacks and the question of terrorism.

Additionally, the U.K. continued to play a central role in the stabilization of Sierra Leone. Jonathan Riley, the then British brigadier commanding in Sierra Leone, pledged in January that British troops would stay until the RUF was either defeated militarily or diplomatically. The U.K. also continued its commitment to rebuild the Sierra Leonean army and police. From June 2000 through September, some six hundred British troops were involved in training 8,500 Sierra Leonean Army soldiers. After September 2001, the 360 U.K. military personnel who remained would continue to play a major role in advising and directing military operations, including the staffing of key positions within the Sierra Leonean defense headquarters. Other sectors which benefited from British aid included demobilization programs, human rights and civil society groups, rehabilitation of the legal system, humanitarian aid and programs, and the restoration of local government. Concerns remained, however, that among the newly-trained soldiers were many human rights abusers.

International Development Minister Clare Short showed unusual interest in the DRC. In early August, she made a focused three-day visit to the country. On top of her agenda was the role the United Kingdom could play in supporting the demobilization and reintegration of armed groups in the region. In previous years, she had focused her attention principally on Rwanda and Uganda—problematically offering uncritical support for those governments.

France

France reiterated previous statements of the main elements of its rethought Africa policy: loyalty to a tradition of commitment and solidarity, modernization of France's cooperation machinery, and the opening up of France's policy to embrace the whole of the continent. In April, Prime Minister Lionel Jospin insisted that his country's approach marked a new era: a break with the imperialist past and a new pragmatism which would be based on noninterference in domestic African issues. During an official visit to South Africa, Prime Minister Jospin insisted that Paris had decided to break with its networks of influence in its former colonies. South Africa, he said, was a country he called "a strategic axis not only in French African policy but also in French international policy." His statements were supposedly put to the test by an attempted coup d'état in the Central African Republic. France did not intervene in Bangui. However, France was also reluctant to openly criticize "old friends," or apply diplomatic pressure aimed at improving human rights in former French colonies, including Burkina Faso, Togo, and Côte d'Ivoire (where new president Laurent Gbagbo's longstanding links to socialist politicians in Paris protected him from serious pressure to ensure accountability for election atrocities).

France's military training program in Africa, the *Renforcement des Capacités Africaines de Maintien de la Paix* (Recamp), continued. In May, military officers and diplomats from fifteen African countries and twenty non-African partners met to prepare for a military exercise scheduled for Tanzania in February 2002, the first big Recamp event in non-francophone southern Africa. Britain, previously skeptical about the initiative, also attended; future U.S. cooperation was discussed, with its own Africa Crisis Response Initiative up for review. However, Recamp did not effectively screen trainees for the purpose of excluding known human rights abusers.

International Monetary Fund and World Bank

In February 2001, the heads of the International Monetary Fund (IMF) and World Bank undertook an unprecedented tour of Africa, visiting Kenya, Mali, Nigeria, and Tanzania, and meeting leaders from most of sub-Saharan Africa. The Bank's vice-president for Africa asserted, "We are working with Africa very differently from the way we have worked in the past," underlining a shift in jargon of the Bretton Woods institutions over the previous two years from the predominance of "structural adjustment" to "poverty reduction."

The two institutions worked more proactively toward rapid implementation of the Highly Indebted Poor Countries (HIPC) program in twenty-three countries, nineteen of which were in Africa. Benin, Burkina Faso, Cameroon, Chad, Gambia, Guinea, Guinea-Bissau, Madagascar, Malawi, Mali, Mauritania, Mozambique, Niger, Rwanda, Senegal, São Tomé and Príncipe, Tanzania, Uganda, Zambia reached their "decision point," at which it was decided that they qualified for relief under the enhanced HIPC Initiative. The twenty-three countries were receiving relief which could amount to some U.S. $34 billion over time. Uganda and Mozambique reached "completion point," indicating they had established a track record of good performance under the original HIPC initiative and qualified for additional relief. Zambia ($2.5 billion), Tanzania ($2 billion), Mozambique ($2 billion), Cameroon ($1.3 billion) and Uganda ($1 billion) topped the December 2000 list of the African countries receiving the greatest dollar value of committed debt relief.

Guinea-Bissau had the greatest percentage of debt reduction, at over 80 percent. Yet the World Bank itself acknowledged that any benefits expected from HIPC would likely be wiped out by a worldwide slump in commodity prices. In the wake of the September 11 attacks, the IMF gave assurances that it would be ready to make additional resources available to African countries experiencing problems as a result of a downturn in the world economy.

The IMF, backed by the U.S. and U.K., refused to renew lending to Kenya in August, citing corruption. In September, responding to the crisis in Zimbabwe, the IMF announced that it had barred the country from future IMF loans or use of its general resources. An agreement with Nigeria, however, was extended in August, despite the failure of the government to observe the conditions set, and both the World Bank and IMF ramped up their support for the DRC. They facilitated the preparation of the government's program for a meeting of bilateral and multilateral donors in early July in Paris. In late July, the IMF approved a staff-monitored program and a U.S. $50 million grant for the economic recovery program. The two institutions also expressed willingness to assist the DRC to address its debt of U.S. $800 million owed to them.

The World Bank, under the leadership of James Wolfensohn, came to see HIV/AIDS as one of the central issues it had to address. However, instead of the debt reduction hoped for in severely AIDS-affected countries, the bank played an old tune, offering U.S. $500 million in additional loans for sub-Saharan Africa, to be used almost exclusively for prevention.

United States

Even before the September 11 attacks, Africa had low expectations of the new U.S. administration under President George W. Bush. During his campaign for the presidency Bush barely mentioned Africa. When specifically asked about his vision for the continent, his reply was terse: "While Africa may be important, it doesn't fit into the national strategic interests, as far as I can see them."

But after coming into office, the administration's approach was somewhat nuanced. Confronted by the continuing armed conflicts that ravaged large parts of Africa, including the wars in Angola, Burundi, DRC, Liberia, and Sierra Leone, the administration started sending signals that it would continue to play a role in resolving Africa's crises and in particular would seek to play a more neutral role in the Great Lakes wars. But U.S interest in peacemaking or peacekeeping remained minimal and official statements still focused mainly on trade and investment, revealing a fundamental lack of engagement with human rights issues. However, the administration exhibited some interest in training African armies to perform peacekeeping functions, and the U.S. trained battalions during the year from Ghana, Nigeria, and Senegal, and prepared to train troops from Guinea. Walter Kansteiner, assistant secretary of state for African affairs, told Congress at his May confirmation hearing: "Sub-Saharan Africa is a priority for this administration. We are not immune from Africa's problems," and proceeded to list them as being the spread of HIV/AIDS, rampant poverty, and civil strife. In line with this tack, it was not surprising that senior U.S. officials argued that the mandate of UNAMSIL, the

U.N. peacekeeping force in Sierra Leone, should be extended not because of the civilian population at risk, but because of the criminal networks in the country that would undermine U.S. economic and political interests.

Secretary of State Colin Powell undertook a trip to the region in May, visiting Mali, Uganda, Kenya, and South Africa. Powell stated: "We cannot ignore any place in the world, and Africa is a huge continent in great need—so we have to be engaged." A major focus of the trip was HIV/AIDS. He also discussed regional conflicts, including with leaders of the DRC and Sudan, but the broad message throughout the trip appeared to be that Africa's future depended on the actions of its own leaders, not the international community. Echoing the administration's plans to use trade as a major tool and to send aid primarily to countries it viewed as making economic and political progress, Powell said, "Money loves security and stability." The United States Trade Representative for Africa revisited this theme in a speech to the Congressional Black Caucus on September 28, when he reiterated the administration's belief that the Africa Growth and Opportunity Act (AGOA) was the primary vehicle for U.S. trade and development in Africa. This underlined the continuity in Africa policy since the Clinton administration. Although there was a change in attitude and style towards Africa, the strategic priorities remained the same, namely economic. For the Bush team, this implied greater interest in free trade and open markets; though the concessions to Africa offered by AGOA were in fact limited.

Notwithstanding Colin Powell's vow of engagement, in practice the Bush administration remained detached from African issues, seemingly preferring, with the exception of Sudan, to defer to the Europeans, or to the so-called anchor states of South Africa and Nigeria. Sudan galvanized sustained high-level attention because of a powerful coalition of religious and conservative forces that pressured the administration to take a stronger line against the Khartoum government. The establishment in September of the position of special envoy to Sudan mirrored that pressure. President Bush named former U.S. Senator John Danforth to the position, saying, "Sudan is a disaster for all human rights. We must turn the eyes of the world upon the atrocities in Sudan."

The withdrawal of the U.S. delegation from the World Conference Against Racism, Racial Discrimination, Xenophobia and Related Intolerance, held in South Africa from August 31 to September 8, showed disregard for African activists as well as the efforts devoted to the event within the region. What could have been an excellent opportunity for the U.S. to contribute to the understanding and remedy of such serious issues as discrimination against refugees, sexism, and the disproportionate impact of HIV/AIDS on people of color resulted instead in disappointment.

In the wake of the September attacks, it was likely that the administration's interest would be focused on the Horn and East Africa (embracing Sudan, Eritrea, Ethiopia, Kenya, Somalia, and Tanzania). Sudan was reported to have offered extensive cooperation with the U.S., including sharing intelligence on the al-Qaeda network. Reports suggested that beyond Afghanistan, Somalia might be a target of U.S. military operations in pursuit of al-Qaeda cells. That would significantly reshape U.S. relations with the subregion, with potentially serious human rights implications. Throughout the continent, there was concern that enhanced cooperation with the U.S. on the terrorism agenda would silence criticism of allies' attacks on domestic political enemies. National security adviser Condoleezza Rice insisted that in building alliances, it was "clear our job is to make certain that we draw a line in all our discussions between legitimate dissent or legitimate movements for the rights of minorities, and the fact that there may be international terrorism in various parts of the world." However, past conduct by the U.S. on making such human rights issues a priority—prior to the September attacks when the stakes for the U.S. were much lower—did not back her assurances.

For example, in the case of Ethiopia, the U.S. had rarely spoken out and exerted no meaningful pressure when abuses—including excessive force against demonstrators, silencing of dissent, and the violent repression of minorities in restless regions—were perpetrated by the government. On the contrary, the government was rewarded with generous aid packages. In the wake of September 11, exchanges between Ethiopia and the U.S. increased, but were focused exclusively on antiterrorism rather than any human rights concerns. In one of the only three telephone calls to African leaders reported prior to launching the strikes against Afghanistan, President Bush spoke with Prime Minister Meles of Ethiopia on October 5, thanking him for his offer to cooperate in the campaign against terrorism and discussing his intent to take action against terrorists and their sanctuaries. Mainstreaming human rights considerations was not on the agenda.

Colin Powell, during his whirlwind tour of Africa, had praised democratic trends in Kenya but emphasized the importance of constitutional rule, hinting at Kenya's need for a thorough constitutional review. His comments were widely viewed by observers as a diplomatic way of saying that President Moi should step down from the presidency in 2002, as he was required to do so by the constitution. But September 11 might have pushed such concerns to the back burner. According to a White House press release, the president spoke with President Moi of Kenya on October 5, emphasizing the need for cooperation on many fronts—financial, intelligence, diplomatic, and military. He suggested further talks between the United States and Kenya on how to meet the challenges ahead. Again, there appeared to be no room for valuing human rights as integral to regional security.

When a State Department spokesperson was asked about the implications of coalition making for U.S. policy regarding Sudan, he responded that cooperation with the U.S. would not relieve Sudan of its responsibility to terminate its abusive domestic practices, including denial of humanitarian access, bombing attacks on humanitarian operations and civilian targets, and religious discrimination. The spokesperson contended that all those issues remained firmly fixed on the U.S agenda despite an alignment with Sudan to fight terror. It remained to be seen, however, whether the demands of the terrorism coalition would override human rights and humanitarian concerns, in this and other cases.

THE WORK OF HUMAN RIGHTS WATCH

While focusing on areas of prolonged conflict, Human Rights Watch continued to cover all of sub-Saharan Africa and to expand monitoring of French-speaking countries. We carried out research and advocacy on Angola, Burundi, Côte d'Ivoire,

Democratic Republic of Congo (DRC), Eritrea, Ethiopia, Guinea-Conakry, Kenya, Liberia, Nigeria, Mozambique, Rwanda, Sierra Leone, South Africa, Sudan, Tanzania, Uganda, Zambia, and Zimbabwe. Additionally, the Africa division tackled cross-country, thematic research on arms flows, natural resources and corporate responsibility, national human rights commissions, and the rights of children, women, refugees, and the internally displaced. We also increased the level and scope of our monitoring of non-state actors, placing special focus on the violence perpetrated by rebel forces, and practical methods to influence them through dialogue and third country leverage.

We fielded investigative and advocacy missions to Angola, Burundi, Côte d'Ivoire, DRC, Gambia, Guinea-Conakry, Kenya, Nigeria, Rwanda, South Africa, Tanzania, Uganda, Zambia, and Zimbabwe. Human Rights Watch maintained field offices in Kigali, Rwanda; Freetown, Sierra Leone; and Bujumbura, Burundi.

Human Rights Watch continued its strong collaboration with national human rights organizations. Behind the scenes, we continued to build the capacity of local NGOs to effect change on the human rights record in their countries. When human rights defenders were harassed, Human Rights Watch pushed for diplomatic measures to end the problem. In October 2001, Human Rights Watch published a briefing paper, *Freedom of Association at Risk: The Proposed NGO Bill and Current Restrictions on NGOs in Uganda,* about a new law before the Ugandan parliament that would severely limit or curtail the rights of NGOs whose work did not conform with "government policies or plans."

The Great Lakes region remained a priority, as the conflict in the DRC continued to involve and spill over into all neighboring states. In meetings with senior officials in Washington, New York, Brussels, Berlin, London, and in the region, and in presentations to United Nations bodies, Human Rights Watch continued to highlight the exploitation of resources and illegal importation of arms that added fuel to the conflagration. In a March 2001 report, *Uganda in Eastern DRC: Fueling Political and Ethnic Strife,* we explicated the role of Uganda in escalating the conflict in eastern Congo, and called on the Ugandan government and rebel groups to alleviate the suffering they were causing there.

Enhancing the organization's work on economic and social rights, Human Rights Watch published two reports addressing the indivisibility of human rights. In *Uprooting the Rural Poor in Rwanda,* we detailed the government practice of forced villagization and dispossession of land of tens of thousands of impoverished Hutu and Tutsi in the countryside. In *Unequal Protection: The State Response to Violent Crime on South African Farms,* we highlighted rural violence and abuses against farm workers. Another report on South Africa, *Scared at School: Sexual Violence Against Girls in South African Schools,* complemented previous work on violence against women in South Africa by considering the danger girls faced in schools as a violation of the right to education.

Human Rights Watch extended its Africa-wide advocacy through the publication of a major report on the performance of government-sponsored human rights commissions, *Protectors or Pretenders? Government Human Rights Commissions in Africa.* The study reported on the often disappointing record of these commissions, which had received large sums of money for their creation from the donor community. The report found that many commissions did more to deflect international criticisms of their government than to solve human rights problems, but also singled out the commissions of Uganda, Ghana, and South Africa as exceptions. The study was widely circulated amongst donors to national human rights institutions—including the Office of the U.N. High Commissioner for Human Rights and the United Nations Development Program—as well as to high-level government officials and the human rights commissions themselves, and catalyzed a larger debate about the roles and expectations of such commissions.

Violence surrounding elections was a particular focus of the division during the year, with a report on the manipulation of the electoral system and accompanying violence in Uganda (*Uganda: Not a Level Playing Field*) and a detailed report on Côte d'Ivoire (*The New Racism: The Political Manipulation of Ethnicity in Côte d'Ivoire*) published at the time of the World Conference Against Racism in Durban. The latter report chronicled wide-scale torture, murder, and rape, and the official manipulation of ethnic tensions during presidential and parliamentary elections in Côte d'Ivoire in late 2000, garnering intense media interest. Human Rights Watch also alerted the international community to governmental interference and irregularities in local elections in Rwanda.

Throughout the year we remained active on international justice issues. Human Rights Watch experts took part in genocide trials in Belgium and at the International Criminal Tribunal for Rwanda (ICTR) in Arusha, Tanzania, acting as expert witnesses on the human rights situation in the Rwanda. We also called upon the international community to invest in the future of Sierra Leone by funding its special court for the prosecution of crimes related to the decade long conflict.

Human Rights Watch intervened regularly to protest abuse of refugees and internally displaced. Our report on the treatment of refugees in Guinea, *Refugees Still at Risk: Continuing Refugee Protection Concerns in Guinea*, documented harassment and assault of Sierra Leonean and Liberian refugees by Guinean security personnel and civilians, leading to changes in the provisions for those in refugee camps there.

ANGOLA

HUMAN RIGHTS DEVELOPMENTS

Civil war persisted in Angola, accompanied by a dramatic escalation of violations of the laws of war. The National Union for the Total Independence of Angola (UNITA), a rebel group led by Jonas Savimbi, killed, abducted, and terrorized civilians with impunity. Government forces abused civilians during forced relocations and beat or killed civilians displaced in the course of looting, extortion, and forced recruitment of boys and men.

The situation worsened since the breakdown of the Lusaka Peace Protocol in mid-1998 when UNITA resumed fighting. In 2001, the numbers of internally displaced persons grew to over four million, and some 435,000 Angolan refugees lived in camps in the Democratic Republic of Congo (DRC), Zambia, and Namibia. Within Angola, security was limited to areas within a narrow perimeter around the government-controlled provincial capitals and the major municipalities, making safe land travel almost impossible. Humanitarian aid delivered by air only reached 10 to 15 percent of Angola. Ambushes of civilians and humanitarian workers increased, preventing travel by humanitarian ground convoys and impeding delivery of aid to thousands in desperate need.

UNITA stepped up hit-and-run tactics against civilians. Rebels used terror as a policy, to obtain supplies and coerce and intimidate civilians. Indiscriminate killings, mutilation of limbs or ears, and beatings were used by rebels to punish suspected government sympathizers or as a warning against betraying UNITA. UNITA continued to forcibly recruit men and teenage boys to fight. Girls were held in sexual slavery and used as a source of forced labor.

In an apparent bid for international attention, UNITA struck against government targets several times while foreign officials visited Angola. For instance, in early May the visiting United Nations (U.N.) secretary general's special adviser for Africa, Ibrahim Gambari, commented that "Progress is being made to find solutions for the conflict and to end war in Angola." But on May 5 the rebels attacked Caxito, a provincial capital sixty kilometers north of the capital, Luanda, killing more than 150 people and kidnapping sixty children from a Danish-run orphanage. After an international outcry, rebels handed over the children to a Catholic mission.

Similarly, during a visit by a U.S. delegation, the Consortium for Electoral and Political Processes Strengthening (CEPPS), there to evaluate conditions for national elections, UNITA blew up a train 130 kilometers from Luanda. Passengers fleeing the flames were ambushed, leaving 256 dead and more than 170 wounded. During the last week of August alone, rebels killed 268 civilians. On August 31, they ambushed a bus near Cacolo, thirty kilometers from Malanje, and set the bus on fire with passengers still alive inside, killing fifty-three passengers.UNITA deliberately targeted humanitarian workers and aircraft. On April 15, they looted a warehouse belonging to relief organizations in Benguela province. In June, rebels launched missiles towards two planes carrying relief supplies near the cities of Kuito and Luena. That same month, they attacked the city of Uige, forcing evacuation of U.N. and other humanitarian workers. Civilian vehicles were also ambushed in Bie, Benguela, Huila, Cuanza Sul, Cuanza Norte and Malanje provinces. During a May 14 attack on a truck convoy in Benguela, two people were killed and fifty kidnapped.

In late 2000, government forces mounted an attack on UNITA forces in central Angola. Fighting reached neighboring Namibia, with Namibian troops taking part. In November, a government assault in Malanje aimed at controlling towns near the DRC border drove many civilians to Malanje's provincial capital. UNITA regained control of the area in February and March, leading the government to undertake another campaign in April. When no displaced civilians appeared, concerns arose over their safety. Also in February, UNITA forces held the town of Quibaxe in Bengo province, killing and abducting many civilians and causing others to flee. An estimated 8,000 people from Quibaxe were missing.

Unprecedented numbers of internally displaced persons were registered in twelve of the eighteen provinces throughout the year, with an average of 30,000 new arrivals each month. The most affected areas were Golungo Alto, Caxito, Mussende, Camacupa Cuemba, and Matala. Humanitarian services were overburdened. In Matala, in January, for instance, some 28,000 displaced persons were living in desperate conditions and the average of seventy new arrivals registering daily found no food, shelter, or health care. In September, there were some 60,000 newly displaced with 24,000 in the provinces of Cuando Cubango, Moxico, Luanda Sul and Norte, and 10,000 in Bie province alone. As of early October, there were 160,000 in Kuito and 60,000 in Camacupa and Catabola. Eight people died daily in Cuemba from lack of food and medicine.

The internally displaced primarily suffered abuses at the hands of UNITA. Yet allegations of abuse by government forces continued, ranging from forced relocation to killing and looting. Violations occurred mainly during military operations and while army and police implemented "limpeza" ("cleansing") operations near recently recaptured towns, to clear the area of the local residents, ostensibly for their safety, but thereby depriving UNITA of a potential source of food and labor. During cleansing operations, government troops forced families to move from the area carrying goods looted by the army; those who refused were beaten or killed. Allegations of soldiers raping women during these operations were confirmed in Moxico and Malanje provinces.

Those driven from their home areas by government forces were in many cases first moved to the government-controlled municipalities. Conditions for the displaced in these areas were often terrible, with insufficient assistance, sanitation, health services, and security. In addition to extortion, the army also forced displaced persons to accompany government troops to search for food in mined or otherwise insecure areas. When the numbers in the municipalities became overwhelming, the government relocated the displaced women, elderly, and children to internally displaced camps on the outskirts of the provincial capitals under government control. Men and adolescent boys were often forced to remain in combat areas to fight.

Gains were made in strengthening the legal framework to protect the internally displaced—a new law, the Norms for the Resettlement of the Internally Displaced, was passed in January 2001, and several other plans of action were drafted. However, practical mechanisms for their implementation were not put in place, particularly at the provincial and municipal levels. Many of the internally displaced camps were located at the outskirts of government-controlled towns, serving in effect as a human shield or buffer zone against UNITA attacks. The internally displaced were regularly subjected to assaults at the hands of the security forces in the camps and served as a source of exploitable labor by nearby landowners. Regular looting and extortion by the security forces of the displaced populations provided a source of goods, including food, to the security forces, which were often not paid for months.

A continuing flow of military arms and equipment sustained the conflict. On February 26, Spanish authorities intercepted a Georgian freighter in the Canary Islands en route to Angola, carrying an undeclared 636-ton cargo of Russian-made weapons. On September 30, a shipment of five hundred anti-tank rockets from Iran bound for Angola was seized at Bratislava airport. Two days later, the Angolan army uncovered a large cache of weapons close to the Mavinga airport.

In one positive development, government use of antipersonnel mines appeared to decline in 2001. Nevertheless, troops reportedly laid mines at night around defensive positions, removing them in the morning. UNITA continued to lay mines to prevent residents from fleeing to government-held areas or to keep them from reaching their fields. Rebels also used anti-vehicle mines to interrupt transportation and ambush humanitarian convoys and civilian vehicles. 70 percent of the casualties were civilians, and more than half were displaced people fleeing fighting.

Freedom of expression in Angola remained a concern. Restrictions on journalists continued, despite assurances by the vice minister of social communications, who met with the Committee to Protect Journalists in October 2000 and May 2001. On July 7, Gilberto Neto, a reporter for the independent weekly *Folha 8*, and Philippe Lebillon, a researcher from the London-based Overseas Development Institute, were arrested at an airport in Malanje province and escorted back to Luanda. During interrogation at the National Directorate of Criminal Investigation, their documentation and equipment were confiscated.

Neto was also blocked from leaving the country at Luanda International Airport on August 23. He was charged with endangering state security and defaming the police. (He had reported in 1999 on a police raid on the independent, church-affiliated Radio Ecclesia.) The charges were not pursued in court. In an earlier case in December 2000, immigration authorities at Luanda Airport prevented Raphael Marques, a free-lance journalist, from leaving Angola. They confiscated his passport and he was sent home without explanation, although he carried a provincial court order lifting any travel restriction against him. In July, several reporters, including British Broadcasting Corporation (BBC) correspondents, faced obstacles in covering the violent forcible relocation of residents from the Boa Vista district of Luanda. On the positive side, Radio Ecclesia resumed broadcasting countrywide. That same month, the director of Radio Morena in Benguela was dismissed following a broadcast about a UNITA attack.

While authorities allowed some open discussion of public affairs, especially through the privately owned media, it cracked down on opposition political parties by denying freedom of association and assembly, in some cases violently. In December 2000, the army seriously injured a Catholic deacon suspected of being a sympathizer of the separatist Front for the Liberation of the Cabinda Enclave (FLEC) and beat other members of the church. A month later, members of the army and police beat, arrested and detained eight members of the Party for Democracy and Progress in Angola (PADPA) for protesting against the government. In March, local authorities blocked the National Front for the Liberation of Angola (FNLA) from activities in Bie. In three other cases, UNITA-Renovada representatives were threatened, arrested, and tortured. The provincial secretary of the Party for Social Renovation (PRS) was detained and four militants of the Democratic Party for the Progress of the Angolan National Alliance (PDP-ANA) were detained and interrogated about their political activities. In April, the Provincial Government of Luanda dismissed a petition by church groups to organize a march on peace and human rights, and in July it refused to allow a demonstration by Boa Vista residents, citing security concerns.

DEFENDING HUMAN RIGHTS

Human rights activity increased, mainly in the capital, as the government allowed civic and church groups to discuss human rights violations and concerns about the war—for example in conferences held by two organizations, the Open Society and the Women's Movement for Peace and Development. However, the ability of human rights organizations to function outside the capital was greatly constrained by insecurity, and no human rights groups were able to obtain access to or function in UNITA-held territory. In October, D. Zacarias Camuenho, president of the Catholic Bishops' Conference of Angola and Sao Tome and a member of the Inter-Ecclesiastical Committee for Peace in Angola (COIEPA), was awarded the 2001 Sakharov Human Rights Prize by the European parliament, signaling the growing importance of the churches as a possible mediator between the two parties in the conflict. In July, COIEPA launched a sensitization campaign to end the war, while the Open Society and the Catholic Pro Peace Movement followed suit with an antiwar campaign in September.

Medicines Sans Frontieres released a report in November 2000 titled "Angola: Behind the Façade of Normalization, Manipulation, Violence and Abandoned Populations" detailing the heavy price paid by civilians in the conflict. The report highlighted the increasing violence and policy of terror by both sides, but mainly blamed UNITA. Oxfam echoed those condemnations in a September 2001 report on the catastrophic humanitarian situation of Angolans.

THE ROLE OF THE INTERNATIONAL COMMUNITY

An economic reform program agreed on by the International Monetary Fund, the World Bank, and the government of Angola in April 2000 was designed to monitor oil revenues. Angola is the second largest oil exporter in sub-Saharan Africa and gains significant revenues from its oil exports. Dampening hopes for greater government transparency and accountability, the government failed to publish required auditing reports, despite two deadline extensions. (See Business and Human Rights.)

International donors continued to criticize the government's chronic underfunding of humanitarian services for its citizens, and in recent years donor support for humanitarian operations was reduced. Donors urged the Angolan government to use its substantial revenues from oil sales on humanitarian services rather than on military spending. Additionally, with the changing military situation, the move away from conventional warfare to counterinsurgency strategies was expected to reduce military spending by the government.

United Nations

The U.N. continued to support the Angolan government's efforts to resolve the conflict. The U.N. reiterated its call to UNITA to fully implement its commitments under the 1994 Lusaka Protocol. A number of U.N. Security Council sanctions on UNITA remained in force, including an arms and petroleum embargo in force since 1993, prohibitions on diamond trading, prohibition on travel of senior UNITA officials outside Angola, and a freeze on UNITA's financial assets. The U.N.'s Monitoring Mechanism that verified compliance was extended again in October 2001.

In April and October, the Sanctions Committee's Independent Panel of Experts issued reports concluding that UNITA retained vast quantities of weapons hidden throughout Angola. The panel identified at least sixteen diamond companies responsible for sanctions busting. The report made clear that efforts to reduce the illicit diamond trade fueling the war, including U.N. sanctions, met with little success. Angola's so-called "blood diamonds" represented 5 percent of the world's rough diamond trade, with a value of U.S.$420 million a year. Smuggled through Burkina Faso, Congo, Cyprus, South Africa, Tanzania, or Zambia, these diamonds ended up in cutting centers in Belgium, India, and Israel.

Two high-level U.N. visits were made to Angola during the year. When the secretary-general's senior adviser Ibrahim Gambari visited in May, he strongly condemned UNITA, stating that it was "solely responsible for the war in Angola," and pledged U.N. assistance for reconstruction efforts. In April the special coordinator of the Network on Internal Displacement, Dennis MacNamara, visited Angola and noted the need for the U.N. to strengthen its overall capacity to address serious gaps in assistance and protection to the internally displaced.

The U.N. Office in Angola (UNOA) continued to implement capacity-building projects such as improving access to the judicial system, increasing human rights awareness through legal counseling, and supporting media programs. The appointment of a new director in July to head UNOA's human rights division was followed by the office's internal reorganization and the preparation of a strategic plan of action.

European Union

The European Union (E.U.) maintained a focus on trade and oil sales, rather than on human rights abuses. In its 2001 annual human rights report, the E.U. condemned UNITA's abuses and called on the Angolan government to assume greater responsibility for protecting displaced populations. It also recommended that the U.N. create a permanent group of independent experts to follow diamond trafficking in violation of the U.N. sanctions.

Human rights issues were also not high on the agenda of the "troika" monitors of the 1994 Lusaka Peace Agreement—Portugal, Russia, and the U.S. Since 1998, Portugal has increased export of light weapons and ammunitions, including to Angola, in violation of the E.U. code of conduct that prevents arms sales to conflict countries where human rights are extensively violated.

United States

Good relations between Luanda and Washington concentrated largely on improving trade and investment. Angola rose in importance for the U.S. due to its vast oil resources. In ten years, the U.S. is projected to rely on Angola for 15 percent of its oil. In May, the first trade mission to Angola since September 1997 examined possibilities of corporate partnerships in the areas of data processing, industry, water systems, environment and conservation, transportation, aviation, legal services, shipping, and banking.

However, the U.S. did not always disregard human rights in relation to trade. According to the president's 2001 report on the implementation of the African Growth and Opportunity Act (AGOA), prepared by the U.S. Trade Representative, Angola did not receive AGOA beneficiary country designation due to "concerns related to corruption, labor and human rights." The report cited extrajudicial executions by security forces and scorched-earth policies by certain army units, including burning villages and killing civilians in Cuando Cubango and Lunda Sul provinces, as well as government repression of independent media. Angola was one of only ten countries that sought to participate in AGOA but was denied.

The U.S. gave some aid for humanitarian assistance and civil society activities, although it did not play a strong role in efforts to end the war. U.S. development and humanitarian assistance was over U.S. $39 million for FY 2001.

BURUNDI

HUMAN RIGHTS DEVELOPMENTS

A transitional government installed November 1 inherited a civil war in which both governmental and rebel forces were killing, raping, and otherwise injuring civilians and destroying their property. Civilian casualties in 2001, however, were fewer than in the previous seven years of warfare, in part because there were fewer large-scale massacres than in the past. The government greatly expanded a program of civil defense, giving arms training and access to weapons to thousands of civilians. According to authorities the program was meant partly to curb increases in crime but instead it led to more exactions on ordinary people. Along with theft and looting, rape increased sharply in many areas where large numbers of soldiers were posted. Hundreds of detainees were released in 2000 and early 2001 but hundreds more replaced them in the over-crowded jails by year's end. Courts functioned slowly and badly whether handling current cases or those resulting from ethnically-based killings in 1993 and 1994.

By establishing the transitional government, the former government and opposition political parties implemented a key provision of the Arusha Accord of August 2000. But the two major rebel movements, the Forces for the Defense of Democracy (Forces pour la défense de la démocratie, FDD) and the Forces for National Liberation (Forces pour la Liberation Nationale, FNL), had not signed the agreement and stepped up attacks just before and after the new government took power. Some 130 civilians and scores of government soldiers and rebels were slain in the first weeks of November as combat increased in many parts of the country. Although the new government incorporated some opposition leaders recently returned from exile, it failed to win a cease-fire in discussions with rebels held in October and November. International actors invested considerable energy in trying to end the war, with South African troops, funded by Belgium, providing security deemed necessary to establishing the new government.

Shortly after taking power, the new government signed the optional protocol to the Convention on the Rights of the Child which establishes eighteen as the minimum age for forced recruitment, conscription, or participation in armed conflict, so confirming an order of the outgoing government that children under eighteen should not be recruited for the army. But the government observed no such rule for the civil defense program, where children as young as fourteen were enrolled this year. The rebels recruited and in some cases abducted children for military service. In mid-November, the FDD kidnapped several hundred school children, the youngest thirteen years old, apparently to use them as soldiers. The majority escaped, but at the end of November a dozen remained in rebel hands.

The war in Burundi was intertwined with conflicts in the neighboring Democratic Republic of Congo (DRC) and Rwanda (see Democratic Republic of Congo and Rwanda). For several years Burundian rebels, particularly those of the FDD, had launched attacks inside Burundi from bases in the DRC. The Congolese government supported them in return for help fighting a rebel movement against it backed by neighboring Rwanda. During the year, thousands of rebel combatants came home, hastened by signs that the Congolese government was moving towards ending its own war. Hundreds of Rwandans, also previously based in the Congo and engaged in war against the Rwandan government, came into Burundi as well, perhaps to assist Burundian comrades, perhaps to prepare an assault against Rwanda. By late in the year, soldiers of the Rwandan Patriotic Army had begun fighting rebels of both groups inside Burundi. Burundian rebels based in Tanzania frequently crossed the border to raid communities inside Burundi, leading to an increase in tensions between Burundi and Tanzania which military authorities from both countries tried to calm in the latter half of the year.

Military officers opposed to President Pierre Buyoya and the terms of the Arusha Accord attempted two unsuccessful coups, one in April, the other in July. Forces loyal to the president foiled the attempts and arrested those responsible, thirty of whom were detained in the first case, some one hundred in the second. As of this writing, their detentions had not been confirmed by magistrates, a violation of legal procedure.

During the year combat intensified in the provinces of Bujumbura-rural, Cibitoke, and Bubanza in the north and in Bururi, Makamba, and Rutana in the south. In February, FNL combatants entrenched in the hills around Bujumbura took control of the Kinama neighborhood of the capital for nearly two weeks. Dozens of civilians were killed or wounded during the combat and thousands more displaced. In early April, government soldiers killed at least twenty-five civilians, including one two-year-old child, when they searched houses in Rubirizi, Mutimbuzi commune, for suspected rebels shortly after FNL combatants attacked military posts in the area. That same month, other soldiers reportedly fired on civilians in a bar in Gitega, assuming them to be rebel supporters. They killed eleven and wounded three. After an FDD attack in late June, government soldiers fired from a boat in Lake Tanganyika on the village of Rubindi, killing five civilians and seriously wounding several others. Soldiers attempting to repel FNL attacks on their posts in the vicinity of Mageyo, near Bujumbura, on September 20 killed nineteen civilians and wounded at least eighteen. Although one officer was heard to order his men not to fire at civilians, soldiers "shot at anything which moved," according to one witness. On October 4, FNL combatants shot and killed at least eight soldiers who were drinking in a bar at Muzinda market in Bubanza province. Other soldiers from nearby posts then took reprisals, firing indiscriminately on civilians in the area and looting and burning their homes and shops. One baby was shot on her mother's back as the mother was fleeing and an estimated eight other persons were also killed by soldiers. Soldiers killed at least thirteen civilians, ten of them women and children, on October 25 in Bubanza province after an attack by FNL combatants in the area. On October 30, soldiers killed forty-two civilians, eighteen of them women and children, in apparent reprisal killings after an FNL attack in Maramvya, Bujumbura-rural province. Government soldiers killed an estimated twenty civilians and wounded six others in an air attack on the Congolese village of Mwaba, which they supposed to be a FDD base. During the year several civilians were killed and many others were maimed by mines in Burundi, apparently laid by government soldiers throughout the countryside.

Hundreds of civilians died from rebel fire during combat or were slain in ambushes and robberies or were deliberately targeted for having supposedly assisted the government. In one of the worst cases, FNL rebels ambushed a bus from Rwanda near Mageyo in late December 2000. According to witnesses, they separated the passengers by ethnic group and killed twenty persons, all Tutsi or those who appeared Tutsi and one English woman. Several other persons were wounded and left for dead. Rebels, presumably of the FNL, murdered a university student and his uncle, a former soldier, in Bujumbura on September 8. FDD rebels killed civilians in ambushes on roads in the southern provinces and in raids in the eastern provinces launched from Tanzanian bases. In April, thousands of FDD rebels moved through eastern and central Burundi from the Tanzanian frontier to the Kibira forest, killing more than a dozen civilians and burning hundreds of houses, shops, health centers, and schools. In late April, FDD combatants reportedly murdered the communal administrator of Gisagara commune, Cankuzo province, and his family as well as five other civilians and in mid-November, they killed an administrator and two other civilians in Mutumba, Karuzi province. In May, FDD combatants abducted six workers of the international humanitarian agency Memisa in Makamba province and took them into Tanzania before releasing them several days later. In June, rebels, apparently FDD, killed the driver of a vehicle of the humanitarian agency Children's Aid Direct in Bubanza province and briefly detained other employees. In November, FDD combatants killed at least thirteen civilians in ambushes in eastern Burundi and on November 4 they killed another eighteen civilians in an attack on Munini in Bururi province.

In several cases unidentified assailants used grenades to attack markets or places of business. In late August, four persons were killed and more than fifty injured at Kinama market in Bujumbura.

Women reported dozens of rapes and cases of sexual torture by soldiers, many in areas in or near the part of Bujumbura taken briefly by rebels, after their withdrawal in early March. Rebels abducted scores of women to provide sexual and domestic services in their camps. Both government soldiers and rebels forced civilians to transport goods or wounded members of their forces or to do other labor in combat zones, putting them at risk of injury or death.

Authorities recruited thousands of children and young men, the vast majority of them Hutu, to expand the "Guardians of the Peace," a purportedly civilian force established with no clear legal authority or regulations. The "Guardians," many of whom were obliged to serve against their will, ordinarily operated at the direction of soldiers who also provided them with firearms to use on duty. First active in the northwest and south, "Guardians" were organized this year in most other provinces. Some guarded communities, displaced persons camps, and roads; others engaged in combat, often sent in advance of regular troops and thus exposed to greater risk of injury or death. Minimally trained and unpaid, many lived by extorting money or goods from the people they were supposed to protect. Several killed or raped local residents. Authorities also provided weapons training in urban areas, usually to Tutsi residents, and encouraged them to patrol their own neighborhoods.

The economic situation worsened, the result of years of war and stagnation exacerbated by the exhaustion of emergency funds provided by the World Bank and the European Union. With firearms easily available, armed robbery increased in the form of ambushes and attacks on homes, sometimes injuring or killing residents. Often assailants wore military uniform and could have been soldiers, rebels, or neither. Authorities proved ineffective both in halting and in prosecuting such crimes.

As stipulated by the Arusha Accord, the government drafted laws concerning genocide and provisional immunity from prosecution for certain crimes related to the 1993-1994 events. As of this writing, the legislature was still debating the terms of laws deemed a necessary precursor to the establishment of the transitional government on November 1. The accord also provided for a commission of experts comprising both international jurists and Burundians to examine the cases of political prisoners. It was due to begin work in November.

Lack of resources, difficulties with travel due to insecurity, and demoralization related to uncertainty about the future contributed to the sluggish performance of the prosecution and courts. As of mid-year, the criminal courts dealing with the ethnically-related killings of 1993-1994 had sat only once and sessions ordinarily held by itinerant courts had not been convened at all. Many cases were adjourned because judicial personnel or witnesses were not present. Judicial reforms implemented in 2000 resulted in the provisional liberation of hundreds of detainees that year, but the rate slowed noticeably during 2001. Some fifty prisoners over the age of seventy and some twenty minors were provisionally released. Although some prosecutors and police tried to follow the new regulations, others flouted measures meant to limit arbitrary detention and the use of torture. Particularly in the aftermath of the FNL occupation of part of Bujumbura, authorities detained and tortured dozens of persons whom they suspected of supporting the rebels. In several cases, persons tortured by soldiers, the police, or "Guardians of the Peace" died from their injuries. Dozens of persons were held in miserable conditions in illegal places of detention, particularly in military camps. In a number of cases authorities who had arbitrarily detained persons released them after obliging them to pay a "fine" for unspecified offenses.

Some 9,000 persons were held in prisons, about 75 percent of them awaiting trial, most accused of crimes related to the massacres of 1993-1994. Conditions improved slightly in a few prisons, largely as a result of efforts by the International Committee of the Red Cross and a local organization, the Association Burundaise de Défense des Prisonniers (ABDP), but remained very poor in others.

In 2000, the government officially closed the regroupment camps which had been established in the name of security several years before. Hundreds of thousands of persons who had been held against their will returned home, but more than 370,000 remained in camps because they feared continuing combat in their home regions. In some areas soldiers and "Guardians" demanded services from camp residents, such as transporting supplies or fetching water, or prevented them from going to work their fields unless they paid for the privilege.

Burundian authorities detained or forced back to the Congo several dozen Congolese, some of whom had recognized refugee status in the country, apparently at the request of the Rally for Congolese Democracy (RDC), the Rwandan-backed rebel authorities in eastern Congo. In May communal authorities sent more than one hundred Congolese back over the border without regard to the risks they might run in returning home. In October, authorities detained a Congolese human rights activist for nearly a week but released him after extensive protests from local and international colleagues.

On several occasions, authorities detained members of political parties or other organizations opposed to government policy. Fearing detention, the head of Pouvoir d' Auto-Dèfense Amasekanya, a Tutsi militia group, took refuge for several weeks in the office of the U.N. High Commissioner for Human Rights. A spokesman for a party opposed to President Buyoya was arrested after giving a press conference and was charged with insulting the head of state.

Authorities permitted the establishment of African Public Radio, the second major private station to operate in Burundi, but soldiers harassed its journalists, occasionally confiscating briefly their vehicles and cameras. In November, agents of the special investigations bureau detained and beat an African Public Radio journalist after he reported on the arrival of South African troops to facilitate installation of the new government. He was released after paying a fine. In March, two journalists of the other private station, Radio Bonesha, were detained and one was fined for broadcasting an interview with a rebel spokesperson.

DEFENDING HUMAN RIGHTS

Local and international human rights organizations functioned with little interference from the government. The leading human rights organization, Ligue Iteka, expanded its activities throughout the country, adding monitors to deal with economic and social rights and established a web site to disseminate its information. In one case Iteka monitors were threatened and harassed by soldiers while investigating alleged abuses. ABDP monitored prison conditions, helped detainees with judicial assistance, and organized a conference on torture where several victims spoke out publicly about their abuse by authorities.

In April, members were named to a national human rights commission that had been established the previous year. All were governmental representatives from the office of the president and vice-presidents and various ministries. At the time of writing, the commission had not published any reports.

THE ROLE OF THE INTERNATIONAL COMMUNITY

Representatives of other governments and of the United Nations, the Organization of African Unity, the European Union (E.U.), and other bodies followed the situation in Burundi closely, many of them concerned to avoid a repetition of previous massive slaughter in Burundi and of the genocide that devastated Rwanda. In addition to making numerous public statements denouncing human rights abuses and encouraging peace, they invested millions of dollars and untold diplomatic effort in negotiations for the Arusha Accord and in getting it implemented. In December 2000 donors pledged some U.S. $440 million in previously promised and new aid to help restart the economy. Little of this aid was delivered as donors awaited the installation of the new government, but in late November 2001 the E.U. agreed to deliver U.S. $58 million to rebuild infrastructure, deliver health services, and assist economic recovery, resuming development assistance halted since 1997 because of the war.

In mid-2001 officials at the U.S. National Security Council and State Department debated options, including the possible deployment of U.S. troops, should Burundi explode into large-scale violence. In the wake of the September 11 attacks, however, it became clear that the U.S. would at most fund military intervention by others. The U.S. provided $1 million in development assistance for fiscal year 2001, $3.5 million for justice under the Great Lakes Justice Initiative, and $5.8 million in food assistance.

In October, South Africa agreed to provide troops for a protection force demanded by opposition politicians before they would return to join the transitional government and Belgium pledged $5 million for their expenses with a promise to secure another $17 million from the E.U. The South African troops were supposed to be joined by others from Senegal, Nigeria, and Ghana and eventually to be replaced by a Burundian force that would be composed half of Tutsi, half of Hutu.

The U.N. special rapporteur for Burundi, Marie-Therese Keita Boucoum, visited the country twice and issued strong denunciations of human rights abuses. The field office of the High Commissioner for Human Rights, hampered by lack of funds and personnel, helped provide judicial assistance to the accused, monitored prison conditions, and undertook educational activities. It addressed abuses with authorities but published no reports locally.

The U.N. High Commission for Refugees also suffered funding cuts, hampering provision of its services, including protection, for refugees just at a time when increasing numbers of Rwandans and Congolese sought their assistance and when planning was needed for the hundreds of thousands of refugees who may return home if the war ends.

Relevant Human Rights Watch Reports

To Protect the People: The Government-Sponsored "Self-Defense" Program in Burundi, 12/01.

DEMOCRATIC REPUBLIC OF CONGO (DRC)

HUMAN RIGHTS DEVELOPMENTS

With the accession of Joseph Kabila as president of the Democratic Republic of Congo (DRC), hopes were raised in January for an end to the disastrous war that has cost more than two million lives. During the four years of war, all parties routinely attacked civilians, killing, raping, and maiming thousands. Hundreds of thousands of civilians died of hunger, diseases, or exposure as a result of the war. Belligerents this year implemented some terms of the 1999 Lusaka Accords meant to end the war: troops disengaged along the front lines, some Ugandan and Rwandan government soldiers returned home, some 1,500 Rwandan rebels laid down their arms, and United Nations troops (U.N. Organization Mission in Congo, MONUC) began monitoring compliance with the accord. But late in the year fighting still raged almost daily in the eastern provinces and the inter-Congolese dialogue among Congolese actors about the future of their country was suspended days after it began. The DRC government, supported by Zimbabwe, Angola, and Namibia, controlled the western half of the country. Rebel movements, the most important being the Congolese Rally for Democracy (RCD), backed by Rwanda, and RCD-Kisangani and the Movement for the Liberation of the Congo (MLC), both backed by Uganda, controlled the east. The Congolese government and rebel authorities declared support for political openness and Kabila implemented some reforms, but all continued to limit dissent and harass and punish journalists and human rights defenders.

Rwanda and Uganda originally claimed their troops were in Congo to fight armed groups hostile to their governments and based in the DRC. But by 2001 they seemed equally concerned to control resources, trade routes, and access to tax revenues. A U.N. Security Council expert panel reported extensive exploitation of Congolese resources by Rwandans and Ugandans, acting in both public and private capacities, underlining the importance of economic motives for the war. In November, the panel confirmed these findings and also criticized the massive exploitation of DRC resources by Kabila's allies, particularly Zimbabwe. Belgium, named in the report, set up a parliamentary commission to inquire into the role of its nationals in this exploitation.

In eastern DRC various armed groups continued the war, often acting as proxies for governments. Those which generally benefited from the support of the Congo government included Mai-Mai, militia hostile to all foreign presence; Rwandan rebels, including a nucleus of those who participated in the 1994 genocide in Rwanda, formed into the Army for the Liberation of Rwanda (ALIR) in the north and the Democratic Forces for the Liberation of Rwanda (FDLR) in the south; and Burundian rebels, usually fighting as part of the Forces for the Defense of Democracy (FDD). Those supported by Rwanda and Uganda included the armed groups linked the different branches of the RCD and MLC. In addition Rwandan army and RCD forces supported the militia of the Banyamulenge, a people generally associated with the Tutsi of Rwanda, and Ugandan forces frequently backed the Hema in their two-year-long conflict with neighboring Lendu over control of land. In the worst recent episode of this conflict which has cost some 15,000 lives, approximately four hundred Hema and Lendu were killed in Bunia in January. Burundian army troops also operated in the southern part of eastern DRC, attacking Burundian rebels and collaborating with RCD and Rwandan army soldiers.

Mai-Mai represented a diverse group of autonomous actors, some of whom opportunistically switched alliances. By September their groups had gained such importance that government and RCD alike tried to incorporate Mai-Mai into their delegations to the inter-Congolese dialogue but Mai-Mai maintained they should participate on their own.

All parties to the war abducted and recruited children to be trained and deployed as soldiers, as members of local militia or civil defense forces, or as workers attached to military units.

President Kabila, chosen by consensus among leading domestic and foreign players rather than by any constitutional mechanism, inherited autocratic powers from his father, the late President Laurent-Desiré Kabila. According to Decree Law No. 3 of 1997, all executive, legislative, and judicial powers rest in his hands. Kabila promised human rights reforms but delivered relatively little. He did impose a moratorium on the execution of death sentences in March which was still in effect in late November and in May he began demobilizing child soldiers from the Congolese army. But the security agencies continued the numerous abuses for which they were notorious in the past. Government agents were allegedly responsible for the summary execution of eleven Lebanese just after the assassination of the elder Kabila. Agents of the National Security Agency and the Military Detection of Antipatriotic Activities (DEMIAP) played an important part in investigations of the assassination. This occurred under the aegis of a commission set up in February and including Congolese and representatives of foreign allies of the government. The commission exercised unlimited power to interrogate and arrest suspects and afforded them no due process guarantees. Many detained by the commission were reportedly tortured and some were "disappeared." The worst abuses occurred in unofficial detention places run by the security agencies, including the death of one detainee from torture in mid-April. Bending to domestic and international outcry at abuses linked to the investigation, Kabila closed down unofficial places of detention and ordered detainees transferred to Kinshasa central prison. In September, authorities released some two hundred people detained mostly in connection with the investigation.

Kabila's promises to limit the powers of the abusive Court of Military Order brought no reform by late October. In November 2000, the court found former presidential security adviser Anselme Masasu and eight of his subordinates guilty of conspiracy and ordered their execution, a sentence which was carried out before the moratorium mentioned above. In September 2001, in Katanga province, the court sentenced eight people to death and eighteen others to between five and twenty years imprisonment on charges of plotting to overthrow the government. All were said to have been tortured and to have had no legal counsel before the trial. There is no appeal to decisions by this court.

Officials in the Ministry of Interior and some provincial governors obstructed political party activities despite the promulgation of a new law in May that purported to liberalize political life. Leaders of opposition parties refused to acknowledge the new law. Police on July 30 arrested and beat participants in an opposition march in support of the peace process.

In areas under Rwandan government control, the RCD attempted to legitimate its de facto control by declaring eastern Congo a "federal state" and by establishing regional legislative assemblies. Many local leaders rejected these initiatives as preparatory moves towards secession. Anxious about challenges to their legitimacy, RCD authorities detained scores of Uvira residents, including leaders of civil society, when they sought to boycott a celebration of the August 2 anniversary of the RCD rebellion. Soldiers accused detainees of supporting the Mai-Mai and beat several of them, one so severely as to require hospitalization. In other areas as well, RCD and Rwandan soldiers routinely held persons accused of backing the Mai-Mai in military detention centers, private houses, or shipping containers and tortured and otherwise mistreated them. Several were reported to have "disappeared" while in custody. In Kisangani, RCD authorities denounced journalists and activists of the peace movement on the radio and at rallies, calling them traitors allied with hostile foreigners. After Radio Amani, owned by the Catholic Church, broadcast programs seen by the authorities as critical, agents of the Department of Security and Intelligence abducted and severely beat the clergyman who headed the Catholic Justice and Peace Commission. Authorities prohibited other civil society leaders from traveling and harassed them by sending soldiers to their homes at night.

This year, however, the RCD permitted Radio Mandeleo, banned two years before, to resume broadcasting.

Determined to avert any demonstration that might turn critical, RCD authorities banned public events planned by women's organizations to celebrate International Woman's Day on March 8. In September RCD soldiers broke up a demonstration of Bukavu residents who wanted to show support for a recent announcement that the Congo government would pay three years back pay to state employees. RCD soldiers shot into the crowd and killed one fourteen-year-old boy.

In areas under Ugandan control, Ugandan soldiers and their local allies arbitrarily detained, ill-treated, or tortured political opponents, holding some in pits underground.

Banyamulenge militia, Rwandan rebels, and Mai-Mai attacked persons whom they suspected of supporting their opponents, killing and maiming civilians and destroying or pillaging their property. In May, Mai-Mai abducted twenty-six foreign nationals who worked for a logging company, but later released them all. In early September Mai-Mai in the area of Butembo ambushed a vehicle carrying two local civil society leaders who sought to mediate between their group and another. The assailants killed two Mai-Mai from the rival group and badly beat one of the civil society leaders.

Throughout eastern DRC armed men from various governmental and rebel forces have raped and otherwise sexually tortured thousands of women and girls.

DEFENDING HUMAN RIGHTS

Dozens of Congolese NGOs and other civil society organizations documented and reported on human rights abuses by all parties and the larger human toll of the war. Many NGOs also provided assistance to victims of abuses and advocated on their behalf. Government and rebel authorities generally ignored their pleas and mirrored each other in clamping down on vocal rights defenders, often by accusing them of being enemy agents.

The government detained human rights activists Golden Misabiko and N'sii Luanda for months without charges in connection with the Kabila assassination but released them in September. Once free Misabiko said that he and other prisoners had been tortured and inhumanely treated and that some had "disappeared."

At a national human rights conference in June government delegates and civil society participants from throughout the country adopted a Congolese Charter of Human Rights and a National Plan of Action on human rights. The government in May authorized the reopening of the Kinshasa office of the African Association for the Defense of Human Rights (ASAHDO), a leading human rights organization which it had closed in May 1998.

RCD officials frequently summoned and publicly threatened leading members of Heritiers de la Justice, a human rights NGO in Bukavu. They warned members of the Goma-based Center for Research on the Environment, Democracy, and Human Rights (CREDDHO) not to divulge information to foreigners and made death threats against them. The RCD subjected human rights defenders and women activists to similar treatment in Kisangani.

In an early October press conference in the Ugandan-controlled town of Beni, Hangi Bin Talent, the local representative of ASADHO, asked officials of the local RCD branch (Congolese Rally for Democracy-Movement for Liberation, RCD-ML) about the recent multiplication of underground detention cells. In response, RCD-ML officials ordered him detained in such a cell, where he was severely beaten for two days.

THE ROLE OF THE INTERNATIONAL COMMUNITY

The international community welcomed Kabila's overtures towards peace and reform, ready to end the Congo's decade of relative isolation. But donors reengaged cautiously, unwilling to encourage Kabila to entrench himself as unelected head of state. International leaders denounced human rights abuses and supported the peacekeeping force to help assure an end to the war that was thought to be the source of many of these abuses. They also called for accountability but established no mechanism to assure it.

United Nations

Both U.N. Secretary-General Kofi Annan and the Security Council devoted much attention to ending the DRC war and frequently denounced human rights abuses and the humanitarian crisis spawned by it. In an effort to be well informed about the situation in the DRC, eleven ambassadors of the council visited the region and all members attended an Arria-formula briefing in which representatives of Human Rights Watch and other nongovernmental organizations presented analyses of the war.

Yet the council hesitated to commit significant resources to a war whose end was not yet sure. It voted in February in resolution 1341 to deploy only 2,300 MONUC troops, about half the number originally foreseen. Although the resolution condemned war-related atrocities and reminded all parties that they were obligated to protect civilians, it gave no mandate for civilian protection to MONUC.

In addressing the council in late May, the secretary-general spoke of the importance of accountability for past crimes in establishing a lasting peace in the region. The council extended the mandate for MONUC for a year in mid-June and itself affirmed in resolution 1355 the importance of accountability. In his mid-October report to the Security Council, the secretary-general denounced human rights abuses in some detail and again called for accountability in the DRC. The council's adoption of resolution 1376 in November launched phase III of MONUC, requiring the demilitarization of Kisangani, the restoration of freedom of movement throughout the country, and the full cooperation of the belligerents with MONUC's activities.

Roberto Garretón, then special rapporteur on the situation of human rights in the DRC, issued damning reports on abuses by government and rebels alike after his two missions to DRC in March and June. During his tenure, he briefed the Security Council several times on abuses in the DRC and in the speech marking the end of his tenure he too called for accountability for past crimes in the DRC. The Field Office of the High Commissioner for Human Rights continued to play a prominent role in monitoring conditions in the country, assisting government reform initiatives and supporting local rights groups.

In early December, child protection officers attached to MONUC and UNICEF reported that Congolese children had been sent from Bunia to Kampala, Uganda's capital, for military training. In mid-December, the Security Council urged that these children be demobilized and sent home for rehabilitation, steps which were taken several months later after continued pressure from MONUC, UNICEF, Human Rights Watch, and other organizations.

In April, a U.N. panel of experts reported to the Security Council that the governments of Uganda, Rwanda, and Burundi were illegally exploiting natural resources and other forms of wealth of the DRC. The report also found that foreign forces allied with the Congolese government were profiting from the conflict. This exploitation had especially exacerbated the suffering of the population in parts of eastern Congo occupied by the Ugandan and Rwandan armies. The governments named contested the report and the Security Council extended the mandate of the panel for three months to supplement its information.

European Union

Soon after being installed as president, Kabila visited Paris, Brussels, London, and Bonn as well as Washington and New York, promising at each stop to cooperate with the U.N., to facilitate the internal political dialogue, and to return the country to the rule of law.

On a visit to the DRC in June, Belgian Prime Minister Guy Verhofstad responded to Kabila's assurances by announcing a new aid package totaling U.S. $18 million dedicated to health, education and infrastructure. In inaugurating his country's presidency of the E.U. in July, Verhofstad called for greater attention to the DRC. The E.U. council of ministers in March approved a provisional allocation of about U.S. $100 million for health, education, justice, and road repair programs, but had insisted Congo could access the funds only after achieving real progress in the inter-Congolese dialogue. During a July visit to the DRC, Paul Nielson, the E.U.'s commissioner for development and humanitarian affairs, stated that E.U. structural assistance would be delivered only after consensus had been achieved among the Congolese. He indicated that part of the E.U. allocation would also go to finance the reintegration of armed groups in eastern Congo, a program for which the United Kingdom also pledged funds. In late November, an E.U. delegation headed by Belgian Foreign Minister Louis Michel visited the DRC and other countries involved in the war to promote peace.

In July, the European Parliament urged making the DRC a priority for the E.U. It urged foreign forces to withdraw from Congo, condemned the plundering of Congo's national wealth, and appealed to the World Bank and the International Monitory Fund (IMF) to stop supporting the countries implicated in that plunder.

Donor Community

Kabila initiated reforms including the floating of the Congolese franc, the decontrol of prices, the improvement of collection of state revenues, and the commitment to balance the state budget which rapidly strengthened the economy. Impressed by the improvement, bilateral and multilateral donors in early July noted that Congo had U.S. $280 million of programs underway and pledged further assistance of U.S. $240 million before the end of the year, subject to adherence to the Lusaka Accords and improved security for the population.

To encourage the new government, the World Bank and the IMF arranged relay loans to address its debt to them of U.S. $800 million. Both provided assistance to the government in preparing for the July donor meeting and the IMF helped plan a program which was expected to spur increased levels of international assistance, starting with the IMF's own heavily indebted poor countries (HIPC) debt-relief initiative. The World Bank in late July approved a U.S. $50 million grant for the economic recovery program.

United States

The significant political changes that took place in Kinshasa in January coincided with the installation of George W. Bush as the U.S. president. As the Clinton administration drew to a close, its "new leaders" policy had lost credibility as those once thought to be beacons of hope, such as the presidents of Rwanda and Uganda, were more and more identified with serious human rights abuses and deadly wars. The Bush administration made no dramatic changes, but pressed Uganda and Rwanda more firmly to adhere to the Lusaka agreement in withdrawing their forces. On November 10, President Bush discussed with visiting President Kabila the state of the Congolese economy, humanitarian issues, and the nature of the war. Despite this and earlier indications that the Congo crisis would attract high-level attention, the State Department issued only one public statement on the DRC by late October compared to twenty-five issued over the same period the year before. The September 11 attacks on the U.S. and the focus on building an international anti-terrorism coalition contributed to further diminishing U.S. attention on central Africa.

In recognition of the growing misery in the DRC, however, the U.S. tripled its humanitarian assistance in 2001 to approximately U.S. $80 million, most of it for food and other emergency supplies, immunization programs, and refugee relief. It also spent some U.S. $5 million on judicial programs under the Great Lakes justice initiative.

Relevant Human Rights Watch Reports:

Reluctant Recruits: Children and Adults Forcibly Recruited for Military Service in North Kivu, 5/01
Uganda in Eastern DRC: Fueling Political and Ethnic Strife, 3/01

ERITREA

HUMAN RIGHTS DEVELOPMENTS

A border war with Ethiopia that began in 1998 was a disaster for Eritrea. The war, which ended with a cease-fire in mid-2000 and a peace agreement in December 2000, displaced over a quarter of the population; seriously undermined the country's economy; and achieved no military gains. About 20,000 Eritreans died during the war and the Ethiopian army advanced to within one hundred kilometers of Asmara, the capital. (See also Ethiopia.)

After October 2000, civil liberties became the latest victims of that war. Critics of government policy were jailed without charges, the small independent press was closed, and university students who challenged a compulsory summer work program were subjected to harsh treatment and to jail.

Since the country achieved independence from Ethiopia in 1993, after a thirty-year armed struggle, all governmental power had been held by the leading force in the fight for independence, the Eritrean People Liberation Front, and its post-independence incarnation, the People's Front for Democracy and Justice (PFDJ). The leader of the PFDJ, Isayas Afwerki, had been president of the country since independence. A constitution, with provisions creating civil liberties, was adopted in 1997 but was never implemented. Elections for the new National Assembly were scheduled for 1998 but were postponed indefinitely after the outbreak of the war with Ethiopia. As a result, president Isayas governed by proclamation, unrestrained by a transitional national assembly that met infrequently. In mid-2001, the government circulated a draft Proclamation on the Formation of Political Parties and Organizations and an Eritrean Electoral Law Proclamation. No electoral politics were permitted and presidential rule was essentially unfettered pending adoption of both measures.

There was no effective mechanism for questioning, much less challenging, government policy and operations. In October 2000, thirteen academics and professionals sent the president a letter suggesting a "critical review" of post-independence development. The letter stated that the war raised "grave questions" about the government's conduct domestically and internationally. Although sent privately to the president, its contents soon became known. The president met with the group but rejected its criticisms. In February 2001, the president removed the minister of local government after he questioned the president's leadership and requested meetings of the PFDJ's central and national councils, which had met only twice during the two-year war with Ethiopia.

Criticism of presidential rule gathered force in May 2001, when fifteen of the seventy-five-member central council of the PFDJ published an open letter demanding reforms. This "Group of 15" urged full application of the constitution, multi-party elections, abolition of the non-judicial Special Court (discussed below), and other reforms. Among the signatories were the former defense minister, other former ministers and ambassadors, and three generals.

In July, the government arrested University of Asmara student union president Semere Kesete for having protested the government's management of the university's mandatory summer work program. (The university was the only institution of higher education in the country). The work program supplemented a compulsory national service program in which many of University of Asmara students participated during the border war with Ethiopia. When about four hundred students protested the arrest of their leader on August 10, the government rounded them up and sent them to a work camp in Wia, near the Red Sea port of Massawa, where daytime temperatures exceed well over 100 degrees Fahrenheit (38 degrees Celsius).

The government later coerced 1,700 other students into joining the camp by threatening to deny them registration for the new academic year. Two students died of heat stroke, which the government attributed to "lack of adequate logistical support" at the camp. In September, police used clubs to break up a demonstration of mothers of the students who were protesting their treatment at Wia. Most of the students were released after signing a form letter of apology, and the university reopened on October 1, 2001. About twenty students who refused to sign the letter remained under arrest, including student council president Semere. All but Semere were released without charged in early November. Semere remained in detention without being charged—despite a penal code provision requiring charges to be brought within thirty days of arrest.

On September 18 and 19, 2001, the government arrested eleven signatories of the Group of 15's May letter. Only three members abroad for medical or business reasons and one who had retracted his signature avoided arrest. Those arrested had not been charged as of early November. However, government and PFDJ spokesmen publicly accused them of plotting to create "opposition cells" in the army and other governmental institutions; establishing relations with "neighboring countries"; and cooperating with outlawed groups. A presidential spokesman said that these were illegal acts that "jeopardized the nation's sovereignty." After the Group of 15 arrests, the government reportedly arrested four to five dozen other prominent individuals, including elderly businessmen who had tried to act as intermediaries between the group and the president. All of those arrested were held incommunicado and information about their whereabouts was withheld from the public and from their families.

The accusations leveled at the Group of 15 members were sufficiently grave to fall within the jurisdiction of a secret Special Court established by presidential decree in 1996–although at the time of writing charges had not been brought. The court's membership consisted of three military senior officers without legal training who reported directly to the Ministry of Defense. Defendants had no right to counsel or to appeal. In January 2001, the president issued a decree creating a Special Committee of Investigation to investigate "crimes against the state" as a complement to the Special Court. Among its members were the minister of justice and the head of the Eritrean intelligence service.

The civil court system was not independent. It was administered as part of the Ministry of Justice and depended on the ministry for logistical and financial support. In mid-2001, the chief justice was fired after he complained about executive interference in the work of the judiciary. Moreover, court decisions could be reviewed by the Special Court.

On September 19, the second day of the Group of 15 arrests, the government withdrew the licenses of the country's eight independent newspapers on the grounds that they had violated the 1996 Press Proclamation and were undermining national unity. The minister of information (who had previously served as security chief) announced he would review each newspaper to determine whether it could reopen. As of early November 2001, none had reopened. Suppression of the independent press left the government's newspaper, television, and radio outlets as the only public sources of information. Even before the mass closings, the government had frequently harried the private press by detaining journalists, explaining that they had been called to perform national service. After ten journalists were reportedly arrested in September, authorities again said that they had been called for military service, but observers noted that at least two were exempt from national service because of age or their status as veterans.

DEFENDING HUMAN RIGHTS

The Eritrean government tolerated the operation of only one human rights organization, Citizens for Peace in Eritrea, which strictly limited its advocacy to the rights of war victims.

The transitional civil code and the constitution prohibited discrimination against women and the government had traditionally advocated improving the status of women. The draft election law proclamation reserved 30 percent of parliamentary seats for women and made women eligible to contest the other 70 percent. The government had a record of taking a firm stance against domestic violence.

THE ROLE OF THE INTERNATIONAL COMMUNITY

In September 2001, the World Bank, the European Union, and individual E.U. members pledged U.S. $130 million in loans and grants to help Eritrea demobilize 200,000 of its soldiers by early 2003. Financial assistance from the E.U. was jeopardized, however, when the government expelled the E.U. representative, the Italian ambassador, after he delivered a demarche from the E.U. expressing concern about the deterioration in human rights protections. Ambassadors from other E.U. states were promptly recalled for consultation. The government said the expulsion was unrelated to the protest.

On the day the United States protested the arrests of the Group of 15 and press closings in early October, Eritrea seized two local U.S. embassy employees in what it said were unrelated arrests. The U.S., which in FY 2001 provided Eritrea with $10.219 million in development and child survival assistance, and another $155,000 under the IMET military training program, cancelled joint military exercises planned for November. The Foreign Ministry issued a press release expressing "puzzle[ment]" over "negative statements" issued by several countries: "The Government of Eritrea particularly finds inexplicable the attempts to 'whitewash' crimes against the nation's security and sovereignty and present it as advocacy for democratic reform."

But protest over the shrinking liberties in Eritrea was not limited to its international partners alone. The government by year-end faced the prospect of losing U.S. $300 million that it annually collected from Eritreans living abroad in taxes and donations due to widening discontent in the diaspora about the deteriorating conditions at home.

In mid-2001, Sudan, Eritrea, and the United Nations High Commissioner for Refugees reached agreement to repatriate most of the estimated 250,000 Eritreans who fled to Sudan during the pre-independence fighting as well as the 1998-2000 war. Under the agreement, refugees from the more recent fighting would be repatriated by the end of 2001; 160,000 others would follow by the beginning of 2002.

The war with Ethiopia internally displaced as many as 960,000 Eritreans. At the end of September 2001, 44,000 were still living in temporary camps. Their return was hampered by fields strewn with landmines, the absence of basic social services in their home districts, and general insecurity along the still disputed border with Ethiopia. (See Ethiopia).

ETHIOPIA

HUMAN RIGHTS DEVELOPMENTS

There was a marked deterioration of civil liberties in Ethiopia during 2001 in the wake of (and partially as a result of) the war with Eritrea. The government jailed civil rights advocates, political rivals, students, and journalists without formal charges, and police used lethal force against unarmed civilians. In July, the foreign minister told journalists that conditions in Ethiopia were not conducive for liberal democracy. The minister of education acknowledged that Ethiopia's justice system had major deficiencies. Government agencies, she said, interfered in the justice system. The system also often abused its authority and lacked transparency and accountability.

The judiciary, with rare exceptions, was complicit in the government's violations of human rights. The courts routinely granted extensions allowing individuals to be held in detention without formal charges and without bail while the police "investigated," usually at a snail's pace. Rarely did they inquire into the need for holding suspects in custody. Court hearings convened every several weeks, only to have the court uncritically permit the police to investigate for months. Court cases historically lasted for years, during which time activists and government critics, apparently held only for their nonviolent criticism of the government, endured harsh detention conditions. Sometimes charges were eventually brought; sometimes prisoners were released after months of captivity without charge or trial.

Although the war with Eritrea ended with a cease-fire in June 2000, and a comprehensive Peace Agreement in December 2000, disputes over its prosecution and conclusion continued to simmer within the political elite and the enmity created permeated relations between the two countries. In March, twelve central committee members of the Tigray People's Liberation Front (TPLF), the lead party in the government coalition, the Ethiopian Peoples' Revolutionary Democratic Front (EPRDF), issued a twelve-point critique of Prime Minister Meles Zenawi's policies. The dissenters, joined by members of other government parties, complained that the government had concluded a premature and unfavorable peace agreement. They also protested the government's economic liberalization policies and accused the prime minister of corruption.

The government's initial response to this dissent in its own ranks was political. It fired a number of ministers and generals, including the minister of defense Siye Abraha, and organized successful recall petitions for members of parliament who supported the dissidents. Later in the year, the EPRDF constituent parties purged their leadership and ranks of those who had participated in criticism of the government. That included Ethiopia's (largely ceremonial) president, Negaso Gidada, who was expelled from the central committee of his party, the Oromo People's Democratic Organization (OPDO). When Negaso's term expired in October 2001, parliament unanimously voted Girma Woldegiorgis president for a six-year term and endorsed a new government.

Against the background of political dissent and stalemated war, university students in April 2001 protested the government's interference with academic freedom. The students' main demands were permission to republish a banned student magazine, dismissal of two university administrators closely affiliated with the government, and removal of security troops stationed inside the university campus. While the government initially conceded the first two demands, it did not commit to a schedule for removing the security forces. When students continued to press their demands, the minister of education issued an ultimatum threatening students who did not return to classes with arrest. The security forces' efforts to enforce the ultimatum set off clashes on April 17 and 18 that quickly got out of hand as nonstudents joined in the protests. In suppressing the protest, the police used excessive force, including live ammunition, and conducted massive arrests. At the end of the two days, over forty civilians, primarily students, had been killed and another four hundred injured. Other campuses also witnessed antigovernment protests.

The government immediately detained almost 2,000 students; although most were quickly released, several hundred were shipped to prisons two hundred kilometers or more from the capital. Aside from those arrested, over one hundred students fled to Kenya and another seventy or so to Djibouti.

Also arrested in the weeks following the police crackdown on the students were members of two opposition parties, the All-Amhara People's Organization (AAPO) and the Ethiopians' Democratic Party (EDP). Over four hundred AAPO members were arrested between April and June. According to the party, most of those taken into custody were candidates in local elections. Over one hundred EDP members were arrested. The police claimed that the AAPO and EDP members had "a clear role in the violence" and had been active in organizing "hooligans" to riot.

Because of the mass arrests, prisons became severely overcrowded. While no independent observers were allowed in to monitor prison conditions, prisoners who were subsequently released complained of poor sanitation, leading to the proliferation of water- and air-borne diseases such as typhoid, dysentery, and tuberculosis. Four prisoners were reported to have died, including AAPO member Gebrehana Wolde Medhin. Although the government claimed that he had died of tuberculosis, AAPO asserted that he had died as a result of severe beatings, noting that the family had never been informed that he was hospitalized and the body had not been returned to the family.

In early July, the government announced that it released about a hundred of those arrested in connection with the April events. They had not been charged but were nevertheless held two months or more. Another 150 were released on bail. The government acknowledged continuing to imprison sixteen, but the number of students actually being held remained unconfirmed. Although the government released thirty-two of the AAPO detainees in July (two on bail), at least six remained in jail without charges as of early November 2001. Of the hundred or so EDP members, ninety were released without charges. Four others were released on bail. Seven, however, remained in custody without charge as of November 2001.

In June 2001, the government amended its "anti-corruption" law to prohibit bail for anyone charged with corruption by the police. The amendment was immediately applied to former colleagues of the prime minister who had been purged from the EPRDF's constituent parties. Most prominent among those arrested was former defense minister Siye. He and seven co-defendants were arrested in mid-June. In an unusual move, the court ordered Siye's release on bail but he was rearrested outside the courthouse. In mid-August, a court ineffectually gave the police a "last" two-week extension to complete the investigation. The two weeks came and went without charges or release. In late October, almost five months after their arrests, Siye and his co-defendants were charged with corruption. Bail was denied.

The amended anti-corruption law was also applied to another prominent dissident politician, Abate Kisho, the former president of the province known as the Southern Nations, Nationality and People's State. He was arrested in late July for allegedly steering contracts to a defendant in the Siye case. He claimed that the acts for which the police arrested him predated the laws he is alleged to have violated but he was kept in custody for four months without charge. Article 22.1 of the Ethiopian constitution, echoes article 11.2 of the Universal Declaration of Human Rights by providing that no one may be convicted "on account of any act or omission which did not constitute a criminal offense" at the time it was committed and no heavier penalty may be imposed than was applicable when the offense took place. In late October 2001, Kisho was charged with having used his office to make illegal purchases.

Governmental pressure on the courts was exemplified by the treatment of judges who attempted to act independently. One EDP member arrested in April was the party's secretary general, Lidetu Ayalew. A court ordered his release in early June but he was rearrested two weeks later and accused by the police of having used his mobile phone to coordinate the student protests. He, however, was not the only one to be sanctioned. Charges were also brought against the three judges who formed the court panel ordering his release. Lidetu was released again in mid-July without formal charges, after seventy days in jail.

The government also arrested about a dozen businessmen under the anti-corruption law. They, too, were jailed for months without formal charges and their financial assets businesses were frozen. Several of those arrested had no obvious political ties.

Incarceration without trial for months at a time paled in comparison with the treatment of officials of and accused collaborators with the former dictatorship, the Derg, and those arrested on suspicion of assisting insurrectionary groups. Most of the alleged Derg officials were arrested in 1991. In October, the Amhara State court acquitted twenty-three more Derg defendants and sentenced two to sixteen years. Ethiopian courts by then had handed down 1,181 verdicts, acquitting 375. After a full decade, 2,200 defendants had not been brought to trial. Since 1999, the federal government has held 1,200 individuals in Oromiya State suspected of assisting the Oromo Liberation Front. Half of those had not been charged. The federal prosecutor's office attributed the delays in bringing them to trial or releasing them to the lack of trained police and prosecuting personnel and the lack of other resources.

Journalists working for the independent press were often the victims of harassment because of their reporting. Ethiopia has permitted an independent press to operate, but in the past Prime Minister Meles Zenawi had described it as a "gutter press," and denied the reporters access to official news and briefings. In what passed for "improvement" in October, the government announced that it would grant "responsible and constructive" independent newspapers access to its information. Control of all television and radio broadcasting remained in the hands of the government and the ruling EPRDF. As of October 2001, only one journalist remained in jail, the publisher of a defunct weekly, *Akturot*, but there remained pending charges against eighty journalists from earlier reporting. The jailed journalist was arrested for inciting violence by having published an article two years earlier quoting a retired general who predicted the overthrow of the government. He was also accused of defamation for publishing an article about alleged corruption at a government-owned factory. In addition, short-term detention was still alarmingly frequent. For example, two journalists were jailed in May and June for articles written years earlier alleging corruption by church officials and at the Ethiopian Electric Power Company, respectively. In July, the government arrested journalists from eight publications after the foreign minister complained he had been defamed by their reports that he had had a falling out with the prime minister. In July, an editor was jailed for 1999 articles claiming that a regional official and that some of the president's security detail had defected. About two dozen journalists lived in exile, including three who fled in 2001.

Opposing political parties have also been hampered in their legitimate activities, even apart from the mass arrests following the April disturbances. The EDP was denied a permit to hold its convention in Addis Ababa in August. AAPO directed its six elected *woreda* (district) representatives in Addis Ababa not to participate in district councils as a protest against what it claimed were rigged local elections. The EDP, while not directing its ten woreda representatives to boycott the district councils, also asserted that the elections had been tainted.

The Eritrean war sapped economic resources that could have been used to improve the conditions of the civilian population and its baleful aftermaths linger. The Ethiopian government announced that the war cost the impoverished country U.S. $3 billion, including the expense of prosecuting the war and the expense of rebuilding and resettlement once the war ended. A local research institute reported that the war had a devastating impact on civilian life through displacement, loss of livestock and stored food grains, and the destruction of houses, social infrastructure, and commercial enterprises. The institute estimated the cost of lost social infrastructure alone to be well over $200 million. Income also dropped as tourism and international investment and aid fell.

The end of the war has enabled Ethiopia to decrease its security budget by 20 percent, to U.S. $350 million, but the country remained plagued by military threats from ethnically-based separatist groups, especially in the Oromiya, Somali, Southern Nations, and Benishangul-Gumuz states. Local skirmishes in which government and rebel troops (and civilians) were killed and wounded continued to occur occasionally. These small but deadly battles sometimes led to mass arrests of local inhabitants suspected of abetting the rebels. They, too, have historically been held for months or years without charges or trial.

The cease-fire ended the fighting but not the animosity between the two countries. In June, Ethiopia forcibly expelled 772 people it identified as Eritreans from its territory without prior notification to the International Committee of the Red Cross as anticipated under article 2 of the truce agreement. In August, it announced suspension of prisoner-of-war exchanges with Eritrea until it received information about a missing fighter pilot. Exchanges resumed in October when Eritrea released twenty-four Ethiopians "for health reasons" and Ethiopia reciprocated with the release of twenty-three Eritrean POWs, also "for health reasons." With the October releases, 653 Ethiopian and 879 Eritrean POWs had been repatriated but about 350 Ethiopians and 1750 Eritreans still remained in POW detention camps as of early November 2001. Voluntary civilian repatriation between the two countries progressed more smoothly. During the war, about 345,000 civilians fled the fighting. Most escaped to internal exile but others were trapped behind enemy lines as the war front shifted. In November, the International Committee of the Red Cross reported it had repatriated almost 55,000 Ethiopian civilians from Eritrea since 1998. In July, it had reported the repatriation of 1,000 Eritrean civilians from Ethiopia.

DEFENDING HUMAN RIGHTS

In early May, about two weeks after the police actions involving university students, the police arrested two leading human liberties activists, Professor Mesfin Woldemariam and Dr. Berhanu Nega. They were both charged with having incited the students to riot. The government produced no evidence then or since to substantiate the claims. Mesfin was the founder and first president of the Ethiopian Human Rights Council (EHRCO). On the day of the arrests, the government raided and sealed the EHRCO offices. EHRCO was founded in 1991 to promote democracy, human rights, and the rule of law, and to document human rights abuses. The government refused to recognize the EHRCO until May 1999, and often harassed those engaged in its monitoring activities. While in prison, Mesfin and Berhanu began a hunger strike. This, together with considerable international publicity and pressure, may have facilitated their release on bail in June after a month of captivity. After their release, the EHRCO was allowed to reopen.

Harassment of organizations established to monitor and advance civil liberties also extended to other activists. In August, the Ethiopian Women Lawyers Association (EWLA) mounted a peaceful demonstration with several hundred participants to demand that rape laws be strengthened and more aggressively enforced. At about the same time, it received extensive media coverage for its letter to a local newspaper protesting the ministry of justice's failure to prosecute an alleged sexual assault by the son of a prominent family. Shortly thereafter, the ministry of justice suspended EWLA's charter and froze its bank accounts. It announced that EWLA's activity's exceeded its charter, without offering details. In mid-October, a trial court ordered the release of ELWA's frozen accounts and the Justice Ministry—under a new minister—restored ELWA's license.

In May, a court acquitted eight founding members of the Human Rights League after three-and-a-half years' detention on unsubstantiated charges of involvement in terrorist activities. The Human Rights League was a monitoring group founded in 1996 by prominent members of the Oromo community that the government never allowed to function. Other groups that government harassment forced underground or into exile in past years included the Ogaden Human Rights Committee, the Solidarity Committee for Ethiopian Political Prisoners, and the Oromo Ex-Prisoners for Human Rights.

Both the Ethiopian constitution and legislation empower parliament to create a Human Rights Commission and an ombudsman. Neither had yet been established.

THE ROLE OF THE INTERNATIONAL COMMUNITY

The economic cost of the war was a key factor in pressing both Ethiopia and Eritrea to conclude the December 2000 peace agreement. The Ethiopian government subsequently received generous aid packages, even as it used lethal force against demonstrators, silenced dissent, and violently repressed minorities in restless regions. Contributing to the international community's muted criticism of these practices was the apparent perception that the dissenters were "hardliners," and the government's was the "moderate" camp.

The dissenters considered the government's espousing of a free-market economy and its partnership with international financial institutions a betrayal of the TPLF's ideological roots. In a strong sign of support for the government's policies, the IMF in March approved a U.S. $112 million loan, and agreed to back Ethiopia's poverty reduction program. Likewise, a meeting of Ethiopia's donors in early April agreed to reschedule or cancel 70 percent of U.S. $430 million in foreign debts.

United Nations

Implementation of the peace agreement progressed relatively well, but both parties repeatedly showed intransigence. The Security Council in Resolution 1369 (2001) passed in September extended the mandate of the United Nations Mission in Ethiopia and Eritrea (UNMEE)—a mission to monitor and help implement the cease-fire agreement—to March 15, 2002, and called on the parties to settle all outstanding issues. These included Ethiopia's reluctance to supply maps detailing the location of its minefields in Eritrea. About 70,000 internally-displaced Eritreans still could not be resettled because of the danger of land mines. Both countries balked at engaging in bilateral talks. Eritrea was accused of infiltrating militia into its side of the buffer zone in violation of the cease-fire agreement but confirmation was difficult because Eritrea restricted the movement of UNMEE monitors. UNMEE reported that no Ethiopian troops remained in the temporary security zone separating the two countries. While matters could improve in 2002 when a boundary commission demarks a permanent boundary, both sides expressed dissatisfaction with the commission's interim findings.

Both countries continued to evict those identified as the other's nationals, causing great suffering to the victims and their kin, and blatantly violating international human rights norms in the process. Of concern also was the slow pace in implementing the agreement's compensation provisions for war-related losses.

A committee established pursuant to Security Council Resolution 1298 (2000) that imposed an arms embargo on the two parties complained in a May letter to the council that it had no monitoring arm and was thus constrained in carrying out its mandate of ensuring the effective implementation of the embargo. The Security Council lifted the ban in May. By contrast, the European Union in March renewed the arms embargo it imposed on Ethiopia and Eritrea in March 1999.

The United Nations Committee on the Rights of the Child gave Ethiopia a mixed review in 2001. It applauded the government's adoption of a new Family Code. It also welcomed the interim prohibition on the use of corporal punishment in schools but expressed disappointment that the ban had not been implemented. It identified ongoing abuses in violation of Ethiopia's own constitution. Many children continued to be subject to the adult justice system because neither a juvenile court nor a juvenile detention facility existed outside the capital; children were often exploited for child labor; and large numbers of children lived and worked in the streets without access to education, health care, or nutrition. The U.N. report echoed an April EHRCO report on the "frighteningly increasing number" of abandoned children in Ethiopian cities. In addition, rapes of young girls were common; even when reported, they were usually lightly punished, if at all.

United States

The U.S. continued to show reluctance to speak out publicly against rampant human rights abuses in Ethiopia, with a noticeable exception in April when its embassy in Addis Ababa denounced the use of excessive force against demonstrators. Further, while the U.S. had initially sponsored the U.N.'s yearlong arms embargo adopted on May 17, 2000, the outgoing Clinton administration attempted, but failed, to get the ban lifted in the weeks that followed the signature of the peace agreement in December 2000. The U.N. allowed the ban to expire in May, but warned the parties it would take action if they resumed fighting. And despite the close U.S. alliance with Ethiopia and Eritrea, the U.S. throughout the war put insufficient pressures on countries supplying the belligerents, including Bulgaria, China, France, Russia, and others, to stem the flow of arms.

In the wake of the September 11 attacks on New York and Washington, the Horn of Africa appeared poised to gain prominence in a U.S. foreign policy focused on building a global coalition against international terrorism. Following the attacks, the Ethiopian government had accused the Islamist group Al-Itihad Al-Islami, which fought for the autonomy of Ethiopia's Somali regional state from base in Somalia, of having links to the Bin Laden network. The Bush administration sought to freeze the assets of that group. President Bush called Prime Minister Meles in early October and thanked him for his offer to cooperate in the U.S. campaign. U.S. assistance to Ethiopia totaled U.S. $146 million in FY 2001, most of which was earmarked for food assistance and child survival programs.

KENYA

HUMAN RIGHTS DEVELOPMENTS

Amid an ongoing political crisis, constitutional reform remained critical to Kenya's future and promised to grow in urgency with the approach of the 2002 national election. From January 2001, when the chairman of the government-appointed Kenya Constitutional Review Commission was sworn in, progress on substantive issues was bogged down in controversy about its composition and the administration of its finances, and dissipated the public hopes initially vested in it. The repeated efforts of the ruling Kenya African National Union (KANU) to control the commission, to exclude or reduce significantly the input of civil society groups, and to use police to prevent or violently disrupt civic education gatherings or political opposition meetings further dashed public expectations.

In June 2001, the commission promised a draft of a new constitution by June and then September 2002. Both dates were viewed as unrealistic. The political opposition and civil society groups expressed concerns that the process would be rushed through to completion without sufficient civic education or participation, or if it proved patently impossible to meet the deadline that President Daniel arap Moi would seize the opportunity to introduce "interim reforms" by decree. Overshadowing reform efforts was the question of whether or not President Moi would step down in 2002 in accordance with the existing constitution's two-term limit. When the ruling party and an opposition party merged in June, some saw the move as a stratagem by Moi to stay in power after the 2002 election.

There was one hopeful development in May, when President Moi agreed to include civil society representatives within the constitutional review commission. This concession ended the stalemate that had existed since 1999, when the Ufungamano group, a coalition of the political opposition and civil society, boycotted the parliamentary committee originally charged with the task of reviewing the constitution. As of August 2001, the expanded twenty-seven-member commission, which included members put forward by civil society groups, was gathering views from citizens on how they want to be involved in the review process.

In addition to the debate over constitutional review, there were important discussions over the grant of amnesty for economic and political crimes and over a motion in parliament to establish a Truth and Reconciliation Commission to explore human rights violations since 1966. But there was a lack of consensus in parliament on the need to confront past abuses: the motion was defeated.

Meanwhile, high-ranking government and ruling party officials continued unabated to sponsor or permit violence against opposition activists, with police cracking down on government critics in numerous incidents, and state-protected youth gangs attacking political opposition rallies. For example, police in February in Kisii town beat up James Orengo, a member of parliament (MP) and leader of *Muungano wa Mageuzi* (Peoples Movement for Change), a coalition of opposition and civil society organizations, along with two other MPs in Kisii town. President Moi accused Mageuzi leaders of plotting to overthrow the government, setting the stage for further police harassment. At a May opposition rally, police arrested two MPs on "treason" charges for allegedly threatening the president, who then ordered police to tape record all political speeches at rallies. The same month, there was a petrol bomb attack on opposition leader Mwai Kibaki during a rally in a predominantly KANU area. In July, democracy activists were beaten and arrested when police violently broke up a Nairobi prayer meeting and a political rally commemorating Kenya's struggle to restore multiparty democracy.

Sporadic clashes between members of ethnic groups allied to the ruling party and those perceived to support the opposition continued in the run-up to the 2002 election, adding to the toll of numerous deaths and hundreds of thousands displaced in "ethnic" violence. The government was slow to respond with anything more than restrictions on freedom of association and assembly, all targeted against the opposition. As of October, the report delivered to President Moi almost two years before by the presidential Commission on the Ethnic Clashes (known as "the Akiwumi Commission") had still not been published.

As rates of violent crime climbed, reports of police corruption, harassment, use of excessive force, and unlawful confinement were routine. The capital erupted in violence for two days in February when police attacked street hawkers, firing into crowds. In June, the government responded to a mounting public outcry with a plan to overhaul Kenya's police. Yet the next month, police extrajudicially executed seven suspects in cold blood and in public view after hauling them off a Nairobi bus. Kenya's notorious prisons promised some improvement under a new commissioner, who warned wardens not to use torture and instituted rights to medical care, visitors, and letter writing.

The picture was mixed on freedom of expression. While newspapers published unhindered, police routinely harassed journalists. After the beating of a female *Nation TV* reporter in January, the International Press Institute condemned Kenyan police attacks on journalists. While the number of independent broadcasters grew, the granting of government licenses and the allocation of frequencies were irregular. Some stations, especially those outside cities, waited long periods before they were able to air their programs. The state-run Kenya Broadcasting Corporation was the only media outlet allowed to broadcast nationwide, while most newly licensed FM stations had limited reach, mostly to Nairobi and its environs. In July, a group of public and private media owners was formed to draft a comprehensive broadcasting policy.

In a positive move, the government outlawed caning in schools and introduced a bill on children's rights in parliament. But the parliamentary debate was poorly attended and the bill was not passed. Student strikes over educational conditions hit 118 schools, closing down half of them. The Kenyan government took little or no action to address the plight of over a million children orphaned and otherwise affected by AIDS in Kenya. Many of these children were living in poverty, and were at high risk of engaging in hazardous work or losing property that might be the key to their future protection (See Children's Rights.)

DEFENDING HUMAN RIGHTS

Although human rights groups operated openly, President Moi kept up a verbal offensive against nongovernmental organizations (NGOs), characterizing them as enemies of the state. In March, President Moi warned Kenyans to be wary of NGOs "pretending to fight for human rights," accusing "con men who have formed NGOs calling themselves human rights activists," of wanting to "destabilize the country" and to "cause confusion through foreign-funded seminars."

In October, seventy-one members of the nongovernmental group Release Political Prisoners (RPP) were detained for several days and charged with holding an illegal meeting. The group had been commemorating Mau Mau day to honor those who had fought for Kenya's independence from British colonial rule. The police stormed the compound, assaulted people, and used teargas to break up the peaceful gathering.

On the other hand, the government's traditionally ineffective Standing Committee on Human Rights, created by the president in 1996, showed new vigor in stepping up pressure for police reform. It condemned torture and recommended that police officers receive compulsory human rights training. The committee also blamed "trigger-happy" police for a pattern of shootings of unarmed civilians and subsequent cover-ups. Most importantly, in June the committee published its findings that prison wardens had murdered six death-row inmates who had died last year. As a result the chair of the Standing Committee was charged by the judge with contempt of court for being in breach of judicial rules that prevent comment on a pending case. A draft bill to strengthen the independence of the Standing Committee, pending since the previous year, had not been considered by parliament as of November 2001.

THE ROLE OF THE INTERNATIONAL COMMUNITY

Corruption remained the key sticking point with Kenya's international donors, who negotiated with the government over aid pegged to anti-corruption legislation. With donors focused on corruption and economic reform, human rights issues largely took a back seat. The major exception to this was in March, when nineteen diplomatic missions called on Kenya to respect political freedom during the constitutional review process. The statement drew an angry rebuke from President Moi, who warned donors to stay out of the process.

Donors' concerns about Kenya's plummeting economy deepened. Government mismanagement and endemic corruption remained, causing a further drop in the average Kenyan's standard of living. Echoing its first-ever negative growth rate of the year before, the country's United Nations human development ranking sank to 123 out of 162 countries.

Many of the loans pledged by the International Monetary Fund (IMF) (U.S. $198 million), and the World Bank (U.S. $150 million) remained suspended due to the lack of progress on anti-corruption efforts. In December 2000, the IMF suspended its funding until the moribund Kenya Anti-Corruption Authority (KACA) resumed work. The World Bank also suspended some development loans. In August, hopes dimmed for resumption of IMF funding when Parliament failed to pass a fresh anti-corruption bill, despite personal lobbying by President Moi. The Constitutional Amendment Bill would have entrenched the new KACA in the constitution. Opponents of the bill charged that it was too weak and saw in Moi's advocacy of it a cynical attempt to please donors without engaging in genuine reform. In response, Moi immediately ordered the police to investigate corruption cases pending before the KACA. Without a special session of parliament called by the president, the bill could not be reintroduced and voted on again until March 2002.

Awaiting action were two other bills the IMF had also tied to renewed funding: a Code of Ethics bill for public servants and an Economic Crimes bill. In July, the IMF expressed satisfaction with the latter, which it helped draft, but flagged its dismay with its most controversial clause—a blanket amnesty for all economic crimes committed before December 1, 1997. President Moi and his cabinet approved the amnesty measure, which was sharply criticized.

After initially wooing donors for renewed funding, a backlash against the international pressure built among KANU politicians, increasing tension between the donor community and the government. In March, soon after a meeting with World Bank and IMF officials, the president fired the health minister and his assistant for mounting a stinging attack on the two institutions. That month, the World Bank issued a scathing report on ten African countries, including Kenya, which the report charged was not serious about reform. Transparency International, a Berlin-based watchdog group, ranked Kenya the fourth most corrupt country in the world according to the perceptions of international business.

Shortly after, anti-corruption efforts were dealt a blow with the firing of Richard Leakey in March, following twenty-one dramatic months as head of Kenya's civil service. President Moi had lured Leakey from the opposition camp and appointed him and his "Dream Team" to streamline the civil service, root out corruption, and revive the economy. Leakey's appointment was instrumental in obtaining the pledges of renewed assistance from the international financial institutions. In Leakey's short time in office, he was successful in reinvigorating the anti-corruption initiative and tightening the economy. Resentful of the clout he wielded, a group of parliamentarians pushed for Leakey's ouster.

European Union

European Union (E.U.) representatives also pegged disbursement of future funds to progress in fighting corruption, following a May meeting with President Moi. While commending Kenya on progress in constitutional review, they said the E.U. attached particular importance to effective preparation for the coming national election. They also expressed concern over violations of freedom of speech and assembly, treatment of suspects and prisoners, and an increase in extrajudicial executions. Denmark announced it would not increase aid until significant progress was made on governance and fighting corruption, and called for respect for human rights. And the United Kingdom, a traditionally staunch supporter of the Moi government, issued two warnings that it would halt funding if reforms continued to slip.

United States

President Moi held high level meetings with President George Bush and Secretary of State Colin Powell, and used the opportunity to appeal for United States intervention for renewed IMF and World Bank funding. In May, Powell visited Kenya and pledged U.S. $8 million to fight AIDS and urged economic reform efforts. Powell stressed that the U.S. would closely watch the 2002 elections, and underscored the importance of democratization. The State Department issued a formal statement in August urging passage of anti-corruption legislation. On June 27, President Bush and Vice President Dick Cheney met with Moi in Washington, and encouraged him to ensure continued progress on democratization and economic reform. However, in the aftermath of the September 11 attacks, anti-terrorism efforts came to the forefront of U.S. policy regarding Kenya. In October, Powell met with Kenyan foreign minister Christopher Obure on Kenya's cooperation in anti-terrorism efforts. In November, President Bush met again with President Moi; this time the discussion centered around anti-terrorism efforts and peace initiatives for Sudan and Somalia.

Other concerns included regional conflict and proliferation of small arms, which the State Department warned had reached crisis proportions. President Moi stepped up efforts to control arms flows by ordering his security and immigration departments to get involved. Unfortunately, the government's attempts resulted in renewed harassment and indiscriminate crackdowns against refugees in Kenya.

The U.S. responded to outrage over the previous year's shooting of Father John Kaiser by sending a Federal Bureau of Investigations (FBI) team to investigate. Kaiser, a U.S. citizen, was a Catholic parish priest in the Rift Valley and a human rights activist. He was an outspoken critic of government sponsored "ethnic" violence. The FBI's finding of suicide created an uproar among Kenya's clergy and human rights community, who were convinced he was murdered. U.S. Senator Paul Wellstone called for a new inquiry that took into account findings of the U.S. Embassy's own investigation. "Reports of ethnic cleansing, provocation of land clashes, rapes of young women, and harassment of priests and human rights workers are widespread," Wellstone said in June.

U.S. assistance to Kenya in FY 2001 was approximately U.S. $66.7 million, including development assistance, child survival, and food aid, and some $450,000 in International Military Education and Training (IMET) funding.

Relevant Human Rights Watch Reports:

In the Shadow of Death: HIV/AIDS and Children's Rights in Kenya, 6/01

LIBERIA

HUMAN RIGHTS DEVELOPMENTS

Continued violence threatened to plunge Liberia back into civil war after nearly five years of shaky transition to peace. Fierce fighting continued to rage in the country's north since the start of a rebel incursion in July 2000, the fifth serious outbreak of violence since the 1997 elections that ended the civil war. The fighting and repression blocked recovery efforts with the nation's economy in tatters, 80 percent of the workforce unemployed and 80 percent illiteracy. Basic services such as health care, communications, electricity, and the public supply of drinking water remained extremely limited. Public and private institutions deteriorated amid widespread corruption and fear.

Fighting between government forces and the rebel group, Liberians United for Reconciliation and Democracy (LURD), intensified in northern Lofa County. Amid the violence, widespread human rights abuses took place against civilians, including women and children. Liberian government troops and rebels alike detained, tortured, or killed hundreds of civilians, raping women and girls at will, and forcing men and boys to fight. Reports by Amnesty International found that government security forces—especially the Anti-Terrorist Unit (ATU), a security force accountable only to President Taylor—detained, tortured, or executed more than two hundred civilians suspected of supporting rebels, raping some of them. The government denied these allegations and took no steps to investigate, punish, or end the abuses. In April 2001, President Taylor called up 15,000 former fighters from the faction he had led during the civil war to combat the growing rebel threat. As of September, fighting had spread southward to within sixty miles of the capital, Monrovia.

Responding to the rebel action, government repression of civil society continued to intensify. President Taylor's government functioned without accountability, independent of an ineffective judiciary and legislature that operated in fear of the executive. Ethnic Mandingo citizens, whom the government indiscriminately accused of supporting the rebels, faced growing discrimination, arbitrary arrests, and violence based solely on their ethnicity. In March, state security troops stormed the University of Liberia in Monrovia, assaulting and arresting unarmed students meeting to raise legal fees for detained journalists. More than forty students were reportedly tortured and female students raped in the raid by the ATU and the Special Operation Division, a special police unit. More than fifteen student leaders from the University of Liberia went into exile in May following the justice minister's public claim that rebel collaborators operated from their campus. In August, in an attempt to allay growing criticism, President Taylor freed three of thirteen prominent ethnic Krahn leaders imprisoned on treason charges since 1998, pardoned exiled opposition leaders, and announced an amnesty for rebels who disarmed.

Press censorship and arrests of journalists continued, as President Taylor and other high-ranking officials blamed them for negative international publicity. In February, four journalists from the *Daily* newspaper were arrested and held for over a month on espionage charges following a report questioning government spending on helicopter repairs. The government shut down four independent newspapers in connection with the report. Harassment continued with the arrest in August of the editor of the *Monrovia Guardian* following an article on police brutality. The information minister announced in April that all war-related reports had to be cleared by him. The government also tightened restrictions on foreign journalists.

With most Liberians dependent on radio for their news, government silencing of independent radio broadcasts deprived them of information. In August, President Taylor banned all radio stations but the three currently licensed—his private Liberian Communications Network and two others that only operated infrequently. At the same time, he refused to lift a ban on Veritas, a station of Liberia's Roman Catholic Church, and the independent Star radio.

The violence was part of a growing subregional struggle over control of diamonds and other resources. In 2001, President Taylor shifted his commercial focus from diamonds to logging, relying on the same men who organized the arms-for-diamonds trade to export timber and ship weapons from Monrovia to Sierra Leone. Illustrating the corruption at the heart of the Taylor government, two of the individuals involved in diamond trading sat on the board of directors of the Liberian Forestry Development Authority that oversees logging. A Strategic Commodities Act reportedly passed secretly in 2000 gave President Taylor "the sole power to execute, negotiate and conclude all commercial contracts or agreements with any foreign or domestic investor" for designated commodities, including timber and diamonds. The act was challenged as unconstitutional by the legal community.

Divisions and tensions in the subregion deepened as the internal conflicts within Liberia, Sierra Leone, and Guinea continued to spill across the borders. Guinea and Liberia accused each other of supporting armed anti-government rebels, and the Sierra Leonean government accused Liberia of providing support to the Sierra Leonean rebel group, the Revolutionary United Front (RUF).

The insecurity and violence in the subregion displaced thousands of Liberians. Humanitarian agencies estimated in July 2001 that more than 40,000 persons had been newly displaced in Lofa County since April. In the country's six internally displaced camps, about 70 percent were women and children who had fled south into areas with scarce food, clean water, shelter, or medical assistance. An unknown number remained in areas inaccessible to humanitarian workers, and without assistance in unsafe conditions in forests and villages.

Liberians also fled across the borders. In 2001, some 15,000 Liberians fled to Sierra Leone and nearly 5,000 to Ivory Coast. Although some Liberians were able to flee into Guinea, the Guinean government officially closed the border to Liberian refugees from Lofa County following cross-border fighting between Liberian, Guinean, and Sierra Leonean rebel and government forces in late 2000. This cross-border fighting also affected a longstanding Liberian refugee population that had been in Guinea for the past decade. Guinean security and civilians also targeted refugees for attack following xenophobic statements by President Lansana Conte in September 2000. In early 2001, as the violence at the border subsided, the Office of the U.N. High Commissioner for Refugees (UNHCR) and the Guinean government relocated some 60,000 refugees (largely Sierra Leoneans) to inland camps in Guinea. In May 2001, the relocation program ended and an unknown number of refugees chose to remain at the embattled border.

DEFENDING HUMAN RIGHTS

Following the escalation of fighting in Lofa County and a stinging December 2000 U.N. report on Liberian support of Sierra Leonean rebels, the government intensified attacks on human rights groups. Liberian security forces harassed, arrested, and tortured perceived critics, and human rights activists continued to flee the country in fear of government reprisals. Despite the threats, a small but dedicated human rights community continued to work in Liberia.

The leader of the Catholic Church's Justice and Peace Commission, a key human rights defender, said in March that he had received threats from "prominent individuals" in retaliation for a report critical of the government's human rights record. The commission's premises, which had been the object of previous attacks by security forces, were burglarized a few months later. Despite the climate of fear, human rights organizations persisted in their activities. By contrast, the government's National Human Rights Commission was inactive.

Thompson Ade-Bayo, a human rights activist who had been in hiding for a week, was arrested and detained by the police in September. He was wanted for criticizing as illegal the government's anti-terrorist security unit, which he had described as functioning like President Taylor's private army.

Lawyers in the Liberian National Bar Association came under attack for speaking out against the lack of due process in the courts. In October, two lawyers—Marcus Jones, vice president of the Liberia National Bar and Ishmael Campbell, president of the Montserrado County Bar—were ordered detained by the House of Representatives and fined after they protested its order for the detention of their colleague and Bar Association president Emmanuel Wureh. Wureh was detained for contempt of court in late September, but was released the first week of October after a week-long boycott of courts by lawyers. The two lawyers had called the House of Representative's order "unconstitutional" and urged a boycott of the courts. Although the two paid the fine, they were informed that they would be detained until March 2002 unless they retracted their statement. On October 11, lawyers started a second round of boycotts to protest the continued detention of their two colleagues.

THE ROLE OF THE INTERNATIONAL COMMUNITY

A downturn in foreign aid for development and relief efforts created a humanitarian crisis. Relief organizations struggling to help Liberians displaced by war expressed strong concerns over dwindling resources. Donors stayed away, accusing the Taylor government's of human rights violations, poor economic policies, and continuing involvement in arms smuggling.

United Nations

The U.N. Security Council played an active role in attempting to end the arms-for-diamonds trade in Liberia and the subregion. In December 2000, the U.N. panel monitoring compliance with the arms embargo placed on supplies to the RUF in Sierra Leone reported that the Liberian logging industry played a key role in arms trafficking. In May, the Security Council imposed a ban on Liberian diamond exports (believed in fact to derive mostly from Sierra Leone), as well as an arms embargo on Liberia itself, and a ban on foreign travel by President Taylor and more than 130 senior government officials and their spouses. An October 2001 report for the Security Council prepared by the Independent Panel of Experts found that illegal arms shipments to Liberia continued despite the arms embargo.

In response to the international scrutiny, the government made some gestures. In January, it grounded all aircraft registered in Liberia to review their legality, following accusations that Liberian-registered airplanes were flying arms to Sierra Leone. In March, Liberia banned diamond exports as well as imports of uncertified rough diamonds. However, arms continued to flow, financed by the unregulated trade in Liberian timber, which was not affected by any sanctions. A Danish trading company, however, announced in July that it would stop selling Liberian timber in Europe.

On August 14, 2001, the U.N. Committee on the Elimination of Racial Discrimination expressed concern about "reports of extrajudicial killings, allegations of torture, including rape, and the lack of accountability of perpetrators, including government security forces, for these abuses." On August 16, 2001, the U.N. Security Council publicly stressed "the need for human rights abuses to cease by whatever parties they are committed" in Liberia. In contrast, the U.N. Office in Liberia (UNOL) Peace-building Support Office played little or no active role in addressing the growing repression and abuses in Liberia.

European Union

In July the E.U. agreed to open consultations with the Liberian government about the worsening situation in human rights, democratic principles, and the rule of law, citing "serious cases of corruption" as the primary impetus for the move. It was the first time the commission proposed using articles 96 and 97 of the Cotonou Agreement signed in Benin in June 2000 by the E.U. and the African, Caribbean, and Pacific (ACP) nations. The E.U. expressed concerns over a "significantly deteriorated" political situation, threats to freedom of the press, attacks on human rights activists, and mismanagement of public funds. In October, European Union (E.U.) envoy Hans Dahlgren visited Liberia, Sierra Leone, and Guinea to examine prospects for peace and security in the region, and to formulate an E.U. policy on the crisis in the region.

The biggest aid donor to Liberia since the civil war ended, the E.U. suspended approximately U.S. $50 million in aid in 2000 to pressure the Taylor government to cut its support to RUF rebels. In May 2001, E.U. member states approved a 25-million-euro (approximately U.S. $22 million) program to assist programs for resettling refugees and displaced people.

United States

Relations between the U.S. and Liberia further deteriorated as President Taylor's role in fueling the war in Sierra Leone became more evident. Following U.N. sanctions in May, the U.S. prohibited the importation of Liberian rough diamonds. The Bush administration continued the Clinton policy of isolating Taylor politically and diplomatically, although the U.S. was less public in its approach. Administration officials stressed that until Taylor ceased efforts to destabilize the subregion, including his support for the RUF in Sierra Leone, U.S. policy would remain unchanged.

After the E.U., the U.S. was Liberia's largest donor, providing one-third of the country's total assistance. From 1997 to 2000, the USAID program focused on the resettlement of refugees and internally displaced persons and a modest, but less successful, democracy and governance program. In August, USAID reported that "the oppressive and irresponsible Charles Taylor government has overshadowed these achievements and alienated its citizens and the donor community." The agency continued to support delivery of food and health care services in 2001, but planned to put greater emphasis on strengthening civil society.

NIGERIA

HUMAN RIGHTS DEVELOPMENTS

Halfway through the four-year term of Olusegun Obasanjo's presidency, the overall human rights picture in Nigeria was mixed. There were investigations into past abuses but alarming developments, in particular recurring violence between ethnic or religious groups in several parts of the country. The military responded to attacks on its own personnel with indiscriminate killings of civilians. Political tension increased in the run-up to elections scheduled for 2003. Nigerians were expressing disillusion with the lack of fundamental change since the advent of a civilian government in 1999. The legacy of decades of repressive military rule was still keenly felt. The police were not only ineffective in maintaining law and order, but also responsible for serious human rights violations themselves.

Corruption remained rampant, despite the creation of an anti-corruption commission and adoption of anti-corruption legislation in 2000. However, the government took steps to recover some of the wealth appropriated by senior members of former governments, in particular that of Sani Abacha (1993-1998), and asked other governments to freeze some of their assets abroad.

The commission set up in 1999 to investigate human rights abuses committed under previous governments, chaired by Chukwudifu Oputa (known as the Oputa panel), received over 10,000 submissions, of which it was only able to consider around two hundred; these included numerous testimonies of killings, rape, and other abuses by the security forces against Ogoni civilians in the oil-producing Niger Delta region in 1993-1994. The commission held public hearings in Lagos, Abuja, Port Harcourt, Kano, and Enugu. Its summons to former heads of state Abdulsalami Abubakar, Ibrahim Babangida, and Muhammad Buhari was the focus of much attention. By October, when the commission concluded its hearings, none of them had agreed to testify. President Obasanjo himself appeared before the panel in September in connection with events during his first presidency as military ruler (1976-1979). The Oputa panel was under-resourced and had limited powers: it could only make recommendations, not ensure arrests or prosecutions. Nevertheless, it played an important role in beginning to erode the decades of impunity of human rights violators in Nigeria. Its hearings were televised and closely followed by the public, raising awareness of human rights and the principle of accountability.

In contrast, little action was taken by the government to investigate human rights abuses committed since it came to power. There was still no public investigation into the Nigerian military's November 1999 massacre of hundreds of civilians and widespread destruction in the town of Odi in Bayelsa State. President Obasanjo visited Odi in March 2001, but no one was brought to justice for these abuses. In August, the National Human Rights Commission (NHRC) called on the government to speed up the reconstruction and rehabilitation of Odi.

Members of the security forces were responsible for numerous extrajudicial executions, including a series of massacres by the military in Benue State in October. On October 22 and 23, soldiers killed more than two hundred (and possibly many more) civilians of the Tiv ethnic group in Gbagi, Zaki-Biam, and several other villages, and engaged in widespread destruction of homes and property. The soldiers, who were apparently acting in revenge for the murder of nineteen soldiers attributed to a Tiv armed group less than two weeks earlier, gathered villagers for a "meeting" then opened fire on them indiscriminately. Senior government and military officials including President Obasanjo initially sought to excuse the military's actions by claiming that they were acting in self-defense.

When confronted with real or suspected common criminals, the police in many cases appeared to make little attempt to arrest the suspects. They shot on sight suspected armed robbers, alleged members of ethnic militia, and youth in the Niger Delta region accused of plundering oil, vandalizing facilities, or obstructing oil production. Detainees were also shot dead while in police custody. There were reports of police brutality including beatings and arbitrary arrests when police broke up rallies of opposition groups.

The police clamped down on the activities of the Movement for the Actualization of the Sovereign State of Biafra (MASSOB), a group which advocates autonomy for the Igbo people. MASSOB meetings were repeatedly and violently broken up by police, their offices raided, and hundreds of MASSOB members arrested; many were detained without charge. Their leader, Ralph Uwazuruike, was arrested several times. Police summarily executed several MASSOB members, in particular during a police attack on their office in Okigwe in Abia state, in February, when at least ten MASSOB members were reportedly killed.

The police were ineffective in controlling the high crime rate. The inadequate size of the force, low morale, poor working conditions, and insufficient training all encouraged corruption and brutality within the police force and reinforced its lack of respect among the population. The government announced a major reform and expansion of the police, including plans to increase its numbers by tens of thousands as part of a five year program, and launched a campaign to improve its image.

Civilian "vigilante" groups were seen by some as the answer to, or a substitute for, the inability of the police to reduce crime levels. Despite the violence and brutality that characterized many of their operations, some of these groups, for example in Anambra and Lagos states, enjoyed the active and public support of their state governor. The Bakassi Boys in the south-east and the O'odua People's Congress (OPC) in the south-west were responsible for scores of deaths of alleged armed robbers. When apprehending suspected criminals, they often killed them on the spot. The Bakassi Boys also burned and mutilated their victims and systematically tortured detainees in their custody with impunity and, in some cases, on the effective authority of the state governor. In several southeastern states, the Bakassi Boys were used to target suspected political opponents and critics, as well as to settle scores and intervene in private disputes.

Members of the OPC, a more explicitly political group claiming to advocate for the Yoruba cause and officially banned in 1999, had many violent clashes with the police, attacking police stations and killing and injuring policemen. The police response, in turn, was heavy-handed. Many real or suspected OPC members were arrested and several killed. In August, prominent OPC leader Ganiyu Adams was arrested and charged with several offences including murder, torture, arson, and armed robbery; he was released in November.

In the north, civilian groups were used by the state authorities to enforce Sharia (Islamic law) in those states which had extended its application to criminal law. Some administered instant punishments to those caught violating Sharia law. In January, the governor of Zamfara state announced that he was giving powers of arrest and prosecution to local Islamic "vigilante" groups as the police had failed in their duties.

Sharia criminal courts handed down judgments in several northern states; until 1999, they had operated only for personal status law. Punishments amounting to cruel, inhuman, and degrading treatment included floggings and amputations, for offenses ranging from extra-marital sex to consumption or sale of alcohol, or theft. Floggings were carried out in public, sometimes immediately after the sentence was handed down by the court, apparently disregarding the right to appeal. The victims included minors, such as a seventeen-year-old mother convicted for pre-marital sex who was flogged in Zamfara state in January, less than a month after giving birth. In June, a court in Kebbi state ordered that a fifteen-year-old boy's hand be amputated after he was found guilty of theft; it was not known whether the sentence was carried out. At least two people were sentenced to death by stoning, including a pregnant woman in Sokoto; by November these death sentences had not been carried out.

While government officials repeatedly stated that Sharia law only applied to Muslims, it inevitably had consequences for Christians living in the northern states. On several occasions, civilian groups attacked establishments owned by Christians and destroyed consignments of alcohol. Rules such as those that forbid women from traveling with men in public vehicles were applied to Christians as well as Muslims. In January, a group claiming to enforce Sharia flogged a Christian man for selling alcohol.

There were several waves of serious inter-communal violence in various parts of the country. In the central state of Nasarawa, between one hundred and two hundred people were killed in June and July in clashes between the Tiv and several other ethnic groups; tens of thousands fleeing the violence were internally displaced. There had been earlier spates of violence in this area, particularly during April and May. In July and August, violence broke out between Christians and Muslims in Tafawa Balewa in Bauchi state, apparently in response to the introduction of Sharia there. In September, more than 1,000 people were estimated to have been killed in violence between Muslims and Christians in Jos, Plateau State; Human Rights Watch researchers who visited Jos in October gathered eyewitness testimony of the violence from both communities. In October, further violence erupted in the northern city of Kano following protests at the United States attacks on Afghanistan.

The Niger Delta continued to experience tension between different ethnic groups. There was also continuing conflict between local communities and the oil companies operating in the area, as well as government representatives. Communities continued to complain bitterly about the absence of local benefits from the exploitation of natural resources and lack of compensation for damage to the environment. The creation by the government of a Nigeria Delta Development Commission in 2000 did little to pacify them and was not very effective. There were several incidents in which security personnel posted at oil facilities shot and wounded or killed young men protesting oil production. Other protesters were arrested.

There were widespread violations of the rights of women and children. Reports were common of trafficking of Nigerian women and teenage girls for prostitution or slavery, to other West African countries as well as to Europe. In some cases trafficked women or girls were deported back to Nigeria. In June, a report by the International Labour Organization (ILO) identified a number of states in Nigeria as central points for child trafficking, both in terms of supplying and receiving children as well as acting as transit routes. There were also reports of trafficking of boys and girls under the age of ten for child labor. Government officials repeatedly declared their resolve to stamp out trafficking. A number of alleged traffickers were arrested, but overall, the practice remained entrenched, despite initiatives by several governmental and nongovernmental bodies, including the Presidential Task Force on Human Trafficking and Child Labour.

While female genital mutilation remained a common practice, some states took welcome steps to eradicate it. The Rivers State House of Assembly passed a bill to abolish female circumcision. There were moves towards adopting similar legislation in Delta State. In March, it was reported that the Enugu State House of Assembly passed a bill to protect women from traditional practices which are considered physically, psychologically, or emotionally harmful to them.

Prison conditions remained poor and sometimes life-threatening, despite government promises to release funds for improvements as part of longer-term prison reform plans. Prisons were congested, with inadequate facilities and very limited access to medical care. More than two-thirds of detainees were held without trial, many having spent several years in detention. Torture and ill-treatment were widespread, especially in police custody.

DEFENDING HUMAN RIGHTS

A broad range of nongovernmental organizations continued to work actively on a variety of issues including freedom of expression, women's rights, and proposals for reform of law enforcement agencies and the judiciary. They were generally able to carry out their activities without hindrance or obstruction from the authorities. Likewise, journalists were mostly able to report critically and encourage public debate, including on sensitive issues. The NGO Media Rights Agenda, along with journalists' groups, initiated discussion of proposals for a draft law which would harmonize laws governing the media and enshrine freedom of expression in the legislation.

The National Human Rights Commission, a government-appointed body created in 1996, suffered from a lack of resources and complained of difficulties in compelling alleged human rights violators to cooperate with its investigations. Nevertheless it attempted to carry out a range of activities as part of an ambitious national program, including several workshops with nongovernmental human rights organizations.

THE ROLE OF THE INTERNATIONAL COMMUNITY

United States

Nigeria, the fifth largest supplier of U.S. crude oil imports in 2000, assumed further importance to the United States as a leader in West Africa and throughout the continent, often referred to by U.S. officials as an "anchor state." U.S. policy focused on supporting democratic and economic reform, including civil-military relations and police reform, but rarely including public criticism on human rights grounds.

U.S. assistance to the Nigerian military came in two main forms. Military Professional Resources International (MPRI), a consulting firm on contract with the U.S. government, carried out a retraining and restructuring program as part of the Nigerian government's plans to reform the army. The stated aims of the program, initially paid for by the U.S. Agency for International Development (USAID) along with the Nigerian government, included restoring greater civilian control over the military. A separate military training program conducted by United States Special Forces and designed for peacekeeping duty in Sierra Leone, known as Operation Focus Relief, involved training and equipment for five Nigerian battalions. The training was reportedly aimed at enhancing combat skills and strengthening command and control, and included a human rights component; the equipment included small arms, communications equipment and vehicles. However, the program lacked an effective monitoring and accountability component, a serious shortcoming given the history of abuses by the Nigerian military.

The United States, in part through USAID, was one of the major bilateral donors to Nigeria, with an annual USAID budget of U.S. $20 million for support to democracy and good governance and economic reform. The program of the Office of Transition Initiatives (OTI), set up by USAID to assist Nigeria's transition towards reconciliation and democracy, concluded in 2001. It sponsored workshops on various themes including election-related violence, conflict management, and relations between police and local communities. Its annual budget was U.S. $6 million; the majority of its grants were allocated to nongovernmental organizations and civil society groups.

The U.S. Department of State country report on human rights practices for 2000 provided an accurate assessment of the human rights situation; it stated that the Nigerian government's human rights record remained poor, while commenting on some improvements. It highlighted extrajudicial executions and excessive use of force by the police and military, prolonged pre-trial detention, violence between ethnic and religious groups, and violations of the rights of women as some of the main human rights problems.

In May, the U.S. Commission on International Religious Freedom published a report in which it expressed heightened concern about violent clashes between Nigerian Muslims and Christians in 2000 and threats to religious freedom, including reports of discrimination against Muslims in the south and Christians in the north. The report commented on tensions sparked off by the extension of Sharia law. A report on religious freedom published by the U.S. Department of State in October also commented on a deterioration of religious freedom particularly in northern states.

President Obasanjo visited the United States in May 2001 to meet President George W. Bush and other U.S. government officials, and again in November to discuss anti-terrorism measures. After the September 11 attacks on the United States, President Bush called President Obasanjo to brief him on U.S. actions.

European Union

The United Kingdom was the main country providing assistance to Nigeria. The Department for International Development (DFID) had an extensive program and identified safety, security, and access to justice as priority themes. In January, a workshop in Abuja on justice sector reform was sponsored jointly by DFID and USAID. The European Commission also funded a variety of projects to promote democracy and justice.

In September, the United Kingdom and Nigeria signed a Memorandum of Understanding on military cooperation, under which advice on training and re-equipment would be supplied to the Nigerian armed forces through British personnel on secondment to the Nigerian Ministry of Defense. President Obasanjo visited the United Kingdom in September for a meeting of several African heads of state called by British Prime Minister Tony Blair.

In August a re-admission agreement was signed between the Irish and Nigerian governments to facilitate the deportation of Nigerians whose claims for asylum in Ireland had been turned down, as well as other Nigerian immigrants rejected by Ireland. The Irish Government denied claims that the deal was linked to an increase in Irish aid to Nigeria.

The European Union (E.U.) itself worked towards strengthening relations with Nigeria. A special joint meeting on Nigeria of the Africa Working Group and the Africa, Caribbean and Pacific Working Group was held in March. It resulted in a Common Position on Nigeria that will constitute the basis for regular political dialogue, aimed at supporting consolidation of democracy, respect for human rights, the rule of law, and good governance. In January, the E.U. condemned the use of corporal punishment in the flogging sentence imposed on a seventeen-year-old girl in Zamfara state.

World Bank and International Monetary Fund (IMF)

In 2001 two World Bank projects were approved: a community-based poverty reduction project for U.S. $60 million and a privatization support project for U.S. $114.3 million. Two projects were approved for 2002, including a U.S. $90.3 million HIV/AIDS project.

NGOs in the Niger Delta complained to the World Bank about a decision to establish the Niger Delta Contractor Revolving Credit Facility, a controversial scheme set up by the International Finance Corporation (part of the World Bank Group) in conjunction with Shell. The complaint centered around the absence of consultation with local communities about the benefits of the scheme, which was intended to relieve poverty by providing credit facilities to Nigerian contractors working with Shell, and lack of confidence in Shell in the light of the company's past environmental and human rights record.

Representatives of the International Monetary Fund (IMF) visited Nigeria. In a review of Nigeria's economy, the IMF expressed concern about macroeconomic imbalances, increased inflation and foreign exchange instability.

RWANDA

HUMAN RIGHTS DEVELOPMENTS

Rwanda appeared to be moving towards greater democracy by decentralizing the administration, drafting a new constitution, and holding local elections. But at the same time the government suppressed a new political party and imposed new limits on civil society. The dominant Rwandan Patriotic Front (RPF) was permitted to recruit extensively while other political parties were banned from any local activities. Justice for the 1994 genocide that killed at least half a million Tutsi advanced slowly in both national and international jurisdictions. Elections for judges under a new system of "popular" justice called *gacaca* spurred hopes of faster resolution of the cases of over 100,000 people still jailed on accusations of genocide, but trials under the new system were unlikely before mid-2002.

Rwanda professed commitment to ending the war in neighboring Congo, but its troops, allied with the Congolese Rally for Democracy (RCD), intensified combat in the eastern provinces of North and South Kivu during September and October. At the same time Rwandan troops were reported fighting rebels inside Burundi, some of them Rwandan, some Burundian, and late in the year troop movements fed speculation about possible war with Uganda.

Rwandan army soldiers assisted their RCD allies in abducting and forcibly recruiting children and men to serve in the RCD armed forces. Rwandan military and civilian authorities continued to use some children as part of the official paramilitary Local Defense Force which sometimes engaged in combat.

From May through July, Rwandan troops fought and defeated the rebel Rwandan Liberation Army (ALIR) which had crossed from bases in the Democratic Republic of Congo (DRC) into northwestern Rwanda. The Rwandan army reportedly killed some 2,000 combatants and captured about the same number who were then detained for "re-education" in "solidarity" camps. In contrast to previous practices, neither Rwandan government soldiers nor ALIR rebels targeted civilians during these months of combat. The ALIR forces had several hundred child soldiers in their ranks, some of whom served in combat. In September and October, rebel combatants fought several skirmishes with Rwandan army soldiers in southwestern Rwanda. Assailants, said by the government to be rebels, ambushed a vehicle in that region and killed one passenger.

In March, Rwandans voted, generally without incident, for district councils. A complicated system of indirect elections gave disproportionate importance to the vote of officials, many of whom had taken office since 1999. In some places RPF representatives and some officials manipulated the registration of candidates, some 45 percent of whom ran unopposed. Party and administrative officials also exerted pressure on voters in some cases, ordinarily in favor of the incumbent. More than 80 percent of incumbent district mayors were re-elected. The law organizing these local elections prohibited political party activity in apparent violation of the constitution. Parties generally observed a moratorium on grass-roots activities, as demanded by the RPF. Ignoring both the electoral law and the moratorium, the RPF recruited new members and did electoral campaigning in some areas. It was not called to account for its activities.

While a commission worked to prepare a new constitution which would supposedly guarantee political freedoms, the government did not honor those guaranteed under the existing fundamental law. In June, former president Pasteur Bizimungu sought to organize a new political party, as permitted by the current constitution. But the government declared the party illegal and twice put Bizimungu under house arrest for brief periods after he had spoken with journalists. Street gangs attacked Bizimungu and another prominent supporter of the new party and several other founding members were threatened and felt obliged to resign to protect themselves.

Others said to have been critical of the government were assassinated or fled the country. A well-known military officer and diplomat, Alphonse Mbayire, was shot in the head twenty-eight times by a RPF soldier in February. Although the assassin was identified by several eyewitnesses, he escaped arrest. At least two other military officers "disappeared" during the year. One, Major Alexis Ruzindana, was believed to have been assassinated as well. Both Mbayire and Ruzindana were reportedly suspected of dissatisfaction with the government and of contacts with dissidents outside the country. These killings resembled that of leading genocide survivor Assiel Kabera in 2000, a crime for which no one was charged.

A military officer of the former government's army, taken into custody by Rwandan military authorities in the DRC last year, was later traced to military detention facilities in Gisenyi and Kigali, but subsequently "disappeared." Civilians last known to have been in custody also "disappeared" during the year, including a Congolese tailor last known to have been detained in a military camp in May. A farmer from Kigali Rural was reportedly last seen at the home of an influential member of the RPF in February 2001 with whom he had a dispute. His family received no official help in locating him.

A number of dissaffected RPA soldiers fled to Uganda where the Rwandan government said they were organizing rebel forces to attack it. Rwanda accused Uganda of aiding these efforts, one of the reasons for heightened tensions and rumors of war between Rwanda and Uganda near the end of the year. In April, seven jurists were detained for several weeks without charge, all of them returned former refugees from Uganda and reportedly accused of links with Rwandan dissidents there.

Several prominent civilians known to have been critical of the government also fled Rwanda. They included a former cabinet minister who was Hutu and a bank president who was Tutsi. In the latter case, the government accused the financier of fraud and sought his arrest on an international warrant. A colonel suspected of having favored Bizimungu's new party was arrested when the new party was suppressed; he was convicted of financial misconduct in a family affair and sentenced to prison. A former parliamentarian who was arrested on charges of fraud in 2000 shortly after he issued a statement criticizing the government remained in prison without trial.

In April, the government published a new law giving authorities broad powers to control the management, finances, and projects of local and international non-governmental organizations. Ministerial directives to implement the law, under discussion at the end of the year, seemed meant to tighten control further. Authorities sent police to disrupt meetings of two human rights organizations in June and August. Security agents detained and interrogated representatives of the Rwanda Debt Relief Network in September after they made critical statements about poverty in Rwanda. Authorities accused these civil society actors of representing political parties and of inciting ethnic divisions.

The government permitted numerous journals to publish, some of them representing independent voices, and granted the Voice of America FM broadcast rights in Rwanda. But security agents called in staff of one critical newspaper twelve times for questioning and the journal ceased publication of its English edition. Rwandan journalists who interviewed Bizimungu when he tried to establish his new party were questioned by security agents and intimidated into handing over a tape recording of the interview. Authorities also threatened action against the British Broadcasting Corporation after it aired an interview with Bizimungu.

With well over 100,000 persons still detained on accusations of genocide, the government gave new attention to improving the delivery of justice. In April, the gov-ernment published a law creating more than 11,000 jurisdictions for gacaca, an innovative system of popular justice. Supposedly inspired by the spirit of local conflict-resolution practices, the system in fact reflects the highly centralized administrative system and will work from materials prepared by prosecutors. According to the law, neither accused nor victim has the right to counsel. Nor has the accused any right to appeal the categorization of his or her crime into one of four levels of gravity, a designation with major consequences for punishment. Those assigned to category one by gacaca jurisdictions are to be tried in regular courts and will likely be sentenced to death if found guilty. Despite the absence of some basic guarantees of due process, the innovative system offered the only hope of trial within the foreseeable future for the tens of thousands now suffering inhumane conditions in prisons and communal lockups. The election of more than 200,000 gacaca judges in October raised expectations that trials would soon begin, but proceedings seemed unlikely before mid-2002 at the earliest. Judges must be trained and prosecutors, over-burdened with work in the regular courts, must prepare case files and summaries of them from which the gacaca jurisdictions will work. The legislature must pass a law on the indemnization of victims and authorities must work out implementation of the community labor which may be imposed as punishment on the guilty.

Throughout the year authorities made some efforts to deal with the thousands of detainees who still have no specific charges against them, sometimes after seven years in prison. Prosecutors continued the practice begun in late 2000 of bringing such persons before their home communities to ask for testimonies against them, in the absence of which the persons were provisionally freed. Hundreds were liberated in this way. Authorities also encouraged detainees to confess in a plea-bargaining procedure which was meant to shorten trials but seemed unlikely to speed proceedings greatly since prosecutors must establish the validity of each confession and over 15,000 confessions awaited examination.

As of March 2001, 5,310 persons had been tried on charges of genocide in the formal court system, some 17 percent of whom were acquitted. Courts worked at a slightly faster pace in the two last years and sentenced fewer of the convicted to death. From 1996 to 1999 more than 30 percent of those found guilty were sentenced to die, but in 2000 only 8.5 percent received this penalty and no one was executed. Despite the widespread prevalence of rape during the genocide, few accused have been tried on this charge, in part because the predominantly male judicial personnel showed little concern for such prosecutions, in part because victims hesitated to come forward.

Hundreds of minors under the age of fourteen at the time of their supposed crime and as such not criminally responsible under Rwandan law were held in prison on charges of genocide until December 2000. After years of promises, authorities finally released over four hundred to a "solidarity camp" for re-education. Hundreds of others remained illegally in detention until September 2001 when they were sent for "re-education;" they were released in November. Thousands of detainees who were aged fourteen to eighteen at the time of their alleged crimes remained in detention. Although supposed to benefit from priority in processing, most did not.

In several cases persons tried, acquitted, and released were later re-arrested after public protest against the verdicts. Eight detainees acquitted in Butare in December 2000 were never released and were to be tried a second time on "new facts." In November 2001, one died, still in detention. Magistrates involved in their acquittal were transferred to other posts with the result that no judgments in genocide cases were issued in that jurisdiction in the first quarter of 2001. Three judges arrested in 2000 on charges of genocide remained in jail; two had served on panels that had acquitted accused persons in well-publicized cases prior to their own arrests.

Authorities recognized corruption in the judiciary as widespread and serious and called on judicial personnel to reform. Both prosecutors and judges were accused of accepting bribes, either to free the accused or to assure their conviction regardless of guilt.

In March the attorney general issued a revised list of category one genocide suspects, those charged with the worst crimes. Some eight hundred persons had been added to the previous list issued in 1999, bringing the total to nearly 2,900. Among the additions was Pierre-Celestin Rwigema, prime minister of Rwanda from 1995 to 2000 and currently living in exile. Also listed was Col. Pierre Habimana of the former Rwandan army, in the hands of Rwandan authorities since July 2001 but not yet charged with genocide as of late 2001.

Authorities did little to protect children from abuse and exploitation and in the capital local officials supervised a harsh campaign to rid Kigali of thousands of street children. Police and members of the Local Defense Force forcibly rounded up the children and sometimes beat them before detaining them in ill-equipped centers. An estimated 400,000 orphans lived in child-headed households or in unofficial fostering arrangements. Many were exploited as domestic laborers or lost their property to adults.

The government debated a new policy on land holdings while at the local level disputes over acquisition of large holdings by the powerful continued. Authorities slowed implementation of the forced villagization which had displaced hundreds of thousands of persons in previous years.

DEFENDING HUMAN RIGHTS

Authorities harassed the Rwandan League for the Promotion and Defense of Human Rights (LIPRODHOR), the most important human rights organization in the country, after it published a press release criticizing conditions at one prison. A journalist lost his job at the national radio after giving an internationally-broadcast interview about the press release. Authorities threatened a LIPRODHOR representative with arrest in one province and banned educational programs by the organization in three provinces. Government officials attempted to interfere in staffing decisions and blocked disbursement of funds granted LIPRODHOR by an international agency.

Police disrupted an initial meeting of a new human rights organization, Justice and Peace, but authorities later permitted the new group to meet.

The National Human Rights Commission expanded both staff and activities. In its first substantial report on the human rights situation, the commission showed some independence from authorities and detailed a number of cases of abuses.

THE ROLE OF THE INTERNATIONAL COMMUNITY

As the international community became increasingly critical of the Rwandan role in the Congo war, the U.N. Security Council in October called upon Rwanda and other signatories to the Lusaka Accords to implement their commitments, including withdrawing their troops. The council also urged all parties to end their continuing human rights abuses. In April a panel of experts named by the Security Council published a report documenting the illegal exploitation of Congolese resources by Rwandans and other foreign actors and suggesting that economic rather than security considerations explained the continued presence of Rwandan troops in the eastern DRC. After those criticized contested the findings, the Security Council mandated a second report. Issued in November, it confirmed the original conclusions regarding Rwandan conduct and added new criticism of Zimbabwe and others.

The U.N. Commission on Human Rights ended the mandate of its special representative for Rwanda. The result of extensive lobbying by Rwandan delegates, this decision underestimated the gravity of continuing human rights abuses in Rwanda.

The European Union pressed for an end to the Congo war, sending a high level delegation to the region in November. It budgeted some $100 million in assistance to Rwanda for 2000-2001 but not all of that amount was spent. It granted $1.2 million to the National Human Rights Commission to help it monitor gacaca proceedings.

Despite reservations about Rwandan involvement in the Congo war, international actors expressed continued confidence in the Rwandan domestic political and economic situation. The International Monetary Fund (IMF) released U.S.$ 12 million for a three year poverty reduction plan and the World Bank, the IMF, the African Development Fund, and the International Fund for Agricultural Development cancelled $25 million of Rwandan foreign debt. France, in the past critical of the Rwandan government, showed new willingness to support such international aid measures after Foreign Minister Herbert Vedrine was well received in Kigali. Germany granted $16.8 million for development and China granted $3.6 million and forgave more than $16 million in Rwandan debt. The United Kingdom, still the most enthusiastic supporter of the Rwandan government, continued its ten-year program of $70 million in general budget support.

In the United States the Bush administration adopted a more neutral position in the Great Lakes crisis coincidental with its general reduction of engagement elsewhere in Africa and joined other donors in criticizing Rwandan involvement in the Congo war. Embassy staff closely monitored the conduct of both Rwandan troops and ALIR rebels during the combat in northwestern Rwanda in May through July, thus encouraging observation of international humanitarian law. Permitted to establish FM service for the Voice of America (VOA) in Rwanda, the U.S. failed to criticize publicly government intimidation of the press even though a VOA journalist was among those harassed. Although State Department officials privately expressed more reservations about the Rwandan government than in the past, the U.S. provided $14 million in development assistance and another $1.5 million under the Great Lakes Justice Initiative.

The International Criminal Tribunal for Rwanda had fifty-two persons in custody, eight of whom had been tried and convicted of genocide. One accused person was acquitted in 2001. The tribunal continued to suffer from serious management problems and was increasingly criticized for its expense and delays in delivering justice. A Belgian court found four persons guilty of genocide in the first jury trial held anywhere in connection with the 1994 slaughter and sentenced them to prison terms ranging from twelve to twenty years.

Relevant Human Rights Watch Reports:

Uprooting the Rural Poor in Rwanda, 5/01

SIERRA LEONE

HUMAN RIGHTS DEVELOPMENTS

Three agreements between the Sierra Leonean government and the rebel Revolutionary United Front (RUF) contributed to an improvement in the human rights situation in Sierra Leone in 2001. The first, signed in Abuja, Nigeria in November 2000, led to a ceasefire. The second and third agreements, signed in

May 2001, committed both parties to restart the disarmament process, provide for the reestablishment of government authority in former rebel held areas, and release all child combatants and abductees. Military pressure on the RUF by both the Guinean army, which responded to RUF cross-border raids by launching ground and air attacks into Sierra Leone, and the British-trained and led Sierra Leonean army, contributed to this process. Over 16,700 United Nations peace-keepers deployed into RUF strongholds, including the diamond-rich Kono District, and over 29,300 combatants were disarmed. The release of over 3,000 child soldiers, abductees, and separated children by the RUF and by pro-government civil defense militias was one of the most positive human rights developments of the year. However, serious violations, which often involved victims and perpetrators not only from Sierra Leone but also from neighboring Liberia and Guinea, were persistent and served to highlight the region's conflicts. The government extended its own mandate, but announced that elections due in 2001 would take place on May 14, 2002.

In 2001, Sierra Leone ratified the Mine Ban Treaty, the Convention against Torture, and the optional protocols to the Convention on the Rights of the Child on the involvement of children in armed conflict and on the sale of children, child prostitution, and child pornography.

Within government-controlled areas, pro-government militias committed numerous human rights violations with impunity. In the southern city of Bo, Kamajor militiamen intimidated and threatened police officers attempting to question several Kamajor suspects, forcing the police to later release them. There were numerous cases of sexual assault by Kamajor militiamen, including gang rape and the rape of children. Members of civil defense militias returning from refugee camps in Guinea through RUF-held areas attacked, looted, and burned several villages, and in June massacred at least twenty-two civilians, including nine children, in Yiriai village, in northern Koinadugu District, in what was the worst single atrocity of the year.

From January through November 2001, the government released 137 detainees, including thirteen children, who since May 2000 had been held without charge under the 1991 State of Emergency Act. However, scores remained in detention and were systematically denied the right to counsel and to have contact with their families. The whereabouts of RUF leader Foday Sankoh remained undisclosed. At least ten RUF prisoners died in custody. In December 2000, the International Committee of the Red Cross received government authorization to visit detention facilities, although its delegates were again excluded for some two months following a March 14 riot over poor prison conditions within Freetown's central prison.

The human rights picture within RUF-held areas improved somewhat relative to previous years. Some RUF commanders attempted to discipline combatants who committed abuses. Nevertheless, RUF forces, often acting together with Liberian government troops, committed scores of serious abuses including rape, murder, abduction, and subjection to forced labor. The victims of these abuses included Sierra Leoneans returning from refugee camps in Guinea; Guinean civilians, attacked during a campaign of cross-border raids from September 2000 through April 2001; and Liberians fleeing renewed fighting in Lofa county from April 2001.

The RUF abducted at least one hundred Guineans, including children and the elderly, and held them in Kailahun for up to five months. UNHCR and other aid agencies were on a few occasions refused permission to evacuate sick and severely malnourished refugees. Refugees were very often forced to work in exchange for permission to leave rebel held areas. Scores of refugees died of illness and hundreds suffered moderate to severe malnourishment. While the RUF released or demobilized more than 1,500 male child combatants, they were reluctant to release Sierra Leonean and Guinean female abductees, most of whom were suspected of having been sexually abused.

Fighting between the RUF and civil defense militias in the east of the country in June through August 2001 left tens of civilians dead. In June and July, RUF combatants attacked several villages, including Porpon, in which they killed at least three children, hacked off the ear of one man, and abducted at least sixteen civilians. On July 19, RUF combatants attacked Henekuma village and massacred at least ten civilians. There were several reports of members of pro-government militias having been tortured and summarily executed by the RUF, including the October 2000 execution of ten militiamen in Kambia District, and the May 2001 execution of two militiamen in Kono. In July, RUF rebels cut off the ear and severed the Achilles tendons of a militiaman captured in Koinadugu District.

From September 2000 through April 2001, RUF rebels and Liberian government forces acting together attacked refugee camps and villages just across the border with Guinea, then home to several hundred thousand Sierra Leonean and Liberian refugees. Following the attacks, Guinean security forces and the local population retaliated against the refugees, frequently looting, extorting, raping, and unlawfully detaining them. At least eleven refugees were tortured or beaten to death while detained within the Forecariah Prison in Southwestern Guinean, and several more detainees died of illness and starvation.

Guinean forces responded to RUF raids into Guinea by killing and wounding dozens of civilians in indiscriminate helicopter and artillery attacks against rebel-held areas of Sierra Leone in northern Kambia, Bombali, and Koinadugu districts. At least forty-two civilians, including eleven children, were killed during at least thirteen attacks between September 2000 and April 2001. Guinean troops also conducted several ground attacks during which several civilians were gunned down, several girls and women were raped, and houses were set on fire. Captured RUF combatants were summarily executed and at least eighteen RUF detainees "disappeared" following capture. In March 2001, Guinean troops amputated the hands of several RUF combatants detained during attacks on the towns of Kychom and Kasiri.

There were two reported cases of rape by U.N. peacekeepers, one involving a Guinean soldier accused of raping a twelve-year-old girl in Bo, and another involving a Nigerian. Both were at this writing under investigation. There were also reports of excessive use of force and illegal detention of civilians by Nigerian peacekeepers. In the most serious incident, in July 2001, the peacekeepers beat and in some cases tortured civilians they had detained after a riot in Port Loko. Following a UNAMSIL board of inquiry, disciplinary action was taken against two peacekeepers, including one lieutenant.

DEFENDING HUMAN RIGHTS

Numerous nongovernmental human rights organizations operated in Sierra Leone, including the Campaign for Good Governance, Forum of Conscience, and Network Movement for Peace and Justice. Thirty-three of these groups were part of a coalition called the National Forum for Human Rights (NFHR) whose purpose was coordination and technical advice to the member groups. The establishment of government control over previously inaccessible areas allowed human rights groups to start operating outside the capital Freetown. However, most of these lacked proper funding, expertise, and institutional support. Most of their activities focused on human rights education for the public and preparing the groundwork for the planned Truth and Reconciliation Commission (TRC). As in past years, these groups did very little monitoring of continuing human rights abuses. Local human rights groups denounced the indiscriminate attack on civilians by a Guinean helicopter gunship, and governmental failure to provide due process for RUF prisoners, but in general remained reluctant to document and publicly denounce persistent abuses by either rebel or government forces.

The TRC mandated under the 1999 Lome Peace Accord, was yet to be set up, though its establishment was a priority for both local human rights groups and the U.N. Mission in Sierra Leone (UNAMSIL) human rights section. The formation of an autonomous, quasi-judicial national human rights commission, also provided for in the 1999 Lomé Peace Accord, was slow and received little national or international attention. Legislation to establish the commission had yet to be presented to parliament.

Meanwhile, the existing governmental body, the National Commission for Democracy and Human Rights (NCDHR), formed in 1996, was severely constrained by lack of funds. It did little or no monitoring or documentation of human rights violations. Its activities consisted of human rights and civic education, and raising public awareness about the role of the TRC. It also continued to run a successful legal aid clinic for indigents.

THE ROLE OF THE INTERNATIONAL COMMUNITY

The activities of all key members of the international community were aimed at salvaging the fragile peace process shattered by the RUF in May 2000. Pressing human rights concerns received inadequate attention.

United Nations

UNAMSIL's budget for 2001 was an estimated U.S.$744 million. Security Council Resolution 1346, passed in March 2001, mandated that UNAMSIL's troop strength be increased from 13,000, to 17,500. At regular U.N.-chaired meetings between the RUF and the Sierra Leonean government, UNAMSIL failed to aggressively interpret the part of its mandate that allowed for the protection of civilians or to emphasize concerns regarding ongoing violations against civilians. Members of the UNAMSIL human rights section were, for most of the year, not allowed to attend these meetings. The number of UNAMSIL human rights monitors—mandated in 2000 to be fourteen—was in mid-2001 increased to twenty by the Department of Peacekeeping Operations, but as of this writing, the unit never operated with more than fifteen. For most of the year the unit concentrated on conducting human rights education, and preparation for the TRC, rather than monitoring ongoing violations. However, the unit did complete thorough reports on RUF and Civil Defense Forces (CDF) violence in the east and on prison conditions, but lacked a regular channel for disseminating information.

On August 14, 2000, the Security Council adopted Resolution 1315, which authorized the secretary-general to enter into negotiations with the government of Sierra Leone to establish a Special Court for Sierra Leone, using both international and Sierra Leonean law, judges, and prosecutors, to bring the perpetrators of the most serious violations since 1996 to justice. At this writing, the draft statute for the court was yet to be finalized and, despite considerable efforts on the part of the secretary-general, funds for its operation were yet to be secured. By May 2001, the lack of member state contributions for the original budget of U.S.$114 (for the first three years) led to budget revision. On June 14, 2001, the secretary-general submitted a revised three-year budget of U.S.$56.8 million. On July 24, 2001, the Security Council approved the plans to go ahead with the Special Court despite a shortfall of one million dollars for the first year and forty million dollars for the next two years. A Sierra Leonean government proposal that the temporal jurisdiction of the court be extended back to 1991, the commencement of the war, was not supported.

In 2000, the U.N. Security Council adopted Resolution 1306, which imposed an eighteen month ban on the trade in rough diamonds from Sierra Leone that did not have a government certificate, and mandated setting up a five-person panel of experts to look into violations of sanctions and the link between the trade in diamonds and arms. On December 20, 2000, the findings of the panel of experts were published in a report which implicated, among others, the governments of Liberia, Burkina Faso, United Arab Emirates, and Belgium in facilitating illicit arms and diamond sales to the RUF. On March 7, 2001, the Security Council voted unanimously in support of Resolution 1343, which placed a global ban on the direct or indirect import of all rough diamonds from Liberia, and placed an international travel ban on senior member of the Liberian government. The ban came into effect two months later. On March 26, the U.N. secretary-general appointed a Panel of Experts to investigate any violations of the sanctions and possible links between the exploitation of natural resources and the fuelling of the conflict.

On October 30, the Panel of Experts published its findings. The panel found widespread violations of sanctions against Liberia and recommended that the council impose an arms embargo on all rebel groups in Mano River Union countries, extend the Liberian arms embargo and the rough diamonds sanctions and urged all U.N. members to stop supplying weapons to Guinea and Sierra Leone. The panel also focused on the importance of timber revenues for the government, and called for the U.N. to impose a ban on all log exports from Liberia starting in July 2002.

Several high-level U.N. officials visited Sierra Leone, including Deputy Secretary-General Louise Frechette who visited in April, and Undersecretary-General of United Nations Peacekeeping Operations Hedi Annabi, in May. An August visit by U.N. Special Rapporteur on Violence against Women Radhika Coomaraswamy resulted in a call for more donor support to help victims of sexual violence.

UNHCR struggled to respond to the subregional crisis. After visiting the area in February 2001, High Commissioner Ruud Lubbers proposed a policy of humanitarian corridors for Sierra Leonean refugees in Guinea to return through rebel-held territory. However, following international criticism, it was decided rather to relocate the refugees to camps further within Guinea.

Organization of African Unity (OAU) and Economic Community of West African States (ECOWAS)

Responding to the unfolding regional crisis brought on by cross-border raids, the ECOWAS Defense and Security Commission in December 2000 proposed to deploy a force of some 1,700 troops to secure the borders between Guinea, Sierra Leone, and Liberia. Although the OAU endorsed this plan in May, Guinea argued that the protection and monitoring mandate of the force was too weak. When neither Guinea nor Liberia had signed the status of forces agreement, and after ECOWAS heads of states insisted upon Security Council involvement and funding, the plan was dropped.

Nevertheless, members of the ECOWAS Committee of Six on Sierra Leone conducted considerable shuttle diplomacy aimed at restarting the Sierra Leonean peace process and seeking a diplomatic solution to the regional crisis. Together with the United Nations, ECOWAS was directly involved in securing the November 2000 Abuja Ceasefire Agreement, and a subsequent meeting in Abuja in May 2001 which committed the RUF and government to start disarming. During an extraordinary ECOWAS summit in Abuja, Nigeria on April 11, an ECOWAS mediation committee, comprising the presidents of Mali, Nigeria, and Togo was set up to encourage dialogue between the Mano River countries.

Ethiopian Kingsley Mamabolo, who was appointed the OAU special envoy to Sierra Leone in June 2000, made several low-profile visits to Sierra Leone, and representatives from the OAU were present as observers in several key meetings surrounding the Sierra Leonean peace process.

European Union

In February 2001, the European Parliament issued a resolution on the situation in the Mano River Union strongly condemning cross-border incursions by all sides and urging all parties to respect the human rights of refugees, civilians, and humanitarian workers. In May, Hans Dahlgren, the Swedish State Secretary for Foreign Affairs, led an eight-member European Union Ministerial Delegation to the Mano

River countries. In July, Dahlgren was appointed E.U. special envoy in the Mano River region.

Since 1995 the European Commission has allocated more than 135 million ECU (U.S.$120 million) to Sierra Leone for development, good governance, social-economic infrastructure, child protection programs, and health and rehabilitation projects over five years. In March 2001, the European Community granted 11 million ECU (U.S.$9.7 million) to be distributed through the community's Humanitarian Office (ECHO) for humanitarian assistance in Sierra Leone, specifically to help the internally displaced, women, children, and the disabled. In May, 4.5 million ECU was dispatched to help Sierra Leonean and Liberian refugees in Guinea, and in October, an additional 5.1 million ECU was dispatched, much of it to be channeled through UNHCR, for refugees, returnees and IDP's within the Mano River Union.

At this writing, the E.U. itself has not contributed to the Sierra Leone Special Court. E.U. officials maintain that their contributions should focus on rehabilitation and reintegration, including vocational skills and education for returning refugees and IDP's. However, a number of member states contributed, including Denmark, Germany, the Netherlands, Sweden and the United Kingdom.

United Kingdom

The United Kingdom continued to play a pivotal role in political and military developments in Sierra Leone. In January, Jonathan Riley, the British brigadier commanding in Sierra Leone, pledged that British troops would stay until the RUF was either defeated militarily or diplomatically. The U.K. also continued its commitment to rebuild and restructure the Sierra Leonean Army and the Sierra Leonean Police. From June 2000 through September 2001, some six hundred British troops were involved in training 8,500 Sierra Leonean Army soldiers. After September 2001, the 360 U.K. military personnel who remained continued to play a major role in advising and directing military operations, including the staffing of key positions within the Sierra Leonean Defense Headquarters. They also helped administer a program to train up to 3,000 ex-RUF and CDF combatants selected to join the new SLA. In coordination with the commonwealth secretariat, the U.K. provided officers and funds for training and administration of the Sierra Leonean police, including the secondment of the inspector general.

U.K. assistance to Sierra Leone since April 2001 was estimated to be 84.5 million pounds sterling, including funding for demobilization and reintegration programs, training and equipment for the army and police, human rights and civil society groups, rehabilitation of the legal system, humanitarian aid, and helping to restore the local Paramount Chiefs.

United States

U.S. policy on Sierra Leone revolved around ending external support for the RUF, supporting the British military actions, and providing humanitarian support. The U.S. pledge of U.S. $15 million over three years to the proposed Special Court for Sierra Leone was the largest of any contributing nation. The U.S. total human-itarian and emergency contribution in FY 2001, including grants to aid agencies, UNHCR, and World Food Programme through USAID for food relief, assistance to refugees, and development programs was U.S. $75 million.

After the May 2000 breakdown in the peace process, former U.S. president Bill Clinton initiated a program called Operation Focus Relief (OFR) to train and equip seven battalions of West African troops for peacekeeping with the U.N. in Sierra Leone. The training was conducted by U.S. Special Forces. The first phase of the program trained two Nigerian battalions that were deployed in January 2001 to serve with UNAMSIL. The second phase, which ended in August, trained troops from Ghana and Senegal. The third phase, which will be completed before the end of 2001, involved three further Nigerian battalions. For FY 2001, OFR was bud-geted at U.S. $24 million in peacekeeping funds, as well as U.S. $32 million in Department of Defense funds for equipment and transportation. The U.S. also deployed three military officers to work with the Sierra Leone army as part of the British training program. These officers, as well as other U.S. Embassy officials, had some responsibility for monitoring the performance of the U.S.-trained troops.

In addition to OFR, in June the administration notified Congress of its intention to provide U.S. $3 million in nonlethal training and equipment to the Guinean mil-itary to assist that country in defending against the destabilizing activities of the RUF and Charles Taylor in Liberia. Congressional concerns about abuses by the Guinean military led to additional reporting and monitoring requirements. At this writing, however, the program had not yet begun.

SOUTH AFRICA

HUMAN RIGHTS DEVELOPMENTS

President Thabo Mbeki led a government dominated by the African National Congress (ANC), though the Inkatha Freedom Party (IFP) remained a junior part-ner. Apparently reflecting divisions within the ruling party, Minister for Safety and Security Steve Tshwete announced in April that the police would investigate bizarre allegations of a conspiracy against the president led by three prominent members of the ANC. The Congress of South African Trades Unions (COSATU) and many other commentators expressed concern about the use of state resources for politi-cal purposes. Tensions within the tripartite alliance of the ANC, COSATU, and the South African Communist Party (SACP) also increased on other fronts during the year. In August, COSATU staged a two-day general strike in protest at the govern-ment's policies of privatization. A major investigation into corruption in relation to government arms purchases led to the arrest of former ANC chief whip Tony Yengeni in October; other arrests were expected. Later that month, the opposition

Democratic Alliance split into its constituent parts, the Democratic Party and the New National Party (NNP), provoked by clashes between the parties in the Western Cape. An alliance between the ANC and the NNP (a reincarnation of the party of government between 1948 and 1994) was mooted.

The Truth and Reconciliation Commission (TRC) continued hearing applications for amnesty until May 31, when its work was formally ended. The mandate of the TRC itself was extended only to complete the final two volumes of its report. The government stated that legislation setting the framework for reparations to the victims would be introduced to parliament in 2002. Also wrapping up business from the past, the trial of Wouter Basson, a chemical weapons expert with the old South African army, continued throughout 2001.

In November 2000, South Africa ratified the treaty to establish an International Criminal Court; legislation to bring it into effect domestically was introduced to parliament in July 2001. The Promotion of Access to Information Act came into effect in March 2001, adding flesh to the constitutional right to access government and privately held information. The Protected Disclosure Act, designed to shield "whistle-blowers," came into effect February. Among notable decisions, the Constitutional Court ruled in May that the South African government's deportation to the U.S. of Mohamed Khalfan, a suspect in the 1998 bombing of the U.S. embassies in Nairobi and Dar es Salaam, was unlawful. The court found that South Africa should have sought assurances from the U.S. government that Khalfan would not be subject to the death penalty.

In July, there were scenes uncomfortably reminiscent of the past when the government evicted squatters from land outside Johannesburg who had been "sold" plots by the opposition Pan Africanist Congress (PAC). In response to these developments, and land invasions taking place in Zimbabwe, the Democratic Alliance joined with the PAC in demanding a national debate on South Africa's land reform program.

Torture and ill-treatment of criminal suspects by the police remained a serious problem. The Independent Complaints Directorate (ICD), set up in 1997 to investigate or oversee the investigation of complaints against the police, reported 650 deaths in custody or as a result of police action during the year to March 2001, a slight decrease on the previous year. The number of complaints lodged with the ICD increased by 11 percent, to 4,863. Encouragingly, the ICD reported that there had been a decrease in allegations of torture. In November 2000, a booklet titled "The ABC of Human Rights and Policing," produced with funding from the Danish Embassy, was launched and distributed among police officers.

In July, Minister Tshwete announced that the government intended to increase the size of the police force from 121,000 to 127,000 over the next three years. In May, the minister announced progress in carrying out a review of police collection of crime statistics, and that publication of those statistics, suspended since July 2000, would be resumed at the end of the third quarter of 2001. Trial projects to establish "community safety forums" were launched in the Western Cape, involving all sectors of government in improving safety and security, and not only the police. In January 2001, it was announced that all specialized units within the police would be phased out, and their personnel redeployed to priority crime units at local police stations. New metropolitan police forces were launched in Johannesburg and Tshwane (the greater Pretoria area).

In February 2001, the first of sixty planned government-funded legal assistance centers opened in Benoni, outside Johannesburg. A new management team was installed at the Legal Aid Board in the same month, leading to hopes that the improvements since Mohammed Navsa took over as chairman of the board would continue. In October, the board announced a range of cooperative agreements aimed at improving access to legal services among the poor. However, a backlog of court cases continued to plague the system despite government initiatives to clear it, contributing to the crisis of overcrowding in prisons. Following several strikes, large increases in pay to prosecutors were awarded in July, backdated to January. The office of the National Director for Public Prosecutions (NDPP) and its elite crime fighting unit known as the Scorpions, carried out investigations of high priority crimes; tensions between the Scorpions and the regular police were reported.

At the end of 2000, South Africa's prisons held 160,003 people, a slight fall on the previous year; approved prison accommodation grew from 99,834 to 101,991, and four additional prisons were under construction. In March 2001, the minister of correctional services signed a contract with a private company, the Ikwezi Consortium, to design, build, and operate a maximum security prison in Bloemfontein, the first such contract in South Africa. More than 55,000 of those being held were awaiting trial, of whom almost 13,000 had been locked up for more than six months. More than 4,000 were under eighteen years of age; legislation and practical measures to improve the situation of children charged with violent crimes was still not in place. By April 2001, the total prison population had risen again to 172,000, of whom 64,000 were awaiting trial, according to a report to parliament by Inspecting Judge Johannes Fagan. Draft legislation aimed at improving the parole system was tabled in Parliament in February 2001. Assaults on prisoners by warders and other prisoners remained serious problems, including widespread prisoner-on-prisoner rape: a spokesperson for the inspecting judge estimated that 70 to 80 percent of all suspects were sodomized by fellow prisoners before they were even officially charged. In October 2000, it was revealed that AIDS-related deaths in South African prisons had increased by 300 percent from 1995 to 1999. The doctor in charge of medical services for prisoners in Cape Town's Pollsmoor prison stated that conditions in the prison represented a health hazard for the Western Cape.

In November, legislation was approved by parliament to regulate South Africa's private security industry, long plagued with allegations of abuse. Vigilante violence remained a serious problem, with groups such as People Against Gangsterism and Drugs (PAGAD) and Mapogo a Mathamaga responsible for beatings and execution-style murders. A witness due to testify in a trial of PAGAD members was shot dead in April. "Taxi violence" between rival operators of minibus taxis continued; reports implicated members of the police in this violence. In KwaZulu-Natal, long standing tensions between the ANC and IFP broke out into violence at different times. In May, a workshop organized by the Parliamentary Participation Unit in rural KwaZulu-Natal was disrupted by a group of thirty-five IFP supporters who claimed that the unit had not gained IFP consent to hold the meeting in their area.

Violence against women and girls, including sexual violence, remained a very serious problem. Human Rights Watch published a report in March concluding that rape and other sexual violence were part of the normal environment for girls in schools, as well as in the wider community. In September 2001, a report from the Eastern Cape legislature's standing committee on education detailed horrific abuse by teachers at the province's schools. In March, the ICD reported for the first time to parliament on its duties to monitor the implementation by police of the Domestic Violence Act, and noted serious deficiencies at many police stations. In August, National Police Commissioner Jackie Selebi said that violence against women was a priority crime for the police, but that the Domestic Violence Act was effectively not enforceable. In August, the Constitutional Court handed down an important decision ruling that the state's duty to protect the security of women could form the basis of a case for damages. The case considered involved a woman who had been raped by a man out on bail on charges of attempting to rape another woman; it was referred back to the High Court for rehearing on the facts. The Recognition of Customary Marriages Act came into effect in November 2000, bringing the protection of the law to people in such unions. In the same month, Molo Songololo, an NGO, launched a report on the trafficking of children within South Africa for the purposes of sexual exploitation, identifying this as a serious but unquantified problem to which the state response was wholly inadequate. Another study, published in January 2001, suggested that child poverty was increasing, contributing to children's vulnerability to such exploitation. In August, the Pretoria High Court ruled that sections of the Sexual Offences Act banning prostitution were unconstitutional.

Violence on commercial farms—documented in an August Human Rights Watch report—remained a high profile issue. Commercial farmers, highly vulnerable to violent crime, called for greater security force protection, while organizations representing farm workers denounced assaults on farm workers. In October, the government held a conference on rural safety, focusing on several aspects of crime in commercial farming areas. In the same month, commercial farmers in the Western Cape launched a code of conduct committing farmers to promoting "decent livelihoods" for their workers.

Widespread xenophobia led to violence against foreigners on several occasions, including attacks on Zimbabweans resident in a squatter camp in Gauteng in October, in which seventy-four shacks were gutted by fire. Police were deployed to patrol the settlement. In May, the Department of Home Affairs agreed to withdraw a directive to immigration officers to refuse asylum to applicants who had transited a "safe" third country before reaching South Africa, in a settlement following a court application by the NGO Lawyers for Human Rights. In the same month, the department began to issue new identity documents to refugees, in accordance with the 1998 Refugees Act. In June, the department was defeated in court, when the Constitutional Court upheld the High Court's declaration that two sections of the existing Aliens Control Act relating to applications for work permits for foreign spouses of South African citizens were unconstitutional. In June, the department tabled in parliament a new draft of a long-awaited Immigration Bill; but by November it had yet to make any progress.

In April, the Pharmaceutical Manufacturers' Association of South Africa withdrew a case from the Pretoria High Court that it had brought against the government to strike down legislative provisions that would allow the government to produce or import anti-retroviral drugs at low cost. However, the government did not go on to announce any plans to make such drugs available in public hospitals. The government also opposed in court a legal challenge brought by the Treatment Action Campaign (TAC) to require the government to supply in the public health sector anti-retroviral drugs to prevent mother-to-child transmission. President Mbeki continued to question the link between HIV and AIDS, but spoke less on the subject than in previous years. In October, a report by the Medical Research Council was published, indicating that in 2000, 40 percent of adult deaths and 25 percent of total deaths in South Africa were HIV-related, thus contradicting a statement by President Mbeki that violence was the main cause of death.

DEFENDING HUMAN RIGHTS

South Africa's vigorous human rights community continued to monitor adherence to national and international standards. Occasional government hostility to NGO criticism was counteracted by strong collaboration in government-NGO partnerships elsewhere. The constitutionally mandated South African Human Rights Commission (SAHRC) criticized the government for often ignoring its recommendations. The commission took a high profile on issues related to racism, including in programs related to the World Conference Against Racism, held in Durban, in August and September. In July, it announced a major investigation into human rights violations on commercial farms. In May, a new set of commissioners joined the Commission on Gender Equality (CGE), also established by constitutional mandate. In August, the CGE hosted a national gender summit.

THE ROLE OF THE INTERNATIONAL COMMUNITY

South Africa's pivotal position in the continent was underlined during the year by several high profile visits to South Africa by foreign leaders (including Japanese Prime Minister Yoshiro Mori, during the first visit by a Japanese head of government to sub-Saharan Africa), and President Mbeki's involvement in a number of key initiatives, including the New Partnership for Africa's Development (NEPAD) launched at the OAU summit in July. In October, South Africa deployed seven hundred soldiers to Burundi, as part of a peacekeeping force to protect the transitional government. In August and September, South Africa hosted the World Conference Against Racism.

United States

Outgoing Secretary of State Madeleine Albright visited South Africa in December 2000, as did her successor Colin Powell in May 2001. In June 2001 President Mbeki visited the U.S., his second visit as head of state, and met with President

Bush. The two leaders reaffirmed "excellent ties" between the two countries and signed treaties related to the fight against international crime, including on extradition. However, the U.S./South Africa bi-national commission set up under President Clinton was scrapped. Following the September 11 attacks, South Africa stated that it would cooperate with U.S. efforts to bring the culprits to justice, but that any action taken should be based on "thorough investigation and incontrovertible evidence."

The U.S. Agency for International Development (USAID) program for South Africa funded projects worth U.S. $46.68 million to South Africa in 2000, and projected spending $50 million in 2001. The critical areas for funding in 2001 identified in a December 2000 declaration on development assistance included job creation, the criminal justice system, HIV/AIDS, education, and small business development.

European Union

Several European heads of government visited South Africa during the year. In these and other discussions, E.U. member states indicated their commitment to NEPAD, and reliance on South Africa as leader in the region.

The E.U. Foundation for Human Rights in South Africa continued funding human rights projects, with funds from the European Commission's Program for Reconstruction and Development in South Africa. The E.U. remained South Africa's largest donor, having given an average 125 million euro per year for development since 1994. Individual E.U. member states also made bilateral contributions to human rights initiatives.

Britain in particular continued its close ties to South Africa. In June, President Mbeki visited the U.K. for meetings with Prime Minister Tony Blair and other ministers, including a meeting of the U.K.-South Africa bilateral forum. Blair and Mbeki published a joint article committing resources to development in Africa. The presence of the British Military Advisory and Training Team (BMATT) in South Africa was extended to 2003.

Relevant Human Rights Watch Reports:

Unequal Protection: The State Response to Violent Crime on South African Farms, 8/01

Scared at School: Sexual Violence Against Girls in South African Schools, 3/01

SUDAN

HUMAN RIGHTS DEVELOPMENTS

Despite openings in the political arena, the human rights situation in Sudan was grim. The government kept in force a state of emergency to suppress Islamist and other opposition to the ruling Islamist party. It was increasingly aggressive in pursuing the eighteen-year civil war, particularly in southern oil fields where its militias and army forcibly displaced thousands of residents. The war reflected a failure among Sudanese to agree on the role of religion in government, tolerance of diversity, and sharing of resources between the marginalized majority and the politically dominant Arab-Muslim minority. As Sudan comprised 35 million people divided into nineteen major African and Arab ethnic groups, about 70 percent Muslim and the rest Christian and traditional believers, lack of tolerance was an invitation to strife.

President Omar El Bashir's ruling National Congress (NC) party won the December 2000 presidential and legislative elections, which were boycotted by all the main opposition parties and excluded those living in rebel-held areas. That month the government amended the National Security Act permitting suspects to be detained indefinitely without charge and denied judicial review for up to six months. It extended the state of emergency through a second year, until December 31, 2001.

In late December 2000, security forces arrested seven civilian members of the opposition National Democratic Alliance (NDA) while they met with a U.S. diplomat. The NDA had not registered a political party registration required an oath of allegiance to the ruling party's goals. The NDA civilians in Khartoum had ties to the military wing of the NDA, operating from exile, but their presence and low-key meetings in Khartoum were usually ignored by the authorities, who sought to woo the entire organization and its component parties back from exile. Charges of treason (carrying the death penalty) and threatening the existing government were brought against the NDA members. Defense lawyers protested numerous violations of fair trial rights.

Government opponents in the People's National Congress (PNC), a NC splinter party founded by Islamist political leader Hassan Turabi in 2000, were also harassed and jailed, but not charged with any crime. In February 2001, Turabi signed a memorandum of understanding with the rebel Sudan People's Liberation Movement/Army (SPLM/A), and called on Sudanese to rise against El Bashir. Security forces arrested Turabi and at least twenty other PNC leaders. Turabi was charged with crimes punishable by death or life imprisonment, and authorities periodically rounded up PNC members.

After September 11, the Sudan government dismissed the charges against the NDA members, Turabi, and other PNC members, and freed all but Turabi—who remained under house arrest. Some thirty-five PNC activists were rearrested at their post-release press conference.

Reports of torture and ill-treatment continued. A Sudatel employee fleeing the July 2001 SPLA capture of Raga reportedly was beaten daily and was given little food or water after his detention by government forces. Security forces reportedly pulled out the fingernails of another man detained during the same exodus. Security forces in Juba reportedly continued to use a large metal shipping container as a detention cell, a years-long practice that subjected detainees to life-threatening heat.

The two English-language newspapers in Khartoum, *Khartoum Monitor* and *Nile Courier,* provided a political forum for southerners. The *Khartoum Monitor* was periodically suspended by security forces or by the Press National Council, however, and on April 12, 2001, security forces briefly detained its editor-in-chief Alfred Taban at a church-called news conference. In February 2001, a Sudanese court fined the independent *Al Rai Al Akhar* newspaper an astounding U.S. $390,000, and fined the editor and a journalist another $5,800 or three months in jail each, for libeling local government. A government censor was permanently based in all newspaper offices. Censorship of English-language newspapers was tightened during the visit of the ACP-EU mission, and papers were forbidden to publish blank spaces indicating where censorship was imposed.

The government harassed and discriminated against Christians. In April 2001, police injured and briefly detained Christians demonstrating against a government order transferring an Easter service (convoked by a visiting German evangelist) from Khartoum to a suburb. The following day police teargassed students protesting these arrests outside All Saints' Episcopal church, then stormed the protest meeting inside the church, damaging windows and chairs, and tear-gassing the interior; three were seriously injured and fifty-seven arrested on this second day of disturbances. They had no legal representation at their trial the following day, which lasted less than one hour. The six girls detained and several boys were flogged; the rest were sentenced to twenty days in jail each.

Half of the Omdurman headquarters of the Episcopal Church of Sudan was illegally occupied by the ministry of health of Khartoum State, which continued its two-year battle to take over the other half of this church's freehold plot. Churches complained that Christian students undergoing obligatory military training in camps near Khartoum were denied their right to worship, in contrast to Muslim students. The law against apostasy—banning Muslims from conversion to another religion—was enforced on several occasions. In June 2001, security arrested an alleged convert to Christianity and held him incommunicado for three months, while reportedly torturing him and demanding that he reconvert to Islam.

In the north, destitute southern women continued to brew and sell traditional southern alcoholic drinks, for which they were arrested. More than nine hundred women were held in the Women's Prison in Omdurman (designed for two hundred) as of December 2000 in grossly poor conditions. The prison also housed southern women with twenty-year sentences for dealing in cannabis, and women sentenced, sometimes for indeterminate periods, for financial crimes.

On June 23, 2001, the authorities raided a workshop on "Democracy and Gender Issues" organized by the Gender Centre in Khartoum. Four speakers were arrested and released the same night. All participants in the workshop were interrogated about their political affiliations and their addresses were taken.

The most severe abuses occurred in the civil war fought in the south, the central Nuba Mountains, and the east. The Sudan government and its ethnic militias continued to displace, starve, abduct, rape, and kill civilians outright—while burning, and bombing, villages, churches, hospitals, and schools.

The rebel-held Nuba Mountains were hit especially hard in 2001. In May 2001, the government attacked the region, bombing extensively and burning down six villages, resulting in the displacement of more than 15,000 people. According to the Nuba relief office, an estimated 400,000 people were in SPLA-controlled territory as of June 2001, cut off from rest of rebel-held Sudan, with the lives of more than 50,000 displaced and 30,000 others unable to harvest crops at risk because of government attacks. The government persistently denied humanitarian access to civilians in the SPLA-held Nuba Mountains, through flight denials and shelling of airstrips used for unapproved relief deliveries. After years of negotiations, the U.N. in October 2001 succeeded in making the first-ever delivery there of relief with government permission. Another month of delivery was promised by the government, with no guarantee of access on an as-needed basis.

Following the brief capture of Kassala in eastern Sudan by opposition NDA forces (mostly SPLA) in November 2000, security forces arrested and reportedly tortured hundreds of southerners living in Kassala, in some cases extrajudicially executing them, according to the exiled Sudan Human Rights Organization.

Oil exploration and development in concession areas in Upper Nile exacerbated the conflict, with continuing displacement of civilians. Some 40,000-55,000 Nuer were displaced from the oilfields in the first half of 2001, according to two different reports, by government and its Nuer militias which were fighting the SPLA and its Nuer commanders. Often fighting resulted from government efforts to claim and to clear the people from the land, using its Nuer militias to push fellow Nuer out of the oilfields. More dependable government soldiers and *mujaheeden* then guarded construction equipment for roads, pipelines, drilling, and other oil infrastructure. Each oil facility was given a twenty-four hour guard of soldiers; up to four hundred soldiers were at Timsa, a location attacked by the SPLA in early 2001. The government imposed a long-term relief flight ban on most oil field areas in inaccessible Western Upper Nile (except for garrison towns), making the situation for civilians there even more acute.

Government use of new, heavier arms, including surface-to-surface missiles and helicopter gunships, and high-altitude Antonov bombing of southern and Nuba operations took a toll on the civilian population. Government aerial bombing destroyed the Episcopal Cathedral in Lui, Eastern Equatoria on December 29, 2000. Despite government pledges to stop bombing civilians and civilian structures, more bombing raids occurred: Tali, a center for relief food distribution in Eastern Equatoria, was bombed three times in December 2000, twice in January 2001, and again in May 2001. In June 2001, government Antonovs bombed three towns in Bahr El Ghazal, including one in which a World Food Program (WFP) relief operation was underway. Such attacks targeting relief deliveries in progress were increasing. Although bombing seemed to decline in September 2001, government planes bombed the little civilian village of Mangayat, twenty-five miles outside of rebel-held Raga in October on three different days, while WFP deliveries were in progress to aid an estimated 20,000 displaced people. The WFP gave up its attempt to distribute food.

Although the government of Sudan signed the 1997 Mine Ban Treaty, it did not ratify it and had not begun to destroy its stockpiled antipersonnel land mines. There were strong indications that both government and rebel forces in Sudan continued to use antipersonnel mines, but the government denied its forces did so. In October 2001, the SPLA signed an agreement at an NGO conference in Geneva to ban the use, production, storage, or transfer of antipersonnel land mines in its territory. Small arms and ammunition were produced by three new arms factories near Khartoum in partnership with Chinese companies, using government oil revenue.

Recruitment of boys aged sixteen and seventeen into the Popular Defence Force, a government Islamist militia, proceeded as government policy, and occasional press-gangs seized even younger children for this military service. The government-backed ethnic militias also recruited child soldiers in the south, sometimes forcibly, as did rebel groups. The SPLA admitted in 2000 it had about 10,000 child soldiers. Following an agreement with the SPLA, in February 2001 UNICEF began demobilizing some 3,000 SPLA child soldiers from northern Bahr El Ghazal. The children were disarmed and given schooling in transition camps, and by late August returned to their villages of origin. Some NGOs questioned the effectiveness of the program because, with no real job or school opportunities, the demobilized boys were likely to go back to the SPLA to survive. In late October, UNICEF said it was ready for another phase of demobilization, involving 1,000 children. The SPLA said it still had more than 7,000 child soldiers within its ranks.

Government army and militia forces continued to abduct women and children during ongoing raids in the south, mostly in northern Bahr El Ghazal and often in connection with the military train they accompanied to Wau, a garrison town. The Committee to Eradicate the Abduction of Women and Children (CEAWC), created by the government, was ineffective: the government admitted that abductors, even from among their own forces, were seldom prosecuted, although it announced in November 2001 its intention to set up a tribunal to try the abductors. UNICEF said 670 children were reunited with their families and 270 retrieved children were in CEAWC transit facilities, but retrievals had stalled. The Geneva-based solidarity organization Christian Solidarity International (CSI) claimed that between 1995 and 2001 it had "bought back" 56,000 enslaved Sudanese during sporadic CSI visits to SPLA territory. CSI estimated that there were an additional 200,000 enslaved in northern Sudan. (The CSI estimates doubled from 100,000 in 2000, without explanation.)

The Sudan government stopped supplying the Lord's Resistance Army (LRA), a Ugandan rebel group with a horrendous human rights record, in 2001 pursuant to an agreement with Uganda. The LRA subsequently began forcibly looting food from southern Sudanese, thousands of whom took refuge in Nimele and in northern Ugandan refugee camps. An LRA ambush on a relief agency vehicle traveling from northern Uganda to southern Sudan killed six Sudanese.

The SPLA openly opposed a broadening of civil society when it prevented civilians in its territory from attending two south-south peace and reconciliation conferences convened by the New Sudan Council of Churches (NSCC) in 2001. The NSCC and others condemned the SPLA's violations of freedom of movement, association, and speech. The Africa-Caribbean-Pacific-European Union (ACP-E.U.) mission noted that the SPLA's record on human rights was "far from being acceptable." The U.N. special rapporteur also criticized the SPLA.

In late February 2001, Nuer SPLA commander Peter Gatdet attacked and set fire to Nyal in Western Upper Nile, the base of the Riek Machar Nuer faction and a U.N. relief hub. The SPLA sponsored the attack. The U.S. government forcefully condemned the attack. Abuses proliferated as the forces of Nuer leader Riek Machar, lacking material support, allied themselves alternatively with the government or the SPLA, and sought to reestablish their control over their home territory.

DEFENDING HUMAN RIGHTS

The Sudan government persecuted human rights defenders. Ghazi Suleiman and Ali Mahmoud Hassanein, well-known advocates and human rights activists, were detained without charge by security forces from December 9, 2000 until February 17, 2001, after they condemned the arrests. Suleiman was reportedly tortured, sustaining a head injury and being hospitalized twice during detention The principal lawyer/advocate for the NDA defendants, Mustafa Abdel Gadir, was arrested and interrogated on the eve of the trial which started in May. On March 11, 2001, security forces arrested director Dr. Nageed Nagmeldin el Toum and two staff members from the Amal Centre, where free medical treatment and assistance to victims of torture and other human rights violations was provided. The staffers were released the same day but Dr. Nageed, former president of the banned Doctors' Union, was not released until March 29, 2001, after an international campaign. The confiscated office equipment was returned and the center reopened on June 27, 2001, the day before the ACP-EU visit. Another associate of Amal, Faisal el Bagir Mohamed, a journalist and human rights advocate, was detained without charges from June 13 to 26, 2001. On November 2, 2001, four lawyers/advocates and two members of the Sudanese Communist Party (banned) were detained and released within a few days and told to report daily to Security offices. All members of the loose coalition National Alliance for the Restoration of Democracy, it was believed that their detention was in connection with the upcoming bar association elections in December 2001. The last such elections were held in 1997 and were reportedly accompanied by widespread fraud on the part of the ruling party. One lawyer who failed to report on time to the Security offices was beaten with hoses and knotted wire when he arrived. Others were made to stand outside in the hot sun for two hours, a common form of ill-treatment in Sudan.

THE ROLE OF THE INTERNATIONAL COMMUNITY

United Nations

The U.N. Security Council in late September 2001 lifted sanctions imposed in 1996 because of Sudan's noncompliance with an Ethiopian extradition warrant for three suspects sought for attempted assassination of the Egyptian president. The United States abstained on the issue. The sanctions had required member states to reduce the number of Sudanese diplomatic personnel and restrict the travel of Sudanese government officials in their respective countries, though they were not generally enforced.

Although Sudan was reelected to its seat on the U.N. Commission on Human Rights in April 2001, reports by the special rapporteur on human rights in Sudan to the commission in April and to the General Assembly in October warned that human rights in Sudan were worsening in many respects, and that oil development was exacerbating the conflict.

United States

Oil and religion combined to bring Sudan higher up on the agenda of the new U.S. administration in 2001. It was the main African issue on which President Bush expressed interest. and Secretary of State Colin Powell remarked that "There is perhaps no greater tragedy on the face of the earth today than the tragedy unfolding in the Sudan."

Stringent prohibitions on U.S. citizens doing business with Sudan under a Clinton administration executive order remained in place. The Bush administration in May 2001 appointed Andrew Natsios, newly-named head of U.S. Agency for International Development, as the president's special envoy to Sudan for humanitarian issues. In early September, the president named former senator John Danforth his special envoy for peace in Sudan.

Natsios headed a U.S. delegation to Khartoum in July 2001 and announced U.S. emergency relief for drought victims in western Sudan, the first such aid to government-controlled areas for years. Total U.S. humanitarian assistance to Sudan for the year October 2000-September 2001 was U.S. $161 million.

In mid-2001, the State Department contracted with a U.S.-based contractor, Dyncorp, to assist the NDA (consisting of military and civilian wings) to set up offices and improve its "negotiating skills." The state department claimed none of the funding allocated would be used for "nonlethal" aid to the SPLA (defining "nonlethal aid" to include dual-use supplies such as boots, communications equipment, and tents).

Before September 11, U.S. policy on Sudan was a contested domestic issue between some members of Congress and conservative and religious rights groups—who sought to isolate Khartoum and aid the SPLA—and moderates in the administration, the business community, and elsewhere who argued that the isolation policy had not worked. After September 11, the antiterrorism agenda trumped this contest.

Following the September 11 attacks, the Sudan government opportunistically announced its cooperation with the U.S. on terrorism. According to the U.S. government, U.S. counterterrorism teams had been in Sudan for more than a year already, and had been receiving "satisfactory" cooperation from the Sudan government. In late September, the Sudan government reportedly deported several persons sought by the U.S. for terrorist activities or associations, but the details were not publicly released; Khartoum continued to deny any such cooperation to the domestic and Arabic press.

The Bush administration maintained, however, that it would persist with its full agenda of human rights issues requiring Sudan's resolution before normalization of relations. The U.S. strongly protested Sudan government's three days' bombings of a relief operation in October 2001.

European Union

The European Union (E.U.) began a political dialogue in November 1999 with the Sudan government, with regular meetings between E.U. ambassadors in Khartoum and government officials. An ACP-E.U. Joint Parliamentary Assembly mission to Sudan in June-July 2001, reported disappointment with the government's lack of cooperation in the dialogue since the end of 2000. It noted several areas of human rights concerns that were discussed but not addressed by the government, such as detention without charge, press freedom, abduction and forced labor, and bombing.

The E.U. maintained its arms embargo on Sudan, but without any enforcement mechanism. There were no E.U. restrictions on its members' investments in the Sudan oil industry. In June, however, the E.U. presidency stated concern at renewed SPLA military activity in Bahr El Ghazal—the capture of Raga—and the Sudan government's resumption of aerial bombings in response. A group of nations, predominantly European, formed the International Partners' Forum Working Group to provide funding and diplomatic support for the efforts of the east African Inter-Governmental Authority on Development (IGAD). IGAD peace negotiations between the Sudan government and the SPLA foundered nevertheless.

In May 2001, a broad coalition of European NGOs formed the European Campaign on Oil in Sudan to lobby European governments and companies in the oil business in Sudan to pull out of Sudan, because of the Sudan government's gross human rights abuses.

Africa

The Sudan government used its new oil resources—and more than U.S. $ 400 million in extra revenue—to strengthen its position in the Horn of Africa. In June 2001, Sudan and Ethiopia announced a project to supply Ethiopia with Sudanese gasoline and kerosene equivalent to 85 percent of the country's needs for the year 2002. Ethiopia, previously supportive of Sudanese rebels, had already cut relations with them.

Kenya was to import tax-free Sudanese oil through its port Mombasa until the

Kenyan churches strongly protested. In July 2001, Kenyan authorities banned delivery of Sudan oil shipments to Kenya, causing Sudan to threaten that it might stop importing Kenyan tea and coffee. The situation remains unresolved.

South Africa's state-owned oil company Soekor denied reports that it too intended to explore for Sudanese oil, after South African churches denounced reported Soekor meetings on the topic.

AMERICAS

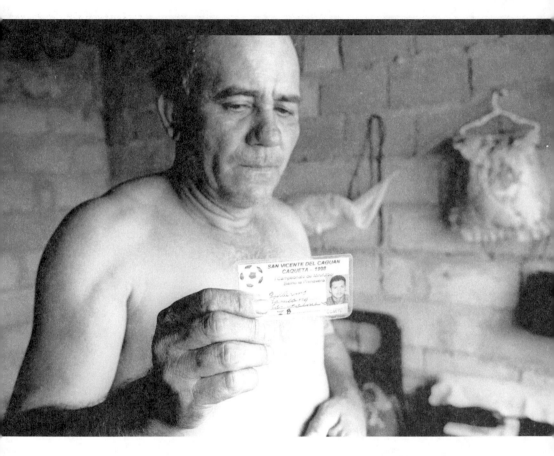

A father shows a soccer club identification card of his "disappeared" son in Colombia.

AMERICAS OVERVIEW

HUMAN RIGHTS DEVELOPMENTS

Although the year was dominated by the human rights tragedy in Colombia, other parts of Latin America experienced positive change. With presidential balloting in April, Peru finally closed the door on the undemocratic and discredited administration of former President Alberto Fujimori. Mexico, having just ended seven decades of one-party rule, took several steps toward reform. And a number of different countries made meaningful progress in the area of truth, justice, and accountability. Still, all over Latin America and the Caribbean, chronic problems such as police brutality, deplorable prison conditions, domestic violence, and labor right abuses went largely unaddressed.

The human rights situation in Colombia deteriorated markedly over the course of the year, with civilians bearing the brunt of the country's violent armed conflict. In the first ten months of 2001, the office of the Public Advocate recorded ninety-two massacres, defined as the killing of three or more people at the same place and at the same time. Paramilitary groups linked to the security forces were responsible for the bulk of the killings, followed by guerrillas. The country's epidemic of kidnappings, half committed by leftist guerrilla forces, showed no sign of abating. Children, some as young as thirteen, were recruited into the irregular armed forces—guerrillas and paramilitaries—that played a primary role in the conflict. An estimated two million Colombians were internally displaced, with at least 300,000 reported displaced in 2001, the highest number ever in a single year. Human rights defenders, trade unionists, journalists, government investigators, and community leaders continued to be killed because of their work.

In Peru, the fall of the Fujimori government in late 2000 brought new hope for democracy and human rights. Both the interim administration of Valentín Paniagua and the new government of President Alejandro Toledo took important steps to strengthen democratic institutions and the rule of law, while also taking aim at long neglected human rights problems.

Haiti remained mired in political turmoil stemming from fraudulent elections held in 2000. Despite the vigorous efforts of international negotiators to reach a solution to the crisis, the lack of progress discouraged donor states, leaving hundreds of millions of dollars in international aid frozen.

Chile's indictment of Augusto Pinochet was an important landmark in Latin America's efforts to achieve accountability for past human rights violations, even though the trial of the former military ruler was later terminated on the grounds of poor health. Equally significant was the decision of Argentine Federal Judge Gabriel

Cavallo to strike down the country's amnesty laws, a ruling that was later affirmed by a Buenos Aires appellate tribunal. In Peru, a truth commission was established to investigate responsibility for the systematic human rights violations and guerrilla abuses committed during the country's twenty-two year internal armed conflict, which began in 1980. The commission was mandated to investigate violations of collective rights of Peru's Andean and native communities as well as violations of individual rights such as extrajudicial executions, torture, and "disappearances." The large number of Latin American governments having signed or ratified the Rome Statute of the International Criminal Court (ICC) was further encouraging proof of the strength of the regional impetus toward justice.

In Mexico, as of this writing, President Vicente Fox had yet to establish a promised truth commission to examine past human rights abuses. Fox did, however, order his government to grant public access to files on "disappearances" that took place in the 1970s and 1980s. In November, after the country's National Human Rights Commission presented him with a study documenting the military's role in the forced disappearance and torture of hundreds of suspected leftists in the 1970s, Fox announced that he would name a special prosecutor to investigate the crimes. The commission report represented the Mexican government's first official acknowledgment of responsibility for the abuses, but it did not name the estimated seventy-four public officials said to be personally implicated in them.

Police violence, frequent in many Latin American countries, was of particular concern in Venezuela and Argentina. According to the Buenos Aires-based Center for Legal and Social Studies (Centro de Estudios Legales y Sociales, CELS), police in Argentina killed some 266 people in the last six months of 2000 and the first six months of 2001. While most of these killings were officially attributed to shootouts with suspected criminals, investigations by human rights groups suggested that many deaths resulted from the excessive use of lethal force by the police, or were deliberate executions. A disturbing recent development in Venezuela was the emergence in some states of organized death squads with ties to the police.

Prisoners throughout the region frequently suffered inhumane treatment, with particularly abusive prison and jail conditions found in Venezuela, Brazil, Haiti, Panama, Colombia, and El Salvador. The continued growth of inmate populations exacerbated overcrowding, at the root of a host of other problems. Yet, all over the region, prisons and jails were not crammed with convicted prisoners, but instead with pretrial detainees, turning the presumption of innocence on its head. In February, a large-scale inmate riot at Brazil's Carandirú prison ended bloodily, bringing momentary public attention to the country's chronic prison abuses. Fifteen prisoners were killed during and after the rioting, most by riot police, and some in circumstances suggesting extrajudicial executions. In November, similarly, prisoners in Haiti's National Penitentiary claimed that prison officials deliberately killed unarmed inmates in quelling prison unrest.

The use of capital punishment was of particular concern in the English-speaking Caribbean, where countries such as Trinidad and Tobago, Jamaica, and Barbados retained the death penalty. In August, Trinidad and Tobago sentenced ten men to hang for a single murder. One positive development occurred in April, when the Eastern Caribbean Court of Appeal, which has jurisdiction over some Caribbean countries, ruled that the mandatory death penalty was unconstitutional.

In May, Chilean President Ricardo Lagos signed a law that substituted life in prison for the death penalty. Chile's legal reform left Guatemala and Cuba as the only Spanish-speaking countries in the region to fully apply the death penalty, although several others reserved the right to execute persons convicted of treason during wartime or of other extraordinary offenses. Guatemala not only retained the death penalty, but by imposing it in cases of non-fatal kidnappings it contravened the American Convention on Human Rights.

Chile also made important strides toward protecting freedom of expression by repealing article 6b of the State Security Law, a repressive and antediluvian penal statute that had protected public authorities from criticism. In Panama, in contrast, the government had yet to reform the draconian press laws inherited from military rule. More than fifty journalists reportedly faced criminal charges for defamation or "contempt of authority," with several being convicted of those offenses over the course of the year. In May, for example, journalist Marcelino Rodríguez of *El Siglo* was sentenced to sixteen months in prison, commutable to a fine of U.S. $1,000, after being convicted of libel of a public employee.

Throughout Latin American and the Caribbean, workers continued to suffer myriad violations of internationally recognized labor rights. Common abuses included the worst forms of child labor, employment discrimination, and violations of the right to freedom of association. In some cases, violations were perpetuated by the government's failure to enforce domestic labor legislation and, in other cases, national labor laws fell short of international labor standards. The result was the same, however: governmental omissions that allowed employers to violate workers' rights with impunity.

In Ecuador, children as young as eight labored for long hours on banana plantations in unsafe and unhealthy working conditions. In Guatemala, women workers in the maquila sector often faced pregnancy-based discrimination. And in Brazil, according to a 2001 International Labor Organization report, the government's failure to apply effective sanctions, the slow judicial process, impunity for perpetrators, and lack of intra-governmental coordination impeded the eradication of "degrading working conditions and debt bondage" in the rural sector.

Workers' right to organize—the internationally sanctioned tool for demanding better working conditions and respect for labor rights—was obstructed or violated throughout the region. In Mexico, legitimate organizing activity was frequently hindered by collective bargaining agreements negotiated between management and pro-business, non-independent unions. In other cases, workers were impeded from organizing by employers' hiring practices, including the use of subcontractors and "permanent temporary" workers. Although employers benefited from subcontracted workers' labor and often even controlled their employment terms and conditions, employers were not required to bargain collectively with the subcontracted workers because, legally, the subcontractor was the employer. Similarly, employers hired workers for months or years on end using consecutive temporary employment contracts, creating a "permanent temporary" workforce without job stability and too afraid to organize. Such tactics inhibited worker organization, for example, in Ecuador's banana sector, where the banana worker affiliation rate, at roughly 1 percent, was exceptionally low.

In other cases, workers' right to organize was violated through direct anti-union discrimination, including the harassment, demotion, or dismissal of union members and sympathizers. In the most serious cases, union leaders and their supporters risked assassination. Colombia led the world in such assassinations, with 112 trade unionists killed in 2000, and 125 killed in the first ten months of 2001, according to Colombia's largest trade union organization. In March 2001, the Governing Body of the International Labor Organization (ILO) criticized the Colombian authorities' failure to prosecute the perpetrators of such crimes and to implement adequate security measures to protect trade union officials and members.

Many women in the region faced daily violence and discrimination, perpetuated by their governments' failure to take meaningful action to protect women from abuse. Domestic violence remained a particularly salient issue in many countries, with men beating their wives and other female family members with little fear of criminal prosecution.

Some positive steps were taken to improve women's legal status, but much remained to be done. In August, the Brazilian Congress approved a new civil code that recognized men's and women's equality before the law. The new code did away with the expression "paternal power," replacing it with the gender-neutral concept of "the power of the family." Under the reformed code, women were to have equal authority with men in family affairs. In other countries, however, women still did not enjoy full legal equality with men, despite constitutional provisions granting both sexes equal rights. The Chilean civil code continued to grant husbands primary control over household decisions and property. The civil codes of countries such as Argentina, Mexico, and Colombia set lower marrying ages for girls than for boys. Venezuelan women were barred from remarrying until ten months after a divorce or annulment, unless they proved they were not pregnant.

Gays, lesbians, and transgender people were also particularly vulnerable to violations of their human rights. In several countries, police singled out gay people and transvestites for abuses. In Mexico, transvestites in Monterrey, the capital of Nuevo Leon state, faced arbitrary arrest, extortion, and physical violence. Even more frequently around the region, criminal justice authorities failed to respond to crimes against gays and transvestites. A series of killings of gay men in Colima, Mexico, went unpunished and inadequately investigated. "It's as if [the gay community] doesn't enjoy the protection of the law," commented Max Mejía, a Colima-based gay rights activist.

Yet over the course of the year significant advances were made in the area of gay rights. In an important legal victory, the Association of New Men and Women Association of Panama (Asociación Hombres y Mujeres Nuevos de Panamá, AHMNP) finally obtained legal recognition by the government. In other places, laws were passed to protect the rights of sexual minorities or legislation was drafted on the issue. The Brazilian state of Minas Gerais passed a measure in October 2001 adding sexual orientation as a protected status to existing anti-discrimination legislation. In November 2000, the city council of Niteroi, in Rio de Janeiro, Brazil, passed an ordinance barring discrimination based on sexual orientation. A similar draft bill was presented to Mexican President Vicente Fox and the leaders of Mexico's political parties in November 2001, a first step toward passing federal legislation on the topic.

DEFENDING HUMAN RIGHTS

The strength of the human rights movement in Latin America and the Caribbean was evidenced by, among other things, the multitude of local and regional nongovernmental organizations dedicated to the issue. Made up of talented and committed lawyers, activists, community leaders, and others, these groups worked to put human rights principles into practice locally. In some countries, the work of nongovernmental groups was supplemented by that of permanent national human right commissions, ad hoc parliamentary bodies, and other government organs.

The public in many Latin American countries, having lived through repressive military governments, recognized the importance of human rights principles. Nonetheless, human rights defenders were frequently stigmatized for protecting the rights of unpopular groups, particularly criminal suspects.

In several countries, including Colombia, Guatemala, Haiti, Mexico, and Brazil, individual activists faced intimidation, assault, and sometimes death for their advocacy of human rights. Colombia remained the most dangerous country for human rights defenders. According to the Colombian Commission of Jurists, eleven defenders were killed there in the first ten months of 2001. Government investigators handling prosecutions of paramilitary leaders were also at risk, as were witnesses in such cases.

The brutal murder of Mexican human rights lawyer Digna Ochoa in October 2001 further underscored the dangers that these frontline defenders of fundamental rights endure. Next to Ochoa's body was a note that warned members of the human rights center where Ochoa had worked for several years that the same could happen to them.

THE ROLE OF THE INTERNATIONAL COMMUNITY

United Nations

The United Nations did not have a particularly high profile on human rights issues in Latin America and the Caribbean, although specific problems and situations received attention. Colombia remained, appropriately, the primary recipient of the U.N.'s efforts in the region. The country's human rights and humanitarian crisis was on the agenda of a number of U.N. bodies.

With the departure in February of the U.N. mission in Haiti, only Colombia and Guatemala still hosted a long-term U.N. human rights field presence. In Guatemala, the United Nations verification mission, known as MINUGUA, played a central role in monitoring compliance with the country's 1996 peace accords. In Colombia, the U.N. maintained a field office of the High Commissioner for Human Rights, which did important work despite poor cooperation from Colombian government officials. The U.N. High Commissioner for Refugees also had field offices in Colombia, with an operational capacity in the Urabá and Middle Magdalena regions as well as the department of Putumayo. Jan Egeland, the special adviser on Colombia to the U.N. Secretary-General, frequently visited Colombia to assist in peace talks

Three Latin American countries—Colombia, Cuba, and Haiti—were on the agenda at the fifty-seventh session of the Commission on Human Rights. The result, with regard to Cuba, was a resolution criticizing the government's continuing human rights violations. Haiti was the subject of a chairperson's statement that focused on electoral issues and the political crisis. For Colombia, the subject of a special segment of the Commission, the High Commissioner for Human Rights presented her annual report on human rights conditions.

U.N. thematic mechanisms visiting the Americas region included the special representative of the Secretary-General on human rights defenders, who visited Colombia, and the special rapporteur on the independence of judges and lawyers, who visited Guatemala. In addition, the various U.N. treaty bodies examined the human rights records of a number of Latin American and Caribbean states.

Organization of American States (OAS)

On the diplomatic front, the Organization of American States (OAS) was extremely active in trying to negotiate a solution to the political crisis in Haiti. As of November, however, these efforts had not borne fruit.

In September, the OAS Permanent Council approved the Inter-American Democratic Charter, which was subsequently ratified by the foreign ministers of OAS member states at a special general assembly in Lima. The charter attempts to set out the essential elements of representative democracy, citing, among other features, respect for human rights and fundamental freedoms; the rule of law; the holding of periodic free and fair elections based on secret balloting and universal suffrage; a multi-party system; the separation of powers; freedom of expression and of the press; and the constitutional subordination of all state institutions to a legally constituted civilian authority. Designed to protect democracy in the region, the charter codifies the OAS's power to suspend member states deemed undemocratic and sets up mechanisms for responding to coups and other threats against democracy.

The Inter-American Court of Human Rights and the Inter-American Commission on Human Rights—both OAS human rights bodies—heard a number of important cases in 2001. In addition to cases relating to the American Convention on Human Rights, the two bodies had jurisdiction to consider violations of five other regional conventions and protocols pertaining to forced disappearance, the death penalty, violence against women, torture, and social and economic rights. At a special session held in December 2000, the Commission approved new rules of procedure, which took effect on May 1, 2001.

In April, the Inter-American Commission on Human Rights issued its first decision on the issue of violence against women. Ruling in a case brought by Maria da Penha, a Brazilian woman who was repeatedly beaten by her husband and finally left paraplegic, the Commission found Brazil to be responsible for numerous rights violations. Besides recommending that the perpetrator be prosecuted and the victim be adequately compensated, the commission concluded that Brazil should adopt measures to remedy the problem of state tolerance of domestic violence against women.

In January, Peru's Congress overturned an earlier resolution, made in 1999 under the Fujimori government, by which it had voted to remove Peru from the jurisdiction of the Inter-American Court of Human Rights. (The Court had already declared the earlier resolution to be inadmissible.)

European Union

The European Union (E.U.) gave its continuing support to efforts to address the region's most pressing human rights and humanitarian problems, including, most notably, the armed conflict in Colombia. The E.U. provided financial support for the Colombian peace process and for the humanitarian assistance of displaced persons. E.U. representatives expressed concern, however, regarding slowdowns in the peace process, mounting violence, and the failure of parties to the conflict to respect basic humanitarian law norms.

Cuba remained the only Latin American country that did not have a cooperation agreement with the European Union. An E.U. visit to Cuba in late November 2001, however, appeared to promise improved E.U.-Cuba relations, possibly signaling a future change in the E.U.'s "common position" on Cuba. Because of the Haitian government's failure to remedy the results of the country's seriously flawed 2000 elections, E.U. economic cooperation with Haiti remained suspended as of November.

Several Western European countries played a critical role in promoting accountability in Latin American and the Caribbean. European courts, continuing the "Pinochet precedent," heard criminal cases against the perpetrators of past human rights crimes, including the systematic abuses that took place in Argentina and Chile in the 1970s. Through the mechanism of universal jurisdiction, by which a country's national courts are empowered to adjudicate human rights crimes committed on another country's territory—and also through the passive personality principle, which recognizes a country's legal interest in crimes committed against its nationals—European courts adjudicated a number of criminal cases in which Latin American high officials and former high officials were defendants.

Courts in Spain, Italy, France, and Germany continued to prosecute, or to seek to prosecute, members of the Argentine armed forces implicated in "dirty war" abuses. The Argentine government, however, did not cooperate in these efforts. Asserting the principle of territoriality—that only Argentine courts had jurisdiction over the crimes at issue—the government failed to comply with the European extradition requests. This argument, which ignored the interest of all states in prosecuting gross violations of human rights, was particularly unconvincing in light of the impunity enjoyed for decades by the perpetrators of human rights crimes in Argentina.

Most disappointingly, Argentina refused to extradite former navy officer Alfredo Astiz, a notorious intelligence operative during military rule. Astiz was arrested and detained for a few weeks in July until the Argentine Foreign Ministry denied extradition requests made by Italian and French judges.

Another setback was the dismissal in December 2000 of a suit in Spain against

Guatemala's former military ruler, Gen. Efraín Ríos Montt, and several other military officials. The case, filed a year previously, was thrown out of court on the ground that the petitioners had not exhausted the possibility of prosecuting the defendants in Guatemala. Yet, given Ríos Montt's continuing power in Guatemala, the ability of the Guatemala courts to manage such a case was questionable. (Facing daunting obstacles, a group of indigenous Maya Indians sued Ríos Montt and others in Guatemala in June for crimes committed during military rule.)

In an important and encouraging new trend, the Mexican government became a strong regional voice in favor of accountability by ratifying the extradition to Spain of Ricardo Miguel Cavallo, a former Argentine navy officer. Cavallo, a member of a notorious naval task force implicated in numerous "disappearances," had been living and working in Mexico. In January, a Mexican district court ruled in favor of Spain's extradition request, and in February Mexican Foreign Minister Jorge Castañeda authorized the extradition. As of November, Cavallo's appeal against the extradition order was pending.

In November, a French judge issued international arrest warrants for fifteen Chileans implicated in the torture and "disappearance" of four French citizens in Chile during the Pinochet era. The suspects included retired Gen. Manuel Contreras, former head of Pinochet's secret police, and four other former generals. Since Chile and France did not have an extradition agreement, the targets of the arrest warrants, all believed to be in Chile, would probably only face arrest if they were to leave the country.

The Belgian courts, too, played a part in the trend toward foreign prosecutions. In October, Cuban exiles filed suit in Brussels against President Fidel Castro and other high Cuban officials. Their criminal complaint, which had not been ruled upon at this writing, described torture and other abuses suffered by political prisoners, as well as Cuba's downing of two planes in 1996.

United States

The Latin America policies of the Bush administration, in its first year in office, did not differ meaningfully from those of the previous administration. The United States under President Bush took a selective interest in the region, focusing primarily on trade and drug issues. The U.S. did not take the lead in promoting human rights in Latin America, nor were U.S. representatives especially vocal on the topic.

In 2001, as in 2000, Colombia was the Latin American country that received the greater part of the U.S. government's attention and funding. The United States continued to push a drug control strategy based on aerial eradication, providing the funding for Colombian counter-narcotics military battalions. In January, President Clinton, under a questionable reading of the relevant legislation, dispersed a second tranche of the military aid passed the previous year. The Bush administration sought an additional U.S. $400 million for Colombia for fiscal year 2002. But in a clear improvement over the previous year's legislation, the draft legislation before Congress as of this writing did not contain presidential waiver authority for its human rights conditions. In other words, Colombia would have to show concrete progress in breaking military-paramilitary ties to be eligible to receive aid.

In early September, the United States named the Colombian paramilitary alliance—the United Self Defense Group of Colombia (Autodefensas Unidas de Colombia, AUC)—as a "foreign terrorist organization" under U.S. law. Among other legal consequences, the designation requires U.S. banks to block the group's funds.

Peru's downing of a civilian aircraft during a U.S.-Peruvian surveillance operation on April 20 caused the joint drug interdiction program to be suspended. Although the plane's pilot survived the crash of the small Cessna, two others were killed in the incident: Veronica Bowers, a missionary, and her infant daughter. A joint U.S.-Peruvian report released by the State Department in August put the blame for the tragedy on lax procedures and the failure of the Peruvian pilot to give proper warning.

By nominating Otto Reich, a Cuban-American anti-communist, to be assistant secretary of state, President Bush signaled an apparent unwillingness to modify the U.S. economic embargo against Cuba. In July, when Bush suspended certain provisions under the Helms-Burton sanctions law, he publicly reaffirmed his administration's commitment to maintaining the embargo. Nonetheless, a milestone in U.S.-Cuban economic relations was reached with the sale to Cuba of some $30 million in food and medicine by U.S. companies in October. Made necessary after Hurricane Michelle devastated the island, they were the first U.S. sales to Cuba since the imposition of the embargo in 1962.

THE WORK OF HUMAN RIGHTS WATCH

The Americas division of Human Rights Watch kept abreast of human rights developments around the region through frequent visits, close contact with local activists, and intensive monitoring of the media and other information sources. The division sought not only to identify the most pressing problems of the countries in which it worked, but also to understand the root causes of violations and to formulate strategies for addressing them. It campaigned vigorously to put a stop to violations, relying on targeted advocacy with policy-makers, careful coordination with like-minded groups, and outreach to the broader public via the media and the internet.

While the Americas division responded quickly to fast-breaking events, it also gave sustained attention to chronic, long-term problems. Among the issues the division worked on in 2001 were military-paramilitary links and violations of international humanitarian law in Colombia; the Pinochet prosecution and freedom of expression in Chile; military abuses, violence against sexual minorities, and labor rights in Mexico; political violence and impunity in Haiti; accountability in Argentina; freedom of association and child labor in Ecuador; the treatment of Haitian immigrants and Dominico-Haitians in the Dominican Republic; police violence in Jamaica; accountability in Peru; the protection of NGOs and human rights defenders in Guatemala; and overall human rights conditions in Cuba.

Over the course of the year, the Americas division fielded investigative and advocacy missions to nearly a dozen countries. In addition to brief two- or three-day advocacy visits, the division's researchers conducted longer fact-finding investigations in Argentina, Chile, Colombia, the Dominican Republic, Ecuador, Haiti, Mexico, Peru, and Venezuela, with the division sending, in some cases, more than one mission to a single country. With the information collected during these trips, the Americas division prepared detailed reports and other materials to document the problems under review.

Besides disseminating information via written materials, Human Rights Watch directly addressed high-level government officials and representatives of relevant regional and international bodies, conveying our human rights concerns in a firm, concise, and timely way. In several countries, Human Rights Watch representatives held meetings with presidents and other top government officials. In meetings, as well as in correspondence and written statements, the Americas division made specific recommendations for improving human rights conditions.

As the region's gravest human rights crisis, Colombia was the major focus of the Americas division during 2001. The division's work in support of human rights in Colombia had three tracks: pressing for change within the country, working to influence U.S. policy toward Colombia, and promoting U.N. and other international efforts.

Because all parties to the conflict in Colombia were guilty of serious violations, the division examined not only government abuses but also those committed by non-state actors. In a twenty-page letter sent in July to Manuel Marulanda, the commander-in-chief of the Revolutionary Armed Forces of Colombia-People's Army (Fuerzas Armadas Revolucionarias de Colombia-Ejército del Pueblo, FARC-EP), the executive director of the Americas division assessed the FARC-EP's actions by the standards of international humanitarian law. The letter set out the FARC-EP's responsibility for serious violations, including killings of civilians, cruel and inhuman treatment of captured combatants, abductions of civilians, hostage-taking, the use of child soldiers, grossly unfair trials, and forced displacement of civilians. It also cited the FARC-EP's continuing use of prohibited weapons, including gas cylinder bombs, and its attacks against medical workers and facilities. The FARC-EP's public response to the letter did not counter the substance of these findings, but only attacked Human Rights Watch's integrity as an independent monitor. Later in the year, the findings of Human Rights Watch's letter were incorporated into a report, *Beyond Negotiation: International Humanitarian Law and its Application to the Conduct of the FARC-EP.*

In October, Human Rights Watch issued a report on another critical aspect of the Colombia crisis. Titled *The "Sixth Division": Military-Paramilitary Ties and U.S. Policy in Colombia,* and launched at a press conference in Bogotá, the report documented continuing close ties between Colombian military and police detachments, and paramilitary groups. The report received extensive local and international media coverage; the press conference was carried live on Colombian television. Prior to the report's release, Human Rights Watch representatives discussed human rights concerns in meetings with top Colombian officials, including President Andrés Pastrana. Because *The "Sixth Division"* also addressed U.S. policy, its findings were influential with regard to U.S. aid to Colombia, and it was extensively cited during Senate hearings on the issue.

Human Rights Watch celebrated a major victory a month after the release of its March report on free expression in Chile, when repressive defamation legislation criticized in the report was repealed. The timing of Human Rights Watch's report, and the organization's targeted advocacy—which included an hour-long meeting with Chilean President Ricardo Lagos—were instrumental in creating momentum for the law's repeal. The report, *Progress Stalled: Setbacks in Freedom of Expression Reform*, was a follow-up to a 1998 report on the same topic, illustrating the value of sustained advocacy on a single issue.

The Americas division continued to draw attention to labor rights violations in the region. In April, the division issued a comprehensive study showing how Mexico, the United States, and Canada have failed to fulfill their obligations under the labor side accord of the North American Free Trade Agreement (NAFTA). Released on the eve of the Summit of the Americas in Québec, the report called for the creation of an independent oversight agency to spur remedial action for workers' rights violations.

To facilitate the broad dissemination of its findings in Latin America, the Americas division put a high priority on translating its materials into Spanish (and Portuguese, in some instances) and posting them on the Human Rights Watch website. With materials arranged chronologically by country and by issue, the Spanish-language website, in particular, presented a detailed picture of human rights conditions in the region. Visitor traffic to the Spanish-language pages expanded rapidly over the course of the year, drawn by the comprehensive and timely selection of materials. By year's end, Spanish-language visitors constituted Human Rights Watch's largest non-English audience.

ARGENTINA

Preoccupied by a deep economic crisis, the government of President Fernando de la Rúa did little to promote human rights. An escalation of police abuses in the province of Buenos Aires came to public attention in October 2001, leading to the immediate dismissal of Buenos Aires police and justice officials. The courts made important strides toward bringing to justice those responsible for the gross human rights violations committed during the period of military rule (1976-1983). President de la Rúa scarcely commented on these developments. Instead of supporting these efforts to break impunity, his ministry of defense backed Argentina's increasingly questioned amnesty laws and the government rejected requests for the extradition of former human rights violators to stand trial in Europe.

HUMAN RIGHTS DEVELOPMENTS

Police engaged in operations to combat urban crime committed serious human rights violations. Evidence emerged during the year that the Buenos Aires police harassed and threatened minors for denouncing maltreatment and torture in police stations. Some were later shot dead in suspicious incidents officially described as firefights.

According to the nongovernmental Center for Legal and Social Studies (Centro de Estudios Legales y Sociales, CELS), police killed some 266 people in the last six months of 2000 and the first six months of 2001, many of them teenagers from poor urban areas. The police attributed most civilian killings to exchanges of gunfire, but investigations by human rights groups suggested that many deaths were the result of excessive use of lethal force by the police, or deliberate executions. During the first six months of 2001, fifteen minors were killed and eighteen wounded in shooting incidents in Greater Buenos Aires, according to CELS. Some adolescents appeared to have been deliberately killed in reprisal for denouncing that they had been tortured or maltreated while previously in police custody. In October 2001, the Buenos Aires provincial Supreme Court expressed concern about the death of sixty young people in "alleged shootouts" in 1999 and 2000 after they had filed complaints of torture. Many had received death threats before they were killed. The provincial security minister, former police commissioner Ramón Verón, replied to the allegations by saying that it was "almost a sport" for young people to denounce torture. Provincial governor Carlos Ruckauf, who was elected in 1999 on a tough anti-crime platform, immediately replaced him and the province's minister of justice. Verón's successor, Juan José Alvarez, admitted that "one or two" cases of police killings following complaints of torture had been recently confirmed.

A court was investigating the killing of fourteen-year-old Gastón Galván and sixteen-year-old Miguel Burgos, whose bodies were found in April by a roadside on the outskirts of Buenos Aires. Their hands and feet were tied, their bodies had multiple bullet wounds, and one of them had a plastic bag tied over his head. The police maintained that the deaths were the result of a gang dispute, but the youths' relatives said that police from the area had been constantly harassing the boys. A prosecutor revealed that, before they were killed, the youths had told a judge that police attached to a police station in Don Torcuato, Buenos Aires province, had tortured them. At the end of October, five Don Torcuato policemen, who were suspected of reprisal killings of minors who had denounced torture, were removed from their posts.

Ill-treatment was common in police stations where young offenders were held in overcrowded and squalid conditions. Methods of torture reported including beatings, hooding with plastic bags almost to the point of suffocation, and the use of electric shock batons on sensitive parts of the body, techniques in widespread use when Argentina was under military rule. These practices were most frequently reported in the populous greater Buenos Aires area. In July, Mario Coriolano, the chief state defense attorney attached to the criminal appeals court in the province of Buenos Aires, issued a report to the provincial Supreme Court giving details of more than six hundred complaints of ill-treatment and torture made from March 2000 until July 2001. By late October the court had information on more than 1,000 cases. In August, four respected federal judges publicly expressed concern about the prevalence of torture, asserting that the practice had become systematic in both police stations and prisons.

Twenty-four-year-old Javier Villanueva, for example, was arrested on October 21, 2001, while driving a stolen car in Lomas de Zamora, Buenos Aires province. After the prosecutor interviewing him noticed suspicious marks on his body he ordered that Villanueva be examined by a doctor, who found that he had lesions consistent with electric shock torture. The prosecutor ordered an immediate inspection of the police station in which Villanueva had been held; where an electric cable was found which Villaneuva alleged had been used to torture him. Six officers attached to the Lomas de Zamora precinct, one of those most frequently mentioned in complaints, were detained and charged with torture and obstructing justice.

In July, President Fernando de la Rúa confirmed his intention to introduce in the Chamber of Deputies a bill to reform the country's criminal defamation law, an undertaking he made in response to several cases under consideration by the Inter-American Commission on Human Rights. The bill, proposed by the nongovernmental press freedom advocacy group Periodistas, aimed to eliminate criminal defamation in the case of public figures, and to make "actual malice" the basic standard for adjudicating defamation suits. At this writing, presentation of the bill was still awaited. Provincial and municipal authorities and members of the Senate, meanwhile, continued to use existing laws to crack down on press critics. In the province of Santiago del Estero, whose government was controlled by the Peronist Justicialista party, the El Liberal newspaper was the target of at least eleven civil suits brought by 4,000 members of the party's Women's Branch, about which the newspaper had published critical reports in 2000. As a result, a provincial court ordered the seizure of more than 500,000 pesos (approximately U.S. $500,000) of the newspaper's assets, threatening its survival. The newspaper, with the largest print-run in the province, also faced discrimination in the granting of government advertising, and several of its journalists were harassed.

Public officials continued to file criminal suits to deter press reports of malfeasance, but in several cases higher courts found in favor of the journalists, appealing to constitutional principles protecting the publication of information in the public interest. In July, the federal appeals court dismissed charges of violation of confidentiality against journalist Marcelo Bonelli, of the newspaper Clarín, for revealing details of the tax returns of a former manager of the state pensions fund. In September, another chamber of the same court dismissed a criminal libel complaint filed by the same official against Bartolomé Mitre, director of the newspaper La Nación, for reporting on a criminal investigation in progress against him for a questioned contract.

The Supreme Court, however, cited privacy norms to justify penalties against a magazine for publishing information of clear public interest. In September, the Supreme Court upheld a lower court decision awarding criminal damages against the weekly news magazine Noticias for reporting in 1994 and 1995 that former president Carlos Menem had an illegitimate son by a congresswoman with whom he had an affair in the 1980s, and that he had used his office to advance her political career. The court found the magazine to have violated Menem's right to privacy, even though neither he nor the courts questioned the truth of the allegations.

Federal and provincial judges continued to investigate "disappearances" and extrajudicial executions committed during the era of military rule (1976-1983), in so-called "truth trials." The hearings sought to establish the truth about the crimes even though those responsible could not be prosecuted or convicted because of amnesty laws passed in 1986 and 1987. Former chief of state Jorge Videla, junta member Admiral Emilio Massera, and former commander of the First Army Corps Carlos Guillermo Suárez Mason were among a dozen retired officers held under house arrest on charges of ordering the theft of babies born to mothers in secret detention and their handover for adoption to military families. These crimes had been expressly excluded from the amnesty laws.

On June 20, Videla appeared in court to be questioned on charges of illicit association, illegal arrest, and torture. He was accused of participating in Operation Condor, a secret plan devised by Southern Cone military governments to kidnap, exchange, or "disappear" political refugees from neighboring states. Two months previously, investigating Judge Rodolfo Canicoba had issued an international warrant for the arrest and extradition of former Paraguayan dictator Alfredo Stroessner, now in exile in Brasilia, and of Manuel Contreras, the former chief of the DINA, Pinochet's secret police, in Chile. An early example of Operation Condor was the car-bomb assassination of Chilean General Carlos Prats and his wife in Buenos Aires in September 1974. In November 2000, the Sixth Federal Oral Court in Buenos Aires sentenced former Chilean intelligence agent Enrique Arancibia Clavel, a resident of Buenos Aires, to life imprisonment as an accomplice in the crime. Investigating judge María Servini de Cubría was seeking the extradition from Chile of former dictator Augusto Pinochet, Manuel Contreras, and five former DINA officers, for planning and carrying out the assassinations. (See Chile.)

In a landmark decision in March, federal judge Gabriel Cavallo became the first Argentine judge to declare the amnesty laws unconstitutional and null. Judge Cavallo was investigating the theft of Claudia Poblete, who was eight months old when she and her parents José Poblete Roa and Gertrudis Hlaczik, "disappeared" after a military task force abducted them in November 1978. The 188-page ruling, solidly based on international human rights law and precedents in Argentine jurisprudence, argued that the "full-stop" and "due obedience" laws of 1986 and 1987 violated articles 29 and 118 of the Argentine constitution, and conflicted with Argentina's obligation to bring to justice those responsible for crimes against humanity. The two police agents accused of stealing Claudia Poblete and illegally giving her in adoption were the first officers to be charged for "disappearances" since 1987. On November 9, a three-judge panel of the Buenos Aires Federal Court unanimously rejected the defendants' appeal, confirming both the charges and the nullity of the amnesty laws. The trial's future depended on the Supreme Court ratifying the Federal Court's ruling, which would create a precedent for scores of other cases to be opened.

While the government nominally supported the truth and baby theft trials, it opposed any change in the *status quo* defined by the amnesty laws. In a speech in March at a military ceremony in Córdoba, Defense Minister Jaunarena contended that the prolongation of the trials was not beneficial for anyone, neither for the victims nor those who might be accused. Jaunarena's predecessor as defense minister, Ricardo López Murphy, supported the army when, in the same month, 663 officers in active service presented a *habeas data* demand against CELS, demanding that it turn over information that might implicate the officers in human rights abuse. The army's chief of staff, Gen. Ricardo Brinzoni, who was believed to have authorized the legal action, was himself the object of a criminal complaint filed by CELS in May for his alleged involvement in a notorious massacre of twenty-two political prisoners in Margarita Belén, Chaco province, on December 13, 1976. On Army Day, May 29, President De la Rúa publicly defended Brinzoni in a ceremony attended by members of the military juntas.

DEFENDING HUMAN RIGHTS

Lawyers and human rights activists continued to face death threats and harassment. On November 7, Matilde Bruera, a human rights lawyer in Rosario, province of Santa Fe, received an anonymous message with the words "Bruera, we are going to kill you with a bullet through your head." During June and October she had received similar threats. Other human rights lawyers, including Juan Roberto Coria, Lindolfo Bertinat, Vildor Garavelli, María Eugenia Caggiano, and Juan Lewis suffered break-ins or received threats apparently connected to the opening of a "truth trial" in Rosario.

In October 2000, Carlos Varela, Alejandro Acosta, and Diego Lavado, lawyers representing relatives of the victim of a police killing, suffered a break-in at their office in Mendoza. The desk computers were opened, the hard drives removed, and a laptop computer was stolen. They reported another break-in at the end of the year. The under-secretary for human rights at the Ministry of Justice arranged for the three to be given police protection.

THE ROLE OF THE INTERNATIONAL COMMUNITY

United Nations

In November 2000, the Human Rights Committee issued its concluding observations on Argentina's report under article 40 of the International Covenant on Civil and Political Rights. The committee recommended that "gross violations of civil and political rights during military rule should be prosecutable for as long as necessary, with applicability as far back in time as necessary to bring their perpetrators to justice." In its concluding observations on Argentina's report under article 9 of the International Convention on the Elimination of All Forms of Discrimination, the Committee on the Elimination of Racial Discrimination expressed concern over reports of racist police brutality.

European Union

Courts in Spain, Italy, France, and Germany continued to try, or seek the extradition of, members of the Argentine armed forces for the "disappearance" of their citizens during military rule. In July, Alfredo Astiz, a former agent attached to the Navy Mechanics School (ESMA), gave himself up to Buenos Aires police after federal judge María Servini de Cubría ordered his arrest at the request of Italian judge Claudio Tortora, for the "disappearance" in 1976 of three Italian citizens. Italy filed an extradition request, and while Astiz was in custody, France also requested his extradition. A French court had sentenced Astiz to life imprisonment in absentia in 1990 for the "disappearance" of two French nuns, Alice Domon and Leonie Duquet, a crime for which Astiz had been spared trial in Argentina under the due obedience law.

In August, the Ministry of Foreign Affairs refused to extradite Astiz, claiming that only Argentine courts had jurisdiction for crimes committed in Argentina. While influential Argentine judges and jurists had assimilated the doctrine of international jurisdiction for crimes against humanity, the government was unwilling to allow the courts to decide such cases on their legal merits. Since there were no charges pending against him in Argentina, Astiz was immediately released. In contrast to its position on the Astiz case, Argentina took a positive step toward combating impunity by ratifying the Rome Treaty for the International Criminal Court (ICC).

In December 2000, Rome's Second Criminal Court sentenced Gen. Carlos Guillermo Suárez Mason, commander of the First Army Corps from 1976 until 1980, and Gen. Santiago Omar Riveros, to life imprisonment, *in absentia*, on charges of kidnapping, torture, and premeditated murder. Five naval officers received lesser sentences. In July, a court in Nuremberg, Germany, issued an international warrant for Suárez's arrest in connection with the murder of German sociologist Elisabeth Kaesermann, who was the victim of an extrajudicial execution in May 1977 in Argentina.

In January, Mexican Judge Jesús Guadalupe Luna Altamirano accepted a petition from Spain for the extradition of Ricardo Miguel Cavallo, a member of the notorious 3.3.2 task force that operated out of ESMA. Cavallo had been detained in August 2000 at Cancún airport, after Spanish judge Baltazar Garzón issued an international warrant for his arrest on charges of genocide, terrorism, and torture. In February, Mexican Foreign Minister Jorge Castañeda authorized the extradition. The decision was the first by a Latin American country to put into practice the principle of universal jurisdiction. Again, Argentina expressed opposition: Defense Minister Ricardo López Murphy asserted that no country "should be recognized as having the capacity to be a court of appeals for decisions freely adopted by Argentines." As of October, Cavallo remained in custody in Mexico awaiting the results of a judicial appeal against his extradition.

United States

In response to requests by Argentine human rights groups and judges in Europe and Argentina, then-Secretary of State Madeleine Albright promised in November 2000 to declassify State Department documents on "disappearances," the theft of babies, and Operation Condor. It was understood that, unlike the celebrated Chile revelations in 2000, the release would not include Central Intelligence Agency or

Defense Department files. The documents were still awaited at the end of October 2001.

In August, Argentine Judge Rodolfo Canicoba sent a letter rogatory to the State Department requesting a deposition by former Secretary of State Henry Kissinger to aid the judge's investigation of Operation Condor. In addition, French judge Roger Le Loire requested Kissinger's cooperation with judicial inquiries into the "disappearance" in Argentina of French nationals. Although de-classified documents showed that Kissinger was informed about Operation Condor, he did not contribute any information to the French or Argentine courts. The *Washington Times* on August 1 quoted an unnamed White House source as saying that the courts' demands were "unjust and ridiculous."

Relevant Human Rights Watch Reports:

Reluctant Partner: The Argentine Government's Failure to Back Trials of Human Rights Violators, 12/01

BRASIL

HUMAN RIGHTS DEVELOPMENTS

Extrajudicial killings, ill-treatment, and torture continued to be Brazil's most serious human rights problems, with police and prison officials being the primary perpetrators of these abuses. In addition, land reform activists and indigenous people involved in land disputes were harassed, assaulted and killed in circumstances that suggested the acquiescence of public authorities. From police stations to prisons, and from urban centers to the vast territories of Brazil's interior, those responsible for abuses enjoyed widespread impunity. Efforts by the government to address these problems consistently fell short of achieving significant change.

In a landmark ruling, Col. Ubiratan Guimarães—the first military police officer of the rank of colonel or above to be criminally prosecuted in a civilian court—was found responsible for a massacre that left 111 inmates dead after a 1992 prison riot. On June 30, Colonel Guimarães received a 632-year sentence for his role in leading a military police squad that quelled a riot at Carandirú, Brazil's largest prison complex. Police under his command had opened fire on prisoners, many of whom were in their cells, using machine guns and semi-automatic weapons. Subsequent investigations confirmed that the vast majority of the victims died as a result of gunshot wounds, principally to the head and thorax regions. No police were killed in the operation.

While the verdict represented a welcome departure from Brazil's long-standing tradition of impunity, the final outcome of the prosecution remained uncertain. Guimarães was immediately freed after sentencing pending his appeal, which was likely to take at least another year, and he was allowed to continue in his post as director of a private security firm. Another eighty-five military police implicated in the killings were also to be tried, although no trial date had been set as of this writing.

The case shone a spotlight on the brutality of the country's prisons, still a pressing concern. Just months before the trial, in February, another inmate riot at Carandirú had turned bloody, leaving fifteen prisoners dead. Most were killed by riot police, some in circumstances suggesting extrajudicial executions. The uprising quickly spread to several other states, paralyzing the overburdened prison system and grabbing headlines worldwide. Conditions remained subhuman in most of the country's prisons, jails, and police lockups, and riots and escape attempts were frequent.

After the February rioting at Carandirú, officials from the Justice Ministry promised to close the prison, although the closure date was later pushed back repeatedly. Announced plans to build eleven new detention facilities around the state of São Paulo would, according to state prison officials, create space for 8,256 prisoners, including some 7,200 to be transferred from Carandirú. Yet with the total number of inmates growing by approximately nine hundred each year, the problem of insufficient space appeared unlikely to be resolved.

On March 11, police allegedly fired rubber bullets on juvenile detainees after a riot in Unit 30 of the São Paulo state juvenile detention facilities (Fundação Estadual para o Bem-Estar do Menor, FEBEM), in Franco da Rocha. The uprising left one prison guard dead, and thirty-three young inmates wounded. According to reports, after the juveniles had been subdued, police poured powdered soap and pepper on their open wounds. Angered by the death of their colleague, guards beat a priest called in by the state to negotiate with the inmates.

Torture remained a "systematic and widespread" practice in detention facilities, according to a report issued at the end of March by Sir Nigel Rodley, the U.N. special rapporteur on torture. The U.N. report, which corroborated years of research by Brazilian and international human rights organizations, found that state agents routinely commit acts of torture during all phases of detention, including police investigations, short- and long-term imprisonment, and in centers for juvenile offenders. In addition to describing the overcrowded and unhealthy conditions discovered during the special rapporteur's visit to five Brazilian states and the national capital, the report included an appendix detailing 348 cases of torture in eighteen Brazilian states.

Police abuse outside of the detention context also remained a serious concern. Deaths resulting from the excessive use of force by police, or in circumstances suggesting extrajudicial executions, continued throughout the country. Despite the widespread nature of the abuses, only five of Brazil's twenty-seven states had an office of police ombudsman (ouvidoria) to receive complaints of police brutality and monitor police actions. Low wages, poor training, and inadequate equipment all contributed to the widespread corruption and violence of the police forces. In July, a massive police strike to protest these problems in Bahia state resulted in a rash of looting and killings, which were only halted when the army was called in to restore control.

According to the São Paulo police ombudsman, military police in that state killed 272 people in the first half of 2001, an average of three killings every two days. While shocking, these numbers actually represented a decrease from comparable figures from 2000. Most victims of police killings had no prior criminal record. Notably, black and dark-skinned people were disproportionately subject to fatal police shootings.

A particularly egregious case of police violence in Mato Grosso state involved a minor, fifteen-year-old Nilson Pedro da Silva. According to reports, da Silva was killed in the pre-dawn hours of March 30, shot in the head and stomach by military police. Da Silva was apparently unarmed and did not resist arrest. Another young man, Ronilson Oliveira Ferreira, age nineteen, was shot in the leg, but managed to escape. A camera crew from a local television station, TV Cidade, caught the incident on film. The two soldiers involved in the incident, identified in news reports as Macedo César Filho and Denis Coutinho, were dismissed from their posts but not incarcerated. Rights groups urged Mato Grosso state authorities to prosecute the officers and to offer Oliveira the security of the state's witness protection program.

A hauntingly similar case from 1999 went unpunished. On August 27, 1999, Daniel Silva Cartarino, age fifteen, Vando Almeida Araújo, age twenty, and a sixteen-year-old now known as AAS were arrested by military police in the city of São Bernardo do Campo, made to strip naked, and shot, execution style. AAS was able to escape by pretending to be dead. He later identified the police officers and was granted entry into the São Paulo state witness protection program. In July, police officers Ivair Roberto de Souza, Isaías Mendonça Silva, Wagner Augusto Pinheiro, and Emerson Roberto de Sisto were acquitted of the killings. Officials from the Public Ministry in São Bernardo do Campo said that they would appeal the case to the Supreme Court.

Justice in a case involving 149 military police accused of killing nineteen landless peasants and wounding sixty-six others also remained elusive. The incident occurred in April 1996, in Eldorado dos Carajás, during a protest roadblock organized by members of the Landless Movement (Movimento dos Sem Terra, MST). Charges against the three commanding officers were dropped by a jury in August 1999, a decision that was later reversed by the Pará state Justice Tribunal. A retrial was originally set for May 2001, but was suspended after judge Eva Coelho de Amaral barred the entry into evidence of a report thought to discredit police claims that protesters fired the first shots. Under pressure from civil society and the human rights community, the judge later ruled that the report was admissible in the proceedings, but ordered a counter-investigation that was expected to delay the trial even further.

Although the case of Eldorado dos Carajás was the most high profile example of rural violence, killings and threats against rural workers were frequent throughout the year. According to the Pastoral Land Commission (Comissão Pastoral da Terra, CPT), 1,532 people were assassinated in rural areas from 1988 to September 2001, among them workers, religious agents, lawyers, and labor leaders. In most of these cases, those responsible were never brought to justice. In the state of Pará, where many of the violations were concentrated, the CPT counted six people killed in the four-month period from April to August, hundreds more imprisoned, and more than 1,500 families displaced in military police operations. The majority of displaced families had been occupying areas of land for more than two years and had registered to take legal title to the land.

In one of the many serious attacks against rural activists and landless peasants in southern Pará state, José Pinheiro de Lima, his wife, and their fifteen-year-old son were killed by gunmen in their home in Morada Nova, Marabá, on July 9. The murders came just five days after another peasant worker, Manoel Messias Colono de Souza, was shot dead on a nearby farm. Following the killings, federal police sent a team to Marabá to help with the investigation, four months after they had themselves alerted state authorities about death threats against Lima, a leader in the movement to expropriate land on the Fazenda São Raimundo. Later that month, the former owner of the Fazenda São Raimundo, who had lost title to his land due to Lima's efforts, was arrested for ordering the killing.

On August 25, Ademir Alfeu Federicci was murdered in his home in Altamira, in western Pará state. Federicci, a coordinator for the Movement for the Development of the Transamazon and the Xingu Area (Movimento pelo Desenvolvimento da Transamazônica e do Xingu), worked to promote sustainable development in the region. Although police called his killing the result of an armed robbery, Federicci's leadership in the fight against dam construction, illegal logging, and corruption, made a political motive appear more likely.

Indigenous people were also a frequent target in land disputes, and they continued to be moved off their land, threatened, and killed. According to a report released by Guarani leaders, in November 2000 members of the Guarani community were fired on by police allegedly hired by a cattle rancher who had taken over their land. Among those injured was a baby, who was hit in the head by a rubber bullet. In February, the then-president of the Human Rights Committee of the Chamber of Representatives, Marcos Rolim, reported several cases of alleged sexual abuse by army soldiers against Yanomami women in the Surucucus region of the Amazon.

On August 23, indigenous leader Francisco de Assis Santana was murdered in Pesqueira, Pernambuco, apparently in connection with his struggles for Xucuru land rights in the territory, demarcated as an official reserve in April 2001. De Assis Santana, known as "Chico Quelé," was killed in an ambush as he made his way to a meeting with an authority from the country's indigenous rights organization (Fundaçao Nacional do Indio, FUNAI).

Attacks against and harassment of lesbians and gays were also of concern. The Gay Association of Bahia, a gay rights advocacy group, reported frequent murders of gay men, claiming that less than 10 percent of such crimes were successfully prosecuted in the courts. But in February, in an encouraging development, José Nilson Pereira da Silva and Juliano Filipini Sabino were sentenced to twenty-one years in prison for beating a gay man to death. José Edson Neris da Silva and his partner Dario Pereira were attacked in downtown São Paulo in February 2000, apparently because they were holding hands. Neris da Silva died as a result of the attack. A third suspect was acquitted of the murder but convicted of assault, while a fourth was sentenced to three years and four months in prison for attempted murder.

Freedom of expression was undermined by violence against journalists, censorship, exorbitantly high lawsuits against the press, and proposed gag laws. On August 16, the day before he was to testify in a defamation trial brought by two municipal officials whom he had accused of misappropriating funds, journalist Mário Coelho de Almeida Filho was murdered. According to reports, Coelho, who lived in Magé, in the state of Rio de Janeiro, had been threatened because of his writing, and a company linked to one of the municipal officials had recently tried to buy his silence. In September, a retired military police officer was arrested for the crime; the officer had previously served as a bodyguard for the daughter of one of the two municipal officials.

On July 21, Judge Ana Paula Braga Alencastro ordered the confiscation of the next day's issue of the newspaper *Tribuna Popular*, published in São Lourenço do Sul, in the state of Rio Grande do Sul. The confiscation was carried out at the request of a local prefect whose administrative improprieties were described in an article to be published that day. The Inter American Press Association condemned the action as an act of "prior censorship."

Efforts to extend the "Pinochet precedent" to Brazil were initiated, part of an international movement to bring former dictators to justice. In December 2000, a Paraguayan judge issued a detention order against former Paraguayan ruler Gen. Alfredo Stroessner, whose thirty-five-year reign was characterized by human rights abuses such as political killings and "disappearances." As of this writing, however, Stroessner continued to enjoy immunity in Brasília, where he was granted political asylum and has lived since 1989.

Brazil's aggressive efforts to combat the HIV/AIDS pandemic were one positive element in its overall human rights picture, with the country's national HIV/AIDS program being rightly hailed as a model. Although the country had the highest number of AIDS-affected persons in Latin America, mortality from AIDS declined sharply over the past few years as the government ensured that persons with HIV had access to a treatment regimen based on generic drugs.

DEFENDING HUMAN RIGHTS

The president of the Pastoral Land Commission (Commisão Pastoral da Terra, CPT) in Paraná, Dinísio Vandressi, reportedly received several death threats over the course of the year. On May 24, members of congress asked the Justice Ministry to intervene to ensure the protection of Vandressi and his family.

Father Júlio Lancellotti of the Catholic Church's Youth Pastoral was assaulted by FEBEM guards during the March 11 rioting at the Franco da Rocha youth detention facility. Although Lacellotti had been invited by the state to negotiate with inmates, his arrival was greeted not by officials, but by a group of prison guards who were angry over a colleague's death in the uprising. The priest was hit in the face by guards, and the cross he was wearing around his neck was ripped off.

THE ROLE OF THE INTERNATIONAL COMMUNITY

United Nations

As described above, the report of the U.N. special rapporteur on torture was comprehensive, forceful, and accurate. Following a recommendation contained in the U.N. report, and under pressure from human rights organizations, the government invited the U.N. special rapporteur on extrajudicial executions, Dr. Asma Jahangir, to visit Brazil. She was expected to begin research in the country in early 2002.

In May, the Committee against Torture reviewed Brazil's record of implementing the Convention against Torture and Other Cruel, Inhuman or Degrading Treatment or Punishment. The committee noted the "remarkably frank and self-critical character" of the Brazilian government's report on implementation. Among other things, the committee expressed concern over the frequency of torture and inhuman treatment, and the impunity enjoyed by the perpetrators of such acts.

Organization of American States (OAS)

In 2001, the Brazilian government began directly negotiating with parties involved in litigation before the Inter-American Court of Human Rights. The initiative was welcomed as a sign of increased government cooperation and as a means to obtain faster results in remedying human rights violations. According to the Brazil office of the nongovernmental Center for Justice and International Law (CEJIL), Brazil conducted direct negotiations in six cases pending before the Inter-American Court.

In April, the Inter-American Commission on Human Rights decided the case of Maria da Penha. It was the first case involving Brazil that the Inter-American Commission had accepted based on violations of the Inter-American Convention on the Prevention, Punishment and Eradication of Violence against Women. Da Penha had been repeatedly beaten by her husband, Marco Antônio Heredia Viveiros. The beatings culminated, in 1983, in an attempted homicide that left her paraplegic. In its ground-breaking decision, the commission found numerous rights violations and recommended that Brazil adopt measures to remedy the problem of state tolerance of domestic violence against women.

United States

The United States, Brazil's main trade partner, remained the major source of direct foreign investment, including investment by a number of major U.S. companies. Brazil was not, however, a major recipient of direct U.S. foreign assistance. The State Department's chapter on Brazil in its *Country Reports on Human Rights Practices for 2000* fairly portrayed the country's human rights situation.

Under pressure from pharmaceutical companies, the United States had initiated a trade dispute with Brazil, complaining that the Brazilian authorities violated patent protections in manufacturing and distributing generic anti-AIDS drugs. In late June, however, the U.S. government dropped its objections to Brazil's successful anti-AIDS effort.

European Union

Bilateral trade between Brazil and the members of the European Union (E.U.) remained substantial, with Brazil being the E.U.'s principal market in Latin America. The E.U. committed 150 million euros to cooperation projects in Brazil in 2000.

CHILE

The landmark indictment of former dictator Gen. Augusto Pinochet and its confirmation by the Santiago Appeals Court were the year's signal human rights achievements. Yet the suspension of criminal proceedings against Pinochet in July, ostensibly for medical reasons, undermined hopes that all Chileans were genuinely equal before the law.

Encouraging, but partial, progress was also made in the area of freedom of expression. Congress repealed several objectionable provisions of the State Security Law, and took steps toward ending film censorship.

HUMAN RIGHTS DEVELOPMENTS

On December 1, 2001, Judge Juan Guzmán indicted Pinochet on eighteen counts of aggravated kidnapping and fifty-seven counts of homicide. The former dictator was accused of ordering killings committed by the "Caravan of Death," a helicopter-borne military squad that toured the country in October 1973, removing political prisoners from their cells and secretly executing them. Pinochet's lawyers appealed the indictment, arguing that Judge Guzmán had failed to take a deposition from Pinochet before charging him, as the law required. On December 20, the Supreme Court upheld the appeal, annulled the indictment, and ordered Judge Guzmán to question Pinochet within twenty days. The court did not make it a requirement, as Pinochet's lawyers had urged, that Pinochet undergo medical tests *before* the deposition. Six days later, however, the Supreme Court issued a "clarification" of its earlier ruling that said that the medical tests had to be conducted beforehand, giving Pinochet's defense another opportunity to fend off criminal charges.

Between January 10 and 13, a team of six psychiatrists and neurologists, with one expert observer from either side, examined and tested Pinochet at the military hospital. They found him to be suffering from "light to moderate" sub cortical dementia caused by a series of mild strokes (in their final report, they termed the dementia "moderate"). Reviewing the team's report, Judge Guzmán concluded that

Pinochet's disability was not severe enough for him to be exempted from trial since under Chilean law defendants must be found to be "mad" or "demented" before trial proceedings are suspended for mental health reasons. On January 23 the judge finally obtained Pinochet's deposition at his Santiago residence. Five days later he indicted Pinochet a second time, placing him under house arrest.

Chilean society, though it was divided over Pinochet's legacy, absorbed this momentous episode without violence or political instability. Nor did the political branches of government put overt pressure on the courts. Nonetheless, it was no secret that the government hoped to see Pinochet eventually exempted from trial on humanitarian grounds.

On March 8, a Santiago Appeals Court panel confirmed Pinochet's indictment, but reduced the charges against him from kidnapping and murder to concealment of the crimes. Both sides appealed. A week later, another panel of the court permitted Pinochet to be released on bail. It also ordered Judge Guzmán to take Pinochet's fingerprints and photographs, a formal requirement in Chile following criminal indictment. Pinochet's defense lawyers insisted that even this brief procedure would endanger the defendant's health. They made strenuous efforts to delay the procedure in the hope that the case would be closed on health grounds and finger-printing would be unnecessary. Eventually, they succeeded: on July 9, the Sixth Chamber of the Santiago Appeals Court suspended the proceedings, ruling by two votes to one that Pinochet was too infirm to stand trial.

The appellate court ruled that if the terms "madness" or "dementia" (grounds for exemption from trial under the code of penal procedures in force) were inter-preted in the light of modern medical science (as the court believed they should be) Pinochet's condition should bar his trial. Moreover, the court held, to try Pinochet in his condition would violate the due process guarantees of the Chilean constitu-tion and its new code of penal procedures.

The decision gave norms of due process precedence over written laws for the first time in Chilean legal history. It also relied in part on a code of penal procedures that had not yet entered into force in Santiago, where Pinochet's trial was to be held. (In December 2000, the new code of penal procedures entered into force in Chile's Fourth and Ninth regions, but it was not scheduled to become effective in Santiago until 2004. The code allowed judges to suspend trials if the due process rights of a defendant cannot be guaranteed). Prominent justice officials, including represen-tatives of the Council for the Defense of the State and the Public Defender (Defen-sor Público Penal), declared that the application of the new code in Santiago was illegal and unconstitutional.

Subsequent court rulings confirmed fears that the Sixth Chamber's decision was a special concession to Pinochet, and not would benefit other mentally challenged defendants. In July, the Legal Assistance Corporation, which provides free legal rep-resentation to poor defendants, asked a different panel of the Santiago Appeals Court to grant the same rights to a hundred of its clients who were facing trial on a variety of felony charges. The court rejected the petition on grounds that the new penal procedures code was not in force. As of this writing the Supreme Court was due to hear the petitioners' appeal, as well as an appeal alleging the Sixth Chamber's misapplication of the new code in the Pinochet case.

Continued progress was made in other prosecutions of Pinochet-era officials. In August, Judge Sergio Muñoz charged sixteen army officers, most of them members of the Army Intelligence Directorate (Dirección de Inteligencia del Ejército, DINE), with the 1982 murder of trade unionist Tucapel Jiménez. Among the accused were four retired army generals. The investigation, which had been thwarted for years, progressed rapidly after Judge Muñoz took over the case in 2000 and several of the soldiers confessed. Interior Ministry officials confirmed that judges and police officers investigating human rights violations committed during the Pinochet era had been followed and threatened by individuals believed to be former members of the National Information Center (Central Nacional de Informaciones, CNI), a secret police force that operated during the 1980s.

In January, the armed forces and uniformed police, whose representatives had participated in a civil-military roundtable initiated in August 1999, acknowledged for the first time that the bodies of 151 prisoners who "disappeared" after the September 1973 military coup had been thrown from aircraft into the sea, rivers, and lakes of Chile. Unfortunately, the importance of the revelation was overshadowed by numerous errors in the information provided by the military regarding two hundred "disappearance" cases. The errors added to the trauma of relatives of the "disappeared," and confirmed the expectations of many relatives who had opposed the civil-military dialogue from the outset.

Out of two hundred victims whose fate was revealed, the final resting place of forty-nine was given with sufficient precision to make it possible, in theory, to find their remains. Yet in more than fifty cases the dates given for the arrest and death of the victim did not tally with the facts known to human rights organizations. The body of trade unionist Juan Rivera Matus, described in the round table list as having been thrown into the sea near the port of San Antonio, was found in April buried in an army compound at Fort Arteaga. Some dental fragments and pieces of bone found in a disused mineshaft near Santiago were believed to belong to Communist Party leaders Horacio Cepeda and Fernando Ortíz, detained in December 1976, and whose bodies were listed in the armed forces document as having been buried at the site. However, relatives still awaited conclusive identification in October. After months of searching, investigators could not find the remains of four other party members whose bodies, according to the Navy, were also thrown down the shaft. The discovery only of small bone fragments suggested that the mine had been visited at some subsequent date and skeletal remains removed to conceal the crime.

After years of debate, Congress finally enacted reforms benefiting freedom of expression, although many legal restraints remained in place. In April, it repealed article 6b of the State Security Law, a 1958 statute that allowed top judges, military chiefs and members of congress to bring charges of contempt of authority against their press critics.

Other provisions of the State Security Law—including article 16, which allowed the seizure of publications considered insulting by public officials—were also abolished. Legislators refused to accept more sweeping reforms, including a government proposal to repeal three articles of the criminal code that cover defamation and libel of public officials in terms similar to article 6b.

Journalist Alejandra Matus, who left Chile to avoid arrest in April 1999 after her book *The Black Book of Chilean Justice* was seized under article 16, returned to the country for the first time in July. During her visit she petitioned the Santiago Appeals Court to allow the distribution of her book, since the law under which it had been confiscated was no longer in force. The court rejected her writ, and in August the Supreme Court dismissed her appeal of the rejection. In October, however, appeals court judge Rubén Ballesteros finally lifted the ban on the book and ordered the confiscated copies returned to the publisher. He also suspended Matus's prosecution on other charges related to the book.

The State Security Law amendments were part of a comprehensive new law regulating the press and protecting the rights of journalists, first proposed by the Aylwin government in 1993. It shielded journalists from having to reveal their sources, and stripped courts of the power to gag press reporting of controversial criminal cases. It also stripped military courts of jurisdiction over cases involving criticism of the military. However, the law was by no means a panacea ending all of Chile's freedom of expression restrictions, and in some areas it made matters worse. For example, it discriminated against journalists without recognized university degrees. And even with the reforms, Chile's privacy laws failed to sufficiently protect those responsible for disclosures in the public interest.

In July, Congress approved a constitutional amendment eliminating prior censorship of the cinema. The reform was expected to come into force as soon as Congress approved a bill changing the powers and composition of the film classification council. That bill, introduced by President Lagos in March, restricted the council's powers to the certification of films for age-group suitability, and eliminated the representation of the armed forces and the police on the council.

On May 20, twenty-six inmates died in a prison fire in the northern city of Iquique. Prison officials were reported to have mistaken the fire for a riot and failed to call the fire brigade in time to rescue the victims, while fire-fighting equipment in the prison failed to work. The prison, constructed for a maximum of 1,000 inmates, held 1,700 at the time of the tragedy. Minister of Justice José Antonio Gómez announced that the government was planning to build ten new prisons to alleviate overcrowding.

On May 28, President Lagos signed into law the abolition of capital punishment. The death penalty was replaced by life imprisonment, with a minimum forty-year prison sentence for the most serious crimes. The new code of penal procedures entered into force in two regions in December 2000, replacing written with oral proceedings and strengthening the due process rights of defendants. The new code was scheduled to enter force progressively across the country.

DEFENDING HUMAN RIGHTS

Attorneys representing relatives of the victims in the "Caravan of Death" case litigated tirelessly to hold Pinochet accountable for the crimes committed by the military death squad. The Council for the Defense of the State, an autonomous body representing the interests of the state, made itself a party to this and several other human rights cases.

Relatives of the "disappeared" and other human rights defenders did not report any direct threats or harassment, in contrast to previous years. However, a website believed to be linked to former members of the CNI, the military government's intelligence agency, carried spiteful attacks on the president of the Association of Relatives of the "Disappeared," Viviana Díaz, and publicized her private address and telephone number.

THE ROLE OF THE INTERNATIONAL COMMUNITY

Organization of American States (OAS)

In February, the Inter-American Court of Human Rights found that Chile had violated article 13 of the American Convention on Human Rights by refusing to allow the public exhibition of Martin Scorsese's film *The Last Temptation of Christ*. The court ruled that Chile must amend its domestic law to eliminate prior censorship and allow the film to be screened. The decision, which was unanimous, was the court's first ruling in a contentious case involving freedom of expression, and its first ruling against Chile.

United States

In November 2000 the Clinton administration fulfilled its promise to release more than 16,000 secret documents on U.S.-Chilean relations before and after the military coup that brought General Pinochet to power in September 1973. The release included some seven hundred Central Intelligence Agency (CIA) records, which the CIA's Directorate of Operations agreed to release only after pressure from the White House. These dealt with covert operations to prevent the election of President Salvador Allende, to destabilize his government, and to bolster that of Pinochet.

On the basis of new information from the declassified documents, in October and December 2000, Judge Guzmán opened investigations into the "disappearance" and murder of two North Americans, Boris Weisfeiler and Charles Horman. Weisfeiler, a Russian-born mathematician, "disappeared" in January 1985 while hiking in southern Chile. Horman was executed in the National Stadium days after the military coup. In July, Judge Guzmán sent a letter rogatory to the State Department, requesting depositions on the case from former Secretary of State Henry Kissinger and from officials of the U.S. embassy in Chile at the time of the coup.

Argentina

In October 2001, Manuel Contreras (former director of Pinochet's secret police, the DINA), and five former DINA agents were arrested in Chile at the request of Argentine federal judge María Servini de Cubría, pending a hearing on their extradition to Argentina. They had been charged in Argentina for the 1974 assassination in Buenos Aires of former Gen. Carlos Prats and his wife Sofia Cuthbert, but the Chilean Supreme Court had earlier denied their extradition on procedural grounds. In August, the Supreme Court had rejected Judge Servini's request that Pinochet be extradited for ordering the assassination.

In April, Argentine federal judge Rodolfo Canicoba issued another international warrant for the arrest of Manuel Contreras with a view to his extradition for organizing Operation Condor, a secret plan of South American military governments to track, kidnap, murder, or illegally deport persons seeking refuge from repression in neighboring countries. In July, Justice Alberto Chaigneau of the Chilean Supreme Court ordered that Contreras be placed under house arrest. The following month the Santiago Appeals Court denied Contreras' bail request. Chilean Supreme Court judge Domingo Kokisch denied a similar request by the Argentine judge for the arrest, pending extradition, of General Pinochet. In both the Prats and Condor cases the Chilean courts held that Pinochet still preserved his parliamentary immunity from prosecution. Unless the Supreme Court lifted his immunity, Pinochet could not be questioned or charged in either case, a necessary prerequisite to his extradition.

Relevant Human Rights Watch Reports:

Progress Stalled: Setbacks in Freedom of Expression Reform, 3/01

COLOMBIA

Negotiations between the government and leftist guerrillas reached an impasse in 2001 as both sides traded accusations of bad faith and broken promises. Political violence increased for the second consecutive year and became increasingly urban, with clashes and selective killings occurring in cities. Colombians continued to flee their homes and even their country in record numbers, facing hunger, the elements, and disease in desperate efforts to save themselves and their families.

In the first ten months of the year, the office of the Public Advocate (Defensoría del Pueblo) recorded ninety-two massacres, which they defined as the killing of three or more people at the same place and at the same time. Most were linked to paramilitary groups, followed by guerrillas. Both paramilitaries and guerrillas reportedly moved with ease throughout the country, including via helicopter.

One of the year's worst massacres occurred on January 17, in Chengue, Sucre. Witnesses told government investigators that several Colombian navy units looked the other way as heavily armed paramilitaries traveled past them to the village. Paramilitaries assembled villagers in two groups, the *Washington Post* later reported. "Then, one by one, they killed the men by crushing their heads with heavy stones and a sledgehammer. When it was over, twenty-four men lay dead in pools of blood. Two more were found later in shallow graves. As the troops left, they set fire to the village."

The authorities subsequently arrested Navy Sergeant Rubén Darío Rojas and charged him with supplying weapons to paramilitaries and helping coordinate the attack. Colombia's Internal Affairs agency (Procuraduría) filed disciplinary charges against Navy Brig. Gen. Rodrigo Quiñones and five other security force officers for allegedly ignoring detailed information received in advance about paramilitary movements near Chengue. At the time, Quiñones was the commander of the first Naval Brigade. Despite the charges, he was later promoted to the post of navy chief of staff.

As the Chengue case showed, certain military units and police detachments continued to promote, work with, support, profit from, and tolerate paramilitary groups, treating them as a force allied to and compatible with their own. At their most brazen, these relationships involved active coordination during military operations between government and paramilitary units; communication via radios, cellular telephones, and beepers; the sharing of intelligence, including the names of suspected guerrilla collaborators; the sharing of fighters, including active-duty soldiers serving in paramilitary units and paramilitary commanders lodging on military bases; the sharing of vehicles, including army trucks used to transport paramilitary fighters; coordination of army roadblocks, which routinely let heavily-armed paramilitary fighters pass; and payments made from paramilitaries to military officers for their support.

Overall, President Andrés Pastrana and his defense ministers failed to take effective action to establish control over the security forces and break their persistent ties to paramilitary groups. Even as President Pastrana publicly deplored atrocities, the high-ranking officers he commanded failed to take steps necessary to prevent killings by suspending security force members suspected of abuses, ensuring that their cases were handed over to civilian judicial authorities for investigation and prosecution, and pursuing and arresting paramilitary leaders.

Paramilitaries allied under the umbrella United Self Defense Group of Colombia (Autodefensas Unidas de Colombia, AUC) expanded their radius of action and troop strength in 2001. In June, AUC commander Carlos Castaño announced that he had relinquished military leadership and dedicated himself to organizing its political wing. Since 1996, the group had grown by over 560 percent, according to Castaño, who claimed a force of over 11,000 fighters. In some situations, as with the temporary seizure of a community of displaced people in Esperanza en Dios and Nueva Vida, Chocó, paramilitaries reportedly operated with as many as eight hundred troops at a time. Large concentrations of paramilitaries were rarely challenged by the Colombian security forces.

Over a period of a week in early July, in the town of Peque, Antioquia, over five hundred armed and uniformed paramilitaries blockaded roads, occupied municipal buildings, looted, cut all outside communication, and prevented food and medicines from being shipped in, according to the Public Advocate's office. Over 5,000 Colombians were forced to flee. When the paramilitaries left, church workers counted at least nine dead and another ten people "disappeared," several of them children. As a local official said: "The state abandoned us. This was a massacre foretold. We alerted the regional government the paramilitaries were coming and they didn't send help."

During much of 2000, the AUC paid monthly salaries to local army and police officials based on rank in the department of Putumayo, where U.S.-funded and trained counternarcotics battalions were deployed. In the state of Cauca, soldiers moonlighting as paramilitaries earned up to $500 per month. These salaries far exceeded the average Colombian's monthly income.

Mayors, municipal officials, governors, human rights groups, the Public Advocate's office and even some police detachments regularly informed the appropriate authorities about credible threats by paramilitaries or even massacres that were taking place. An early warning system paid for by the United States and administered by the office of the Public Advocate registered twenty separate warnings nationwide between June, when the system began to function, and September. But rarely did the government take effective action to prevent atrocities. Of the warnings that were received, eleven incidents resulted either in killings being committed or the continued, pronounced presence of armed groups that threatened civilians.

Paramilitaries were linked to the murders of Colombians working to foster peace, among them three congressmen. On June 2, armed men believed to be paramilitaries seized Kimy Pernía Domicó, a leader of the Emberá-Katío community in the department of Córdoba, who remained "disappeared" at this writing. Three weeks after he was abducted, another Emberá-Katío leader who had been active in calls for Domicó's release was abducted by presumed paramilitaries and later killed. As these killings showed, certain groups faced special risks, among them indigenous groups, trade unionists, journalists, human rights defenders, and peace advocates.

The security forces were also directly implicated in abuses. In May, it was revealed that a combined police-army unit had illegally tapped over 2,000 telephone lines in the city of Medellín, many belonging to nongovernmental and human rights groups. The police officer who apparently helped place the taps was killed in April in circumstances that remained unclear.

Prosecutors implicated a former Colombian army major and an active duty police captain along with Carlos Castaño in the December 21, 2000, attack on trade union leader Wilson Borja, who was seriously wounded. In the first ten months of 2001, 125 trade unionists were murdered according to the Central Workers Union (Central Unitaria de Trabajadores, CUT), which represents most Colombian unions.

With the stated goal of furthering peace talks, the government continued to allow the Revolutionary Armed Forces of Colombia-People's Army (Fuerzas Armadas Revolucionarias de Colombia-Ejército del Pueblo, FARC-EP) to maintain control over a Switzerland-sized area in southern Colombia. During the year, the two sides agreed on a prisoner exchange that led to the release of 364 captured members of the police and military forces, and fourteen imprisoned FARC-EP members. Several freed officers reported that FARC-EP guerrillas abused them during captivity. Colombian National Police (CNP) Col. Álvaro León Acosta, captured on April 5, 2000, suffered from serious ailments and excruciating pain stemming from an untreated back injury. Other captives reported jungle diseases, including malaria, fungi, constant diarrhea because of contaminated water, and leishmaniasis, which can be fatal if untreated. Guerrillas never allowed the International Committee of the Red Cross (ICRC) or other independent groups to visit captured combatants, dozens of whom remained in the group's custody.

Criticism of the FARC-EP intensified as evidence mounted that the group used its area of control not only to warehouse prisoners and kidnaped civilians, but also to plan and mount attacks, including assaults that caused civilian casualties. The FARC-EP frequently used indiscriminate weapons, specifically gas cylinder bombs.

The FARC-EP continued to kill civilians throughout Colombia, with human rights groups reporting 197 such killings in the first ten months of the year. Among the victims was former culture minister Consuelo Araújo Noguera, abducted by the FARC-EP on September 24. The wife of Colombia's Internal Affairs director, Araújo Noguera was apparently executed by guerrillas during a Colombian army rescue attempt. Other victims included Paez leader Cristóbal Secué Escué, a former president of the Cauca Indigenous Regional Council (Consejo Regional Indígena del Cauca, CRIC), who was shot on June 25 near his home in Corinto, Cauca. The FARC-EP accused Paez communities of forming "civic guards" that were like para-military groups, a charge indigenous leaders denied. Secué was, at the time of the killing, serving as a judge investigating several alleged murders by FARC-EP guer-rillas.

Kidnaping remained a source of income and political pressure for the FARC-EP. In July, the group carried out its first mass kidnaping from an apartment building, seizing sixteen people after blowing the doors off a residence in Neiva, Huila. Among those kidnaped were children as young as five years old. Six people were later released.

After Human Rights Watch wrote to FARC-EP leader Manuel Marulanda to protest these violations, he dismissed the letter as "Yankee interventionism, dis-guised as a humanitarian action."

For its part, the Camilist Union-National Liberation Army (Unión Camilista-Ejército de Liberación Nacional, UC-ELN) violated international humanitarian law by launching indiscriminate attacks and committing kidnapings. After the gov-ernment suspended talks with the group on August 7, the UC-ELN set off a series of car and package bombs in the department of Antioquia, including the city of Medellín, killing passers-by and destroying electrical towers and public buses. Two weeks earlier, over fifteen UC-ELN guerrillas died when bombs they were placing along a road exploded in the truck carrying them.

There were some advances on accountability, principally by the office of the attorney general under the direction of Alfonso Gómez Méndez, who completed his four-year term in July. On May 25, prosecutors seized valuable information related to paramilitary financing networks and communications in the city of Montería, Córdoba, long considered an AUC stronghold. During the raid, prose-cutors searched the home of Salvatore Mancuso, a Montería native who was said to be the AUC's military commander. In part, the investigation focused on how landowners and business people in the region donated heavily to the AUC.

The attorney general's office also pursued important cases involving laws of war violations, among them the murder in December 29, 2000, of Congressman Diego Turbay and six others outside Florencia, Caquetá. The massacre took place as Tur-bay, chair of the Peace Commission in Colombia's House of Representatives, and his companions were headed toward a meeting with guerrilla leaders in Los Pozos. The FARC-EP denied committing this massacre, but the attorney general opened a formal investigation of alleged guerrillas based on testimonies of captured gunmen and other evidence.

New Attorney General Luis Osorio set a disturbing precedent when he forced the resignation of the director of the Human Rights Unit, the former director of the Human Rights Unit, and the former head of the Technical Investigations Unit (Cuerpo Técnico de Investigaciones, CTI) during his first hours in office. This change in leadership and the message it sent threatened to reverse or hamper important investigations and led to a slowdown or suspension of important cases, including the Chengue massacre.

Osorio objected to the unit's decision to order the July 23 arrest of Gen. (ret.) Rito Alejo del Río for his alleged support of paramilitary groups while in command of the army's Seventeenth Brigade in Carepa, Antioquia, between 1995 and 1997. Del Río was among the officers dismissed from the army by President Pastrana because of his poor human rights record. Also, the United States canceled his visa to the United States because of his alleged involvement in acts of terrorism and drug trafficking.

The Security and National Defense Law that President Pastrana signed on August 13 threatened to reinforce impunity for human rights abuses. The law gave the security forces judicial police powers under certain circumstances and severely restricted the ability of civilian investigators to initiate disciplinary investigations against security force personnel for human rights violations committed during operations. Also, the law limited the obligation of the armed forces to inform judicial authorities about the detention of suspects, increasing the risk of torture.

Since the president signed a new military penal code in 2000 that allowed military commanders to dismiss subordinates implicated in a wide range of crime, the Defense Ministry claimed that over five hundred people had been removed from the service. However, the government provided no information indicating the reason for the dismissals, which could range from incompetence to involvement in human rights crimes. In addition, there was no evidence that any of these individuals subsequently faced criminal investigations for human rights violations. Meanwhile, officers charged with abuses remained on active duty and in charge of groups in the field.

The Colombian government also argued that it arrested hundreds of paramilitaries and dismissed their military supporters. However, arrests were mainly of low-ranking individuals, some of whom were speedily released.

Landmines were a threat to civilians throughout Colombia. According to the Colombian army and independent landmine monitors, the total number of landmines in Colombia was estimated at 130,000. Deaths and injuries resulting from their use were up sharply. Through mid-July 2001, the Colombian Campaign Against Land Mines recorded eighty-eight people killed or maimed by landmines, mostly farmers and their children. Colombia has signed but not yet ratified the 1999 Ottawa Convention banning the use, stockpiling, and export of landmines.

Forced displacement continued to increase, with at least 300,000 Colombians reported displaced in 2001, the highest number ever in a single year. Increasingly, Colombians applied for exit visas to travel abroad and applied for political asylum in other countries.

Kofi Asomani, the United Nations special coordinator on internal displacement of the Office for the Coordination of Humanitarian Affairs, visited Colombia in August and concluded that the conflict had "catastrophic consequences" for the civilian population. Despite government programs meant to assist the displaced,

Asomani found that they continued to suffer extreme hardship, living in over-crowded and unsanitary conditions with limited access to basic services.

DEFENDING HUMAN RIGHTS

Colombia continued to be an extremely dangerous place for human rights defenders as well as for government investigators handling human rights and international humanitarian law investigations. In the first ten months of 2001, eleven defenders were killed according to the CCJ.

Among the victims was lawyer Alma Rosa Jaramillo Lafourie, who worked with the Middle Magdalena Development and Peace Program (Programa de Desarrollo y Paz del Magdalena Medio, PDPMM). Seized by presumed paramilitaries in Morales, in the department of Bolívar, on June 29, locals found her body two days later dumped in a rural area. According to associates, Jaramillo was tortured before being executed. Another PDPMM colleague, Eduardo Estrada, was murdered in similar circumstances on July 18 in the town of San Pablo, Bolívar. Colombia's Pacific coast was also dangerous. On September 19, armed men shot and killed Roman Catholic nun and human rights defender Yolanda Cerón Delgado in front of a church in Tumaco, Nariño.

Paramilitaries intensified an announced campaign to murder prosecutors and investigators of cases that implicated paramilitary leaders. During 2001, seven government investigators were murdered by alleged paramilitary gunmen. Among them were the three investigators who worked most closely on the investigation of the Chengue massacre. Several key witnesses to important cases were also killed while in government custody or while in the process of supplying information to prosecutors. The office in Colombia of the U.N. High Commissioner for Human Rights (UNHCHR) called these killings "a systematic campaign of retaliation and intimidation" by those seeking "total impunity for the most serious crimes committed in the country."

Human rights defenders were among the main targets of the paramilitary advance in Barrancabermeja that began in December 2000. Members of the Regional Committee for the Defense of Human Rights and the Popular Women's Organization (Organización Femenina Popular, OFP) received multiple death threats by telephone and in person, and paramilitaries destroyed a house they used to hold events. "The paramilitaries are not just killing us physically, they are also killing our ability to organize, to be community leaders," said Yolanda Becerra, OFP president. "We have been forced to shut down projects outside the city, because the paramilitaries have banned us from traveling by river."

Some government offices attempted to protect threatened defenders, supplying bodyguards, bulletproof reinforcement for offices, and an emergency response network operated by handheld radios. The CNP Human Rights office and the Interior Ministry, in particular, took steps to protect defenders and to investigate specific allegations of police collaboration with paramilitary groups. The Interior Ministry provided protection or relocation assistance to 747 people between May and mid-September of 2001.

In many instances, however, government response was slow, nonexistent, or abusive. For example, the commander of the Barrancabermeja-based CNP, Col. José Miguel Villar Jiménez, attacked human rights groups by claiming that they had their "origin in [guerrillas], which attempt to throw mud on the good work that is done constantly with reports and information that also has an echo in the different international Non-Governmental Organizations."

THE ROLE OF THE INTERNATIONAL COMMUNITY

The international community played a prominent role in efforts to resolve Colombia's conflict. France, Switzerland, Cuba, Mexico, Venezuela, Norway, Spain, Italy, Canada, and Sweden agreed to meet every two weeks with the FARC-EP and act as "facilitator countries" for the peace process.

United Nations

The office of the UNHCHR continued to operate in Colombia, despite poor cooperation from Colombian government officials. As High Commissioner Mary Robinson noted in the office's annual report, "the overwhelming majority of Governmental responses to Office communications about specific cases and situations (such as early warnings) have been unsatisfactory, inoperative and purely bureaucratic." The end result, she emphasized, was that "the potential of the Office has been greatly underutilized by the Government."

Before announcing his departure at year's end, Jan Egeland, the special adviser on Colombia to the United Nations Secretary-General, frequently visited Colombia to assist in peace talks, but was prevented by the government from remaining in the country for more than eight days at a time.

Special representative of the secretary-general on human rights defenders, Hina Jilani, undertook a fact-finding mission to Colombia in October at the invitation of the Colombian government. It ended bitterly, after Jilani raised questions about the new Attorney General and his commitment to prosecuting cases involving high-ranking military officers.

European Union

Political relations with the European Union were strengthened in 2001. In March, E.U. Foreign Affairs Commissioner Chris Patten met with President Pastrana in Colombia. Shortly after, Patten announced a 3 million euro aid package in support of the displaced population and the launching of an Andean regional human rights program.

In July, the European Union expressed deep concern at mounting violence, in particular the holding up of a U.N. vehicle and the abduction of one it its Colombian occupants, former Meta department governor Alan Jara, as well as three German aid workers. The FARC-EP acknowledged abducting the workers in a communiqué. The incidents, the E.U. stated, "seriously jeopardize the peace process and openly flout elementary principles of international law." In October, one of the German hostages escaped and the remaining two were later released. Jara remained in FARC-EP custody as of this writing.

Spanish authorities detained Carlos Arturo Marulanda, the former Colombian ambassador to the European Union, on charges that he supported paramilitary groups that killed and threatened farmers in the department of Cesar. A Colombian judge ordered the arrest after receiving information that allegedly linked the diplomat directly to paramilitary support. Marulanda remained in Spain at this writing awaiting the outcome of extradition hearings.

United States

The United States continued to focus on the aerial eradication of drug-producing crops and was increasingly and publicly skeptical of the peace process. U.S. State Department spokesman Philip Reeker charged in August that the FARC-EP was "misusing the demilitarized zone to abuse prisoners, engage in narcotics trafficking and, for example, reportedly receive training from the Irish Republican Army," referring to three Irish nationals charged in Colombia in August with helping train guerrillas. At the same time, U.S. Ambassador Anne Patterson made several important public statements in support of human rights.

Despite such concerns, the United States remained Colombia's largest foreign donor. It also increased military aid to Colombia's neighbors, in an effort to strengthen border controls against both armed groups and trafficking.

In March, Secretary of State Colin Powell announced to the U.S. Congress that he would seek another $400 million for Colombia for fiscal year (FY) 2002, roughly equivalent to the amount Colombia received in 2000 and in 2001. At this writing, the legislation contained human rights conditions and no waiver authority, meaning that Colombia would have to show concrete progress in breaking ties between the security forces and paramilitaries in order to receive aid. A day before his planned visit to Colombia, suspended after the September 11 attacks on the World Trade Center and Pentagon, Secretary Powell also announced that the United States had put the AUC on the administration's list of terrorist groups, along with the FARC-EP and UC-ELN, allowing U.S. officials to suspend the U.S.-based accounts of people who contributed to the group.

Between 1998 and 2001, eleven Colombian Army units were vetted for human rights problems and approved to receive U.S. security assistance. In addition, all CNP counternarcotics units, the Colombian Air Force, the Colombian Navy, and the Colombian Marines were cleared to receive U.S. assistance.

Although human rights continued to be cited as an important policy concern, the U.S. violated the spirit of its own laws and in some cases downplayed evidence of ties between the Colombian armed forces and paramilitary groups in order to continue funding abusive units. Compelling evidence emerged, in particular, of ties between paramilitaries and Colombian military units deployed in the U.S. antinarcotics campaign in southern Colombia, showing that U.S.-vetted, -funded, and -trained troops were mixing freely with units that maintained close ties with paramilitaries.

This occurred in the case of the First and Second Counternarcotics Battalions.

On their first joint deployment in December 2000, these battalions depended heavily on the army's Twenty-Fourth Brigade for support and logistical assistance, particularly with regard to intelligence, civic-military outreach, and psychological operations. Yet there was abundant and credible evidence to show that the Twenty-Fourth Brigade regularly worked with and supported paramilitary groups in the department of Putumayo. Indeed, the Twenty-Fourth Brigade hosted counternarcotics battalion troops at its facilities in La Hormiga—a town where, according to witnesses, paramilitaries and Colombian Army troops were indistinguishable.

The application of human rights conditions proved inconsistent if a unit was considered key to U.S. strategy, with embassy officials openly acknowledging that they applied conditions in a subjective manner. In certain cases, if a unit was considered important enough to drug war objectives, the U.S. circumvented its own human rights law to continue funding and training it.

One example was Combat Air Command No. 1 (Comando Aéreo de Combate No. 1), part of the Colombian Air Force. The State Department did not suspend this unit from receiving security assistance despite credible evidence that one of its helicopter crews committed a serious violation in the village of Santo Domingo, near Arauca, in 1998, by bombing a house where civilians had taken shelter. At the time of this writing, almost three years after the incident, no military personnel had been effectively investigated or disciplined for an attack that killed seven children and eleven adults. Throughout, Combat Air Command No. 1 continued to be authorized to receive U.S. security assistance and training.

A report prepared by the U.S. General Accounting Office concluded that farmers displaced by the U.S.-funded anti-drug campaign received little assistance beyond the first ninety days of their displacement. Under the U.S. aid plan, U.S. $37 million was set aside to deal with displaced persons, particularly those affected by eradication efforts in the south of Colombia.

The United States took some positive steps with regard to human rights in Colombia. The foreign aid bill approved by the U.S. Congress for FY 2002 contained strong human rights conditions on security assistance with no waiver authority, a clear improvement over previous legislation. The U.S. Agency for International Development (USAID) made grants to seven human rights groups in Colombia totaling over $575,000. USAID also contributed assistance to 176,000 people forcibly displaced by aerial eradication and political violence and supported a $2.5 million program for ex-combatant children. However, proposed aid for the attorney general's Human Rights Unit was diverted to buy expensive equipment that only marginally benefited this office, which continued to face serious problems in getting prosecutors to the sites of crimes and providing them with even minimal protection. In 2000 and the first three months of 2001—a fifteen-month period— the attorney general's Human Rights Unit and advisers from the Internal Affairs agency received only U.S. $65,763 from USAID. That worked out to less than the average amount of U.S. military assistance spent in Colombia in two hours of a single day.

The annual country report on human rights issued by the State Department accurately reflected the situation in Colombia, giving a detailed and grim picture of abuses. As importantly, U.S. Amb. Anne Patterson began a long-overdue policy of speaking out on the human rights situation and expressing concern over specific cases. Her timely telephone call to the army commander of a Barrancabermeja battalion in December 2000 was a critical factor in spurring the Colombian authorities to act to address the paramilitary advance. She also publicly supported the UNHCHR in Colombia, speaking out on the importance of their work at critical moments.

Relevant Human Rights Watch Reports:

The "Sixth Division": Military-Paramilitary Ties and U.S. Policy in Colombia, 9/01

Beyond Negotiation: International Humanitarian Law and its Application to the Conduct of the FARC-EP, 8/01

CUBA

HUMAN RIGHTS DEVELOPMENTS

The Cuban government's intolerance of democracy and free expression remained unique in the region. A one-party state, Cuba restricted nearly all avenues of political dissent. Although dissidents occasionally faced criminal prosecution, the government relied more frequently on short-term detentions, house arrest, travel restrictions, threats, surveillance, politically-motivated dismissals from employment, and other forms of harassment.

Cuba's restrictions on human rights were undergirded by the country's legal and institutional structure. The rights to freedom of expression, association, assembly, movement, and of the press were strictly limited under Cuban law. By criminalizing enemy propaganda, the spreading of "unauthorized news," and insult to patriotic symbols, the government curbed freedom of speech under the guise of protecting state security. The authorities also imprisoned or ordered the surveillance of individuals who had committed no illegal act, relying upon laws penalizing "dangerousness" (estado peligroso) and allowing for "official warning" (advertencia oficial). The government-controlled courts undermined the right to fair trial by restricting the right to a defense, and frequently failed to observe the few due process rights available to defendants under domestic law.

In July, the Cuban Commission for Human Rights and National Reconciliation (Comisión Cubana de Derechos Humanos y Reconciliación Nacional), a respected Havana-based nongovernmental group, released a partial list of political prisoners that included 246 cases they considered to be reliably documented. Some of the prisoners named on the list were serving extremely long sentences—twenty or more years for crimes such as "rebellion" and "sabotage," offenses broadly defined by Cuban courts—while others were serving short sentences for "contempt of authority" (desacato) or public disorder.

The government continued to prosecute people for "illegal exit" if they attempted to leave the island without first obtaining official permission to do so. Such permission was sometimes denied arbitrarily, or made contingent on the purchase of an expensive exit permit. In June, Pedro Riera Escalante, a former Cuban consul and intelligence officer in Mexico City, was sentenced by a military court to six years in prison for leaving Cuba illegally, using false documents, and bribing officials to allow his departure. Riera Escalante had broken with his government and sought political asylum in Mexico, but he was forcibly deported by the Mexican authorities in October.

Even though his three co-defendants were released in May 2000, dissident leader Vladimiro Roca Antúnez remained incarcerated as of November, serving his last year of a five-year sentence. The four, then members of the Internal Dissidents Working Group (Grupo de Trabajo de la Disidencia Interna, GTDI), were convicted of "acts against the security of the state" in March 1999, after having been detained since July 1997. Their detention followed the GTDI's release of an analytical paper on the Cuban economy, human rights, and democracy.

Another prominent activist who was still behind bars as of November was thirty-nine-year-old Dr. Oscar Elías Biscet González. Biscet received a three-year prison sentence in February 2000 for protests that included turning the Cuban flag upside-down and carrying anti-abortion placards. The president of the Lawton Human Rights Foundation, an independent organization, Biscet was convicted of dishonoring patriotic symbols, public disorder, and instigating delinquency. In detention since November 1999, he had reportedly been mistreated by prison authorities and kept in poor conditions, causing weight loss and dental problems. In April, Biscet was reportedly made to share a cell with a mentally disordered inmate.

José Orlando González Bridon, leader of the Confederation of Democratic Workers of Cuba, an unofficial union, was sentenced to two years of imprisonment in May for "spreading false news." The charges stemmed from an article he published on an Internet site in August 2000 that criticized local police for negligence in the death of another labor rights activist. In November 2000, shortly before he was detained, González Bridon took part in a protest rally in which he and other dissidents chanted "Down with Fidel!" as they symbolically buried the Cuban constitution and penal code in small coffins. Prosecutors had originally requested a seven-year sentence for González Bridon. Although they reduced their petition to one year, the trial court added a year to the sentence after finding him guilty. Later, on appeal, the sentence was cut back to a year. González Bridon was released on conditional liberty on November 22, three weeks before the expiration of his sentence. (Cuban law allows for conditional liberty contingent on good behavior after half of a prisoner's sentence has been served.)

Another person who left prison slightly early was Julia Cecilia Delgado, released on October 19. Delgado, an independent librarian and president of a nongovernmental group, had been serving a one-year sentence for "disrespect." Delgado was one of about two hundred people who were detained in early December 2000, in a wave of arrests probably meant to discourage public gatherings on December 10, International Human Rights Day. Pro-democracy activist Angel Moya Acosta, prosecuted at the same time, was believed to be finishing his one-year sentence in December.

Cecilio Monteagudo Sánchez, a member of the unofficial Democratic Solidarity Party (Partido Solidaridad Democrática), was released from prison in June. He had been convicted of "enemy propaganda" and sentenced to four years of imprisonment in 1998. Cuban police originally detained him in September 1997, after he had drafted, but not published, a document calling for abstention from local elections.

Much more frequent than actual criminal prosecutions were arrests and short-term detentions. The most prominent case began on January 12, when Czech citizens Jan Bubenik and Ivan Pilip were detained after meeting with independent Cuban journalists in the province of Ciego de Avila. Bubenik, a former student activist, and Pilip, a legislator and former Czech government finance minister, were held for nearly four weeks, as the Cuban authorities considered prosecuting them on charges of acting against state security. The two were released in early February after intensive diplomatic efforts by European officials.

A blind dissident, Juan Carlos Gonzalez Leyva, was reportedly stopped and roughed up by members of the Cuban secret police on January 16, along with two of his colleagues. Over the course of the year, dozens of other dissidents and human rights activists reported being arrested and detained for brief periods, such as a few hours or overnight. On some occasions, detainees were threatened or insulted, or their homes were searched.

Whether detained for political or common crimes, inmates were subjected to abusive prison conditions. Prisoners frequently suffered malnourishment and languished in overcrowded cells without appropriate medical attention. Some endured physical and sexual abuse, typically by other inmates with the acquiescence of guards, or long periods in punitive isolation cells. Prison authorities insisted that all detainees participate in politically oriented "re-education" sessions or face punishment. Political prisoners who denounced the poor conditions of imprisonment were frequently punished with solitary confinement, restricted visits, or denial of medical treatment.

Cuba maintained the death penalty for a large number of offences. In June, Justice Minister Roberto Diaz Sotolongo said that "for humanitarian reasons" Cuba preferred not to employ capital punishment, but that the penalty served as a warning to drug traffickers. Penal code changes dating from the late 1990s had extended capital punishment to cases of drug trafficking with aggravating circumstances.

In April, Elizardo Sánchez of the Cuban Commission for Human Rights and National Reconciliation announced that the death penalty had not been applied in Cuba over the past year. "We are seeing a moratorium on the death penalty, but we should move on to its abolition," Sánchez reportedly explained. Two Salvadorans convicted of taking part in a wave of bombings of tourist installations in Havana were on death row, having been confined there since 1998. Some twenty other prisoners were also reportedly on death row, although this could not be verified as the authorities did not provide public information on death sentences and executions.

The authorities maintained strict controls on the press, barring local independent news coverage and taking steps to limit foreign reporting. As of November, independent journalist Bernardo Arévalo Padrón, director of the news agency Linea Sur Press, remained behind bars, having been denied conditional release. He was serving a six-year sentence for "insulting" President Castro, imposed in

November 1997. In January, independent journalist Jesús Joel Díaz Hernández, who had been serving a four-year sentence for "dangerousness," was granted conditional release.

The authorities routinely detained and questioned independent journalists, monitored their telephone calls and visitors, restricted their travel, and put them under house arrest to prevent coverage of certain events. In May, in recognition of such tactics, the Committee to Protect Journalists (CPJ), a U.S.-based press freedom group, named President Fidel Castro as one of the Ten Worst Enemies of the Press for 2001.

To prevent negative foreign media coverage, Cuban authorities continued to deny visas to certain disfavored foreign journalists. In January, President Castro accused some reporters of "transmitting insults and lies," suggesting that Cuba might consider canceling their employers' license to operate in Cuba. "We have tolerated for years reporters who intentionally and deliberately insult the leaders of the revolution and me," Castro said.

The government maintained considerable control over religious expression, but in general religious institutions and their leaders enjoyed a degree of autonomy not permitted other bodies. Several religious-run groups distributed humanitarian aid and carried out social programs. Yet the government continued to slow the entry of foreign priests and nuns and to bar religious institutions from running schools (although religious instruction was allowed). In contrast to the first decades after the Cuban Revolution, discrimination against overtly religious persons was rare.

The government recognized only one labor union, the Worker's Central of Cuba (Central de Trabajadores de Cuba, CTC). Independent labor unions were denied formal status and their members were harassed. Workers employed in businesses backed by foreign investment remained under tight government control. Under restrictive labor laws, the authorities had a prominent role in the selection, payment, and dismissal of workers, effectively denying workers the right to bargain directly with employers over benefits, promotions, and wages. Cuba also continued to use prison labor for agricultural camps and ran clothing assembly and other factories in its prisons. The authorities' insistence that political prisoners work without pay in poor conditions violated international labor standards.

DEFENDING HUMAN RIGHTS

Human rights defenders were systematically harassed. The authorities routinely used surveillance, phone tapping, and intimidation in its efforts to restrict independent monitoring of the government's human rights practices. In some instances, they employed arbitrary searches, short-term arrests, evictions, travel restrictions, politically-motivated dismissals from employment, threats and other forms of harassment against local activists.

Although the U.N. special rapporteur on violence against women was permitted to visit in 1999, the government generally barred international human rights and humanitarian monitors from the country. The International Committee of the Red Cross (ICRC) has not been allowed to conduct prison visits in Cuba since 1989, making Cuba the only country in the region to deny the organization such access.

THE ROLE OF THE INTERNATIONAL COMMUNITY

United Nations

At its fifty-seventh session in April, the U.N. Commission on Human Rights passed a resolution expressing concern about continuing human rights violations in Cuba, the ninth such resolution passed since 1991, and urged the government to invite the U.N. special rapporteurs on torture and on freedom of expression to visit the country.

In the resolution, the Commission noted that Cuba had made "no satisfactory improvements" in the area of human rights. It expressed particular concern at the "continued repression of members of the political opposition," as well as about the "detention of dissidents and all other persons detained or imprisoned for peacefully expressing their political, religious and social views and for exercising their right to full and equal participation in public affairs." An early draft of the resolution criticized the U.S. economic embargo on Cuba, but that language was omitted from the final version.

The resolution, which was sponsored by the Czech Republic, passed by a 22-20 vote, with a number of abstentions.

European Union

Cuba remained the only Latin American country that did not have a cooperation agreement with the European Union. The E.U. "common position" on Cuba, adopted in 1996 and extended in June 2001, made full economic cooperation conditional on reforms toward greater democracy and human rights protection. A number of E.U. members, however, were in favor of revisiting the common position and establishing closer ties with Cuba free of any conditions. Already, European countries accounted for almost half of Cuba's foreign trade, and more than 180 European companies operated on the island.

Visiting Brussels in July, Cuban Foreign Minister Felipe Pérez Roque appealed for a review of E.U. policy toward Cuba. A few months later, E.U. officials announced that the European Union favored resuming the political dialogue with Cuba and permitting the island to join the Cotonou Agreement, which governs the E.U.'s aid relationships with African, Caribbean, and Pacific states. Belgian Foreign Minister Louis Michel, holding the rotating presidency of the E.U. Council, had visited Havana in August, meeting with high Cuban officials as well as political dissidents. On returning to Europe, he expressed support for strengthening contacts with Cuba. Political talks between the European Union and Cuba were scheduled to take place at the end of November.

In early October, Cuban exiles filed a lawsuit in Brussels against President Fidel Castro and other high Cuban officials under a law that empowers Belgian courts to hear cases of genocide and crimes against humanity, regardless of where the incidents occurred. The lead plaintiff in the case was José Basulto, president of the Miami-based group Brothers to the Rescue. Another plaintiff was Eugenio de Sosa Chabau, a former newspaper editor who spent twenty years in prison after the Cuban Revolution. The complaint described torture and other abuses suffered by political prisoners, including a 1960 incident in which a prisoner allegedly received electric shocks to his head and testicles.

Latin America and the Organization of American States (OAS)

Venezuelan President Hugo Chavez remained Cuba's most reliable ally in the region, with his country being the only one in Latin American (besides Cuba itself) to vote against the U.N. resolution on Cuba's human rights conditions. Several other countries in the region abstained from the vote, while four—Argentina, Costa Rica, Guatemala, and Uruguay—voted in favor of the resolution.

Cuba reacted strongly to the U.N. vote, lashing out at the Latin American countries that voted for the censure. In February, prior to the Geneva session, Cuba's official daily *Granma* accused Argentina of seeking U.S. economic assistance in exchange for voting against Cuba at the United Nations. President Castro accused Argentine President Fernando de la Rúa of "licking the Yankees' boots," leading Argentina to temporarily withdraw its ambassador from Cuba. After the Geneva vote, Castro again attacked Argentina and described Costa Rica as playing the role of "a lackey—something more than a lackey—a servant" of the United States. He also claimed that Guatemala only went along with the vote because of heavy U.S. pressure.

The latter part of the year saw movement toward eliminating the last vestiges of Cuba's diplomatic isolation in the region. In September, Honduras opened an interests section in Havana, a likely first step toward full diplomatic relations. The Honduran move left El Salvador as the only Latin American country with no diplomatic relations with the island. Cuba's diplomatic estrangement from other Latin American states dated from 1961, when the Organization of American States suspended its membership. In August, in a speech before the OAS Permanent Council, Venezuelan Foreign Minister Luis Alfonso Davila pointedly called for the "complete integration" of the hemisphere, arguing that no country should be isolated.

United States

The devastation wrought by Hurricane Michelle opened a crack in the U.S. economic embargo on Cuba, with U.S. companies selling food and medicine to Havana in November 2001 to offset losses and replenish stocks used in the island's worst storm in half a century. The sales, valued by a U.S. official at about U.S. $30 million, represented the first commercial transactions between the two countries since the embargo was put in place. Authorities in Washington had originally offered to provide Cuba with disaster relief aid, but Cuban officials, declining the aid offer, expressed interest in buying food, medicine, and other necessities.

A law enacted in 2000 allowed food sales to Cuba, and an earlier law allowed the export of medicines. Yet, because the law on food sales barred U.S. government or private financing of the sales, Cuban officials had previously criticized it, saying that they would refrain from buying food until the embargo was lifted. This year's purchase represented a departure from that position, but one that Cuban officials insisted was exceptional. "We have no reason to see [the sales] as a policy shift, rather as something that happened because of a hurricane that doesn't happen every month in Cuba," explained Cuban Vice-President Carlos Lage.

In May, Senator Jesse Helms and Senator Joseph Lieberman introduced draft legislation in Congress to allocate up to $100 million over four years to assist dissidents, opposition groups, political prisoners, and other nongovernmental voices in Cuba. The bill, known as the Cuban Solidarity Act of 2001, was criticized by some of its potential beneficiaries, who feared that receiving U.S. government aid would damage their credibility and help discredit their views. A parallel bill had been introduced in the House in March. Both versions of the draft legislation were still under review by congressional committees as of November.

A Cuban émigré, Eriberto Mederos, faced denaturalization proceedings in Florida at the end of the year. Mederos could be stripped of his U.S. citizenship because of allegations by another Cuban-American who accused Mederos of torturing him when he was a political prisoner in Cuba in the 1960s. According to the former prisoner, Mederos subjected him to painful electrical shock treatments that lacked any medical justification.

GUATEMALA

HUMAN RIGHTS DEVELOPMENTS

Aside from the successful conclusion of one landmark trial, Guatemala made little progress in addressing persistent human rights problems, with certain conditions worsening. State agents were responsible for some abuses, while others were carried out by non-state actors who were able to operate with impunity because their crimes were not adequately investigated. There were increased reports of threats and violence targeting human rights advocates, labor leaders, judges, prosecutors and journalists. Meanwhile, the army's continued influence over the civilian government was evidenced by President Alfonso Portillo's decision to postpone the dismantling of the Presidential Guard (Estado Mayor Presidencial, EMP), an elite army corps associated with past human rights violations. The 1996 peace accords had called for the dismantling of the EMP.

One positive development was the successful prosecution of those responsible for the murder of Bishop Juan Gerardi, who was bludgeoned to death in April 1998, two days after he released the Catholic Church's report on human rights abuses during Guatemala's internal conflict which ended in 1996. In June, a three-judge tribunal found retired army Col. Byron Lima Estrada and his son, army Capt. Byron Lima Oliva, guilty of murder. The two men were sentenced to thirty years in prison. Also convicted were former presidential bodyguard José Obdulio Villanueva and Roman Catholic priest Mario Orantes, who received sentences of thirty years and twenty years respectively.

A major obstacle to investigating and prosecuting human rights violations committed by the army was the intimidation of prosecutors, judges and witnesses through terror tactics. In this, the Gerardi trial was no exception. From the outset, key participants in the case were subjected to "systematic" and "planned" harassment that "intensified in the key procedural moments" of the trial, according to the United Nations Verification Mission in Guatemala (Misión de Verificación de las Naciones Unidas en Guatemala, MINUGUA). One judge, one prosecutor, and several witnesses fled the country before the trial got underway after receiving death threats. In January, Luis García Pontaza, a potential defense witness with links to organized crime, was found dead in a Guatemala City jail. Prior to his death, he told MINUGUA that he had resisted pressure from the EMP to testify that certain individuals linked to the Catholic Church had been involved in the Bishop's murder. One of the trial judges, Yasmín Barrios Aguilar, reported that two strangers attempted to break into her home a week before the trial and on March 21, the day before the oral debate was scheduled to begin, grenades were exploded at the back of her home. The special prosecutor for the case, Leopoldo Zeissig, reported receiving anonymous telephoned threats and being tailed by strangers. After the trial concluded, he fled the country, as did another witness.

While the trial's outcome represented an enormous advance for the country, there was little or no progress made in several of the other high-profile human rights cases before the Guatemalan courts. The prosecution of soldiers implicated in the 1995 massacre in Xamán, department of Alta Verapaz, remained in its preliminary stages six years after the crime, and there were no advances in the prosecution, begun in 1994, of soldiers accused of perpetrating the 1982 massacre in Dos Erres, department of Petén. After years of delay the trial of military officers accused of ordering the 1990 assassination of anthropologist Myrna Mack was set to begin in October 2001.

Impunity also remained a serious problem in less prominent cases. MINUGUA documented hundreds of human rights abuses during the year, the majority of which it attributed to the failure of government authorities to investigate and punish the perpetrators adequately. One case that exemplified this pattern of failure involved the family of retired Gen. Otto Pérez Molina, who had helped to negotiate the 1996 peace accords and was preparing to launch a new political party. In November 2000, unknown assailants in an automobile shot and wounded his daughter-in-law. Then, in February 2001, assailants attacked and wounded his daughter and, moments later, shot and killed the driver of a car traveling next to one his wife was driving. Yet, the authorities mounted no serious investigation into the case, failing even to take testimony from an army officer who witnessed the fatal attack. The general's family left the country for their own safety. Francisco Arnoldo Aguilar, whose wife was the driver killed in the February attack, pressed for an official investigation and urged the creation of a citizens' group to combat impunity. In May, however, he was assassinated in front of his home in circumstances that, MINUGUA said, ruled out robbery as a motive. The authorities nonetheless insisted that it was a common crime.

The authorities also failed to take strong action against anti-union violence that undermined workers' right to freedom of association. In March, twenty-four men were tried for a 1999 incident in which five leaders of the Union of Banana Workers of Izabal (Sindicato de Trabajadores Bananeros de Izabal, SITRABI) were held at gunpoint, ordered to quit the union and their jobs, and call off a planned work stoppage in protest against the firing of 918 banana workers in violation of a collective bargaining agreement. They were indicted on lesser charges of false imprisonment and coercion, however, rather than for kidnapping or other crimes that carry a mandatory prison sentence. All but two were convicted; they received three-and-a-half year prison sentences but these were immediately commuted upon payment of fines. With these men again at large, the five SITRABI leaders feared for their safety and that of their families, and fled the country.

The absence of effective law enforcement and the high incidence of common crime contributed to a climate of insecurity, and the continued use of lynching as a form of vigilante justice. MINUGUA documented eighty-eight lynchings between July 2000 and June 2001, resulting in thirty-seven deaths. Local authorities often played a role in inciting and perpetrating lynchings.

Officers of the National Civilian Police (Policía Nacional Civil, PNC) were responsible for numerous human rights violations, including extrajudicial executions and torture, and for obstructing justice. In October 2000, Rolando Barillas Herrera was detained by two PNC agents in Gualán, Zacapa, brought to a station, and put in cell at midnight. At 5:00 a.m., Barillas was found dead from asphyxiation. A forensic exam found signs of beating and ruled out suicide. Yet, a year later, government investigators still had not identified those responsible for the killing. In April 2001, the PNC detained Julio Alberto Casasola and William Cotom Rodas in Quetzaltenango, having allegedly caught them in the process of stealing a car. The two were tortured and then transferred to a prison. The next day, Casasola was brought to a hospital where he died as a result of the blows he had received from the police.

There was a marked increase in threats made against people who challenged the actions of public authorities. In March, the president of the Constitutional Court, Judge Conchita Mazariegos, reported that she had received threatening phone calls and that shots had been fired at her house. Earlier that month, the Constitutional Court had lifted the immunity of members of Congress, including Gen. Efraín Ríos Montt, so that they could face prosecution for illegally altering the text of a law after it had been voted on by Congress. Three days before the attack on Judge Mazariegos's home, the court had ruled unconstitutional a decree passed by General Ríos Montt's party that would allow him and his colleagues to retain their congressional seats during their prosecution.

Also in March, several members of Congress who defected from the ruling Guatemalan Republican Front party (Frente Republicana Guatemalteca, FRG), reported being subject to threats and acts of intimidation. These politicians had joined the opposition National Unity of Hope party (Unidad Nacional de la Esperanza, UNE). The UNE's offices had previously been raided in August 2000 by people who stole documents and left threatening messages behind.

One journalist was killed; others harassed and threatened, apparently to influence their reporting. Radio journalist Jorge Mynor Alegría was assassinated by unknown assailants in September in the port city of Puerto Barrios, department of

Izabal. A colleague said that before his killing Alegría had rejected an attempt by local municipal authorities to bribe him to stop criticizing local corruption in his broadcasts. Other journalists received threats, including Claudia Méndez Villaseñor of *El Periódico*, who reported receiving telephone threats from two government officials in January when she was investigating alleged government corruption. In March, Silvia Gereda and Martín Juárez, two other *El Periódico* journalists reported receiving death threats and being assaulted. Juárez told MINUGUA that a car followed him for two hours before he was intercepted and forced to stop by another car, whose occupants then got out and pointed a gun at his head and threatened to kill him. The same month, Gustavo Soberanis of *Siglo XXI*, was threatened with a firearm by the comptroller of the president's office (*Contralor General de Cuentas*) when he tried to interview him about its expenses. Journalists in the departments of Zacapa, Quetzaltenango, and Chiqimula also reported receiving death threats. In June, the Public Ministry created a Special Prosecutor's Office for the Protection of Journalists and Unionized Workers (Fiscalía Especial para la Protección a Periodistas y Sindicalistas).

Union leaders also continued to be subject to threats. In February, union leaders who organized a work stoppage in the Puerto Barrios harbor received threats and were later fired. In May and June, union leaders in two Izabal banana plantations were also subject to firings and death threats. And during the year, union members were threatened and subject to discriminatory firing by municipal mayors in several towns throughout the country.

Discrimination remained a problem for indigenous people who made up roughly half the country's population. They faced unequal access to education, justice, health and other government services. According to MINUGUA, the government's record with regard to implementing the 1996 peace accords was particularly poor in the area of indigenous people's rights.

Guatemala continued to violate its international treaty obligations in its application of the death penalty. In November 2001, twenty-eight prisoners were on death row. Thirteen of them had been sentenced for kidnappings that did not result in death, a crime that was not a capital offense when the American Convention on Human Rights entered into force. Because the American Convention prohibited extending the death penalty to cover additional crimes, Guatemala's Constitutional Court ruled in October 2000 that the laws extending the death penalty to non-fatal kidnappings violated Guatemala's obligations under the Convention. In June, however, a newly constituted court overturned that earlier ruling.

In October 2000, Guatemala ratified the Additional Protocol to the American Convention on Social, Economic and Cultural Rights, and in November 2000 it ratified the Additional Protocol to the American Convention on Human Rights in the Area of Economic, Social and Cultural Rights.

DEFENDING HUMAN RIGHTS

In 2001, Guatemala experienced an alarming rise in the number of threats and incidents of harassment and targeted violence against human rights advocates.

MINUGUA documented 171 such cases between July 2000 and June 2001 and concluded that they were the result of "systematic action."

In November 2000, the Rigoberta Menchú Foundation received threats in the days leading up to a ruling by Spain's highest court (the Audiencia Nacional de España) on a genocide case that the foundation had brought before it. In May, two members of the organization Relatives of the Detained-Disappeared of Guatemala (Familiares de Detenidos-Desaparecidos de Guatemala, FAMDEGUA) were assaulted outside their Guatemala City office. Two armed men forced their way into their car and interrogated them about the organization's work while driving them around the city, before releasing the two FAMDEGUA activists and escaping in their car. The Center for Studies, Information and Basis for Social Action (Centro de Estudios, Investigación y Bases para la Acción Social, CEIBAS) reported that its office was repeatedly burgled between February and May, and the Association for Justice and Reconciliation (Asociación Justicia y Reconciliación, AJR) reported that its president was attacked and wounded by a man with a knife, who threatened him and other witnesses in a criminal complaint that the organization had brought against General Ríos Montt and other former military commanders for genocide and crimes against humanity. In June, an Amnesty International representative undertaking research on human rights in Guatemala was the victim of an apparent abduction attempt by unidentified assailants in her Guatemala City hotel.

THE ROLE OF THE INTERNATIONAL COMMUNITY

The international community continued to play a prominent role in monitoring the Guatemalan government's compliance with the 1996 peace accords and with international human rights norms. The United Nations and the Organization of American States provided mechanisms to which Guatemalans could denounce human rights abuses by the government. The United States also monitored Guatemala's human rights record, though its responses to this record varied, with the Senate penalizing its shortcomings while the United States Trade Representative rewarded its perceived gains.

United Nations and
the Organization of American States (OAS)

The United Nations verification mission, MINUGUA, continued its institution-building activities as well as playing a central role in monitoring compliance with the peace accords. MINUGUA's reports contained detailed human rights analyses and indicated that significant aspects of the accords remained unimplemented. In September, MINUGUA issued a human rights report for the period July 2000 to June 2001, and at other times it issued communiqués on specific human rights abuses.

The U.N. special rapporteur on the independence of judges and lawyers, Param Cumaraswamy, visited Guatemala in May and found that the climate of insecurity for members of the legal community continued to undermine the rule of law. He noted that recommendations he made after a 1999 visit had been largely ignored by government authorities.

In November 2000, the Committee against Torture expressed concern about a "deterioration" of the human-rights situation in Guatemala, and recommended, among other things, that independent commissions be established to monitor the performance of the police and to investigate cases of kidnapping and "disappearances."

In May, the Committee on the Rights of the Child met with the Guatemalan government to discuss its implementation of the Rights of the Child. The committee expressed concern that violence against children was increasing in Guatemala and urged the government to adopt legislation that would protect the children's rights.

In July, the Human Rights Committee, responding to a report submitted by the Guatemala government, commended Guatemala for providing resources for human rights institutions, yet expressed concern at ongoing "glaring and systematic violations." It recommended that the Guatemalan government give priority to investigating and bringing to justice the perpetrators of human rights violations.

The Inter-American Commission on Human Rights issued four case reports on Guatemala. In one, it urged the government to reform provisions of the civil code that imposed unequal spousal and familial obligations on women and men. In the other three, it called for the government to investigate and punish extrajudicial executions, forced disappearances and other serious human rights violations committed by the security forces during the 1980s and 1990s, and to compensate victims' families.

United States

In July, the United States Senate voted to maintain a ban on regular military training and funding for Guatemala's military. The report that accompanied the Senate foreign operations bill cited the Guatemalan government's failure to dismantle the EMP and to address the deteriorating human rights situation.

In October 2000, the United States Trade Representative (USTR) took the unprecedented step of initiating a review of Guatemala's status as a beneficiary of the U.S. Generalized System of Preferences (GSP) largely in response to the failure of government authorities to adequately punish anti-union violence. A review examines a country's compliance with certain internationally-recognized workers' rights to determine its eligibility for GSP tariff benefits. In May 2001, the Bush administration's new USTR lifted the review of Guatemala's beneficiary status, citing as positive government steps the reinstatement of illegally dismissed banana workers, and the conviction of the twenty-two gunmen involved in the October 13, 1999 incident. In fact, the banana workers' reinstatement was the result of a negotiated settlement between the workers and management not governmental intervention.

HAITI

W orsening human rights conditions, mounting political turmoil, and a declining economy marked President Jean-Bertrand's Aristide first year back in office. The investigation into the murder of crusading journalist Jean Dominique reached a standstill, with the judge assigned to the case receiving little cooperation from the police and other government bodies. The work of human rights defenders became increasingly dangerous, as several received serious death threats.

HUMAN RIGHTS DEVELOPMENTS

Aristide won the presidency in November 2000, in an election that was boycotted by credible opposition candidates because of the government's failure to remedy the deeply flawed results of the May 2000 legislative and local elections. The Organization of American States (OAS) and other international observers refused to monitor the November balloting, in which Aristide faced no serious challengers.

During meetings with U.S. Special Envoy Tony Lake in December 2000, Aristide committed to undertaking a series of steps to address the country's serious problems. The reforms he promised—which included remedying the results of the May 2000 elections, professionalizing the police and judiciary, and strengthening democratic institutions—were urgently needed. Unfortunately, over the course of the year, Aristide showed little inclination to follow through on his promises.

Despite many millions in international aid hanging in the balance, progress toward resolving Haiti's political crisis was painfully slow. As of late November, no agreement had yet been reached between Fanmi Lavalas, the party of President Aristide, and the Democratic Convergence, the main opposition coalition. Talks in October brokered by OAS envoy Luigi Einaudi, the latest in a long series of negotiations, broke down almost immediately. Although the two sides had tentatively agreed to hold new legislative elections in November 2002, they were unable to resolve other areas of disagreement.

The country's polarization raised the spectre of political violence. In early January, a month before Aristide's inauguration, leaders of so-called popular organizations that supported Fanmi Lavalas made violent threats against a number of opposition figures. Speaking at a press conference at the church of Saint Jean Bosco, Aristide's former parish, Paul Raymond and René Civil referred to a list of opposition leaders, religious figures, journalists, and others who they said were opposed to Aristide's inauguration. They warned the people on the list to change their position within three days or face violent retaliation.

With Aristide's inauguration and the opposition's declaration of a "parallel government," political instability continued. There were several outbreaks of violent unrest over the course of the year. In mid-March, angry mobs staged street demonstrations and erected burning barricades in parts of Port-au-Prince to protest opposition claims that the government lacked legitimacy. The office of the main opposition coalition was firebombed, as pro-government demonstrators called for the arrest of the opposition's self-styled "president," Gerard Gourgue.

At the end of the March wave of violence, which spread to other Haitian cities as well, at least four people had been killed and many more injured. Police inaction in the face of violent demonstrations by armed gangs raised doubts about the government's interest in quelling the unrest.

A chain of attacks on police stations on July 28, characterized by the government as a coup attempt, led to a crackdown on the opposition. Although the motives and circumstances of the attacks were unclear, it was undisputed that armed men clad in the uniform of Haiti's disbanded army seized the national police academy for several hours and later tried to take over several police stations in central Haiti. Seven people were killed, including five police. At least forty people were arrested in the wake of the attacks, including many members of the Democratic Convergence. A number of the arrests were made without a judicial warrant, leading a coalition of local human rights groups to complain that the arrestees' prolonged detention was "arbitrary and illegal."

Earlier in the year, several hundred former army officers had held demonstrations to demand the restoration of the army, which was dissolved by President Aristide in 1995. Many believed that the July attacks were carried out by such former officers.

In mid-November, large scale rioting broke out in Cap Haitien, Haiti's second largest city, following a call by the main opposition coalition for a two-day general strike to pressure President Aristide and his political allies to relinquish power. The previous week, smaller demonstrations were held in Petit-Goave and Gonaives, coastal towns west of the capital.

Although in the first half of the year there were encouraging signs of progress in the investigation into the April 2000 killings of journalist Jean Dominique and security guard Jean Claude Louissant, by November the case appeared stalled. Investigating Judge Claudy Gassant, citing safety concerns, announced that he would not accept the renewal of his appointment to the case, set to expire in January 2002. Earlier, in June, Judge Gassant had resigned from the case because of security threats and a lack of government protection. He fled to the United States at that time but returned after a few weeks, when the minister of justice promised to provide armed bodyguards and other security guarantees. Gassant faced death threats and intimidation because of his work.

Stymied by a lack of cooperation from police and other officials, Gassant was unable even to question some of his top suspects. Arrest warrants issued against Paul Raymond, René Civil, Richard Solomon, and Franck Joseph had no effect, with the suspects moving freely about the capital. Another leading suspect, Senator Dany Toussaint, benefited from parliamentary immunity. As of November, more than three months after receiving Judge Gassant's request that Toussaint's immunity be lifted, the Senate had yet to make any decision on the question. Indeed, the parliamentary commission charged with examining the request did not even meet until five weeks after the request was made.

In early November, one of Dominique's suspected killers was lynched by an angry mob in Léogane, a town southwest of the capital. He was the second suspect in the case to die before being questioned. The killing, which police apparently allowed to take place, further hindered the investigation of the case. Judge Gassant, who witnessed the murder, announced two days later his decision to leave the case.

Ivorian journalist Abdoulaye Guedeouengue—who was abducted, beaten, and robbed in May—had been investigating the Dominique murder at the time of his capture. He was reportedly warned by the kidnappers to stop looking into the case.

As the Guedeouengue case indicated, the media came under increasing pressure to limit its reporting. On October 12, Jean Robert Delciné, a journalist with Radio Haiti Inter, was hit by police while investigating a police killing in Cite Soleil. Other Radio Haiti Inter journalists also reported threats and harassment over the course of the year, in some instances by men believed to be police. On October 2, members of a so-called popular organization close to Fanmi Lavalas threatened radio journalist Jean-Marie Mayard, telling him that he would be a "dead man" if his reporting did not favor the Aristide government. According to Reporters without Borders, a France-based international press freedom organization, ten journalists were threatened or attacked by people connected to Fanmi Lavalas during the first ten months of the year.

The justice system remained largely dysfunctional, with many crimes going unpunished. In June, in a speech to police, President Aristide announced a "zero tolerance" crime policy, stating that it was not necessary to bring criminals to court. His words were widely interpreted by Haitians as an invitation to vigilante justice and police violence. Human rights groups reported that in the months following the speech, dozens of suspected thieves were killed by mobs.

The increasing politicization of the Haitian National Police (HNP) raised additional concerns. The reluctance of police to intervene in certain situations to prevent political violence, typically when opposition supporters were in danger, was frequently in evidence. In an open letter to the police leadership sent in October, the nongovernmental National Coalition for Haitian Rights (NCHR) deplored the HNP's lack of political neutrality. The letter drew attention to the failure of the police to arrest certain criminal suspects pursuant to valid arrest orders and, in contrast, the willingness of the police to arbitrarily arrest others. It also claimed that several police officers, previously dismissed for involvement in serious human rights violations, had been reintegrated into the force.

Accountability for past abuses remained elusive. Although the success of the Raboteau trial in 2000 raised hopes of further such prosecutions, the prospect of achieving justice for many other notorious crimes seemed remote. In a letter sent on August 28, the seventh anniversary of the assassination of Father Jean Marie Vincent, NCHR criticized what it called the "systematisation of impunity."

Former Gen. Prosper Avril, who headed the country's government for two years after a 1988 coup, was arrested on May 28 on charges of assault, torture and illegal arrest. Avril's rule was characterized by egregious human rights abuses. Although efforts to prosecute such crimes were all too rare in Haiti, the circumstances and timing of Avril's arrest suggested that it was politically motivated. The arrest was made on the basis of a 1996 warrant that had been ignored for years; it was acted upon only after Avril attended a highly-publicized meeting of the main opposition coalition. A number of political figures who were tortured under Avril's government, but had since joined the current opposition, were unwilling to testify against Avril regarding past abuses. In June, a court of appeals judge ordered that Avril be freed, but the head of the public prosecutor's office refused to sign the release form, blocking the defendant's release.

Prison conditions remained dire, with the country's desperately overcrowded prisons and jails being largely filled with pretrial detainees. Detention facilities lacked the necessary infrastructure and many failed to provide medical care, sufficient food, or even potable water. A study of the prison system published by the Vera Institute for Justice found "a serious problem of malnutrition." In mid-November, five prisoners were killed by police who were putting down a riot at the National Penitentiary in Port-au-Prince.

Of all Latin American and Caribbean countries, Haiti continued to have the highest prevalence of HIV/AIDS, although treatment was largely unavailable. According to UNICEF, some 74,000 Haitian children were orphaned because of the AIDS pandemic. Many of the orphans were themselves HIV-positive.

Determined to escape Haiti's dire conditions, thousands of Haitians tried to leave the country in overcrowded and rickety boats. Many of them, hoping to reach the United States, were intercepted by U.S. coast guard cutters and immediately repatriated, while an unknown number died at sea.

DEFENDING HUMAN RIGHTS

Human rights defenders came under increasing pressure in 2001, with several receiving death threats. In October, both NCHR and the Platform for Haitian Human Rights Organizations (POHDH) were threatened following the publication of a strongly-worded letter from NCHR to the police leadership.

Pierre Espérance, the director of NCHR in Haiti, also received several menacing calls in August. The different callers warned him that if NCHR continued to press for justice in the Jean Dominique case, he would be eliminated. Espérance had reason to take such threats seriously, having suffered an assassination attempt in 1999.

THE ROLE OF THE INTERNATIONAL COMMUNITY

At this writing, some U.S. $500 million in international aid remained frozen, reflecting donor governments' impatience with Haiti's inability to resolve the political crisis.

United Nations

In November 2000, U.N. Secretary-General Kofi Annan recommended against renewing the mandate of the United Nations International Civilian Support Mission in Haiti (MICAH). In an usually critical report to the General Assembly, he noted that over the previous several months, "Haiti's political and electoral crisis has deepened, polarising its political class and civil society." In light of such conditions he concluded that MICAH's ability to function successfully was limited. MICAH's mandate ended on February 6, the day before President Aristide entered office.

In July, Secretary-General Annan reiterated that the resolution of the political crisis was a prerequisite for the resumption of aid to Haiti.

Adama Dieng, the United Nations independent expert on the human rights situation in Haiti, issued his last report on conditions in Haiti in January. In it, he drew attention to the deterioration of the system of justice, noting the "politicization of the police, arbitrary arrests, prolonged detention without trial, the climate of violence and also the deplorable health conditions in the prisons." Dieng, who resigned from his post to work for the Rwanda war crimes tribunal, had not been replaced as of November.

The U.N. Commission on Human Rights, issuing a chairperson's statement in April, called upon the Haitian government to thoroughly investigate politically motivated crimes, including the murder of journalist Jean Dominique; to prosecute the perpetrators of such crimes; to institute legal proceedings against perpetrators of human rights violations identified by the National Commission for Truth and Justice; and to ensure the neutrality of the police.

Organization of American States (OAS)

As in 1999, Luigi Einaudi, assistant secretary-general of the Organization of American States (OAS), carried out intensive efforts to break Haiti's political deadlock. He made a number of trips to Haiti, including in February, April, May, June, and October. In May and June, Einaudi visited Haiti in the company of OAS Secretary General Cesar Gaviria. Their efforts to mediate the crisis did not, however, bear fruit.

In early October, the OAS established a new "Group of Friends on Haiti"—made up of Canada, Argentina, the Bahamas, Belize, Chile, Guatemala, Mexico, the Dominican Republic, United States, and Venezuela—in hopes of restarting the stalled negotiations.

United States

In September, on the tenth anniversary of the military coup that drove him from power, President Aristide announced that the United States had returned thousands of pages of documents gathered from the offices of the Haitian military and the paramilitary Revolutionary Front for the Advancement and Progress of Haiti (FRAPH). The documents, which detailed paramilitary abuses after the 1991 coup, had been seized by U.S. forces in September 1994. It was believed, however, that the names of U.S. citizens had been excised from the returned documents, a condition that previous Haitian administrations had publicly rejected.

The failure of the United States to extradite Emmanuel "Toto" Constant, former FRAPH leader, continued to thwart Haitians' hopes for justice for past abuses. Constant, previously an informer for the Central Intelligence Agency, remained in Queens, New York, having been extended protection from deportation. Other members of the coup-era high command were also resident in the United States.

European Union

Finding that "respect for democratic principles has not yet been re-established in Haiti," in January the European Union (E.U.) terminated consultations with Haiti that had been initiated under the Cotonou Agreement, an aid pact linking the E.U. with African, Caribbean, and Pacific states. As a result, all direct budget aid to Haiti was suspended.

MEXICO

HUMAN RIGHTS DEVELOPMENTS

By ending seven decades of one-party rule in Mexico, the election of President Vicente Fox in 2000 created an historic opportunity to tackle the country's long-standing human rights problems. In his inaugural address, President Fox promised to seize this opportunity and, in the following months, his administration took encouraging steps toward that end. However, by November, significant progress was still needed in a variety of areas.

President Fox appointed several people known for their promotion of human rights to his cabinet, including Foreign Minister Jorge G. Castañeda and National Security Adviser Adolfo Aguilar Zínser. He also created a new post, the special ambassador for human rights and democracy, to which he appointed Mariclaire Acosta, for years one of the country's most outspoken human rights advocates. (In September, the position was reconfigured as deputy minister for Human Rights and Democracy within the Ministry of Foreign Relations.)

The Fox administration made a crucial break with Mexico's past by opening the country to international scrutiny by human rights monitors. In December, Fox announced that he would eliminate visa restrictions that had made it difficult for foreign monitors to gain access to the country on short notice. In March, addressing the U.N. Commission on Human Rights, Foreign Minister Castañeda extended "a permanent invitation to the representatives of international human rights mechanisms to visit Mexico." In May, the Foreign Ministry co-sponsored a seminar with the office of the United Nations High Commissioner on Human Rights on procedures for investigating torture. In July, it invited the president of the Inter-American Commission on Human Rights to visit Mexico to examine the government's compliance with past commission recommendations.

Under Fox's leadership, Mexico became more active in promoting the concept of the universality of human rights principles, a notion that was anathema to previous Mexican governments. In February, the foreign minister authorized the extradition of former Argentine navy officer Ricardo Miguel Cavallo to face charges in Spain for atrocities committed during Argentina's "dirty war." Cavallo filed a judicial appeal challenging the constitutionality of the foreign minister's ruling, and at this writing a ruling on the appeal was pending.

In October, the Foreign Ministry began working with congressional leaders to secure the ratification of the Rome Statute for the International Criminal Court, together with a reform of the Mexican constitution that would allow international tribunals, in some instances, to exercise jurisdiction over Mexican citizens. The Foreign Ministry also sought the ratification of several other international human rights treaties, including the Inter-American Convention on Forced Disappearance of Persons; the Convention on the Non-Applicability of Statutory Limitations to War Crimes and Crimes Against Humanity; the Optional Protocol to the Convention on the Rights of the Child on the sale of children, child prostitution, and child pornography; and the Optional Protocol to the Convention on the Rights of the Child on the involvement of children in armed conflicts. Finally, the ministry sought ratification of a treaty recognizing the competence of the U.N. Human Rights Committee to hear individual communications.

In addition to assuming new international human rights obligations, the government promised to promote respect for human rights abroad—in particular, the rights of Mexican citizens residing in the United States. President Fox's February meeting with U.S. President George W. Bush led to the creation of a working group consisting of top officials of both governments with the aim of achieving safe, legal, and humane migration. In October, the Presidential Office for Mexicans Abroad announced that it had reached an agreement with municipal health authorities in U.S. cities to ensure that Mexicans would receive medical attention regardless of their residency status. The National Human Rights Commission (Comisión Nacional de Derechos Humanos, CNDH), the government's autonomous human rights ombudsman, also made migrants' rights a priority.

Unfortunately, the strides made in Mexican foreign policy were not matched on the domestic front, where President Fox promised to intervene in several high profile human rights cases. One was that of General José Francisco Gallardo, who was jailed in 1993 after he openly called for the creation of a military human rights ombudsman's office. In 1997, the Inter-American Commission on Human Rights (IACHR) called for Gallardo's immediate release; yet, as of late 2001, Gallardo remained in jail. In February, his family petitioned the Supreme Court to order the president to comply with the IACHR's recommendation. A court ruling was pending at this writing.

A second case involved peasant environmentalists Teodoro Cabrera García and Rodolfo Montiel Flores, who were illegally detained and apparently tortured by soldiers in May 1999 and then convicted of drug and weapons crimes in August 2000 on the basis of evidence that was planted on them at the time of their detention. In January, President Fox promised that his government would conduct a thorough investigation of the case. The Foreign Ministry's human rights office provided legal advice to the lawyers handling a judicial appeal on behalf of Montiel and Cabrera. In July, a federal appeals court upheld the conviction of Cabrera and Montiel and they remained in prison until November, when President Fox issued an order for their release as a demonstration of his government's commitment to human rights norms. The investigation of the torture allegations was left to the military prosecutor's office, which had an extremely poor record of probing abuses by the military.

Little progress was made in addressing the underlying problems of the justice system that gave rise to cases like these. Judicial oversight of police practices was seriously inadequate. Judges cited legal precedents that vitiated human rights guarantees by accepting the use of evidence obtained through violations. The lenient sentences given to convicted torturers served to reinforce the climate of impunity.

Soldiers involved in counternarcotics operations also committed abuses against civilians. In January, soldiers on patrol near the town of Lindavista in Guerrero state shot at two unarmed civilians, killing fourteen-year-old Esteban Martínez Nazario. In August, the Baja California state human rights prosecutor's office reported that soldiers had been caught carrying out illegal detentions without arrest warrants. In October, the Center for Border Studies and Promotion of Human Rights reported complaints of illegal detentions carried out by soldiers in the Tamaulipas.

Under Mexican law, cases involving army abuses were subject to military rather than civilian jurisdiction. The military justice system, however, did not adequately investigate and prosecute alleged abuses by the army. Its operations generally lacked transparency and accountability. Following the January killing in Lindavista, however, military authorities did arrest and begin proceedings against five soldiers and an army officer. But this was exceptional and it occurred only after local people took the extraordinary measure of surrounding the army camp and refusing to allow anyone to leave until the killing was investigated. After a day-long siege, army and state government officials arrived and signed an agreement to investigate the shooting and punish those responsible. According to Lindavista residents, the boy who died was the seventh member of the community to be killed by soldiers in recent years, but his was the first case to be investigated. However, residents who organized the protest afterwards reported receiving threats from military personnel.

There was considerable debate within the Fox government over how to address past human rights violations, such as the 1968 massacre of student protestors in Mexico City, and the 1997 massacre of villagers in Acteal, Chiapas. In his inaugural address in December 2000, the president promised to establish a truth commission to investigate violations committed under previous governments. In the months that followed, however, his administration sent mixed signals about whether it would pursue the plan, with Secretary of Government Santiago Creel Miranda openly opposing the idea.

Another area requiring attention was the protection of labor rights. Mexico failed to guarantee free and fair union elections, despite the previous government's May 2000 pledge "to promote the use of eligible voter lists and secret ballot elections" as a step toward this. For example, at the Duro Bag Manufacturing Corporation in Río Bravo, union elections in March were conducted by open ballot, with workers required to vote aloud in front of company management and representatives of the company-favored Revolutionary Confederation of Workers and Peasants (CROC).

Legitimate labor organizing activity continued to be obstructed by collective bargaining agreements negotiated between management and pro-business, non-independent unions. These agreements frequently failed to provide worker benefits beyond the minimum standards mandated by Mexican legislation, and workers often only learned of the agreements when they grew discontented and attempted to organize independent unions. However, when workers sought to displace non-independent unions, they often suffered anti-union discrimination. In early January 2001, for example, five workers at the Kukdong International México S.A. de C.V. ("Kukdong") apparel factory in Puebla were discharged, allegedly for asserting workplace grievances and attempting to organize an independent union to replace the CROC. A week later, a majority of the Kukdong workforce began a work stoppage in solidarity with the fired workers. When the stoppage ended, many of the workers who had participated were denied reinstatement by Kukdong and CROC representatives. A concerted campaign on behalf of the workers was mounted by labor and nongovernmental organizations (NGOs) in the United States and Mexico, and largely in response to this effort, multinational corporate buyers began to exert pressure on Kukdong management to address the situation. From mid-February, most workers were allowed to return to the factory, and by September, workers had established an independent union and signed a collective agreement with the company (which had changed its name to Mex Mode).

Certain sections of the population were more vulnerable to rights violations. Among the most vulnerable groups, according to CNDH President José Luis Soberanes, were migrants and indigenous people. Gays and lesbians were also targeted for abuse. In August, for instance, gay activist César Salazar Gongora was kidnapped in the city of Merida, Yucatan, by three young men who raped him, beat him with a stone, cut his ear with a knife and then abandoned him in a nearby village. Salazar Gongora submitted a complaint to local prosecutors. In the days that followed he received dozens of phone calls threatening him with death for reporting the crime. An investigation was launched, but according to local rights advocates, it made no headway until Salazar Gongora, his lawyer and two gay rights advocates met with the state's attorney general and obtained from him a promise to replace the investigator attached to the case.

DEFENDING HUMAN RIGHTS

In October 2001, human rights lawyer Digna Ochoa was found shot to death in her Mexico City office. A note left by her side warned members of the Miguel Agustín Pro Juarez Human Rights Center, where Ochoa had worked for several years, that the same could happen to them. Ochoa had been subject to repeated threats in recent years because of her work on high profile human rights cases. (Among the people she had defended were alleged guerrillas jailed during the 1990s, and environmental activists Rodolfo Montiel and Teodoro Cabrera Garcia.) She was abducted twice in 1999 and, on the second occasion, interrogated by her assailants. The Zedillo government had failed to conduct thorough investigations of these incidents.

In 1999, the Inter-American Court of Human Rights had ordered the Mexican government to take special measures to protect the lives of Ochoa and her colleagues. Ochoa received police protection until she left the country in 2000 to work in the United States, but the protection lapsed upon her return to Mexico in April 2001. The Fox government promised to take all possible steps to bring those responsible to justice.

In addition to showing increased openness to international human rights monitors, the Fox government was more willing than its predecessors to consult its critics at home. In March, the Foreign Ministry's human rights office arranged a meeting between the commission that coordinates the human rights agendas of distinct government ministries and a wide range of human rights organizations. It then developed a proposal, based largely on the recommendations of the NGOs, for a "Dialogue Mechanism" that would allow NGOs to contribute to the design and implementation of Mexican human rights policy. At this writing, the proposal had not been implemented.

THE ROLE OF THE INTERNATIONAL COMMUNITY

United Nations

In May, U.N. special rapporteur on the independence of judges and lawyers Param Cumaraswamy visited Mexico to assess the justice system. He met the attorney general, the presidents of the CNDH and the Supreme Court, and other senior officials, as well as NGO representatives. He reported that impunity remained a serious problem within the Mexican judicial system.

Organization of American States (OAS)

In July, the IACHR president Claudio Grossman visited Mexico to assess the new government's compliance with past commission recommendations. Working with the Foreign Ministry's human rights office, the IACHR obtained amicable resolutions in several pending cases. It also issued two new case reports on Mexico and accepted a further case for consideration.

United States

In January, in its annual human rights report, the U.S. Department of State criticized "widespread impunity" that "continues to be a serious problem among the security forces" and noted that the government's efforts to improve human rights "continued to meet with limited success." Despite these criticisms, however, in its relations with Mexico, the U.S. focused less on strong bilateral action to promote human rights than on issues such as economic relations, immigration control, and narcotics.

In April, the U.S. National Administrative Office (NAO)—one of the three national agencies established under the labor side agreement of the North American Free Trade Agreement (NAFTA) to investigate charges of labor rights violation in member countries—released a report in which it confirmed allegations made by workers in two auto parts factories in Tamaulipas of chemical exposure and injuries from poor ergonomic conditions. The report found that the Mexican government had failed to fulfill its obligations under NAFTA's labor side accord to ensure safe working conditions. Specifically, the Mexican authorities had failed to conduct meaningful workplace inspections, to respond to workers who filed complaints with government agencies, and to provide proper compensation to workers for work-related injuries and illnesses. The NAO recommended ministerial consultations between the U.S and Mexican governments to discuss Mexico's failure to meet its obligations. If these consultations failed to resolve the matter, a panel could be convened to determine appropriate actions, including economic sanctions against the Mexican government. Under the labor side accord, economic sanctions could only be applied if a government was found to have persistently failed to enforce its domestic labor laws in three areas: occupational safety and health, child labor, and minimum wage.

Most of the other twenty-three cases submitted since NAFTA went into effect involved primarily the right to freedom of association, which can lead, at most, to an NAO request for intergovernmental consultation. In the absence of a more effective enforcement mechanism, the labor side accord had a limited impact on workers rights in Mexico.

Relevant Human Rights Watch Reports:

Military Injustice: Mexico's Failure to Punish Army Abuses, 12/01
Trading Away Rights: The Unfulfilled Promise of NAFTA's Labor Side Agreement, 4/01

PERU

HUMAN RIGHTS DEVELOPMENTS

In a series of dramatic developments in late 2000, the repressive and discredited government of President Alberto Fujimori disintegrated, generating new hope for democracy and human rights. Although Peru was faced with the legacy of a decade of authoritarian rule, both the interim administration of Valentín Paniagua and the new government of President Alejandro Toledo took important steps in 2001 to strengthen democratic institutions and the rule of law, while starting to address long neglected human rights problems.

In November 2000, after Fujimori had gained a third consecutive term of office in widely discredited elections held the previous May, his government collapsed in the midst of a major political corruption scandal. Fujimori fled to Japan, his parents' native country, from where he submitted his resignation by fax. The Peruvian

Congress declared Fujimori morally unfit for office and appointed its president, Valentín Paniagua, to head a caretaker government. Paniagua's eight-month transitional government achieved notable advances for human rights. It leveled the playing field for new presidential elections, held in April 2001. A special prosecutor, whom Fujimori had appointed in his final month in office, began to unravel a vast web of corruption spun by Fujimori's former advisor Vladimiro Montesinos. Paniagua formed a truth commission to investigate responsibility for the systematic human rights violations and guerrilla abuses committed during Peru's twenty-year counter-insurgency war, beginning in 1980. His government also took steps to improve prison conditions, and speeded up the release of people falsely convicted or charged with crimes of terrorism by Fujimori's widely condemned anti-terrorism courts.

On July 28, 2001, President Alejandro Toledo was sworn in after narrowly defeating Alán García's bid for a second mandate in a run-off vote in June (García had been president from 1985-1990). Toledo, who had led the opposition against Fujimori for two years, said that his government was committed to fully reestablishing human rights, accountability, and the rule of law, and he appointed former members of Peru's nongovernmental human rights community to his cabinet.

Both the interim administration and the Toledo government took important steps to bring members of the Fujimori government to justice for human rights violations and corruption. On June 23, Vladimiro Montesinos, the disgraced former *de facto* chief of the National Intelligence Service (Servicio de Inteligencia Nacional, SIN) and virtual co-ruler of Peru with President Fujimori, was arrested in Caracas, Venezuela, after eight months on the run. After an unsuccessful attempt to obtain asylum in Panama in September 2000, Montesinos had returned clandestinely to Peru in October, evaded capture, and escaped by yacht to Venezuela. Venezuela deported Montesinos to Peru, where he was imprisoned pending trial on charges of corruption and human rights violations.

In May, special prosecutor José Ugaz reported that seventy-four former government officials, judges, legislators and businessmen were being held on a wide range of corruption charges, and that U.S. $153 million held in foreign bank accounts by Montesinos and his cronies had been frozen. By November, more than 1,000 people were under investigation for corruption, according to a senior judicial official. Many were exposed by the discovery and exhibition in Congress of secret videos filmed by Montesinos at the SIN's Lima headquarters, showing them accepting bribes from the former intelligence chief. Those detained included former army commanders Gen. Nicolás de Bari Hermoza Ríos and Gen. José Villanueva Ruesta, during whose command the army had come under Montesinos' indirect control. Altogether, more than thirty senior military officers were accused of corruption, drug trafficking, wiretapping of government opponents, extrajudicial executions, and other crimes. Nineteen of them were in detention or under house arrest in October 2001.

On August 27, Congress voted unanimously to remove Fujimori's immunity from prosecution as head of state. On September 5, Attorney General Nelly Calderón filed charges against him of murder, causing grave injuries, and "disappearances." Fujimori was accused of being co-author, along with Montesinos, of the extrajudicial execution in 1991 of fifteen people, including an eight-year-old child, at a fund-raising party in a poor tenement in Lima's Barrios Altos district, and the "disappearance" in 1992 of nine students and a professor from La Cantuta University. Both crimes were attributed to the Colina Group, a paramilitary death squad answering to Montesinos as *de facto* head of the SIN, for which Fujimori exercised ultimate responsibility. By June, nineteen alleged Colina Group members were already facing charges for the Barrios Altos massacre, including several who had been released in 1995 under two sweeping amnesty laws approved by the Fujimori-controlled Congress. On September 13, Supreme Court justice José Luis Lecaros issued an international warrant to Interpol for Fujimori's arrest, pending the submission to Japan of a formal extradition request. The Japanese government, which had swiftly recognized Fujimori's claim to Japanese nationality, stated repeatedly that its laws prohibited the extradition of its citizens.

The truth commission established by interim President Paniagua in June got off to a slow start due to initial disagreements over its composition. Human rights groups criticized the Paniagua cabinet's decision to include a former pro-Fujimori congresswoman, Beatriz Alva Hart, in the seven-person commission, headed by the rector of the Catholic University, Salomón Lerner. After taking office, President Toledo finally confirmed Hart in her post, and he himself appointed five extra members, including a retired army general. The commission was mandated to investigate violations of the collective rights of Peru's Andean and native communities as well as violations of individual rights such as extrajudicial executions, torture, and "disappearances." It was also empowered to hold public hearings, and to name those it found responsible for abuses and human rights violations. Although government officials were required by law to provide support to and cooperate with the commission, it was not given powers to subpoena them to testify. The commission had plans to establish regional offices to collect information in the rural zones most affected by the armed conflict.

Abuses by guerrilla groups continued. Although states of emergency were no longer in force in any part of the country, isolated pockets of armed guerrilla activity were still reported. In the Alta Huallaga region in Huánuco and San Martín departments, Shining Path (Sendero Luminoso) guerrillas murdered fourteen civilian non-combatants in separate incidents in March. The victims were alleged to have been former guerrillas or sympathizers who their captors accused of collaborating with the government. Remnants of the Shining Path also continued to operate, reportedly in alliance with cocaine traffickers, in the jungle regions of Junín and Ucayali. Concerns continued that Asháninka Indians were being forcibly recruited and forced to work for the guerrillas. On August 7, four policemen on a mission to intercept a Shining Path column were killed after being ambushed by guerrillas in the jungle near Satipo. The Shining Path was reported to have kidnapped fifteen Asháninkas, whose names were not given for fear of reprisals. Incidents like these confronted the new government with the challenge of mounting an effective response to terrorism while avoiding the human rights abuses of earlier years.

There was steady progress in securing the release of scores of prisoners falsely accused or unjustly convicted of terrorism under the anti-terrorism laws introduced by the Fujimori government in 1992. Between November 2000 and mid-July, the government issued 144 pardons and commuted fifty-two sentences on the recommendations of an ad-hoc commission appointed by Fujimori to vet petitions for a presidential pardon. Nongovernmental human rights groups, which had themselves forwarded applications for pardons, however, urged the government to approve releases more quickly. By early August, more than one hundred cases presented by human rights organizations and the churches still awaited government approval. The situation of hundreds of peasants still affected by terrorism arrest warrants dating back for years was somewhat eased by a law passed in June permitting judges to suspend the investigation, or to allow prisoners to testify voluntarily without being detained.

By October, the government had not announced any plans to review the s entences and trials of more than 2,000 prisoners who had been convicted of terrorism or treason by anti-terrorism courts. These courts' procedures systematically violated due process and had been internationally condemned. In May, however, the Supreme Council of Military Justice, Peru's highest military court, announced that four Chilean members of the Tupac Amaru Revolutionary Movement (Movimiento Revolucionario Tupac Amaru, MRTA), who had been sentenced to life imprisonment for treason in 1994 by a "faceless" military court, would receive a new trial in a civilian court. The decision promised to put into effect a 1999 ruling by the Inter-American Court of Human Rights, which Fujimori had cited as a pretext for withdrawing Peru from the court's jurisdiction. In June, a civilian anti-terrorism court presided over by Judge Marcos Ibazeta re-tried U.S. citizen Lori Berenson, who had been sentenced in 1996 by a faceless military court to life imprisonment for treason. Berenson had been found guilty of participating in a foiled plot to take members of Congress hostage in order to obtain the release of MRTA prisoners. After a three-month trial in open court, at which her defense counsel was permitted to cross-examine witnesses, Berenson received a twenty-year sentence for collaborating with the group.

Some positive measures were taken to tackle Peru's inhumane prison conditions, another legacy of years of neglect of basic human rights. Overcrowding was severe, with more than 27,000 prisoners occupying facilities built for a maximum of 20,000. Long sentences and the habit of incarcerating offenders before trial contributed to the problem. The problem of overcrowding was compounded by insufficient food, poor hygiene, and inadequate medical services. More than half the prisons had seriously inadequate infrastructure and facilities. At the beginning of the year, two-thirds of the prisons were controlled by the police rather than by trained prison officers. Extortion and violence by guards was common.

Inmates convicted on serious charges, such as drug trafficking and terrorism, were not entitled to any remission for good conduct. Moreover, for years prisoners convicted of acts of terrorism had been kept locked up all day with minimal access to recreation areas and rights to family visits. In March, the Ministry of Justice introduced new rules allowing prisoners out of their cells between 6:00 am and 6:00 pm, more frequent and longer visits by relatives, and access to defense lawyers in private. Regulations were expected to enter force in September 2001 establishing this as a uniform regime for all inmates. Despite these advances, no action was taken to close down the isolated high-security prison of Challapalca, located at

14,000 feet in the Andes near Puno, whose oxygen-thin air and freezing temperatures made it a serious health hazard. Although some inmates were moved to other facilities, fifty continued to be held there.

Press freedom benefited almost immediately from the collapse of the Fujimori government and the dismantling of the SIN in September 2000. In December 2000, for example, Baruch Ivcher, owner of Channel 2-Frecuencia Latina, who was stripped of his Peruvian nationality in 1997 and deprived of his controlling shares in the station because of its reporting of abuses committed by the SIN, returned from exile and a court later restored his ownership of the company. Several media owners were facing charges, however, for accepting bribes from Montesinos in exchange for favoring the Fujimori government.

In the provinces, journalists continued to face threats and legal action in retaliation for critical coverage of local authorities and politicians. Local radio was particularly vulnerable. Of thirty complaints monitored from January to July by the Press and Society Institute (Instituto Prensa y Sociedad, IPYS), a non-governmental press freedom advocacy group, twenty-eight were received from outside Lima, and twenty-two affected radio stations. In February, the Human Rights Ombudsman presented to Congress a bill to repeal article 374 of the Criminal Code that penalizes defamation of public authorities. The bill was still under consideration at the time of writing.

DEFENDING HUMAN RIGHTS

Both the Paniagua and Toledo governments expressed support and appreciation for the work of human rights monitors. Human rights organizations made a vital contribution to the public debate in the transitional months before Toledo's election. Both governments appointed human rights advocates with long experience in nongovernmental organizations to their cabinets. The organizations grouped together in the widely respected National Human Rights Coordinating Group (Coordinadora Nacional de Derechos Humanos, CNDDHH) successfully advocated that a truth commission be appointed before the elected president took office in July, and it obtained the agreement of both candidates to support the initiative. In September, President Toledo appointed CNDDHH's executive director, Sofía Macher, as a member of the commission.

The Human Rights Ombudsman's office published in November 2000 a comprehensive report on "disappearances" between 1980 and 1996. Basing its data mainly on files from the Attorney General's office, the report documented 4,022 cases of "disappearance" in which the fate of the victims was still unknown. In an update published in November 2001, the ombudsman put the total number at 6,362, including cases recorded by human rights groups but not officially reported.

In November 2000, the offices of two CNDDHH member organizations, Peace and Hope (Paz y Esperanza) and the Human Rights Commission (Comisión de Derechos Humanos, COMISEDH), suffered break-ins and the theft of data storage equipment. The burglaries occurred soon after the CNDDHH filed a criminal complaint against those responsible for the Barrios Altos and La Cantuta massacres.

THE ROLE OF THE INTERNATIONAL COMMUNITY

United Nations

The Human Rights Committee (HRC) criticized abuses in the administration of justice. In its concluding observations on Peru's report under article 40 of the International Covenant on Civil and Political Rights, published in November 2000, the HRC called for the government to "review and repeal the 1995 amnesty laws, which help create an atmosphere of impunity." The committee also recommended that Peru "establish an effective mechanism for the review of all sentences imposed by the military courts for the offences of terrorism and treason," and expressed concern about prison conditions.

Organization of American States (OAS)

The human rights bodies of the Organization of American States (OAS) helped redress some of the abuses of the Fujimori era and promote justice for the victims, while Peru demonstrated a new commitment to comply with the OAS's recommendations. On January 18, Peru's Congress overturned a July 1999 resolution not to recognize the jurisdiction of the Inter-American Court of Human Rights, a resolution that the court had declared to be inadmissible. In February, the court ordered Peru to facilitate the return to Baruch Ivcher of his majority shares in the Channel 2-Frecuencia Latina television network, and pay him damages and compensation totaling U.S. $70,000. In compliance with recommendations made by the Inter-American Commission on Human Rights in December 1998, Peru reinstated three members of the Constitutional Court who had been dismissed in 1997 for opposing Fujimori's re-election plans.

In a landmark decision in March, the Inter-American Court ruled unanimously that the application of the 1995 amnesty laws to the Barrios Altos case was incompatible with the American Convention on Human Rights and therefore without legal effect. It urged Peru to hold accountable those responsible and to compensate the victims. Within days of the decision, Peruvian police detained several alleged former members of the Colina death squad on murder charges, including two former generals. In September, the Inter-American Court responded to a request by the Peruvian government for clarification of the scope of the Barrios Altos decision, by affirming that application of the amnesty laws to any other case of human rights violation would also violate the American Convention. In October, the Supreme Council of Military Justice annulled its 1995 decision applying the amnesty laws to the Barrios Altos and La Cantuta cases.

European Union

E.U. financial assistance to Peru was suspended in 1999-2000 under the Fujimori government. In 2001, aid programs were reestablished, primarily focusing on institutional and judicial reform, and the fight against poverty.

United States

Amid scandalous revelations about the criminal activities of Vladimiro Montesinos, the U.S. press published details about Montesinos' long association with the U.S. Central Intelligence Agency (CIA) and his pivotal role in U.S. anti-drug efforts in Peru. In September 2000, the *Washington Post* reported that the CIA defended Montesinos in inter-agency reviews and dismissed as "unproven and irrelevant" reports that he had "orchestrated" human rights violations in the early 1990s. The United States maintained its association with Montesinos well into 2000, according to the newspaper, until evidence emerged that Fujimori's advisor had been involved in the illegal sale of assault rifles to left-wing guerrillas in Colombia. In June, the National Security Archive (NSA), a U.S. non-governmental freedom of information advocacy group, published documents declassified under the Freedom of Information Act about the U.S.'s early links with Montesinos in the 1970s. Other documents showed that the U.S. received reports of Montesinos' growing influence over Fujimori as early as 1990. Apparently following a top-level decision finally to break off ties with Montesinos, the Federal Bureau of Investigations gave Peruvian police vital assistance in apprehending him in Caracas in June.

In July, Human Rights Watch wrote to President George W. Bush to express concern about the shooting down of a plane during a joint U.S.-Peruvian drug surveillance operation on April 20, causing the deaths of Veronica Bowers, a missionary, and her infant daughter. Human Rights Watch urged that surveillance pilots be issued with clear instructions not to use lethal force in the absence of an imminent threat of violence. A joint U.S.-Peruvian report released by the State Department in August put the blame for the tragedy on lax procedures and the failure of the Peruvian pilot to give proper warning.

VENEZUELA

As in the past, the most pressing human rights issues facing the government of President Hugo Chávez involved crime and the criminal justice system. High levels of violent crime placed great stress on public institutions, whose level of professionalism was often low. Corruption and violence in the police forces and the prison system remained endemic, while the judiciary—under-funded, inefficient, and often corrupt—was incapable of dispensing justice in an efficient manner.

The extrajudicial execution of criminal suspects by police continued to be a major human rights problem. A disturbing recent development was the emergence in some states of organized death squads, acting with impunity and even publishing their hit lists in local newspapers.

President Chávez's frequent outbursts against his political and media critics, coupled with his authoritarian style of governance, raised fears of encroachments on civil liberties and free expression. However, as in previous years, Chávez's rhetoric was generally more aggressive than his actions.

HUMAN RIGHTS DEVELOPMENTS

In the state of Portuguesa, a death squad composed of off-duty members of the state police and National Guard was believed responsible for up to one hundred killings of criminal suspects over the last two years, mainly in the cities of Acarigua and Araure. Calling itself the "extermination group," it selected its victims from lists of wanted criminals openly published in the press. Given the apparent indifference of the state government, police, and judges to the incidents, the killers reportedly took to operating in broad daylight aboard police patrol cars. According to press reports, they extorted large sums of money from those on their hit list and killed them if they were unable to pay up.

In October 2000, members of the group murdered twenty-three-year-old Jimmy Rodríguez, a third year law student, and his friend César Agray Meléndez. Both were well known locally and neither was believed to have criminal connections. In May, Rodríguez' father, José Ramón Rodríguez, who had campaigned publicly to bring his son's killers to justice, was himself gunned down. A few days later, Belmiro Gutiérrez, one of the principal witnesses in the Rodríguez-Agray killings, was also murdered. In July, the government sent two prosecutors and large contingent of police from Caracas to investigate these incidents. Many witnesses received death threats.

Human rights groups accused Rodrigo Pérez Pérez, the chief of public security of the Portuguesa state government, and the former chief of the State Police, Carlos Navarro, of complicity in the activities of the death squad, but neither had been charged by October. At least six state police officers, however, were arrested in connection with the killings. On September 25 a large National Guard and police contingent, acting on the orders of the attorney general, Isaías Rodríguez, raided the state police headquarters. According to the press, they found that four of the six detained officers were not in their cells, which contained liquor and cell phones. The police also reportedly found illegal weapons, drugs, and the registration documents of stolen cars in the building.

In June, Attorney General Isaías Rodríguez announced that the government was also investigating death squad activity in the states of Yaracuy, Miranda, Anzoátegui, and in metropolitan Caracas. The nongovernmental human rights group Venezuelan Program for Education and Action on Human Rights (Programa Venezolano de Educación-Acción en Derechos Humanos, PROVEA) denounced a pattern of extrajudicial killings in the states of Barinas (with thirty-two such deaths between January 2000 and June 2001), and Zulia, where ninety-eight people died in "clashes" with police in 2000, and forty-three in the first four months of 2001. Police often attempted to disguise deliberate killings by claiming that the victims were killed in firefights.

In July, the Supreme Court granted a habeas corpus writ filed on behalf of

Roberto Javier Hernández Paz, who "disappeared" after intelligence agents arrested him in his home in the state of Vargas in December 1999. The court ordered the prosecutor to renew investigations into Hernández' "disappearance" and bring to justice those responsible. Hernández was one of four people who "disappeared" when intelligence agents and army paratroopers committed serious abuses during efforts to control looting during flooding in Vargas state. In September the public prosecutor brought charges of enforced disappearance against Jose Yañez Casimiro, a DISIP officer implicated in the "disappearance" of Oscar Blanco Romero, and against Justiniano Martínez Carreño for covering up Blanco's illegal arrest.

The progressive new code of penal procedures, introduced in 1999 under the government of Rafael Caldera, came under fire as the public security crisis worsened. With the code being scapegoated for the weaknesses of law enforcement, calls multiplied for its reform, in particular, to tighten its provisions on parole and pretrial release, and to eliminate jury trials.

Prison conditions remained inhumane and, because of inter-prisoner violence, often life-threatening. Despite a significant reduction in the numbers of prisoners awaiting trial, levels of inmate violence were extremely high, abetted by insufficient staffing and equipment, widespread corruption among guards, and the unchecked entry into prisons of narcotics and firearms. In March, two prisoners died and forty-one were wounded in a gun battle between rival gangs in the El Rodeo prison in Miranda state. One of the dead, Edgard Alexander Bazán, was killed when he picked up a hand grenade another prisoner had thrown toward him. The prison with the worst record of inmate violence was Yare I, in Miranda state, where at least twenty inmates died in separate incidents from April to August, as gangs competed to control the market in drugs and weapons.

Venezuela's treatment of refugees from neighboring Colombia raised serious concerns. In October 2000, Venezuelan authorities forcibly returned at least seven asylum seekers who had fled paramilitary violence in their villages, having barred access to the group by the United Nations High Commissioner for Refugees (UNHCR). In February human rights and church groups expressed concern about the plight of hundreds of Colombians who had crossed into Zulia state to escape political violence in Colombia. The refugees, whose presence both the Venezuelan and Colombian governments initially denied, were reported to be undocumented and suffering from malnutrition and disease. In March, the Inter-American Commission on Human Rights issued an urgent appeal to the Venezuelan government not to return the 287 refugees and to guarantee their safety, provide them with humanitarian assistance, and consider their applications for refugee status.

In August, the National Assembly approved an Organic Law on Refugees and Asylum Seekers, drafted with the participation of nongovernmental human rights groups. The new law prohibited the forcible return of asylum seekers and established a National Commission for Refugees to consider asylum applications. According to PROVEA, more than one hundred such applications had been awaiting consideration since July 1999.

President Chávez's authoritarian tendencies continued to reveal themselves in efforts to undermine civil society institutions such as labor unions and the press.

Yet, even as Chávez threatened severe measures—as in May when he proposed declaring a state of emergency—his actions were rarely as drastic as his more alarmist critics expected.

On December 3, 2000, at Chávez's behest, the government held, and won, a national referendum to remove the leadership of the country's discredited trade union federations. The proposal was in breach of treaty obligations mandating that the government respect the autonomy of labor organizations. After repeated postponements, new union elections held under the auspices of the National Electoral Council, a state body, were scheduled for October.

Although press freedom was generally respected, Chávez continued to deliver blistering attacks on his press critics in his weekly television show and other public appearances, as well as in calls placed by him to radio and television networks. Chávez's aversion to criticism was also evident in his June announcement that "foreigners who come here to slander Venezuela will be expelled." His words were believed to be a reaction to comments made during a visit to Venezuela by Peruvian presidential candidate Lourdes Flores, who had compared Chávez's government to that of deposed President Alberto Fujimori of Peru.

Also in June, the Supreme Court issued a decision interpreting a controversial clause in Venezuela's new constitution, a document drafted under Chávez' direction. In a much-criticized ruling, the court found that article 58 of the constitution guaranteeing the right to "timely, truthful, and impartial information" imposed enforceable obligations on the media. The court held that media outlets must avoid "publishing false news or news that is manipulated with half truths; disinformation that denies the opportunity to know the reality of the news; and speculation or biased information to obtain a goal with regard to someone or something." The court also concluded that article 58 required publications to be ideologically pluralistic unless their editorial line was made explicit.

The Supreme Court ruling raised fears that article 58 would be used to gag press critics of the government. Indeed, in October, the National Commission of Telecommunications (Comisión Nacional de Telecomunicaciones, CONATEL) began an investigation into the conduct of the Venezuelan television network Globovisión, for allegedly having broadcast "false, misleading or tendentious information," an offense under Venezuela's Radiocommunications Regulations. In September, the network aired the statement of a taxi driver who claimed that nine colleagues had been killed by criminals, when in fact only one had died. President Chavez urged the station to "reflect before it is too late," and threatened to "apply mechanisms for the defense of the national interest, the truth, and public order." For its error, which it promptly corrected, the station was potentially liable to a fine or the suspension of its broadcasting license.

On January 7, members of the Directorate of Military Intelligence (Dirección de Inteligencia Militar, DIM) detained lawyer and academic Pablo Aure Sánchez in response to a letter he wrote ridiculing the army that was published in a national newspaper. Aure was stripped of his clothes and spent the night in a cramped cell without access to a toilet. Although he was released for health reasons three days later, Aure faced charges under an article 505 of the code of military justice, which mandates a three- to five-year sentence for anyone who "insults, offends or disparages the armed forces." Disregarding objections made by the attorney general and the human rights ombudsman, who argued that military jurisdiction over civilians was unconstitutional, the military prosecutor refused to turn the case over to the civilian courts.

On June 24, Venezuelan military intelligence agents arrested Vladimiro Montesinos, the shadowy head of Peru's National Intelligence Service and the power behind the throne of deposed President Alberto Fujimori, in Caracas. Montesinos was promptly deported to Peru, where he was imprisoned on charges of corruption and human rights abuse. Since Montesinos fled Peru amidst a bribery scandal in October 2000, persistent rumors had circulated that he was hiding in Venezuela with the protection of government officials. The strongest suspicions centered on members of the Directorate of Intelligence and Prevention Services (Dirección de los Servicios de Inteligencia y Prevención, DISIP) and on its director, Eliecer Otaiza, who was fired by Chávez days before Montesinos' arrest. However, investigations by the Attorney General's Office and two parliamentary commissions of inquiry failed to clarify questions regarding the government's involvement.

DEFENDING HUMAN RIGHTS

The year began with positive overtures by the Chávez government toward human rights groups, but little real cooperation resulted. In January, Human Rights Watch was present as an observer at a meeting on public security convened by Minister of the Interior and Justice Luis Alfonso Dávila with representatives of the Venezuelan human rights community, and attended by cabinet ministers, the attorney general, the president of the Supreme Court, and the human rights ombudsman. The participants agreed to form a permanent advisory commission to ensure an ongoing dialogue between the government and human rights groups, particularly on crime control policy. However, by October the proposal had not been implemented.

In January, the press reported that Liliana Ortega, executive director of the respected Committee of Relatives of Victims of the Events of February-March 1989 (Comité de Familiares de los Víctimas de los Sucesos de Febrero-Marzo de 1989, COFAVIC), was on a list of persons under investigation by DISIP for "plotting against the government." The following month, however, DISIP's director denied the allegations.

THE ROLE OF THE INTERNATIONAL COMMUNITY

United Nations

In March the Human Rights Committee reviewed Venezuela's record of compliance with the International Covenant on Civil and Political Rights. In its concluding observations, the committee expressed grave concern at reports of "disappearances" and extrajudicial executions, and regarding the failure of the state authorities to investigate them and bring those responsible to justice. It also urged Venezuela to pass a law codifying torture as a crime, and expressed concern that the extended reform of the judiciary could threaten its independence. In May, the Committee on Economic, Social and Cultural Rights called on Venezuela to ratify the 1951 Convention on the Status of Refugees and to issue asylum applicants with appropriate documentation. It considered that Venezuela's failure to do so "seriously hinders their enjoyment of economic, social and cultural rights, including the rights to work, health and education."

Organization of American States (OAS)

In its annual report for the year 2000, the Inter-American Commission on Human Rights expressed concern about restrictions on freedom of expression in Venezuela. The special rapporteur on freedom of expression raised the case of Pablo Aure as an example of the continuing problems posed by contempt of authority laws.

In February the Inter-American Commission on Human Rights issued an urgent appeal to the Venezuelan government with regard to criminal defamation proceedings targeting journalist Pablo López Ulacio. The proceedings, brought by a prominent businessman whom Ulacio had accused of corrupt business practices, were flawed by the evident partiality of the judges. Yet the government failed to take the measures requested by the commission, and in July a Caracas judge issued another order for López' arrest.

Venezuela also continued to flout a 1996 ruling of the Inter-American Court on Human Rights. The court had ordered Venezuela to compensate the relatives of fourteen fishermen extrajudicially executed at El Amparo in Apure state in October 1988, and to bring to justice those responsible.

United States

Neither the Clinton nor Bush administrations commented publicly on human rights. The State Department's *Country Reports on Human Rights Practices for 2000* highlighted the problem of extrajudicial executions and "disappearances," noting that the perpetrators acted with "near impunity." High-level Venezuelan officials, including Defense Minister José Vicente Rangel and Foreign Minister Luis Alfonso Dávila, criticized the report.

ASIA

Mourners pay tribute to civilians who were killed when they tried to attend a pro-referendum rally in Banda Aceh, Indonesia. © 2000 JACQUELINE KOCH

ASIA OVERVIEW

The entire Asian region suffered a political earthquake in the aftermath of the September 11 attacks on the United States. Afghanistan was the epicenter, but the aftershocks threw domestic politics and international relations into upheaval.

All countries in the region condemned the September 11 attacks, and in response to the Bush administration's challenge, "Are you with us or against us?" most governments, including North Korea, lined up cautiously on the U.S. side. Governments from India to China found, in measures to counteract terrorism, new justifications for longstanding repression. Real enthusiasm, however, was only evident in the Philippines, Malaysia, Taiwan, and South Korea, and by November, most Asian leaders were finding that a pro-U.S. position had political costs at home.

Indonesian and Malaysian leaders found that support from important domestic constituencies could be jeopardized if they seemed to be unconditionally supportive of the U.S. bombing of a fellow Muslim-majority nation. By November, Indonesian President Megawati was pleading with President Bush to end the bombing before Ramadan, the Muslim fasting month, began. In South Asia, India was clearly worried about the U.S. embrace of Pakistan and the implications for Pakistani mischief in Kashmir, while Pakistan's President Musharraf worried about how he could use alliance with the U.S. to achieve political and economic goals (halting the U.S. embrace of India, securing the lifting of economic sanctions against Pakistan) while keeping Islamist forces at bay. For China, the question was how a war on terrorism could be used to intensify a campaign against splittists in Xinjiang without the U.S. threatening Chinese interests in Central Asia. China and the Koreas, mindful of Japanese atrocities against their peoples in World War II, were concerned about how Japan's offer of logistical support for U.S. forces might strengthen forces on Japan's pro-military right.

But these were all government reactions. The popular reactions across the region were if anything more important, given the increasing importance of civil society in most Asian countries. In general, there were widespread expressions of sympathy both for victims of the September 11 attacks as well as for Afghan civilians. Large demonstrations against the U.S. airstrikes erupted in October across Bangladesh, India, Sri Lanka, Malaysia, Indonesia, and elsewhere. (Anti-U.S. sentiment in China after September 11 was actively suppressed by the Chinese government through controls on the media and the Internet.) In some cases, these protests reflected the successful portrayal by conservative Muslims of the U.S. effort as an attack on Islam, but they also expressed a broader discomfort within civil society about the perceived disproportionate use of power by the U.S. in a devastated country. Intellectuals throughout the region also raised the issue of how U.S. policies, particularly in the Middle East, had alienated important segments of the Muslim community.

FRAGILE DEMOCRATIC TRANSITIONS

The September 11 attacks eclipsed many of the human rights issues that had dominated the first nine months of the year. These included the fragility of democratic transitions in the region and the dilemmas posed by partial democratization in the absence of strong political institutions—or in the presence of strong militaries.

Fair elections produced disastrous leaders in Southeast Asia: Joseph Estrada, a corrupt ex-movie star, ousted from the Philippines presidency in January by Gloria Macapagal Arroyo, and Abdurrahman Wahid, a nearly blind cleric, ousted from the Indonesian presidency in July. Estrada remained highly popular among the country's poor, and his ouster after military-backed protests from the elite and middle class in Manila was semi-legal at best. The question arose, which was the greater danger to Philippine democracy, a shady president with underworld connections who systematically looted the national treasury but who was nevertheless the choice of the people, or his less than constitutional ouster? The crisis showed Philippine political leaders and institutions at their worst: a malleable parliament, a weak judiciary, and new president whose first instinct in May, in the face of protests from pro-Estrada forces, was to declare a state of rebellion to arrest political opponents.

In Thailand the dilemma was similar but less stark. In January, the Thai Rak Thai party, led by Thaksin Shinawatra, won a majority of parliamentary seats in the January 6 national election, making Thaksin prime minister. But ten days before the vote, Thaksin, a telecommunications tycoon, was indicted by the National Counter-Corruption Committee (NCCC) on charges of failing to fully declare his financial assets as required by law when he held a previous government post. If the Constitutional Court upheld the indictment, banning Thaksin from public office for five years, the Thai political system could have been thrown into serious crisis. If it did not, despite apparently strong evidence of unrevealed wealth, the independence of the court and Thailand's battle against high-level graft and corruption would be undermined. Which was worse? The court voted eight to seven not to uphold the indictment, to the disappointment of political reformers and yet to the relief of many who feared that democracy would be poorly served by a prolonged period of uncertainty and instability.

President Abdurrahman Wahid, Indonesia's great hope for furthering democratization, proved to be entirely unsuited for the job. He listened to no one, ignored major crises, and in the end, tried unsuccessfully to use the military against the parliament that was trying to impeach him on corruption grounds. But the alternative was either a return to former President Soeharto's party, Golkar, or support for Vice-President Megawati Sukarnoputri, whose party had the most seats in the Indonesian parliament and who had extensive army backing. On human rights issues, the choice came down to one of incompetence versus lack of political will. Which was worse, a president who could not make the justice system work or one who would not even try? Much of the human rights and reformist community preferred the former, but when that same inability and inattention to political and economic problems began to lead to a nostalgia in some circles for authoritarianism, Indonesia's democratic experiment was in trouble.

In Cambodia, targeted political assassinations, while few in number, continued to discourage many grassroots candidates from running in Cambodia's long-delayed commune elections, scheduled for early 2002.

Nepal's shaky transition to democracy, begun in 1990, underwent its most severe test with the assassination of almost the entire royal family by the crown prince in June 2001. The prince later shot himself. Like Thailand and Cambodia, the monarchy in Nepal has been an anchor for the transition, and the murdered King Birendra had helped hold the country together through the collapse of ten governments in ten years combined with a growing Maoist insurgency. The unpopularity of the new king, an economic crisis in an already desperately poor country, and the growing clout of the rebels all suggested that Nepal's democratic transition would face further trials in 2002.

In Pakistan, the problem was somewhat different. President Pervez Musharraf had abruptly halted Pakistan's flailing attempts at democratization when he overthrew the corrupt Nawaz Sharif in a military coup in October 1999. Some Pakistanis at the time saw a temporary loss of civil liberties as an acceptable price to pay for getting rid of politicians whose desire for power seemed motivated primarily by greed. But human rights defenders and reformers accurately predicted that once taken away, these liberties were going to be hard to restore. By September 11, Musharraf, despite international condemnation of the coup, had shown no hurry to hold elections. Human rights activists and political reformers pointed out that the political vacuum was only encouraging the growth of religious extremism, all the more so after the U.S. war against the Taliban provided a potent rallying point for the Islamic right. The U.S. and British embrace of Musharraf in their anti-terrorism coalition effectively ended any international pressure for the restoration of democracy in Pakistan.

While nothing could be further from democratic transition than North Korea, the importance of that country's slight opening to the outside world in late 2000 and 2001, apparently driven by the need to earn foreign exchange, should not be underestimated. In February, during a visit by a European Union delegation, North Korean officials agreed to a human rights dialogue with the E.U.

INTERNATIONAL JUSTICE

International justice for war crimes and crimes against humanity was an issue throughout Asia during the year, but it was often a case of local NGOs, foreign governments, and international rights organizations trying to force unwilling governments to act. The Cambodian parliament passed a law in August to set up a tribunal to try former Khmer Rouge leaders, and the same month in Indonesia, all legal hurdles blocking the establishment of an ad hoc tribunal on East Timor were cleared, but neither court was functioning by the end of November. Political will to proceed with indictments was noticeably absent. In East Timor, local NGOs by September 2001 were demanding an international tribunal to try Indonesian officers and the militia commanders they had created and armed, but it was not just Indonesian leaders who showed little interest in justice. East Timorese leaders also made clear that punishing past abuses was not for them a priority.

The issue of war crimes by Japan during World War II continued to fester. China and Korea, whose populations suffered terribly under Japanese occupation, were outraged in August by Japanese Prime Minister Koizumi's visit to a shrine honoring Japanese war heroes. The issue of "comfort women"—women forced to provide sexual services to Japanese soldiers—returned to center stage with a people's tribunal convened in Tokyo in December 2000.

Accountability for past abuses was becoming an issue in Afghanistan by late 2001, with respect to crimes not only by the Taliban but by individual commanders in the Northern Alliance (United Front) and by *mujahideen* outside that alliance, and by Soviet commanders during their decade-long occupation of the country. Efforts were underway to being a war crimes case against a former Afghan commander living in London.

By mid-November, Cambodia was close to becoming the first country in East or South Asia to ratify the Rome Statute of the International Criminal Court.

VIOLENCE, REFUGEES, AND
THE INTERNALLY DISPLACED

Asia continued to be wracked by outbreaks of war and ethnic and communal strife, producing widespread human rights violations and massive new populations of refugees and the displaced. As all eyes were focused on the humanitarian crisis in Afghanistan in November 2001, with estimates of the displaced in the hundreds of thousands as winter approached, it was also important to remember the 850,000 to one million internally displaced in Indonesia; more than 800,000 in Sri Lanka; some 600,000 to one million in Burma, and an estimated half million displaced in India. In most cases, access to humanitarian aid and protection for the displaced was difficult, either because of government obstruction or security concerns.

Refugee populations were also large, with an estimated 200,000 Burmese in Thailand, 120,000 Burmese in Bangladesh, and about 100,000 refugees from Bhutan in Nepal. An estimated 135,000 new refugees from Afghanistan had arrived in Pakistan after September 11. In West Timor, an estimated 60,000 to 80,000 East Timorese remained after the forcible expulsions of 1999, but the rate of voluntary return picked up sharply after the peaceful elections in East Timor in August.

If would-be refugees managed to cross into another country, access to aid was usually easier, but some governments deliberately closed their borders to asylum-seekers. By the time the American bombing campaign in Afghanistan began, for examples, all of Afghanistan's neighbors had shut their borders, citing security concerns, inability to handle a new influx, and in some cases, U.S. pressure. By November, Pakistan, already host to some two and a half million Afghan refugees, had relented somewhat and was allowing fifteen new camps to be built inside its borders, but under conditions that raised serious protection concerns for the new arrivals.

The other country in the region that closed its borders to asylum-seekers was Australia. In August, when his political popularity was at an all-time low, Prime Minister John Howard decided to capitalize on anti-immigrant sentiment by very noisily denying asylum to more than four hundred mostly Afghan refugees who had nearly drowned in Indonesian waters and had been picked up by a Norwegian freighter and brought to Australian waters near Christmas Island. Howard refused to let them land and reversed his political fortunes, winning a third term in mid-November on the basis of hardline policies and new legislation that violated Australia's obligations under international refugee law.

Asylum-seekers also had a difficult time in Japan. Only twenty-two asylum-seekers were granted refugee status in Japan in 2000, and the figures for 2001, to be published in 2002, were not expected to be any greater.

In addition to violence, repression and discrimination were factors leading Asians to flee their own countries. China's Uighurs fled to Kyrgyzstan and Kazakhstan, from which they were occasionally sent back, and even to Pakistan; some Tibetans continued to try and reach Nepal.

Beginning in February, more than 1,000 ethnic highlanders from Vietnam, known collectively as Montagnards, fled to Cambodia after Vietnamese police crushed a public protest over land-grabbing and controls on freedom of religion. While Cambodia agreed to provide temporary asylum to the Montagnards at two United Nations High Commissioner for Refugees (UNHCR) sites, Cambodian officials violated the principle of *non-refoulement* several times during the year when they forcibly returned large groups of Montagnards back to Vietnam, where many were arrested and beaten.

North Koreans fled to China largely to look for food and work. They could face severe punishment in North Korea on charges of illegal departure if returned. Chinese authorities reportedly sent many back to unclear fates. Estimates of the number of North Koreans in China ranged from South Korean government figures of ten to thirty thousand to estimates ten times higher from nongovernmental sources. The problem drew international attention in June when a family of seven North Koreans sought refuge in the UNHCR office in Beijing. They were eventually allowed to leave for South Korea via the Philippines.

Bhutanese refugees spent a tenth year in exile in camps in southeast Nepal, deprived of their right to return home. Despite the start in early 2001 of a joint verification program by the governments of Nepal and Bhutan to ascertain the status of these refugees, progress was slow, and no refugees had returned as of late November.

INTERNAL SECURITY LAWS

Even before September 11, internal security legislation was being widely abused in many Asian countries. In China, several academics and business people based in the West were detained under laws preventing the disclosure of state secrets. In Malaysia, Prime Minister Mahathir made increasing use of the draconian Internal Security Act to arrest members of the political opposition. In Indonesia, laws once used to detain critics of former President Soeharto made an unwelcome comeback, particularly clauses of the Criminal Code punishing spreading hatred toward government officials. In South Korea, little progress was made toward amending the hated National Security Law. In August, seven activists of a pro-reunification organization were arrested in Seoul for having illicitly contacted members of the North Korean Youth League before attending a meeting of the League in Pyongyang.

In India, government officials used the post-September focus on terrorism to push for a new Prevention of Terrorism Ordinance, that would give police sweeping powers of arrest and detention. It would reinstate a modified version of the hated Terrorist and Disruptive Activities (Prevention) Act or TADA which was repealed in 1995 after years of abuse against suspected rebels and anti-government activists.

HUMAN RIGHTS DEFENDERS

Asian human rights activists continued to play a high-profile international role, and in some cases, paid a high price for doing so. At least nine human rights defenders in the region were killed between November 2000 and November 2001, seven of them from Aceh, Indonesia. Many more faced intimidation or arrest, and the trial of Malaysian human rights defender Irene Fernandez entered its sixth year in Kuala Lumpur.

At the World Conference Against Racism, Racial Discrimination, Xenophobia and Related Intolerance (WCAR), Asian activists succeeded in getting international attention to the issue of caste discrimination, not just in Asia but around the world.

Human rights in Singapore took a step forward with the approval in October 2001 of the Think Centre, an independent organization committed to the expansion of civil liberties, as a fully registered society under Singaporean law. Founder James Gomez had faced pressure during the year for holding rallies without permits, but no legal action was taken against him.

Long established regional nongovernmental organizations such as Forum Asia and the Asian Commission on Human Rights campaigned actively for Asian ratification of the treaty establishing an International Criminal Court and for the repeal of the Internal Security Act in Malaysia. They also worked with other groups in the region to promote better protection of human rights defenders. The Asian Migrant Centre based in Hong Kong had a campaign in seven Asian countries for the ratification of the International Convention on the Protection of the Rights of All Migrant Workers and Members of Their Families. The Asia Monitor Resource Centre took a leading role in documenting labor practices and implementation of corporate codes of conduct throughout East and Southeast Asia. The Bangkok-based South East Asia Press Alliance (SEAPA) was an effective advocate for journalists in the region, helping raise the profile of the beleaguered malaysiakini.com, an electronic news service that the Malaysian government shut down; assist the new East Timorese journalists association in getting started; and protest threats against the daily newspaper in Banda Aceh by rebels unhappy with the paper's content.

In November 2001, three hundred activists from Bangladesh, India, Nepal, Pakistan, and Sri Lanka formed a new group called South Asians for Human Rights.

National human rights commissions in the region had their ups and downs. SUHAKAM in Malaysia took a stronger position than many expected in criticizing government abuses against demonstrators and Internal Security Act arrests; Komnas HAM in Indonesia came more and more under the control of obstructionists anxious to prevent serious human rights investigations.

On April 30, the Korean National Assembly passed a law establishing a national human rights commission, scheduled to begin work in November 2001. The body was empowered to investigate a broad range of human rights violations and provide compensation to victims. Its mandate covered discrimination, including sexual, racial, religious, and against the mentally or physically handicapped. The bill also included provisions dealing with cases of unlawful arrest, torture, intimidation, punishment, and detention of citizens by public service personnel, including employees of psychiatric hospitals.

THE ROLE OF THE INTERNATIONAL COMMUNITY

The stance of the international community toward Asia shifted dramatically after September 11. It was not just terrorism that was suddenly front and center on the international agenda; the humanitarian crisis in Afghanistan, all but forgotten before mid-September, suddenly became an issue as television screens across the world focused on the plight of refugees, the displaced, and the near-starving.

With that attention came new questions about mixing military and humanitarian missions, exemplified by U.S. food drops inside Afghanistan; tradeoffs between security and refugee protection as Afghanistan's neighbors closed their borders; and the extent to which failure to address humanitarian issues in the past might have contributed to the rise of religious extremism. These questions had a relevance not just for Afghanistan but for conflict-ridden areas of Asia more generally.

The crisis in Afghanistan highlighted once again the lack of regional institutions in Asia that have any capacity for dispute resolution, peacekeeping, human rights monitoring, or administration of justice. The Association of South East Asian Nations (ASEAN) remained weakened by Indonesia's ongoing internal troubles, and the South Asian Association for Regional Cooperation (SAARC) never functioned effectively, largely because of hostility between India and Pakistan.

That left, as always, the United Nations. Just as the U.N. began to wind down its operations in East Timor, it appeared poised to take on a major new role in Afghanistan, although exactly what that role would be was not clear as of late November.

In general, the large, amorphous organizations set up to discuss trade issues (Asia-Pacific Economic Cooperation or APEC for Asia and North America and the Asia Europe Meeting or ASEM for Asia and the European Union) were useful largely as a setting for informal high-level bilateral meetings and symbolic shows of solidarity. The APEC summit in October in Shanghai, for example, became a forum for building alliances against terrorism.

In September 2001, the European Commission adopted a new strategy for enhanced partnership with Asia that focused on six areas, including peace and security, and the promotion of democracy, governance, and the rule of law. The strategy called for the European Union (E.U.) to play a more active role in conflict prevention in Asia and strengthen an E.U.-Asia dialogue on issues such as asylum and immigration. It also cited the much-criticized E.U.-China human rights dialogue as a model of constructive exchanges.

Japan was eager to contribute to the counter-terrorism effort. Despite worries in East Asia about Japan's expanded military role, the Koizumi government pushed through the Diet a bill to allow Japanese self-defense forces to supply logistical support in Afghanistan in non-combat areas. Japan also provided humanitarian assistance for refugees in Pakistan and planned to co-host with the U.S. an international conference on Afghanistan's reconstruction. On human rights concerns in Asia, Japan was most active diplomatically in Indonesia, and least willing to push rights concerns with China and Malaysia.

Some donor meetings convened by the World Bank were useful forums to raise human rights concerns, such as the donor conferences on Cambodia and Sri Lanka. Donors at the annual meeting of the Consultative Group on Indonesia in November 2001 were frank about unhappiness with Indonesia's lack of progress fighting corruption. In general, views of civil society organizations were increasingly solicited prior to these meetings.

THE WORK OF HUMAN RIGHTS WATCH

Throughout the year, the Asia Division focused in particular on five countries: Afghanistan, Cambodia, China, India, and Indonesia, with additional monitoring of human rights developments across the region.

The human rights situation in Afghanistan had been a priority all year, with a major effort having gone into documenting massacres by the Taliban in the Hazarajat region in January and again in June. Following the September 11 attacks, Human Rights Watch launched a major emergency project to monitor violations of human rights and international humanitarian law in Afghanistan, using the model employed earlier in Chechnya and Kosovo. A Human Rights Watch team arrived in Pakistan in October.

Work on Indonesia focused on Aceh and Papua, with reports and numerous updates produced on both. In both areas, Human Rights Watch worked closely with local rights organizations. Staff conducted two training sessions, in May and August, in human rights documentation for some three dozen human rights activists from Aceh.

The WCAR provided a focal point for work in India where an international campaign against caste violence and discrimination continued to gather strength. Despite hard lobbying by the Indian government to keep caste off the agenda of the conference, the Dalit (untouchable) delegation succeeded in getting international media coverage and direct acknowledgment from U.N. Secretary-General Kofi Annan.

The flight to Cambodia of Montagnard refugees from Vietnam led to intensive advocacy work by Human Rights Watch to persuade both the Cambodian government and the UNHCR to protect the refugees from refoulement. Without that advocacy, there would have been no protection; even with it, Cambodian authorities forcibly deported several hundred Montagnards. Human Rights Watch later received first-hand reports that some of those who had been deported were subsequently detained and tortured.

In the U.S., Human Rights Watch focused on the development of strategies to effectively engage the incoming Bush administration on human rights in Asia. The administration tended to be far more preoccupied with security and economic relations than with human rights, especially in South and East Asia, and to emphasize religious freedom over other concerns. Human Rights Watch also met regularly with corporations in the U.S. and Japan, to explore ways in which corporate leverage might be used to address concerns in Indonesia and China. Advocacy work on China was particularly challenging, given the decline in effectiveness of the U.N. Commission on Human Rights in Geneva as a vehicle for raising concerns about the country's human rights practices, and as Beijing's "dialogue" strategy deflected pressure from the E.U., Canada, Australia, and other key countries. Research on China focused on the arrest and detention of Falungong supporters and on repression in Tibet and Xinjiang.

AFGHANISTAN

Events in Afghanistan were changing daily as this report went to press. Before the September 11 terror attacks on the United States (U.S.), the main human rights concerns in Afghanistan were collective punishment by Taliban forces of civilians in areas that the opposition Northern Alliance (United Front) had briefly occupied or attempted to capture; systematic discrimination against women; harassment of international aid agency staff and other abuses; and continued arms supplies to parties responsible for human rights violations. After September 11, concerns focused on violations of the laws of war, including summary executions of prisoners by the Northern Alliance and use of cluster bombs by the U.S.; protection of millions of refugees and internally displaced; ensuring accountability for human rights violations; and instituting human rights safeguards for the future, including to protect women's rights.

Beginning on October 7 Taliban-held territory in Afghanistan became the focus of a U.S.-led military campaign to destroy the al-Qaeda network of Osama bin Laden, whom the U.S. accused of planning the September 11 attacks, and remove from power the core Taliban leadership that had sheltered bin Laden since 1997.

By late November, the Northern Alliance (United Front), backed by a U.S.

bombing campaign, had recaptured virtually all of northern Afghanistan, and Taliban rule was rapidly collapsing in the south. The demise of the Taliban brought with it the immediate prospect of greater personal freedoms and opportunities for women. It also portended a return to the political fragmentation that marked the country before the Taliban's rise, and the reemergence of many of the same warlords whose fighting and disregard for international humanitarian law devastated Kabul between 1992 and 1996. Against this backdrop, the United Nations was seeking to broker negotiations among different Afghan factions for the creation of a viable transitional government.

The U.S. airstrikes against Taliban military targets entailed an undetermined number of civilian casualties, at least some of which resulted from mistargeting. The airstrikes also contributed to the humanitarian crisis, with thousands of Afghans fleeing their homes. Their flight swelled the ranks of hundreds of thousands who were already internally displaced because of drought, war, and conflict-related violence.

HUMAN RIGHTS DEVELOPMENTS

Systematic human rights abuses were committed by both Taliban and anti-Taliban forces. By late October, questions had also arisen as to whether any of the civilian casualties caused by the U.S. bombing campaign were possible violations of international humanitarian law, although there were no clear answers at the time this report went to press.

Reprisal Killings by the Taliban

In several areas of northern and central Afghanistan, Taliban forces subjected local civilians to a ruthless and systematic policy of collective punishment. Summary executions, the deliberate destruction of homes, and confiscation of farmland were recurrent practices in these campaigns. The Taliban's victims overwhelmingly belonged to ethnic minority groups predominating in those areas, including Aymaqs, Hazaras, and Uzbeks. The groups were suspected of supporting forces linked to the Northern Alliance in the Afghan civil war.

After retaking Yakaolang district in the central highland region of Hazarajat from Hizb-i Wahdat and Harakat-i Islami, two Shi'a Muslim parties in the Northern Alliance, on January 8, Taliban troops detained and then massacred at least 170 male residents of the town, all of them noncombatants. The men were herded to assembly points in the center of the district and several outlying areas, and then shot by firing squad in public view. The two Shi'a parties regained control of Yakaolang at the end of January, permitting human rights investigators to independently document the killings that had taken place. The Taliban retook the district in early May and carried out isolated killings of civilians; most of Yakaolang's civilian population, however, fled in advance to the surrounding hills.

On June 5, Hizb-i Wahdat recaptured Yakaolang but it fell again to the Taliban on June 10. Mullah Dadaullah, a Kabul-based Taliban commander implicated in previous abuses against civilians, was in charge of what the Taliban's official news agency termed a "mopping up operation." Over a two-day period, his troops burned over 4,000 houses, shops, and public buildings in central and eastern Yakaolang, including a medical clinic, twelve mosques and prayer halls, and the main *madrassa*, or Islamic seminary. As the Taliban troops retreated, they continued to burn villages and to detain and kill civilians. Some civilians were killed while trying to escape, and a number of detainees were held for a period of forced labor.

A number of villages around the town of Khwajaghar in Takhar province also changed hands several times. Taliban forces occupied the area from January 13 to 23. After Northern Alliance forces had taken control of the area, they discovered mass graves of civilians who had apparently been shot with their hands bound. Human rights investigators reported that at least thirty-four ethnic Uzbek civilians had been summarily executed and that forty-five others had been detained and were unaccounted for.

To the north of Bamiyan, in Zari district, Balkh province, similar reprisals were carried out by Taliban forces against ethnic Uzbek civilians in late May 2001. While most civilians fled to the hills, many of those who remained or who returned were reported to have been killed by Taliban forces reoccupying the district. There were also credible reports from Ghowr of summary executions, looting, and the large-scale burning of villages by Taliban forces between late June and mid-October.

Discrimination Against Women

Taliban decrees continued to restrict women's movement, behavior, and dress. In public, women were required under threat of severe punishment to wear the *chadari*, an all-enveloping garment, and to be accompanied by a close male relative at all times. Violations of the dress code, in particular, could result in public beatings and lashing by the Religious Police, who wielded leather batons reinforced with metal studs. Women were not permitted to work outside the home except in the area of health care, and girls over eight years old were not permitted to attend school. The decrees contributed to an illiteracy level for women of over 90 percent, while the restrictions on mobility meant that women did not enjoy satisfactory access to health care.

International relief agencies grappled with more rigorous enforcement of Taliban prohibitions on women working outside the home as well as heightened surveillance of the personal conduct of their employees. In May, an impasse between the Taliban and the U.N.'s World Food Program (WFP) over employing Afghan women to conduct household surveys threatened to close down bakeries feeding 300,000 vulnerable households in Kabul. On several occasions during the same month, police from the Ministry for the Prevention of Vice and Promotion of Virtue raided hospitals, beating several staff members and forcing the facilities to suspend surgical operations because male and female staff allegedly mixed in the dining area and operating wards. The Taliban also prohibited all female aid workers from driving cars.

As the Northern Alliance established control over areas once under the Taliban, Afghan women became able to move about freely in public. In Kabul, women were able to register to return to medical school for the first time in five years. At the same time, however, the Northern Alliance's interior minister, Younis Qanooni, citing security concerns, ordered the cancellation of a planned women's freedom march through the streets of Kabul. (See Women's Human Rights.)

Other Taliban Violations

The Taliban's increasingly confrontational posture toward the international community included moves that appeared calculated to provoke an international outcry. These included attacks on the country's architectural heritage as well as the proposal of laws discriminating against religious minorities.

On March 11, Taliban forces in Bamiyan destroyed two enormous statues of the Buddha, thirty-eight to fifty-three meters high, that had been carved into sandstone cliffs overlooking the city in the second and fifth centuries, A.D. A BBC report on the destruction, which included an interview with a prominent Afghan living outside the country, led to the expulsion of the BBC reporter from Taliban-controlled Afghanistan in April.

In May, the Kabul-based Council of the Ulema promulgated a new order requiring Afghan Hindus to wear distinctive clothing. Taliban representatives stated that the measure was intended to protect Hindus from being stopped by the religious police, although most local Hindus who interacted with the authorities already carried documentation attesting to their religious identity. The order met with widespread international condemnation, and subsequently appeared to have been withdrawn.

Also in May, the Taliban imposed new restrictions on foreign workers, placing them under the jurisdiction of the religious police of the Ministry for the Prevention of Vice and Promotion of Virtue, and requiring that they sign a letter undertaking not to violate prohibitions on adultery, consuming pork and alcohol, and proselytizing. Those found in violation could be imprisoned or deported. Twenty-four staff members of the German relief agency Shelter Now, including eight foreigners, were arrested by the Taliban on August 6, on charges of proselytising. They were brought to trial in September. The foreign detainees were freed on November 15, when Northern Alliance forces took control of Ghazni, where they were then being held.

Security conditions for humanitarian aid agencies worsened sharply after September 11. On October 16, Taliban soldiers seized WFP food warehouses in Kabul and Kandahar, taking control of some 7,000 tons of food. Human Rights Watch also received credible reports of other incidents involving looting of vehicles and office equipment, as well as assaults on aid agency staff, from the Taliban-controlled cities of Kandahar, Kabul, Jalalabad, and Mazar-i-Sharif. While most of those responsible for the attacks appeared to be Taliban fighters, non-Afghan fighters (known in Afghanistan as "foreign guests") and rogue armed elements also appeared to have been involved.

On October 26, Taliban forces captured and executed Abdul Haq, a veteran commander from eastern Afghanistan who had returned to build opposition to the Taliban among local ethnic Pashtun commanders. Also executed were his nephew,

Izzatullah and another companion, Commander Haji Dauran. The fate of eight others who were arrested by the Taliban following a confrontation between Abdul Haq and the Taliban was unknown.

Violations by Anti-Taliban Forces

There were several reported rights abuses by Northern Alliance forces in the wake of the Taliban retreat from Mazar-i-Sharif, Herat, Kunduz, and Kabul in November 2001. Scattered reports from aid agencies, refugees, and news correspondents indicated that Northern Alliance forces in newly captured areas summarily executed a significant number of Taliban troops who had surrendered or were captured, and engaged in looting of humanitarian aid compounds and commercial stores. In Mazar-i-Sharif, in early November, the siege of a school compound in which several hundred Pakistani Taliban fighters had taken refuge ended with the entire school being repeatedly shelled, killing the entire force inside. There were conflicting reports about whether some of the Pakistani Taliban forces attempted to surrender before the compound was shelled. In addition, there were outstanding questions about the events surrounding a prison riot in Mazar-i-Sharif which began on November 25. All of the prisoners, at least 120 and perhaps twice that many, were reportedly killed in the suppression of the riot, which entailed the use of Northern Alliance artillery and tank fire, and bombardment of parts of the prison by U.S. air support. In southern Afghanistan, a Northern Alliance commander claimed to have executed 160 captured Taliban fighters, according to a November 28 Reuters report.

United States Bombing Campaign

The US-led military campaign in Afghanistan began on October 7. In two separate incidents investigated by Human Rights Watch researchers, civilians were killed by bombs that had either been mistargeted or went astray. On October 21, at least twenty-three civilians, the majority of them young children, were killed when U.S. bombs hit a remote Afghan village located near a Taliban military base in Thori, Urozgan province. The following day, at least twenty-five, and possibly as many as thirty-five, Afghan civilians were killed when U.S. airplanes first bombed and then strafed the village of Chowkar-Karez, near Kandahar.

On October 22, nine people died in the village of Shakar Qala near Herat after U.S. warplanes dropped cluster munitions in the area. Eight died instantly and a ninth was killed after picking up one of the bombs, according to a U.N. demining team which visited the village after the attack. Human Rights Watch called for a global moratorium on use of cluster bombs, which have a wide dispersal pattern and cannot be targeted precisely, urging the U.S. to desist from using them in Afghanistan. Cluster bombs also have a high initial failure rate, resulting in numerous explosive "duds" that pose the same post-conflict problem as antipersonnel landmines.

Other bombing raids hit facilities belonging to U.N. agencies and the International Committee of the Red Cross (ICRC). On October 9, U.S. bombs hit an office of a U.N.-backed demining agency in Kabul, killing four security guards. On October 16, U.S. bombs also struck the ICRC warehouses in Kabul, destroying supplies and injuring at least one worker. The ICRC said that it had provided the U.S. the locations of its facilities in Afghanistan before the bombing campaign began. Despite further consultations between the ICRC and U.S., the same compound was struck again by U.S. forces on October 26. According to the ICRC, food and non-food items meant for 55,000 people in Kabul were destroyed in the second attack.

Internal Displacement

Hundreds of thousands of Afghans were displaced during the year from their homes within Afghanistan, adding to the ranks of the millions displaced in previous years. Before September 11, the leading causes of displacement were food and water shortages, localized persecution by Taliban or Northern Alliance authorities, security concerns stemming from fighting between the Taliban and the Northern Alliance, and systematic destruction of homes and farmland by Taliban forces.

Most displaced families moved toward urban areas, especially Herat, Mazar-i-Sharif, Kunduz, and Kabul in Taliban-held areas, and Faizabad in the Northern Alliance held areas. In many parts of the north and west, displaced persons ultimately settled in unorganized and unsanitary camps without adequate shelter. Scores of these spontaneous camps sprung up outside Mazar-i-Sharif, Kunduz, and Pul-e-Khumri. Most of the displaced were forced to beg food and even water from other Afghan families, many of whom were themselves struggling to survive. Several independent reports from the north indicated that some families resorted to marrying off their daughters at young ages (between six and twelve years) for reduced dowries, essentially selling their children to survive. Other reports indicated that Taliban soldiers occasionally abducted young women from camps for the displaced. (See Refugees, Asylum Seekers, Migrants, and Internally Displaced Persons.)

DEFENDING HUMAN RIGHTS

A number of Afghan human rights groups operated from Pakistan and issued reports on rights violations inside Afghanistan and against Afghan refugees in Pakistan. In October a new group, Citizen's Against War Criminals, which included relatives and survivors of various civilian massacres, formed and issued statements calling for a war crimes tribunal for Afghanistan.

THE ROLE OF THE INTERNATIONAL COMMUNITY

United Nations

The U.N.'s peacemaking efforts—which had previously been thwarted by Taliban opposition to power-sharing—were revitalized after the rapid collapse of Taliban rule throughout most of Afghanistan in November 2001. The U.N. secretary-general's special representative to Afghanistan, Lakhdar Brahimi, who was appointed in October to oversee the U.N.'s political and humanitarian work in the country, convened a meeting in Bonn, Germany on November 27 of the Northern Alliance and three Afghan exile political groupings. As this report went to press, the meeting had made progress on a formula to establish an interim ruling council, to be followed by the convening of a *loya jirga* or Grand National Assembly that would elect a transitional government. The Northern Alliance, however, had rejected proposals to deploy an international peacekeeping force in Afghanistan.

The Taliban's collapse also enabled officers from the Civil Affairs Unit of the U.N. Special Mission to Afghanistan (UNSMA) to resume work in some areas of the country. Following the Security Council-mandated closure of the Taliban's diplomatic offices abroad, in February the Taliban ordered the UNSMA to close its offices in territory under its control. After negotiations with the Taliban, UNSMA closed most of its offices in May, thereby curtailing much of the monitoring capacity of its Civil Affairs Unit.

A sanctions monitoring team was appointed on September 18, pursuant to U.N. Security Council Resolution 1333 in December 2000 which imposed an arms embargo on the Taliban, banned travel outside Afghanistan by Taliban officials of deputy ministerial rank, and ordered the closing of Taliban offices abroad. An earlier resolution had imposed an international flight ban on the Afghan airline Ariana and frozen overseas assets of the Taliban. After September 11, the Security Council issued resolutions calling on states to cooperate in preventing and suppressing terrorism (resolution 1373); supporting the establishment of a transitional administration that would lead in turn to the formation of a "broad-based, multi-ethnic and fully representative" Afghan government (resolution 1378). Resolution 1378 also said that the transitional administration should respect the human rights of all Afghans and called on all Afghan armed forces to refrain from reprisals.

Various U.N. human rights mechanisms directed greater attention toward civilian massacres in Afghanistan and the flow of arms to the warring parties. Early in 2001, the U.N. Commission on Human Rights, in resolution 2000/13, noted reports about the January 2001 mass killings of ethnic Hazaras in Yakaolang and urged an immediate end to the supply of arms and other military support, including providing foreign military personnel, to all parties to the conflict. The Commission's special rapporteur on Afghanistan, Kamal Hossain, included in his sixth report extensive details of both the January 2001 massacre and the Taliban's subsequent destruction of villages in Yakaolang and western Bamiyan in June 2001. He also recommended a comprehensive arms embargo on Afghanistan.

In November, U.N. High Commissioner for Human Rights Mary Robinson seconded a full-time human rights officer to a task force in New York that was meant to facilitate a coordinated U.N. response to the crisis in Afghanistan. The United Nations High Commissioner for Refugees (UNHCR) was also actively engaged with the Afghanistan crisis. (See Refugees, Asylum Seekers, Migrants, and Internally Displaced Persons.)

Military Assistance

At a meeting in Tehran on December 28, 2000, Russia and Iran agreed to launch a new long-term program of political and military co-operation, including closer ties over Central Asia and in Afghanistan, where both sides had supplied arms and other assistance to factions opposing the Taliban. Such supplies increased after September 11. Beginning in October, the U.S. also began to supply Northern Alliance factions with food, ammunition, and air support.

The Taliban's principal supporter, Pakistan, continued to provide military support throughout the first half of the year. In direct violation of U.N. sanctions, in April and May 2001 as many as thirty trucks a day were crossing the Pakistan border, Human Rights Watch sources reported; sources inside Afghanistan reported that some of these convoys were carrying artillery shells, tank rounds, and rocket-propelled grenades. Shipments of fuel and other military supplies reportedly continued through September. (See Arms.) After joining the U.S.-led anti-terrorism coalition in early October, President Pervez Musharraf reshuffled Pakistan's army corps command, marginalizing several officers with close ties to the Taliban.

Donor Countries

The increasingly bitter confrontation between humanitarian organizations and the Taliban led many donors to exert pressure on the Taliban to ease its restrictions. At a meeting in Islamabad in June, the Afghanistan Support Group (ASG), a joint funding group made up of various donor governments and U.N. agencies, issued a statement urging the Taliban to co-operate with aid agencies working in the country or risk having vital humanitarian projects come to a halt.

International aid to Afghanistan in 2001 before September 11 amounted to approximately U.S. $300 million. These funds were devoted primarily to short-term humanitarian projects and demining programs and to a lesser extent to development programs in agriculture, health, education, and income generation.

Following September 11, several countries have pledged additional emergency funds for humanitarian projects in Afghanistan. Two main funding conferences met to discuss future long-term funding plans for Afghanistan. A joint development conference hosted by the World Bank, the United Nations Development Program, and the Asia Development Bank, geared toward long-term economic development, commenced on November 27. The ASG convened a meeting that was geared toward humanitarian assistance but which also provided a forum for discussing long-term development strategies.

Detailed planning during both meetings was made difficult by uncertainty over the future Afghan government; and questions about how long current military activities in Afghanistan would continue. Nevertheless, participants noted in position papers the need for a comprehensive funding program going beyond the immediate humanitarian needs of the country. Donors at an ASG meeting in August were told by several U.N. and nongovernmental agencies of the need for increased funding in development areas not previously funded in Afghanistan, including programs for rebuilding civil society and civil infrastructure, among them rule of law mechanisms and educational, health, and banking systems.

Relevant Human Rights Watch Reports:

Humanity Denied: Systematic Violations of Women's Rights in Afghanistan, 10/01
The Crisis of Impunity: The Role of Pakistan, Russia, and Iran in Fueling the Civil War, 7/01
Massacres of Hazaras in Afghanistan, 2/01

BURMA

There were signs of a political thaw early in the year and, for the first time in years, hopes that the government might lift some of its stifling controls on civil and political rights. By November, however, the only progress had been limited political prisoner releases and easing of pressures on some opposition politicians in Rangoon. There was no sign of fundamental changes in law or policy, and grave human rights violations remained unaddressed.

HUMAN RIGHTS DEVELOPMENTS

Upon his return from a January visit to Rangoon, new United Nations Special Representative for Myanmar Razali Ismail revealed that Lieutenant General Khin Nyunt, one of the top three leaders of the ruling State Peace and Development Council (SPDC), and Aung San Suu Kyi, the head of the opposition National League for Democracy (NLD), had been engaged in talks about a political settlement since October 2000. The talks, the first since 1994, were largely attributed to the efforts of Ismail, who had worked behind the scenes to promote dialogue. The talks continued throughout much of 2001, though representatives of minority groups were not invited to participate.

In an apparent goodwill gesture connected to the talks, the SPDC periodically released small groups of political prisoners, 182 of whom had been freed by November. They included NLD chairman Aung Shwe and vice-chairman Tin Oo; fifty-four NLD members who had been elected to parliament in the aborted 1990 elections; journalist San San Nweh; and members of a comedy troupe, The Moustache Brothers, who had been held since January 1996 for political satire.

Even with these releases, over 1,000 prisoners remained in prison for their political beliefs, including 1988 student leader Min Ko Naing and NLD political strategist Win Tin. More than fifty had completed their sentences but continued to be detained by the SPDC using article 10a of the penal code, which gives authorities broad discretion to extend incarceration. Four political prisoners—Mya Shwe,

Maung Maung Aye, Sithu, and Khin Maung Myint—died in prison during the year, and the Emergency Provisions Act, the security law most frequently used to charge and imprison political prisoners, remained in use.

The SPDC continued to stringently restrict freedom of association and assembly nationwide, but initiated some limited confidence-building measures in conjunction with the political talks that eased conditions slightly. In June, authorities permitted the NLD to reopen its headquarters and eighteen of forty-two Rangoon ward-level offices; another three ward-level offices were allowed to reopen later in the year. On June 19, some four hundred supporters of Aung San Suu Kyi were permitted to gather to celebrate her birthday and on September 27 around five hundred NLD sympathizers were able to gather to celebrate the anniversary of its founding, though on both occasions NLD Secretary General Aung San Sui Kyi remained confined to her home. Burmese intelligence continued to monitor NLD leaders, however, and to attend many NLD meetings in Rangoon.

Outside Rangoon, there was no relaxation and hundreds of NLD local offices remained closed by the authorities, as were those of other political parties that had secured seats in the 1990 election, such as the Shan Nationalities League for Democracy, the National Democratic Party for Human Rights, and the Mon National Democratic Front, which were effectively unable to function.

The press was largely state run and strictly censored. The government did not renew the license of the Burmese language magazine *Thintbawa* in December 2000 after one of its editors, Tin Maung Than, was accused of copying and circulating a speech by Deputy Minister for National Planning and Development Brigadier General Zaw Tun. The speech was sharply critical of the SPDC's economic policy. Detained on August 13, 2000, Tin Maung Than was held for four days, questioned, and forced to sign a document acknowledging that he would be prosecuted if circulation of the speech turned out to be "a political plot." Fearing that he could be imprisoned, he fled to Thailand in December 2000.

Some 140,000 Burmese displaced by decades of conflict and ongoing political repression continued to live in refugee camps in Bangladesh and Thailand, and hundreds of thousands more lived as internally displaced people within Burma or outside camps in Bangladesh, India, and Thailand.

Life in conflict affected areas, where the Burmese army sought to deny ethnic minority insurgents all sources of support, remained particularly grim. Villagers continued to be forcibly relocated, and those suspected of aiding guerrillas were tortured and sometimes killed. In January, government soldiers extrajudicially executed three ethnic minority Palaung men in Ho Ha village in Shan State after a search for weapons turned up an old carbine rifle that villagers used for hunting. In another case in early 2001, soldiers deployed in Shan State tortured and interrogated one man by setting light to his mustache and burning his mouth and another by holding a flame to his eye.

The army forbade villagers whom they forcibly relocated in Shan, Kayah (Karenni), and Karen State from returning to their fields. Villagers were required to obtain a pass to move between major towns under government control and curfews were enforced in many areas. The army continued to uproot villagers and consolidate them in larger, government-controlled towns, though on a reduced scale compared to the mid-1990s. In January, the army reportedly displaced some 30,000 villagers in Karen State when it burned villages in its dry season offensive against the insurgent Karen National Union. In Shan State, hundreds of people were forced to move during Burmese army attacks on the Shan State Army-South in February and March. Many joined the estimated hundreds of thousands of internally displaced villagers in ethnic minority states while others fled to Thailand.

The SPDC continued to deny full citizenship rights to ethnic and religious minority Rohingya villagers, leaving many of them stateless and subject to severe restrictions on their freedom of movement, right to own land, and access to education. In February, violence between Buddhist and Muslim communities in the Arakan State capital Sittwe reportedly resulted in over a dozen deaths, and led to further regulation of movement by Rohingya and other Muslims within and out of Arakan, impeding their access to markets and health care. In Prome (Pyi), Pegu town, and Hanthada, night curfews were introduced following communal clashes in October.

The authorities continued to use forced labor. On October 27, 2000, following the visit of a technical mission from the International Labour Organization (ILO), the SPDC issued an order banning all government officers from requisitioning labor, and circulated it to local level authorities. Even so, refugees told Human Rights Watch that they had no knowledge of it, indicating that the policy was not being aggressively implemented. At its November 2000 meeting, the ILO's governing body, concluding that the new order was insufficient and that the SPDC had still not taken adequate steps to end forced labor, recommended penalties to force compliance. One called on other governments, United Nations agencies, and corporations to scrutinize their relationships with the SPDC to ensure that none of their activities contributed to the perpetuation of forced labor. In response, several member states submitted reports on this to the ILO in March 2001.

In February 2001, refugees from Shan State arriving in Thailand reported that they were continuing to face demands from the Burmese army to construct roads and military bases, clear and plant fields for local battalions, and porter for troops on patrol. Reports of forced labor were also received from other states and divisions throughout the year. In November, ILO experts submitted a report on their visit a month earlier, concluding that though the government had widely circulated its order banning forced labor, implementation and enforcement remained weak. The ILO governing body in its November meeting recommended an ILO presence in Burma to work with the SPDC to address those weaknesses.

As of mid-November, Human Rights Watch knew of no cases in which the government had prosecuted anyone for violating the ban on forced labor.

DEFENDING HUMAN RIGHTS

The SPDC did not permit local human rights groups to operate in Burma and those human rights and democracy organizations that did function had to do so from abroad.

THE ROLE OF THE INTERNATIONAL COMMUNITY

The talks between Aung San Suu Kyi and the government and release of political prisoners were welcomed by the international community. Some governments moved towards resuming or offering to provide aid to Burma in order to encourage further progress, while others maintained sanctions.

The United Nations was particularly active. Special Representative Razali Ismail visited the country in January, June, and August to facilitate the dialogue between the SPDC and the NLD, and for the first time since 1995, the government permitted a visit by the United Nations special rapporteur on Myanmar. The new rapporteur, Paulo Sergio Pinheiro, made a brief visit in April and met with SPDC representatives, Aung San Suu Kyi, and local aid workers. In a report to the U.N. in August, he welcomed the talks and prisoner releases but pointed to the need to address other important rights issues, including the need for a humanitarian space to relieve villagers affected by conflict. He made a second visit Burma in October and presented his conclusions to the U.N. General Assembly (Third Committee) in early November.

The United Nations High Commissioner for Refugees (UNHCR) maintained a presence in northern Arakan State to protect and reintegrate hundreds of thousands of Rohingya returnees. UNHCR requested access to eastern parts of Burma, but received no reply from the SPDC.

Japan stepped up its policy of engagement with a decision to offer major new aid to Burma. Though officially justified on humanitarian grounds, the move was widely seen as a political gesture to reward the SPDC for the dialogue. In April, Japanese officials promised approximately U.S. $29 million to upgrade Baluchaung no. 2 hydroelectric power plant in Kayah (Karenni state). A survey mission went to Burma in August; by November, the cabinet had not yet approved disbursement of the funds. The aid decision was widely criticized as premature in view of Burmese government failure to end forced labor and other major abuses.

In May, Japan's Federation of Economic Organizations (Keidanren) held two days of discussions with the SPDC on ways to improve trade and investment between the two countries, though most Japanese companies remained reluctant to invest.

Japanese officials publicly praised Burma's release of political prisoners at several points during the year. In July, Foreign Minister Makiko Tanaka, during an Association of Southeast Asian Nations (ASEAN) conference in Vietnam, said Burma "should develop as quickly as possible into a country with which we can cooperate," hinting that more aid might be forthcoming if the dialogue led to substantive progress. In October she said it was important that the SPDC "take steps to allow freedom of activities for political parties beginning with the NLD."

Australia welcomed the release of political prisoners and continued its engagement policy. On May 25, John Howard's government announced that it would renew its Human Rights Initiative, providing training for Burmese officials with the ultimate goal of establishing a national human rights commission. Australia planned to allocate approximately Au $140,000 to hold four training sessions, one of which was to be held in Mandalay. Former Australian human rights commissioner and director of the program, Chris Sidoti, stated that Aung San Suu Kyi had expressed support for the training.

The E.U. held to its basic sanctions policy on Burma, while offering the carrot of humanitarian aid. An E.U. "troika" mission visited Burma in January and described the dialogue between the SPDC and Aung San Sui Kyi as "the most interesting development since 1990." E.U. External Affairs Commissioner Chris Patten told the July ASEAN meeting in Hanoi that the SPDC would have to make more "significant progress" before the E.U. would consider lifting sanctions. In October, when reviewing its common position on Burma, the E.U. symbolically eased its sanctions by agreeing that Burma's foreign minister could attend an E.U.-ASEAN meeting in 2002, and stressed its "readiness to accompany the deepening of the reconciliation process with humanitarian assistance."

Speculation that the Bush administration would lift sanctions on Burma had not proved correct by November 2001. The U.S. welcomed the talks but renewed regulations that ban travel to the U.S. by top Burmese officials, prohibited new U.S. investment in Burma, and continued to block lending to Burma by the World Bank and other international financial institutions.

In December 2000, the U.S. Defense Department ordered an immediate halt to the import of clothing made in Burma after a news report disclosed that in October 2000 alone nearly $140,000 of apparel was purchased from Burma for sale to U.S. military personnel, dependents, and U.S. government employees overseas. In May 2001, a bill was introduced in the U.S. Senate to ban private retailers from importing apparel from Burma, but the legislation was never voted on.

In February, Deputy Assistant Secretary of State Ralph Boyce visited Burma and met with Aung San Suu Kyi and Lt. Gen. Khin Nyunt to discuss the Razali-initiated dialogue, which he called a "welcome development." Secretary of State Colin Powell met with Razali in September and expressed his support for Razali's mission, while emphasizing the need for results.

Various ASEAN members expressed support for the talks between the SPDC and Aung San Suu Kyi. Malaysia deepened its political and economic. Prime Minister Mahathir Mohammed visited Burma in January and Malaysian economic delegations followed, while Senior General Than Shwe and Lt. Gen. Khin Nyunt paid a return visit to Malaysia in September to discuss bilateral trade and other issues.

The new Thai government of Thaksin Shinawatra also sought to improve relations. However Thai efforts to do this suffered a six-month setback when the Thai and Burmese armies engaged in skirmishes in February and March after a Burmese military unit entered Thai territory. The Thai government also blamed Burma for one of its main national security concerns, the flood of methamphetamines entering Thailand, an illegal trade involving both the Burmese military and its aligned militia, the United Wa State Army, allegedly the top narcotics producer in Burma's portion of the Golden Triangle. The armed confrontation led to high level official exchanges, including a visit to Burma in June by Prime Minister Thaksin, and in early September, a trip to Bangkok by Lt. Gen. Khin Nyunt. By October, relations had apparently improved, with talks shifting to trade and improving communication links between the two countries.

CAMBODIA

ambodia's human rights record during 2001 included progress on some
issues as well as several disappointing setbacks. By mid-November, Cambodia was close to becoming the first Southeast Asian country to ratify the Rome
Statute of the International Criminal Court (ICC), but the government continued
its efforts to dilute the power of a tribunal to bring the Khmer Rouge to justice.
While advocacy organizations benefited from relaxed policies on freedom of association, political violence increased. The government risked angering its long-time
ally Vietnam by affording temporary asylum to ethnic minority asylum seekers
from Vietnam, thereby meeting its obligations as a signatory to the 1951 Refugee
Convention. At the same time, provincial Cambodian officials periodically
deported dozens of asylum seekers back to Vietnam, violating the fundamental
principle of *non-refoulement.* Prison conditions remained poor and torture continued to be used by police and prison officials with impunity. Social and environmental rights increasingly emerged as an issue. Hundreds of villagers organized to
protect community fisheries, forests, and other natural resources from abusive
exploitation by government agencies or officially sanctioned companies.

HUMAN RIGHTS DEVELOPMENTS

Political violence increased and preparations began for long overdue local elections, scheduled for February 2002 in Cambodia's 1,600 communes, or subdistricts.
In the elections, existing commune chiefs, mostly appointed by the ruling Cambodian People's Party (CPP), were to be replaced with popularly elected commune
councils. In September, the Cambodian Human Rights Action Committee, a coalition of eighteen nongovernmental organizations (NGOs), documented eighty-two
cases of political threats and violence since the beginning of the year, most of them
directed at the opposition Sam Rainsy Party (SRP).

By November, at least four likely commune candidates had been shot dead and
two others wounded. SRP commune candidate Uch Horn was killed on June 30 in
Kompong Speu. He had previously complained to two local human rights organizations and the U.N. that he had received death threats. On July 1, Soeung Sem, a
commune candidate for the royalist Funcinpec Party, survived a shooting in Pur-
sat, but Funcinpec candidate Meas Soy was shot and killed on July 17 in Kompong
Chhnang. SRP activist Toch Savoeun was shot and killed on August 23 by two
unidentified gunmen at his home in Siem Reap. On November 5, SRP candidate
Sam Sophear was beaten to death by five unknown assailants in Battambang. While
Cambodian human rights groups and the Cambodia Office of the U.N. High Commissioner for Human Rights (COHCHR) determined that at least three of the
killings were politically motivated, local officials attributed the murders to personal
disputes.

In August, after a barrage of criticism from donor countries, human rights groups and the U.N., the government established a Central Security Office comprising representatives from the interior and defense ministries, national police, military, and the National Election Commission (NEC), to address electoral violence. By mid-November, the office was still inactive.

There were reports of vote buying as early as August. The Committee for Free and Fair Elections (Comfrel), a Cambodian NGO, reported that CPP activists in Takeo and Banteay Meanchey provinces were promising gifts to voters in exchange for pledges of loyalty to the CPP. In September, Comfrel reported widespread confiscation of voter registration cards by CPP officials and accused the CPP of pressuring people in many provinces to sign documents pledging to vote for the CPP.

Local authorities and in some cases uniformed police officers carried out voter opinion surveys on behalf of the CPP, distributing forms with lists of names and photographs of possible candidates. Election monitoring NGOs charged that this was in violation of the Commune Election Law, which calls for government institutions to be politically neutral.

Moves Toward a Khmer Rouge Tribunal

Progress toward establishing a tribunal to bring former members of the Khmer Rouge to justice was slow. In July 2000, the government had agreed on legislation with the U.N. that would establish a "mixed tribunal" presided over by both Cambodian and international judges and co-prosecutors. However, the legislation sent to the Cambodian National Assembly in January 2001 differed markedly from what had been agreed on, most notably deleting the provision that prior amnesties would not be a bar to prosecution. This had been designed to ensure that key people, such as former Khmer Rouge Foreign Minister Ieng Sary, granted a royal pardon in 1996, could still be brought to justice.

The U.N.'s Office of Legal Affairs sent a strongly worded letter to the Cambodian government in January, calling for clarifications or changes to seventeen of the forty-eight articles in the draft law. In June, U.N. Secretary-General Kofi Annan stressed that the Cambodian law should accord with the previous agreements, but Prime Minister Hun Sen's response was that Cambodia would conduct its own tribunal if the U.N. refused to participate.

In August, the National Assembly passed the tribunal legislation as proposed by the government. By October, the U.N. had still to agree and sign a Memorandum of Understanding with the Cambodian government, one of the final steps toward actually establishing the court. It was clear, however, that former members of the Khmer Rouge were becoming apprehensive. In August, the Democratic National Union Movement (DNUM), a group loyal to Ieng Sary, urged the government not to prosecute their leader, and former Khmer Rouge leader Khieu Samphan issued a seven-page public letter in which he offered an unusual apology to the Cambodian people.

Cambodia's judicial system remained weak and far from independent, with numerous court decisions influenced by corruption or apparent political influence. The high-profile trials in June and October of sixty alleged members of the Cambodian Freedom Fighters (CFF) fell short of international standards for fairness. Most of the defendants were arrested without warrants and had little or no access to their lawyers while in pre-trial detention, which exceeded the legal limit of six months. After the first day of the trial of the first thirty-two defendants in June, most of the lawyers for the accused boycotted the proceedings, citing breaches of proper procedures. Five lawyers subsequently received anonymous threats of violence against them if they did not return to the courtroom. The judge appointed two new lawyers to act for all of the accused, and refused to delay the hearing, leaving these lawyers with no opportunity to meet their clients or prepare an adequate defense. On June 22, all but two of the first group of accused were convicted of terrorism and membership in an illegal armed group, and given sentences ranging from three years to life in prison. Another twenty-six defendants were convicted in the October trial.

In September 2001, more than fifty additional CFF suspects were arrested in the provinces and Phnom Penh. Human rights groups expressed concern that the government's response to the CFF's November 2000 attack in Phnom Penh could be used as a pretext to intimidate opposition party members, particularly as the commune election campaign began to get underway.

Two political killings resulted in trials. On March 15, the Kampot provincial court found commune chief Im Nan, a CPP member, and three accomplices guilty of the murder of Funcinpec commune candidate Pak Choeun in June 2000. On October 12, a former soldier, Sang Rin, and another accused were convicted of the murder of SRP member Uch Horn at a trial in the Kompong Speu provincial court. In both cases rights groups held that the murders were politically motivated; the courts, however, attributed both murders to retaliation for the victims' alleged use of "black magic."

Refugee Influx

Beginning in March, a slow but steady stream of refugees from Vietnam entered Cambodia's eastern Mondolkiri and Ratanakiri provinces. They were indigenous minority people from Vietnam's Central Highlands, known collectively as Montagnards, who were displaced by a Vietnamese government crackdown in February. (See Vietnam.) On March 23, Cambodian police arrested twenty-four Montagnards in Mondolkiri and took them to the municipal Gendarmerie headquarters in Phnom Penh, where they detained them for several weeks. Prime Minister Hun Sen initially threatened to deport the group, saying he did not want Cambodia to become a haven for other countries' political opponents. After considerable international pressure, Cambodia agreed to allow United Nations High Commissioner for Refugees (UNHCR) representatives to interview the Montagnards on March 31, and by April, thirty-eight Montagnards were resettled in the United States.

In the following months, more than 1,000 Montagnards crossed the border to Cambodia. Provincial officials forcibly returned several hundred back to Vietnam and in May attempted to arrest and deport several refugees under UNHCR protection. After negotiations between UNHCR and the government, and pressure from several foreign embassies, Cambodia agreed to provide temporary asylum to Montagnards fleeing Vietnam at two sites operated by UNHCR. As of October, the number of Montagnards asylum seekers in Cambodia had swelled to more than seven hundred.

Unlike in neighboring Laos and Vietnam, recent years have seen the development of a thriving civil society in Cambodia and the emergence of hundreds of local NGOs. The government generally does not obstruct public meetings. In June, however, the Council of Ministers banned a public forum on the country's border disputes, organized by the Students Movement for Democracy, on grounds that it could confuse the public by raising disagreements with the government's National Committee on Border Disputes.

For the most part, rallies and demonstrations were allowed, although demonstrators were sometimes dispersed by police or by counter-demonstrators organized by the government. As in previous years, hundreds of farmers from the countryside periodically gathered in front of the National Assembly to demand resolution of land or fishing conflicts or appeal for flood and food relief. In February, scuffles broke out in Siem Reap at the SRP's annual congress, when counter-demonstrators were trucked in to disrupt the proceedings. Police used water cannons to disperse a Buddhist ceremony organized to mark the end of the SRP's congress, reportedly because the SRP lacked proper authorization to hold the ceremony.

In May, more than seven hundred market vendors in Siem Reap demonstrated against a provincial decision to evict them from the provincial market and construct a new market where vendors would be charged higher rents. Cambodian human rights groups urged the provincial authorities to organize a public forum to resolve the dispute. Instead, on July 9, police and soldiers surrounded the market, firing in the air and forcibly removed the vendors, at least fourteen of whom were beaten, handcuffed and temporarily detained by provincial military police. Several SRP parliamentarians observing the process were also assaulted. In August, Hun Sen supported a proposal for negotiations to resume between the vendors and representatives of the market developers.

Cambodian television stations were still owned fully or partly by the government, which continued to deny a broadcast license to the opposition SRP on the grounds that no frequencies were available. In February, Sam Rainsy announced plans to start broadcasting a one-hour radio program from an un-named Asian country. Only one independent radio station, Sambok Kmum (Beehive), broadcast during the year. The NEC's media monitoring subcommittee primarily focused on the political content of voter education materials produced by election NGOs, rather than the denial of access to the airwaves by opposition parties during the election campaign. NGO leaders were occasionally featured on radio and television programs to discuss social issues.

More than two dozen privately owned newspapers were published, including some affiliated with opposition groups. Foreign Minister Hor Nam Hong sued three journalists from the English-language *Cambodia Daily* for defamation after they published an article in January that examined his alleged role in the Khmer Rouge regime. In September, the Phnom Penh municipal court ordered the journalists to pay U.S. $6,500 in compensation to Hor Nam Hong and a $1,280 fine to the government. Both sides appealed the decision. In August, the Ministry of Information banned a Khmer-language book written by Sam Rainsy entitled "Light of Justice," saying that it made false allegations about the government. In response, Rainsy filed a complaint against the banning in the Phnom Penh municipal court in September.

The Ministry of Information revived a media subdecree, in the works since 1996. It included provisions for the licensing of newspapers and defined vague terms used in the 1994 Press Law, including national security and political stability. As a result of pressure from journalist associations and human rights groups, several provisions were dropped from the original draft subdecree, including requirements that publishers certify that they have 2.5 million riel (about U.S. $640) in the bank and health certificates showing they have no mental problems.

Freedom of expression came under threat in September, when the Ministry of Cults and Religion issued a decision forbidding political discussions in the country's mosques following the September 11 attacks in the United States as well as a controversial leadership split in a mosque near Phnom Penh. In October, Hun Sen reversed the ministry's decision.

Prison conditions continued to be poor, with many facilities seriously overcrowded and lacking adequate medical care, food, and water. At least six prisoners died within a two-month period in Prey Sar prison in Phnom Penh because of insufficient food and medication, according to a report by a Cambodian human rights organization. The use of shackles was reported in prisons in Kompong Som and Kompong Cham. Pre-trial detention beyond the legal limit of six months was common.

Torture continued to be used with impunity, particularly by police officers attempting to extract confessions from suspects in custody. Police also failed to intervene to stop violence against women either in the home, where domestic abuse was considered a family matter, or in the sex industry, which is often supported and protected by members of the military, police or other government officials.

Cambodian human rights organizations increasingly gave attention to social and environmental rights. Villagers filed complaints protesting the confiscation by military officers and local officials of natural resources that rural communities depend on for their livelihoods - such as bamboo, tree resin, and rattan. They also protested the government's granting of concessions to exploit such resources. Environmental and human rights advocates worked to draft a Community Forest Subdecree that would protect community user rights to forests that villagers rely upon for collection of forest products. In April, the Department of Forestry issued an instruction calling for the temporary suspension, in all forest concessions, of cutting of all trees from which people collect resin.

Positive steps were taken during the year to protect community fisheries, on which a huge percentage of Cambodians depend. In late 2000 Hun Sen announced that fishing lots would be taken away from large concessionaires and returned to local people. He subsequently dismissed the director of the Department of Fisheries for not implementing the decision. The department involved local communities in developing legislation to protect community fisheries, setting a positive precedent for local participation in natural resource management. Despite these efforts, poor implementation of policies at the local level, reflected in the confiscation of community fishing lots by fishery department officials, continued to pose a problem in some areas.

Land conflicts also remained a major issue throughout the country. Legal Aid of Cambodia (LAC), a local NGO, reported that its land-related caseload involved 7,000 families, or 35,000 people, with the vast majority of the conflicts involving military commanders or provincial and local officials. In one high-profile case, indigenous minority villagers in Ratanakiri province filed a lawsuit seeking to protect their rights to 1,250 hectares of village land that they said had been fraudulently obtained by a representative of a military general. Villagers were given bags of salt and promises of development in return for their thumbprints on documents that—without their knowledge—transferred ownership of their ancestral lands to the general. In a decision in March, the Ratanakiri provincial court ruled against the villagers' civil complaint. With the help of LAC the villagers then took the case to the Appeals Court in Phnom Penh, but it had not been heard by November. In July, the National Assembly passed a new land law, drafted with the input of NGOs and local communities, designed to stem the widespread practice of land grabbing.

DEFENDING HUMAN RIGHTS

Several dozen Cambodian human rights organizations were active throughout the country investigating violations, monitoring prison conditions, observing trials, and conducting human rights education. In addition, three large NGOs specializing in election observation monitored voter registration and the commune election process. Overall, the atmosphere for NGOs was less threatening than in previous years. Several times during the year, however, public officials issued strongly worded warnings to NGOs. In the months following the November 2000 CFF attack in Phnom Penh, human rights groups and their leaders came under strong criticism from officials when the groups called for due process to be followed in the arrests and trial of alleged CFF members. In several speeches Prime Minister Hun Sen charged that NGOs were hiding terrorists "under their logos" and threatened them with arrest.

Global Witness, which has served as an independent monitor within the government's Forest Crime Monitoring and Reporting project since 1999, came under fire in January when it released a report critical of illegal logging and resource rights abuses just prior to an international donor meeting. Government officials said Global Witness should have given them the opportunity to review and comment on the report before it was publicized. Prime Minister Hun Sen threatened to expel the group from Cambodia but relented after pressure from donors. In June, Global Witness signed an agreement with the government on new reporting procedures shortly before the annual donor meeting.

In July, Hun Sen criticized the Human Rights Action Committee for its statements deploring the rise in political violence. He said the burden of proof was on the NGOs to show that the killings of commune candidates were politically motivated.

In October, the acting director of the Cambodian League for the Promotion and

Defense of Human Rights (Licadho), a local human rights group, faced criminal charges when a court accepted a complaint by the adoptive parents of a seven-year-old girl whom Licadho was housing. Licadho previously had sought child abuse charges against the adoptive parents and had been granted temporarily lawful custody of the child. Cambodian and international rights groups expressed concern that the initiation of criminal proceedings appeared to be without foundation and aimed at intimidating Licadho. As of November, the case had not yet been heard.

THE ROLE OF THE INTERNATIONAL COMMUNITY

The Cambodia Office of the High Commissioner for Human Rights (COHCHR) maintained a field operation in Phnom Penh and several provinces. The U.N. Secretary General's Special Representative for Human Rights in Cambodia, Peter Leuprecht, made several visits to Cambodia during the year, and called for increased foreign aid while urging the government to address broad issues of poverty, violence, corruption, and lawlessness. During Leuprecht's June trip, he expressed reservations about the Khmer Rouge tribunal bill that had been passed by the National Assembly. In August he condemned mounting political violence against commune candidates and urged the government to cease its involvement in election-related opinion surveys. He constantly pressed the government to formalize its memorandum of understanding with COHCHR so as to extend its mandate, last renewed in March 2000, and to address the security concerns of COHCHR's Cambodian staff.

Relations between the government and the UNHCR were strained at times, particularly over the issue of refoulement of Montagnard asylum seekers to Vietnam.

Major Donors

Donors pledged U.S. $560 million at the World Bank chaired Consultative Group meeting, hosted by Japan in June. Most donors praised the Cambodian government's efforts to improve political stability and the economy, although some raised human rights concerns as well. A study on key governance issues prepared for the Asian Development Bank, released in May, criticized corruption, lack of government transparency and weaknesses in the judiciary, and called for concrete reforms as a precondition for assistance. In August, the World Bank approved a U.S. $18.4 million loan to demobilize 30,000 soldiers and reintegrate them to civilian life.

China increasingly became a key player in Cambodia. In May, visiting Chinese Prime Minister Li Peng told Hun Sen that China would consider aid requests totaling U.S. $60 million to assist road construction and demobilization.

Several donors, including Japan, Australia, and the European Union (E.U.), were expected to help meet the costs of the commune elections. In July, an E.U. delegation called for an intimidation-free environment before and during the election. In a meeting with Deputy Prime Minister Sarkheng in September, the U.S., U.K.,

Canadian, Swedish and other ambassadors expressed concern over the low rate of voter registration and pressed for extension of the registration period. On September 6, the European Parliament passed a resolution deploring political violence and calling for E.U. observers to monitor the commune elections.

A number of donor countries expressed interest in funding the Khmer Rouge Tribunal or nominating judges to participate in the proceedings once a final agreement is reached. Japan was expected to contribute an estimated U.S. $60 million. Judges from Australia, France, India, Japan, Russia, the United Kingdom and the United States were considered candidates to preside over the trials, along with Cambodia judges. China, which was one of the Khmer rouge's main financial backers, was not expected to participate.

The U.S. took a strong stand on the Montagnard refugee issue, swiftly resettling thirty-eight Montagnards in the U.S. in April and consistently pressing for protection of asylum seekers by both UNHCR and Cambodian authorities. In August, the Ministry of Foreign Affairs issued a strongly worded response after the U.S. ambassador criticized government corruption at a public forum, charging that "inflammatory words inciting revolt against the royal government of Cambodia" had been used.

Cambodia's relations with Vietnam were tense at times over the Montagnard issue. During a visit to Cambodia in July, Vietnamese Public Security Minister Le Minh Huong signed a bilateral agreement with Deputy Prime Minister Sar Kheng on cooperation to stem illegal immigration, drug smuggling and organized crime. In November, Vietnamese and Cambodian officials were slated to sign several agreements, including one on border and immigration issues, during a visit to Phnom Penh by Vietnamese President Tan Duc Luong.

CHINA AND TIBET

The Chinese leadership's preoccupation with stability in the face of continued economic and social upheaval fueled an increase in human rights violations. China's increasingly prominent international profile, symbolized in 2001 by its entry into the World Trade Organization (WTO) and by Beijing's successful bid to host the 2008 Olympics, was accompanied by tightened controls on fundamental freedoms. The leadership turned to trusted tools, limiting free expression by arresting academics, closing newspapers and magazines, strictly controlling Internet content, and utilizing a refurbished Strike Hard campaign to circumvent legal safeguards for criminal suspects and alleged separatists, terrorists, and so-called religious extremists. In its campaign to eradicate Falungong, Chinese officials imprisoned thousands of practitioners and used torture and psychological pressure to force recantations. Legal experts continued the work of professionalizing the legal system but authorities in too many cases invoked "rule of law" to justify repressive politics. After the September 11 attacks in the United States, Chinese officials used concern with global terrorism as justification for crackdowns in Tibet and Xinjiang.

HUMAN RIGHTS DEVELOPMENTS

Starting in late 2000, authorities began tightening existing restrictions on the circulation of information, limiting the space available to academics, journalists and Internet users. Attacks on academic researchers may have been partly a response to the January 2001 publication of the *Tiananmen Papers*, a collection of government documents spirited out of China which described in detail the role played by Chinese leaders at the time of the historic June 1989 crackdown.

In December 2000, Guangdong's publicity bureau told newspapers and journals not to publish articles by eleven prominent scholars. In June 2001, one of those named, economist He Qinglian, fearing imminent arrest, fled China. Although her 1998 book, *China's Pitfalls*, had been widely praised by the Communist leadership for its exposé of corruption, she later angered authorities when she publicized the widening income gap in the country.

Between February and September, four Chinese academics who were either naturalized U.S. citizens or permanent U.S. residents were arrested, tried on charges of spying for Taiwan, and then deported. The four were Dr. Gao Zhan, a scholar at American University in Washington; journalist and writer Wu Jianmin; Qin Guangguang, a former editor and scholar; and Dr. Li Shaomin, a naturalized U.S. citizen teaching in Hong Kong. Sichuan native Xu Zerong, a Hong Kong resident since 1987, detained in June 2000, was still in custody in November 2001.

Scholars were also affected when the Chinese Academy of Social Sciences rescinded invitations to foreign and Taiwan scholars to participate in an August 2001 conference on income disparities. In November 2000, authorities cancelled an officially sponsored poets' meeting in Guangxi province after it became known that dissident poets, some of whom helped underground colleagues publish, were expected to attend. Three organizers were detained. In May, police in Hunan province raided a political reading club that had attracted teachers and intellectuals, and detained several participants including the founder.

Restrictions on information flows also affected HIV-AIDS research and reporting. In May, Beijing prohibited Dr. Gao Yaojie, who had helped publicize the role of unsanitary blood collection stations in the spread of the disease, from traveling to the U.S. to receive an award. Earlier, Henan health officials had accused her of being used by "anti-Chinese forces;" local officials, who often profited from the sale of blood, had warned her not to speak out. In July, village cadres refused to allow her to enter their AIDS-ridden villages.

Media regulations were also tightened. In November, the Communist Party's top publicity official signaled a new policy when he told a meeting of journalists that "the broad masses of journalists must be in strict agreement with the central committee with President Jiang Zemin at its core," a warning repeated in January by Jiang himself. The same month, a Party Central Propaganda Department internal circular warned that any newspaper, television channel, or radio station would be closed if it acted independently to publish stories on sensitive or taboo topics such as domestic politics, national unity, or social stability. The regulations instituted a new warning system; after three citations, a media outlet was subject to closure.

By June, the Party had instituted a stricter regime. A decree expanded taboo content to include speculation on leadership changes, calls for political reforms, criticism of Party policies including those related to ethnic minorities or religion, and rejection of the guiding role of Marxism-Leninism and Mao-Deng theories, among many other categories. The decree forbade independent reporting on major corruption scandals, major criminal cases, and human and natural disasters and threatened immediate shutdown for violators. The government also ordered a nationwide campaign to educate journalists in "Marxist news ideology."

In the immediate aftermath of the September 11 attacks in New York and Washington, the Chinese Communist Party's Central Committee Propaganda Department ordered news media to refrain from playing up the incident, relaying foreign news photos or reports, holding forums, or publishing news commentaries without permission. Chinese youth had welcomed the attacks on Internet postings and officials said the restrictions were needed to prevent damage to U.S.-China relations.

Authorities routinely prohibited the domestic press from reporting on incidents it considered damaging to China's image. After a military truck blew up in Xinjiang in November 2000, three journalists were sanctioned for "violat[ing] news discipline and reveal[ing] a lot of detailed information" before Xinhua, the official news agency, printed the official line on the incident. News media in China are required to use Xinhua reports on any stories that local or central propaganda authorities deem sensitive. In June, Yao Xiaohong, head of news for *Dushi Consumer Daily* in Jiangxi province, was dismissed after reporting an illegal kidney transplant from an executed prisoner. In October, under pressure from central government publicity authorities, he was fired from his new job at the *Yangcheng Evening News* in Guangdong province. Jiang Weiping, a Dalian, Liaoning province journalist who had exposed corruption, received a nine-year prison sentence in September 2001 for "leaking state secrets."

Chinese authorities moved against publications as well as individual journalists. In May, *Today's Celebrities* was peremptorily closed for printing articles about corruption and the Cultural Revolution (1966-76). In June, authorities replaced the acting editor and other editorial staff at *Southern Weekend* (*Nanfang Zhoumuo*), China's most outspoken news publication after the magazine published a series of articles blaming the government for problems in rural areas. Officials also closed the *Guangxi Business Daily*, which had operated for two years as an independent, privately-owned paper, when it refused to merge with the *Guanxi Daily*. In Jiangsu province, officials ordered the immediate suspension of the *Business Morning Daily* after it suggested that President Jiang's policies had advanced Shanghai's development at the expense of other cities.

In August, party leaders associated with Jiang used publishing regulations to shutter an opposition party faction, suspending the theoretical journal *Seeking Truth*, (*Zhenli de Zhuiqui*) which had opposed Jiang's proposal to allow private entrepreneurs to become party members, and tightening control over *Mainstream* (*Zhongliu*) and *Contemporary Thoughts*, also affiliated with opposition factions.

That same month, the State Council announced revised "Regulations on Printing," which included a sweeping provision forbidding publication of reactionary, erotic, or superstitious materials or "any other" material forbidden by the state. In early November 2000, courts sentenced ten people to prison terms ranging from five years to life for illegally printing and selling books about such topics as the Chinese intelligence community and the film community. In September, tens of thousands of Falungong publications were among some 500,000 documents confiscated in Anhui province.

The foreign press was also muzzled. In early March, after *Time* ran a story on Falungong, Beijing banned future newsstand sales of the magazine. In June, five security officers beat an *Agence France Presse* reporter after he photographed a protestor outside a "Three Tenors" concert held to support Beijing's Olympic bid. In July, government officials in Beijing prohibited the U.S. CBS television network from transmitting video footage for a story about Falungong. Chinese authorities banned the October 29 issue of *Newsweek* when it ran a cover story on corruption.

China Central Television also reneged on a July agreement to air in full U.S. Secretary of State Colin Powell's Beijing interview. It cut one-fifth of his remarks, including those defending U.S. criticism of Beijing's human rights record.

Other moves to tighten information flows and increase government control included the construction of new jamming facilities aimed at preventing ethnic groups in Tibet and Xinjiang from receiving news from overseas "hostile radio stations." In May, the State Administration of Radio, Film, and Television ordered all cable TV networks folded into provincial or municipal broadcasting networks. In July and August, the State Press and Publications Administration announced plans to set up publishing conglomerates to consolidate control of magazines and newspapers.

Stringent regulations on rapidly growing Internet use came into effect in November 2000. New regulations required general portal sites to get their news solely from state-controlled media, required that bulletin board services and chatrooms limit postings to approved topics, and made monitoring of postings routine. A month later, Chinese authorities increased the number of Internet police to more than 300,000. In January 2001, a new regulation made it a capital crime to send "secret" or "reactionary" information over the Internet. In February, software called Internet Police 100, capable of "capturing" computer screens and "casting" them onto screens at local public security bureaus, was released in versions that could be installed in homes, cafés, and schools. But even with some sixty sets of regulations in force, President Jiang in July decried the spread of "pernicious information" over the Web and called the existing legal framework inadequate.

Chinese regulations limited news postings on the websites of U.S.-based companies operating in China. The English chatroom of SOHU.com, partly owned by Dow Jones, posted a list of issues prohibited on the Internet by Chinese law, including criticism of the Chinese constitution, topics which damage China's reputation, discussion that undermines China's religious policy, and "any discussion and promotion of content which PRC laws prohibit." The posting continues: "If you are a Chinese national and willingly choose to break these laws, SOHU.com is legally obligated to report you to the Public Security Bureau." An internal AOL memo recommended that if AOL were asked what it would do if the Chinese government demanded records relating to political dissidents, AOL staff should respond "It is our policy to abide by the laws of the country in which we offer services."

Chinese officials stopped licensing new Internet cafes beginning in April while public security departments checked more than 55,000 cafes. In October, officials announced that more than 17,000 had been closed. Internet bulletin boards, chat rooms, and online magazines, including university-based sites and those catering to journalists, were also closed. Sites that were normally blocked, such as those of U.S. newspapers, were unblocked during the Asia-Pacific Economic Cooperation (APEC) summit in Shanghai in mid-October, but blocked again as soon as the conference was over.

At least sixteen people were arrested or sentenced in 2001 for using the Internet to send information or express views that the leadership disliked. Four others were tried at the end of September on charges of subversion for organizing a new youth organization and publishing articles about political reform. As of mid-November, there was still no information available on the outcome of Huang Qi's secret trial in August 2001. Huang was charged with subversion for featuring articles about democracy on his website.

Political dissidents continued to be persecuted, including members of the banned China Democracy Party. Activists associated with the Southern Mongolian Democratic Alliance, which seeks to promote Mongolian traditions and cultural values, and farmers in the Three Gorges dam area protesting corruption associated with resettlement in the dam basin were also monitored and in some cases arrested and sentenced on spurious charges.

On April 3, 2001, President Jiang initiated a three-month Strike Hard (*yan da*) campaign. Stressing the need to safeguard social stability and the reform process, he asked that improvements in fighting crime be made with "two tough hands." The campaign featured hastily processed cases, denial of due process rights, summary trials, harsh sentences, mass sentencing rallies, and an upsurge in executions. Although the use of torture to elicit confessions was illegal, such confessions, admissible in court, were officially acknowledged. Li Kuisheng, a prominent lawyer in Zhengzhou, Henan, was finally cleared of all charges and released in January 2001. He had been arrested in November 1998 after defending a client fighting corruption charges, and under torture had "confessed" to fabricating evidence.

Provinces and municipalities, in a kind of bizarre competition, reported regularly on their compliance with the campaign. Their accounts included totals of those apprehended, sentenced, and executed, and information on the kinds of crimes committed. Capital sentences were imposed for some sixty offenses including, in addition to violent acts, economic crimes, drug trafficking, smuggling, arms dealing, racketeering, counterfeiting, poaching, pimping, robbery, and theft. During the first month of Strike Hard, some 10,000 people were arrested and at least five hundred executed. By the end of October, at least 1,800 people had been executed, at least double that number had received death sentences, and officials had announced they would continue the campaign at least through June 2002 with increased "intensity."

Despite the Strike Hard campaign, officials in some areas implicitly acknowledged unfairness in the criminal justice system. In November 2000, Liaoning officials announced that prosecutions in some cities would be based on proof rather than confessions, thus guaranteeing suspects' right to remain silent during criminal interrogation. In January, the vice-president of the Supreme People's Court admitted to corruption within the legal system, including intentional errors of judgment, forged court papers, and bribe taking. In June, the Supreme People's Procuratorate issued six new regulations to prevent violations in the handling of cases and acknowledged Communist Party interference in sensitive cases. However, in August, in Luoyang, Henan province, judges who heard the cases of twenty-three defendants charged in a fire that killed 309 people said they would not release their findings until they had talked to provincial leaders.

China continued to crack down on groups it labeled cults and on independent religious organizations. Falungong continued to experience the harshest repression, with thousands of practitioners assigned to "reeducation through labor" camps and more than 350 imprisoned, many for nothing more than printing leaflets or recruiting followers for protests . On June 11, the Supreme People's Court and the Supreme People's Procuratorate issued a new interpretation of cult provisions in the Criminal Law to make it easier to punish practitioners on a wide variety of charges. Authorities also targeted other so-called cults, among them Zhonggong, Xiang Gong, Guanyin Famin, and Kuangmin Zhaimen, sentencing their leaders, closing down their offices, and seizing their publications.

A few weeks before Christmas 2000, hundreds of "illegal" Protestant and Catholic churches and Buddhist and Taoist temples and shrines in Wenzhou were demolished. In March and April, several dozen house church leaders in Hubei province were detained; in May, twelve others were administratively sentenced in Inner Mongolia. Beijing also instituted a special study group to bring Christianity "into line with socialism" through reinterpretation of basic beliefs. The continuing government-ordered merger of Catholic dioceses, a move that went unrecognized by Rome, also signaled Beijing's determination to run the church in accord with its own needs. In October, after Pope John Paul expressed regrets for Catholic Church errors committed during the "colonial period" and expressed hope of normalized relations, Chinese religious officials responded by demanding that the Vatican first sever its ties with Taiwan, refrain from "using the pretext of religious issues to meddle in Chinese internal affairs," and apologize for last year's canonization of "foreign missionaries and their followers who committed notorious crimes in China." Detentions in 2001 included those of several elderly influential bishops and priests. One priest, Father Lu, was sentenced administratively in April to three years' reeducation through labor for refusing to join the official Catholic Patriotic Association and continuing to preach the gospel and celebrate Mass. In May, the Chinese government leveled the grave of Bishop Fan Xueyan, a prominent "underground" bishop who died in 1992, to prevent Catholics from paying their respects.

Reports of clashes between police and workers and farmers protesting layoffs, unpaid wages and benefits, corruption, and relocation problems continued throughout the year. In April, police in Yuntang, Jiangxi arrested five villagers who had been leading a three-year protest against new taxes, then stormed the village killing two unarmed protestors and injuring some thirty-eight others. In October, police in Qingdao, Shandong detained protestors demonstrating against the city's failure to honor its commitment to provide appropriate housing for residents displaced by a real estate project.

Labor activists also continued to be targeted. In one prominent case, Li Wangyang, imprisoned from 1989 to 2000 for labor activism, was sentenced in September to a new ten-year prison term after petitioning for compensation for mistreatment suffered while serving the prior term. Li's sister received a three-year administrative sentence on June 7 for publicizing her brother's case.

In October 2001, authorities passed a new Trade Union Law requiring enterprises with more than twenty-five workers to establish a union and prohibiting management personnel from holding important union positions, but only government-affiliated unions were mentioned in the law and the right to strike was not guaranteed. Also in October, authorities revised residential regulations to allow rural residents to apply for residence in some small cities and towns so long as they could first find jobs and homes. In most cities, however, continuance of the existing permit system left migrants open to abuses by their employers, the police, and private security guards. Most migrant parents, even if legally registered, could not afford school fees for regular city schools, forcing them to send their children back to the countryside, keep them out of school, or send them to inferior "migrant" schools. Before the start of classes in September, officials closed fifty migrant schools in one Beijing district.

Tibet

China revised its overall Tibetan policy in June 2001, the fourth such change since it took command of the region in 1950. Goals for 2001-2006 included accelerated economic development and tightened control over alleged "secessionist" activities. During a July visit, Vice-President Hu Jintao stated that it was "essential to fight unequivocally against separatist activities by the Dalai clique and anti-China forces in the world."

Efforts to engage the Chinese leadership in a dialogue with representatives of the Dalai Lama were unsuccessful in 2001. Following the Dalai Lama's criticism of Chinese policy during a speech to the European Parliament general assembly on October 24, Chinese officials reiterated their position that talks could take place only if the Dalai Lama renounced his "separatist stand" and openly acknowledged that Tibet was an inalienable part of China, Taiwan merely a province, and "the government of the People's Republic of China the sole legitimate government representing the whole of China."

At the beginning of the Tibetan New Year in February, government workers, cadres, and school children were banned from attending prayer festivals at monasteries or from contributing to temples and monasteries. During Monlam Chemo, formerly a festival of great religious significance, monks at Lhasa's major monasteries were not permitted to leave their respective complexes, and government authorities banned certain rites.

The Strike Hard campaign in Tibet had a decidedly political focus. At a May meeting in Lhasa, capital of the Tibet Autonomous Region (TAR), courts were ordered to carry out the campaign forcefully against "those whose crimes endanger state security," and "those who guide people illegally across borders," in other words, against those who help Tibetans reach Nepal or Dharamsala, India, the Dalai Lama's home in exile. During the first month of the campaign, 254 people were caught trying to leave or reenter the TAR, many allegedly carrying "reactionary propaganda materials." In June, police in the Lhasa region detained hundreds of Tibetans who burned incense, said prayers, or threw *tsampa* (roasted barley) into the air in defiance of an order banning celebration of the Dalai Lama's birthday. Some twenty Tibetans were arrested or sentenced in 2001 for "splittist" activities. In October, at least three foreign tourists and three Tibetans were detained in Lhasa in October for displaying the banned Tibetan flag and shouting pro-independence slogans.

Authorities cut back the number of nuns and monks from 8,000 to 1,400 at the Buddhist Study Center Larung Gar near Serthar in Sichuan province, destroying their housing as they left. A similar order was put into effect at Yachen, another encampment in Sichuan. Authorities continued to deny access to the Panchen Lama, the second most important figure in Tibetan Buddhism. The boy, now twelve years old, disappeared from public view in 1995 after Beijing chose another child as the reincarnation. Chadrel Rinpoche, the senior lama who led the search, was still in prison. He was last seen in mid-May 1995 shortly before he was sentenced to a six-year prison term.

Xinjiang

Even before September 18, when the Chinese government publicly equated Uighur calls for autonomy or independence with global terrorism, Beijing had instituted strict measures to crush "separatism" and "religious extremism" in Xinjiang. In April, at the beginning of the nationwide Strike Hard campaign, Ablat Abdureshit, chairman of the region, was explicit as to targets in Xinjiang: "national splittists," "violent terrorists," and "religious extremists." At the same time, the leadership reiterated its determination to develop the region economically. Both campaigns were entrusted to patriotic Party cadres working at the grassroots, kept in check by a local law passed in May threatening punishment should they sympathize with Uighur aims. In June, the Shanghai Cooperation Organization (formerly the Shanghai Five), composed of China, Russia and four republics in Central Asia, reiterated its pledge of cooperation to combat "terrorism, separatism and extremists" and to establish "a regular anti-terrorist structure."

Efforts to bring religious practices under the aegis of the state included the April formation of a China Islamic Affairs Steering Committee under the administration of the Islamic Association of China. The members, sixteen senior China-based experts on Islam, interpreted religious doctrines in accordance with Chinese law, drafted sermon pamphlets, and worked to bring Islam into conformity with Chinese political ideology. An imam "patriotic reeducation" campaign, begun in March, assigned some 8,000 religious leaders to twenty-day sessions stressing patriotism, upholding Party leadership, combating separatism, and the like. In a number of cases, mosques were leveled, clerics arrested, and "illegal" books and audio cassettes confiscated.

Although there were credible reports of violence by Uighur separatists in Xinjiang, strict Chinese controls on information coming from the region often made it impossible to know whether particular individuals had indeed committed criminal acts or whether they were being punished for exercising their rights to free political expression, association, or assembly. Typical charges included "splittism," subverting state power, setting up an organization to establish Islamic rule, stockpiling weapons, endangering social order, and printing anti-government literature. There were also new reports of torture, forced confessions, unfair trial procedures, and collective punishment. In November 2000, Abdulelil Abdumejit died while serving a sentence for the anti-Chinese riots in Yining in 1997. Supporters claim he died from beatings and torture; the state claims he died from his refusal to follow an appropriate medical regime.

The Strike Hard campaign exacerbated the rate of arrests and sentencing. Within three months of the campaign's start in April, Xinjiang police reported that they had arrested 605 suspects, destroyed six separatist and terrorist organizations, and, in conjunction with the procuracy, held more than one hundred rallies before 300,000 spectators to parade "criminals" and announce sentences before a public expected to signify approval. Rebiya Kadeer, a Uighur businesswoman sentenced to an eight-year prison term in March 2000 for sending local newspapers to her husband in the U.S., continued to be limited to one family visit every three months. Rebiya's four sons, one of whom was released from a "reeducation through labor" camp in February, continued to be subjected to harassment and surveillance.

Hong Kong

Hong Kong authorities continued to defer to Beijing on a range of important questions. In July, Hong Kong's legislature, of which elected members are a minority, passed legislation acknowledging Beijing's power to remove Hong Kong's chief executive, even though the Basic Law, which governs Hong Kong-mainland relations, is silent on the question. Although many observers noted a continuing trend toward media self-censorship and other pressures on civil liberties, the year was also significant for what did not happen. Despite surveillance and escalating rhetoric, the Hong Kong government did not ban Falungong or enact an anti-cult law. After losing a "right of abode" case in Hong Kong's high court, authorities did not seek reinterpretation from Beijing as they had in May 1999. Finally, government and university officials did not block Li Shaomin, convicted in July on the mainland of spying for Taiwan and subsequently deported, from returning and resuming his teaching duties at the City University of Hong Kong.

DEFENDING HUMAN RIGHTS

No independent watchdog organizations were permitted in China; in Hong Kong there was a vibrant NGO community functioning without any apparent government interference.

THE ROLE OF THE INTERNATIONAL COMMUNITY

United Nations

On February 28, China ratified the International Covenant on Economic, Social and Cultural Rights but took a reservation on the right to freely organize and join trade unions. In May, the International Labor Organization signed an agreement to provide assistance with social security, job retraining, and worker health and safety concerns, but did not address the right of free association. China still had not ratified the International Covenant on Civil and Political Rights, which it signed in 1998.

Mary Robinson, the U.N. High Commissioner for Human Rights, visited Beijing in February and November for workshops on punishment of minor crimes and human rights education, respectively. In her November visit, Robinson also met with Jiang Zemin, pressed for access for the U.N. special rapporteur on torture, warned China not to use the war on terrorism to justify its crackdown in Xinjiang, and signed a Memorandum of Understanding for expanded technical cooperation. In August, the U.N. held a workshop in Beijing on human rights and the police.

On April 19, the U.N. Commission on Human Rights adopted China's no-action motion, twenty-three to seventeen with twelve abstentions and one absence, blocking debate of a U.S.-sponsored resolution critical of China's rights record. No other governments co-sponsored the resolution.

In August, the U.N. Committee on the Elimination of Racial Discrimination issued "concluding observations" following review of China's report on its implementation of the convention. The committee expressed concern about restrictions on freedom of religion for national minorities in Tibet and Xinjiang, and discrimination in education, particularly in Tibet. In May, the Committee reviewed Hong Kong's record under the Convention, noting the SAR's failure to enact an anti-racial discrimination law.

Olympics

China waged an aggressive campaign on behalf of Beijing's bid to host the Olympics in 2008. Human rights were raised in the international debate leading up to the July 17 decision in Moscow to award the games to Beijing, but the IOC set no human rights preconditions and ignored appeals from Human Rights Watch and others to set up an independent monitoring committee. Chinese officials publicly pledged to allow foreign journalists covering the games unrestricted access to the country.

United States

The Bush administration's policy towards China shifted from a confrontational posture early on, to cordial by mid-year, to cooperative in the post-September 11 climate. Bush put a heavy emphasis on religious freedom. But after September 11, it was unclear how effectively the administration would balance human rights concerns, trade, and cooperation with China on anti-terrorism initiatives.

The early months of the Bush administration were marked by tensions over arms sales to Taiwan and detentions of China scholars. When Vice Premier Qian Qichen visited Washington to meet Bush in March to smooth relations, Bush raised specific cases of detained academics. A low point came in April when Chinese forces captured a U.S. Navy spy plane and its crew.

The administration embraced expanded trade with China, and supported China's formal entry into membership of the World Trade Organization on November 10 at the Doha, Qatar ministerial meeting. The National People's Congress had not ratified the accession agreement by mid-November.

A Congressional-Executive Commission on China was established mid-year; it was required under legislation enacted in October 2000 giving China permanent normal trade relations (PNTR). It had nine members each from the House and Senate, and representatives from the departments of State, Commerce, and Labor. The commission was charged with monitoring human rights, rule of law, labor rights, and religious freedom in China and with making U.S. policy recommendations. But its first report, due in October 2001, was delayed until 2002, and the Commission held no meetings or hearings during the year.

The administration and Congress were active in pressing for consular access to detained China scholars and for their prompt release and return to the U.S. The high profile cases of Gao Zhan and Li Shaomin were resolved just days before Secretary Powell's Beijing visit in July.

During his visit, Powell announced resumption of a U.S.-China human rights dialogue, which China had suspended following the NATO bombing of its Belgrade embassy in 1999. A dialogue meeting held from October 9-11 in Washington, DC produced no immediate results.

In late October, Bush met Jiang Zemin for the first time for bilateral talks at the Shanghai APEC summit. Bush reportedly raised human rights issues, urged dialogue with the Dalai Lama, and publicly said that no government should use the anti-terrorism campaign "as an excuse to persecute minorities within their borders." When U.S. military strikes began against Afghanistan, China had appealed for international support for its crackdown in Xinjiang.

Canada, European Union, and Japan

During trade meetings in China in February, Canadian Prime Minister Jean Chretien raised human rights concerns in Tibet and the crackdown on Falungong, and the two countries held a human rights dialogue in July.

The European Union, under public pressure to show more progress from its human rights dialogues with China—nine had taken place since 1997—made public in January a set of objectives including China's ratification of U.N. covenants, cooperation with U.N. human rights mechanisms, restrictions on the use of the death penalty, and international access to prisoners in Tibet and Xinjiang. In February, the Swedish presidency presided over an E.U.-China rights dialogue and the E.U. held a seminar on the death penalty in Beijing in May.

In late May, in advance of the Asia-Europe Meeting of E.U. and Asian foreign ministers in Beijing, the E.U. Council published a revised policy statement on China, declaring that the E.U. must increase its engagement. Chris Patten, E.U. Commissioner for External Affairs, argued that expanded contacts would "support China's transition to an open society based upon the rule of law and respect for human rights."

A China-E.U. summit took place in Brussels on September 5, led by Belgian Prime Minister Guy Verhofstadt and Premier Zhu Rongji. Talks focused on China's prospective WTO membership, illegal immigration and trafficking of Chinese to Europe, and the treatment of North Korean refugees in China. The two sides affirmed their interest in continuing the human rights dialogue, although Zhu insisted that China's human rights record was the best it had ever been.

Japanese policy towards China was marked by tensions over a decision to allow the former Taiwanese president permission to come to Japan for medical treatment in April, Chinese outrage over official approval of Japanese history textbooks that sanitized Japan's record during World War II, and a visit to a war shrine by new Japanese Prime Minister Junichiro Koizumi in August. The prime minister went to China in early October, in advance of the APEC summit, to apologize to the Chinese "victims of aggression" and to explain new legislation allowing Japan's Self Defense Forces to give logistical support for U.S. attacks in Afghanistan. Another session in Japan's bilateral human rights dialogue with China was agreed to in principle, but as of November, no meeting had taken place.

World Bank

In fiscal year 2001, the World Bank gave over U.S. $787 million in loans to China, mainly for environmental and infrastructure projects. In fiscal year 2002, which began in July, it estimated that approximately $950 million in new projects would be approved. The Bank also continued to fund transportation projects in Xinjiang and gave small grants to government-sponsored "NGOs," including groups working on HIV-AIDS and environmental initiatives. It made some efforts to expand its consultation process with local communities and international NGOs in designing new projects, but did not provide new financial support for legal and judicial reform or use its policy dialogue with China to promote anti-corruption initiatives.

EAST TIMOR

East Timor made steady progress toward self-government, with full independence scheduled for May 20, 2002. Under the auspices of the U.N. Transitional Administration in East Timor (UNTAET), it held a peaceful election in August for a constituent assembly whose delegates then proceeded to discuss and debate the nature of the new state: how it would be structured, how power would be shared, what fundamental rights would be guaranteed. In September, an all-East Timorese Council of Ministers was appointed as the effective cabinet. The guerrilla force, Falintil, was transformed during the year into a component of the new East Timorese Defence Force. Policing was increasingly turned over to local graduates of the East Timorese police academy. In October, an East Timorese replaced a Tanzanian expatriate as general prosecutor.

The slow pace of justice continued to be a source of frustration for East Timorese jurists, human rights advocates, and victims alike, with much of the blame focused on UNTAET's Serious Crimes Unit. Nevertheless, prosecutions for serious crimes committed in 1999 did take place, with the first conviction in November 2001 of a former militia leader for crimes against humanity.

East Timorese who fled or were forcibly expelled to West Timor in 1999 began to return home in greater numbers. In May, a fifteen-year-old East Timorese girl was rescued and returned to East Timor from West Timor where she had been held in sexual slavery in a militia-controlled camp. Following the August election, the rate of return increased, with more than 3,000 people returning in October. Although reports continued of militia leaders in the West Timor camps intimidating refugees and spreading disinformation to discourage them from returning, their hold over the camps seemed to be steadily declining.

HUMAN RIGHTS DEVELOPMENTS

East Timor took a giant step toward independence with a widely praised election on August 30, 2001, the second anniversary of the referendum that produced a vote to separate from Indonesia—and devastating violence. The election for a constituent assembly involved sixteen parties competing for eighty-eight seats. Nearly the entire eligible voting population registered and participated, with almost none of the political violence that had been widely predicted. Prior to the elections, in June, the National Council of East Timorese Resistance (CNRT), the pro-independence coalition that had dominated East Timor's political life for the last two years, quietly dissolved itself to make way for a more competitive political system.

Justice for the 1999 violence in East Timor continued to be elusive. By late November, the office of the general prosecutor in Dili, the capital, had filed thirty-three indictments for serious crimes, four of which involved crimes against humanity. But many of the more than seventy suspects named in the indictments were militia members or Indonesian army officers living in Indonesia, and unlikely to be prosecuted there, let alone extradited to East Timor.

The sentences handed down by the panel of East Timorese and international judges in the Dili District Court reflected the seriousness of the crimes. On January 25, Joao Fernandes became the first person convicted of murder in connection with the 1999 violence. He received a sentence of twelve years. (He then escaped, but was eventually recaptured.) Augostino da Costa, who was convicted in July of killing a local employee of the United Nations Mission in East Timor (UNAMET) on August 31, 1999, received a fifteen-year prison sentence. Defendants who cooperated fully with the court and were shown to have themselves been under threat of death from their commanders when they killed were given similarly heavy sentences.

While such terms for serious crimes would ordinarily have occasioned little comment, some senior East Timorese officials, including Xanana Gusmao, former resistance leader and East Timor's president-in-waiting, questioned whether prosecuting East Timorese served the interests of justice when the Indonesian architects of the 1999 violence were not even indicted.

The Serious Crimes Unit's need to clear the backlog of cases, involving long-detained suspects, also meant that investigators and prosecutors had no time to prepare cases against top militia commanders believed to have been responsible for crimes against humanity—cases which should have been prepared as a top priority when UNTAET first arrived in Dili. This meant that some commanders, such as Cancio de Carvalho and his brother, Nemencio, could negotiate their return to East Timor from West Timor on the understanding they would face trial, yet without any serious prospect of prosecution.

Criticism of the Serious Crimes Unit surfaced repeatedly during the year, notably poor administration and weakness of its senior staff, and several good prosecutors and investigators left in frustration.

Problems also continued with the Dili court due to its lack of good interpreters, poor or nonexistent translations of dossiers, inadequate court reporters, and inexperienced defense counsel and other court personnel. In Baucau, East Timor's second largest city, the district court was briefly closed in May after assaults on a judge and prosecutor. Court personnel complained that the U.N. police had failed to provide adequate security in the face of threats, apparently from people unhappy with court decisions.

On October 4, a U.S. Federal Court judge ruled in response to a lawsuit based on the Alien Torts Claim Act that Indonesian General Johny Lumintang should pay damages of U.S. $66 million for his role in the human rights violations committed by the Indonesian army following the August 30, 1999, referendum in East Timor.

On October 16, during a seminar in Dili on "Justice and Accountability in East Timor," East Timorese nongovernmental organizations called for an international ad hoc tribunal to be set up to prosecute war crimes and crimes against humanity in East Timor occurring after Indonesia's 1975 invasion of the country. One week later, on October 23, Jakarta's chief justice of the Supreme Court promised that the long-delayed ad hoc human rights court to try the East Timor cases would be up and running in Jakarta by December.

In April East Timor's provisional legislature, the National Council, approved the establishment of a Truth, Reception, and Reconciliation. It was designed both to facilitate the return of former militia members from West Timor and to ease the burden on the formal judicial system by allowing those responsible for less serious crimes, such as arson, to confess their crimes before a commission panel and receive a punishment of community service.

There were some instances of attacks on Muslims during the year, but they were quickly condemned by East Timorese and UNTAET officials. On January 1 and 2, 2001, stones were thrown at Muslims living in the An-Nur mosque in Dili, and on March 7, the mosque in Baucau was destroyed.

A long-awaited labor law was finally passed by the National Council in July. Drafted with the help of the International Labor Organization, it established a system of labor relations in accordance with ILO standards.

DEFENDING HUMAN RIGHTS

East Timor's human rights defenders operated freely and played an active role in lobbying UNTAET and transitional government institutions. In July, the country's premier human rights organization, Yayasan Hak, led an effort to challenge UNTAET regulations that it felt compromised the independence of the judiciary in East Timor; the regulations were changed as a result. There were no attacks on human rights defenders. UNTAET's Human Rights Unit provided human rights training programs for East Timorese NGOs.

THE ROLE OF THE INTERNATIONAL COMMUNITY

Australia continued to play a particularly significant role in the reconstruction of East Timor given its proximity to the new country, and Japan was the largest single donor. East Timor in general, however, enjoyed strong support from the international donor community.

In November 2000 and June 2001, international donor conferences were held in Dili with the specific aim of providing assistance to the East Timorese Defence Force. Australia was expected to provide major aid to the new force; lusophone countries were prominently represented at the conference, including Portugal, Angola, and Mozambique.

The E.U., U.S., Canada, and Australia were among the most active donors with regard to supporting justice projects.

Portugal and the lusophone countries, notably Brazil, continued to provide important assistance to East Timor, particularly in the field of education and culture. Some three hundred students from East Timor went to Portugal for post-high school studies, and some 150 Portuguese schoolteachers arrived in East Timor.

United Nations

The United Nations administered East Timor for a second year, and despite criticism within East Timor of some aspects of its role there, it continued to be seen as a major peace-keeping success story. Given the enormity of the task at hand, UNTAET, the U.N. Security Council, the international donor community, and above all, the East Timorese themselves deserved credit for the enormous progress made in institution- and capacity-building. One question outstanding at the end of the year, however, was what human rights role the United Nations would have post-independence; it appeared by November that the Office of the High Commissioner for Human Rights had secured agreement for a team of human rights monitors to be assigned to East Timor after UNTAET formally comes to an end.

The Security Council continued to take an active interest in East Timor. In November 2000, in the aftermath of the killings of three workers from the U.N. High Commissioner for Refugees office in Atambua, West Timor, a Security Council delegation visited Indonesia and East Timor. In January 2001, through resolution 1338, the Security Council voted to extend UNTAET's mandate through January 2002. On November 1, the Council endorsed May 20, 2002, as the date for East Timor's independence and agreed to keep peacekeepers, some civilian staff, and police trainers in East Timor for up to two years after independence.

United States

In February, legislation was introduced in both houses of the U.S. Congress to facilitate East Timor's transition to independence through assistance for democracy building, support for reconciliation programs, steps to enhance trade and investment, and training of self defense forces. The bill was incorporated into the State Department authorization legislation for fiscal year (FY) 2002; final adoption, which was expected, was pending in late November. In the FY 2002 foreign operations appropriations bill, the U.S. Congress renewed and strengthened human rights conditions on International Military Education and Training (IMET) and government military sales to Indonesia. One condition was progress on accountability for abuses committed in East Timor.

Xanana Gusmao visited Washington, D.C. in May and met U.S. Secretary of State Colin Powell. In August, James Kelly, U.S. assistant secretary of state for East Asia and the Pacific, visited East Timor. He used the opportunity to criticize the Indonesian government for its lack of progress on accountability for abuses committed in East Timor in 1999.

European Union

The European Commission remained one of East Timor's major donors. In addition to providing significant humanitarian and development aid during the year, the European Union also fielded the largest delegation of observers—thirty members in all—for the constituent assembly elections in August.

Japan

Japan supported the creation in Indonesia of an ad hoc human rights court for East Timor. In August and September, it sent monitors to East Timor and provided $ 1.19 million in emergency grants to the United Nations Development Program (UNDP) to assist with monitoring and training of local election administrators in Indonesia. In November 2001, it decided to dispatch seven hundred members of Japan's Self-Defense Forces to East Timor as peacekeepers, mainly for operations in areas bordering West Timor; an assessment mission was due to visit East Timor later in the month to finalize plans for the deployment. East Timorese NGOs opposed the deployment on the grounds that Japan had never compensated East Timorese victims of atrocities during World War II.

World Bank

The World Bank continued to play an instrumental role in financing development and reconstruction projects through the Trust Fund for East Timor (TFET). TFET is administered jointly by World Bank and the Asian Development Bank. World Bank personnel have also been active in working with East Timorese leaders on setting benchmarks for political and economic goals, for the transition to independence and beyond. UNDP was active in supporting programs to assist the electoral process and to aid the administration of justice.

INDIA

In 2001, India held steadfast to its distinction as the region's most stable and vibrant democracy even as its neighbors underwent dramatic and often violent shifts in power. With the onset of the war in Afghanistan, and as relations with Pakistan deteriorated and violence in Kashmir and elsewhere escalated, the Indian government faced heightened national security concerns. Some measures taken in response, including the cabinet approval of the Prevention of Terrorism Ordinance, came under sharp attack by various sectors of Indian civil society for opportunistically curtailing civil liberties in the name of fighting terrorism. Increased violence in the state of Uttar Pradesh, where the Hindu nationalist Bharatiya Janata Party (BJP) hopes to achieve a comeback election victory early in 2002, highlighted the dangerous results of exploiting communal and caste tensions for political ends.

Police violence, attacks on the country's minority communities including Muslims, Christians, Dalits and tribals, and violence against women continued to be serious problems, though some positive steps were taken to help better ensure women's and children's rights. Human rights defenders came under legislative assault through changes to laws and procedures aimed at restricting their ability to travel, hold conferences, and receive foreign funds. The U.N. World Conference Against Racism, Racial Discrimination, Xenophobia and Related Intolerance (WCAR), held in South Africa from August 31 to September 8, paved the way for unprecedented international as well as national scrutiny of the problem of caste discrimination.

HUMAN RIGHTS DEVELOPMENTS

On January 26, a devastating earthquake rocked the northwest state of Gujarat, the country's worst natural disaster in recent history. Within days at least 30,000 were declared dead and over one million were left homeless. While the government allocated equal amounts of monetary compensation and food supplies to members of all communities, Dalit (so-called untouchable) and Muslim populations did not have the same access to adequate shelter, electricity, running water, and other supplies available to others. Upper-caste families in Kutch refused to live alongside Dalits in temporary settlements built by Rapid Action Forces. As a result, hundreds of tents lay empty while Dalits were required to live in makeshift shelters. Even relief kitchens for the two communities had to be kept separate as the higher castes refused to share resources with those they considered "diseased." According to local NGOs, several thousand Dalit homes were also left out of government reconstruction surveys. In October, Gujarat Chief Minister Keshubhai Patel resigned, in part because of criticism about the slow pace of relief and rehabilitation following the earthquake.

Dalit communities continued to suffer systemic discrimination and violence. In a number of cases, police were complicit in the attacks or used excessive force against Dalits when they organized to respond to the attacks, rendering legal protections meaningless. Violence was particularly acute in Uttar Pradesh and Bihar, and those responsible were rarely brought to justice by the authorities.

On February 19, a group of Thakurs (an upper-caste community) in Lucknow, Uttar Pradesh, assaulted a Dalit laborer following a wage dispute. The perpetrators entered the victim's home and pinned him down while the employer urinated in his mouth. On June 12, assailants beat a Dalit man and then pushed his wife into a fire, burning her to death. The incident was quickly followed by a spate of violence, including a June 14 rampage led by seven Thakurs who killed five members of a Dalit family, including three women and a ten year-old girl. In Aligarh, Uttar Pradesh in June a Dalit woman and her five children were burnt alive, allegedly by the staff of a brick kiln operating unit which had employed the woman and her husband as bonded laborers.

Conditions in Bihar continued to be marred by a caste war involving rival leftist factions and upper-caste private militias. In January, fifty houses were set ablaze and four Dalits were killed in a gun battle. On February 3, rival gangs gunned down twelve Dalit youths, killing nine of them, and subsequently set their homes on fire; on April 18, militants belonging to the Maoist Communist Center killed fourteen Dalits. In August, a village in Patna was attacked, killing six Dalit women and children.

Dalits also continued to face considerable opposition in exercising their political rights. On October 16 in Dharmapuri district, Tamil Nadu, an entire Dalit village was razed after Dalits dared to nominate their own candidate to the post of village council president. More than 140 houses were destroyed by members of the upper-caste community in the area, rendering eight hundred Dalits homeless. Many were also physically assaulted during the attacks. One pregnant woman was kicked in the stomach, aborted her child, and died later that day. Police charged protesting Dalit villagers with batons and arrested more than twenty-two Dalits while the upper-caste attackers remained at-large.

Social prohibitions on marriages between higher and lower-caste community members remained in place and were often reinforced through the threat of social ostracism and punitive violence. On August 6, 2001, an upper-caste Brahmin boy and a lower-caste Jat girl in Uttar Pradesh were dragged to the roof of a house and publicly hanged by members of their own families as hundreds of spectators looked on. The public lynching was punishment for refusing to end an inter-caste relationship. Also in August, a forty-year-old Dalit woman was paraded naked in Bellary, Karnataka after being accused of helping a fifteen-year-old upper-caste girl elope with her lower-caste fiancé.

Dalits were often beaten or fined for participating in religious ceremonies. On April 3 in Bargarh, Orissa, for example, a Dalit was fined Rs. 4,000 (U.S. $83.42) and beaten for entering a Hindu temple. On June 2 in Bhadkiyan, Rajasthan, an upper-caste man beat to death a sixty-five-year-old Dalit man with an iron bar for daring to pray outside the temple of the village deity.

Attacks on churches and members of the Christian clergy by members of right wing Hindu groups including the Bajrang Dal, the Vishwa Hindu Parishad (VHP), and the Rashtriya Swayamsevak Sangh (RSS), collectively known as the *sangh parivar* continued, peaking in July and August. Christians in Orissa, Gujarat, Rajasthan, Maharastra, Uttar Pradesh and Madhya Pradesh were hardest hit.

On November 26, 2000, four hundred VHP activists in Gujarat desecrated and took over a church, replacing the church's cross with Hindu idols and hoisting their signature saffron flag. The mob also drove out eighty Christian families from the area, confining them to a nearby forest until they embraced Hinduism.

At St. Anna High School in Bokaro district, Bihar, a dozen armed men assaulted the principal and three nuns, and raped the school cook on December 3, 2000. In Tamil Nadu a nun was murdered on January 21, 2001, in the state's Salem district. On January 23, in Rampur district, Uttar Pradesh, a nun was hospitalized after sustaining serious head injuries. Two simultaneous attacks on Christian missionaries on August 6 in Madhya Pradesh and Maharashtra drew sharp condemnation from the All India Christian Council and the Catholic Bishops' Conference of India.

From March 16-18, Muslim youth in Kanpur, Uttar Pradesh clashed with state police during protests over the burning of a Koran in New Delhi by Hindu radicals. When protesters began to burn an effigy of Prime Minister Atal Bihari Vajpayee, police responded with tear gas and the crowd turned violent. Police then opened fire as rioters began burning shops and hurling crude bombs. By the end of three days of riots, fourteen people were dead, dozens injured, and eighty-nine arrested. Six mosques were damaged, Muslim homes were looted, and the authorities had imposed a round-the-clock curfew. In the wake of the violence, human rights groups charged the police with using excessive force against Muslim demonstrators and looting and plundering Muslim shops and homes.

In the hopes of achieving a comeback victory in assembly elections scheduled for early 2002 in Uttar Pradesh, India's most populous state, the BJP and its allies amplified calls to build a temple to the Hindu god Ram at the site of the Babri Masjid, a mosque in the city of Ayodhya whose demolition sparked the infamous 1992-1993 Bombay riots in which thousands of people, most notably Muslims, were killed. In 2001, many feared that the re-energized Ram temple campaign would lead to more violence and bloodshed between the state's Hindu and Muslim communities.

In July, a crowd of three hundred people demolished a sixteenth century mosque at Asind near Bhilwara, Rajasthan and built a makeshift Hindu temple in its place. The mob was encouraged by VHP and RSS activists.

The government took some positive steps to prosecute perpetrators of violence against members of minority religious communities. In May, the Jhabua district court in Madhya Pradesh sentenced ten men to life in prison for the September 1998 gang-rape of four Christian nuns. Prosecution of Dara Singh, accused in the 1999 murder of Australian missionary Graham Staines and his two sons in Orissa, also continued, with several witnesses testifying that Singh played a key role in insti-gating the murder.

There was little progress, however, in many other cases, including those of indi-viduals indicted by the Srikrishna Commission for their role in the 1992-93 Bom-bay riots. One exception occurred in August, however, when a special task force filed charges against former police commissioner R.D. Tyagi and seventeen police-men for their role in 1993 riots in the city.

Control over natural resources continued to be the source of violence against tribal communities in Orissa. On December 16, 2000, three tribals were killed in Maikanch village, Rayagada district, in clashes with the police over the villagers' opposition to a proposed private aluminum plant in the area. A fact-finding team, which included retired Chief Justice D.S. Tewatia, claimed that the attack was pre-planned and demanded a judicial probe, alleging that an administrative inquiry ordered by the state government was a "cover-up operation." On October 30, 2001, in Rangabhatti village, three tribals were killed and over fifty were injured when police reportedly opened fire on a gathering of four hundred tribals. The tribals were protesting against the June 24 killing of two people by an armed mob of 3,000 in Jambodora, a Dalit village. Two more people were killed by police in Raigarhar, Nabrangpur district on November 11, when over 8,000 women held a rally to protest the October 30 incident.

Violence against women, including rape, kidnapping, dowry deaths, domestic violence, female foeticide, sexual harassment, and trafficking continued unabated, though authorities did take some positive steps in response.

In April, the Supreme Court directed prosecutors to enforce existing laws ban-ning the use of prenatal diagnostic techniques to determine the sex of the fetus and authorities warned doctors that their names would be removed from the register of the Medical Council of India if they were found to be practicing female foeticide. In June, authorities announced new legislative measures to safeguard women's rights, including a new Domestic Violence Prevention Bill.

There were also positive developments for children's rights. In September, the government announced that a seven-member national commission for children, headed by a retired Supreme Court judge, would be established to implement pro-tections for children enshrined in the Indian constitution. A meeting between Indian and Bangladeshi border guards in October resulted in agreements to strengthen cooperation to stop the trafficking of women and children across the border. According to human rights groups, about 20,000 women and children were trafficked to India from Bangladesh annually. Also in October, the state govern-ment of Rajasthan, in an attempt to make child marriage illegal, approved legisla-tion requiring all couples to register marriages with authorities.

In mid-November, the government was considering enacting a modified ver-sion of the Terrorist and Disruptive Activities (Prevention) Act (TADA), notori-ous for facilitating tens of thousands of politically motivated detentions, torture, and other human rights violations against Muslims, Sikhs, Dalits, trade union activists, and political opponents in the late 1980s and early 1990s. The new proposed Prevention of Terrorism Ordinance (POTO) set forth a broad definition of terrorism that included acts of violence or disruption of essential services carried out with "intent to threaten the unity and integrity of India or to strike terror in any part of the people." It also made it a crime not to provide authorities with "information relating to any terrorist activity," and allowed for up to three months of preventive detention without charge. The ordinance came under sharp attack from civil rights groups, academics, lawyers, opposition parties, media organizations, and both religious and secular institutions. The National Human Rights Commission also maintained that existing laws were sufficient to fight the threat of terrorism.

Freedom of assembly nationwide suffered following the beginning of U.S.-led air strikes in Afghanistan on October 7, with student groups and organizations protesting India's backing of the U.S.-led campaign facing increased harassment from the police. On October 28, seven anti-U.S. protestors were killed when police opened fire on demonstrators in Malegaon, Maharashtra. Local police reportedly had tried to prevent a small group of Muslim protestors from distributing leaflets calling on people to boycott U.S.-made goods and to oppose air strikes in Afghanistan. Authorities claimed that protestors began throwing stones, leading first to a police baton-charge and then police shooting. Three more people were killed the following night when protestors tried to block the main road connecting Malegaon to the capital, Delhi. Police said they used baton charges and tear gas to disperse the crowd and only fired at protestors when that failed.

The government drew sharp criticism from numerous minority groups for selectively banning the Students Islamic Movement of India (SIMI) as part of its post-September 11 actions to counter terrorism while ignoring the "anti-national" activities of right-wing Hindu groups. At least four people were killed when police opened fire on a protest in Lucknow on September 27 following the arrest of some SIMI activists.

Insurgency and increased ethnic violence took a heavy toll in Assam and other northeastern states. In January, the United Liberation Front (ULFA) of Assam that advocates the establishment of a "sovereign socialist Assam" by armed force was blamed for a number of killings and bombings to disrupt elections and protest Republic Day celebrations. The group was also believed responsible for killing a ruling party leader, ten activists, and six political leaders in the run-up to elections in May. Indian federal troops killed at least five ULFA militants in response. In June, protestors opposed to any concessions to Naga rebels in Manipur burned the state legislature building and a former chief minister's home after the government extended a truce with the rebels.

The conflict in Kashmir remained a flashpoint for violence, as all parties failed to protect civilian non-combatants. On November 19, 2000, Prime Minister Vajpayee declared a unilateral ceasefire, but, shortly thereafter, Jammu and Kashmir police chief A.K. Suri announced that the ceasefire would not affect police counterinsurgency operations. Indian security personnel continued to target Muslim citizens suspected of supporting guerrillas. Arbitrary arrests, torture, and staged "encounter killings" were reported throughout the year, both when the ceasefire was in effect and after it was lifted on May 23, 2001.

India, like Pakistan, continued to deny political rights and to restrict freedoms of expression and assembly in Jammu and Kashmir. At least six people were killed when security personnel opened fire on demonstrators in Haigam and Maisuma in February. On February 15 in Haigam, forty kilometers north of Srinagar, five people were killed when Indian troops opened fire on demonstrators protesting the alleged killing of pro-independence activist Jalil Ahmed Shah in police custody the day before. In Maisuma, Srinagar on February 16, one person was killed in a similar incident. In both cases the police maintained that they were firing in self-defense.

On May 10, seventeen journalists were beaten by troops of the Indian Border Security Force (BSF) in Magam. The assault took place while the journalists were covering a suicide bomb attack against a BSF camp. The officers implicated were subsequently recalled from Kashmir but as of mid-November no disciplinary action had been taken against them.

July also witnessed a dramatic upsurge in violence in Kashmir with almost two hundred reported deaths in the week following the failed Agra summit between Prime Minister Vajpayee and Pakistani President Pervez Musharraf. On July 22, fifteen Hindu villagers were killed by suspected Islamic militants in Doda district. The attacks came a day after thirteen Hindus were killed while on pilgrimage.

Tensions flared up again after the September 11 attacks on the United States. On October 1, at least thirty-eight people were killed when a suicide attacker drove a hijacked government jeep to the main entrance of the state assembly in Srinagar and detonated explosives loaded in the car. The Pakistan-based Jaish-e Mohammad militant group claimed responsibility for the attack but then retracted the following day.

In the weeks that followed, numerous militants and security personnel were killed in tit-for-tat attacks while tensions heated up along the Line of Control between the Indian and Pakistan-controlled portions of the territory.

DEFENDING HUMAN RIGHTS

The brutal killings of two members of the Andhra Pradesh Civil Liberties Committee (APCLC) within a period of four months sent shock waves throughout the human rights community. In November 2000, T. Puroshottam, Joint Secretary of APCLC was stabbed to death by a group of unidentified men. Puroshottam had been a leading monitor of police abuses. In February 2001, Azam Ali, the district secretary of the Nalgonda branch of APCLC, was hacked to death by two sword-wielding youth. Despite demands from human rights organizations and allegations that police hired former members of armed groups to carry out the attacks, by November 2001 the government had yet to conduct any judicial inquiry.

On July 7 police raided the offices of Bharosa Trust and the Naz Foundation International in Lucknow, organizations that work on HIV/AIDS prevention, arresting several staff members. Although subsequently released on bail, the staff members were charged under article 377 of the Indian Penal Code, a provision that prohibits "carnal intercourse against the order of nature." Article 377 has been used repeatedly to justify discrimination and police brutality against gay, lesbian, and bisexual individuals.

The Narmada Bachao Andolan (NBA), one of India's largest peoples' movements, continued to protest the construction of large dams on the Narmada river in central India. Protesters highlighting the impact of the project on millions of river valley residents and the government's failure to adequately rehabilitate affected families continued to face harassment, police abuse, and contempt charges.

The work of rights activists was also hindered by restrictive laws and regulations. In July, the Supreme Court upheld the validity of a Union Home Ministry order requiring that organizations obtain clearance from the ministry before holding international conferences, seminars or workshops if the subject matter was "political, semi-political, communal or religious in nature or is related to human rights." On October 23, President K.R. Narayanan signed an ordinance empowering both central and state governments to suspend the passports and travel documents of any suspected terrorist, militant or "anti-national element," or any person suspected of having links with terrorist organizations. At this writing, a bill amending the Indian Passports Act, 1967 to reflect these changes was being considered during Indian parliament's winter session. Many human rights activists have been labeled by authorities as "anti-national elements."

The National Human Rights Commission continued to highlight the need for more effective implementation of laws on bonded labor and manual scavenging and issued several directives to state governments to compensate the victims of police and military atrocities. In total, the commission received 71,685 complaints alleging human rights violations in 2000-2001, 41,984 of which were from Uttar Pradesh. State human rights commissions were also set up in Maharashtra and Chattisgarh.

THE ROLE OF THE INTERNATIONAL COMMUNITY

United Nations

The year saw a much-heightened international focus on the plight of India's 160 million Dalits. In August 2001, U.N. Subcommission on the Promotion and Protection of Human Rights expert R.K.W. Goonesekere presented a working paper on work and descent-based discrimination, or caste discrimination, to the subcommission's fifty-third session. The presentation of the paper, and the ensuing debate amongst subcommission experts that followed, marked the first time that caste discrimination worldwide was treated as a serious rights violation by a U.N. human rights body.

The WCAR held in Durban, South Africa in September, was a watershed for the Dalit movement and for the rights of "untouchables" and other so-called lower-caste communities worldwide. The Dalit contingent of more than 160 activists, led by India's National Campaign for Dalit Human Rights, was one of the largest at the conference and drew strong international support from governments, India's National Human Rights Commission, and U.N. Secretary-General Kofi Annan. Dalit NGO efforts met with considerable resistance from the Indian government, which maintained that caste discrimination was an internal matter and used its political and economic leverage to censor any mention of caste in WCAR documents. In the run up to the conference, journalists, anthropologists, political parties, and others in India joined an increasingly mainstream debate on caste discrimination as an issue of international concern. The conference also highlighted caste discrimination as a global phenomenon affecting many Asian and African countries.

United States

The U.S. walked a tightrope in its relations with India and Pakistan following the September 11 attacks. India lobbied hard to ensure that the U.S.' campaign against terrorism would include militants in Kashmir.

After September 11, the Bush White House accelerated the Clinton administration's moves towards closer political and economic relations with India. On September 22, the U.S. lifted the sanctions imposed against India and Pakistan in the wake of nuclear testing by both nations in May 1998, allowing resumption of military equipment sales. The administration planned to increase funding for international military education and training (IMET) of Indian officers from $500,000 to $650,000 in the fiscal year 2002. It also planned a boost in bilateral economic assistance from $5 million to $7 million.

On November 9 President Bush met with Prime Minister Vajpayee. The U.S. renewed its offer to facilitate talks between India and Pakistan on Kashmir but made no public comments on the Prevention of Terrorism Ordinance.

The U.S. Commission on International Religious Freedom urged the Indian government in May 2001 to more swiftly and explicitly condemn and counteract increasing violence directed towards Christian populations. The panel voiced concern that the government's lack of decisive action created an atmosphere that invited inter-religious violence.

European Union

The E.U. welcomed the July Agra summit between India and Pakistan. Although the summit did not reach any resolution, the E.U. urged both countries to continue their dialogue—a dialogue that seemed far out of reach by mid-November.

In its annual Human Rights Report, the European Parliament called upon the E.U. to investigate the extent to which its policies "contribute to the abolition of caste discrimination and the practice of untouchability in India" and "to formulate strategies to counter the widespread practice [of caste discrimination]." A subsequent parliamentary resolution expressed regret that the final declaration of the World Conference Against Racism failed to highlight caste discrimination.

At this writing, the E.U. and India were preparing for a second annual summit to be held in New Delhi on November 23.

Japan

On October 26 Japan announced that it too would lift sanctions against India and Pakistan imposed after the 1998 nuclear tests, citing both countries'"efforts to contribute to strengthening the international coalition against terrorism" and increased instability in the region as a result of U.S.-led military strikes in Afghanistan.

World Bank

India continued to be the World Bank's largest borrower. In June 2001 the World Bank sanctioned four loans and credits to the government of India totaling U.S. $913.8 million, for a total lending of U.S. $2.5 billion for the fiscal year (FY) 2001.

The U.S. Foreign Aid Bill for the FY 2002 instructed the United States executive director at the World Bank to vote against any water or sewage project in India that did not prohibit the use of scavenger labor. Though prohibited by law, the government of India employs a majority of the country's estimated one million Dalit manual scavengers for the cleaning of non-flush public latrines.

In an August meeting in Delhi, Indian groups joined trade union leaders from Pakistan, Bangladesh, Sri Lanka, and Nepal to formulate a regional stance against IMF and World Bank policies that reduce jobs and increase layoffs. Over 160 delegates took part in the four-day seminar that also focused on the impact of the World Trade Organization on the developing world.

Relevant Human Rights Watch Reports:

Caste Discrimination: A Global Concern, 8/01

INDONESIA

Indonesia had another turbulent year, marked by a power struggle in Jakarta and an escalation in regional conflicts. The war in Aceh and an outbreak of communal violence in West Kalimantan produced the most civilian casualties, but conflicts in the Moluccas, Central Sulawesi, and Papua continued to simmer. By October, the number of displaced persons remained well over one million, half of them from the Moluccas.

The government made no serious efforts to address past or current abuses, new human rights legislation notwithstanding. The number of political prisoners rose steadily during the year, with many peaceful political activists charged with "spreading hatred toward the government," an offense associated with the government of former president Soeharto. The justice system remained a shambles.

Defending human rights remained a dangerous occupation, particularly in Aceh, where at least seven rights workers were killed.

Indonesia's bilateral donors showed concern over the regional conflicts, but their main focus was the long drawn-out struggle in Jakarta between the parliament and President Abdurrahman Wahid. That conflict ended peacefully in late July with Wahid's impeachment and the accession to the presidency of Megawati Sukarnoputri. A combination of relief over the transition, delight over some key cabinet appointees, and strategic and economic interests led many donors to rush to support the new administration.

In late 2001, widespread protests in Indonesian cities against the U.S. bombing of Afghanistan, accompanied by some intimidation of Westerners, underscored the difficulties President Megawati faced in balancing domestic political constituencies with external pressures.

HUMAN RIGHTS DEVELOPMENTS

The power struggle between President Abdurrahman Wahid and the Indonesian parliament consumed so much energy of the political elite that all of the country's major problems were left to fester. The Indonesian parliament, following decidedly unclear constitutional guidelines, formally censured Wahid on February 1 and again on April 30 over two financial scandals. At the end of May, the attorney-general ruled there was no evidence of presidential involvement in the scandals, but the parliament continued the de facto impeachment process on grounds of presidential incompetence. On July 23, the People's Consultative Assembly, Indonesia's highest legislative body, ignored a decree from Wahid disbanding parliament and convened a special session during which those present voted unanimously to remove Wahid and replace him with Megawati.

Megawati's first cabinet had some strengths, but her choice of attorney-general was poor. The new minister, M.A. Rahman, was a career prosecutor known for obstructing human rights cases, particularly with regard to East Timor.

The appointment continued a pattern of one step forward, two steps back that marked successive governments' approach to accountability. In November 2000, the parliament passed Law No. 26 setting up new courts to try cases of serious human rights violations. For the first time, crimes against humanity, war crimes, and other crimes of a "widespread or systematic" nature were incorporated into Indonesian law. The law established new courts to try such cases prospectively and provided for the establishment of "ad hoc" courts to prosecute serious human rights abuses that had occurred before the law took effect, including the 1999 East Timor cases.

But President Wahid's attorney-general, Marzuki Darusman, dithered and by the time the Wahid government fell, had failed to set up the courts or proceed with a single prosecution. His accomplice in procrastination was M.A. Rahman, appointed by Megawati to succeed him. As of October 2001, prosecutors for the new courts had been named, as had some but not all of the judges. Indictments were promised for December.

Other problems with accountability surfaced. The Indonesian National Human Rights Commission, known as Komnas-HAM, had been one of the most courageous defenders of human rights during the late Soeharto years. Ironically, it began to lose its critical edge under the democratically-elected Abdurrahman Wahid. Law No. 26 gave Komnas-HAM, rather than the police, responsibility for initial investigations into cases of serious human rights violations, but leading obstructionists within Komnas-HAM itself increasingly blocked action on key cases. A bill in the parliament to set up a national truth and reconciliation commission along the lines of the South African model remained undiscussed as of late 2001. With no interest in prosecutions on the part of the president, the attorney general, or the minister of justice, let alone the military, prospects for accountability looked bleaker than ever.

Aceh

The situation in Aceh deteriorated sharply during the year, and a six-hour visit in September by Megawati to the area made little difference. The 2001 death toll had topped 1,300 by September, and while most of the deaths were civilians killed in the course of military operations, the rebel Free Aceh Movement (Gerakan Aceh Merdeka or GAM) was also responsible for serious abuses.

In early November 2000, Indonesian security forces tried to prevent a rally organized by the Information Center for a Referendum on Aceh (Sentral Informasi Referendum Aceh or SIRA) in the provincial capital, Banda Aceh. They blocked people from reaching the city, including by shooting at sea and land transport; arrested and beat up members of the organizing committee; and raided offices of nongovernmental organizations (NGOs) in the lead-up to the rally. On November 20, the head of SIRA, Muhammad Nazar, was arrested on charges of "spreading hatred" for having hung banners in favor of a referendum and against the Indonesian military during a campus rally the previous August. He was convicted in March 2001 and sentenced to ten months in prison. With time served, he was released in October.

On December 6, 2000, four workers for an organization called Rehabilitation Action for Torture Victims of Aceh or RATA, were stopped outside Lhokseumawe, North Aceh, and abducted by a group of armed soldiers and civilians. Two men and a woman were executed; a fourth escaped and gave testimony identifying several of the killers. Later that month, four civilians and four military men were arrested. The civilians "escaped"—they were almost certainly let go with official connivance—from a police barracks in Medan, North Sumatra on March 22, 2001. One of them was back in Aceh in June, terrorizing local activists. The soldiers reportedly remained in the military police detention center in Medan as of October. Efforts by some within Komnas-HAM to have the RATA murders treated as serious enough to warrant prosecution by the new human rights courts were blocked by some of their own colleagues, and the prosecutor in Banda Aceh maintained in May that he lacked enough evidence to proceed with a trial.

On March 29, a human rights lawyer, Suprin Sulaiman, together with his client, Teungku Kamal, and a driver, Amiruddin, were shot dead shortly after leaving the

South Aceh district police station where Tgk. Kamal had been summoned as a suspect in criminal defamation of the police. In February, he had allegedly helped NGOs rescue five women that they believed were victims of sexual assault by the paramilitary police, Brimob. The women were brought to Banda Aceh where their case was widely covered by the local press. As they were returning home, the police took them into custody, whereupon they changed their stories, saying they had been forced by GAM to accuse the police. The police began targeting all NGO workers and journalists involved in the initial rescue and publicity efforts and formally named several as suspects. They did not proceed with any investigation into the deaths of the three men in South Aceh.

On April 11, President Wahid issued President Instruction (Inpres) No. 4, which effectively authorized increased police-military operations in Aceh. The instruction was issued following the closure of Exxon-Mobil gasfields in North Aceh because of security threats. The decree was roundly denounced in Aceh and the call for its revocation became a rallying cry for political activists province-wide.

Even before Inpres No.4 was issued, the security forces made a practice of retaliatory burnings of houses and shops to punish GAM attacks. On February 28, 2001, GAM took control briefly of the town of Idi Rayeuk in East Aceh. After military forces retook the town of 15,000, they burned it to the ground, causing massive displacement. Similar arson attacks took place throughout the year, despite the fact that on May 22, Brig. Gen. Zamroni, the commander of military operations in Aceh, formally forbade the practice.

In June, an eruption of violence in central Aceh led to hundreds of civilian deaths. It started with a GAM attack on the night of June 5-6 on Javanese settlers, killing more than forty. The next days and weeks saw a ferocious counterattack by the military working in collaboration with a local militia. By early July some 150 people had been confirmed dead by the Indonesian Red Cross and more than eight hundred houses had been burned to the ground.

On August 9, a massacre of thirty-one Acehnese workers took place on the Bumi Flora palm oil plantation in Julok, East Aceh. While both sides blamed each other for the killing, the evidence accumulated by late September suggested that Indonesian security forces were responsible and were intimidating potential witnesses. Reports by fact-finding teams sent by the district government and Komnas-HAM had not been made public by late 2001.

In addition to the killings noted above, several high-profile murders took place that remained unsolved by the end of November. On May 10, 2001, Major General (ret.) Haji Djohan, local leader of Golkar, the former ruling party, was gunned down outside his home in Banda Aceh. On September 1, Zaini Sulaiman, a member of the provincial parliament representing the United Development Party (known as PPP) was slain in front of his home by unidentified armed men. On September 6, Dayan Dawood, the rector of Banda Aceh's Syiah Kuala University, was killed as he was driving home from work in an official car. Neither side acknowledged responsibility for the killings.

Local parliamentarians faced threats from both sides. A legislator from East Aceh, Ghazali Usman, was abducted by GAM after having been named a member of the government fact-finding team looking into the Julok massacre. He had not been released by early November. Schoolteachers were also targeted. The Indonesian teachers' association noted in September that 135 of its members had been victims of violence in Aceh over the previous two years. Dozens of elementary schools were burned down during the year.

Banda Aceh's main newspaper, *Serambi Indonesia*, was forced to close twice during the year because of GAM threats, once in June and once in August.

Efforts at dialogue proved fruitless. Negotiations between the Indonesian government and GAM, facilitated by the Geneva-based Centre for Humanitarian Dialogue, foundered on mutual lack of trust and effectively broke down in early July when. Indonesia unilaterally withdrew from a security monitoring team. Later that month, police in Banda Aceh arrested six GAM negotiators despite government guarantees of their security. Five of the negotiators were conditionally released on August 29 but the charges against them were not dropped; one continued to be held as of October on the grounds that he held a false passport. New talks were scheduled for early November, but GAM refused to participate unless the Indonesian government dropped its case against the negotiators.

President Megawati signed a law giving autonomy to Aceh on August 11 and made that implementation of that law the centerpiece of her Aceh policy. But the law, changing the name of the province to Nanggroe Aceh Daroessalam (NAD), did not appear to have widespread support, especially as there was little consultation in Aceh before it was passed.

Papua

Conditions in Papua also continued to worsen. Although the Indonesian government made important political overtures, including a promise of substantial autonomy, to Papuan leaders in response to an all-Papua congress in June 2000, it also returned to a hardline approach.

In late 2000 and throughout 2001, Indonesian security forces intimidated and at times attacked civilians in areas where rebels of the Free Papua Movement (Organisasi Papua Merdeka or OPM) were believed to be active. They at times used indiscriminate or excessive force against pro-independence demonstrators: two Papuans were killed in Fakfak on December 1, 2000, eight in Merauke on December 2, and four in the highland town of Tiom on December 16, all during clashes between pro-independence demonstrators and security forces. Authorities also increased surveillance and harassment of prominent civil society leaders and banned peaceful pro-independence expression. Several activists were put on trial in Wamena, Jayapura, and Jakarta, many of them under the same "spreading hatred" laws used in Aceh.

One of the most highly publicized incidents took place in Abepura, near the provincial capital, on December 7, 2000. After two police officers and a security guard were killed in an early morning raid apparently carried out by pro-independence Papuan highlanders, police retaliated by rounding up scores of sleeping students (mostly highlanders) and other Papuans, beating and torturing many of them for much of the next thirty-six hours. One student was shot and killed, two more died as a result of beatings, and dozens sustained serious injuries. The case became the subject of a high profile investigation that led investigators to issue a hard-hitting report naming twenty-six police officers as suspects, but no charges were filed and the future of the prosecution remained in doubt as of mid-November 2001.

The worst violence occurred in the Wasior area of Manokwari district, triggered by the murder on April 6 of three plantation workers. Plantation officials claimed the perpetrators were rebels. Security forces responded by launching violent "sweeps" or raids in nearby villages which, according to local rights monitors, left six civilians dead by mid-May. On June 13, five police officers and a logging company employee were killed in an attack police blamed on the rebels, prompting renewed sweeps. By mid-November, there had been dozens of new arrests, several reports of torture, and thousands of people in the region had fled their homes fearing retaliation. Local monitors in November also reported security crackdowns in Ilaga and near Timika following clashes between rebels and security forces.

The Indonesian parliament passed the Papuan autonomy bill on October 23, giving Papuans a greater say in provincial government and allowing provincial authorities to retain 80 percent of local forestry and fishery revenues and 70 percent of oil, gas, and mining revenues. Papuan political leaders, however, continued to demand independence. On November 10, Theys Eluay, a leading Papuan independence leader was abducted and killed outside Jayapura; his family blamed security forces, as international and domestic organizations called for an independent inquiry.

Central Kalimantan

An eruption of violence in Central Kalimantan in February 2001 around the logging port of Sampit, Kotawaringin Timur district, led to indigenous Dayaks killing some five hundred immigrants from the island of Madura, off the coast of East Java, and displacing more than 150,000 people. Many of the killings involved decapitation, and little distinction was made between men, women, and children. The outbreak had complex roots but appeared to be linked to longstanding economic and social grievances of the Dayaks, competition over local resources, and new opportunities for political mobilization along ethnic lines. Muhamad Usop, a Dayak leader who sought the Central Kalimantan governorship, was arrested on May 4 and held briefly on incitement charges.

As elsewhere in Indonesia, police proved incapable of halting the violence, and the army was sent in, further poisoning relations between the police and army.

Maluku

Christian-Muslim violence continued to erupt sporadically in the Moluccas. The government made no effort to remove Laskar Jihad, the Java-based Muslim militia that arrived in the province by the thousands in 2000. Its members continued to be responsible for human rights violations. In early 2001, evidence emerged of Laskar Jihad forcing several hundred Christians from Teor, Ceram and the island of Kesui to convert to Islam and circumcising men and women alike. On May 4, the

Wahid government finally took action against the head of Laskar Jihad, Jafar Umar Thalib, but not for any of his actions as commander of a private army. Instead, he was charged with murder for sentencing one of his followers to execution by stoning and having a crowd proceed to kill the confessed adulterer. The arrest appeared to prompt a new wave of violence that killed eighteen Christians by the end of May. On June 14, a botched raid by an army battalion on a Laskar Jihad post left twenty-two Muslims dead. On August 8, Megawati's vice-president, Hamzah Haz, made a point of meeting with Jafar Umar Thalib and Laskar Jihad members. While he urged them to abide by the constitution, the meeting gave the group new legitimacy.

In June, Alex Manuputty, the Christian militia leader and founder of the Front for Maluku Sovereignty, was arrested on charges of rebellion. He was sentenced to four months in November.

East and West Timor

No one was brought to justice by November for the 1999 crimes in East Timor. Half-hearted efforts by the attorney general's office during the year to set up an ad hoc tribunal to try people originally named in September 2000 as suspected perpetrators of serious crimes came to nothing. The tribunal needed a recommendation from the parliament to the president and then a presidential instruction. When President Wahid finally issued the instruction in April, it only allowed for prosecution of crimes occurring after the August 30, 1999 referendum. After protests, the instruction was returned to the Ministry of Justice for rewriting. The reworded decree was issued in August by President Megawati in one of her first acts after taking office, but it remained flawed, as it only allowed for prosecution of two cases from before August 30, 1999, that the attorney general's office had deemed a priority. It thus weakened the possibility of examining the whole pattern of state policy that would be critical to establishing a crimes against humanity case.

In the meantime, the six alleged killers of the three United Nations High Commissioner for Refugees (UNHCR) workers, murdered in Atambua, West Timor, on September 6, 2000 were brought to trial in January 2001. On May 4, they were sentenced to prison terms ranging from ten to twenty months. They had only been accused of assault, apparently at the direction of the man who became Megawati's attorney general, M.A. Rahman, but even that charge could have resulted in a twelve-year sentence. The leniency of the sentences was widely condemned internationally.

Eurico Gutteres, the East Timorese militia leader responsible for much of the 1999 violence in the city of Dili, was charged in relation to another incident in Atambua that took place on September 24, 2000 shortly after the UNHCR killings. Accused of incitement for resisting efforts of authorities to disarm the militias, he was sentenced to six months in prison by the North Jakarta district court on April 30, 2001, but, credited with time spent under house arrest, he served only twenty-three days before being released.

Little progress was made toward addressing the 1999 violence in East Timor. As of September, some 50,000 East Timorese remained in West Timor. A June 6, 2001 registration of that population conducted by the Indonesian government found that 98.2 percent wished to stay in Indonesia, but it was unclear to what extent the refugees had access to relevant information and felt able to answer freely. Only the views of "heads of households"—usually men—were surveyed. Many refugees were expected to return in the aftermath of the peaceful election in East Timor on August 30.

DEFENDING HUMAN RIGHTS

At least seven human rights defenders were killed in Aceh between November 2000 and October 2001, including the three RATA workers mentioned above. Muhamad Efendi Malikon, thirty-five, secretary of a human rights organization called Care Forum for Human Rights—East Aceh (Forum Peduli HAM-Aceh Timur) was killed on February 28 in Peukan Langsa village, Langsa Timur subdistrict, East Aceh. His body was found shortly after the vehicle in which he was riding was stopped at a checkpoint by the paramilitary police, Brimob. At the time, he was carrying a substantial amount of money to turn over to widows whose husbands had been the victims of human rights violations in 1991.

Suprin Sulaiman, a lawyer with Koalisi-HAM in South Aceh, was killed on March 29 after accompanying his client to an interrogation session by police. (See above.)

Yusuf Usman, another member of Forum-Peduli HAM-Aceh Timor, was killed on September 8. Jafar Syehdo, fifty-seven, a volunteer with the Indonesian Red Cross (Palang Merah Indonesia, PMI) was found shot to death on October 3 in Bireun. The PMI is the only humanitarian organization with a province-wide field operation; among its tasks is the recovery of bodies of victims of the conflict.

No progress was made in the investigation of the death of Jafar Siddiq Hamzah, human rights lawyer and founder of the International Forum on Aceh, whose stabbed body was found north of Medan, North Sumatra in September 2000.

Acehnese human rights monitors trying to investigate abuses were routinely hampered by the security forces, sometimes through short-term detention.

THE ROLE OF THE INTERNATIONAL COMMUNITY

International attention focused largely on the power struggle over the presidency, the economy, the transition to democracy, and regional conflicts. Donors continued to express frustration, often publicly, at Indonesia's failure to make headway in bringing human rights abusers to justice, particularly in relation to the 1999 violence in East Timor and the September 2000 killing of the three UNHCR workers.

The resumption of military aid to Indonesia was a major issue for many donors and their respective publics. In August, the *Jakarta Post* announced that the United Kingdom (U.K.) would resume arms sales to Indonesia, quoting U.K. Foreign Office Minister Ben Bradshaw as saying Britain had accepted Indonesian army assurances that the arms would not be used for internal repression. The U.S. also decided to "re-engage" the army, without, however, resuming sales of lethal weapons.

United Nations

The U.N. Security Council continued to be concerned about Indonesia's failure to make any progress toward accountability for the 1999 violence in East Timor and the situation of East Timorese refugees in West Timor. In a visit to Jakarta in mid-November 2000, a Security Council delegation stressed the need for speedy resolution of the refugee problem and progress in bringing human rights abusers to trial. On May 4, Secretary-General Kofi Annan took the unusual step of issuing a statement expressing outrage at the light sentences handed down by a Jakarta court against the killers of the UNHCR workers.

The U.N.'s Office for the Coordination of Humanitarian Affairs (OCHA) continued to be active in Indonesia. On February 27, it sent two missions to Kalimantan to look into the impact of the Dayak-Madurese violence, particularly as it related to the internally displaced. In late August, OCHA opened a small office in Aceh to coordinate humanitarian aid, and it continued to be active in the Moluccas.

In late 2000, the United Nations Development Program launched a program called "Partnership for Governance Reform" through which it coordinated aid programs from several donors in efforts to strengthen democracy and civil society. Program areas included strengthening of parliamentary institutions; electoral reform; civil society participation; legal and judicial reform; anti-corruption efforts; decentralization and civil society reform; and police reform. The Asian Development Bank, World Bank, and several bilateral donors including the Netherlands and Nordic countries were among the initial donors.

On November 22, 2000, five U.N. human rights experts issued a joint statement of concern about the deteriorating situation in Aceh. Francis Deng, the U.N. special rapporteur for internally displaced persons, visited Indonesia during the last week in September.

Indonesia presented its first report to the Committee against Torture in November 2001; in doing so, it announced that it would ratify the International Covenant on Civil and Political Rights and the International Covenant on Economic, Social, and Cultural Rights by the end of the year.

European Union

The E.U. continued actively to strengthen relations with Indonesia, while also exploring ways to resolve regional conflicts. On December 13, 2000, in response to a proposal from the European Commission to develop closer relations with Indonesia, the European Parliament expressed concern about factors undermining democratization in Indonesia, including lack of accountability for human rights abuses, the continued role of the armed forces in government, and the ongoing conflicts in the Moluccas, Aceh, and Papua. It supported further aid for Indonesia as long as attempts were made to resolve those conflicts, human rights were substantially improved, and the corruption problem was addressed.

In May, the E.U. echoed Kofi Annan's protest over the light sentences given the six men found guilty of the deaths of the UNHCR workers. In a statement issued on May 10, the E.U. welcomed the Indonesian attorney-general's declared intent to appeal the sentences and pointedly recalled Indonesia's earlier commitment to the United Nations Commission on Human Rights that the trials of the suspects be conducted in conformity with international standards of justice and fairness."

The E.U. repeatedly called on Indonesia during the year to implement Security Council Resolution 1319 with regard to disarming the militias in West Timor and facilitating the return of East Timorese there.

United States

Both Congress and the Clinton administration condemned the murders of the UNHCR workers in West Timor, and urged the indictment of senior military officials responsible for the violence in 1999. Accountability in general remained high on the agenda of the U.S. embassy in Jakarta.

The U.S. was actively engaged in supporting dialogue and strengthening civil society in Aceh. In March, the State Department denied reports in the Indonesian press that the U.S. was backing an Indonesian military offensive in order to secure the Exxon-Mobil gasfields, saying that it was instead urging restraint and a "comprehensive political solution." U.S. diplomats repeatedly reiterated their support for Indonesia's territorial integrity.

Megawati Sukarnoputri became the first head of state to visit the U.S. in the aftermath of the September 11 attacks in New York and Washington. Rather than cancel the long-planned visit, the Bush administration used it to secure Indonesia's cooperation in opposing global terrorism. The administration had earlier decided to expand contacts with the TNI, lifting some of the sanctions that had been in place since the East Timor violence in 1999, including a ban on non-lethal commercial arms sales, and used the visit to announce this. Restrictions on foreign military sales (FMS), U.S.-government financed arms sales, and international military education and training (IMET) programs remained in place in accordance with provisions of the so-called Leahy Amendment.

The U.S. also promised bilateral assistance for judicial reform and carried out some limited police training in areas such as crowd control and counternarcotics efforts. The U.S. Export-Import bank gave a U.S. $3.2 million credit to Indonesia in May for police equipment for forensics work.

Indonesia's failure to curb threats against Americans by radical Islamic groups following September 11 led to U.S. protests that its citizens and interests were not being sufficiently protected.

Japan

Japan quietly urged President Wahid to move forward with setting up the ad hoc tribunal on East Timor. While not objecting to military operations in Aceh, Japanese officials urged both Indonesian security forces and GAM to exercise restraint. Japan continued to be Indonesia's largest donor. Its aid programs included some training in community-based policing.

President Megawati visited Japan in September and met with Prime Minister Junichiro Koizumi. The two leaders expressed opposition to terrorism. Megawati asked for Japanese aid and private investment; she also sought rescheduling of Indonesia's debt (more than $2.7 billion) to Japan. Koizumi agreed to consider her requests in advance of the donor conference in November.

Australia

Relations with Indonesia, seriously strained by Australia's role in the East Timor crisis in 1999, improved somewhat with the visit to Canberra by President Wahid in late June 2001—the first visit by an Indonesian president in twenty-six years. According to press reports, he assured Prime Minister John Howard that prosecutions would take place for serious crimes committed in East Timor in 1999.

Prime Minister Howard became the first head of state to visit President Megawati after her accession to the presidency in July. On his return to Australia, Howard declared that the two countries had put their differences over East Timor behind them.

Relations quickly became strained again in August, however, over the issue of asylum-seekers and undocumented migrants seeking to enter Australia from Indonesian waters. Indonesia is not a party to the 1951 Refugee Convention.

International Financial Institutions

In February, the World Bank launched a new three-year country assistance strategy for Indonesia, criticizing the high level of debt and corruption. It announced that it would lend only $492.7 million for fiscal year 2001, down from the average of $1.3 billion annually from 1990-1997. The bank also urged adoption of an agreement with the International Monetary Fund (IMF) that would allow disbursement of a $400 million loan held up since late 2000. The loan was eventually disbursed on September 10, 2001.

President Megawati met with World Bank President James Wolfensohn in September; he stressed the need for progress on legal and judicial reform before the bank could consider increasing its lending.

Relevant Human Rights Watch Reports:

The War in Aceh, 8/01
Violence and Political Impasse in Papua, 7/01

MALAYSIA

The government of Mahathir Mohamed, beginning his third decade as prime minister, continued to crack down hard on potential political challengers, arresting key opposition leaders, banning political rallies, and breaking up public gatherings with force.

The year began with the prime minister's popularity in decline. In November 2000, the ruling coalition suffered a by-election defeat in Mahathir's home district in Kedah state and the government faced increasingly vocal opposition protests. In response, it turned the draconian Internal Security Act (ISA) against its political opponents. Among those targeted under the ISA, which allows detainees to be held indefinitely without charge or public airing of the evidence against them, were minority Shi'a Muslims, supporters of jailed former Deputy Prime Minister Anwar Ibrahim, and youth leaders in the opposition PAS (Partai Islam Se-Malaysia) party, although individuals linked to specific violent acts were also among those detained. In the wake of the September 11 attacks in the United States, authorities used global concern with terrorism to justify their actions.

HUMAN RIGHTS DEVELOPMENTS

The government detained six Shi'a Muslims under the ISA between October 2000 and January 2001, three of whom reportedly were still being held in November. Other ISA detentions of Shi'a Muslims in previous years were said by government officials to be necessary to prevent "religious disharmony" that could damage the nation's political and economic development.

On November 5, 2000, police punched and kicked participants at a peaceful demonstration outside the city of Klang, fired tear gas and water cannons, and arrested 126 people demonstrating in support of Anwar Ibrahim. The National Justice Party (Partai Keadilan Nasional or Keadilan), founded by Anwar's wife, Wan Azizah, had applied for but been denied a permit to hold the demonstration.

In January, nine government opponents were arrested and charged with rioting in the run-up to the November 2000 by-election in Kedah. The nine were accused of trying to prevent busloads of supporters of the ruling coalition (Barisan Nasional), whom they believed were traveling to the area to vote illegally, from reaching the polls.

In January, police also forcibly prevented political speeches and stopped cultural displays at a multi-cultural festival organized by the opposition, despite having issued a permit for the festival. Police also stopped a book launch party at a restaurant attended by more than 1,000 former Labour Party members. The book was a historical account of the leftist party disbanded three decades ago.

In February, police arrested four protestors, including Keadilan Vice-President Tian Chua and columnist/filmmaker Hishammuddin Rais, at a demonstration calling for former Attorney General Mohtar Abdullah to be for abuse of power in conducting the prosecution of Anwar. On February 14, police used tear gas and water cannons to disperse 15,000 to 20,000 people at a Keadilan political rally in Kampung Lahar, held on private property. Police had refused to grant a permit for the rally.

On February 9, Marina Yusoff, former vice president of Keadilan, was fined 5,000 ringgit (approximately U.S. $1,315) for asserting in a speech in September 2000 that the ruling coalition had sparked anti-Chinese riots in 1969 following a local election defeat. On March 5, Keadilan youth leader Mohamed Ezam Mohamed Nor was arrested and subsequently charged with sedition for remarks published in *Mingguan Malaysia* newspaper in which he reportedly stated that he would continue leading street demonstrations until the government was brought down. On March 6, police arrested nine people who held a candlelight vigil for him outside a police station. Ezam was released on bail on March 13, but, as described below, was subsequently rearrested less than a month later under the ISA.

Ethnic violence broke out on March 9 when ethnic Indians and Malays clashed in Kampung Medan, a poor quarter of Kuala Lumpur. Police reported that six people, including five of Indian origin, were killed and over fifty injured. Most of the wounded were also ethnic Indians. Four opposition party leaders jointly challenged the official casualty figures, suggesting the actual figures were higher: in response, the government threatened to charge them with sedition, though no charges were ultimately brought. Indian community representatives continued to demand further investigation.

On April 10-11, just days before public protests planned to mark the second anniversary of the sentencing of former Deputy Prime Minister Anwar Ibrahim, the authorities detained seven opposition leaders under the ISA, then three other people in the following days. Most of the ten, who were all held incommunicado until May 4, were members of Keadilan. The authorities alleged that they were plotting to overthrow the government but produced no evidence to substantiate this. On May 30, in an unusual and courageous ruling Judge Hishamuddin Yunus ordered the release of two ISA detainees on a writ of habeas corpus, and suggested that the parliament should review and either scrap or amend the ISA to reduce its potential for abuse. By mid-November, authorities had released three more detainees, but five had been served with two-year detention orders and were being held at the Kamunting Detention Centre. The five are: Tian Chua, Ezam Mohamed Noor, Hishammuddin Rais, Saari Sungib, and Lokman Nor.

In July, the authorities detained two student activists, Khairul Anuar Ahmad Zainuddin and Mohamad Fuad Mohamad Ikhwan, under the ISA, the former for twenty three days and the latter for ten days.

Also in July, the government banned all political rallies stating that they would undermine the country's security. When PAS subsequently planned a series of meetings to protest the policy, police refused to grant permits and dispersed those who attempted to attend. On August 2-4, police arrested an additional ten people under the ISA, all of whom were affiliated with or supporters of PAS, including four prominent youth leaders. The authorities said the ten belonged to a group that planned to overthrow the government, sometimes labeling the group the Malaysian

Militant Group and sometimes the Malaysian Mojahedin Group. One of those detained, Nik Adli Nik Aziz, was the son of a leading PAS official. The authorities alleged he had received military training in Afghanistan and had learned bomb making from Muslim rebels in the Philippines, but he denied this and PAS leaders emphasized that they used only peaceful, democratic means in their struggle against the ruling coalition. As of mid-November, nine of the ten remained in custody after being served two-year detention orders.

Four days after the September 11 attacks in the United States, Deputy Prime Minister Abdullah Ahman Badawi sought to justify the ISA as providing "an initial preventive measure before threats get beyond control," and on October 10 two other alleged members of the Malaysian Mojahedin Group were detained under the act. PAS leaders, however, dismissed the detentions as a "political ploy" and challenged the government to bring charges and produce the detainees in open court.

The government maintained important restrictions on press freedom. Under the Printing Presses and Publications Act, newspapers were required annually to obtain licenses to publish from the government and those held to have breached the terms of their license could be restricted or shut down. The PAS organ *Harakah*, formerly a biweekly publication, continued to be restricted to two issues per month for allegedly breaching the terms of its license in 2000 by selling to non-PAS members. In March, editions of both *Far Eastern Economic Review* and *Asiaweek*, which had been chronicling the growing opposition to Mahathir and signs of political unrest, were held back by government censors. Mahathir had complained that the photo of him on the cover of an earlier edition of *Asiaweek* had made him look like "an idiot."

Authorities also appeared to be struggling for a way to rein in independent Internet daily malaysiakini.com, winner of an International Press Institute 2001 Press Freedom Award. As part of its effort to promote Malaysia's multimedia corridor, the government had promised there would be no Internet censorship, and Internet sites were exempt from media licensing provisions. Early in the year, ministers accused malaysiakini.com of receiving funds via a Bangkok press group from financier George Soros, long pilloried in the government-controlled Malaysian press as personally responsible for the Asian economic crisis in 1997. On February 11, an information ministry official said that malaysiakini.com would be barred from covering government press conferences "because their credibility is doubtful." On May 23, the deputy home affairs minister told parliament that the government was monitoring "every article" published by malaysiakini.com to ensure that its writings did not upset public order.

The threat of multimillion dollar libel awards against journalists and media publications, said to be the highest such awards among the fifty-four countries of the Commonwealth, also continued to limit press freedom. A Bar Council publication in March noted that, since businessman and one-time Mahathir insider Vincent Tan won a 10 million Ringgit (approximately U.S. $2.2 million) judgment against a group of media defendants in 1994, more than seventy libel cases had been filed against journalists and media defendants, many seeking millions of dollars in damages.

Serious questions remained about the independence of the judiciary. In March, the Kuala Lumpur Bar Committee issued a memorandum concluding that "the administration of justice in Malaysia is in its darkest hour since independence." By early November, however, a number of developments suggested that the appointment in December 2000 of respected jurist Dzaiddin Abdullah as chief justice was beginning to have a positive impact. On March 15, former police chief Abdul Rahim Noor was sentenced for the prison beating of Anwar Ibrahim, though only to a two-month term. In June, a federal court dismissed contempt charges that had been laid against Anwar's lawyer, Zainur Zakaria, when he petitioned for the removal of two of the prosecutors during Anwar's trial. The May 30 decision of Judge Hishamuddin Yunus to order the release of two ISA detainees was also a powerful reassertion of judicial independence.

In another important decision on June 8, high court judge Muhammad Kamil Awang overturned the results of the March 1999 state elections in Likas (Sabah) after finding that the electoral roll included nonexistent voters. (Sabah's three million population includes an estimated 500,000 immigrants, mostly from neighboring Indonesia and the Philippines). The judge also sparked a police investigation into improper judicial interference when he disclosed that one of his superiors had ordered him in 1999 to dismiss the case.

On October 16, prominent human rights lawyer Karpal Singh was put on trial for sedition for comments he had made in January 2000 while lead defense counsel for Anwar Ibrahim. Following reports that increased levels of arsenic had been found in Anwar's blood, Singh had suggested in court that "people in high places" were trying to poison his client. He faced up to three years in jail if convicted.

It was a difficult year for migrant workers. In May, the government announced plans to expel 100,000 illegal migrant workers. Government figures showed that 50,953 illegal immigrants were detained in nationwide operations between January and the end of June. In August, the government announced plans to amend the Immigration Act to punish illegal migrant workers and employers who engage them with imprisonment and caning. Officials justified the measures as necessary to stem the influx of illegal migrants, who they blamed for an increase in serious crime.

DEFENDING HUMAN RIGHTS

Human rights groups continued to play a critical role in investigating and publicizing abuses. In response to the increased use of the ISA, rights groups such as Aliran, Hakam, and Suaram (Suara Rakyat Malaysia) helped form a new umbrella organization called AIM (Abolish ISA Movement), which campaigned actively on behalf of detainees' rights and for repeal of the law. Some human rights workers were among those detained: Badaruddin Ismail (also known as Pak Din), a member of Suaram's secretariat, was among those detained under the ISA. He was released on June 5.

With the government still exerting substantial control over major media outlets, Malaysia's alternative media and rights groups were also important sources of independent information about human rights and related developments.

Malaysia's national human rights commission (Suhakam), established by the government in late 1999, also began to speak out more forcefully, though its performance was uneven. It called for review of the ISA and urged the government, unsuccessfully, to allow Anwar to travel to Germany for surgery for back injuries that he apparently sustained as a result of being beaten in custody. In early August, Suhakam criticized the police in a report on freedom of assembly. The commission said police had refused to grant permits for public gatherings without adequate justification, and had given protestors insufficient time to disperse and used excessive force against them. It called for amendment of the Police Act to remove the police permit system and require only that police be given advance notice of an assembly, to provide that any conditions should not restrict free expression, and to require the police to exercise restraint in dispersing demonstrators. The commission also recommended amendment of the Public Order (Preservation) Act 1958, which it said unduly restricted freedom of assembly. Later in August, Suhakam published the results of its five-month inquiry into police conduct in connection with the November 2000 Keadilan-sponsored rally near Klang. The commission accused the police of using excessive force in crowd control and in the arrest and treatment of detainees. The government said it would study Suhakam's findings and recommendations.

The trial of Irene Fernandez, head of Tenaganita (Women's Force), already the longest trial in Malaysian history, entered its sixth year. Fernandez faced three years in prison if convicted on charges of malicious publishing for her July 1995 memorandum on abuses in immigration detention centers. Several former detainees testified in 2001, corroborating allegations in the report of the existence of torture and sexual abuse in the camps.

THE ROLE OF THE INTERNATIONAL COMMUNITY

The continuing crackdown in Malaysia evoked little international response either in the region, including from Japan, the country's largest bilateral aid donor and one of its most important investors, or from Western governments.

In April 2001, Foreign Minister Syed Hamid complained when a dozen foreign Malaysia-based diplomats attended a private briefing by Wan Azizah on the health of her husband, Anwar Ibrahim. The minister said he would summon the diplomats and explain to them "the actual political situation" in Malaysia.

The Bush administration shifted its position on Malaysia following the September 11 attacks. In late June, Wan Azizah visited Washington and met senior U.S. State Department officials and members of Congress. A few weeks later, Syed met with U.S. Secretary of State Colin Powell and was reportedly told that a meeting between President Bush and Prime Minister Mahathir could take place only if there were progress on Anwar's case and in the treatment of political dissidents. However, when Mahathir and Bush met at the Asia Pacific Economic Cooperation (APEC) summit in Shanghai in late October, Bush reportedly made no public comment on Malaysia's human rights record.

PAKISTAN

General Pervez Musharraf took steps that further consolidated the army's authority and all but ensured that any future government would operate under military tutelage. With media attention focused on internal unrest following Pakistan's break with the Taliban and its public support for the United States-led intervention there, Musharraf's movement toward establishing a controlled democracy faced little international opposition. Musharraf arguably emerged from the political realignment that occurred following the September 11 attacks on the U.S. in a stronger position. He reshuffled the military corps command so as to marginalize key Taliban backers; arrested leaders of religious parties who challenged his authority; and secured a critical rescheduling of Pakistan's debt, donor commitments of new loans, and the lifting of existing sanctions. Nevertheless, the potential domestic fallout from a prolonged U.S. presence in Afghanistan and the possibility of a Northern Alliance-dominated government emerging in Afghanistan left Musharraf clearly discomfited by November.

Mainstream political parties continued to operate under tight constraints. A ban on rallies remained in force, and the authorities detained thousands of political party members and activists to forestall planned demonstrations against government policies and continued military rule. The government used a draconian accountability law that it introduced shortly after the October 1999 coup as leverage in a largely unsuccessful attempt to fashion a pliant party leadership.

HUMAN RIGHTS DEVELOPMENTS

The formation of the multiparty Alliance for the Restoration of Democracy (ARD) on December 3, 2000, posed the first major challenge to military rule and remained a principal target of the Musharraf administration during the first months of the year. The alliance brought together by the country's two largest political organizations—the Pakistan Muslim League (PML) of deposed Prime Minister Nawaz Sharif and the Pakistan People's Party (PPP), led by the self-exiled former prime minister Benazir Bhutto—with the avowed aim of restoring parliamentary government through immediate elections. In an apparent effort to forestall the alliance from pursuing its objectives and to control any restoration of parliamentary government, the Musharraf administration lent tacit support to a group of dissidents within the PML who had broken with Sharif after the coup and who opposed the formation of the alliance.

The National Accountability Ordinance was a key instrument in this effort. The ordinance, enacted in November 1999 ostensibly to facilitate prosecution of officials and other leaders for corruption and other illegal acts, combined unchecked powers of arrest, investigation, and prosecution in a single institution, the National Accountability Bureau (NAB). The ordinance provided for detention of suspects for up to ninety days without charge, abolished bail, and established special accountability courts. Additional provisions required that trials be conducted within thirty days of charges being filed, effectively limiting defendants' ability to arrange an adequate defense, and automatically barred those convicted under the ordinance from holding public office for twenty-one years.

Although linkages could not conclusively be drawn, events suggested that the government withdrew accountability cases against PML leaders or improved conditions of detention in exchange for obtaining their support for the dissident faction or their resignation from party posts. Syed Ghous Ali Shah, who had been held by NAB since his April 2000 acquittal in a plane hijacking conspiracy case against Sharif and his senior aides, resigned as the PML president for Sindh province on March 2, 2001; the move was followed by Shah's transfer from NAB custody to a hospital. On March 8, before new elections for a party president were held, about two hundred pro-dissident activists of the Sindh PML youth wing forcibly occupied the PML office in Karachi. Police were subsequently deployed in the area, but did not interfere with the takeover. Within days of the occupation, an accountability case was withdrawn against the Sindh PML youth wing leader.

In April, the Pakistan Supreme Court ordered the government to modify the ordinance to restore the right to bail and reduce pretrial detention to fifteen days. However, the court order did little to limit the potential for selective application of the law; detention periods could be extended at the court's discretion, and the burden of proof remained on the accused.

The other major devices employed by the government to limit opposition political activity were the Maintenance of Public Order (MPO) ordinance, which broadly prohibited any speech deemed "likely to cause fear or alarm to the public" or "likely to further any activity prejudicial to public safety or the maintenance of public order," and a ban on "political meetings at public places, strikes and processions" that was imposed in March 2000. Officials announced in August that they would lift the ban ninety days before the general elections scheduled to take place in October 2002.

On two separate occasions, authorities arrested hundreds of ARD leaders and activists to forestall planned protests. On March 20, police in Punjab carried out mass arrests to prevent the ARD from holding a rally that had been planned for March 23; ARD leaders said that about two hundred party members were detained in Lahore alone and some 2,500 throughout Punjab. A second rally, planned for May 1 in Karachi, was similarly suppressed. According to the Sindh home secretary, Mukhtar Ahmed, about 850 ARD members had been taken into "protective custody" throughout the province as of April 30. On May 1, protesters clashed with police across Karachi, chanting, waving placards, and throwing stones. Police responded with baton charges and tear gas, arresting three hundred people.

Regional parties were also prevented from holding planned protests. On April 9, police in Karachi used batons, fired tear gas, and arrested about ninety people, many of them women, who were protesting against water shortages in Sindh province. Two days later, police arrested thirty activists of the Muttahida Qaumi Movement (MQM) and Jeay Sindh Qaumi Mahaz (JSQM) after they arrived outside the Karachi Press Club to begin a fast to protest the shortages.

For much of the year, the authorities enforced the ban on political meetings selectively. They prevented mainstream political parties from holding meetings, but allowed religious parties to hold regular meetings and processions in most parts of the country. This changed after September 11, however, when Musharraf announced his administration's support for the U.S.-led anti-terrorism coalition. Religious parties that continued to mobilize protesters in support of the Taliban, or who explicitly challenged Musharraf's authority, faced arrest.

On October 7, North West Frontier Province (NWFP) authorities placed Maulana Fazlur Rehman, leader of the Jamiat Ulema-i Islam (JUI), and Maulana Samiul Haq, leader of a JUI splinter party, under house arrest. On October 22, more than one hundred members of the JUL and the Jamiat-e Islami (JI) were arrested in Sindh, reportedly to thwart plans by the parties to stage a sit-in at Jacobabad, site of a Pakistani air base used by U.S. military personnel. On November 3, authorities placed JI head Qazi Hussain Ahmed under house arrest to prevent him from participating in an anti-U.S. rally in the Bajaur tribal agency bordering Afghanistan. Two days later, the government filed sedition charges against Ahmed; although details of the charges were not specified, Ahmed had two weeks earlier accused the government of working against national interests in a speech in Rawalpindi, near the federal capital.

The withdrawal of government support from the Taliban starting in September and the government's decision to back U.S.-led military action in Afghanistan also triggered public protests in Quetta, the capital of Baluchistan province. On October 8, police clashed with protesters at rallies in Quetta involving some seven to eight thousand demonstrators, many of them Afghan refugees. On October 9, three Afghan refugees were shot dead by police in Kuchlak, a small town close to Quetta, with police reportedly failing to give warnings or use teargas or other means to control the mob before opening fire.

The militarization of civilian institutions, a trend already observable during Nawaz Sharif's second term in office, continued under Musharraf. According to official records cited by the respected Lahore-based weekly *Friday Times*, at the beginning of the year about 175 serving and retired military officers held high-level civilian posts. In addition, Musharraf had established a countrywide network of army monitoring teams to supervise and assist in the functioning of the civilian bureaucracy. The teams were constituted at the provincial, regional, and district levels and consisted of army personnel, Directorate of Military Intelligence personnel, and members of the Inter-Services Intelligence Agency's field units. In practice, local observers claimed, the teams interfered with the autonomy of the civilian bureaucracy and frequently disregarded civil procedure laws.

At the executive level, Musharraf initiated moves that institutionalized his personal authority and formalized the military's role in governance. On June 20, he amended his 1999 Proclamation of Emergency Order, formally dissolving the suspended national and provincial assemblies, and issued a President's Succession Order enabling him to assume the presidency the following day. How long his term of office would last was not clear. Musharraf justified his actions as being necessary to ensure political and economic stability. On July 4, Musharraf issued an order reconstituting the National Security Council (NSC) that he had established immediately after the coup. Under the new guidelines, it would aid and advise the president on "Islamic ideology, national security, sovereignty, integrity, and solidarity of Pakistan." The revamped NSC was to be chaired by the president and consist of the chairmen of the joint chiefs of staff committee; the naval, army, and air force chiefs; provincial governors; and "such other members as may be appointed by the president in his discretion." The government also announced on August 14 that it would promulgate new constitutional amendments in 2002 aimed at introducing checks and balances in government. Officials said that the proposed amendments would be opened for public debate but would be finalized by June 30, 2002 without a public referendum.

In July, the government barred twenty-five candidates from the Jammu and Kashmir Liberation Front (JKLF) from contesting assembly elections in the Pakistan-held portion of Kashmir, known in Pakistan as Azaad Kashmir, after they refused to sign a declaration pledging their support for the accession of Kashmir to Pakistan. Several dozen JKLF supporters were also arrested during protests over the elections.

Candidates associated with the mainstream political parties took the lion's share of the seats in the non-party local government elections, dealing a setback to government ambitions of establishing local bodies that were not bound to provincial political interests and were directly accountable to the federal government. While accepting the need for accountable government at the local level, Pakistani human rights activists faulted the design and implementation of the administration's plan. Election planners had reserved 33 percent of the seats for women in an affirmative effort to increase women's participation in the political process. But during local government elections held on March 21 and July 2 in parts of the North-West Frontier Province, women voters were reportedly threatened and intimidated from voting and running for office by conservative religious activists. The election results in these areas were nevertheless upheld.

Many voters belonging to religious minorities boycotted the local government elections after federal authorities disregarded demands by minority nongovernmental organizations and community leaders to hold the elections on the basis of a joint electorate. Introduced at the national and provincial levels by Pakistan's last military ruler, General Mohammad Zia-ul-Haq, the separate electoral system reserved a limited number of seats for each minority community and limited the franchise of non-Muslim citizens to the seats that had been allotted to their respective communities. The system was widely criticized by minority activists as having contributed to their communities' political marginalization.

Under the Musharraf administration's local government plan, seats were reserved for minorities in districts and sub-divisions of districts where they form 10 percent or more of the population. Of the 210 seats reserved for minorities in Sindh's Larkana division, which had a large Hindu population, only fifty-six declared candidates during the first phase of the local government elections, in December 2000; of those, fifty-two ran unopposed. A similar pattern was observable in several districts of Punjab with significant Christian minorities.

The government promptly condemned an October 28 attack on a Christian congregation in the southern Punjab town of Bahawalpur, and ordered an investigation into the incident. Eighteen people were killed when masked gunmen entered

St. Dominic's Church, locked the doors, and fired at the assembled worshippers. Although Bahawalpur has been scarred by sectarian violence between Sunni and Shi'a Muslims in recent years, human rights investigators said it was the first attack directed at Christians in the area.

In September 2000, the government established the Commission on the Status of Women. Despite its directive to safeguard and promote women's rights, the commission had few powers to implement its mandate and in 2001 made little progress in the way of setting forth concrete recommendations. Human rights activists decried continued impunity and lenient sentences for so-called honor crimes against women, the practice of punishing women said to have brought dishonor to their families.

The government officially closed Pakistan's border with Afghanistan in November 2000, citing an inability to absorb additional refugees. The border remained formally closed throughout 2001, though refugees continued to make their way to Pakistan, with about 200,000 entering the country between September 2000 and September 2001, and a further 150,000 arriving after the start of U.S.-led bombing on October 7. The government attempted at the beginning of the year to prevent the registration of new arrivals, deported thousands of undocumented Afghans who were already living in the country, and sought to uproot a large, established refugee community at Nasir Bagh, near Peshawar. A screening agreement reached with the United Nations High Commissioner for Refugees (UNHCR) in August, after protracted negotiations with the government, was shelved after the September 11 attacks on the U.S. a temporary relocation of UNHCR's international staff. The government subsequently identified a number of sites near the border where it proposed relocating new arrivals from Afghanistan as well as residents from two camps near Peshawar and the transit camp at the Chaman border crossing.

In a welcomed move affecting labor rights, Pakistan, on August 15, ratified International Labor Organization (ILO) Convention No. 182, which called for immediate and effective measures to secure prohibition of the worst forms of child labor, as well as ILO Convention No. 100, concerning equal remuneration for men and women.

DEFENDING HUMAN RIGHTS

Pakistani human rights groups played a vital role in challenging the government's policies toward refugees and, especially in the case of minority NGOs, its retention of the separate electorate.

THE ROLE OF THE INTERNATIONAL COMMUNITY

The international community almost unanimously eased diplomatic and economic sanctions when Pakistan backed the U.S.-led anti-terrorism coalition. Pressure for elections and a return to constitutional rule in 2002 was eased, while key donors made commitments of huge aid packages for Afghan refugee relief and basic economic assistance. Some donors resumed arms sales.

United States

On September 22, the Bush administration, with strong Congressional backing, waived economic sanctions imposed on Pakistan after its 1998 nuclear tests, allowing the U.S. to approve loans at the International Monetary Fund (IMF) and the World Bank. On October 30, President Bush signed legislation giving him authority to waive "democracy sanctions" on Pakistan, imposed following the October 1999 coup, opening the door for the sale and licensing of military equipment through September 30, 2003. However, the administration refused a request from Pakistan to transfer twenty-eight F-16 fighter planes that Pakistan had purchased in the 1980s.

On November 10, President Bush announced more than U.S. $1 billion in U.S. support to Pakistan, including direct budgetary assistance, funds for control of its borders, anti-terrorism assistance, Afghan refugee relief, financial support through the IMF, debt relief, and trade assistance. In September, Washington agreed to reschedule U.S. $379 million of Pakistan's $3 billion debt obligation to the U.S.

President Bush met with President Musharraf at the United Nations in early November. Musharraf repeated his pledge to hold national elections by October 2002. A visit to Pakistan by Secretary of State Colin Powell in mid-October was largely overshadowed by renewed fighting in Kashmir, which ended a ten-month cease-fire.

European Union

On October 17, the U.K. announced a 15 million pound debt relief package to Pakistan to help cope with the Afghan refugee crisis and internal reforms. On November 24, Pakistan signed a new Co-operation Agreement with the European Community, replacing the 1986 agreement. The signing of the agreement had initially been postponed following the October 1999 coup. In a joint declaration, the European Union and Pakistan "reconfirmed their commitment to the respect, protection and promotion of human rights and democratic principles." Pakistan also reiterated "its firm commitment to return to democratic government in accordance with the roadmap announced by President Musharraf on August 14, 2001." Ongoing European Commission development cooperation projects in Pakistan totalled 195 million euros, and were primarily focused on social sector development.

Commonwealth of Nations

In its concluding statement of March 20, 2001, the Commonwealth Ministerial Action Group criticized the restrictions imposed by the Musharraf administration on political parties, including their formal exclusion from the local government elections, and pressed the regime to shorten its electoral timetable and to restore full democratic rule. The ministers agreed that Pakistan should remain suspended from the councils of the Commonwealth pending the restoration of democracy.

On August 21, Commonwealth Secretary General Don McKinnon met with President Musharraf in Islamabad to discuss plans to restore democracy by October 2002. He also met with politicians from the disbanded parliament.

Japan

On October 26, Japan joined the E.U., the U.S., and Canada, and lifted economic sanctions against Pakistan. Japan had frozen new grants and loans, except for humanitarian aid, to Pakistan since the country conducted nuclear tests in 1998.

In September, Tokyo announced it would consider rescheduling some of Pakistan's $500 million debt and offered U.S. $40 million in emergency aid for Pakistan including assistance for refugees. Prior to September 11, Japan had decided to give more than U.S. $70 million in Official Development Assistance (ODA) in the form of grants and soft loans for various health, education, and communication projects.

Foreign Minister Makiko Tanaka met President Musharraf in Islamabad in late November to express support for Pakistan's counter-terrorism efforts and invited him to Tokyo for the ministerial conference on Afghanistan's reconstruction scheduled for early 2002. Tanaka also pledged an additional U.S. $300 million in grant aid to Pakistan over the next two years.

International Financial Institutions

The World Bank on October 24 approved a U.S. $300 million loan to promote privatized banking, and planned to provide additional assistance bringing the total for fiscal year 2002 to about $600 million. The Asian Development Bank announced plans to give Pakistan a total of U.S. $950 million in 2001, increased from $626 million planned prior to September 11. In late October, the U.S. was negotiating with the International Monetary Fund for a line of credit for Pakistan of up to U.S. $1 billion. On October 24, the Islamic Development Bank approved U.S. $25 million to help finance imports of energy products.

Relevant Human Rights Watch Reports:

The Crisis of Impunity: The Role of Pakistan, Russia, and Iran in Fueling the Civil War, 7/01

SRI LANKA

The year was marked by prolonged political infighting in Colombo, renewed clashes between Sri Lankan military forces and the armed separatist Liberation Tigers of Tamil Eelam (the "Tamil Tigers" or LTTE), and stalled peace initiatives. By early November, with the political fate of the People's Alliance government in question and new parliamentary elections called for December 5, pressing human rights problems had again been pushed off the top of the government's agenda.

Renewed fighting in the war, which since 1983 has claimed more than 60,000 lives, left hundreds of civilians dead, many more injured, and thousands newly displaced from their homes. Both the government and LTTE were responsible for serious abuses, including indiscriminate suicide bombings by the LTTE and torture and "disappearances" by government security forces and affiliated paramilitaries. Norway's efforts to bring the two sides to the negotiating table continued until June when the process appeared to stall; no formal talks took place during 2001. Although the government appeared more ready than in previous years to acknowledge past abuses and there was progress in a few specific cases, impunity remained the norm. Draconian security laws continued to facilitate arbitrary arrest, lengthy detention of suspects without trial, and attendant abuses. Restrictions in the north and east, disproportionately affecting Tamil civilians, prevented many displaced persons from reaching work sites to earn a living, attend schools, or seek urgent medical care.

HUMAN RIGHTS DEVELOPMENTS

On April 24, LTTE leader Velupillai Prabhakaran announced the end of a five-month unilateral cease-fire, saying that the government had not reciprocated. Within hours of the cease-fire's end, the Sri Lanka army launched Operation Agni Khiela ("fire ball") seeking to extend its control over the Jaffna peninsula. The army sustained heavy losses. Civilians, caught in the middle of the conflict, faced renewed hardships.

Increased fighting meant renewed displacement. At the end of April, for example, government aerial attacks on the Jaffna peninsula caused some 5,000 civilians to flee from their homes in Pooneryn north, adding to the estimated 800,000 internally displaced people (IDPs) island-wide. Reports of "disappearances" continued to emerge, including one in July that two youths had "disappeared" after being questioned by members of the People's Liberation Organization of Tamil Eelam (PLOTE), which is paid and armed by the government.

New cases of torture were also reported. In January, Sri Lankan Human Rights Commission (HRC) officials reported that anti-terrorism police held Jaffna-based journalist Nadarajah Thiruchelvam in incommunicado detention, beat him with metal pipes, and kept him handcuffed in solitary confinement for twelve days before HRC officials were permitted to visit him. In October, the Hong Kong-based Asian Human Rights Commission reported the torture of Namal Fernando, a social worker, who had been threatened and pistol-whipped by police after being taken from his home near Colombo on October 6. He was reportedly forced to sign a confession, but then was released without charge the following day. His arrest was apparently a case of mistaken identity.

Although fighting was heaviest in the north, civilians were also reported killed and wounded in military operations against LTTE positions in the east, although most accounts were insufficiently detailed to determine if the deaths were avoidable or due to violations of international humanitarian law. Most deaths and injuries in eastern Sri Lanka occurred around Batticaloa, Velaichenai, and in Muttur, south of Trincomalee. In November 2000, homes were reported damaged, a two-year-old child killed, and twelve others injured during army and police shelling north of Batticaloa. Again in late April, eight villagers were reported injured in artillery fire across the Batticaloa lagoon. Three civilians were killed and more than twenty injured in separate incidents in the Valaichenai area in June and July; the army acknowledged two civilian deaths and seven injuries during the July 30 assault.

For its part, the LTTE continued to be responsible for or implicated in serious abuses. On November 7, 2000, newly elected Tamil United Liberation Front (TULF) member of parliament Nirmalan Soundaranayagam was assassinated near Batticaloa. Although his assailant was never identified, the LTTE, believed to have been responsible for the assassination of several other TULF members in previous years, including human rights advocate Neelan Thiruchelvam in July 1999, was the prime suspect.

In April 2001, there were reports that the LTTE had executed three men, M. Kamalanathan, Xavier Albert, and S. Thillainayagam after charging them with murder and rape. On April 24, LTTE members reportedly abducted two Muslim civilians near Valaichenai and held them for ransom. Four workers in a prawn farm and a rice mill from the same area were abducted for ransom on June 1. On May 2, LTTE members and local thugs reportedly killed Sivanesarajah, a young minister for a local church group of the Assembly of God near Vakarai. The human rights organization University Teachers for Human Rights (UTHR) said that the church's emphasis on pacifism had been viewed as a threat to LTTE recruitment.

In July, the United Nations Children's Fund (UNICEF) accused the LTTE of continuing to recruit and deploy child soldiers, some of them as young as twelve. Monitors in the north and east reported a sharp increase in conscription of children by the LTTE though October and said the LTTE had resorted to extortion and threats to families to comply. In an article published September 4, LTTE Batticaloa and Amparai district political leader Karikalan told the Tamil press that a recruitment drive in eastern areas was attracting "large numbers of youth, male and female" and praised parents for bringing their children to enlist. He rejected accusations that the recruitment was forced.

On July 24, the LTTE attacked Katunayake air force base and Colombo's Bandaranaike International Airport, destroying military aircraft and passenger jets. Two civilians, seven security personnel, and fourteen LTTE members were killed. The attack on Sri Lanka's only international airport was both a political and financial blow. It reduced the country's commercial fleet by half, drove up exporters' insurance premiums and damaged tourism.

On October 30, Prime Minister Ratnasiri Wickramanayake narrowly escaped a suicide bombing in Colombo that claimed the lives of three civilians and a police officer and injured many others. On November 15, three former members of a paramilitary group working with a Sri Lankan army intelligence unit were killed and another wounded by a suicide bomber in Batticaloa; one civilian was also killed and eight injured in the attack. The LTTE was suspected in both attacks.

Arbitrary detention and mistreatment of prisoners by police and security forces remained common. A report by human rights lawyer N. Kandasamy indicated that some 18,000 people may have been arrested under emergency regulations and the Prevention of Terrorism Act from January to November 2000. The vast majority were Tamil, some of whom were ordered detained without trial for more than two years. Often the only evidence against them was a confession extracted under torture. Although many such cases were thrown out by courts in 2001 and some torture victims won court-ordered compensation, cases continued to take years to make their way through the court system. Deaths in custody in 2001 included that of Kandaiah Uthayakumar, suspected of smuggling banned commodities in the northern town of Mannar, who died on February 28 after arrest by Navy personnel. His children, who witnessed the arrest, said he had been beaten and strangled by the arresting officers. In late March, a Mannar district judge ordered two naval personnel detained pending investigation.

Government efforts to stem custodial abuse included a new emergency regulation promulgated in May requiring detention centers to provide district courts with a list of all persons in custody every two weeks. Earlier, the government had established a police unit and special committee under the Justice Ministry to investigate complaints of illegal detention and harassment by police and armed forces, and to accelerate the release of victims.

Sexual violence against women by security forces attracted new attention in 2001. The premeditated gang-rape on June 24 of a twenty-eight year old Tamil woman in Colombo by police and army personnel at a security checkpoint sparked widespread protests by Tamil and Muslim political parties and women's rights organizations, and a general strike by shop owners in the north and east on July 6. In the media storm that followed, several other custodial rape cases received new scrutiny and at least one victim of grave sexual abuse was ordered released from custody. Prosecutions in older cases stalled because witnesses were afraid to testify, or, as in the case of Ida Carmelita, raped and murdered in Mannar in July 1999, proceeded extremely slowly.

Pressure on medical officials to cover up evidence of custodial mistreatment was suggested in another case of sexual abuse — the March 19 gang rape and sexual torture by police and naval personnel of two women who had been arrested by anti-subversion police in Mannar. The initial report of the district medical officer concluded there were no signs of mistreatment. After the women's complaints were made public, a second examination was ordered about a week later, the second doctor concluding that the women had been tortured and raped.

Police and military personnel were rarely punished for mistreatment of detainees or failing to abide by legally mandated procedures, such as notifying the HRC of arrests and notifying family members when individuals were detained under special security legislation. No one had been convicted for the crime of torture since Sri Lanka ratified the U.N. Convention Against Torture in 1994 and introduced domestic legislation mandating a seven-year minimum sentence for torture. According to the Attorney General's Office, several prosecutions were pending.

Sri Lankan authorities appeared more willing than in past years to acknowledge official responsibility for atrocities. On January 31, Sri Lankan army personnel in Batticaloa publicly acknowledged their role in large-scale massacres of civilians in the east, mentioning notorious attacks in Kokkaddicholai, Sathurukkondaan, Vanthaarumoolai, and Batticaloa. In February, the attorney general reportedly issued indictments against more than six hundred police and armed forces personnel implicated in "disappearances" that occurred before 1994—many in connection with counterinsurgency operations against the Janatha Vimukthi Peramuna (JVP) organization. On June 28, two soldiers were sentenced to six years in prison and fined Rs. 2,500 (U.S. $27) each for their role in an abduction and murder in 1989.

On March 12, President Chandrika Kumaratunga appointed Justice P.H.K. Kulatilaka to investigate the October 2000 massacre of some twenty-seven youths in the Bindunuwewa Rehabilitation camp. The dead included individuals being held under the Prevention of Terrorism Act and LTTE members, some in their early teens, who had surrendered to authorities. On June 28, the attorney general reported that forty-three suspects had been arrested in connection with the killings. In July, President Kumaratunga announced the formation of a three-member "truth commission" to investigate incidents of ethnic violence between 1981 and 1984, including anti-Tamil riots in July 1983 that killed nearly six hundred people.

Progress was halting or nonexistent in many high profile cases. Some cases were slowed partly by defendants' petitions to move cases out of the north and east for security reasons, including the Mirusuvil massacre case, in which fourteen soldiers were accused of having tortured and murdered Tamil civilians in northern Jaffna in December 2000. In 2001, the case was transferred out of the district to the Anuradhapura District Court. Similarly, while proceedings continued in the trial of soldiers accused of the 1992 massacre of thirty-five Tamil civilians in the eastern village of Mailanthani, the case continued to move slowly following its transfer in 1996 to Colombo, far from key civilian witnesses. The case of five security personnel arrested in connection with the 1999 discovery of fifteen skeletons in Chemmani, thought to be those of persons "disappeared" by the army in 1996, also made little progress.

Official restrictions on war reporting, including provisions imposed in 2000, were relaxed in May 2001, but restrictions on access to areas under LTTE control remained a serious impediment to accurate reporting on the human rights situation in conflict areas. In April, journalist Marie Colvin, writing for the London *Sunday Times* was shot and seriously injured when she defied a government ban on travel to LTTE controlled areas and crossed the line of fire. Certain Sri Lankan journalists also faced arrest, intimidation, and physical threats. The risks were particularly acute for correspondents in the north and east and those covering political events. Between October 2000 and November 2001, one Jaffna-based journalist was killed and at least five others based in the northeast were arrested or threatened by the security forces.

Criminal extortion rings linked to political forces were blamed for increased communal tension in central and eastern Sri Lanka. In May, two people were killed and a large number of shops destroyed when Sinhalese mobs attacked Muslims demonstrators. The demonstrators had been protesting police inaction after thugs with alleged ruling party links publicly tortured a Muslim shopkeeper who had refused to pay protection money. Demonstrations—some violent—spread to Colombo. The government invoked a curfew to prevent further violence and appointed a commission of inquiry. In September Muslim businessmen in the eastern town of Muttur demonstrated against an extortion racket allegedly run by the LTTE. The LTTE reportedly retaliated by burning a passenger ferry providing transport to the area and threatened mortar attacks if demonstrations continued.

Violence continued to plague the political process in the lead-up to parliamentary elections scheduled for December 5. As of November 21, the Police Elections Secretariat said it had received 1028 election-related complaints of violence, including three murders.

DEFENDING HUMAN RIGHTS

Human rights defenders in the capital, Colombo, operated in relative freedom, but individuals and organizations in the north and east faced serious pressure from state forces, armed paramilitary groups, and the LTTE. In some cases, human rights defenders in the east asked that the details of threats made against them—particularly those made by LTTE members and paramilitaries—be kept confidential out of fear of retaliation.

Journalists (see above) and humanitarian aid workers were also attacked. Unknown assailants threw two grenades at the Colombo office of Oxfam in late January and three at the International Committee of the Red Cross (ICRC) office in Muttur on September 6. Although buildings and other properties were damaged, no one was injured in either attack.

Local human rights organizations strongly advocated an end to official impunity and custodial abuse, including violence against women. Sri Lankan human defenders denounced political violence locally, but were also active in international fora in events leading up to the Durban World Conference Against Racism and in the global campaign against the use of child soldiers.

In 2001, rights activists joined academics and other private citizens in Sri Lanka's growing peace movement in denouncing the government's ban on the LTTE and calling on the LTTE and government to commence negotiations. Sri Lanka's flagging business climate, particularly in the wake of the LTTE's attack on Sri Lanka's only international airport, also drove business leaders to renew private efforts to end the war. The Society for Love and Understanding, founded by Ceylinco group chairman Lalith Kotelawala, notified political leaders that it intended to open a dialogue with the LTTE. In September, representatives of more than a dozen of top national business groups and advertising agencies initiated a "Sri Lanka First" campaign advocating civil action to end the war.

Human rights defenders continued to express concern about the work of the HRC, particularly in relation to custodial abuse of detainees. Although HRC officers visited registered places of detention, critics said the commission needed to make more regular visits to prevent abuses. Five years after its establishment, the HRC still had no access to any unregistered place of detention or authority over paramilitary groups, and security forces often failed to report arrests and detentions to the commission as required by law.

THE ROLE OF THE INTERNATIONAL COMMUNITY

The European Union, India, Japan, and the United States strongly supported Norway's efforts to facilitate talks between the Sri Lankan government and the LTTE, and rejected the idea of an independent Tamil state. Many countries, particularly Sri Lanka's donors, criticized human rights and international humanitarian law violations by government forces and the LTTE. Donors also called for greater transparency in the government's financial management and criticized increased military spending and the apparent erosion of democratic structures.

Sri Lanka Development Forum

After political instability delayed the meeting for more than two years, the Sri Lanka Development Forum, a consortium of Sri Lanka's donors convened by the World Bank, met in Paris on December 18-19, 2000 to discuss assistance plans for Sri Lanka. In 1997, Sri Lanka received U.S. $860 million in assistance from donors; it received another $780 million in 1998. But at the December 2000 meeting donors refused to pledge new assistance, calling instead for the government to take concrete steps to end the war with the LTTE, speed up restructuring of the public sector, and account for previous assistance. Donors expressed special concern over the country's disproportionately high level of military expenditure and political interference in development and relief initiatives.

World Bank Vice President for South Asia Mieko Nishimizu described Sri Lanka as a country "in deep crisis, public institutions are politicized, politicians are not accountable, people are not heard and they are isolated." She noted links between poverty, war, and governance problems in the country, and suggested that progress on these fronts would be necessary before development partners would provide additional support.

The European Union emphasized the need for a negotiated end to the war, economic restructuring, and transparency. It made a special call for accountability in the Bindunuwewa rehabilitation camp massacre case. The E.U. cautioned that Sri Lanka's large military budget was jeopardizing the country's development. In 2000, the defense budget consumed about 36 percent of government income or 6 percent of Sri Lanka's GDP. Defense expenditure rose by almost $300 million after the government made additional arms purchases following military defeats in April and May 1999. In 2001, Sri Lanka purchased arms from Israel (the Israeli defense ministry sent a delegation to Colombo in August), the Czech Republic ($2.5 million in tanks, rocket launchers, and other military vehicles), and other countries.

United Kingdom

On February 28, in spite of heavy lobbying by Tamil groups, the LTTE was included on the list of 21 banned organizations proscribed under the U.K.'s Terrorism Act 2000, making it illegal to belong to, support, or raise funds for the LTTE.

United States

Ambassador Ashley Wills outlined the U.S. position on Sri Lanka in a speech in Jaffna on March 7. He said that the U.S. supported an end to the war—"the sooner the better"—and rejected the possibility of a military solution. The U.S. favored a negotiated settlement and supported Norway's efforts to facilitate talks. Wills rejected "the idea of an independent state carved out of Sri Lankan territory" and the LTTE as sole representative of Tamils in Sri Lanka. He acknowledged complaints of discrimination against Tamils in Sri Lanka, saying Tamils must be treated "equally, respectfully and with dignity" within a democratic state. Wills said the U.S. would reconsider its ban on the LTTE if it renounced violence, embraced democratic principles, and entered into negotiations to end the war.

The U.S. continued to provide economic support funds (ESF) for development as well as international military education and training (IMET). The Bush administration requested $3 million in ESF and $275,000 for IMET in fiscal year 2002, the latter a $30,000 increase over the previous year.

United Nations

U.N. agencies, including UNICEF, criticized the LTTE's continued recruitment of child soldiers. U.N. Secretary-General Kofi Annan, in a September report to the U.N. Security Council noted that, despite LTTE commitments, children "continued to be targeted in the ongoing conflict of Sri Lanka." Annan noted that the Sri Lankan government was one of only two to set the minimum age for voluntary enlistment at eighteen and acknowledged efforts in the country to demobilize child soldiers, but said prevention of recruitment and re-enlistment was an overwhelming concern. He stressed the need for adequate resources, structures, and programs to ensure successful reintegration into society of demobilized children.

Hoping to help revive agriculture in Sri Lanka's war-torn north and east, the World Bank in September announced plans to fund renewed U.N. mine clearance efforts in the northern regions, where civilian casualty rates from mines are reported to be among the world's highest. The U.N. began its demining program in July 1999 but fighting in 2000 had halted operations.

VIETNAM

The government's human rights record took several major steps backward during 2001, with religious rights in particular coming under attack. Security forces arrested dozens of ethnic minority Montagnards in a heavy-handed response to a popular protest over land rights in the Central Highlands in February. The authorities detained, arrested or harassed many religious leaders and political dissidents, including members of the banned Unified Buddhist Church of Vietnam, the Hoa Hao Buddhist sect, Roman Catholics, retired Communist Party of Vietnam (CPV) members and military veterans known for their criticism of the party, and ethnic minority Protestants in the northern and central highlands.

The election of new CPV General Secretary Nong Duc Manh, known as a consensus builder, at the Ninth Party Congress in April, raised hopes that Vietnam might step up the pace of reform. These hopes had been largely dashed by October.

HUMAN RIGHTS DEVELOPMENTS

In February 2001, unprecedented mass demonstrations broke out in Gia Lai, Dak Lak, and Kontum provinces in the Central Highlands. Thousands of indigenous minority people known collectively as Montagnards, many of them Christians, gathered to demand greater land rights and religious freedom. In response, authorities sent troops to the region, and police conducted door-to-door searches for suspected leaders of the protests, arresting at least twenty in February alone. Some were beaten, kicked, or shocked with electric truncheons by police officers upon arrest and during interrogation. In many parts of the highlands, the government banned gatherings of more than four people, restricted freedom of movement, and increased its surveillance and harassment of ethnic minority Protestants. Telephone communication to, from, and within the region was cut off for weeks. Diplomats and foreign media were barred from visiting the area, other than a government-sponsored press tour in mid-March and a four-day trip by the U.S. Ambassador in July.

Fearing arrest, more than 1,000 Montagnards fled to Cambodia. (See Cambodia.) In September, the People's Courts in Dak Lak and Gia Lai sentenced fourteen Montagnards to prison sentences ranging from six to twelve years on charges of disrupting security brought under article 89 of the Penal Code. At least ten other Montagnards were sentenced in several district-level trials quietly conducted in Dak Lak and Gia Lai in October, bringing the total tried as of November to at least twenty-four people

Human Rights Watch received reports of security forces burning down several Protestant churches in the Central Highlands. On March 10, heavily-armed police and soldiers, in full riot gear and carrying electric batons, raided Plei Lao village, Chu Se district, Gia Lai where several hundred ethnic Jarai villagers were conducting an all-night prayer meeting. After police officers arrested one young villager, a crowd gathered and pulled the youth from the police jeep. Police and soldiers fired tear gas and then bullets into the crowd. Dozens were wounded by shooting or beating, and at least one villager, Rmah Blin, was killed. The security forces then burned down the church. As of October, at least four of the dozens arrested were believed to remain in detention at T-20 prison in Pleiku. In September, Plei Lao villager Siu Boc was sentenced to eleven years in prison at a trial in Gia Lai. Beginning in June, provincial authorities conducted dozens of ceremonies in the Central Highlands in which Montagnards who had participated in the February demonstrations were forced to read confessions about their alleged wrongdoings and renounce Christianity in front of entire villages, sealing their pledges by mandatory drinking of rice wine mixed with goat's blood.

Throughout Vietnam, the government conducted a systematic campaign of intimidation and surveillance of perceived political opponents. On February 9, academic Ha Sy Phu was placed under administrative detention for two years in Dalat for allegedly collaborating with "hostile forces" abroad. That same month democracy activist Vu Cao Quan was summoned to police headquarters several times after he organized a meeting in Hai Phong to discuss democratic reforms. On April 24, Vu was arrested and detained for ten days after meeting in Hanoi with other democracy activists. On April 26, a squad of policemen in Hanoi went to the home of another well-known dissident, Hoang Minh Chinh, and insisted that he go with them to police headquarters. Hoang Minh Chinh refused and remained under surveillance throughout the year.

In June, security police apprehended Vietnam's most influential dissident, Tran Do, in Ho Chi Minh City (Saigon) and confiscated a draft section of his memoirs. Afterwards, Tran wrote to party leaders and the Vietnam Association of Writers to protest the seizure of his writings.

The government stepped up the harassment in September, when fifteen dissidents were detained in Hanoi, including Pham Que Duong, Hoang Tien, Hoang Minh Chinh, Tran Van Khue, Nguyen Vu Binh, and Nguyen Thanh Giang. On September 2, just before the detentions, Pham Que Duong and Tran Van Khue had submitted a request to the government to form an independent anti-corruption organization. On October 9 Tran Van Khue was officially placed under house arrest for two years under Administrative Detention Decree 31/CP. In February and again in June, Pham Que Duong, Hoang Minh Chinh, and Hoang Tien joined more than a dozen other dissidents in signing joint appeals to CPV officials calling for the repeal of decree 31/CP, which authorizes detention for up to two years without trial.

Police summoned outspoken Buddhist monk Thich Quang Do, the second highest-ranking monk in the banned Unified Church of Vietnam (UBCV), for interrogation several times during the year. On February 4, Thich Quang Do was detained and searched by security police after visiting UBCV's Supreme Patriarch, Thich Huyen Quang, who has been under house arrest in Quang Ngai province since 1982. In June, Thich Quang Do was placed under administrative detention for two years at his pagoda after he announced that he intended to escort Thich Huyen Quang to Ho Chi Minh City for medical treatment. Three other UBCV monks, Thich Khong Tanh, Thich Quang Hue and Thich Tan An, were also detained at the same time. On September 2, Ho Tan Anh, a leader of the banned Buddhist Youth Movement (BYM), which is affiliated with the UBCV, burned himself to death in Danang, reportedly as an act of protest against religious intolerance in Vietnam. Afterwards, police searched the homes of several BYM leaders.

As in past years, the government only allowed religious activities by officially-recognized churches and organizations. In April 2001, the State Bureau of Religious Affairs recognized the Evangelical Church of Vietnam, thus granting legal status to approximately three hundred individual churches in the south but specifically excluding the much more numerous ethnic minority Protestant house churches. Christians in ethnic minority areas were suppressed and pressured to renounce their faith, not only in the Central Highlands but also in the northern provinces of Lai Chau, Lao Cai and Ha Giang. At least sixteen ethnic Hmong were thought to be in prison in Lai Chau, Vinh Phuc and Thanh Ha provinces as of October. In April and June, Ho Chi Minh City police shut down services conducted by outspoken Mennonite pastor Nguyen Hong Quang, who was beaten and detained on August 17, reportedly for operating a school for children without official permission.

In January, Ha Hai, secretary general of the banned Hoa Hao church, was sentenced to five years in prison for violating house arrest orders and "abusing democratic rights." On March 17, Le Quang Liem, Chairman of the Central Council of the Hoa Hao Buddhist Church, was arrested in Ho Chi Minh City. Two days later, Hoa Hao church member Nguyen Thi Thu immolated himself in a protest in Dong Thap province. Other Hoa Hao members sentenced during the year included Ho Van Trong and Truong Van Duc.

Despite a visit by a Vatican delegation to Vietnam in June, little progress was made towards establishing diplomatic ties between Vietnam and the Vatican. Vietnam continued to insist on having final approval over Catholic religious appointments, accepting three Vatican-approved bishops in June but rejecting three others. However, the authorities permitted Catholics to attend an annual celebration mass at the historic Our Lady of La Vang Church in Quang Tri province. In March, Catholic Father Nguyen Van Ly was put under house arrest in Hue and denounced by state media after he submitted written testimony to the U.S. Commission on International Religious Freedom. On May 17, he was arrested after leading a religious service at which he allegedly distributed leaflets. He was charged with violating his house arrest order and inciting public disorder. In October, after a one-day trial by the People's Court in Thua Thien-Hue province, he was sentenced to fifteen years in prison for "undermining the policy of national unity" and violating his probation order under articles 87 and 269 of the Penal Code. At least three members of the Catholic Congregation of the Mother Co-Redemptrix, imprisoned in 1987 for holding training courses and distributing religious books, remained in prison.

Freedom of association continued to be severely restricted, and the formation of independent associations, trade unions, or nongovernmental organizations (NGOs) remained prohibited. The government tolerated a number of small gatherings and "sit-ins" to protest land grabs or corruption. In an unusually large protest in Hanoi in March, five hundred ethnic minority people from northern Son La province gathered outside Ho Chi Minh's mausoleum in Hanoi to put forward their side in a land dispute. Police, who allowed representatives of the delegation to speak with officials, quickly cordoned off the area. Later, as part of security arrangements for the Ninth Party Congress, the prime minister ordered a clampdown on public protests in Hanoi.

Strikes, while rare, increased during the year, mostly directed against foreign and private companies. In the first six months of the year there were more than a dozen strikes in Ho Chi Minh City against foreign-invested companies. In August, more than four hundred garment workers struck in Ho Chi Minh City to claim unpaid wages and protest the alleged beating of a pregnant worker at a South Korean-owned company.

All media remained state-owned and tightly controlled. There were no private newspapers and television was operated solely by the government. Foreign media representatives were required to obtain advance authorization from the Foreign Ministry for all travel outside Hanoi and to clear all interviews with Vietnamese nationals four days in advance. In July a new media decree, 31/2001/ND-CP, took effect. It imposed fines for a variety of offenses, including republishing previously banned stories, intentionally providing false information to the media, and publishing articles containing pornography or "superstitious attitudes."

In August, the government passed a decree that imposed stricter regulations on Internet cafes and imposed fines for illegal Internet usage, while opening up provision of Internet services to privately-owned businesses, including foreign companies. The government continued to maintain strict control over the country's overall gateway to the Internet by controlling the operation of the sole Internet access provider. In addition, the government continued to use firewalls to block access to sites considered objectionable or politically sensitive. In August, Internet access was terminated in Phu Yen province, on the grounds that it could threaten national security.

Prison conditions continued to be extremely harsh. Human Rights Watch received reports of the use of shackles and solitary confinement in cramped, dark cells, and the beating, kicking, and use of electric shock batons on detainees by police officers. In June, the official press reported that more than 17 percent of detainees at Chi Hoa prison in Ho Chi Minh City were held beyond the expiration of their sentences, including one inmate who was still in detention thirteen years after his conviction was overturned on appeal. Police officers routinely arrested and detained suspects without written warrants, and suspects were often held in detention for as long as a year without being formally charged or tried. Decree 31/CP, the administrative detention decree, was used on many occasions to place dissidents under house arrest.

Corruption was identified by the Ninth Party Congress as one of the "four dangers" facing Vietnam. The Central Committee passed new measures to address corruption within the CPV, such as requirements for members to reveal their assets. In July, the Ministry of Public Security proposed to establish a special court to address corruption, saying it threatened to undermine the CPV's authority. In September, six government officials were convicted for corrupt land deals involving the Thang Long water park. While a businessman convicted in the same case was jailed for twenty years, the officials were either released or sentenced to prison terms of a year or less. In mid-November a provincial court opened a trial of twelve people accused of bribery and embezzling money from government development projects in northern Lai Chau province, inhabited primarily by low-income ethnic minorities.

The National Assembly appeared to be more assertive than in previous years. In June, National Assembly members grilled cabinet officials on live television about their progress on previous policy commitments. That same month the assembly rejected a law supported by the minister of planning that would have increased the authority of district courts, reportedly because of concerns that the bill would cause a dramatic increase in the prison population and violations of judicial procedures. Also in June, assembly members questioned safety plans for the party-approved Son La dam project as well as the proposed relocation of hundreds of thousands of people to make way for the dam. Despite the controversy, however, they approved the project in late June.

In July, Prime Minister Phan Van Khai called for the 1992 constitution to be amended, reportedly in order to clarify the role of the judiciary, national assembly, and state bureaucracy, and distribute more decision-making power to local authorities. A nationwide campaign was announced in August to solicit public opinion on the proposal, with the caveat that CPV policies be reflected. A clandestine group called the Vietnam Restoration Party (To Chuc Phuc Hung Vietnam) ignored that caveat and distributed a letter calling for the repeal of article 4 of the constitution, which states that the CPV is "the force leading the State and society."

DEFENDING HUMAN RIGHTS

The government did not allow independent associations or human rights organizations to operate in Vietnam. Contact with international human rights organizations was strongly discouraged and the government continued to refuse to permit international human rights organizations such as Human Rights Watch and Amnesty International to conduct official missions to Vietnam. In October Tran Van Khue, who had proposed to establish an anti-corruption NGO, was placed under house arrest.

THE ROLE OF THE INTERNATIONAL COMMUNITY

Vietnam's increasingly poor human rights record came under international criticism during the year. The government's repression of religious leaders and its crackdown against ethnic minorities in the Central Highlands drew particular fire. At the annual World Bank-sponsored donor meeting in December 2000, Vietnam's donors, while pledging U.S. $2.8 billion in aid, pressed the government to focus more on environmental issues and good governance, in addition to economic reforms. In July, the World Bank signed its largest set of loan agreements with Vietnam, totaling U.S. $520 million, targeted at infrastructure development, economic growth, and poverty reduction. The Asian Development Bank (ADB) announced that its Japan Special Fund would provide U.S. $600,000 for secondary education in rural areas, targeted at ethnic minorities.

United Nations

In August, the U.N. Committee on the Elimination of Racial Discrimination (CERD) issued its Concluding Observations on a report, overdue since 1993, submitted by the Vietnamese government. The committee expressed concerns about religious persecution of ethnic minorities, allegations of forced sterilization of Montagnard women, and the impact of population transfers to areas inhabited by indigenous groups. Relations between the Vietnamese government and the United Nations High Commissioner for Refugees (UNHCR) were often strained during the year over the fact that thirty-eight Montagnards were resettled to the U.S. in April, and the UNHCR's establishment of sites to receive asylum seekers in Cambodia. In July, talks between UNHCR, Vietnam and Cambodia on the possibility of voluntary repatriation of Montagnards from Cambodia broke down when Vietnam refused to grant UNHCR unhindered access to the Central Highlands to monitor the status of returning asylum seekers. In September, Vietnam ratified two optional protocols to the Convention on the Rights of the Child, one on the sale of children, child prostitution and child pornography, and the other on child soldiers.

Japan

Vietnam's largest donor, Japan, provided assistance to conduct legal training programs and reform of the legal system in the specific areas of civil code reform, drafting of the civil procedure code and criminal procedure code, as well as various commercial laws.

European Union

The E.U., Vietnam's second largest donor, was vocal in its support of human rights. In July, the European Parliament adopted an emergency resolution on religious freedom in Vietnam and denounced the persecution of several religious leaders and ethnic minorities in the Central Highlands. That same month E.U. External Affairs Commissioner Chris Patten raised concerns about religious freedom and restrictions on international media based in Vietnam in a meeting with the Vietnamese foreign minister. In talks with CPV Secretary General Nong Duc Manh during an August visit to Vietnam, the foreign minister of Sweden raised the issue of human rights and greater freedom of the press, and even broached the topic of a multiparty system. After an European Commission (EC) meeting in Hanoi in November, an EC spokesman said that Vietnam had made some progress on human rights conditions but that it still had a long way to go.

Several E.U. political figures became the subject of controversy after they visited dissidents in Vietnam. In April, Member of the European Parliament (MEP) Lars Rise of the Norwegian opposition Christian People's Party was detained and deported from Vietnam after visiting several dissidents. In June, Italian MEP Olivier Dupuis was expelled after he tried to stage a sit-in at the monastery where Thich Quang Do lives under house arrest.

United States

Relations between the U.S. and Vietnam were strained at times during the year, but the overall trend was positive. Vietnam reacted defensively, however, to any suggestion that its human rights record could be improved. Several times during the year the Foreign Ministry charged that the U.S. was inciting unrest in Vietnam and interfering in its internal affairs, in particular by sponsoring hearings on religious rights in Vietnam in February and by approving Montagnard resettlement to the United States. U.S. Ambassador Pete Peterson pressed hard for an official visit to the troubled Central Highlands after the February unrest. He secured approval only in July, shortly before he ended his term as ambassador. Peterson was highly critical of some provincial officials for preventing him from talking freely with villagers.

U.S. Assistant Secretary of State James Kelly, the first senior Bush administration official to visit Vietnam, made a strong statement criticizing the arrest of Father Nguyen Van Ly, which occurred during Kelly's visit in May. The seventh round in the U.S.-Vietnam human rights dialogue took place in Hanoi in July, with no tangible results.

In October the Senate passed a resolution approving the Bilateral Trade Agreement between the U.S. and Vietnam. In September, the House approved the Vietnam Human Rights Act, which would link future increases in non-humanitarian aid to progress on human rights. Vietnam reacted strongly against the measure, issuing public statements from the Ministry of Foreign Affairs and the mass party organizations.

Association of South-East Asian Nations (ASEAN)

Fellow ASEAN members made virtually no comment on Vietnam's human rights record during the year. In July, Hanoi hosted the annual ASEAN ministerial meetings, the ASEAN Regional Forum, and the ASEAN Post Ministerial Conference, attended by ASEAN members as well as the U.S., E.U., Canada, Japan, and China.

Vietnam's relations with neighboring Cambodia were tense at times over the issue of the Montagnards, especially when Cambodian Prime Minister Hun Sen defied his long-time ally by refusing to send the first group of twenty-four Montagnard asylum seekers back to Vietnam in March. However, the two countries signed agreements during the year to strengthen border controls, prevent illegal crossings, and train Cambodian police in Vietnam.

EUROPE
AND
CENTRAL ASIA

In Uzbekistan, the parents of Shukrat Parpiev, age thirty-one, display the sheets in which their son's body was returned to them in May 2000. Parpiev died in prison, allegedly from torture.

EUROPE AND CENTRAL ASIA OVERVIEW

Augustus 2001 marked ten years since the failed 1991 coup that presaged the end of the Soviet Union, and the anniversary provoked impatience at the uneven progress on human rights in the region. After the September 11 attacks one month later, impatience turned to regret at the lost opportunities for a more thoroughgoing transition during the interlude between the Cold War and the Anti-terror War.

Many countries in the region had made significant strides since 1991, but abusive authoritarian rule persisted in several, and others still struggled to overcome the ethnic conflict that had engulfed large parts of the disintegrating Soviet Union and Yugoslavia. Looking westward toward eventual integration into the European Union, central and eastern European countries had undertaken important reform, while western Europe had turned inward and become increasingly intolerant of immigration and ethnic diversity. As the year drew to a close, it was not entirely clear what the new post-September 11 era would hold for human rights, but in much the same way the Cold War once distorted the human rights agenda, the prospects for tackling the region's persistent and newly emerging human rights problems seemed suddenly to dim in light of the competing and overriding anti-terrorism imperative.

After September 11, governments from Skopje to Moscow scrambled to cast their own often brutal internal conflicts as part of the new international antiterror-ist cause. With too few exceptions, this opportunism went unchecked. At the same time, Western European leaders ramped up their anti-immigrant rhetoric and fur-ther restricted the rights of migrants, refugees, and asylum seekers, all in the name of fighting terrorism. And criticism of human rights abuse softened, particularly for those states that were strategically important to the U.S.-led military action in Afghanistan. The United States and Uzbekistan announced a "qualitatively new relationship," notwithstanding the latter's brutal crackdown on independent Mus-lims. German Chancellor Gerhard Schroeder urged a reevaluation of Russia's abu-sive war in Chechnya. In November, U.S. President George Bush praised Russian President Vladimir Putin's talk of negotiating peace in Chechnya, with no public mention of continued atrocities perpetrated against Chechens since September 11.

The most alarming developments of the year came in Central Asia, where the transition from the Soviet Union had brought only grinding poverty and ever more repressive governance. After September 11, it was these very governments that became the essential allies of the U.S.-led military campaign in Afghanistan. Of particular concern was the close and apparently unconditional U.S. relationship with Uzbekistan, where Islam Karimov's dictatorship permitted no true opposition political activity, no civil society, and no independent media and locked up and tortured thousands who dared demonstrate independent thinking. U.S. officials argued that the new relationship with Uzbekistan put them in a better position to address their partner's gross violations, but as this report went to press there was no relief from the Uzbek government's assault on its own society. In the two months following September 11, yet another human rights defender was detained, dissidents and religious believers continued to be arrested and tortured—one died in custody—and convictions on trumped-up charges of anti-state activity continued.

Ethnic conflict had attended the breakup of the Soviet Union and Yugoslavia for ten years, and in 2001 its aftermath continued to shape much of the human rights landscape. Russia's transitional record remained marred by the continued grave violations committed by its forces in Chechnya. As the Chechen conflict dragged into its third year, the government's halfhearted peace bid and promised troop reductions made no difference in the lives of Chechen civilians. Sweep operations purportedly aimed at apprehending rebel fighters resulted in widespread looting, arbitrary detention, torture, and an alarming number of "disappearances" of Chechens last seen in Russian custody, with the bodies of some later found dumped or hastily buried in unmarked graves. Chechen fighters were also believed to be behind an increasing number of abuses, including a wave of assassinations of Chechen civil servants and religious leaders seen as cooperating with the Russian government, and the fatal shooting of Viktor Popkov, a leading Russian human rights activist.

Ethnic tensions flared again in the Balkans, this time in southern Serbia and Macedonia. The response of both the implicated governments and the international community differed from past conflicts in the region, reflecting important transitional developments and lessons learned. When an ethnic Albanian rebel group emerged in southern Serbia, it was clear that Slobodan Milosevic was no longer in power in Belgrade. In contrast to Kosovo in 1998, the international community immediately and intensively engaged and worked with a relatively cooperative Serbian government to address the legitimate grievances of the ethnic Albanian community, including through the deployment of a multiethnic police force in the region. In May the rebels disarmed, and displaced ethnic Albanians began returning to the region. The lack of Albanian representation in local government, serious employment discrimination, and sporadic incidents of ethnic violence remained concerns, but the threat of armed conflict had receded for the time being.

Similar success came more slowly in Macedonia, where for months the government insisted upon a military response to its ethnic Albanian insurgency, led by the so-called National Liberation Army (NLA). The government's security operations were characterized by indiscriminate attacks, widespread arbitrary detentions and beatings of ethnic Albanians, some extrajudicial executions, and vigilante violence tolerated and in some instances abetted by the police. The Albanian rebels were also responsible for serious crimes, including the detention and torture of ethnic Macedonians and Serbs and the "disappearance" of at least ten people from NLA-controlled areas. Determined to avoid another drawn-out war and cognizant of Macedonia's strategic location, the international community mounted an intensive peacemaking effort. Guided by E.U. and U.S. special envoys and supported by OSCE and NATO deployments, on August 13 the Macedonian government concluded a framework peace agreement with the main ethnic Albanian political parties. Deep divisions emerged within the government over the peace deal and implementation lagged behind schedule, but in mid-November the Parliament adopted constitutional amendments to grant important new rights to the ethnic Albanian minority. The peace remained fragile, however, with extremists within the government and police working to derail the process and skirmishes continuing between a new Albanian National Army and Macedonian forces, even as Parliament approved the new constitutional provisions.

Accountability for genocide, war crimes, and crimes against humanity remained a high priority in efforts to resolve the ethnic conflicts that have plagued the region. The April 1 detention of former Yugoslav president Slobodan Milosevic and his June 28 transfer to the custody of the Hague tribunal were the high points. While Milosevic stubbornly defied the tribunal and obstructed its proceedings, the prosecutor brought additional charges against him, expanding the Kosovo indictment to include important new charges of sexual violence and adding indictments for war crimes dating from 1991 in Croatia and for genocide and crimes against humanity in the 1992-1995 Bosnia conflict. The discovery in Serbia of new mass graves believed to be filled with the bodies of ethnic Albanians slaughtered during the Kosovo conflict brought unprecedented discussion and reflection in Serbia about its role in the serial wars in Yugoslavia. Cooperation with the tribunal remained a contentious issue, however, pitting Serbian nationalist Yugoslav President Vojislav Kostunica against the more pragmatic Prime Minister of the Republic of Serbia Zoran Djindjic, who saw cooperation as key to obtaining further Western integration and much-needed debt forgiveness. Pragmatism seemed to win the day, with six indictees, in addition to Milosevic, having gone from Yugoslavia to The Hague by the end of November—three by surrender and three by Serb government arrest. In contrast, there was no public progress on accountability for war-time crimes committed by the Kosovo Liberation Army (KLA) against Serbs and others in Kosovo. The ICTY was reportedly investigating crimes there but issued no indictments. In Kosovo, even speaking publicly about such crimes brought warnings of retribution from former KLA members.

With the dramatic developments in Serbia, the most conspicuous haven for war criminals indicted by the tribunal remained the Republika Srpska, the Bosnian Serb-controlled part of Bosnia, where Bosnian Serb wartime leader Radovan Karadzic and other indictees remained at large. NATO troops deployed in Republika Srpska deserved some of the blame for the indicted war criminals' continued impunity, which undermined the tribunal and the six-year-old Dayton/Paris peace process.

Russian officials repeatedly assured their international critics that those responsible for any abuses in Chechnya would be held accountable. On the eve of the March meeting of the U.N. Commission on Human Rights, Russian authorities commenced the high-profile trial of Colonel Yuri Budanov for the killing of Elza Kungaeva in 2000, and in April the Russian Duma presented the Council of Europe Parliamentary Assembly with a list of 358 investigations under way. Unfortunately, careful scrutiny of the Russian government's accountability effort revealed little more than an international public relations campaign. Few of the cases on the list provided to the Council of Europe dealt with the worst abuses in Chechnya. Even fewer had proceeded beyond the initial investigation phase. As of September, only five cases had resulted in active prison sentences for the perpetrators. Budanov never faced rape charges, though forensic evidence showed that Kungaeva had been sexually assaulted prior to her murder. Morever, Budanov appeared likely to be amnestied altogether after a psychiatric institute found that he had been "emotionally distressed" at the time of Kungaeva's murder.

The decade of ethnic conflict in the region was evidenced in the millions who remained displaced in 2001, in some cases years after they originally left home. In Ingushetia, over 140,000 Chechens remained too fearful to return. More than 750,000 remained registered as displaced from Bosnia and Herzegovina, two-thirds of them within the country, and, because many people no longer registered, actual numbers were likely much higher. Though return increased, it remained at a rate that would take years to reverse the "ethnic cleansing" of the territory. Over 200,000 Serbs were too afraid to return to post-war Kosovo, and another 200,000-plus Serbs declined to return to their homes in Croatia. In Turkey, although armed clashes in the southeast essentially ceased in 1999 and the government announced an ambitious return program, few of the 250,000 internally displaced Kurds from that region ventured home. More than 800,000 Azeris remained displaced from Nagorno-Karabakh and the surrounding districts of Azerbaijan, seven years after a 1994 cease-fire. About 280,000 Georgians who fled their homes in Abkhazia when the Georgian army surrendered Sukhumi to Abkhazian separatist forces in 1993 continued to endure displacement in Georgia. Sixty thousand Ossetians and 12,000 Georgians remained displaced from their homes in Georgia and its autonomous territory of South Ossetia after the 1991-1992 fighting between Georgians and Ossetians over South Ossetia.

Neither the affected countries nor the international community demonstrated much determination to tackle this persistent problem, which left millions living in substandard conditions and unable to return to their homes and property. In some cases initial post-war efforts had not been sustained as attention and resources shifted to new crises. In others no attempt at promoting return or restitution was ever made. The prospects for any concerted efforts to enable return became ever more remote once the aftermath of September 11 drew humanitarian attention to a new crisis spot, Afghanistan. The long-term impact of displacement was difficult to assess and varied among countries, yet in many places its effect on postwar reconciliation and the prospects for lasting peace remained a serious cause for concern.

Poverty, conflict, and human rights abuse in the region and beyond drove hundreds of thousands to travel to Western Europe to seek a better life. The inhumane and often deadly conditions they endured to reach their destination spoke volumes of their desperation. Trafficking of women for forced prostitution remained an urgent concern throughout the region. In many countries the victims of trafficking faced prosecution and expulsion while their traffickers, sometimes in cahoots with local police, carried on with their lucrative criminal business. Recent years had seen heightened attention to the problem of trafficking, with high-level meetings convened on the subject at the European Union, OSCE, and Council of Europe. Whether these initiatives would be pursued remained an open question as international attention shifted to the all-consuming antiterrorism effort after September 11.

Western European countries' attempts to address the demands of increased migration often led to more restrictive immigration and asylum laws, with little concern for the rights of vulnerable migrants and refugees. Detention conditions for migrants were grossly substandard in a number of countries, and many detainees were denied basic procedural guarantees in the detention and deportation process. Proposals to hinder migrants' access to basic healthcare and to deny migrant children access to education were hotly debated in several countries.

In the aftermath of September 11, many European countries adopted antiterrorism measures inimical to migrants and refugees. In Hungary, all Afghan refugees were transported to special detention facilities. In Greece, some migrants arriving on ships were denied access to asylum procedures and given fifteen-day expulsion orders. The United Kingdom proposed emergency anti-terrorism legislation that would deny some asylum seekers an individual determination procedure, classify as "terrorist" any foreigners with ill-defined "links" to terrorist organizations, and allow authorities to indefinitely detain them. National governments were spurred on by developments at the E.U. level, where proposals to combat terrorism included a broad definition of terrorism that threatened to undermine freedom of assembly and association and a European arrest warrant that lacked adequate fair trial safeguards.

Racist violence targeting migrants and refugees mounted in Western Europe, particularly in the wake of the September 11 attacks. Politicians failed to curb this abuse, too often encouraging it with inflammatory rhetoric equating the fight against terror with the fight against illegal immigration.

European efforts to come to terms with diversity became ever more critical with the European Union's rapidly approaching eastward expansion, set in motion in the heady, early post-Cold War years. With as many as ten countries to be admitted by 2004, much remained to be done to restructure E.U. institutions, as well as to adjust applicant states' laws to E.U. norms. In the field of human rights, poor treatment of Roma remained a challenge for nearly all applicant states. Turkey's persistent problems relating to torture, free expression, and minority rights kept it as a case apart among applicant states. Its National Program for Accession to the E.U. announced in March and the constitutional amendments adopted in October were both disappointing. The national program was too vague to raise any hope of meaningful change. Not surprisingly then, incommunicado detention, the death penalty, and emergency rule remained in place, and important free expression guarantees were neglected. Having missed these important opportunities for meaningful reform, Turkey continued to face a long road to E.U. membership.

DEFENDING HUMAN RIGHTS

Conditions for human rights defenders varied widely in the region, with activists in some countries free to develop innovative new projects while others struggled just to survive in extremely hostile environments. In Turkmenistan, no independent activist dared undertake any human rights activity. In Belarus, Kyrgyzstan, Turkey, and Uzbekistan, defenders worked under siege, facing a constant threat of harassment, police raids, violent attacks by unknown assailants, arrest, torture, and conviction on trumped-up charges. Under pressure from the U.S. government, Uzbekistan released human rights defenders Mahbuba Kasymova in December 2000 and Ismail Adylov in July 2001. In the course of the year, however, the Uzbek government detained two others, one of whom—Shovruk Ruzimuradov—died in custody.

Defenders also put their lives on the line in Chechnya, where Chechen fighters were believed responsible for the shooting death of Russian human rights activist Viktor Popkov and the January kidnapping of humanitarian aid worker Kenneth Gluck, who was subsequently released unharmed. Russian forces maintained strict control on access to Chechnya for human rights monitors, with most groups, including Human Rights Watch, refused entry to the territory.

Accountability for the murders of defenders remained a low priority for many governments in the region. The United Kingdom again failed to set a positive example in this respect, persistently refusing to establish independent inquiries into the murders in Northern Ireland of human rights lawyers Patrick Finucane and Rosemary Nelson, despite calls to do so from the United Nations, the U.S. government, bar councils across the globe, and many nongovernmental organizations.

Notwithstanding the challenges they faced, rights workers in many countries undertook creative new projects to strengthen protection and build a larger grassroots constituency for human rights. In Turkey, Sanar Yurdatapan's Freedom of Expression Initiative challenged the authorities on their arbitrary restrictions on free speech by enlisting internationally acclaimed authors to republish statements for which the original authors had been prosecuted. Throughout the region the Central and Eastern Europe Bankwatch Network trained and empowered consumer, human rights, and environmental groups to challenge international financial institutions to take into consideration the impact of their operations on local communities. Rights groups, refugee, and migrants organizations joined forces in many European countries to advocate for the fundamental human rights of migrants and refugees, and to highlight anti-immigration policies and inflammatory government rhetoric that often contributed to a hostile climate for these vulnerable groups. An effective coalition of nongovernmental organizations undertook a multiyear effort to promote implementation and enforcement of a new E.U. directive aimed at combating race discrimination. Another alliance of groups came together to battle for victim and witness protection measures in the E.U. Council Framework Decision on Trafficking of Human Beings. These and many other initiatives reflected the creativity and resolve of a resilient civil society that, particularly after September 11, was the region's best hope for positive change.

THE ROLE OF THE INTERNATIONAL COMMUNITY

United Nations

The contentious debate on Chechnya at the U.N. Commission on Human Rights ultimately yielded a strongly worded resolution condemning ongoing violations of international humanitarian law there and pressing for accountability and monitoring by the United Nation's human rights mechanisms. The European Union tabled the resolution but under the Swedish presidency negotiated an alternative consensus chairman's statement with Russia. The United States (supported quietly by some E.U. member states) found the statement too weak and pressed for a vote on the resolution. When the resolution passed, Russia immediately denounced it, refusing to meet any of the demands it contained. Neither the European Union, the resolution's reluctant sponsor, nor the United States, the resolution's ultimate champion, publicly raised its implementation during the year. When U.N. Secretary-General Kofi Annan visited Moscow in May, however, he did urge access for the U.N. human rights mechanisms identified in the resolution.

The United Nations maintained a massive peace implementation operation in Kosovo, the U.N. Interim Administration Mission in Kosovo (UNMIK). Though it gradually shifted certain responsibilities to local authorities, UNMIK, together with the NATO-led peacekeeping force (KFOR), retained responsibility for security and judicial affairs, where its activities did not always meet international human rights standards. In particular, there was a tendency to sacrifice due process guarantees in the name of improvements to the security situation in the province. Trials of several Kosovo Serbs and Roma charged before the Kosovo courts with war crimes and genocide suffered from serious fair trial shortcomings, while the number of international judges and prosecutors remained far below what was needed to address ethnic bias in the administration of justice.

The International Criminal Tribunal for the former Yugoslavia made significant progress toward achieving justice for war crimes committed in the Balkan wars. The detention and transfer of Milosevic was a watershed for the tribunal, whose prosecutor Carla Del Ponte persistently pressed the new Yugoslav government to cooperate. There were important developments in other cases during the year as well. In the first eleven months of 2001 seventeen defendants surrendered or were arrested and transferred to custody in The Hague. Giving the lie to charges of bias against Serbs, the tribunal continued investigations of KLA crimes in Kosovo and issued indictments against Croatian generals Rahim Ademi and Ante Gotovina. The tribunal also created an important precedent with convictions for crimes against humanity and war crimes in the Foca case, the first to focus entirely on rapes and sexual assaults perpetrated against women in wartime. Finally, the tribunal played an important deterrent role by opening an office in Skopje and reminding the parties to the conflict in Macedonia that it had jurisdiction over any war crimes they might commit. In November, Del Ponte announced that the tribunal would be investigating war crimes committed by both government forces and the ethnic Albanian insurgency.

An unqualified success of the U.N. World Conference Against Racism in Durban was the clear articulation of the fundamental rights of refugees and migrants and a wholesale rejection of the anti-immigration, "Fortress Europe" mentality that dominated Western Europe throughout the 1990s. Realizing the gains of the conference with respect to the rights of migrants and refugees promised to be a difficult task, however, particularly in light of the repressive measures taken by many European governments in the aftermath of September 11.

Organization for Security and Cooperation in Europe (OSCE)

The OSCE started the year reeling from an embarrassing December 2000 ministerial meeting where foreign ministers failed to agree on a final communiqué after Russia refused to include any reference to Chechnya. In June 2001, Russia finally permitted the redeployment in Chechnya of the OSCE Assistance Group, a year and a half after the OSCE Istanbul Summit at which then-President Yeltsin agreed to the redeployment. A combination of cumbersome security arrangements and OSCE timidity in pursuing the mandate substantially compromised the mission's potential for curbing ongoing abuse. Even its modest monitoring activities brought intense criticism from the Russian authorities.

The OSCE played an important confidence-building role in Macedonia. In September, 159 new international staff—mostly security monitors and police advisors—were added to the fifty-one already deployed. Adopting an overly restrictive interpretation of its mandate, however, the mission limited its human rights monitoring activities. Particularly disappointing was its failure to report its findings on an August government assault on the village of Ljuboten that left ten ethnic Albanian civilians dead, over a hundred detained and beaten, and scores of houses burnt down. Interior Minister Ljube Boskovski, who was present in Ljuboten the day of the operation, referred to the OSCE's silence as confirmation that the security forces conducted themselves appropriately.

In Kosovo, the OSCE organized municipal and Kosovo assembly elections in line with U.N. resolution 1244, which governs the province. In Albania, the OSCE's Office of Democratic Institutions and Human Rights (ODIHR) published a report that, although diplomatically couched, was critical of the electoral system and government manipulation in the June 24 parliamentary elections.

The OSCE continued to finance antitrafficking projects in the region, focusing primarily on public education campaigns and work by nongovernmental organizations. In addition, with financial support from the government of Germany, the OSCE sponsored a high-level conference on trafficking in human beings in October 2001. Participants made numerous recommendations to member states, but it remained unclear at the time of this writing whether any of those recommendations would be implemented.

Council of Europe

Throughout the year, Council of Europe experts were seconded to the office of President Putin's representative on human rights in Chechnya, Vladimir Kalamanov, and the Parliamentary Assembly pursued a dialogue on Chechnya with the

Russian Duma. Neither effort had significant impact on the ground, disappointing in particular in their failure to press effectively for accountability. When the bodies of fifty-one people—at least sixteen of whom were last seen in Russian custody— were found dumped near the Russian military's Khankala base, bearing evidence of torture and execution, the Council of Europe experts failed even to visit the site or monitor the forensic examination and investigation.

Continuing an unfortunate pattern of decisions on new members, in 2001 the Council of Europe undermined its own standards by admitting states that flagrantly violated them. Following a premature mid-2000 Parliamentary Assembly recommendation that Armenia and Azerbaijan be admitted, the Committee of Ministers delayed their admission until after the November general elections in Azerbaijan. Though Council of Europe officials who monitored the elections found the electoral fraud there scandalous, and a partial repolling did little to remedy the situation, the council admitted both states in late January 2001. Likely setting in motion a similar set of concessions, in September the Political Affairs Committee of the Parliamentary Assembly recommended that Bosnia and Herzegovina be admitted, though few of the conditions for admission identified in 1999 had been fully achieved.

The European Court of Human Rights remained an important source of redress for human rights abuse, though its growing caseload meant justice was often long delayed. It issued an important decision against the United Kingdom for inadequate investigations into the killings of eleven people by security forces and paramilitaries in Northern Ireland and admitted the first two cases against Russia since its admission to the Council of Europe in 1996. The court censured Turkey for, among other things, the conduct of its forces in the southeast and for the unfair 1994 trial that landed four Kurdish parliamentary deputies in prison. In a controversial July decision the Court sided with Turkey over the 1998 closure of the Islamist Welfare Party. Finding that the party's intention to establish Islamic law conflicted with Council of Europe norms, the court effectively endorsed the Turkish government's particular form of secularism, often used to restrict nonviolent expression and other democratic freedoms.

European Union

The European Union's accession process remained a valuable incentive for human rights progress among applicant states. In the European Union's annual assessment of applicant states, only Turkey failed to satisfy the political criteria for admission.

On a number of critical issues, however, the E.U.'s stance undermined human rights principles. The European Union led the international embrace of the new Yugoslav government of Vojislav Kostunica, without regard for his refusal to cooperate with the International Criminal Tribunal for the former Yugoslavia. While the United States demanded Kostunica cooperate or lose assistance, the European Union moved forward to organize a May 31 donors conference. Only the threat of a U.S. no-show caused the European Union to postpone the conference until June 30, by which time the Serb government had been compelled to transfer Milosevic.

A similar myopia infected E.U. policy toward Russia. The European Union and its member states continued their aggressive cultivation of Russian President Vladimir Putin with virtually no public reference to the ongoing abuses in Chechnya. Though it sponsored the resolution on Chechnya at the U.N. Commission on Human Rights, the European Union did almost everything possible to scuttle it.

In the aftermath of the September 11 attacks, the European Union entertained a number of proposed security measures that would not only violate human rights at home, but also undermine the E.U.'s credibility as a champion for human rights abroad. The proposed security measures contained an overbroad definition of "terrorist activity" that could potentially have the same sweeping effect as laws used to silence dissidents in, for example, Turkey and Uzbekistan. Having pressed for conformity with fair trial standards in E.U. applicant states and elsewhere abroad, the European Union itself entertained a proposal for a European arrest warrant that lacked sufficient fair trial guarantees.

United States

In the first eight months of the year, the Bush administration sent the mixed signals of a human rights policy still in formation. On the one hand the administration announced a foreign policy driven by strictly construed and narrowly defined national interests, seeming to foreshadow a retreat from peacekeeping and promoting human rights. After initial equivocation, however, the Bush administration firmly committed to keeping its troops in the Balkans. The arrest and transfer of Slobodan Milosevic and other indicted war criminals in Yugoslavia to the Hague tribunal probably would not have happened, at least for years to come, without concerted U.S. pressure. The United States was also the most principled advocate of a resolution on Chechnya at the U.N. Commission on Human Rights.

After September 11, however, the U.S. anti-terrorism effort threatened to sweep aside the human rights agenda, most notably in relations with key anti-terror allies Russia and Uzbekistan. Once again the United States squandered its leverage to obtain rights improvements when the State Department omitted Uzbekistan from its list of the most egregious violators of human rights. In November, President Bush hosted Russian President Putin for three days in Washington and Texas, with little more than gratuitous reference to ongoing Russian government abuses in Chechnya.

International Financial Institutions

Human rights continued to play an ever more important role in the operations of the international financial institutions, although certain issues remained too controversial for the banks to touch. The European Bank for Reconstruction and Development (EBRD) began to take a more robust approach to its charter mandate to invest only in countries committed to the principles of multiparty democracy. In strongly worded letters to the presidents of Belarus and Turkmenistan, EBRD President Jacques Lemierre threatened both countries with expulsion from the bank unless they started to show some evidence of such a commitment. The bank's approach to democratization issues was, however, uneven. While Turkmenistan and Belarus were censured, Uzbekistan received relatively muted criticism, and plans to hold the 2003 EBRD annual meeting in Tashkent moved forward without any apparent concern for the symbolism of convening in such a repressive environment.

The World Bank continued to emphasize the importance of judicial and legal reform, sponsoring a major conference on the subject in St. Petersburg in July. In its policy dialogue with states, the bank increasingly emphasized the importance of criminal law reform, but it remained hesitant to finance the much-needed reform of Soviet-era criminal codes, which remained a source of rampant corruption and abuse.

At the same time, the international financial institutions resisted calls for them to condition financing in Yugoslavia on the government's cooperation with the ICTY. In the same vein, they refused to link their operations in Russia to improved conditions in Chechnya.

THE WORK OF HUMAN RIGHTS WATCH

Human Rights Watch's work tracked the most serious human rights problems in the region. We gathered testimony about abuse in Chechnya in research missions to neighboring Ingushetia in February and July. In two separate reports, we published our findings on forced disappearances and on the government's botched investigation into the mass grave near the Khankala Russian military base. We also monitored the opening hearings in the Budanov trial. By presenting our research to government officials in national capitals and in Geneva, we helped make the case for the Chechnya resolution adopted at the U.N. Commission on Human Rights. We also successfully pressed the Council of Europe Parliamentary Assembly to enter into a serious dialogue on accountability with its Duma counterparts. When the Duma produced a long list of crimes investigated, our analysis helped policy makers appreciate the holes in the list.

Human Rights Watch also continued to track the government of Uzbekistan's brutal crackdown on independent Muslims, their families, and supporters. In August we published a memorandum on the key aspects of the campaign and pressed the U.S. government to name Uzbekistan a country of particular concern under its International Religious Freedom Act. A December 2000 report described the systematic and increasingly deadly use of torture in Uzbekistan. A second report on Uzbekistan, released in June 2001, highlighted the plight of victims of domestic violence, which Uzbek police and local councils routinely countenanced, advising terrorized victims to return to their husbands. Two years of advocacy on behalf of jailed human rights defenders Mahbuba Kasymova and Ismail Adylov were rewarded with their releases in December 2000 and July 2001, respectively. We honored Adylov at our annual dinner in November 2001, which he attended only after a long struggle to obtain an exit visa from the government of Uzbekistan to visit the United States for the event.

Uzbekistan was not the only country where religious freedom was the focus of our work. In an August memorandum we also documented the escalating violence against non-orthodox religious believers in Georgia. We repeatedly raised the issue in letters to Georgian President Eduard Schevardnadze and urged the U.S. government to take appropriate action under the International Religious Freedom Act.

When conflict erupted in Macedonia, we sent five consecutive research missions to monitor the conduct of both sides and published our findings in a series of press releases and a report on the abusive government operation in Ljuboten. In Skopje, Washington, Brussels, and Vienna, we briefed officials on our findings and recommended an active international human rights monitoring presence and a role for the Hague tribunal.

Building on a decade of research into violations committed in the wars in Bosnia, Croatia, and Kosovo, we pressed for accountability for former Yugoslav President Slobodan Milosevic and others responsible for war crimes. We documented and publicized the Yugoslav government's failure to cooperate with the Hague tribunal. An open letter from Human Rights Watch to Yugoslav President Vojislav Kostunica, published in the Belgrade daily Danas, countered his arguments against the tribunal. After Milosevic's transfer to The Hague, a Human Rights Watch representative attended each of his hearings, providing background and commentary for the media chronicling the proceedings. In October we published a six-hundred-page account of violations of international humanitarian law committed in 1998-1999 in Kosovo, primarily by Serbian and Yugoslav forces, but also by the rebel ethnic-Albanian Kosovo Liberation Army, and, though not of a criminal nature, by NATO. Releasing the report in events in Pristina, Djakovica, and Belgrade, we aimed to contribute to ongoing discussions about justice and reconciliation among Serbs and Albanians.

In Turkey, the ongoing prisons crisis remained a priority, as did advocacy aimed at promoting an ambitious reform agenda for Turkey's E.U. accession process. In June and July we conducted a six-week investigation of the Turkish government's efforts to promote return of those displaced from the southeast and found that its program fell far short of the U.N. Guiding Principles on Internal Displacement. In Albania, a November mission focused on restrictions on freedom of the media.

Finally, we continued our monitoring of the treatment of migrants in Western Europe, publishing the results of a November 2000 investigation in Greece in a series of memoranda and letters highlighting gaps in proposed immigration legislation, inadequate detention conditions for foreigners, and the Greek government's complete failure to address the serious problem of trafficking in women for forced prostitution. Our work on detention conditions in Greece sparked close scrutiny of Greece's record by U.N. and Council of Europe bodies and contributed to a growing civil society engagement on migrant rights issues in Greece. We followed up on the trafficking issue with senior government meetings in Athens in October. Trafficking was also the focus of a midyear research mission to Bosnia and Herzegovina. In July, October, and November 2001, we continued our research on migrant rights issues in Spain, focusing in particular on the law and practice pertaining to migrants who had just arrived or were in detention. After September 11, our research in Western Europe took on a new dimension as we monitored and condemned excessively restrictive security measures proposed at both the E.U. and national levels and their impact on migrants, refugees, and asylum seekers.

ALBANIA

HUMAN RIGHT DEVELOPMENTS

Albania took important steps towards a return to stability in 2001. The overall security situation improved significantly, the political climate cooled off in the run-up to the June 2001 general election, and the economy grew. Serious problems remained, however, with the conduct of elections, police abuses and trafficking of human beings, in particular the trafficking of women and girls for forced prostitution. And in the aftermath of the election, the country faced renewed political tensions as the opposition refused to recognize the outcome of the vote.

In June and July 2001 Albanians voted to elect a new parliament in an extremely protracted four-round election that left a mixed record. The electoral campaign was non-inflammatory and issue-based, and the first day of voting was peaceful. The Central Electoral Commission (CEC) generally acted with greater professionalism and openness than in previous elections. The subsequent rounds were marred, however, by what international observers characterized as increasing police misconduct, biased media coverage, and incidents of electoral fraud, mainly in favor of Socialist Party (SP) candidates.

The most serious irregularities occurred in Lushnja, where political squabbling and technical problems delayed the voting by two weeks. The July 8 ballot in Lushnja became particularly important for three junior parties of the governing coalition, which at the time of the delayed vote still needed several hundred more votes to gain seats under the system of proportional representation. The allocation of nine parliamentary seats turned on the votes of the Lushnja constituency as did the hopes of the SP and its allies to muster the parliamentary super-majority (60 percent) required to elect a new head of state in 2002. These circumstances led to a hotly contested election in Lushnja, where international monitors observed serious flaws on voting day. A majority of the local election commission refused to accept the vote as valid, which prompted the CEC to dismiss the local commission and tabulate the results themselves. The data for some of the polling stations, however, were missing or questionable. While the irregularities in Lushnja and elsewhere may not have compromised the Socialists' right to create a new government, they may have affected the final allocation of seats in parliament as well as the chances for an uncontroversial presidential election in 2002.

Most of the political parties that challenged the decisions of the electoral commissions did so through the courts, in a sign of increased confidence in the democratic process. The courts failed, however, to fully investigate a number of key appeals, including the complaints brought by several political parties about the electoral process in Lushnja. The opposition alliance led by the Democratic Party (DP) refused to recognize the outcome of the June election, and their deputies were still boycotting the new parliament at the time of this writing. Journalists, especially from the opposition media, received harsh sentences during 2001 in criminal libel actions brought by high-level officials.

The performance of the judicial system continued to be a major stumbling block for the consolidation of the rule of law in Albania. Judges were poorly trained to enforce the growing body of new legislation, at times unable to resist outside pressures, and often insensitive to human rights violations. In the first serious effort to curb widespread corruption within the judicial system, the government initiated successful disciplinary actions before the High Council of Justice against more than a dozen judges and prosecutors. An attempt by the government in May 2001 to impeach three judges of Albania's highest court for having allegedly favored a suspected drug dealer failed to pass a vote in Parliament, in part because of the government's inability to substantiate the allegations.

Several cases of torture and other serious abuse by the Albanian police in 2001 highlighted the prevalence of police misconduct, particularly as it concerned children and opposition activists. A particularly egregious case involved an eleven-year-old orphan from Saranda, who was detained on charges later found to be false. While in custody, the child was beaten, cut with a knife, and burned with cigarettes. The DP repeatedly protested the arrests and alleged police beatings of participants in its political rallies, which sometimes turned violent. Azgan Haklaj, the head of the DP branch in Tropoja, was brutally assaulted by the special police in January 2001 after having been arrested for his alleged role in a November 2000 attack on the Tropoja police station.

Trafficking of human beings, including the trafficking of women and girls for forced prostitution, continued unabated in 2001, with Albania serving as both a country of origin and a country of transit for trafficking victims. A report by Save the Children noted that 60 percent of Albanian trafficking victims were minors. Trafficking rings preyed upon Albanian women and children, operating with impunity throughout the country and evading border controls. In 2001 the Albanian government continued to treat trafficking victims as criminals: far more criminal charges were brought against victims of trafficking, who were prosecuted for prostitution, than against traffickers. The government failed to provide even minimal assistance to victims or to support witness protection programs.

DEFENDING HUMAN RIGHTS

In general, human rights organizations operated freely in the country. The Albanian Helsinki Committee focused on the monitoring of general elections and its long-term project on conditions of prisons and police custody. It also looked at allegations of police misconduct and patients' rights in hospitals and mental health centers. The Albanian Human Rights Group also defended the rights of those in police custody, denouncing severe restrictions on the defendants' access to defense counsel. The complaint center created by the group in 1999 saw a significant increase in its activity.

THE ROLE OF THE INTERNATIONAL COMMUNITY

Organization for Security and Cooperation in Europe (OSCE)

The OSCE's Office for Democratic Institutions and Human Rights (ODIHR) maintained a robust monitoring presence throughout the drawn-out general election. The observation mission advised the Central Electoral Commission and played a key role, together with the OSCE Presence in Albania, in mediating election-related disputes between the government and opposition parties. The final ODIHR report on the June general election recommended that a bipartisan parliamentary commission be established to investigate "concerns surrounding [the] elections" and propose remedies. In a rare but encouraging public statement, the OSCE field presence called on the Albanian government to investigate allegations of police abuse.

Council of Europe

The Council of Europe and the European Union continued a joint program to support the reform of the Albanian judiciary. The Council of Europe-based European Commission against Racism and Intolerance published a new report on Albania, finding little awareness in the country on the situation of minority groups and issues of ethnic discrimination, especially regarding the Roma.

European Union

In a move much awaited by the Albanian public, the June 2001 Göteborg summit of the European Union decided to open negotiations with Albania for a Stabilization and Association Agreement, the first step towards E.U. membership. A European Commission study concluded, however, that much remained to be done to improve the performance of the judiciary, tackle systemic corruption, enhance the administration's capacity to implement legislation, and shrink the massive gray economy. In response to a government request for assistance to fight trafficking, several E.U. member states pledged support for the establishment of an antitrafficking center in Vlora.

United States

The United States continued to exercise significant influence over the Albanian government and public opinion. The U.S. government publicly supported the efforts of the Albanian police to restore law and order under difficult circumstances, but the United States failed adequately to condemn human rights violations by police officers. A State Department report on trafficking in persons concluded that the Albanian government "ha[d] not yet made significant efforts to combat" serious forms of trafficking, and that its actions were hampered by "corruption at all levels of government."

ARMENIA

HUMAN RIGHTS DEVELOPMENTS

The trauma of the October 27, 1999, murders in the Parliament continued to dominate politics and public debate in Armenia. The government did little to improve on human rights practices, as torture, abuse in the army, and persecution of religious minorities continued, and growing poverty, combined with corruption, also led to rights abuses. The Council of Europe admitted Armenia in January.

The trial of Nairi Hunanian and other members of the group alleged to have killed the prime minister, speaker of Parliament, and six other deputies during the 1999 shootings began in February. After the opposition voiced suspicions that groups close to the president masterminded the assassinations, Parliament formed a commission to examine the criminal investigation. In July, at the commission's request, forensic experts examined the corpse of suspect Norair Yeghiazarian, who died in pretrial detention in September 2000. They concluded that an electric shock followed by a heart attack killed him. Cellmates claimed that he had an accident with an electric heating device.

Other suspects in the case claimed they were ill-treated or tortured during interrogation. In September journalist and former detainee Nairi Badalian alleged that military prosecutors kept him standing for twelve days and poured hot and cold water over him, to induce him to implicate a presidential adviser in the organization of the shootings.

The flawed criminal procedure code and the willingness of judges to admit coerced evidence abetted the routine police practice of extracting confessions through beatings and other forms of torture. In October 2001, Parliament legislated a minor improvement to the code, reducing from four to three days the time police could detain a person without charge.

An egregious case in September demonstrated the impunity security officials apparently enjoyed in cases of physical abuse. The beaten corpse of Pogos Pogosian was found in the restroom of a Yerevan jazz club, after a visit by President Robert Kocharian accompanied by singer Charles Aznavour. Pogosian was reported to have greeted Aznavour and then made an impertinent remark to President Kocharian, resulting in an assault by the president's bodyguards, who took him away. The bodyguards were suspended, but as of this writing no criminal charges were filed.

Armenian courts continued to deliver death sentences, although the government pledged to adopt a new criminal code abolishing the death penalty within a year of Council of Europe accession. A moratorium on executions remained in place. However, reflecting widespread public calls for the execution of the perpetrators of the October 1999 Parliament killings, Parliament failed to adopt the new draft criminal code, which also would decriminalize consensual homosexual relationships between adults.

Widespread torture, beatings, and noncombat fatalities of soldiers in the army continued. In January, Defense Minister Serge Sarkisian claimed that the number of soldier deaths had declined compared to previous years, with seventy-two fatalities in 2000, eight of which were attributed to border skirmishes with Azerbaijan. Military investigators attributed many soldier deaths to suicide, allegedly doing so to cover up fatalities under a range of circumstances. Physical abuse of new conscripts by officers and older conscripts continued to be systematic. Superiors extorted money or personal belongings from conscripts, abusing those who refused to comply.

In July, the Presidential Commission on Human Rights issued the first challenge by an official body to the widespread practice of torture in the detention facilities under the military procuracy's direction and to the latter's role in fostering impunity for grave human rights abuses in the army. It called also for the suspension of chief military prosecutor Gagik Jahangirian. The commission raised cases in which military police and prosecutors allegedly tortured Mikael Arutiunian by crushing his fingers with pliers and beat another detainee repeatedly on an open foot wound. However, it notably failed to address the wider problem of brutality in army units.

In early September, a special investigating commission established by Prosecutor General Aram Tamazian confirmed several allegations of abuse by the military procuracy, including the case of Suren Grigorian, who was permanently crippled when a group of officers allegedly beat him shortly after he was conscripted at the end of 2000. Military prosecutors had declined to pursue the case and pressured medical staff to misreport his injuries. However, by choosing to reject most allegations the special commission signaled that the military procuracy need not answer for systematic abuse.

In June, Armenia partially implemented a Council of Europe requirement to pardon all sentenced conscientious objectors, by pardoning and releasing thirty-seven Jehovah's Witnesses. However, the authorities flouted the requirement by continuing to arrest, detain, and imprison conscientious objectors. Armenia did not adopt a law on alternative service.

The governmental Council for Religious Affairs continued to deny official registration to the Jehovah's Witnesses and other non-Orthodox Christian faiths. The authorities continued to prosecute a Jehovah's Witnesses organizer, Levon Markarian, for holding "illegal" religious meetings. They charged him under article 244(1) of the criminal code: "infringement of individual and civil rights and freedoms." Because families with children were present at these meetings, the procuracy charged him with enticing children into meetings of an unregistered religion, for which the penalty was a prison sentence of up to five years. A court acquitted him in September, but the prosecutor appealed the decision. Article 244 of the criminal code was a remnant from Khrushchev's antireligious campaign of the early 1960s.

Although Armenia reported its seventh successive year of economic growth, the majority of the population remained in poverty. Disparities of wealth increased, as in previous years, with a small elite exercising much control over resources and political power. The government announced an anticorruption drive, yet corruption investigations remained highly selective and often appeared to be politically motivated. A high-profile case was brought against Ashot Bleian, an opponent of the government and a former presidential candidate, who had mounted a legal challenge on President Kocharian's eligibility to stand for the presidency. In December 2000, a court sentenced Bleian to seven years of imprisonment for embezzlement and abuse of office, although witnesses withdrew incriminating statements in court, claiming that prosecutors obtained them by intimidation or blackmail. Two of Bleian's colleagues were also imprisoned. His sentence was reduced to five years on appeal in May; he was released in July.

In several cases, newspapers and journalists publishing articles critical of the authorities received telephoned threats. Police and tax inspectors investigated the holding company of the newspaper *Fourth Estate* after it fiercely criticized the official investigation into the 1999 parliament killings. The authorities did not appear vigorously to investigate an arson attack on the workshop of freelance journalist Vahan Gukasian, another critic of the official investigation into the 1999 parliament killings. The authorities reacted identically to two antigovernment demonstrations—on October 30, 2000, and September 7, 2001—as police arrested and sentenced the respective organizers to administrative detention, and confiscated journalists' cameras or videotapes. Authorities cut the power to an independent television station's transmitter to prevent the broadcast of news footage of the arrest of October 2000 demonstration organizer Arkady Vartanian.

In a December 2000 report on the state's failure to respond to domestic violence, Minnesota Advocates for Human Rights noted that there was a high degree of social acceptance of domestic violence and that the government did not keep statistics on it. The research, conducted in Yerevan and Gyumri, indicated that the authorities did not view domestic violence as a significant problem and that police often attempted to dissuade women from pressing charges against violent partners. The report cited a Ministry of Internal Affairs official who claimed: "If women are assaulted in their homes, it is not considered a crime. According to Armenian tradition, a man has a right to beat his wife in his home."

Prisons were overcrowded, poorly supplied, and neglected. In June, Parliament approved a general prison amnesty, releasing or reducing the sentences of one-third of the country's estimated 6,000 convicts and detained suspects. The authorities planned to implement the transfer of prisons from the jurisdiction of the Ministry of Internal Affairs to the Ministry of Justice by the end of 2001, as mandated by the Council of Europe, in order to reform and demilitarize the system. However, the transfer of pretrial facilities run by the Ministry of Internal Affairs and the Ministry of National Security, mandated to take place within eighteen months of Council of Europe accession, appeared to be stalled.

DEFENDING HUMAN RIGHTS

There were no reported cases of harassment of human rights defenders in 2001.

THE ROLE OF THE INTERNATIONAL COMMUNITY

United Nations

In November 2000, the Committee against Torture reviewed Armenia's second periodic report. It criticized the report for concentrating overly on projected reforms, such as the draft criminal code, rather than the existing situation, and for failing to respond to the committee's 1996 recommendations. It recommended legislative and practical reforms to address violations of the rights of detainees, particularly regarding access to lawyers, family, and doctors; poor prison conditions; hazing in the army; lack of effective compensation for people tortured by state officials; and the draft criminal code's inadequate definition of torture.

Council of Europe

The Council of Europe did not sufficiently monitor Armenia's observance of the obligations it assumed upon membership, and failed to condemn the ongoing imprisonment of conscientious objectors in violation of Armenia's pledges. The three-year deadline it set for the adoption of a law on alternative service was too lax. A group of experts appointed by the secretary-general visited Armenia in May to investigate cases of alleged political prisoners, concluding that there were none.

In July the Venice Commission of the Council of Europe published its report on the revised draft Armenian constitution, which the government intended to put to a referendum. The commission gave a generally positive assessment of the constitution's treatment of human rights, and proposed further revisions, such as incorporating the abolition of the death penalty.

United States

The State Department's *Country Reports on Human Rights Practices for 2000*, published in February, provided a full and telling portrayal of the human rights situation in Armenia.

International Financial Institutions

The World Bank and the Armenian government co-hosted an international donors' meeting in July, and the bank published its Country Assistance Strategy (CAS). The report emphasized a need for generating conditions for poverty reduction through job creation. The paper cited corruption and outward migration as hampering the business and investment environment. It called for expanded budget allocations to education, health, and to targeted social assistance for vulnerable sectors of the population. In August, President Kocharian publicly took issue with the CAS, disputing its assessment that growth had done nothing to reduce poverty levels. The International Monetary Fund and the World Bank oversaw the government's development of an Interim Poverty Reduction Strategy, for which they earmarked loan credits. In May the World Bank granted U.S. $300,000 for an anticorruption program, to be managed by the Yerevan office of the Organization for Security and Cooperation in Europe.

AZERBAIJAN

HUMAN RIGHTS DEVELOPMENTS

Azerbaijan became a member of the Council of Europe after staging parliamentary elections that the international community and local observers branded as "fraudulent." Having secured its firm grip on the political process and its entreé to European institutions, the government harassed the independent media and political parties and cracked down against protesters with social and economic demands. It resisted pressure to release more than a few dozen political prisoners.

The Council of Europe had conditioned Azerbaijan's admission on, among other things, "free and impartial elections," and delayed its final decision on admission until after the vote. The Azerbaijani authorities failed this requirement spectacularly. The November vote gave the ruling party, Yeni Azerbaycan (New Azerbaijan) a majority in Parliament, again delivering President Heidar Aliev a compliant legislature. Opposition parties such as Musavat, the National Independence Party, and the Democratic Party of Azerbaijan, which enjoy significant support, were virtually excluded.

Repeat elections in eleven of the one hundred districts, urged by the Council of Europe, did not affect the overall result. After a campaign period marred by government interference and intimidation, election officials manipulated turnout figures, falsified vote tallies, and stuffed ballot boxes. The level of fraud prompted the Council of Europe observer mission to comment, "[T]he scale of the infringements doesn't fit into any framework. We've never seen anything like it."

Exploitation of oil and gas resources allegedly secured benefits for a small ruling elite. Transparency International rated Azerbaijan one of the world's five most corrupt countries. The president of the state oil company, SOCAR, twice sued opposition leader Etibar Mamedov for claiming that officials exported one and a half million tons of oil surreptitiously, making it allegedly the country's biggest source of corruption. The broader economy was denuded of government attention and investment. President Aliev's August decree, ordering SOCAR to pay $190,000 per month to assist some of the 800,000 Azeris still displaced by the Nagorno Karabakh conflict, appeared to offer implicit acknowledgement of a link between a small elite's control over oil and gas wealth and poverty in society at large.

Opposition parties' protests against the presidential elections combined with local anger about unemployment and electricity and gas shortages. In November 2000 police clashed with demonstrators in Sheki, and reportedly beat and detained hundreds. In July, a court tried twenty-seven of the protesters, mostly from opposition parties, sentencing most to prison terms of four to six years on charges of instigating public disorder, using violence against police officers, and destruction of property. In January handicapped Karabakh war veterans embarked on a mass hunger strike in Baku to demand pension increases. The government promised to examine their demands, but instead dissolved the Society of Karabakh Invalids, replacing it with a government-controlled entity. On February 19, police stormed the society's Baku headquarters and violently broke up a renewed hunger strike, reportedly beating men on crutches and in wheelchairs. Local authorities began withdrawing concessions that had allowed the handicapped veterans to run shops and minibus services to make a living, and seized all of the society's branch offices and property for the new entity. In July, fifteen were found guilty on charges of participating in public disorders and, absurdly, beating twenty-five policemen, and were given sentences ranging up to six years' imprisonment.

Throughout the year the government harassed opposition parties, intimidated independent media, and deterred social protests, but offered just enough human rights concessions to placate the Council of Europe. In August, after the council had presented the government with a confidential experts' report on alleged political prisoners in Azerbaijan, President Aliev amnestied or reduced the sentences of ninety-five prisoners, including seven of the Karabakh handicapped veterans. The Council of Europe secretary general urged President Aliev to release or grant a new trial to all political prisoners, whom Azerbajiani nongovernmental organizations (NGOs) numbered in the hundreds. The October 17 release of only three recently imprisoned newspapermen drew Council of Europe criticism, which President Aliev's office dismissed as "subjective."

In the second half of 2001 the authorities sharply increased their pressure on the independent media. Tax officials investigated Baku's ABA Television and confiscated equipment, which forced the station's management to shut it down. The authorities withheld licenses from provincial independent broadcasters, closing or fining them at will. In September police in Balakan detained the head of a local television station and shut it down by threatening to imprison him and demolish his home if he attempted to broadcast again.

Local authorities also undermined the production and distribution of independent newspapers. The mayor of Baku ordered the removal of newspaper kiosks belonging to private distribution companies. In September a court ordered the closure of the Baku Printing Press and imprisoned its director on tax charges. He had reduced rates for independent newspapers, challenging the monopolistic high prices for printing and newsprint set by government-controlled enterprises.

State officials used slander laws and obliging courts to close newspapers or issue them crippling fines for publishing articles that alleged government corruption or other misdeeds. In September, after it published a polemical article about state racketeering in which it briefly mentioned the mayor of Baku, a court closed *Bakinskii Bulvar*, gave the editor a suspended prison sentence, imprisoned the owner, and seized his apartment and that of the article's author, who sought asylum abroad. The editor of *Milletin Sesi* (The People's Voice) newspaper was imprisoned after it published an article suggesting a presidential administration official consorted with prostitutes. Both were released on October 17.

Police detained journalists, beat them, and confiscated their equipment as they attempted to cover demonstrations. In several cases unknown assailants beat journalists.

The authorities disrupted opposition parties' activities by making it difficult for them to lease office premises, refusing registration, arresting party officials, and violently breaking up their meetings and demonstrations. In August, police in northern Azerbaijan blocked Musavat deputy Rauf Arifoglu's tour of party branches, and beat and detained local Adalyat party officials on the eve of their leader's visit. Police violently dispersed Democratic Party demonstrations in Baku in April, and in Nakhchivan in September, beating and detaining party members.

An alleged culture of corruption, bullying, and neglect in the army continued to cause deaths unrelated to combat. A former Defense Ministry aide reported that since the 1994 Nagorno Karabakh ceasefire, bullying, accidents, infectious disease, and malnutrition had killed or crippled more than 5,000 soldiers. Eighteen soldiers died in a three-week period in August alone, of suicide, sunstroke, and dehydration. The head of a soldiers' mothers' organization linked the deaths of many soldiers with organized extortion. Some of the dead had earlier asked their families for money to hand over to their officers.

Chiefly young men from poor backgrounds were drafted, and it was widely reported that allegedly, a U.S. $2,000 bribe could assure an exemption from military service on spurious ill-health grounds. Poor and cramped conditions in army barracks exacerbated and spread diseases such as tuberculosis, diphtheria, and typhoid. In November former navy captain Janmirza Mirzoev, who had accused the defense minister of corruption, was sentenced to eight years in prison for his alleged role in a 1993 murder. The only witness said to have offered any evidence against Mirzoev withdrew his testimony in court. The murder charges came after Mirzoev had already endured two years of reported harassment and repeated detentions.

A new criminal code adopted in September 2000 criminalized torture as a specific offence and stipulated a five to ten year prison sentence for officials found to have used torture to extract confessions. However, police continued to torture or ill-treat detainees with relative impunity. The judge who tried the Sheki demonstrators ignored the defendants' assertions that they were tortured or ill-treated in custody. At this writing no police officers had been indicted for the death in custody of SOCAR engineer Ilgar Javadov in Baku in May. Reportedly, a forensic examination established beating as the cause of death, though the police claimed he died jumping from a window.

In a rare exception to the general rule of impunity, and after President Aliev's intervention in the case, a former Baku police station chief was brought to trial in September for his alleged role in torturing to death a factory trade union leader in 1994.

To a limited extent, conditions and incidence of tuberculosis in the prison system ameliorated. In May, Parliament adopted an extradition law that expressly forbade extraditing people to countries where they face torture, in line with Azerbaijan's obligations under the Convention against Torture. But Azerbaijan continued to extradite suspected Chechen fighters to Russia, and in October extradited two terrorism suspects to Egypt, both countries which systematically tortured criminal suspects.

DEFENDING HUMAN RIGHTS

In a positive move, the Ministry of Justice and four human rights NGOs signed an agreement in September to work together on prison reform.

In October 2001 the Ministry of Internal Affairs arbitrarily expelled Mehti Mekhtiyev, the director of the Human Rights Resource Center, an NGO, back to Baku from Nakhchivan, where he was visiting twenty-two beaten and detained members of the Democratic Party.

THE ROLE OF THE INTERNATIONAL COMMUNITY

United Nations

A November 2000 report by the U.N. special rapporteur on torture concluded that torture in Azerbaijan was widespread and that detainees assumed that they would be tortured. The report concluded that this fostered detainees' acquiescence in investigators' demands and arguably constituted mental torture.

In October 2001 the U.N. Human Rights Committee reviewed Azerbaijan's second periodic report. It requested the government to report back within one year on the measures taken to address the committee's principal concerns: inaction on violence against women and trafficking, harassment and prosecutions of journalists and actions forcing closure of media outlets, and serious executive interference in the electoral process.

Organization for Security and Cooperation in Europe (OSCE)

The Organization for Security and Cooperation in Europe (OSCE) fielded an observer mission to the November 2000 parliamentary election. The head of the OSCE's Office for Democratic Institutions and Human Rights described the conduct of the vote as "a crash course in various types of manipulation" in a press conference, yet criticism was muted in the organization's official report. On October 4, 2001 the OSCE representative on freedom of the media expressed alarm at the growing assault on freedom of media in Azerbaijan. The OSCE Minsk Group intensified its efforts to mediate a negotiated solution to the Karabakh conflict.

Council of Europe

The Council of Europe squandered its leverage over Azerbaijan at the beginning of the year by admitting it to membership despite the fraudulent election. By midyear both the secretary general and the Council of Ministers had dispatched human rights fact-finding groups to Azerbaijan. Beginning in September the secretary general expressed concern over the crackdown on independent media and stepped up pressure regarding the unresolved situation of political prisoners.

International Financial Institutions

The International Monetary Fund and the World Bank secured pledges of fiscal transparency, particularly in the handling of oil revenues, and prompted the government to design a strategy to reduce poverty and encourage broad-based growth to enable further lending to take place.

BELARUS

HUMAN RIGHTS DEVELOPMENTS

The September 2001 presidential elections brought an unusual level of international attention to Belarus—but human rights abuses there followed familiar patterns. There were state or state-sanctioned attacks on the independent press, human rights defenders, opposition politicians, nongovernmental organizations (NGOs), and peaceful demonstrators. President Alexander Lukashenka was reelected, although no intergovernmental organization recognized the elections as free and fair.

In June, credible evidence surfaced implicating state agents in the 1999-2000 unsolved "disappearances" of opposition figures Yury Zakharenka, Viktor Gonchar, Anatoly Krasovsky, and Dmitri Zavadsky. Two former procuracy investigators who had fled Belarus in May released documents to support their claims that a special death squad, "Almaz," had assassinated the four men.

The election campaign began inauspiciously, when the Belarusian government prevented Mikhail Chygir, the strongest opposition candidate, from running for president. In December 2000, the Belarusian Supreme Court reversed a decision convicting Chygir of abuse of power, but returned his case to a lower court. The pending investigation precluded Chygir from contesting the September vote.

Detentions of canvassers, police raids on candidates' offices, the denial of opposition access to the state media, and unbalanced election commissions seriously compromised the integrity of the campaign and elections. The opposition united behind Vladimir Goncharik of the Independent Trade Union of Belarus, but had little chance of beating the odds. Opposition and independent NGO representatives were disqualified nearly categorically from district election commissions.

In two July incidents, police in Grodno detained volunteers collecting nomination signatures for independent candidates and confiscated the signature sheets; candidate Valery Levonevsky was also detained.

Police raided four of opposition candidate Semyon Domash's campaign offices in July, confiscating newspapers. On August 25, police raided Goncharik's Mogilev campaign headquarters, seizing election materials and detaining the regional campaign coordinator. Two days later, the Central Election Commission notified Goncharik of campaign violations, such as distributing independent newspapers, and warned him that they would remove him from the ballot for further violations.

On September 2, police in Kobrin detained three schoolboys under fourteen years old for putting up Goncharik posters. Without contacting their parents, police questioned the children and threatened them with imprisonment.

Authorities strongly encouraged "early voting," which allowed ballots to be cast at polling places five days before election day without the presence of monitors, making possible widespread vote fraud. The Belarusian Helsinki Committee (BHC) reported that four universities, including Belarus State University, Belarusian State Medical University, the University of Culture, and the Gomel Cooperative Institute cancelled classes and closed dormitories during election week. Rights groups accused authorities of taking these measures to force students to participate in "early voting" and to leave the cities before planned opposition demonstrations.

On September 10, the BHC filed a complaint with the Central Election Committee documenting more than one hundred pages of election violations and calling for the results to be invalidated. After the Central Election Committee rejected the complaint, the BHC appealed to the Supreme Court, which rejected the case on October 24.

In the pre-election period, Belarusian authorities systematically sought to cripple the independent press by confiscating newspapers and presses, bringing charges against editors and journalists, and detaining individuals for distributing newspapers. In July and August authorities seized printing equipment or newspapers from six different independent newspapers, and in August alone, police detained opposition activists for distributing seven independent newspapers. On election day the websites of several independent media outlets were inexplicably blocked.

Authorities particularly targeted Magic Publishing House, the independent publisher in Minsk of eighteen periodicals. During three raids in January and August, the tax police seized printing equipment, shut down printing presses, and confiscated issues of *Nasha Svaboda* (Our Liberty) and *Rabochy* (The Worker). Authorities installed the deputy director of the State Press Committee as acting director of Magic on August 27, obstructing Magic's independent operations.

The State Press Committee reprimanded the newspapers *Narodnaia Volia* (The People's Will) and *Komsomolskaia Pravda Belarus* on February 14 for publishing an article linking the arrest of opposition leader Mikhail Chygir's son, Alexander, to state harassment of opposition candidates. On February 20, the editors of the Krichev district independent newspapers *Volny Gorod* (Free City) and *Nash Volny Gorod* (Our Free City) were convicted of slander for publishing articles critical of the Russia-Belarus union. On March 13, the State Press Committee annulled the registration of the only Belarusian publication for sexual minorities, *Forum Lambda*.

Valery Shchukin, an opposition politician and journalist, received a three-month prison sentence in March for "malicious hooliganism." The charges derive from Shchukin's attempt in January to attend a press conference, when police violently barred him entry, inflicting serious injuries. Although Shchukin had press credentials, police said the event was open only to journalists from the state-run media.

The Ministry of Justice denied registration to the Youth Front, an opposition organization, on January 3, 2001, citing "irregularities" in its registration documents. On February 19, a Minsk court fined the group's leader, Pavel Syverinets, about U.S. $460 for organizing a demonstration.

Authorities routinely detained peaceful demonstrators of all ages, often under article 167 of the Belarusian administrative code, which prohibits the organizing of unauthorized protests or mass actions. On December 10, 2000, Human Rights Day, peaceful demonstrators were detained under article 167 in five cities. Sergei Bakun of the Brest Youth Front was sentenced to ten days' imprisonment; two United Civic Party activists in Vitebsk were fined the equivalent of U.S. $500 each.

During the annual March 25 Freedom Day demonstrations, twenty-five peaceful demonstrators were detained in Minsk alone. Pavel Syverinets and Ales Byalytski, chair of the Viasna Human Rights Center, were sentenced to fifteen days in prison. Ludmila Griazanova, an opposition politician, was fined approximately U.S. $100. At the rally in Grodno, a seventeen-year-old photojournalist was reportedly detained, beaten, and warned not to file his story.

Activists from the youth movement Zubr faced detention for staging demonstrations, painting anti-Lukashenka graffiti, and distributing opposition materials. Youth activists were detained—and in some cases interrogated—without counsel, fined, or imprisoned, in ten cities. Police detained children in at least four of these cities. On August 14, Zubr reported that a Borisov police officer brutally beat a thirteen-year-old for posting Zubr stickers.

HUMAN RIGHTS DEFENDERS

Authorities used registration regulations, police raids, and web site jamming in attempts to silence human rights groups. The March 2001 Presidential Decree No. 8 further intensified the scrutiny of NGOs by forbidding funding from abroad to any organization involved in democracy, civil society, or election monitoring activities, effectively denying vital assistance to NGOs and independent newspapers.

The Viasna Human Rights Center received written warnings from the Ministry of Justice in December 2000 and August 2001 threatening to revoke its registration for alleged administrative violations. In February, the director of the Brest Association of People with Impaired Hearing was forced to resign for allowing opposition candidate Semyon Domash to hold a campaign meeting in the group's office. In April authorities shut down the Minsk office of the People in Need Foundation, a Czech human rights group, and deported its director. Unknown persons stole computer files and research from the Belarusian Helsinki Committee on March 28 and again on July 9. The items stolen, with other valuables ignored, raised suspicion of state responsibility.

On April 2, the Ministry of Justice refused to register the Legal Defense of Citizens, explaining that the organization's goals were contrary to the official definition of the term "legal assistance."

On July 20, civil rights attorney Vera Stremkovskaia was convicted of slander against the chief investigator in a case against Vasily Starovoitov, whom Stremkovskaia defended. In court, Stremkovskaia had accused the investigator of corruption.

THE ROLE OF THE INTERNATIONAL COMMUNITY

United Nations

In November 2000, the U.N. Committee against Torture issued its third periodic report on Belarus, noting concern about "numerous continuing allegations of torture and other inhumane treatment or punishment" by state officials or with their acquiescence. The report called for the establishment of independent national commissions to investigate torture allegations and human rights abuses.

Organization for Security and Cooperation in Europe (OSCE)

In a concerted effort to discredit the Organization for Security and Cooperation in Europe (OSCE), President Lukashenka personally accused OSCE Advisory and Monitoring Group head Ambassador Hans-Georg Wieck of "espionage." Obstruction by Belarusian authorities forced the OSCE to abandon the planned full-fledged observation mission. A limited observation mission was deployed, although two observers were denied visas. On September 3, Lukashenka threatened to expel both Ambassador Wieck and the U.S. ambassador to Belarus.

On September 10, the OSCE declared that the September 9 presidential elections failed to meet OSCE standards. The preliminary report on the elections, however, praised the "growing pluralistic civil society"; called on the authorities, civil society, and the OSCE to begin a period of cooperation despite "recent disputes"; and deplored the international isolation of Belarus. Both Freimut Duvé, representative for freedom of the media, and Gerard Stoudmann, director of the Office of Democratic Institutions and Human Rights, cancelled planned visits to Belarus when several of their staff members were refused visas.

Council of Europe

In January 2001, the Parliamentary Assembly of the Council of Europe (PACE) voted against restoring special guest status to Belarus due to the "unsatisfactory" parliamentary elections and lack of respect for free and fair elections, rule of law, and human rights. A PACE delegation observed the September presidential elections. On September 10, the Council of Europe issued a joint statement with the OSCE and the European Union, calling the campaign and election undemocratic.

European Union

In its public statements, the European Union strongly supported the OSCE and the international election monitoring mission. A European Parliament delegation served as short-term observers. On September 11, the European Union announced that it would not normalize relations with Belarus in light of election violations.

United States

The United States followed closely the presidential campaign and elections in

Belarus, issuing statements harshly criticizing authorities' treatment of the inde-pendent media, civil society, opposition candidates, and election monitors. The State Department also called for investigation into the "disappearances" of Zakharenko, Gonchar, Krasovsky, and Zavadsky. On September 10, the State Department declared the presidential elections undemocratic, citing the OSCE's findings.

The State Department's first annual report on trafficking in persons, released in July, assigned Belarus the lowest of three possible ratings, citing corruption, lack of programs to assist victims and witnesses, detention of victims during investigation, prosecution of victims for violations of other laws, and the criminal code's light penalty for trafficking.

International Financial Institutions

In June, the World Bank approved a $22.6 million loan to Belarus, the first since 1994, to install and update heating, lighting, and insulation in 450 schools and hos-pitals. The World Bank held the negotiations "in connection with serious achieve-ments in social and economic spheres which were reached by the Belarusian government last year."

The European Bank for Reconstruction and Development (EBRD), in an April 2001 letter to President Lukashenka, expressed concern over Belarus's failure to comply with the EBRD's required commitments to multi-party democracy and pluralism. The letter stated that the bank's future operations in Belarus would be reviewed after the fall presidential elections.

BOSNIA AND HERZEGOVINA

HUMAN RIGHTS DEVELOPMENTS

The return of displaced persons and refugees remained the principal unresolved rights issue confronting the people of Bosnia and Herzegovina. The major political development was the formation of non-ethnic-nationalist governments at the national level and in one of Bosnia's two constitutive entities, the Federation of Bosnia and Herzegovina. The ethnic nationalists continued, however, to exercise effective power in majority Croat cantons in the federation. In the other entity, Republika Srpska, Serbian nationalists remained a leading political force.

Bosnian nongovernmental organizations reported that the general elections held on November 11, 2000, were the best-organized elections since the 1995 sign-ing of the Dayton/Paris Peace Agreement. An "open list" system was used in elec-tions for the federal House of Representatives, entity parliaments, and the cantonal assemblies in the federation. The system enabled Bosniacs and Croats in the feder-ation to vote for candidates from the other ethnic group. The more numerous

Bosniacs were thus able to influence the election of Croat candidates. Unsatisfied with the electoral law, the main political party of Bosnian Croats—the Croat Democratic Union (HDZ)—organized an ad hoc referendum on Croat self-rule on the same day as general elections. The party also refused to cooperate with the implementation of election results.

On February 22, Bosnia's central parliament elected a cabinet (Council of Ministers) composed solely of the members of a moderate seven-party grouping dubbed the Alliance for Change. On March 12, the federation Parliament also elected an Alliance for Change government. On March 3, HDZ and its nationalist allies proclaimed self-governance in the territory inhabited by a Croat majority. The efforts to establish self-rule suffered a decisive blow on April 18, when Stabilization Force (SFOR) troops and OHR entered the main branch of the Hercegovacka Bank in Mostar. International auditors blocked the HDZ's access to funds in the bank, thereby cutting off the sources of funding for the Croat self-governance initiative. By mid-June, Croat soldiers who had left the joint federation army at HDZ's invitation renewed their contracts with the federation army.

As the security situation and political climate for return improved, the U.N. High Commissioner for Refugees (UNHCR) registered 56,683 returns of minorities during the first nine months of 2001, an increase of almost 100 percent over the same period in 2000. Most returns continued to be to in rural areas. The return of minorities was still not self-sustaining, however, as returnees continued to face scant employment opportunities and great obstacles to education for minority children. The international community continued to fail to respond adequately to the increased interest in return, with reconstruction funds falling far short of the amount needed. Although rates of property repossession by returnees grew in comparison to previous years, urban return remained modest.

While the security situation generally improved, serious incidents of ethnically motivated violence continued to occur. In a dozen cases in Republika Srpska and, less frequently, in the Croat parts of the federation, unknown perpetrators blew up or set fire to reconstructed returnee houses, shot at returnees, or planted explosive devices under their cars. On January 24, Zijada Zulkic, a forty-nine-year-old Bosniac woman from Banja Luka, was found dead in her apartment with a bullet wound. On May 7, some 4,000 Serbs beat and stoned three hundred elderly Bosniacs who came to Banja Luka for a ceremony to mark the reconstruction of Ferhadija mosque. At least eight people were taken to the Banja Luka hospital for medical treatment. One of them, Murat Badic, aged sixty-one, died on May 26 of head injuries. On July 12, a sixteen-year-old Bosniac returnee, Meliha Duric, was shot dead by an unknown assailant in the village of Damdzici, near Vlasenica in Republika Srpska. In November, Seid Mutapcic, a Bosniac returnee, was killed in Pale in Republika Srpska. Again the motive and perpetrators were unknown, but the crime was disturbing to the returnee community.

On April 6, an organized riot took place in west Mostar, Grude, Siroki Brijeg, Medjugorje, and Tomislavgrad, during an abortive international audit of the Hercegovacka Bank offices. A mob beat twenty-one members of SFOR and the Office of the High Representative tasked with implementation of civilian aspects of the peace process; two gunmen in Grude took eight investigators hostage and threatened to execute one of them. On May 5, Republika Srpska police in Trebinje did little to prevent several hundred Serb nationalists from throwing rocks and bottles at a delegation of state and international officials who came for a ceremony to mark the reconstruction of a mosque.

Independent journalists received explicit threats from nationalists in both entities. The Bosnian Helsinki Committee reported that journalist Ljuba Djikic from Tomislavgrad was threatened with lynching after her son Ivica Djikic, also a journalist, expressed his opinion about the situation in Croat-controlled parts of the federation. Mika Damjanovic, a journalist of the Sarajevo daily "Dnevni Avaz" and reporter-cameraman of the Federation TV, was attacked in Orasje by an HDZ activist who accused Damjanovic of being a "Croatian traitor." A bomb exploded in the doorway of an apartment belonging to journalist Zoran Soviljs, causing only property damage. The International Police Task Force concluded that his coverage of trafficking and prostitution had motivated the attack. In April the Organization for Security and Cooperation in Europe's Free Media Helpline registered an alarming increase in complaints from radio and television stations in Croat-dominated areas about pressure, threats, and intimidation of editors and staff made by the HDZ and other Croat self-rule supporters.

SFOR apprehended two war crimes suspects, both indicted by the International Criminal Tribunal for the former Yugoslavia (ICTY) in connection with crimes committed in Srebrenica in July 1995: Col. Dragan Obrenovic was arrested on April 15, and Col. Vidoje Blagojevic on August 10. NATO officials repeatedly claimed that NATO did not always know the whereabouts of indicted wartime Bosnian Serb leader Radovan Karadzic and former Serb army commander Ratko Mladic. In the alternative, NATO officials suggested that the two were in the Federal Republic of Yugoslavia and thus out of reach of NATO troops.

On August 4, the federation government surrendered to the tribunal three Bosniac officers of the Bosnia and Herzegovina army, Enver Hadzihasanovic, Mehmed Alagic, and Amir Kubura, charged with war crimes against Bosnian Croats and Serbs during the 1992-1995 war. Bosnian Minister for Refugees Sefer Halilovic surrendered to the tribunal voluntarily on September 25. The Republika Srpska had still not apprehended and surrendered to the tribunal a single war crime indictee. The Tribunal Office of the Prosecutor stated in October that at least seventeen indictees were at large in Republika Srpska. Two indicted Bosnian Serbs, former Republika Srpska president Biljana Plavsic and Serb Army officer Dragan Jokic, voluntarily surrendered to the tribunal, on January 10 and August 15 respectively. On October 2, the Republika Srpska National Assembly adopted a law on cooperation with the tribunal.

DEFENDING HUMAN RIGHTS

Local and international human rights organizations were generally free to monitor and report on the human rights situation. Due to concern for researchers' safety, however, some organizations were unwilling to conduct research into corruption in the country. The Helsinki Committee for Human Rights in Bosnia and

Herzegovina and the Helsinki Committee in Republika Srpska continued to be among the leading human rights groups in the country. The office of the Ombudsman for Republika Srpska became fully operative in November 2000. A similar institution had already been in existence in the federation. Most decisions by the national Human Rights Chamber, Bosnia's human rights court, pertained to repossession of houses and apartments by their pre-war owners.

Lara, an antitrafficking NGO in Bijeljina, continued to offer assistance to women trafficked into Republika Srpska for forced prostitution and received threats after launching a nationwide antitrafficking campaign.

THE ROLE OF THE INTERNATIONAL COMMUNITY

Office of the High Representative (OHR)

On June 21, the Peace Implementation Council Steering Board extended the mandate of High Representative Wolfgang Petritsch for another year. Responding to the March 3 proclamation of Croat self-governance in Bosnia and Herzegovina, on March 7 Petritsch removed Bosnian Croat leader Ante Jelavic from his seat in the national Presidency and barred him from holding any official or elected public office or post within political parties. Between March and June, the high representative also dismissed three leading HDZ politicians and four top-ranking police officials in Croat canton seven because of their obstruction of the implementation of the Dayton/Paris Peace Agreement. The overall number of dismissals declined in comparison to the previous year, reflecting the OHR-advocated principle of ownership, whereby indigenous actors—rather than international supervisors—were to take the initiative in the implementation of laws.

United Nations

In a resolution adopted June 21, the Security Council extended the mandate of the United Nations Mission in Bosnia and Herzegovina (UNMIBH), including the International Police Task Force (IPTF), for an additional twelve-month period. The IPTF strength (around 1,800) remained below the authorized number of 2,057. UNMIBH completed registration of all Bosnian police personnel in May 2001 and granted provisional authorization to over 9,300 officers to exercise police powers. Twenty-three police officers had their authorization withdrawn for professional misconduct or for human rights violations. UNMIBH expected that by late 2002 all law enforcement officials would have been appropriately vetted prior to receiving UNMIBH final certification.

In February, UNMIBH dismissed the police chief and the chief of the crime department in Bratunac, a municipality in Republika Srpska where incidents against Bosniac returnees were frequent. In May, UNMIBH also dismissed six top-ranking police officials in the Croat part of the federation who refused to accept the authority of the federal Ministry of Interior during the Croat self-rule campaign.

The U.N. Commission on Human Rights adopted a resolution on April 18 on human rights in parts of southeastern Europe, in which it welcomed the establishment of non-nationalist parties in Bosnia and in the federation and condemned the continued harassment of minority returnees. The chairman of the Commission appointed Jose Cutileiro of Portugal as a special representative to examine the situation of human rights in Bosnia and Herzegovina and in the Federal Republic of Yugoslavia.

In the first conviction on genocide charges before the U.N. International Criminal Tribunal for the former Yugoslavia (ICTY), Bosnian Serb Army General Radislav Krstic was sentenced on August 2 to forty-six years in prison. The tribunal found Krstic responsible for the murder of between 7,000 and 8,000 Bosnian Muslim men and boys after the fall of Srebrenica in July 1995. On February 22, the ICTY convicted Bosnian Serbs Dragoljub Kunarac, Radomir Kovac, and Zoran Vukovic for rape, torture, and enslavement committed in Foca during the Bosnian war. This case marked the first time in history that an international tribunal brought charges expressly for crimes of sexual violence against women. The decision also marked the first time that the ICTY found rape and enslavement to be crimes against humanity. On August 1, the tribunal sentenced Stevan Todorovic, former police chief in Bosanski Samac, to ten years in prison for persecution of Bosniacs and Croats in 1992. Bosnian Croats Dario Kordic and Mario Cerkez were sentenced on February 26 to prison sentences for crimes committed against Bosniac civilians in 1992 and 1993.

Organization for Security and Cooperation in Europe (OSCE)

The OSCE-chaired Provisional Election Commission (PEC) organized general elections on November 11, 2000. In response to the illegal referendum on Croat self-rule on the day of the elections, the PEC's Election Appeals Sub-Commission (EASC) nullified the mandates of the two HDZ candidates who received the most votes among the party's candidates for each of five cantonal assemblies. The EASC also banned reallocation of their mandates to other candidates. The EASC ceased operations in April 2001 as part of the process of transferring responsibilities from the PEC to the permanent Bosnia and Herzegovina election commission, which commenced its work on November 20, 2001.

On April 10, the OSCE Mission released its 2000 Free Media Help Line report, including a detailed review of cases reported to the Help Line in 2000. The report established that the most cases of threats and intimidation reported in 2000 were committed by government or public officials (34.6 percent), followed by anonymous and unaffiliated individuals (with 25 percent each).

Council of Europe

At a November 2000 session the Committee of Ministers of the Council of Europe welcomed the progress achieved by Bosnia and Herzegovina toward meeting the criteria for accession to the Council of Europe and added that further progress was needed, including the adoption of an electoral law. The ministers in May 2001 invited the newly established governmental structures in the country to accelerate the implementation of the required conditions for membership. The Bosnia and Herzegovina House of Representatives adopted an Election Law on August 21. On September 27, the Political Affairs Committee of the Council of Europe Parliamentary Assembly recommended that the Committee of Ministers invite Bosnia and Herzegovina to become a council member.

European Union

The Presidency of the European Union condemned unilateral moves of the Croat nationalist parties in March to establish a self-governing structure. The Presidency also supported the decision of the high representative to remove Bosnian Croat leader Ante Jelavic from his post in the Bosnian presidency. At meetings in May and June in Brussels, the E.U. General Affairs Council condemned all forms of separatism and nationalist violence in Bosnia and Herzegovina and supported the high representative's responses to these developments. During a visit to Sarajevo in May, Chris Patten, the E.U. External Relations Commissioner, and Anna Lindh, Foreign Minister of Sweden (which held the E.U. Presidency at the time), stated that Bosnia's accession to the Council of Europe was a precondition to further negotiations on a stabilization and association agreement with the European Union.

United States

During the year, the United States reduced its contingent in the Stabilization Force from 4,400 troops to 3,300. A spokesman for the U.S. contingent stated in early October that U.S. troops in Bosnia would not be pulled out to engage in the U.S.-led military campaign in Afghanistan. State Department officials refused to meet with Republika Srpska President Mirko Sarovic and Vice President Dragan Cavic during their visit to Washington in April. Sarovic and Cavic are leaders of the Serbian Democratic Party, which was founded by indicted war criminal Radovan Karadzic. The United States also endorsed the elections of a non-nationalist national government and expressed support for the decision of the High Representative to dismiss Ante Jelavic from office.

DynCorp, Inc., the U.S. contractor responsible for employing U.S. IPTF officers and SFOR contractors, faced two lawsuits for wrongful termination after dismissing two DynCorp employees who raised allegations that DynCorp personnel had engaged in human trafficking-related activities. The lawsuits were still pending at the time of this writing.

BULGARIA

HUMAN RIGHTS DEVELOPMENTS

The election of a new government in June offered the promise of reform, but Bulgaria's human rights record remained poor in 2001. Roma faced official and private discrimination and abuse. Police misconduct and inadequate prison conditions marred the criminal justice system. Respect for free expression worsened as the outgoing government sought to silence critical broadcasting at the state radio station. Constraints on religious freedom remained a cause for concern. Some progress was made in curbing the illegal arms trade and destroying surplus small arms, but more remained to be done to consolidate gains and halt irresponsible arms supplies.

The victory of the newly formed National Movement Simeon II (Nacionalno Dvisenie Simeon Tvori, NDSV) party in the June 17 parliamentary elections took center stage in 2001. The party, headed by former king Simeon II (who took office as the new prime minister), won half of all parliamentary seats in an election international monitors characterized as largely free and fair. The NDSV formed a coalition government with the predominantly Turkish Movement for Rights and Freedoms (Dvishenie za Prava i Svobody, DPS). As of October, however, the change in government had made little impact on the serious human rights challenges facing the country.

The plight of Bulgaria's Roma remained a key concern. Roma were beaten by police in at least five cases, including a June 26 assault at Pleven police station in which a Rom suspect was allegedly tortured with electricity. Private individuals beat and shot at Roma on numerous occasions. The abuses sometimes occurred in the context of trespass or petty theft by Roma. Police and prosecutors generally failed to conduct serious investigations into the attacks. Four Roma were killed in the month of June, including two men shot dead by a security guard in Mogila on June 29. As of October 7, there had been no detentions in connection with the four deaths.

Bulgaria continued to lack a comprehensive antidiscrimination law. A study released by the Open Society Institute in September confirmed the broad scale of discrimination against Roma in the provision of housing, social services and health care. There were encouraging signs in April, however, when Petar Stoyanov, then-president of Bulgaria, gave his support to the full desegregation of Roma schools, following the success of a pilot project in Vidin. The Ministry of Education began consultations with Roma school administrators about desegregation in July.

Roma sometimes faced pressure to leave their homes. Arsonists burned down a Romany home in Sofia on March 15. In August, villagers from Oriahovica formed a committee to prevent Roma families from registering as residents of the village. Oriahovica was the scene of attacks on three Roma homes in December 2000, when a middle-aged Roma couple was beaten. Many Roma living in Stezherovo village fled in August after five hundred residents drew up a petition calling for the expulsion of all Roma from the village.

Human rights groups continued to receive credible reports of the excessive use of force by members of the police and security services. Rules of engagement allowing the use of deadly force to stop unarmed suspects fleeing provided part of the explanation. Disturbing incidents included the death of an unarmed twenty-one-year-old army conscript, shot repeatedly in the chest by a military police officer on July 22, the killing of a sixteen-year-old girl in Sofia by an off-duty police officer on January 31, and the November 2000 death of a sixteen-year-old Iraqi boy, shot by border guards as he tried to enter Bulgaria.

Conditions in prison and police detention remained alarming. The Bulgarian Helsinki Committee reported severe overcrowding, inadequate food and sanitation in prisons as well as excessive periods of pre-trial detention and beatings and other ill-treatment in police custody. Inmates protested poor conditions in August, taking over the roof of Sofia's central prison, and carrying out hunger strikes in Varna.

Women's human rights continued to be inadequately protected. Bulgaria lacked anti-sex discrimination legislation. The state response to trafficking in persons fell below minimum international standards with women victims frequently facing police hostility.

Freedom of expression came under renewed threat, with the attempted murder of a journalist in December 2000, problematic criminal defamation laws, and government interference at the state radio, Bulgarian National Radio (BNR). In February the government-dominated National Radio and Television Council appointed Ivan Borislavov as BNR director-general. The decision was widely regarded as an attempt to silence BNR's criticism of state authorities, especially by the popular *Horizint* (Horizon) program, whose staff were quickly replaced with workers loyal to the government. Nineteen journalists were dismissed from the station in the protests that followed. Borislavov resigned prior to an April 9 Supreme Court ruling invalidating his appointment, but his successor continued to dismiss staff on questionable grounds and refused to negotiate with protesters. The May appointment of a new director-general Polya Stancheva, resolved the crisis, and the journalists were reinstated. An August decision by the incoming government to restrict journalists' access at the Council of Ministers raised questions about its commitment to free expression.

Minority religious groups faced official restrictions and societal hostility. The much-criticized draft denominations law regulating the status of religious groups failed to pass in the outgoing Parliament leaving repressive communist-era legislation in force. In March, the European Court of Human Rights admitted a case against Bulgaria brought by a Muslim permanent resident over his expulsion from the country in July 1999 for "illegal religious activity," following the court's October 2000 judgment against Bulgaria for expelling Muslims on similar grounds.

Bulgaria announced in January that by December 2000 it had destroyed its stockpile of antipersonnel landmines in accordance with the 1997 Mine Ban Treaty, to which it is a state party. Bulgaria also took steps to tighten arms export controls, such as by banning arms sales to twenty countries, most under U.N. or E.U. arms embargoes. At the time of this writing, however, it had yet to enact promised legislation institutionalizing other important arms trade reforms, nor to incorporate human rights criteria into such legislation. The new government also gave indications it might reverse some arms trade restrictions to boost exports and protect jobs. Moreover, Bulgaria continued to sell off huge stocks of Soviet-era weapons in anticipation of joining NATO. In October the Bulgarian defense ministry announced it intended to sell nearly two hundred surplus tanks and other heavy weapons to finance purchases of NATO-standard equipment. Past practice, including confirmed 1999 surplus tank sales to Angola, suggested Bulgaria would likely export the weapons to human rights abusers, contrary to government pledges under the 1998 E.U. Code of Conduct on Arms Exports and other agreements. With U.S. financing and under the auspices of NATO's Partnership for Peace program, in August Bulgaria began to destroy large quantities of surplus small arms, especially assault rifles, but no such funds were made available for the responsible disposal of surplus heavy weapons.

DEFENDING HUMAN RIGHTS

There were no reports of government interference in the work of human rights organizations, but two groups representing Roma and Macedonians reported harassment and interference with public education efforts related to minority participation in the March national census.

THE ROLE OF THE INTERNATIONAL COMMUNITY

Organization for Security and Cooperation in Europe (OSCE)

On March 27, Freimut Duvé, the OSCE representative on freedom of the media, voiced concern over the crisis at Bulgarian National Radio, focusing particularly on the dismissal of journalists. On August 31, the OSCE Office for Democratic Institutions and Human Rights issued its final report on the June 17 parliamentary elections, concluding that the elections met OSCE standards, despite overly-restrictive media regulations.

Council of Europe

On May 31, Bulgaria ratified two agreements enhancing its citizen's access to the European Court of Human Rights. The court declared a religious freedom case against Bulgaria admissible in March. Bulgaria settled a case before the court in May, agreeing to expunge the criminal conviction of a conscientious objector who was willing to perform alternative service. In October the court held that Bulgaria had violated a ethnic Macedonian organization's freedom of assembly.

European Union

A September 5 European Parliament resolution emphasized Bulgaria's progress toward E.U. accession but noted the outstanding areas of concern enumerated in the May 28 report from the Parliament's rapporteur on Bulgaria, particularly the limited improvement in conditions for Roma. In its November 2001 regular report on Bulgaria's progress toward E.U. accession, the European Commission highlighted police violence and the limited progress in improving the status of Roma.

United States

There was no public reference to Bulgaria's human rights record when Secretary of State Colin Powell met then-prime minister Ivan Kostov on April 25. The State Department country report on human rights practices for 2000 reflected the main shortcomings in Bulgaria's record.

CROATIA

HUMAN RIGHTS DEVELOPMENTS

President Stipe Mesic's government often failed to confront entrenched ethnic Croat nationalists obstructing reform, particularly on issues of impunity for wartime abuses and the return of Serb refugees. The Parliament approved constitutional changes reducing presidential authority and abolishing the upper house of Parliament in November 2000 and March 2001 respectively. In local elections held throughout the country on May 20 nationalist parties made significant gains in some areas. Police intervention was required in some areas, such as Vojnic, where ethnic Croat nationalist demonstrators tried to keep elected Croatian Serbs from assuming office.

Croatia's first census since 1991 took place on March 31, 2001. Some Croatian Serb organizations protested that the government did not do enough to include Croatian Serb refugees in the Fedral Republic of Yugoslavia and Bosnia and Herzegovina in the count. Serbian Democratic Forum (Srpski Demokratski Forum, SDF), a Croatian NGO, distributed over 50,000 census forms abroad. Comprehensive statistics were not available at this writing, but preliminary results indicated that Croatian Serbs made up approximately 5 percent of the population of 4.38 million in 2001, compared to approximately 12 percent in 1991.

Optimism over the extent of Croatia's cooperation with the International Criminal Tribunal for the former Yugoslavia (ICTY) cooled when the ICTY's chief prosecutor reported to the U.N. Security Council in November 2000 that the government's cooperation was unsatisfactory, particularly in providing access to documents requested by the tribunal.

Demands by opposition parties to cease cooperation with the ICTY resurfaced in June, after the ICTY issued indictments against Croatian generals Rahim Ademi and Ante Gotovina. Opposition rhetoric cooled after the government, standing by its commitment to cooperate with the ICTY, survived a vote of confidence in July. General Ademi, indicted for killing at least thirty-eight people and other abuses committed by troops under his command in the Medak pocket near Gospic in 1993, surrendered voluntarily to the ICTY in July. At the time of writing, General Gotovina, indicted for killings, house destruction, and other abuses against Croatian Serbs in 1995 remained at large. The ICTY also publicly charged Yugoslav and Serb personnel for abuses committed in Croatia in 1991. In October, the ICTY published a previously sealed indictment against four members of the Yugoslav People's Army and Navy for crimes committed during attacks on the Dubrovnik region. Two of them, Pavle Strugar and Miodrag Jokic, surrendered to the tribunal in November. Also in October, the ICTY amended its indictment of former Serbian president Slobodan Milosevic to include charges of war crimes and crimes against humanity for the killings, torture, imprisonment, deportation, and other crimes amounting to persecution of the Croat and other non-Serb population of Croatia in 1991.

Progress was also made on domestic accountability efforts. In February, Croatian authorities expanded their investigation into the killing of approximately forty Croatian Serb civilians in the Gospic area in 1991, naming as a suspect former Croatian Army general Mirko Norac, who reportedly ordered the formation of a firing squad. Protesters took to the streets to oppose General Norac's or ICTY involvement in his trial. The ICTY prosecutor had not indicted General Norac, however, and she decided not to request that the Croatian court cede jurisdiction to the international tribunal. In June, Croatian authorities arrested Fikret Abdic, the leader of the wartime breakaway Bihac pocket of Bosnia-Herzegovina, and charged him with war crimes. Bosnian authorities had long sought his arrest, but his Croatian citizenship prevented his extradition under Croatian law. In August, Croatian authorities in Bjelovar detained four men, accusing them of killing Croatian Serb civilians and prisoners of war in 1991. In September, six former military police were arrested on charges of torturing and killing non-Croat detainees in the Lora military prison in Split in 1991.

Croatian authorities also pursued war-crimes charges against Croatian Serbs. The OSCE noted a substantial increase in such cases, many of which involved defendants arrested pursuant to longstanding dormant indictments. Although some suspects were refugees arrested when attempting to return to Croatia, others had been present in Croatia for years. In many cases charges were subsequently dropped, raising suspicions that the arrests were politically founded and arbitrary. When three men from Glina were arrested in March on the basis of a 1993 war-crimes indictment, the alleged witnesses, who had been tortured at a detention center, were unable to identify any of the three as having been present at the scene of the crimes. At least two of the suspects had been living in Croatia for over a year and one had regularized his status as a returnee with the authorities. Although these men were acquitted, fear of such arrests deterred many Croatian Serb men from returning to Croatia.

Obstacles to the return of Croatian Serb refugees remained a significant human rights concern. Although by August 2001 over 100,000 Croatian Serbs had returned according to the U.N. High Commissioner for Refugees, most were elderly. According to international organizations, significant numbers of these returnees may have again departed for the Federal Republic of Yugoslavia or Bosnia-Herzegovina after only a short stay in Croatia.

Human rights violations contributed to the reluctance of refugees to return and to their renewed flight. While violent attacks on Croatian Serbs continued to decrease in frequency, isolated serious incidents contributed to apprehension about return. Croatian authorities frequently condemned ethnically motivated attacks and opened investigations, but arrests or judicial proceedings did not always follow.

A complicated web of discriminatory and confusing legislation meant that few Croatian Serbs were able to repossess their pre-war homes or obtain government reconstruction assistance. Although the Croatian authorities acknowledged the difficulties and modified some legislation, in many cases these changes simply exacerbated confusion over implementation. For example, the reconstruction law had excluded housing destroyed by "terrorist acts" from reconstruction (a category the authorities often used to describe the tens of thousands of Croatian Serb properties burned and looted following Croatian military operations in 1995). Although this provision of the law was repealed, some county offices refused to consider such applications, claiming that the amended reconstruction legislation contradicted other laws. With few exceptions, courts also failed to rule favorably in repossession cases where the prewar housing had been socially owned and occupancy rights revoked because the residents were absent as refugees or internally displaced persons. There were no mechanisms for compensating people deprived of such property rights.

Even when their property rights were recognized, Croatian Serbs also faced discriminatory practices when attempting to physically repossess their property. For example, in most jurisdictions, officials failed to implement court decisions, particularly with regard to evictions of ethnic Croats from Croatian Serb property. Although the authorities acknowledged this common problem, they failed to condemn even the most flagrant cases, nor did they take action against officials who refused to implement the law.

DEFENDING HUMAN RIGHTS

Croatia's vibrant civil society continued to make an active contribution to public life despite legislation restricting associations. In a serious but isolated incident, lawyer Srdj Jaksic of Dubrovnik, who was known for taking on human rights cases, was shot and injured shortly after his Montenegrin client accused of war crimes was acquitted in December 2000. At the time of writing, there had been no substantial progress in the investigation.

THE ROLE OF THE INTERNATIONAL COMMUNITY

United Nations

The U.N. Commission on Human Rights decided in April 2001 to exclude Croatia from the mandate of its special representative on the former Yugoslavia. The Office of the High Commissioner for Human Rights maintained a field presence in Croatia, however, focusing primarily on technical assistance to the authorities. In March, the Human Rights Committee considered Croatia's initial report on implementation of the International Covenant on Civil and Political Rights. While commending Croatia on constitutional reforms, the committee criticized the continued impunity for killings and torture committed during the armed conflict. The U.N. observer mission in Prevlaka was extended until January 2002. In May, Croatia ratified the Statute of the International Criminal Court.

Organization for Security and Cooperation in Europe (OSCE)

In June, the OSCE Mission to Croatia reported to the Permanent Council on Croatia's progress in meeting its international commitments, highlighting the continuing obstacles to the sustainable return of Croatian Serb refugees. The mission's mandate was extended until December 2001, although staff numbers were reduced in June.

Council of Europe

The European Commission against Racism and Intolerance published its second report on Croatia in July. It found that despite the good will of national authorities, discrimination endured, particularly against Croatian Serbs in war-affected areas, but also against Roma.

European Union

Croatia further advanced its ties to the European Union, in May initialing a Stabilisation and Association Agreement, establishing favorable economic and trade relations and cooperation in justice and internal affairs. The European Union also continued to provide significant reconstruction and development aid to war-affected areas.

United States

Continuing its support for moderate and non-nationalist reforms, the United States funded reconstruction and demining efforts, as well as development and technical assistance. The U.S. Agency for International Development did not directly engage in housing reconstruction, but it did fund community infrastructure and other projects.

CZECH REPUBLIC

HUMAN RIGHTS DEVELOPMENTS

The treatment of the Czech Republic's ethnic Roma minority remained a major stumbling block as it made progress towards membership in the European Union. The government's decision in July to allow British authorities to screen passengers bound for Britain at Prague's airport drew criticism from human rights and civic groups, as well as Czech President Vaclav Havel and speaker of the Czech Parliament Vaclav Klaus, who charged that the checks discriminated against Roma. A journalists' strike at the Czech state-run television network in December 2000 focused attention on political interference in the public media and prompted calls for new legislation to ensure its independence. Policing during the September 2000 World Bank/International Money Fund meetings in Prague drew hundreds of complaints and several lawsuits alleging police ill-treatment, torture, and misconduct. While officials stated that they exercised great caution and rejected all suspicious arms transactions, irresponsible transfers of arms from the Czech Republic continued to be a source of concern in 2001.

De facto discrimination against ethnic Roma in the country remained the most disturbing human rights problem in 2001, affecting access to justice, education, housing, employment, and public services. Little progress was made in implementing the Czech government's long-term strategy to improve the situation of the Romani minority, adopted in June 2000. Racist attacks on Roma continued, but police and prosecutors frequently failed to adequately investigate and prosecute Roma complaints.

The July stabbing death of a thirty-year-old Romani man, Ota Absolon, by a skinhead—racist gang-member—in Svitany, eastern Bohemia, renewed public attention to the failure of state and local authorities to protect minorities victimized by racially motivated violence and abuse. In the Absolon case, the accused was a repeat offender, having received a suspended sentence in 1997 for seriously injuring a Romani man by stabbing him in the stomach. In another incident, forty-five skinheads reportedly attacked a group of twenty Romani men with baseball bats in the town of Novy Bor on April 24, leaving eight Roma injured. According to local Romani representatives, approximately ten Roma and ten skinheads were charged in connection with the incident. The arrested Roma men claimed that they were being punished unjustly for acting out of self-defense. They also criticized the police for failing to pursue Polish and German skinheads who participated in the attack.

The deployment of British immigration officials at Prague's Ruzyne Airport on July 18 drew sharp criticism from human rights groups as discriminatory against Roma. The Czech government agreed to the checks in order to stave off the reintroduction of visa requirements for Czech citizens traveling to the United Kingdom. The agreement was prompted by the wave of mostly-Roma Czech citizens seeking asylum in the U.K. following the introduction of visa-free travel in 1990.

Between January and September 2001, 1,200 asylum claims were filed in the United Kingdom by Czech Roma citizens, none of which were successful.

Before the checks were suspended in early August, British immigration officers had prevented 120 people—the majority of them Roma—from boarding flights to the United Kingdom. The checks were reinstituted on August 27. To bring public attention to the selection process, two undercover reporters for Czech Television (CT), Richard Samko and Nora Novakova, attempted to board a U.K.-bound flight. When questioned by immigration officials, Samko, an ethnic Roma, gave answers identical to those offered by his colleague, a non-Roma Czech. Although both are in their twenties with full-time jobs, carried Czech passports and the same amount in cash, and possessed the numbers and names of people they would be visiting, Samko was denied entrance to the flight. Because most of the Czech citizens claiming asylum in the United Kingdom have been Roma, the Czech Helsinki Committee argued that the checks were designed to discriminate against this group in particular. Such discriminatory checks could deny Czech Roma their right to seek asylum in the United Kingdom.

On December 20, 2000, staff members at Czech Television, the country's public television network, barricaded themselves in the company's newsroom to protest the Czech Television Council's appointment of Jiri Hodac as the station's director. The television journalists accused Hodac of political bias because of his close ties to political leaders. The appointment sparked a widely-supported newscasters' strike, criticism from media organizations abroad, and a demonstration in Prague by some 100,000 people. Despite Hodac's resignation on January 11, journalists continued to call for changes in the law governing the selection of the council to ensure its political independence and public accountability. On January 23, the Czech Parliament passed a bill allowing nongovernmental organizations and civic groups to participate in the nomination of council members. Although a new council was appointed under the new system on May 25, CT employees remained critical of a provision that enabled a parliamentary committee to narrow the list of nominees before submitting it to lawmakers.

In the aftermath of the September 2000 IMF/World Bank summit in Prague (see *World Human Rights Watch World Report 2000*), the U.N. Committee against Torture, the U.N. Human Rights Committee, the European Union, and local and international nongovernmental organizatons expressed concern over alleged police ill-treatment, the arbitrary detention of protesters, and violations of detainees' rights.

Despite numerous pledges to reject arms sales to human rights abusers, areas of armed conflict, and countries that might illegally divert weapons, the Czech Republic continued to supply weapons in all such cases. The Slovak submission to the U.N. arms register indicates that in 2000 (and also in 1999) Czech weapons were supplied via Slovakia to Angola, whose long-running civil war has been marked by gross abuses on both sides. The Czech Republic was a major supplier of weapons to war-torn Sri Lanka. Under a 1999 contract, the Czech Republic in 2000 delivered surplus tanks to Yemen despite concerns that they might be diverted, as had happened a year earlier with tanks from Poland, and initiated negotiations for further arms sales to Yemen. Such sales typically involved surplus Soviet-standard weapons, particularly undesirable following the Czech Republic's accession to NATO in 1999.

There were also allegations of Czech involvement in illegal arms transactions, including a case in April in which a Ukrainian plane carrying Czech weapons was halted at Bulgaria's Burgas airport on suspicion that the weapons were to be delivered to Eritrea, under a U.N. embargo at the time. Following an investigation, the cargo was released for delivery to Georgia, the authorized destination, although there appeared to be discrepancies regarding the weapons carried, which reportedly exceeded that authorized for sale. In June, the Czech Republic, a state party to the 1997 Mine Ban Treaty, reported that it had completed destruction of its stockpile of antipersonnel landmines. A month earlier, at an arms fair in Brno, a Czech company offered antipersonnel landmines for sale in violation of the treaty.

DEFENDING HUMAN RIGHTS

Human rights groups worked freely with little government intervention. In July, following its campaign to bring greater scrutiny to new British immigration controls, the Czech Helsinki Committee was given permission to monitor the checks at Prague's airport. Civic Legal Observers, a nongovernmental organization based in Brno, filed twenty-six criminal complaints and four constitutional complaints against police officers for alleged abuses during the IMF/World Bank summit. La Strada continued to disseminate information on women's rights, provide social assistance and support to trafficked women, and influence legislation to ensure the protection of women's rights.

THE ROLE OF THE INTERNATIONAL COMMUNITY

United Nations

In July, the U.N. Human Rights Committee concluded that the Czech Republic's antidiscrimination legislation was inadequate. The committee also noted the failure of police and judicial authorities to investigate, prosecute, and punish hate crimes and called on the government to take steps to combat racial violence and incitement and provide proper protection to Roma and other minorities. In May, the U.N. Committee against Torture expressed concern about instances of racism and xenophobia in the Czech Republic, including the increase in racially motivated violence against minority groups.

European Union

In its November 2000 regular report on the accession status of the Czech Republic, the European Commission called on the government to improve the situation of Roma and expressed concern over continued disparities in the earnings of women, who take home on average 25 percent less than men performing similar work.

The European Parliament's rapporteur on the Czech Republic produced a report on the country's accession status in July, expressing concern over political bias at Czech Television and urging the government to take further steps to combat prejudice against Roma. In September, the full Parliament adopted a resolution endorsing the rapporteur's findings.

United States

In its July report on trafficking in persons, the U.S. State Department noted that the Czech Republic's current antitrafficking measures fell short of the minimum international standards. The State Department's report on human rights practices in 2000 expressed concern about the excessive use of force by police, particularly during the IMF/World Bank protests, the failure of police to take sufficient action in cases of threats or attacks against Roma, and skinhead violence against minorities. On International Roma Day (April 8), the U.S. government's Helsinki Commission called on the Czech Republic to make adoption of antidiscrimination laws a priority.

GEORGIA

HUMAN RIGHTS DEVELOPMENTS

Government pressure on a popular independent television station caused mass street protests in late October 2001, to which President Shevardnadze responded by dismissing the entire government. The government's failure to combat crippling levels of corruption, improve living conditions, and resolve the ongoing energy crisis stoked social tension. Law enforcement agencies acquiesced in rising religious violence, and police corruption led to human rights abuses.

Georgian authorities allowed organized groups of civilian militants to conduct a sustained campaign of violent assaults and intimidation against members of several non-Orthodox religious faiths, chiefly Jehovah's Witnesses, Pentacostalists, and Baptists. The assailants broke up religious services, beat congregants, ransacked or looted homes and property, and destroyed religious literature. Vasili Mkalavishvili, a defrocked Georgian Orthodox priest who led most of the attacks, justified them by claiming that charismatic faiths were defiling Georgia's nationhood and religious tradition. He boasted of receiving assistance from the police and security services. Emboldened by the inaction or complicity of prosecutors and police, and by a February Supreme Court decision to deregister the Jehovah's Witnesses as a legal entity in Georgia, the frequency of mob attacks rose in 2001. The Jehovah's Witnesses reported more than forty attacks on their adherents in the first half of the year. Police failed to protect endangered worshippers and in at least one case, played an active role in the attacks. Police on February 27 forced open a gate to a courtyard in Tbilisi where several hundred Jehovah's Witnesses had been worshipping, allowing Mkalavishvili and his followers to rush in and beat the congregants with clubs, large crosses, and Bibles.

The Georgian Orthodox Church did not condemn the attacks, and newspapers and television stations frequently gave Mkalavishvili a platform, legitimizing his group's activities. The Kavkazia television station in particular screened video footage of the attacks supplied by the assailants themselves. The positive publicity and impunity aided the spread of religious violence from Tbilisi into the provinces, where local officials, Orthodox priests and their parishioners, and the neighbors of followers of non-traditional faiths perpetrated attacks. The group Jvari (Cross) began attacking Christian minorities in Rustavi. In March an Orthodox priest on horseback led a crowd of 150 that broke into a private house in Sachkhere and beat Jehovah's Witness worshippers inside.

In at least one case, religious persecution extended to denial of the right to education. In February, staff and fellow pupils of a Tbilisi high school together bullied a sixteen-year-old student into discontinuing his attendance because of his Evangelist beliefs.

On September 3, after months of deliberation, the procuracy indicted Mkalavishvili and his colleague Petre Ivanidze on a limited range of charges relating to just five of their many attacks, but left them at liberty to lead new assaults. On September 24, Mkalavishvili led a rally in Tbilisi, where he called for widening the campaign of religious violence. In the most serious of three attacks that week, Mkalavishvili's supporters and the Jvari group blocked a highway and beat dozens of Jehovah's Witnesses on their way to a planned convention in the southern town of Marneuli. The mob then descended on the convention site, destroying and looting it.

There were widespread reports of torture and ill-treatment in police detention. In September, Council of Europe monitors reported that Interior Minister Kakha Targamadze last year had dismissed such reports, telling them that they were made by "enemies of Georgia." In a positive move toward addressing torture, amendments to the criminal procedure code voted in June reportedly granted witnesses the right to legal representation. It had been common police practice to label detained suspects as "witnesses" in order to deny them access to a lawyer.

Courts continued to convict on the strength of confessions that may have been extracted under torture. The state continued to prevent defendants from obtaining and presenting forensic evidence of torture to the courts by means of procedural restrictions and by not licensing nongovernmental forensic doctors. In July a court hearing the case of Lasha Kartavelishvili, accused of murdering a policeman, refused to admit testimony from independent forensic examiner Maia Nikoleishvili that Kartavelishvili had been tortured in police detention, on the grounds that she did not hold a forensic practitioner's license.

On October 30, 2001, the independent Rustavi 2 television station made an emergency live broadcast of a visit by National Security Ministry officers who were seeking evidence of tax violations. Many interpreted the incident as the culmination of a government campaign of intimidation against the station, and thousands came to demonstrate in its support, precipitating a political crisis. Several days before, Minister Targamadze reportedly threatened to send his men to "destroy" the

TV company. In previous weeks, Rustavi 2's *60 Minutes* current affairs program had broadcast three detailed investigations into alleged Ministry of Interior and procuracy corruption, including an exposé that compelled Targamadze to dismiss the police chief of a Tbilisi district who was captured on a hidden camera initiating the planting of drugs on a suspect to extort money from him. Rustavi 2's management had briefly taken the program off the air in June after state television, the procuracy, and intellectuals close to the government vilified it, and the program staff reportedly received anonymous death threats.

The July assassination of Giorgi Sanaia, the young presenter of Rustavi 2's Night Courier news and discussion program, precipitated national mourning. Facing public suspicion about the role of the security ministries, the government swiftly invited the U.S. Federal Bureau of Investigation to give forensic assistance to the investigation. The police quickly arrested a man previously detained on a fraud charge, yet at this writing prosecutors had not presented sufficient evidence to indict him for Sanaia's murder. Some commentators linked Sanaia's shooting, which appeared to be expertly planned and executed, to purported knowledge or video material he had obtained, allegedly demonstrating links between law enforcement officials with criminals in Georgia's Pankisi Gorge who engaged in kidnappings and the narcotics trade.

Georgian police did not attempt to enforce the rule of law in the Pankisi Gorge, where 7,000 Chechen refugees had lived alongside Kists—Georgian ethnic Chechens—since late 1999. Several Georgians and foreign businessmen, most of them kidnapped in Tbilisi, were believed to be held for ransom in the gorge, which was also the center of the country's illegal drug trade.

Fighting flared in the separatist-controlled region, Abkhazia, in October, as ethnic Chechen fighters launched an assault on breakaway Abkhazian forces in the Kodori Gorge. Some alleged that the security ministries had arranged to ferry the Chechen fighters from the Pankisi Gorge to the Abkhaz border. Several civilians were killed in the fighting. At this writing an international investigative commission was still trying to determine responsibility for the downing of a helicopter belonging to the U.N. Observer Mission in Georgia (UNOMIG) by a missile over the Kodori Gorge, which killed nine.

In Abkhazia's Gali district, Georgian paramilitary insurgents, tacitly supported by the central authorities, and forces representing the Abkhazian separatist authorities both abducted civilians for exchange or ransom. In early November 2001, the latter demanded U.S. $65,000 for the release of four Georgian hunters. Relatives and representatives of victims of Georgia's growing kidnapping problem expressed frustration at the authorities' inactivity in securing their release. In August Tbilisi's new police chief led an operation that freed a Lebanese businessman, held for ransom near the city. However, the police appeared to have known for some time where he was held, and they allowed the kidnappers to escape. In July, ethnic Georgian village militias secured the release of two hostages in the Pankisi Gorge by taking seven Kists hostage for exchange; local authorities tacitly approved of this arrangement.

Young women in some rural areas could not rely on law enforcement officials to protect them from the persisting custom of bride kidnapping. Prosecutors reportedly habitually declined to indict the perpetrators for kidnap or rape, telling the victim or her family instead to reconcile themselves to the fait accompli. Likewise, the authorities' failure to make sustained efforts or adopt legislation against trafficking of women allowed networks fronted by employment and travel agencies to continue to lure women into being trafficked abroad for forced prostitution.

Despite strong pressure by international financial institutions, the government did not implement an agreed anticorruption plan. Justice Minister Mikheil Saakashvili resigned in September after the president declined to support an anticorruption bill that included strong confiscation provisions. Some of the worst corruption involved the siphoning of national resources by powerful clans said to be linked to high-level officials, including a so-called kerosene mafia whose interests were served by the continuing electricity shortages.

The government's serious arrears in paying pensions or wages also affected the armed forces. On May 25 a battalion of national guardsmen mutinied in protest at fourteen-month wage arrears and conditions of near starvation. They seized an Interior Ministry troop base near Tbilisi, but relented after President Shevardnadze met with them and promised to address their complaints.

Electricity shortages provoked street protests in Tbilisi. Together with other resource shortages and high unemployment, they also strained intercommunal relations. Ethnic Georgians displaced from Abkhazia since 1993 blocked a highway in western Georgia in April, protesting local authorities' failure to pay their promised monthly living allowance. In July ethnic Azeris in southern Georgia blocked a highway, protesting lack of electricity, gas, and water supplies. Similar issues generated discontent in the ethnic Armenian populated southern region of Samtskhe-Javakheti, causing tension in Georgia's relations with Armenia.

DEFENDING HUMAN RIGHTS

A wide range of lively and public-spirited human rights nongovernmental organizations were based in the capital, Tbilisi.

THE ROLE OF THE INTERNATIONAL COMMUNITY

United Nations

The UNOMIG continued its efforts to promote dialogue between the government and the de facto authorities in Abkhazia, and to monitor implementation of the 1994 ceasefire agreement. It also brokered hostage exchanges and ransom demands between the de facto Abkhazian authorities and Georgian paramilitary groups operating there.

In May, the U.N. Committee against Torture reviewed Georgia's second periodic report. It called for the establishment of an effective and independent complaints mechanism to address numerous allegations of torture by police, and for a systematic review of all convictions based on confessions that may have been obtained by torture. The Committee on the Elimination of Racial Discrimination expressed concern that Georgian law did not criminalize incitement to racial or religious discrimination.

Council of Europe

Informed by a detailed report compiled by rapporteurs of the Monitoring Committee of the Council of Europe, the Parliamentary Assembly of the Council of Europe adopted a strong resolution in September concluding that Georgia was far from honoring its obligations and commitments to the Council of Europe, and urged the government to adopt a raft of remedial measures. The resolution welcomed President Shevardnadze's April 2000 granting of autonomous status to the autonomous region of Ajara, but did not comment on the entrenched authoritarian rule of Ajaran leader Aslan Abashidze. While the resolution noted strong concern over religious violence in Georgia, the Council of Europe took no other action to address it.

In early July the European Court of Human Rights accepted as a priority case a petition from the Jehovah's Witnesses concerning the failure of the Georgian authorities to provide a remedy in the case of the very first mob attack on their adherents, in 1999. The court presented the Georgian authorities with nine questions, including a request that they account for the actions taken to deal with approximately six hundred criminal complaints submitted to date by Jehovah's Witnesses.

European Union

The E.U.-Georgia Partnership and Cooperation Agreement (PCA) entered into force in July. It provided a framework for E.U. development assistance, aimed at achieving Georgia's economic convergence with the European Union and enhancing regional security. Respect for democracy, principles of international law, and human rights were stipulated as essential elements of the partnership and of the PCA.

United States

The U.S. Department of Justice announced its intention to supply the Ministry of Justice with a modern forensic laboratory, and began training Georgian staff in preparation. The facility was intended to provide alternate sources for the provision of forensic expertise.

The U.S. Commission on International Religious Freedom wrote to President George W. Bush, urging him to raise the Georgian authorities' failure to stop religious violence with President Shevardnadze during his October visit to the United States.

Relevant Human Rights Watch Reports:

Memorandum to the U.S. Government on Religious Violence in the Republic of Georgia, 8/01.

GREECE

HUMAN RIGHTS DEVELOPMENTS

Greece faced criticism for its human rights policies and practices from a range of regional and international actors in 2001. A new immigration bill and the ill-treatment of migrants dominated the human rights landscape and gave rise to a new dimension in rights activism in Greece. In the aftermath of the September 11 attacks in the United States, the Greek authorities further restricted access to asylum procedures for refugees. Ongoing discrimination undermined Greece's progress toward protecting Roma. Resistance to the recognition of ethnic minorities remained a systemic problem, with language rights taking center stage. Criticism of Greece for its poor record on press freedom persisted.

A new immigration bill sparked a heated national debate over immigration policy. A February 2001 draft of the bill lacked an antidiscrimination clause, violated the right to family reunification; failed to address trafficking of persons, failed to acknowledge the basic rights of undocumented migrants, denied undocumented migrant children access to education and health care, and lacked provisions prohibiting the arbitrary detention of migrants or their collective expulsion. After intense lobbying by human rights groups, the law adopted in April contained some improvements, including permission for trafficking victims to remain in Greece pending criminal proceedings against traffickers, access to education and healthcare for undocumented migrant children, the right to challenge immigration detention before an administrative court, and a time limit of three months for the detention of migrants who cannot be returned to their home countries. In August, the independent Data Protection Authority called on the government to scrap a provision of the law requiring hospital staff and hotel employees to notify the police if undocumented migrants sought their services because it violated Greece's privacy protection laws.

Detention centers for foreigners in Athens, Hellenikon, and Piraeus came under fire for grossly substandard conditions. A December 2000 Human Rights Watch investigation at the Alexandras Avenue police station in Athens found severe overcrowding, inadequate sleeping accommodations, no access to exercise or fresh air, limited access to medical care, inadequate amounts of food, and a dirty, roach-infested environment. Migrants who had served their sentences but remained incarcerated at Korydallos Prison in Athens also suffered from severe overcrowding. Human rights groups charged the government with arbitrary detention for indefinitely holding migrants who could not be repatriated to their home countries. In two decisions against Greece in 2001, the European Court of Human Rights held that detention conditions at Alexandras Avenue and at Korydallos Prison amounted to inhuman or degrading treatment. In July 2001, the nongovernmental organization Greek Helsinki Monitor (GHM) lodged a complaint with the Greek ombudsman on behalf of detained foreigners who could not be deported to their home countries, charging that under the new immigration law, any detainee held in excess of three months who could not be deported must be released. As a result of the complaint, seventy detained foreigners were released in late July. In September, GHM lodged another complaint with the ombudsman alleging more illegal detentions of foreigners and substandard conditions in the Hellenikon and Piraeus detention centers.

In June 2001, migrants charged that they were brutally assaulted in a makeshift detention center in Hania, Crete. Hania doctors documented bruises and other signs of beatings on 164 migrants from Afghanistan, Ethiopia, Iraq, Iran, Pakistan, and Turkey. An initial investigation by the Merchant Marine Ministry completed in August found three Port Authority officials accused of the beatings to have engaged in the "irregular execution of duties." The men faced disciplinary proceedings but criminal charges had not been brought by the time of writing. Rights groups charged that authorities downplayed the savagery of the attacks, which they claimed amounted to torture.

Migrants continued to face police sweeps and collective expulsion from Greece without the benefit of procedural safeguards. In a potentially positive development, in February, the Greek ombudsman publicly stated that sweep operations and collective expulsions were illegal.

Trafficking of women for forced prostitution remained a serious problem and the government's response inadequate. Specific concerns included the absence of anti-trafficking legislation, the few prosecutions for crimes related to trafficking, the lack of witness protection programs for trafficking victims, the absence of government-sponsored services for all trafficked women, the detention and prosecution of trafficking victims, and the complicity of police officers in trafficking. A U.S. State Department report released on July 12 gave Greece the lowest rating possible for failing to combat trafficking.

People fleeing the military action in Afghanistan and other refugees and migrants who arrived in Greece in the aftermath of the September 11 attacks in the United States were met with a hostile reception. Fearing a large influx of Afghan refugees, the Greek government severely curtailed access to asylum procedures. In October, Afghan refugees arriving in Athens charged that they were not permitted to lodge asylum claims and were summarily given expulsion orders. The Greek Council for Refugees (GRC) reported that the government had even issued an expulsion order to an Afghani mother with a three-week-old infant. On October 18, the GRC charged that the government was in violation of its obligations under the 1951 Refugee Convention. On November 5, a Turkish ship carrying 714 migrants and refugees from Afghanistan, Iraq, Iran, and Turkey—including women and children—was towed to Zakynthos. The Greek authorities initially refused to permit any of the persons from the ship to apply for asylum and relented only after a firestorm of protest from humanitarian, refugee, and human rights groups.

In May 2001 the Greek government took steps to address discrimination with an action plan for Roma, designed to address health, education and housing needs. The first successful resettlement of a Roma community—from the Gallikos River to Gonou—was overshadowed by the inadequate basic services provided to the resettled Roma community. The self-managed Aghia Sofia settlement established in October 2000 was hailed as an exception to the rule of discrimination against Roma. Praise was short-lived, however, as Roma children immediately faced opposition to their attendance at local schools, in particular from the parents' association of the Halastra Public School, which closed the school in November 2000 in opposition to thirty-two Roma children attending. Problems with access to electricity plagued Aghia Sofia residents throughout 2001 and rights groups charged the state electricity company with discriminatory pricing practices that resulted in power cutoffs.

A January 2001 Greek ombudsman's report found that the municipal authorities' expulsion of Roma and destruction of their homes in the Asproprygos suburb of Athens in July 2000 had violated Greek law. The report recommended that an investigation into the evictions be carried out, but at the time of writing, no investigation had been initiated. In September 2001, municipal authorities demolished six more Romani homes in Asproprygos. The operation was halted only after intervention by the Greek ombudsman and Greek Helsinki Monitor.

In August, the police verbally ordered Roma from the Kalakonero area on Rhodes to vacate their settlement by September 3 or have their homes demolished. No demolition occurred though the residents were informed subsequently by authorities that a process of relocation for the settlement had begun. The Roma filed a complaint with the Greek ombudsman alleging that the pending eviction was illegal because contrary to Greek law the community had received no official relocation plan.

Municipal authorities equipped with a bulldozer entered a Romani settlement in the Glykada Riganokampos area of Patras on August 29 and destroyed four sheds that had housed Romani families. The affected Roma subsequently filed a complaint with the Greek ombudsman alleging that municipal authorities had no right to enter the settlement because the land belonged to the University of Patras.

An international outcry followed the trial of a member of the Society for Aromanian (Vlach) Culture in February on charges of "disseminating false information." Sotiris Blatsas was sentenced to fifteen months in prison and fined 500,000 Greek drachmas (U.S. $1,400) because he distributed a publication of the European Union's European Bureau for Lesser Used Languages (EBLUL) at an Aromanian festival in July 1995. The EBLUL document listed minority languages spoken in Greece. Conservative New Democracy Deputy Eugene Haitidis pressed charges against Blatsas. Numerous intergovernmental and human rights organizations, including EBLUL, condemned the Blatsas conviction as a violation of free expression. After two postponements, an appeal date was set for December 18, 2001.

DEFENDING HUMAN RIGHTS

Human rights groups generally operated without interference from the government. In August the government denied access to the Hellenikon Holding Centre to representatives of Greek Helsinki Monitor who were attempting to verify complaints of substandard detention conditions. The organization filed a complaint with the Greek ombudsman.

THE ROLE OF THE INTERNATIONAL COMMUNITY

United Nations

In its March assessment of Greece's record on discrimination issues, the U.N. Committee on the Elimination of Racial Discrimination failed to acknowledge Greece's systematic discrimination against Roma, Albanian migrants, and other minorities or to make specific recommendations to assist the government in remedying these violations.

In May, however, the U.N. Committee against Torture issued conclusions severely critical of Greece, including findings of the use of excessive or unjustifiable force by police when dealing with minorities and foreigners; harsh detention conditions, in particular the long-term detention of undocumented migrants awaiting deportation and asylum-seekers in police stations without adequate facilities; and severe prison overcrowding. The committee recommended that steps be taken to prevent and punish trafficking of women and other forms of violence against women.

Organization for Security and Cooperation in Europe (OSCE)

In January 2001, the OSCE organized a visit to Greece by representatives of the Ukrainian government to establish a program for the repatriation of Ukrainian women trafficked to Greece. The OSCE expressed concern that Greece had no special mechanism for differentiating between illegal immigrants and trafficking victims.

Council of Europe

In June 2001, the chairperson of the specialist group on Roma and gypsies of the Council of Europe visited Roma communities in Greece and publicly condemned the poor living conditions of many Roma, finding many Roma lived in a situation of "institutionalized apartheid" in Greece.

Twice in 2001 the European Court of Human Rights found Greece had violated the rights of foreigners in detention. In *Dougoz v. Greece* (March), the court found that a Syrian national was held in detention in two police stations (Alexandras Avenue and Drapetsona) in conditions amounting to inhuman or degrading treatment and that the detainee was not afforded an effective opportunity to challenge his detention. A U.K. national brought the charges in *Peers v. Greece* (April), in which the court held that detention conditions in Korydallos Prison amounted to inhuman, or degrading treatment.

European Union

An April European Parliament report on the exercise of fundamental freedoms in the European Union criticized Greece for discrimination and ill-treatment of the Turkish, Roma, and Albanian minorities, and the failure of Greek authorities to abide by final judicial decisions.

In February 2001, the Council of the European Bureau for Lesser Used Languages (EBLUL) expressed deep concern over the conviction of Sotiris Blatsas for distributing EBLUL literature and called the conviction an apparent violation of free expression.

United States

In its first annual trafficking in persons report, issued in July 2001, the State Department gave Greece the lowest rating possible—along with Burma, Pakistan, Russia, Saudi Arabia, Sudan, and Turkey—for failing to combat trafficking, to acknowledge publicly that trafficking is a problem, to implement comprehensive antitrafficking legislation, to prosecute traffickers, to punish traffickers when they were tried, or to address corruption in the police and border control, which the report called "a major problem."

The U. S. State Department's *Country Reports on Human Rights Practices for 2000* noted that human rights problems in Greece included substandard detention conditions and occasions of arbitrary detention for foreigners awaiting deportation; the failure to combat trafficking of women for forced prostitution and police corruption in trafficking; ongoing discrimination against minorities, in particular Roma; and continuing abusive prosecutions under Greece's criminal defamation laws.

Relevant Human Rights Watch Reports:

Trafficking of Migrant Women for Forced Prostitution into Greece, 7/01
Human Rights Watch Critique of Greek Immigration Bill, 2/01
Urgent Concerns: Conditions of Detention for Foreigners in Greece, 12/00

HUNGARY

HUMAN RIGHTS DEVELOPMENTS

While the majority of Hungarian citizens enjoyed a full measure of civil and political rights and the benefits of a modernizing economy, those on society's margins continued to face discrimination and abuse. The poor treatment of the country's Roma remained the key concern, despite E.U.-funded government efforts to improve their status, while anti-Semitism and hostility towards gays persisted. Prison overcrowding and police misconduct continued to draw international criticism. Despite some improvements, the state response to violence against women remained inadequate. Asylum seekers faced long periods of detention before their claims were heard, and few were granted refugee status.

The situation for many Hungarian Roma remained precarious. With average life expectancy ten years shorter than the rest of the population and an unemployment rate ten times higher than the national average, Roma faced discrimination in employment, housing, education, and the criminal justice system, as well as physical attacks. The French government's decision in March to grant asylum to fifteen Hungarian Roma underscored the gravity of their difficulties. The fifteen were part of a group who fled from the Hungarian village of Zamoly to Strasbourg during 2000 to escape threats, physical attacks and the destruction of their homes. Applications from ten other Zamoly Roma were rejected by French authorities, while others remained pending at time of this writing.

Police misconduct against Roma continued. On February 9, police officers raided a Roma settlement in the village of Bag. Four Roma were beaten, including an eight-year-old boy. An April 24 police raid on a Roma family party in Budapest left one family member hospitalized and four more injured. The police response to reports of violence against Roma was also a concern. The European Roma Rights Center reported that five Roma men were shot at and threatened in the village of Fiserbocsa on May 5, allegedly in the presence of a police officer. After several failed attempts to register a complaint about the attack with police in nearby Kiskoros, one of the men, Pal Sztoja, returned to the police station on May 10 with a hidden camera to report the incident. The officer refused to take down the complaint, threatened to beat Sztojka and said it was unfortunate he had not been killed in the shooting.

On June 17, gasoline bombs were thrown at the home of Jozsef Ajtai, the head of the Roma Minority Self-Government in Hencida village. Two of Ajtai's daughters suffered burns from the attack. Gasoline bombs were also thrown at two houses in the village of Jaszladany on June 5, one belonging to a Roma family. No one was injured.

Discrimination against Roma remained pervasive. On January 30, a Roma man was prevented from checking onto a flight to Canada by Hungarian airline staff who claimed he lacked proof of sufficient funds for his stay. His ethnic Hungarian wife and child were permitted to check in. The denial appeared linked to the large numbers of Hungarian Roma seeking asylum in Canada. On February 21, a primary school biology teacher in the village of Erdotelek told pupils that "Gypsies" were characterized by a "special odor" and were generally either unemployed or in prison. The leader of the Roma Minority Self-Government in Erdotelek reportedly received death threats after complaints to the mayor about the teacher.

Some positive steps were taken to improve the status of Roma during 2001, notably the March 8 decision by the state radio and television board to grant a permanent license to the Budapest-based Radio C, Hungary's first Roma-run radio station. In May, the government launched an E.U.-backed program aimed at improving infrastructure in Romany settlements and combating discrimination.

Discrimination was also evident in continuing anti-Semitic programming on state radio and anti-Jewish comments by the vice-president of the parliamentary Hungarian Truth and Life Party. In July, a district mayor in Budapest sought to ban gay and lesbian groups from participating in an popular music festival. Although the government signed the antidiscrimination protocol of the European Convention on Human Rights in November 2000, it again failed to introduce a comprehensive domestic antidiscrimination law, even after Parliament adopted legislation granting freedom of movement and access to social welfare programs to the estimated five million ethnic Hungarians living in neighboring countries.

Prison conditions remained a concern. A comprehensive report on Hungary released by the European Committee for the Prevention of Torture (CPT) on March 29 identified overcrowding and limited access to work and exercise facilities as key difficulties, echoing the findings of the Hungarian Helsinki Committee's prison monitoring program. The CPT also flagged shortcomings in the treatment of pre-trial police detention, including reports of beatings by police and delays in access to legal counsel.

Hungary remained a popular transit country for asylum seekers and migrants, and a country of origin, transit, and destination for trafficking. Despite some improvements in the asylum system, many asylum seekers endured lengthy detention periods while their claims were adjudicated. Few of those accepted as having valid claims were granted refugee status, with most given "authorization to stay," granting little assistance other than protection from *refoulement* for one year, renewable after review. In late September, authorities transferred all Afghan asylum seekers and refugees to guarded facilities in Debrecen and Szombatheley, citing concern for the refugees' safety. Human rights groups believed the measure was motivated by fear of terrorism after the September 11 attacks on the U.S. and violated Hungarian law.

Following the suspicious death of a thirty-year-old refugee from Cameroon during his deportation by police on December 18, 2000, the Hungarian Helsinki Committee called for an investigation into the cause of death, which an official autopsy identified as a heart attack. Authorities failed to investigate the complaint.

The state response to human trafficking remained poor, with uneven enforcement of antitrafficking legislation, inadequate victim support services, and frequent police hostility toward women victims. Victims of domestic violence and sexual assault in Hungary faced a biased legal system and a lack of support services.

The appointment of prominent member of the ruling Fidesz party, Karoly Mendreczky, as president of Hungarian Television (Magyar Televizio), on July 12, raised questions about the state broadcaster's editorial independence, despite Mendreczky's resignation from the party prior to taking up his new post.

DEFENDING HUMAN RIGHTS

There were no reports of government interference in the work of human organizations, although Roma community leaders who stood up for minority rights sometimes faced harassment and violence.

THE ROLE OF THE INTERNATIONAL COMMUNITY

United Nations

Hungarian Foreign Minister Janos Martonyi addressed the U.N. Commission on Human Rights on March 30, emphasizing Hungary's support for a binding convention on the rights of minorities. On November 6, the Hungarian Parliament ratified the statute of the International Criminal Court.

Council of Europe

The Committee for the Prevention of Torture report and Hungary's response to it were both published on March 29. On September 17, the Advisory Committee on National Minorities published its opinion on Hungary, noting much progress but also deep concern about the plight of Roma. Hungary signed Protocol 12 of the European Convention on November 4, 2000.

European Union

Hungary continued to be regarded as a front-runner for early accession to the European Union. During a visit to Hungary on April 5, European Commission President Romano Prodi highlighted the treatment of Roma as an area for further progress. Discrimination against Roma was also flagged in a May report by Luis Queiro, the European Parliament's rapporteur on Hungary, and reflected in the resolution on Hungary adopted by the full Parliament on September 5. The November 2001 regular report from the European Commission on Hungary's progress toward E.U. accession identified a need for greater government commitment to improve the lot of Roma.

United States

Secretary of State Colin Powell made no public reference to human rights in Hungary during a meeting with Foreign Minister Janos Martonyi in Washington DC on May 1 or during his visit to Budapest on May 28-30 for a meeting of North Atlantic Treaty Organization foreign ministers. Outgoing Secretary of State Madeline Albright did raise discrimination against Roma with Minister Martonyi in Budapest in December 2000. The State Department country report on human rights practices in Hungary for 2000 reflected difficulties faced by Roma and concerns over police misconduct, and its July trafficking report criticized Hungary for failing to meet minimum standards.

KAZAKHSTAN

HUMAN RIGHTS DEVELOPMENTS

As allegations of corruption against top Kazakh officials persisted in the international press, the government continued to tighten control over political life and the media in 2001. Journalists, editors, and opposition party activists critical of the government, especially of corruption, faced attacks, criminal charges, and other forms of persecution. At the same time, a government tax amnesty came into effect for those who transferred money from abroad back to Kazakhstan. Opposition parties said the measure legalized money laundering. In a progressive move, authorities lifted the longstanding requirement that citizens request an exit visa to leave the country.

The government resisted calls for electoral reform and hounded the political opposition. Former prime minister Akezhan Kazhegeldin, Nazarbaev's one-time rival and leader of the Republican People's Party of Kazakhstan (RNPK), was tried in absentia on charges of corruption and tax evasion and sentenced to ten years' imprisonment in September. On July 15, Kazakh officials prevented Amirzhan Qosanov, the acting chair of the RNPK's executive committee, together with opposition journalist Yermurat Bapi, from boarding a flight to the United States. They were due to testify at a U.S. congressional hearing on human rights in Central Asia. At the hearing itself, a Kazakh embassy official attempted to subpoena Kazhegeldin for a criminal trial in Kazakhstan.

The deputy chairman of the Azamat (Citizen) Party, Platon Pak, was hospitalized on January 30, after three unidentified people broke into his apartment and stabbed him. In February, unidentified assailants beat Alexander Shushannikov, of the Lad Slavic Movement, in the town of Ust-Kamenogorsk.

The government did not fulfill President Nazarbaev's pledge to implement recommendations made in 1999 by the Organization for Security and Cooperation in Europe (OSCE) on electoral reform. The lack of progress on electoral reforms prompted four opposition parties in February to withdraw from a joint working group with the government, organized with the support of the OSCE, on electoral reform. One party also withdrew from a roundtable discussion on electoral reform in May, citing the government's failure to adopt a new elections law.

In February, Temirtas Tleulesov, an author of two books on corruption in Shymkent, was tried in absentia and sentenced to two years of imprisonment for "hooliganism." The charges arose out of a 1999 incident in which bank security guards seriously beat Tleulesov in Shymkent. Following Tleulesov's conviction, the municipal authorities reportedly banned demonstrations planned for February 22 in support of the author.

The independent print and broadcast media suffered constant harassment and repression. Marina Soloveva, the former director of Ust-Kamenogorsk independent television, was attacked on March 6 by several men, resulting in a broken arm. Police investigators decided that no crime had taken place and charged Soloveva with making false accusations. Gulzhan Ergalieva, a journalist affiliated with the political opposition, and her husband and son were severely beaten and robbed in their Almaty home on March 1. Shortly before this incident, Ergalieva had strongly criticized the government's participation in an electoral reform working group.

Yermurat Bapi, the editor-in-chief of the independent newspaper *SolDat* (whose name is a variant of *Dat*, Let Me Speak, a paper closed last year) was found guilty on April 3 of insulting the honor and dignity of President Nazarbaev. He was sentenced to a one-year prison term, but was released under a general amnesty. The charges related to an article published alleging that President Nazarbaev and other Kazakh officials had been funneling millions of U.S. dollars from Kazakhstan into Swiss bank accounts. The authorities confiscated the edition of the newspaper before distribution. No publishing house would print *SolDat* for eight months prior to the trial.

Bigeldy Gabdullin, editor of the opposition newspaper *XXI Vek* (21st Century), faced criminal defamation charges following the publication in October 2000 of two articles alleging corruption by President Nazarbaev. However, on April 6 the prosecutor's office issued a press release stating that it had dropped the case. Reportedly, *XXI Vek* has not been able to resume publication. On January 18, the staff of *Respublika-2000* again received violent threats after the publication of an article about corruption; in September 2000, its editor-in-chief, Lira Baisetova, was beaten after the newspaper had published a similar article.

On April 17, the Parliament passed restrictive amendments to the Law on Mass Media, which had been severely criticized by local and international organizations, including the OSCE. The law brought Internet sites under its regulation and limited the transmission of foreign television and radio programs, requiring foreign material to be reduced to 20 percent of all available airtime by January 2003. The legislation sparked protests by private television stations that relied heavily on the retransmission of Russian television and could force the closure of smaller stations.

Intolerance of nontraditional religious groups continued throughout the country. In March, two Baptists from Atyrau faced fabricated criminal charges, which church members claimed were aimed at stopping their missionary activity. In Kulsary, a small Baptist church received a prosecutor's order, dated May 2, declaring the church illegal due to lack of registration. Three U.S. students found guilty of illegal missionary activity were fined and ordered to leave the country. The Taraz procuracy sought, unsuccessfully, to ban Jehovah's Witnesses' activity.

Following the general crackdown in the region against independent Islam, four alleged members of Hizb ut-Tahrir were arrested while distributing leaflets calling for the reestablishment of an Islamic Caliphate in Central Asia. On May 10, two of the defendants were sentenced to twenty-two and seventeen months' imprisonment, respectively, and the two others were released under a general amnesty.

Prison conditions remained horrific in Kazakhstan, which had one of the highest rates of imprisonment in the world. Even after an amnesty early in the year reportedly led to the release of 26,729 prisoners, the prison population in 2001 grew to 84,000 by the end of April.

On April 13, prosecutors in Kyrgyzstan reportedly announced that they had arrested a man on charges of selling Kyrgyz citizens as "slaves" to work on plantations in Kazakhstan. A former plantation laborer claimed in the press that thousands of Kyrgyz citizens were being used as slaves in Kazakhstan.

DEFENDING HUMAN RIGHTS

The body of a leading Uigur activist, Dilbrim Samsakova, was found in June, following her "disappearance" several weeks earlier. Her injuries indicated that she died from a blow to the head. Samsakova had been working to prevent the extradition to China of the widow and children of a Uighur suspected of violent political activism who was killed during a police operation in Almaty last year. She observed the trial of four Uighurs charged with "terrorism" in Kyrgyzstan earlier this year.

THE ROLE OF THE INTERNATIONAL COMMUNITY

United Nations

In May, the U.N. Committee against Torture considered Kazakhstan's initial report and expressed concern about allegations of torture by law enforcement officials, the lack of investigation into allegations of torture, the insufficient level of independence of the judiciary, and the overcrowding and inadequate access to medical care in prisons and pre-trial detention centers.

In January, the U.N. Committee on the Elimination of Discrimination against Women delivered concluding observations on Kazakhstan's initial report. The committee commended the government for the high levels of education among women, but expressed concern over a wide range of issues, including stereotyped attitudes towards women, the prevalence of violence against women and girls, trafficking in women and girls, and the rise in unemployment and poverty of women. A coalition of women's human rights nongovernmental organizations submitted a report to the committee, recommending that the government introduce training programs to combat trafficking and provide trafficking victims with witness protection and support programs.

Organization for Security and Cooperation in Europe (OSCE)

In June, the OSCE chairman-in-office, Mircea Geoana, visited Kazakhstan, meeting with President Nazarbaev and others. Although Geoana stated that human rights must be developed along with economic, politico-military, and environmental factors, he expressed approval at the pragmatic approach to democratization adopted by the current Kazakh authorities. The OSCE ran a series of roundtable discussions on electoral reform. (See above.) Training sessions were held for local nongovernmental organizations on human rights monitoring and the development of leadership for the promotion of women's rights.

European Union

The European Commission made a formal protest to the Kazakh authorities following the introduction of the new media laws in April 2001. The European Union held the third meeting of its Cooperation Council with Kazakhstan in July, during which it praised Kazakhstan for strong economic growth in 2000 and 2001 but failed publicly to raise concerns about specific human rights abuses.

Council of Europe

The Political Affairs Committee of the Parliamentary Assembly of the Council of Europe continued to consider Kazakhstan's 1999 application for observer status.

United States

In a July 18 congressional hearing in Washington, a State Department representative stated that although there had been economic progress in Kazakhstan, steps towards democracy had been reversed.

The administration requested U.S. $51.5 million in assistance for Kazakhstan for 2002, with some of the requested funds to be used for the purchase of military equipment under the Foreign Military Financing Program.

International Financial Institutions

When the president of the European Bank for Reconstruction and Development (EBRD) visited Kazakhstan in June, he stated that the country deserved more cooperation with the EBRD. He reportedly praised the economic reform process, and did not raise concerns over issues of corruption or human rights which were at odds with the EBRD's founding charter. The EBRD expected to invest about $212 million in projects in 2001.

In February, the World Bank's Board of Executive Directors supported a new Country Assistance Strategy for Kazakhstan for 2001-2003. Depending on progress in reforms, the bank was to lend between $270 and $820 million over three years. If realized, this could make Kazakhstan the largest recipient of bank funding in Central Asia.

In its December 2000 assessment of the economy, the International Monetary Fund recommended that the government "ensure further transparency of the oil sector's operations and its linkages with public finance" in order to encourage fiscal management and "public accountability" over the government's use of oil revenues. It also recommended that the proposed oil stabilization fund that is meant to maximize the benefits of oil revenues and protect the economy from an unstable revenue stream "be based on the principles of transparency and public accountability." Previously, the Kazakh government had been criticized and investigated for allegedly corrupt dealings within its oil sector.

KYRGYZSTAN

HUMAN RIGHTS DEVELOPMENTS

The deterioration in respect for human rights that had dominated the lead-up to the October 2000 reelection of President Askar Akaev continued unabated in

2001. The government harassed the political opposition, independent media, and human rights defenders. Government measures responding to the year 2000 incursions by the Islamic Movement of Uzbekistan (IMU) into Kyrgyzstan violated the rights of certain ethnic minorities and religious groups.

In January, Gen. Felix Kulov, President Akaev's rival in the elections and leader of the opposition Ar-Namys (Dignity) party, was sentenced to seven years of imprisonment on charges of abuse of office, even though he had been acquitted of these charges in August 2000. Kulov had intended to contest the October 2000 elections. The international community criticized his retrial as politically motivated. On July 17, new charges of embezzlement were brought against Kulov.

President Akaev on August 20 pardoned Topchubek Turgunaliev, a political activist and founder of Kyrgyzstan's Guild of Prisoners of Conscience. He was released after almost a year in prison on trumped-up charges of plotting an assassination attempt on President Akaev.

After a wave of criticism by community and opposition leaders, President Akaev on August 16 ordered a review of a draft law that would have banned religious and other political parties and put new restrictions on nongovernmental organizations (NGOs).

Progress in press freedoms in early 2001 proved to be ephemeral. For example, at least two new independent newspapers were registered in the first six months of the year. But on April 5, the Ministry of Justice, apparently seeking to tighten state control over the media, required all outlets to reregister by July 1. It later annulled the registration of the newly created media outlets that reregistered after April 5, declaring that new media could not be registered until September 1; it later moved the date to October 1. The editors of several deregistered newspapers attempted, unsuccessfully, to sue the ministry.

Samagan Orozaliev, a journalist, was arrested on May 28 in Jalal-Abad province when he was investigating allegations of local corruption. Orozaliev was held in pretrial detention on charges of taking a bribe. On July 31, he was reportedly hospitalized, under police guard, due to heart problems. On November 1, a court sentenced Orozaliev to nine years in prison and confiscation of property, and his driver, Mukhtar Topchiev, to eight years for, among other things, illegal weapons possession. They claimed police had fabricated charges against them, and had planted evidence in their car. As of this writing, lawyers were preparing to appeal the verdict. In March, the Supreme Court reinstated a conviction against journalist Moldosali Ibraimov that had been quashed in 2000. The court gave him a two-year suspended sentence on libel charges, which related to allegations of corruption in the judiciary.

The opposition newspaper *Asaba* (The Standard) was declared bankrupt on April 20, after losing a court battle over the repayment of a loan and receiving an unprecedented U.S. $100,000 fine for libel of a member of Parliament. The government-controlled Uchkun publishing house repeatedly refused to publish the newspaper *Res Publica*, as a result of, according to the paper's editor, an edition containing an article about the financial dealings of President Akaev's wife.

In a positive move, the procuracy dropped charges of divulging state secrets against the editor and a journalist of the independent newspaper *Delo No* (Case Number), relating to an article on the trial of Felix Kulov in May. In April, however, the editor was fined for insulting an employee of the National Security Service in an interview he gave.

In another positive move, the Supreme Arbitration Court upheld an appeal by Osh TV, an Uzbek language station, ordering the court of first instance to reconsider its decision to force the station to change frequencies. The change would have led to the closure of the station viewed by the ethnic Uzbek population in the region.

Police used force to disperse protesters, and arrested protest organizers. An opposition leader and journalist were fined, along with three members of the Ar-Namys party, for organizing an unsanctioned rally in Bishkek on April 13. Klara Ajibeka, chairwoman of the Communist Party, was arrested, convicted, and fined for delivering a speech at an unsanctioned June 12 picket in support of Kulov. Police prevented approximately 1,000 demonstrators from gathering in Bishkek's main square for a May 1 rally and protest. Also on May 1, in Jalal-Abad, three human rights activists were convicted and fined for taking part in an unsanctioned rally. On August 10 police in Osh reportedly arrested fifteen women after dispersing a demonstration of about two hundred women merchants who were protesting the local authorities' decision to stop street trade in the city center.

Kyrgyzstan's participation in the regional push against Islamic "extremism" heightened the atmosphere of repression for both independent adherents of Islam and the Uigur minority in Kyrgyzstan. On April 18, the government required special religious schools to obtain a license from the State Commission for Religious Affairs. According to government statistics, between thirty-seven and fifty people in southern Kyrgyzstan were imprisoned for disseminating "extremist" religious materials in the first five months of 2001; more comprehensive figures were not available. The Kyrgyz Committee for Human Rights (KCHR) monitored a trial on July 13 of five alleged Hizb ut-Tahrir (Party of Liberation) members who were charged with disseminating "extremist" leaflets. The men received sentences of from two to five years of imprisonment.

A military court sentenced to death two men on June 19 for their participation in armed clashes between IMU fighters and government troops in August 2000. It is not known what legal standards of proof or due process the military court applied. As of this writing, the defendants' appeal was being considered.

In late July several armed clashes occurred in the southern border region of Kyrgyzstan, although it is unconfirmed that these involved the IMU. The extent of the clashes is unknown, since the government denied several reports that its troops were engaged in ongoing fighting.

Landmines laid by Uzbekistan in Kyrgyz territory in response to the IMU incursions into both countries have killed at least one person and injured several others this year. The two countries have been negotiating over the removal of the mines.

Four ethnic Uigurs and one other man stood trial on March 12 on charges related to two bombing incidents in the city of Osh in 1998. Four of the men were sentenced to death and one to twenty-five years of imprisonment. The defendants' lawyer reportedly stated that the trial began without warning and that even though she was hospitalized at the time, the court refused an adjournment. Thus, her clients had no legal representation. A previous sentence against the five had been overturned for lack of evidence.

Despite a presidential moratorium on death penalty, effective until December 2001, courts continued to hand down death sentences. It remains unclear whether such sentences will be carried out after that date.

Prison conditions remained abysmal due to lack of food, clothing, heating, and medicine. A group of prisoners' relatives sent an appeal to the Kyrgyz authorities and the international community describing prison conditions of starvation and disease.

Police continued to ignore reports of domestic violence as the Kyrgyz government failed to implement the 1999 recommendation of the U.N. Committee on the Elimination of Discrimination against Women to provide for law enforcement officials' training on violence against women.

DEFENDING HUMAN RIGHTS

The KCHR faced continuing persecution in 2001. Bolot Tynaliev, a member of the KCHR, was reportedly threatened with a knife by five men on January 27. The men stole his KCHR files and warned him to stop his human rights work. On June 27, Numanjan Arkabaev, the KCHR coordinator for Osh province, was arrested and charged with defamation and attempting to overthrow the government. He was released from custody on July 18, after having spent two weeks on a hunger strike. The National Security Service later dropped the charges.

On September 17, Abdymamat Kadyrbekov, a member of the KCHR in Jalal-Abad, received a three-year suspended prison sentence on charges of "hooliganism." On October 7, according to the KCHR, masked men burst into Kadyrbekov's house and caused him severe injuries, warning him not file a complaint about his sentence.

Albert Korgoldoev, also a member of the KCHR in Jalal-Abad, faced criminal charges related to his monitoring of the presidential elections results in October 2000; he fled the country in February. According to the KCHR, Kyrgyz authorities confiscated property from their organization's head office in Bishkek in late May.

The director of the Kara-Sui Human Rights Center, Ravshan Gapirov, was arrested on November 13 and charged with "hooliganism" and swindling. He remained in custody until his trial on February 28, when he received a two-year prison sentence. On May 7, his sentence was reduced to a fine and he was released. On September 14, after a verbal dispute with the Kara-Sui procuracy, he was detained. On October 24 Gapirov was sentenced to thirteen years of imprisonment for "hooliganism" and insulting state officials.

An unidentified man attacked Tolekan Ismailova, the head of the NGO Coalition for Democracy and Civil Society, outside her home on March 13. She was hit on the head and momentarily lost consciousness. The previous day she had strongly criticized the Kyrgyz government at a round table discussion.

THE ROLE OF THE INTERNATIONAL COMMUNITY

United Nations

The special representative of the U.N. secretary general on human rights defenders, Hina Jilani, visited Kyrgyzstan in August. During her trip she stated her concerns that basic civil rights were not being systematically observed. Kyrgyz authorities refused to allow her to meet with Turgunaliev, who was in a prison hospital at the time. Kyrgyzstan was included in the 2001 report of the special rapporteur on torture, which cited allegations of excessive police violence against peaceful demonstrators, torture of detainees, and horrific conditions in places of detention.

Organization for Security and Cooperation in Europe (OSCE)

The OSCE report on the October 2000 presidential elections found that they, "despite some positive features," failed to comply with Kyrgyzstan's OSCE commitments. In March, the OSCE representative on freedom of the media, Freimut Duvé, met with President Akaev to express regret at the worsening media situation in the country. In April, the OSCE secretary general visited Kyrgyzstan and met with President Akaev in a closed meeting. The stated aim of the visit was to assess and discuss security and stability in the region. In June, after meeting with President Akaev and others, the OSCE chair announced that he had advised the Kyrgyz leadership that in order to improve the country's tarnished image, the legislature should adopt new laws on human rights, the media, religious freedom, and the status of refugees.

European Union

At the E.U.-Kyrgyzstan Cooperation Council meeting in July, the European Union reiterated its concern about aspects of democratization, such as media freedom. The European Union also raised concerns about recent developments surrounding the KCHR, while it welcomed the suspension of the death penalty and encouraged its complete abolition.

United States

At a July 18 U.S. congressional hearing, a State Department spokesperson testified that there had been progress on economic reform but that the government had been backsliding on democratic reforms and that there were signs of an escalation in the campaign against peaceful Islamic activities. The Department of State trafficking in persons report, published in July 2001, criticized the Kyrgyz government for failing to respond adequately to trafficking in persons. The report noted that traffickers sent Kyrgyz men, women, and children into situations of forced labor and forced prostitution in Russia, Turkey, Germany, and the United Arab Emirates. U.S. financial assistance to Kyrgyzstan remained fairly constant, at about U.S. $ 33 million.

MACEDONIA

HUMAN RIGHTS DEVELOPMENTS

Macedonia's image as an island of inter-ethnic peace and coexistence in the Balkans was dramatically upset in February 2001 by the emergence of an ethnic Albanian insurgent group, the so-called National Liberation Army (Ushtria Çlirimtare Kombëtare, commonly known as the NLA), and the ensuing months of fighting between the rebels and government forces. Negotiations between the major ethnic Macedonian and ethnic Albanian parties, facilitated by the international community, led to an August 13 peace agreement providing for far-reaching constitutional and political measures aimed at enhancing the status of the sizeable ethnic Albanian minority. In return, the NLA agreed to demobilize and hand over its weapons to a North Atlantic Treaty Organizaation force, deployed in Macedonia at the end of August. In mid-November, after a long delay, a lot of filibustering, and mounting international pressure, the Macedonian Parliament finally adopted the constitutional amendments envisaged by the peace agreement. At the time of writing, however, fears persisted that nationalists within the government and police would still try to derail the peace process and pursue a military solution to the conflict.

There was disagreement as to the causes of the conflict, with NLA leaders claiming that they were fighting to end systematic discrimination against ethnic Albanians by the Macedonian authorities, while the government claimed that the NLA's real goal was control over Macedonian territory. Government officials insisted that Kosovar Albanian radicalism lay behind the conflict, not legitimate grievances of Macedonia's own ethnic Albanians. Support for the insurgency by the country's ethnic Albanians, which was tepid early in the conflict, grew quickly as Macedonian security forces launched increasingly heavy-handed attacks against ethnic Albanian civilians and their villages and towns. As of mid-October, about 25,000 refugees remained in Kosovo, while 53,000 ethnic Albanians and Macedonians were still internally displaced within Macedonia.

Both government forces and the NLA committed serious violations of international humanitarian law in the course of the six-month conflict. The government police forces, whose brutality against Albanians has long been a cause of intense resentment, were responsible for a number of grave assaults against civilians and their property. Following an April government offensive in the Tetovo area, monitors of the Organization for Security and Cooperation in Europe (OSCE) found evidence of widespread and indiscriminate destruction and looting in the village of Selce. More than two hundred ethnic Albanians were arrested in the area, dozens of whom were later treated in the Tetovo hospital for fractures and severe bruising. Also in April, a joint mission of the Macedonian, Norwegian, and Serbian Helsinki Committees reported that some thirty men from Poroj had been arbitrarily arrested and severely beaten by the police, resulting in the hospitalization of six persons. The Helsinki mission and Human Rights Watch separately blamed government forces for the destruction of the Runica hamlet in the Kumanovo area in retaliation for earlier NLA strikes. While the Macedonian government accused the rebels of using villagers in the Tetovo and Kumanovo areas as human shields, it frequently responded with indiscriminate shelling of those same villages.

Torture and abuse of civilian detainees was routinely used by the security forces to obtain information on the NLA and to intimidate ethnic Albanians. Following a May 22 offensive north of Kumanovo, for example, government forces separated ethnic Albanian men fleeing the fighting and took them to the Skopje and Kumanovo police stations, where dozens of them suffered torture and severe ill-treatment. Fear of such practices prevented many civilians trapped in the crossfire from fleeing to safety into government-controlled territory, forcing them instead to venture through dangerous mountain trails into neighboring Kosovo.

The most serious violations by the government forces were committed during a three-day operation in a village north of Skopje. Following a land mine explosion that killed eight government soldiers, the Macedonian police launched a fierce attack on the nearby village of Ljuboten, which was heavily shelled for two days in August 10 and 11, 2001. On August 12, several hundred police entered the village and began a house-to-house assault, killing six ethnic Albanian civilians, burning scores of houses and terrorizing the village population. Two men were summarily executed and another three were shot dead after they attempted to flee their burning home. More than one hundred men and boys from the village were taken to police stations in Skopje, where they were subjected to severe beatings. As of late October, about twenty-four of them were still being detained on charges of participation in the insurgency. Thirty-five-year-old Atullah Qaini died in police custody, his mutilated corpse bearing clear signs of torture. Three other men were beaten unconscious by ethnic Macedonian vigilantes in full view of the police. The minister of the interior, Ljube Boskovski, who was himself present during the operation in Ljuboten on August 12, claimed that the village was an NLA stronghold and that the victims were "terrorists." However, Human Rights Watch researchers who visited the village, and interviewed victims and eyewitnesses of the abuses, found no evidence that there was an NLA presence in Ljuboten during the attack or that any of the villagers put up armed resistance. The police operation appeared to be motivated by nothing more than revenge.

NLA forces were responsible for indiscriminate killings, abductions, and intimidation of ethnic Macedonian and other civilians. In June NLA forces arbitrarily detained and tortured eight elderly ethnic Serb civilians from the village of Matejce, subjecting them to repeated mock executions. On August 7, 2001, uniformed members of the NLA kidnapped a group of construction workers on the Skopje-Tetovo highway, and, holding them for several hours, the NLA fighters severely beat, humiliated and sexually abused them. The NLA was also suspected of being behind the August 26 bombing of an ethnic Macedonian-owned restaurant in Celopek, which left two of the employees dead. About ten persons from NLA-controlled areas were still missing at the time of this writing, despite claims by rebel commanders that the NLA had released all captives before its formal disbandment by the end of August.

Such methods of warfare against civilians were imitated by an array of ethnic Macedonian paramilitary groups, whose members were largely drawn from the police reserves. Local and international press reported that the most active of those groups, including the so-called Lions, Tigers, and Red Berets, were controlled by radicals within the Macedonian police structure. Members of such groups appeared to have led a June 6 riot in Bitola, where dozens of ethnic Albanian homes and shops were burned within a few hours. The local police took no action to stop the attacks; in fact, some police officers took an active part in the rampage. The paramilitary groups continued to intimidate and harass ethnic Albanians even after the signing of the peace agreement, threatening to derail the peace process. In a September 15 incident, five "Red Berets" abducted Muharem Ibrahimi, a Tetovo-based activist with an ethnic Albanian humanitarian organization, and attempted to kill him by throwing him into the Vardar river.

The conflict also took a toll on the press covering the events. International and local journalists, both ethnic Macedonian and ethnic Albanian, faced frequent hostility and occasional violence, mostly from ethnic Macedonian crowds and security forces. Reporters sans Frontières protested in June against the ill-treatment of the Agence France-Presse correspondent Colin Neacsu and his interpreter, who were detained and repeatedly beaten at a Skopje police station. A Macedonian journalist from the *Utrinski Vesnik* newspaper was beaten unconscious by a mob outside Ljuboten on August 10, as were several Swedish journalists trying to enter the village on August 12. Ethnic Albanian journalists, in particular, faced severe security constraints and discrimination, and were frequently denied access to the conflict areas by the police. Albanian language public television broadcasts were interrupted for three weeks as the Albanian language bureau rejected an order to air only translations of programs prepared by the ethnic Macedonian editors.

Two serious incidents raised concerns that communist-era practices of surveillance of the political opposition and civil society continue unabated in Macedonia. In January 2001, the opposition Social Democratic Union (SDSM) presented evidence of the unlawful phone tapping of 150 conversations that had taken place between September and November 2000. Most of those involved, including prominent opposition leaders and journalists, confirmed the authenticity of the recordings. A parliamentary investigation led to the resignation of the minister of the interior, Dosta Dimovska, but stopped short of assigning responsibility for the violations. The issue resurfaced after the signing of the peace agreement, when a telephone conversation between Branko Crvenkovski and Arben Xhaferi, the respective leaders of the SDSM and the Democratic Party of the Albanians, was leaked to a television station that accused the two of conspiracy against national interests.

DEFENDING HUMAN RIGHTS

Human rights organizations generally operated freely in 2001, although security concerns often prevented their members from reaching certain areas of the country. Both ethnic Macedonian and ethnic Albanian organizations faced difficulties in moving across the ethnic divide in the conflict areas. The Helsinki Committee for Human Rights investigated the Ljuboten events and made findings that were consistent with the conclusions of Human Rights Watch. (See above.) However, investigation and reporting by local nongovernmental organizations on human rights abuses committed during the conflict was limited overall and at times one-sided.

THE ROLE OF THE INTERNATIONAL COMMUNITY

In contrast with earlier conflicts in the former Yugoslavia, the international community moved relatively quickly in 2001 to bring the inter-ethnic violence in Macedonia to a halt, and to limit its human costs. The diplomatic efforts of the European Union, the United States, NATO, and the OSCE, all of which appointed special envoys to Macedonia, were critical to the negotiation of the cease-fire and the peace agreement. But while much effort was put into security monitoring and shuttle diplomacy, the investigation of human rights violations committed by both sides was inadequate throughout the conflict. At this writing, the international community stood ready to assist with the implementation of an enduring peace in the country, but more needed to be done to integrate critical human rights dimensions into the process.

United Nations

The U.N. Security Council addressed the Macedonian crisis regularly in 2001. The council supported the timely implementation of the peace agreement and the deployment of a multinational security presence in Macedonia. The U.N. High Commissioner for Refugees (UNHCR) cautioned the Macedonian government at the end of September that the return of the refugees remaining in Kosovo and of the internally displaced persons would require ethnically mixed police patrols in conflict areas. UNHCR-chartered buses facilitated the movement of all communities across ethnic lines and security checkpoints in the troubled Tetovo region. The chief prosecutor of the International Criminal Tribunal for the former Yugoslavia warned both warring sides early in the conflict that the tribunal's jurisdiction extended to the events in Macedonia, and that tribunal staff were on the ground collecting information on serious violations of international humanitarian law.

Organization for Security and Cooperation in Europe (OSCE)

The OSCE committed itself, under the peace agreement, to providing a significant number of monitors to report regularly on security incidents, the return of refugees and trafficking in human beings. OSCE-seconded police experts were tasked with assisting in the implementation of the envisaged police reforms. On October 4, however, the OSCE warned the Macedonian government that single-handed efforts by the police to hastily retake control of formerly NLA-held areas were delaying the deployment of the monitors and were jeopardizing the fragile peace. During the conflict, the OSCE Spillover Monitor Mission to Skopje condemned human rights abuses committed by the NLA forces, but showed reluctance to address the serious violations for which the government security forces were responsible.

North Atlantic Treaty Organization (NATO)

NATO's role in the Macedonian conflict was limited by its members' unwillingness to maintain a long-term security presence in the country. The 4,500-strong NATO force deployed in Macedonia throughout September successfully completed its limited, month-long mission to collect about 4,000 weapons voluntarily handed over by the NLA. Doubts remained, however, as to whether the NLA had surrendered all its weaponry. To avoid a security vacuum created by an early departure, NATO agreed by the end of September to maintain a German-led contingent of seven hundred to 1,000 troops in the country to protect E.U. and OSCE security monitors. The second NATO force was to operate in Macedonia for three months, with the option to extend the mission with the consent of the Macedonian government.

European Union

In April 2001, the European Union and Macedonia signed an Association and Stabilization Agreement that sets the stage for Macedonia's progressive integration into the union within ten years. In October the E.U. pledged to finance a 10.3 million euro (approximately U.S.$9.3 million) program aimed at supporting the implementation of the peace agreement. The program was part of a 24.7 million euro emergency package, and in addition to 42.5 million euros of regular support to Macedonia pledged for 2001. The package was made, however, conditional upon the ratification of all constitutional amendments envisaged by the peace agreement. The European Union maintained that improving the status of the country's ethnic minorities was a requirement of the association process, and it postponed a donors' conference scheduled for October 15, citing Macedonia's delay in the implementation of the agreement.

United States

The United States supported the political and constitutional reforms agreed upon by the Macedonian and ethnic Albanian parties. The U.S. special envoy James Pardew, together with the European Union's Francois Leotard, played an important facilitating role in the negotiation of the peace agreement. Although the United States contributed no troops to the two NATO missions, it provided intelligence and logistical support. The U.S. administration pledged also to support the Macedonian police reform, training of ethnic Albanian police officers, the return of refugees and the new Southeast Europe University, set up to provide higher education in the Albanian language.

Relevant Human Rights Watch Reports:

Crimes Against Civilians: Abuses by Macedonian Forces in Ljuboten, August 10-12, 2001, 9/01

ROMANIA

HUMAN RIGHTS DEVELOPMENTS

Despite making progress toward European Union accession, Romania's human rights record in 2001 remained uneven. Rights groups continued to receive reports of excessive use of force by police. The state response to domestic violence against women and trafficking remained inadequate. No action was taken to remedy constitutional restrictions on free speech. Legislation designed to enhance minority rights was not implemented. Roma continued to experience discrimination in housing, education, medical care, employment, and access to goods and services. Legislative efforts to outlaw discrimination against gays and lesbians had mixed results. Romania came under pressure to improve arms export controls, but enforcement of existing laws continued to be a problem.

There were credible reports of excessive use of force and other misconduct by police officers, including against children. On March 14, fourteen-year-old Vasile Danut was detained and beaten severely by police in Vladesti. On April 5, police in Oradea reportedly attacked sixteen-year-old Ioana Silaghi, and also reportedly intimidated witnesses. Two police officers were accused of beating a suspect to death in Cugir in early July. The introduction of new guidelines on the use of firearms in June, intended to bring police practice into line with U.N. and Council of Europe standards, appeared to have had little effect. After September 11, Parliament suspended consideration of a draft bill curbing police powers to detain citizens for up to twenty-four hours without charge.

Legal protections for victims of domestic violence and trafficking remained inadequate. The Romanian Domestic Violence Victims' Assistance Center reported that a long, complicated procedure and probation system discouraged domestic violence victims from pressing charges against perpetrators. Despite the high level of trafficking through Romania, the Romanian government did little to address the problem.

Constitutional curbs on free expression remained in force in 2001 and were used by authorities to interfere with the work of journalists. Journalists also ran afoul of broad criminal defamation laws, under which prosecutions for slander of public officials could bring imprisonment or fines.

Romania continued to show a half-hearted commitment to the rights of national minorities. The National Minorities Council, meeting for the first time on July 10, 2001, criticized the legislation creating the council for failing to require the executive to consult with it on all legislation pertaining to national minorities. Access to media by national minorities remained limited.

Extremist nationalist parties fueled hostility toward national minorities. The November 2000 elections demonstrated the emerging popularity of the nationalist Greater Romania Party (Partidul România Mare, PRM), which captured one-third of the parliamentary seats. The party leader, Corneliu Vadim Tudor, who received

26 percent of the vote for president in the final round of elections, promised to destroy the "Gypsy mafia." In August the Romanian Prosecutor-general's office began an investigation into the publication of *The Nationalist*, a book that minority leaders said incited racial hatred and anti-Semitism. Although the PRM denied any connection to the book's publication, it was written by a party deputy and endorsed by a top PRM aide.

The problem of discrimination against the Roma population—estimated to number as many as two million—continued to permeate society. A January 2001 European Roma Rights Center investigation found that violations of Roma rights were highly unlikely to be prosecuted, and authorities retaliated against complainants. Roma had their houses raided, and were detained, beaten, and threatened by private citizens and police. On February 1 and 9, 2001, police stopped trains headed for Brasov and detained, fingerprinted, and intimidated some one hundred Roma passengers, and warned them not to enter the city.

On April 25, the government published an ambitious plan for improving conditions for Roma, but Roma activists questioned its lack of detail on reaching the goals identified.

The government took steps to enact legal guarantees for gays and lesbians, but at the time of writing opposition from the Chamber of Deputies cast doubt as to whether sexual orientation would remain protected under pending antidiscrimination legislation.

Notwithstanding legislative efforts to decriminalize homosexuality and ensure the rights of gays and lesbians, gays and lesbians continued to face police harassment. In December 2000, Romanian citizen Adrian Georgescu was called to a police station without explanation. There he was questioned about his sexuality by police officers. After Georgescu publicized this event in January, a police officer admitted on Romanian television that Georgescu had been detained and questioned solely because of his sexual orientation.

A U.N. investigative panel determined in 2000 that Romania was a source of weapons illegally supplied to embargoed rebel forces in Angola from 1996 to 1999. It noted that reforms were needed in Romania to improve controls, as the weapons were authorized for sale to Burkina Faso and Togo on the basis of falsified documents. After taking the important step in mid-2000 of arresting and initiating the prosecution of a Romanian-Israeli arms dealer accused of illegal arms sales, Romanian authorities unexpectedly released him in February and he left the country for Israel. Romanian officials denied he was linked to the Angola case and said the prosecution would continue in his absence. Romania began a major push to export more weapons after sales slumped but said it would revise its arms export laws. Romania ratified the Mine Ban Treaty on November 30, 2000, and the treaty entered into force on May 1. It declared in June that it would destroy stockpiled antipersonnel landmines, which numbered just over one million.

DEFENDING HUMAN RIGHTS

Human Rights Watch received no reports of interference with the work of rights groups in 2001.

THE ROLE OF THE INTERNATIONAL COMMUNITY

Organization for Security and Cooperation in Europe (OSCE)

Despite holding the chairmanship of the OSCE during 2001, Romania's penal and civil codes continued to violate the standards of free expression set by that body. Romania hosted the OSCE Conference on Roma and Sinti Affairs from September 10 to 13.

European Union

The European Parliament's report on Romania's application for E.U. accession welcomed Romania's intention to accelerate negotiations concerning membership but sharply criticized its lack of progress in meeting human rights standards, notably on the rights of children and minorities. The European Commission's 2001 regular report on Romania's progress toward accession recognized significant reforms since the 2000 report, but also urged continued progress, particularly toward implementation of the Roma strategy and antidiscrimination legislation.

United States

The U.S. State Department's first annual report on trafficking in persons categorized Romania as a "Tier-3" country, an indication that it had failed to make significant efforts to bring itself into compliance with minimum international standards. In May, the U.S. Agency for International Development awarded a grant to help fight domestic violence and child abuse in two counties in Romania.

RUSSIAN FEDERATION

HUMAN RIGHTS DEVELOPMENTS

The ongoing conflict in Chechnya and heated debates about press freedom dominated the year. Forced disappearances, torture, and extrajudicial executions by Russian forces were continuing hallmarks of the Chechnya conflict, while Chechen rebel fighters increasingly targeted for murder Chechen civilians seen as cooperating with the Russian government. The media landscape in Moscow underwent major changes as media conglomerate Media Most crumbled. President Vladimir Putin revived movement on judicial and criminal justice reform, which had been stalled for years. The proposed reforms, however, did not fully address the entrenched problems of police torture and prison overcrowding.

The situation in Chechnya remained deadlocked, with more than 75,000 Russian troops deployed in the republic, unable to root out rebel forces. In January, President Putin transferred command over the Chechnya operation from the Ministry of Defense to the Federal Security Service (FSB), and announced a gradual withdrawal of troops. The withdrawal halted in May after 5,000 troops had left the republic.

The new military strategy announced by President Putin, involving small operations against specific rebel leaders, did not affect the conduct of Russian forces with regard to Chechen civilians. They conducted numerous large-scale and targeted sweep operations, detaining countless men, often arbitrarily, looting the homes of civilians, and often wantonly destroying their property. Detainees routinely faced ill-treatment and torture. Many detainees "disappeared," with the bodies of some later discovered in unmarked graves.

The sweep operations in Alkhan-Kala, just southwest of Grozny, were paradigmatic. During a June 19 to 25 operation, which resulted in the death of notorious rebel leader Arbi Baraev, federal forces summarily executed at least six men and detained hundreds, many of whom later reported severe beatings. A sweep in late April resulted in the "disappearance" of twelve men.

The July sweep operations in the villages of Sernovodsk and Assinovskaia, in western Chechnya, were of unprecedented harshness. In response to a mine explosion that killed several policemen, soldiers detained hundreds of villagers, often without even asking for their identity papers. Many were later severely beaten and tortured with electroshock.

Russian forces also commonly detained people outside the context of sweep operations who then "disappeared." In January, for example, police detained Zelimkhan Murdalov in Grozny and took him to a local police station. He has since then been unaccounted for.

In 2001, villagers found numerous unmarked graves containing the corpses of people last seen in Russian custody. The largest—containing fifty-one bodies—was discovered near the main Russian military base in February. Law enforcement agents botched the subsequent investigation. At least sixteen of the people whose bodies were found there and identified had last been seen in Russian forces' custody. Some of the bodies found in this and other unmarked graves showed clear signs of torture.

Chechen fighters were widely believed to be responsible for a wave of assassinations of local civil servants and religious leaders who were reportedly targeted for their cooperation with the Russian government. In 2001, those murdered included at least eighteen leaders of district and town administrations, at least five religious leaders and numerous Chechen police officers, teachers, and lower-ranking civil servants. Several attempts were made on the life of Akhmad Kadyrov, the head of the pro-Russian administration of Chechnya, and one of his deputies was killed.

On January 9, masked gunmen kidnapped humanitarian aid worker Kenneth Gluck, of Médécins sans Frontières, on a road near Starye Atagi. Upon his release, about three weeks later, Gluck's captors handed him a letter signed by rebel leader Shamil Basaev calling the kidnapping a "mistake." On April 18, gunmen in Alkhan-Kala opened fire on Viktor Popkov, a leading Russian human rights activist. Popkov died six week later from his wounds. People close to Popkov believe Chechen fighters were involved in the attack.

About 140,000 internally displaced persons from Chechnya remained in Ingushetia, many in squalid conditions, despite strong pressure from the federal government to return to Chechnya. Those interviewed by Human Rights Watch in July 2001 cited poor security guarantees as the main reason for not returning to Chechnya.

The Russian government continued to resist a meaningful accountability process for human rights violations committed in Chechnya, although the number of investigations rose significantly in 2001. In April, a joint Council of Europe-Russian Duma working group compiled a list of 358 criminal investigations into alleged abuses against civilians. But only about 20 percent of the cases were under active investigation; more than half had been suspended. In "disappearance" cases as many as 79 percent of the investigations had been suspended. The criminal investigations list did not include a single case of torture or ill-treatment. Very few abuse cases had progressed to the courts. Courts issued guilty verdicts against servicemen in eleven cases, five of which resulted in prison sentences.

The only trial against a high-ranking military official, for the murder of a Chechen woman in March 2000, seemed set to end in a minimal sentence. In September, a psychiatric institution found that Col. Yuri Budanov was "emotionally distressed" at the time he murdered Elza Kungaeva, allowing the charge to be reduced to manslaughter and opening the way for him to be amnestied. Earlier, prosecutors had dropped a rape charge despite convincing evidence that she had been sexually assaulted.

Media freedom continued to be under attack in Chechnya. Several journalists were briefly detained or punished for their independent reports, and strict limitations on access to Chechnya for journalists remained in force throughout the year.

On February 21, federal forces detained Anna Politkovskaya of *Novaia Gazeta* (The New Gazette) in Khatuni while she was investigating abuses. Russian forces interrogated her and kept her overnight in a basement on a military base. In December 2000, a court in Dagestan found Andrei Babitskii, a Radio Liberty correspondent who had been detained in Grozny in 2000, guilty of carrying a falsified passport (his captors had not returned his Russian passport) but amnestied him. The Ministry of Press delivered several warnings of possible sanctions to Moscow newspapers and the NTV television station for publishing interviews with rebel leaders.

On November 21, 2000, unidentified gunmen speaking Chechen shot dead freelance cameraman Adam Tepsurkaev in Alkhan-Kala. Tepsurkaev had shot extensive footage of Russian soldiers abusing Chechen civilians. Russian soldiers had earlier detained and tortured Tepsurkaev's younger brother, demanding that Adam Tepsurkaev turn himself in to Russian authorities.

In December 2000, Chechen rebels in Georgia's Pankisi gorge briefly detained three Georgian television journalists on suspicion of cooperating with Russian intelligence services.

During a year of heated debates about press freedom, the media landscape in Moscow underwent major changes as media conglomerate Media Most crumbled. As of this writing, the nationwide broadcast media transmitted a variety of political views.

At the heart of the debates about press freedom were the stormy and convoluted events concerning Media Most and its outlets, in particular its television station, NTV, and radio station, Ekho Moskvy. In April 2001, NTV, the country's largest nonstate-owned television station, came under control of Gazprom, a colossal gas company that is partially owned by the state. The procuracy launched new charges of financial malfeasance against Media Most owner Vladimir Gusinski, and tried, unsuccessfully, to secure his extradition from Spain.

Prosecutors questioned several top Media Most officials and detained its financial director on embezzlement charges. By mid-February, company officials claimed prosecutors and the tax police had conducted no fewer than thirty raids on its offices since the investigation into Gusinsky's affairs began in mid-2000.

Gazprom started its bid to take over NTV when Media Most failed to repay a loan worth several hundred million U.S. dollars. After months of bitter controversy, the two sides reached an agreement whereby the gas giant would not obtain a controlling stake in NTV. However, in early 2001, Gazprom obtained a controlling stake after all when a court froze part of Media Most's shares. In April, Gazprom ousted NTV's board and appointed its own executive director. Part of the NTV team left the company in protest. Gazprom also ordered the closure of Media Most's flagship newspaper, *Sevodnya* (Today), and fired the entire editorial team of its weekly newsmagazine, *Itogi* (The Results).

As of October 2001, the fate of Russia's most popular radio station, Ekho Moskvy, remained undecided. The station's staff had threatened to resign should Gazprom obtain a majority stake. Gazprom, which owned a 52 percent stake, had promised in July to sell 9.5 percent to Ekho Moskvy staff, but by October 2001 the transaction had not taken place.

While Gazprom had legitimate business interests at stake in Media Most, the manner it which it gained control over NTV and the vigor and selectivity of law enforcement agencies' pursuit of Media Most and its owner strongly suggested a political motivation for the takeover. Gusinski had been a vociferous opponent of President Putin.

In Russia's regions, journalists and media outlets continued to face violent attacks—the Glasnost Defense Foundation reported that by late May 2001 at least five journalists had been murdered and thirty-nine violently attacked—but in many cases it was impossible to determine whether attacks were politically motivated. Some journalists in the regions faced prosecution for their professional activities.

In April, police in Belgorod detained journalist and parliamentarian Olga Kitova on charges of slander. Several months earlier Kitova had published an article in *Belgorodskaia Pravda* accusing police officers of torturing several teenagers into confessing that they had sexually molested a classmate. When police tried to bring Kitova, who enjoyed immunity as a member of the local parliament, to the precinct for questioning, she resisted and was, as a result, also charged with resisting arrest and beating police officials. In May, prosecutors released Kitova on her own recognizance. As of this writing, a local court was examining the case.

The FSB continued to chill freedom of expression and academic freedom by pursuing espionage cases involving material that defendants claimed was declassified. In July, military journalist Grigorii Pasko went on trial on espionage charges, after Russia's Supreme Court overturned a 1999 ruling by a Vladivostok court acquitting him. The Vladivostok court had excluded several pieces of evidence, citing falsification by the FSB. Pasko was accused of passing state secrets on the combat readiness of the Russian Pacific Fleet to the Japanese media. As of October 2001, the trial was ongoing.

The trial of Igor Sutyagin, a security and arms control researcher at the U.S.A. and Canada Institute, continued. The FSB arrested Sutyagin in 1999, charging him with passing state secrets to two employees of a British consultancy firm. However, according to his lawyers, Sutyagin never had access to classified materials and had only collated materials available in the public domain.

The FSB brought espionage charges against academic Valentin Danilov, head of the Thermo-Physics Center at a university in Krasnoyarsk. Following the scientist's arrest on February 16, the FSB charged Danilov with passing to a Chinese company state secrets relating to satellite technology. In an open letter to the procuracy, twenty of Danilov's colleagues maintained the information had been declassified in 1992. Danilov's trial was expected to start in late 2001.

The espionage conviction of former diplomat Valentin Moiseev also raised fair trial concerns. The Moscow City Court found Moiseev guilty after erratic court proceedings in which three different judges started hearing the case before being removed from it without clear explanation. A fourth judge eventually sentenced Moiseev to a four-and-a-half-year prison term in August.

In a move that could potentially restrict academic freedom, the presidium of the Russian Academy of Sciences in June issued a directive ordering research institutes to exercise "constant control" over scientists' cooperation with foreigners to avoid espionage. Although the directive did not contain any provisions that explicitly restricted academic freedom or freedom of expression, to many, the foregoing espionage cases indicated that the directive might in practice be applied arbitrarily.

In Moscow, racist attacks by skinheads—extremists known for their shaved heads and violence—continued to be a serious problem, as did racist police harassment. Although President Putin sharply and repeatedly condemned racist violence, his statements were undermined by the absence of efforts to hold police accountable for their harassment of ethnic minorities.

Police routinely extorted bribes from ethnic minorities, particularly Chechens, if their victims lacked a *propiska*, the obligatory residence permit. Police continued to plant ammunition, explosives, or narcotics on Chechens, often seeking large bribes in exchange for not pressing charges.

In late October, a group of skinheads stormed a bazaar on the outskirts of Moscow, killing two vendors from the Caucasus in what appeared to be a racially motivated attack. Police attributed the violence to "hooliganism" after Spain's defeat of Moscow's soccer team. Skinhead violence erupted in April around Adolf

Hitler's birthday, when a group of about 150 skinheads attacked an Azerbaijani market in southwestern Moscow and beat many of the vendors. The next day, skinheads taunted and stabbed to death a young Chechen man in central Moscow.

In August, a group of Russian teenagers, using broken bottles and baseball bats, attacked six African asylum seekers near an office of the United Nations High Commissioner for Refugees in Moscow. One of the Africans died of his wounds several weeks later. A week after the incident, two teenagers warned the U.N. office that "they would . . . declare a real war against the Africans."

Russian law enforcement agencies continued to cooperate with Central Asian governments seeking the extradition of political dissidents in Moscow. In June 2001, police arrested religious dissident Nodir Aliev, who was then extradited to Uzbekistan and sentenced to a seven-year prison term on charges of "undermining the constitutional order" of Uzbekistan. Also in June, police detained Tajik journalist Dodojon Avotulloev on an extradition request from the Tajik government, which sought to prosecute him for insulting the president of Tajikistan. After a week of intense international pressure, the Procuracy General denied the extradition request and released Avotulloev.

For the first time in years, the State Duma seemed set to pass a package of laws that would reform Russia's judiciary and criminal justice system. However, the proposed reforms did not adequately address major rights issues, such as torture and ill-treatment in police stations, overcrowding in prisons, and state indifference to domestic violence and rape.

In June, the State Duma passed a draft criminal procedure code in its second reading, the last step before final adoption. If adopted and signed into law, the code would introduce some long-awaited changes, such as a transfer from the procuracy to the judiciary of the authority to approve arrest and search warrants. However, the draft omitted steps that would help combat torture; for example, detainees would still require a prosecutor's consent for a forensic medical examination. Also, the draft code allowed for law enforcement agencies to seek signed statements from suspects before explaining their rights to them.

The State Duma also adopted amendments to several laws on the judiciary to introduce jury trials throughout Russia and to combat corruption among judges. Under the amendments, jury trials would be introduced in all eighty-nine regions of Russia by 2003. Draft amendments would also facilitate the prosecution of corrupt judges. However, some legal experts warned that the amendments made judges more susceptible to political pressure.

Although Penal Reform International reported that overall numbers of inmates in Russian prison facilities had decreased, overcrowding in pretrial detention remained severe. An important initiative that would have relieved overcrowding by limiting pretrial detention to one year failed, due to resistance from the procuracy.

In the first half of 2001, public officials undermined Russia's moratorium of the death penalty. Russia's justice minister and some members of the State Duma called for the restoration of capital punishment, and an army general called for the public executions of Chechen rebel leaders. However, President Putin very firmly spoke out against the death penalty in July.

THE ROLE OF THE INTERNATIONAL COMMUNITY

United Nations

For a second consecutive year, the U.N. Commission on Human Rights in April adopted a resolution expressing grave concern about human rights violations in Chechnya. The resolution strongly condemned the use of disproportionate force and serious human rights violations by Russia's forces. It called on Russia to investigate all violations of international human rights and humanitarian law, to establish a national commission of inquiry, and to extend invitations to several U.N. special mechanisms. Notably, it fell short of calling for an international commission of inquiry.

At the commission's September 25 session, U.N. High Commissioner for Human Rights Mary Robinson spoke about Russia's noncompliance with the resolution, specifically its failure to create a national commission of inquiry and to issue invitations to special mechanisms. The Russian delegation responded that the Russian Federation does not consider itself bound by the resolution.

In October 2000, the U.N. Human Rights Committee issued its first ruling against Russia since that country recognized in 1991 the individual right to petition. It found that Russian citizen Dmitry Gridin's right to a fair trial had been violated in his 1990 conviction for rape and murder and urged his immediate release from prison.

Organization for Security and Cooperation in Europe (OSCE)

On June 15, the OSCE Assistance Group returned to Chechnya, opening its office in Znamenskoye after working from Moscow for more than two years. The Assistance Group had received a considerable number of human rights complaints and worked with the office of the special representative for human rights in Chechnya, other Russian authorities, and human rights nongovernmental organizations. The failure by the OSCE to make full use of its human rights mandate and to commit sufficient staff to the Assistance Group undermined its effectiveness.

Council of Europe

The Parliamentary Assembly of the Council of Europe continued to monitor closely the situation in Chechnya. In January, it restored the Russian delegation's suspended voting rights, opting for engagement over exclusion. The assembly established a joint working group made up of European and Russian parliamentarians to monitor Russian compliance with Council of Europe requirements. In April, the joint working group provided the assembly with an exhaustive list of all investigations into crimes against civilians committed by servicemen and members of special police forces, an important contribution toward transparency in the accountability process. In July, assembly president Lord Russell-Johnston expressed his concern about continuing abuses. In September, the joint working group reported on Russia's failure to comply with the January assembly resolution and its dissatisfaction with Russian investigations into alleged abuses.

Council of Europe Human Rights Commissioner Alvaro Gil-Robles visited Chechnya in February and pressed the Russian government on investigations into rights abuses. However, he chose not to investigate a mass grave near the Khankala military base, discovered days before his arrival in Chechnya. He opted instead to urge the authorities to share information on the investigation with the office of the president's representative on human rights in Chechnya.

The secretary general of the Council of Europe, Walter Schwimmer, also repeatedly criticized the Russian government for the lack of prompt investigations into human rights abuses in Chechnya.

The Committee for the Prevention of Torture issued a rare public statement strongly criticizing Russia's lack of cooperation with the committee's recommendations. The statement specifically addressed Russian authorities' failure to carry out a thorough and independent inquiry into alleged abuses at the Chernokozovo detention facility in 2000 and to prosecute cases of ill-treatment of detainees in Chechnya.

The European Court of Human Rights declared admissible two applications against Russia for the first time since Russia's accession to the Council of Europe in 1996.

European Union

The European Union wavered on human rights in Chechnya in 2001. In April, the European Union tabled a draft resolution on Chechnya at the U.N. Commission on Human Rights but then tried to negotiate a much weaker chairman's statement. When the United States forced a vote on the draft resolution, the European Union voted in favor. At two E.U.-Russia summits, the European Union reportedly discussed Chechnya issues behind closed doors, but avoided mentioning them in public statements.

In December 2000, the European Parliament passed a resolution on the implementation of the E.U. Common Strategy on Russia. It called for a "double-track" strategy of collaborating with Russia on strengthening the rule of law and democratic structures while "whenever necessary, explicitly condemning human rights violations and the disproportionate use of force, as in the case of Chechnya."

U.K. Prime Minister Tony Blair and German Chancellor Gerhard Schroeder undermined the European Union's efforts in Geneva, repeatedly praising President Putin's leadership but neglecting publicly to raise abuses in Chechnya, including Russia's failure to comply with E.U.-sponsored U.N. resolutions. Following the September 11 attacks in the United States, Chancellor Schroeder called for a "reevaluation" of world opinion on the Chechnya conflict.

United States

The Bush administration repeatedly expressed concern over press freedom in Russia in early 2001 and played a critical role in bringing the Chechnya resolution to a vote the resolution at the Commission on Human Rights in April. However, once the resolution had passed, the Bush administration missed key opportunities to press for Russia's compliance with the resolution's requirements.

In June, President Bush and President Putin held their first summit in Slovenia at which Bush declared his support for Putin's leadership, and forfeited the opportunity to publicly ask for Russia's compliance with the U.N. resolution. Subsequent summits brought no U.S. public criticism of the conduct of the Chechnya campaign.

After the September 11 attacks, the United States actively sought Russia's support for its response. While the administration continued public criticism of the abuses in Chechnya, it did little more to bring Russia to pursue a more vigorous accountability process.

Relevant Human Rights Watch Reports:

Burying the Evidence: The Botched Investigation into a Mass Grave in Chechnya, 5/01

The "Dirty War" in Chechnya: Forced Disappearances, Torture, and Summary Executions, 3/01

SLOVAKIA

HUMAN RIGHTS DEVELOPMENTS

Slovakia made progress during 2001 in its efforts to join the first wave of candidate countries for European Union accession, but its human rights record remained uneven. Roma faced continued violence, discrimination, and police abuse, occasionally with fatal consequences. The state response to discrimination was inadequate, with Roma, gays and lesbians, and domestic violence victims lacking full legal protection. A punitive criminal defamation law impinged on free expression. Reforms were also needed to curb the trade in weapons with human rights abusers.

The July death of a Roma man in police custody demonstrated the vulnerability of Slovakia's Roma population. The deceased, Karol Sendrei, and his two sons were detained after a July 5 altercation between Sendrei and the local mayor in Magnezitovce, in which the mayor and his police-officer son seriously assaulted Sendrei. Following their arrest, Sendrei and his sons were handcuffed to a radiator at the police station in nearby Revuca and beaten throughout the night. Sendrei died from his wounds. Seven people were arrested in connection with the incident, including the mayor and his son, who were charged with causing the death, and two other police officers who face abuse of power charges.

Despite the arrests and assurances from the interior minister that he would ensure that justice would be done and improve police training, Sendrei's death was part of a continuing pattern of police failure to prevent racist violence against Slovak Roma. In a week of incidents, racist gang members beat and harassed Roma in the town of Holic, culminating in an August 13 assault on Milan Daniel that left him needing brain surgery. Roma residents asserted that the police had failed to protect them despite repeated complaints. On August 20, police finally charged two youths with the attack on Daniel. On August 30, Peter Bandur was sentenced to seven years' imprisonment for his part in the beating death of a Roma woman, Anastazia Balasova, a year earlier. (See *Human Right Watch World Report 2001*.) While Bandur was convicted of the more serious crime of racially motivated assault, his two accomplices received three and five years respectively for simple assault (without racist intent).

Roma continued to face discrimination in employment, education, and housing. Hostility on the part of other Slovaks formed part of the problem: a government plan to resettle five homeless Roma families in Medzilaborce was met in February by a protest petition signed by around 2,000 of the town's residents. But the government also failed adequately to implement and fund legal and policy measures to combat anti-Roma discrimination. Positive developments came in the form of the replacement in June of Vincent Danihel, the much-criticized minister for Roma issues, by Klara Orgovanova, and the appointment of Roma parliamentarian Ladislav Fizik as advisor to the interior minster.

Equal treatment for gays and lesbians suffered a setback on July 2, when the National Council (parliament) rejected a proposal prohibiting employment discrimination on the grounds of sexual orientation. There was some progress in official recognition of the rights of national minorities, demonstrated by Slovakia's signing of the European Charter for Regional or Minority Languages on February 20 and expanded Hungarian-language teaching. Antagonism toward minorities remained, however, with the desecration of Hungarian monuments in Kosice in March and Jewish tombstones in Zvolen in July. Anti-domestic violence laws remained inadequate, although the Alliance for Women cooperated with a government criminal law reform committee in efforts to remedy the shortcomings. Victims of rape faced bias in the justice system. Slovakia continued to lack an ombudsman office, although the government approved a draft law creating the post on September 19. At time of this writing, Parliament had yet to vote on the legislation.

Free expression continued to mature in Slovakia, but government officials' use of a criminal defamation law against journalists raised ongoing concerns. The office of the Slovak president brought a criminal defamation suit brought against Ales Kratky, a journalist with the daily *Novy Cas*, over an article questioning the president's fitness for office, leading to formal charges by a state prosecutor on July 2. Kratky faced a prison sentence if convicted. On July 12, the European Court of Human Rights found that a Slovak court's 1992 conviction of writer Lubomir Feldek under the same law, for an article about a government official's war record, was a violation of Feldek's right to free expression under article 10 of the European Convention on Human Rights.

Slovakia's growing popularity as a transit country for asylum seekers and migrants and a country of origin and transit for trafficking accentuated its significant shortcomings in refugee and trafficking policy. Principal concerns were the continued lack of an appeal mechanism for asylum petitions, lack of adequate facilities to house asylum-seekers, and inadequate guarantees against return to a country where individuals face threat of persecution.

Slovakia continued to authorize weapons transfers that risked fueling human rights abuses in recipient countries. For example, it continued to be a major supplier of arms to the highly abusive Angolan government, supplying mostly surplus weapons made redundant by military modernization plans linked to Slovakia's NATO aspirations. United Nations investigators found that Slovakia was the point of origin of weapons that were funneled to Liberia, in violation of a mandatory arms embargo. In addition, Slovakia played a role as a transit country for arms shipments originating in other countries. A weapons shipment from Iran apparently destined for Angola via Slovakia and Israel was impounded at Bratislava airport in September because the cargo was wrongly declared. The Slovak government at this writing had not taken action to close a legal loophole that permits weapons to transit through the country for up to seven days without a government license, nor to incorporate in national law minimum export criteria agreed under the 1998 E.U. Code of Conduct and a November 2000 OSCE agreement on small arms. Slovakia, a state party to the 1997 Mine Ban Treaty, announced on October 18, 2000, that it had completed destruction of its stockpile of antipersonnel landmines.

DEFENDING HUMAN RIGHTS

There were no reports of interference with the work of domestic monitoring or international human rights monitors. In March 2001, the Slovak Helsinki Committee initiated a project to monitor news reporting on minorities. Initial findings were encouraging, with more than 75 percent of news reporting on Roma and ethnic Hungarians assessed as neutral. The European Roma Rights Center continued their efforts to secure civil rights for Slovak Roma, filing suit against Slovakia in the European Court of Human Rights on October 5 on behalf of Lubomir Sarissky, a Roma man who died in police custody in August 1999.

THE ROLE OF THE INTERNATIONAL COMMUNITY

United Nations

In May, the Committee against Torture considered Slovakia's initial report on compliance with the Convention against Torture. The committee expressed concern at police involvement in attacks on Roma, allegations of ill-treatment of detainees in police custody, and the failure of Slovak authorities adequately to respond to police misconduct. The special rapporteur on the independence of judges and lawyers, Dato'Param Cumaraswamy, visited Slovakia in November 2000 to investigate government attempts to remove the president of the Supreme Court,

Dr. Stefan Harabin, in light of ongoing concerns about political interference in the judiciary. The government proposal to remove Dr. Harabin was subsequently defeated by the National Council in December 2000.

Organization for Security and Cooperation in Europe (OSCE)

The death of Karol Sendrei while in police custody was condemned in July by the OSCE contact point for Roma and Sinti. The contact point, Nicolae Gheorghe, emphasized the importance of an effective investigation by the Interior Ministry.

Council of Europe

In addition to signing the minority languages charter (see above) in February, Slovakia allowed publication on July 6 of the Opinion on Slovakia by the Advisory Committee on the Framework Convention on the Protection of National Minorities. The opinion, adopted by the committee in September 2000, noted progress in Slovakia's compliance with the convention but expressed concern about the treatment of Roma. Similar concerns were highlighted by Human Rights Commissioner Alvaro Gil Robles while visiting a Roma settlement in Kosice during his May trip to Slovakia.

European Union

E.U. concern over the plight of Roma remained a sticking point in relations with Slovakia during 2001. After visiting a Roma settlement in Jarovnice during a February trip to Slovakia, E.U. Enlargement Commissioner Guenther Verheugen contrasted Slovakia's overall progress towards accession with its continued discrimination against Roma. The European Parliament's rapporteur on Slovakia, Jan Marinus Wiersma, condemned the death of Karol Sendrei. Discrimination against Roma was also noted in Wiersma's May 8 report to the Parliament's Foreign Affairs Committee on Slovakia's membership application and the related resolution adopted by the full Parliament on September 5. In its regular report on Slovakia's progress toward E.U. accession released in November 2001, the European Commission noted continued concerns about the slow implementation of programs designed to assist Roma.

United States

The State Department country report on human rights practices in Slovakia largely reflected the main developments during 2000, including trafficking, although Slovakia was omitted from the department's July global report on trafficking. The U.S. government's interagency Helsinki Commission maintained its scrutiny of Slovakia's record on Roma issues.

TAJIKISTAN

HUMAN RIGHTS DEVELOPMENTS

Four years after a peace agreement ended Tajikistan's civil war, political violence continued and the government moved closer to single-party rule. It imposed increasing control over political and religious life by obstructing political opposition, arresting citizens on religious grounds, and severely restricting the media. Torture by police and security forces remained endemic.

Assassinations of high-ranking political figures reflected ongoing internal power struggles between and within the parties to the 1997 peace agreement—the government, led by President Emomali Rakhmonov, and the United Tajik Opposition (UTO), now disbanded. On April 11, Deputy Interior Minister Habib Sanginov, a former UTO political representative and key contributor to the peace negotiations, together with two of his bodyguards and driver, was shot by three unidentified assailants in Dushanbe. Sanginov's relatives dismissed the official version for his killing—that Sanginov had refused to repay a loan—and asserted it was connected to his efforts to identify illegal criminal groups with alleged links to the government. Authorities detained and harassed Sanginov's friends and relatives, causing at least one to flee the country. On July 17, gunmen killed Karim Yuldashev, a presidential foreign policy advisor, at his home in the capital. On September 8, Minister of Culture Abdurahim Rahimov was shot by unidentified gunmen outside his home in Dushanbe.

Renewed fighting between former UTO members and government forces in 2001 highlighted continuing distrust between the two sides and shortcomings in the demobilization process envisaged in the 1997 peace agreement. In June, former UTO field commanders based in northeastern Tajikistan took hostage at least four policemen in Teppa Samarkandi and fifteen members of a German humanitarian aid organization in Tavil-Dara. The kidnappers protested the arrest of former UTO members in connection with the murder of Habib Sanginov. All hostages were released unharmed, but a military operation against the rebel fighters ensued. Local legal experts and journalists reported that government forces' indiscriminate fire killed or injured up to eighty civilians, and that Tajik law enforcement agencies beat civilians and looted. Authorities acknowledged six civilian deaths.

UTO representation in the government, mandated by the peace accords, remained at best a formality, as in practice their officials and parliamentary deputies supported official policy and the president on almost all points. In 2001 the government moved to consolidate its de facto single-party control by banning and denying registration to opposition parties. The Adolatkhoh (Justice) party was banned on charges of violation of the law on political parties, and party officials claimed that its supporters had been intimidated by authorities into denying membership in the party. Registration documents for the Social Democratic Party languished with the Ministry of Justice. Pro-government candidates in the December

2000 and May 2001 parliamentary by-elections ran uncontested, as opposition candidates were denied registration on charges of violating electoral procedure.

The government harassed and arrested several members of the Islamic Revival Party (IRP), a key part of the former UTO, claiming they were members of Hizb ut-Tahrir (Party of Liberation), a banned Islamic organization. The IRP claimed that only one of its members supported the organization and that the government was using the crackdown against Hizb ut-Tahrir as a pretext to weaken the IRP.

Courts handed down increasingly severe sentences against scores of Hizb ut-Tahrir members. Whereas in previous years sentences ranged between five and twelve years, on charges of inciting religious hatred, distributing antistate literature, membership in banned organizations, and attempted violent overthrow of the state, in 2001 these charges brought sentences of up to fourteen years of imprisonment. Hizb ut-Tahrir advocated Islamic government and reestablishment of the caliphate by peaceful means.

The government continued severely to restrict freedom of expression. The sole state-owned publishing house for newspapers continued to censor material critical of the government or influential public figures. The authorities "counseled" all media on political content, and enforced pre-publication censorship and burdensome licensing procedures for media outlets. The government granted broadcast licenses to one independent radio station in northern Sugd province, while authorities in Dushanbe continued for a fourth year to deny operating licenses to both independent radio and television stations.

The authorities attempted to punish a foreign-based journalist for his criticism of the government. On July 5, Dodojon Atovullo, exiled editor-in-chief of the opposition newspaper *Charogi Ruz* (Light of Day), was arrested in Moscow, upon the request of Tajik law enforcement agencies. Atovullo had in recent years published articles accusing Tajik authorities of corruption and involvement in narcotics trafficking. Threatened with extradition back to Tajikistan to face charges of sedition and publicly slandering the president, he was released after six days after pressure from other governments and international organizations.

Tajik authorities continued to refuse entry to more than 10,000 Afghanis who fled fighting in northern Afghanistan in late 2000. The government claimed that the presence of armed combatants among the refugees posed too great a security risk to Tajikistan and that the country lacked the necessary economic and social resources to accommodate them. The displaced Afghanis were living in squalid conditions on islands in the Pianj River on the border between the two countries and were at times subjected to crossfire between United Front and Taliban forces. Their numbers steadily increased prior to and during the U.S.-led military offensive in Afghanistan. Authorities also ordered several thousand Afghan refugees already resident in Dushanbe to relocate to areas south and west of the capital to "ensure security and public order in places of settlement." While police harassed refugees following the order, as of this writing there were no reports of refugees having been forcibly relocated. In mid-October Dushanbe authorities closed three Afghan schools, charging that they violated administrative regulations, and refused to issue identity documents to Afghan refugees.

The International Organization for Migration reported that more than a thousand women, including minors, were trafficked in 2000 to the Middle East and Commonwealth of Independent States countries, where they were often employed in the sex industry. Traffickers paid bribes to Tajik law enforcement officials to procure travel documents and facilitate travel arrangements.

Antipersonnel landmines remained a feature of the Tajik landscape in 2001. Most were laid by Uzbek government forces in 2000, in response to the incursions of that year by the Islamic Movement of Uzbekistan through Tajikistan into Uzbekistan and Kyrgyzstan.

DEFENDING HUMAN RIGHTS

Local human rights defenders raised human rights violations in international fora, but the atmosphere of fear and intimidation prevented active monitoring and advocacy within the country. One notable initiative included a roundtable on the death penalty jointly organized by the OSCE and the League of Women Lawyers of Tajikistan. A principal recommendation was a moratorium on the death penalty.

THE ROLE OF THE INTERNATIONAL COMMUNITY

Tajikistan assumed a high profile as the U.S. military counterterrorism campaign in Afghanistan got underway. It was of strategic importance both for humanitarian relief operations in northern Afghanistan, and potentially as a base for U.S. military deployment. International actors seeking to bolster financial assistance to Tajikistan in recognition of its new strategic role made no effort whatsoever to take into account the country's dismal human rights record. Tajikistan was granted membership in NATO's Partnership for Peace program.

United Nations

The U.N. Office of Peace-Building (UNTOP), the United Nation's small peace-building mission that followed six years of peacekeeping operations, made a priority of attracting international assistance for job creation programs for former combatants and improvements of the rule of law. The UNTOP mission's staff included a human rights officer, whose brief, however, did not include human rights monitoring.

The U.N. High Commissioner on Refugees (UNHCR) pursued a wavering policy regarding the displaced Afghanis on the Pianj river islands. In early 2001, the high commissioner requested the Tajik government to create the necessary conditions to admit the displaced, by, among other things, separating combatants from civilians and moving the latter to a safer area. When the authorities refused, UNHCR suspended its own relief operations on the islands in mid-March, also arguing that effective relief could not be delivered until combatants were separated from civilians. UNHCR continued to press the Tajik government on devising a strategy for separating combatants from civilians.

Organization for Security and Cooperation in Europe (OSCE)

The OSCE mission headquarters in Dushanbe and its field offices in Khujand, Shaartuz, Dusti, and Kurgan-Tiube intervened in several individual human rights cases involving torture, rape, murder, and commutation of the death penalty. It monitored policies in southern Khatlon province on employment and access to land that discriminated against the Uzbek minority, visited some of the country's prisons, and did limited trial monitoring. Other notable activities included round tables on the death penalty and trafficking of women and children and the initiation of a project to train prison personnel. The mission also provided legal assistance to Tajiks deported from Uzbekistan and helped to draft new laws on the media to bring them into conformity with international norms. It did not, however, publicly intervene to attempt to prevent the single-party elections in May.

Russia

After the September 11 attacks in the United States, Russia for the first time publicly admitted its longstanding provision of material support to the United Front, delivered via Tajikistan. It also increased this support during the course of the U.S. campaign. Tajikistan's role as a strategic partner in the U.S.-led operation in Afghanistan became possible when Russia cleared the way for U.S. use of Tajikistan's airports.

In October, Russia sent at least 1,500 troops to Tajikistan, adding to the already more than 10,000 Russian border guards stationed along the Tajik-Afghan border, and about 10,000 troops of the 201st Motorized Rifle Division headquartered in Dushanbe.

United States

Tajikistan became a strategic partner in the U.S. government's counter-terrorism campaign when it offered the use of airports by U.S. forces should the need arise, and the United States continued to channel important amounts of humanitarian aid through the country. The State Department's annual report of human rights practices delivered an unbiased and in general accurate account of the human rights situation.

International Financial Institutions

Donor activity increased significantly in 2001, largely in reaction to the recognition of Tajikistan's importance to Central Asian security. A U.N.-sponsored donors' conference in May resulted in pledges of U.S. $430 million for poverty reduction and economic growth in 2001-2002. In addition, the European Bank for Reconstruction and Development contributed $2 million for rehabilitation and $13 million in loans for telecommunications modernization, while the World Bank issued a $50 million tranche of a continuing loan for poverty reduction programs and economic reforms. The Asian Development Bank made a $4.4 million loan for reconstruction of water supply systems. During the course of the U.S.-led military coalition operations in Afghanistan, Germany included Tajikistan on its list of priority countries for development assistance.

TURKEY

HUMAN RIGHTS DEVELOPMENTS

The strongly nationalist ruling coalition of the Democratic Left Party, Nationalist Action Party, and Motherland Party once again failed to enact key reforms in the face of longstanding opposition to these measures by the army and security forces. The government's National Program for Accession to the European Union should have marked a turning point for human rights, but consisted mainly of vague and general undertakings that were clearly designed to delay or avoid significant change. In June the Constitutional Court closed the religious Virtue Party for "actions against the republic's secular principles." An opportunity for significant change was missed in October, when a package of constitutional amendments were enacted that shortened detention periods, but left the death penalty and constraints on freedom of expression on the statute books. Three provinces remained under state of emergency. In December, security forces deliberately killed prisoners resisting transfers to new high security "F-type prisons," and beat them in transit. Thirty-three prisoners died in hunger strikes.

The Turkish government talked about lifting constraints on free expression, but did not take effective legislative action to do so. Those who challenged the official view of the role of religion, ethnicity, and the army were prosecuted and imprisoned. In June, Dr. Fikret Baskaya began serving his third prison term for his writings, a sixteen-month sentence for "separatist propaganda" under article 8 of the Anti-Terror Law, for a 1999 newspaper article about the trial of Kurdistan Workers' Party (PKK) leader Abdullah Öcalan. Ahmet Turan Demir, deputy chairperson of the People's Democracy Party (HADEP) which has a largely Kurdish membership, was committed to Ankara Closed Prison in August to serve a one-year sentence under article 8 of the Anti-Terror Law for a speech at his party's youth congress in 1998.

Military courts tried civilians on charges limiting free expression. In December Sanar Yurdatapan, coordinator of the Freedom of Expression Initiative, and Nevzat Onaran of the Contemporary Journalists' Association were imprisoned by the General Staff Military Court with two-month sentences for "criticizing the institution of military service."

Governors closed exhibitions, banned film shows, and confiscated books and newspapers. In August police confiscated the Women Pensioners' Union booklet *Voice and Courage*, which published speeches from a conference on sexual assault and rape in custody, and officials of the group were charged with "insulting the security forces."

The High Council for Radio and Television (R.T.U.K.) temporarily or permanently suspended scores of independent broadcasters and in August banned BBC World Service and Deutsche Welle on the grounds that they "threatened national security."

Various legal pretexts were used to prevent broadcasting and education in minority languages, calling into question whether the 2001 constitutional amendments ostensibly lifting the broadcasting ban would be fully implemented. Local governors prohibited the use of Kurdish street names and banned plays, cassettes, and films in Kurdish on the grounds that they were "separatist."

The ban on wearing the headscarf was applied with increasing severity against students and civil servants and extended to private universities. A change in regulations prohibited any student wearing a headscarf from sitting for the June university examinations, a move that human rights groups criticized as violating the students' right to freedom of religion, conscience, and thought. Teachers and doctors were also dismissed for wearing the headscarf on duty.

Many lawyers and human rights defenders charged that the use of torture and ill-treatment increased. Detainees in all quarters of the country reported that police or gendarmes inflicted torture by beating, death threats, hosing with cold water, sexual assault, electric shocks, and hanging by the arms. Victims included women and children, and people detained for common criminal offenses as well as State Security Court (SSC) offenses (those involving narcotics and organized crime, political violence, and some nonviolent political offenses). Two people died as a result of beatings during arrest.

The Turkish government refused to abolish incommunicado detention, the principal factor in the persistence of torture in Turkey identified by U.N. and Council of Europe experts. Turkish law continued to permit detention for SSC offenses for up to four days without access to family or lawyers. In practice this was frequently extended. Those held for common criminal offenses were entitled to a lawyer from the first moments of detention but rarely got one. Blindfolding, similarly condemned by international experts, also continued unchecked.

Legal safeguards for children in police custody were frequently ignored. In March, parliamentary deputy Sema Piskinsüt, former president of the Parliamentary Human Rights Commission, estimated that 90 percent of imprisoned children had been tortured in police custody. In January, nine children under the age of fifteen complained that they had been beaten, forced to remain standing for long periods, and deprived of food, drink and sleep while detained in Viransehir in the province of Sanlıurfa in southeast Turkey. Local lawyers complained about the ill-treatment and breach of detention procedures, but as of November 2001 no action had been taken against the responsible police officers. A fifteen-year-old detained in April during an Istanbul demonstration against F-type prisons reported that police officers beat him with wooden sticks about the head and body. Medical examination showed extensive bruising and broken teeth.

Women reported sexual abuse and rape in police custody. The Women's Commission of the Diyarbakır Bar stated in February that over the preceding year it had received complaints of sexual assault or rape by police or gendarmes from 123 women. In July, Health Minister Osman Durmus issued a circular which appeared to circumvent a 1999 ban on "virginity examinations" by providing for the expulsion of female medical students proven to be sexually active or engaged in prostitution. The minister later denied that he had authorized the reinstatement of such examinations, but did not rescind the circular. A sixteen-year-old in Van reported that in June she was taken from a gendarmerie post, where she was being questioned for alleged links with the PKK, to a state hospital and there subjected to a forced "virginity test."

The climate of impunity for torture remained unchanged. Where security personnel were charged and convicted of crimes based on torture, sentences were frequently light or suspended. In February a policeman convicted of torturing a thirteen-year-old boy in Istanbul in 1994 received a suspended sentence of fifteen months' imprisonment and returned to active service. In August the Turkish Parliamentary Human Rights Commission reported that it had forwarded 451 torture cases to local prosecutors, who had responded in only sixty-nine cases. Only one prosecution had been opened. The December 2000 Law on Conditional Release and Suspension of Sentences, resulting in the release of thousands of prisoners held on common criminal charges, also suspended sentences for police officers convicted of ill-treatment under article 245 of the Turkish Criminal Code.

Torturers continued to be protected by the abuse of medical examination procedures. In December, Dr. Nur Birgen, a Forensic Institute official, was convicted of issuing misleading reports that concealed torture. Her three-month prison sentence was commuted to a fine of approximately one U.S. dollar.

HADEP officials Serdar Tanıs and Ebubekir Deniz "disappeared" after being summoned to a gendarmerie station in Silopi, Sırnak province, in January. The authorities first denied and then admitted that the two men "visited" the gendarmerie, but claimed they had left after half an hour.

The Justice Ministry moved forward with its long-planned transfer of prisoners held for SSC offenses from large ward-based prisons to new F-type prisons organized in smaller cells for up to three prisoners. The ministry ignored warnings from nongovernmental and international organizations that the planned F-type regime might amount to cruel, inhuman, and degrading treatment and that the lack of transparency surrounding the prison reform risked exacerbating prisoners' fears. In December, the government launched "Operation Return to Life," sending 10,000 soldiers into twenty ward-based prisons to transfer hunger-striking prisoners into small-group isolation in the newly constructed F-type prisons. The operation left twenty-eight prisoners and two gendarmes dead. Some prisoners burned themselves in protest, but others were deliberately killed by security forces. Gendarmes beat and tortured prisoners during transfer and on arrival at the F-type prisons. Eight male prisoners formally complained that gendarmes anally raped them with truncheons on arrival at Kandıra F-type Prison, but they were not medically examined for three weeks.

Complaints that F-type prison guards maintained discipline through beatings were corroborated by medical evidence in several cases. In February, Sabri Diri made a formal complaint that guards at Tekirdag F-type Prison twice beat him and subjected him to *falaqa* (beating on the soles of the feet) in his single cell. A medical examination delayed for a week showed no signs of ill-treatment but a June medical examination using scintigraphy, an imaging technique, revealed evidence consistent with Sabri Diri's allegation of falaka and beating. As of October 2001, thirty-three prisoners and eight relatives had died in hunger strikes in protest at the F-type regime. More than fifty other hunger strikers suffered severe and permanent brain damage.

More than 250,000 mainly Kurdish villagers remained unable to return to their homes in the southeast, despite the substantial reduction in hostilities between government forces and the PKK in that region. The vast majority had been forced from their homes in the early and mid-1990s by security forces in brutal operations accompanied by torture and "disappearances." A smaller number had fled their villages after repeated PKK attacks. Returns were slow due to apparent official reluctance to repopulate distant rural areas. Where civil authorities granted permission to return, villagers were sometimes turned back by gendarmerie or neighboring communities' paramilitary village guards who had occupied their lands.

Sporadic forced evacuation and house destruction actually continued. Following the death of a gendarme in a landmine explosion near Beytüssebab in Sirnak province in July, gendarmes forcibly evacuated the villages of Asat and Ortaklı.

The decline in attacks by armed illegal political organizations in recent years continued but political killings of civilians continued. In September, a suicide bomb attack by a member of the Revolutionary People's Liberation Party/Front (DHKP/C) in Istanbul killed Australian tourist Amanda Rigg and two Anti-Riot Squad officers. A fifteen-year-old was killed and three other schoolchildren injured in an attack on the extreme right Idealist Hearth in Istanbul. Official reports claimed the attack was committed by the Turkish Communist Labour Party (TKEP).

Asylum seekers were frequently denied proper protection. Under Turkey's geographical reservation to the 1951 Refugee Convention, non-European asylum seekers were required to register with the police so that the U.N. High Commissioner for Refugees (UNHCR) could determine whether they were refugees and eligible for resettlement in a third country. Hundreds of asylum seekers entering the country from Iran and northern Iraq were summarily returned across the borders. Others were arbitrarily refused permission to register or to report weekly to police stations, thereby exposing them to risk of summary return as illegal residents. In July more than two hundred African asylum seekers, including some recognized by UNHCR as refugees, were rounded up in Istanbul. One female member of the group died in custody, while others reported that gendarmes ill-treated, raped, or otherwise sexual assaulted them before forcing them at gunpoint across the Greek border.

Landmines laid by the government along the borders and by both sides in the conflict between the security forces and the PKK, killed at least ten people. In April, however, Turkey declared that it would begin procedures to accede to the Ottawa Convention on the prohibition of production and use of anti-personnel mines.

DEFENDING HUMAN RIGHTS

Prime Minister Bülent Ecevit issued a circular in June that required government authorities to be "tolerant towards civil society organizations," but also said that members of such organizations did not deserve to be called human rights defenders.

Human rights organizations saw little benefit from the circular. In September, police raided the Diyarbakir referral center for the treatment of torture survivors run by the Turkish Human Rights Foundation (TIHV) and carried off computers, patient files, and information about assisting doctors. In March, nineteen participants in a conference on sexual assault and rape in custody were put on trial for "insulting the State authorities" at Beyoglu Criminal Court. Nazli Top, who was tortured and raped with a truncheon in police custody in 1992, was a speaker at the June 2000 conference and a defendant in the ongoing trial.

The F-type prison crisis and associated hunger strikes imposed considerable strain on the human rights community. Government authorities relentlessly persecuted TIHV, Human Rights Association (HRA), and Turkish Medical Association members who were stretching their resources to the limit in order to document abuses, ensure supplies of vitamins and clothing to F-type inmates, and provide support to the relatives of sick, dead, and dying prisoners. Five HRA branches were shut down by local governors because of their work on F-type prisons. HRA members were repeatedly beaten and detained when they tried to make public press statements. The Justice Ministry announced that providing information about the hunger strikes was "supporting terrorism." Accordingly, Ankara HRA branch president Lutfi Demirkapı and eleven others were charged in March under the Anti-Terror Law for their defense of human rights and face possible seven and a half year prison sentences. Their trial at Ankara SSC was under way as of this writing.

In October, *Yeni Safak* (New Dawn) published an April 1998 memorandum from the military's Office of the Chief of General Staff, outlining a military plan to discredit the HRA with false information linking it to the PKK. The military did not deny the April 1998 memorandum's authenticity but claimed it was never implemented. However, an attempt on HRA president Akın Birdal's life in May 1998 was provoked by the type of groundless accusations contemplated in the memorandum. Birdal barely survived the attack, which left him disabled.

THE ROLE OF THE INTERNATIONAL COMMUNITY

United Nations

In January, the U.N. special rapporteur on religious intolerance and discrimination published a report on his 1999 visit to Turkey. The report strongly questioned the Turkish Republic's view of itself as a secular state, stating that the Directorate of Religious Affairs wields "excessive powers of religious management such that religious practice appears to be regimented by the government and Islam is treated as if it were a 'State affair.' "

The report noted that Muslim and non-Muslim religious minorities were not satisfactorily protected and recommended that the U.N. Working Group on Minorities review the effectiveness of safeguards provided by the Treaty of Lausanne, the foundation for Turkey's policies towards minorities. The special rapporteur also urged recognition of the right to conscientious objection.

The February visit of the U.N. special rapporteur on extrajudicial, arbitrary and summary executions included investigations into the "disappearance" of HADEP officials Serdar Tanıs and Abubekir Deniz.

In June the Committee on the Rights of the Child recommended that the Turkish government introduce legislative changes and an awareness campaign in order to combat "honor killings," the murder of women by family members who believe that they have been dishonored by the woman's conduct. The committee was also "extremely concerned" that children were being exposed to torture and ill-treatment as a result of incommunicado police detention.

Council of Europe

The Committee for the Prevention of Torture (C.P.T.) concertedly engaged the Justice Ministry on the violence of the December prison operation, isolation in F-type prisons, and associated hunger strikes. The C.P.T. visited Turkey in December just before the operation, attempting to resolve hunger strikes that started in October. It visited again in January, April, and September.

The Turkish government authorized the committee's publication of all outstanding reports visits dating back to 1990. The C.P.T. did not oppose the change from large wards to cells but emphasized that small-group isolation in F-type prisons was "not acceptable" and urged the Justice Ministry to establish out-of-cell activities and independent monitoring.

In a number of judgments the European Court of Human Rights (ECHR) ruled that Turkish security forces had been responsible for arbitrary house destruction, torture, "disappearance," and extrajudicial execution in their operations in the southeast.

The ECHR's controversial judgment in July rejected the Welfare Party's complaint against closure by the Turkish Constitutional Court for "activities against the principle of secularism" in 1998. The European Court considered that the party leadership's intention to establish Islamic law (*shariah*) conflicted with values embodied in the convention, and that statements by the leadership suggested that it might resort to force in order to gain and retain power. In the same month the court ruled that Kurdish former parliamentary deputies Hatip Dicle, Orhan Dogan, Selim Sadak, and Leyla Zana, sentenced to fifteen years for treason in 1994, had been imprisoned after an unfair trial.

European Union

The E.U. Presidency's May statement on the prison crisis urged the Turkish government to implement "generously and properly" the C.P.T.'s suggested steps and underlined that prison reform was a priority area for meeting the accession criteria. In June, a European Parliament delegation visited Turkey to investigate developments in F-type prisons.

The European Parliament's October 2000 report on the accession process criticized the vagueness of the National Plan and noted that "the signs of openness which are on occasion expressed by governmental authorities may be challenged by military powers, which still have an unusual influence on Turkish politics." The European Commission's November 2001 Regular Report concluded that on human rights, "the situation on the ground has hardly improved."

United States

The State Department's *Country Reports on Human Rights Practices for 2000* surveyed the continuing abuses, giving examples of restrictions on speech and the press, extrajudicial killings and torture. The report blamed incommunicado detention and impunity for the persistence of torture. It documented child labor, violence against women, and spousal abuse.

Its description of "an upsurge in the rate of returns" of displaced Kurdish villagers gave a more optimistic picture than warranted. The conclusion, apparently based on official Turkish government pronouncements, was not borne out by Human Rights Watch investigations. The State Department's *Trafficking in Persons Report* stated that Turkey did not meet the minimum standards nor had it made significant efforts to combat trafficking of women and girls to Turkey for forced prostitution.

Technical issues slowed contractual negotiations on the sale of 145 attack helicopters to Turkey by U.S. manufacturer Bell Textron. This class of equipment was implicated in past human rights violations in Turkey, making the pending sale, which is subject to U.S. Congressional approval, highly controversial in the United States.

Relevant Human Rights Watch Reports:

Small Group Isolation in F-type Prisons and the Violent Transfers of Prisoners to Sincan, Kandira, and Edirne Prisons on December 19, 2000, 4/01

TURKMENISTAN

HUMAN RIGHTS DEVELOPMENTS

In 2001, Turkmenistan isolated itself from the international community and continued to stifle all forms of dissent, to hound religious and ethnic minorities, and to exercise strict control over all media and expression.

President Saparmurad Niazov's cult of personality reached new levels. "President for Life" in the year 2000, in February he declared his intention to remain president only until 2010, when he promised multicandidate elections without opposition candidates. On October 19, the government's highest legislative body declared that *Rukhnama* (Book of the Soul), written by President Niazov, was a holy text, and officials indicated that it would be comparable to the Bible and the Koran.

In January, President Niazov added about 1,000 agents to the National Security Committee (or KNB), bringing their number to 2,500. Successor to the KGB, the KNB exercised truly pervasive surveillance over the population, using intimidation, searches without warrants, arbitrary detention, and torture to dissuade all dissent.

In response to international pressure, Turkmen authorities released in December 2000 two dissidents, Nurberdi Nurmamedov and Pirkuli Tangrikuliev, imprisoned since January 2000 and August 1999, respectively. President Niazov signed a decree pardoning the two after their videotaped statements of "repentance" were broadcast on television.

Mukhmatkuli Aimuradov, a political prisoner since 1994, continued to serve an eighteen-year prison sentence. Notwithstanding his worsening health, the authorities limited family visits and delivery of food parcels and medicines, and denied his petition to have his sentence reduced.

Since 1997, the government has officially allowed only two religious denominations, Sunni Islam and Russian Orthodox Christianity, and viciously persecuted those who followed other faiths, which were considered illegal. Religious persecution worsened after a January 26 presidential speech tasked the KNB with reinvigorating the struggle against "various non-native religious groups intent on fracturing our society." Pentacostalists, Baptists, Jehovah's Witnesses, and Hare Krishnas bore the brunt of this new crackdown. Police and KNB agents interrogated and intimidated worshippers, confiscated their literature, and prevented group worship. The government also continued to deport religious activists who were not citizens of Turkmenistan.

At least fifteen believers were tortured or ill-treated during police and KNB interrogations about their beliefs or "illegal" religious activities. On March 11, KNB agents detained seven Hare Krishnas at a wedding in Mari, and beat them on the soles of their feet to punish them for adherence to an "incorrect" faith. A court sentenced them to five days of detention on trumped-up charges of "hooliganism."

In January 2001, President Niazov claimed that in 2000 law enforcement agents had confiscated 350,000 religious books and 80,000 cassettes that were "incompatible with our faith." In March, authorities banned the sale of Bibles in Russian or Turkmen.

By March the government had closed the last Pentacostalist and Baptist houses of worship. Several families were evicted from their homes in retaliation for praying at unsanctioned gatherings.

In February, Shahgildy Atakov, an imprisoned Baptist pastor convicted in 1999 on unfounded charges of alleged financial misdealings, was transferred in serious condition to a prison hospital in Mary. The authorities had reportedly offered to release Atakov provided he take an oath of allegiance to the president. When he refused, state agents beat him and forcibly medicated him with psychotropic drugs. The government denied Atakov's ill-treatment but ignored diplomats' requests to meet with him. On March 23, Atakov was transferred to the remote Turkmenbashi prison facility. Also in March, his wife, Artigul Atakova, and five children were forcibly relocated to Kaakhka, where local authorities reportedly threatened to deny parental rights to Atakova unless her children participated in the school ritual of swearing allegiance to the president.

At least six Jehovah's Witnesses were serving prison sentences, mostly for conscientious objection to military service. Authorities in some cases reportedly brought new charges against conscientious objectors when they finished out their terms.

Islamic groups also suffered state harassment. On June 25, President Niazov stated that he had ordered the official head Turkmen Muslims to close the last *madrassah* (religious school) in the northern city of Dashoguz. Only the department of theology at Ashgabat University, which is under strict police surveillance, had the right to teach Islamic studies. The Shiite community had been denied registration since 1997, although some communities had permission to gather for prayer on major holidays.

Law enforcement agencies stepped up pressure on nongovernmental organizations (NGOs). In November 2000, a special commission in Turkmenbashi composed of the KNB, procuracy, tax police, and local government officials launched "inspections" to intimidate thirty NGOs that had participated in a seminar on democratization sponsored by the Organization for Security and Cooperation in Europe (OSCE). Umid (Hope), the NGO that had organized the conference, was forced to cease its operations. From July through September, the Ministry of Justice and procuracy repeatedly summoned forty-eight environmental and humanitarian NGOs, some of which had previously been denied registration, to warn them that any activities pursued by unregistered NGOS were illegal.

The government systematically stifled all media freedoms, and imposed prepublication state censorship. The authorities forced people to subscribe to Turkmen newspapers, even if they did not speak Turkmen. In March state libraries were instructed to confiscate the works of about twenty authors who either "inaccurately depicted" the country's history or had emigrated for political reasons.

The government went to extraordinary lengths to block all information about the human toll of the December 6, 2000, earthquake in western Turkmenistan. President Niazov publicly stated that no one had perished, though dozens were reported dead, and declined all foreign assistance.

Beginning in the third quarter of 2000, the government took unprecedented action to curtail freedom of movement. It declared two of Turkmenistan's five provinces "closed"; travel there required a special pass. In several of the country's largest cities, local authorities banned the sale of homes to residents of other cities and strictly enforced *propiska* (obligatory residence permits) rules. Several people were denied permission to travel abroad on political or religious grounds. In 2001, the government gave few visas to foreigners, and in numerous cases KNB agents warned individuals not to issue invitations to their friends and relatives abroad, required for Turkmen visas.

To discourage contact with foreigners, on June 4 President Niazov signed an order requiring a fee of U.S. $50,000 to register a marriage with a foreigner.

President Niazov's grandiose construction projects for Ashgabad required the destruction of many homes, and according to diplomats, homeowners in numerous cases were not paid the full amount of promised compensation, or received nothing. Those who had the right to alternative housing in some case did not receive it.

In December 2001, President Niazov amnestied 11,774 of the country's 19,000 prisoners, but prisons remained overcrowded and horrific. Corruption pervaded the amnesty process.

DEFENDING HUMAN RIGHTS

The government does not allow domestic human rights NGOs. Due to emigration, Russian Community, an unregistered entity, collapsed. The organization had defended the rights of ethnic minorities and assisted them in emigration matters. On May 2, KNB agents interrogated one of its former activists, Viacheslav Mamedov, after he visited the OSCE in Ashgabad. They accused him of giving the OSCE a "political document" and banned him from traveling to the capital to meet with foreigners without first informing them.

THE ROLE OF THE INTERNATIONAL COMMUNITY

United Nations

Turkmenistan declared its support for a U.N.-led campaign against terrorism, and agreed to allow the United Nations to deliver humanitarian aid through its border with Afghanistan.

Organization for Security and Cooperation in Europe (OSCE)

For the fourth year in a row, Turkmenistan failed to sign a substantive Memorandum of Understanding with the OSCE's Office of Democratic Institutions and Human Rights, one of the conditions under which the OSCE had agreed in 1998 to establish a center in Ashgabad. Nonetheless, Chairman-in-office Mircea Geoana met with President Niazov in June 2001 for talks on security and human rights issues, and claimed to have made steps toward "re-engaging Turkmenistan on the human dimension of the OSCE."

In February, the head of the OSCE center in Ashgabad requested permission to visit Shahgildy Atakov, but officials ignored the request. He also publicly noted that President Niazov's decision to hold elections in 2010, while positive in setting a limit to his presidency, effectively cancelled the elections scheduled for 2002. Also in February, OSCE representatives attempted to monitor the trial of Nurberdi Nurmamedov; officials barred them entry, despite having invited them to attend.

Despite hindrances to its operation, the OSCE Center sponsored a number of seminars and events on human rights issues.

European Union

The ratification of the E.U. Partnership and Cooperation Agreement (PCA) with Turkmenistan remain stalled, due to human rights concerns. But the PCA's Interim Agreement extended full trade benefits, squandering the European Union's leverage with Turkmenistan.

After the September attacks in the United States, the European Union began to reevaluate its engagement with Central Asian states bordering on Afghanistan. Within this context Belgian Foreign Minister Louis Michel, representing the E.U. presidency, visited Turkmenistan to discuss cooperation on terrorism, border control, and drug trafficking.

United States

In the post-September 11 context of U.S. policy toward Central Asian states, Turkmenistan's human rights record took second place to its strategic location, sharing a border with Afghanistan. The Bush administration's list of countries of particular concern for religious freedom, released in October, did not include Turkmenistan. In August, the U.S. Commission on International Religious Freedom had recommended its inclusion.

European Bank for Reconstruction and Development (EBRD)

In a letter to President Niazov in July 2001, the EBRD threatened to cut off all activities in Turkmenistan if political and economic reforms were not enacted within a year, citing "grave concerns about the state of democracy and the lagging pace of political and economic transition." The EBRD had ended public sector lending to Turkmenistan in April 2000.

UNITED KINGDOM

HUMAN RIGHTS DEVELOPMENTS

In the aftermath of the September 11 attacks in the United States, the United Kingdom proposed emergency measures that threatened to undermine civil liberties and the rights of refugees and migrants. Three years after the 1998 Multi-Party Agreement was negotiated in Northern Ireland, the agreement's human rights provisions were not yet realized. Contentious outstanding issues included the creation of a representative, accountable police force, and the establishment of public inquiries into the murders of two slain defense lawyers.

On September 27, British Home Secretary David Blunkett suggested that Afghans who might flee their country were not entitled to seek refuge elsewhere.

"There is already a major problem on the Afghan border," he said. "The main aim is to stop people coming from that region and spreading across the world. That is also necessary for reasons of terrorism." Blunkett indicated that in order to prevent terrorism it might be necessary to curb the appeal rights of those refused entry into the United Kingdom. Such measures threatened to prevent asylum seekers from having their claims for refugee status assessed fully and fairly. Most individuals recognized as refugees in the United Kingdom had appealed an initial negative decision.

In October, the British Home Office proposed new security measures—including enhanced police powers; a denial of judicial review for decisions made by the Special Immigration Appeals Commission, which deals with asylum claims of persons suspected of terrorist activities; and provisions for the indefinite administrative detention of those suspected of terrorist activity or associated with terrorist groups or their members. In February, the United Kingdom lifted its derogation from article 5 of the European Convention on Human Rights, which governs the rights of individuals in custody. The indefinite detention proposal would have required the United Kingdom to reinstate the derogation.

On November 12, Home Secretary David Blunkett declared a "state of emergency," a requirement for derogation from certain provisions of the European Convention on Human Rights (ECHR). Blunkett told the *Guardian* that the declaration was a legal technicality—necessary to ensure that certain antiterrorism measures that contravene the ECHR could be implemented—and not a response to any imminent terrorist threat. In a statement to Parliament on October 15, Blunkett stated that "[t]here is no immediate intelligence pointing to a specific threat to the United Kingdom." These public pronouncements raised concern that the United Kingdom sought to derogate from its human rights obligations in the absence of conditions amounting to a bona fide state of emergency.

The Home Office subsequently introduced the Anti-Terrorism, Crime and Security 2001 bill on November 13. The bill included a definition of "international terrorist suspects" that included persons who "have links with a person who is a member of or belongs to an international terrorist group," giving rise to concern that people could be found guilty by association; provided for indefinite detention with limited judicial review for foreigners certified by the Home Secretary as suspected terrorists; and undermined the 1951 Refugee Convention by denying those considered suspects the fundamental right to seek asylum and potentially excluding them from the United Kingdom, or detaining them indefinitely without adequate safeguards. An expedited process was implemented to see the bill to adoption, which was expected by December.

Attacks against Muslims living in the United Kingdom increased dramatically after September 11. On September 17, three white men beat an Afghan taxi driver so severely that he was paralyzed from the neck down. Although such attacks were condemned by the government—with a promise to toughen enforcement of hate crimes legislation—new government calls for antiterrorist measures, more restrictive immigration and asylum controls, and for halting the flow of Afghan refugees into Europe contributed to an increasingly hostile climate toward refugees and migrants in the United Kingdom.

The Northern Ireland peace process faced numerous challenges in 2001. On August 18, the Irish and British governments issued a revised implementation plan for the 1999 Patten Commission report on policing. Although Northern Ireland's Irish nationalist Social Democratic Leadership Party (SDLP) agreed to the plan, the republican party Sinn Fein refused to approve it, citing its failure to incorporate key provisions of the 1998 Patten report, which recommended fundamental reform of policing arrangements. In September, the Northern Ireland Police Board—the policing oversight body—was established with representatives from all the major political parties except Sinn Fein. Without support from Sinn Fein, members of the Catholic minority that identify themselves as republicans or nationalists were less likely to seek jobs in the service.

In June, the Royal Ulster Constabulary introduced "less lethal" plastic bullets into its cache of weapons. Human rights groups and Labor Party MPs argued that scientific evidence indicated the new bullets remained lethal and continued their calls for a total ban on the use of plastic bullets.

Children's right to education was threatened in September in the Ardoyne area of Belfast where local protesters—who identify themselves as Protestant "loyalists" to the U.K.—lobbed a blast bomb, tossed bottles, and shouted sectarian slurs at Holy Cross elementary students, girls aged four to eleven, as they made their way to school. Loyalists issued death threats against some parents. On November 11, a sixteen-year old loyalist protester died after a pipe bomb exploded in his hand. Catholic parents charged the RUC with failing to protect their children adequately. In November, the RUC arrested a nationalist who was videotaping loyalist protests outside the school.

Press outlets continued to suffer setbacks in their efforts to report on the Force Research Unit (FRU), a unit within British Army intelligence alleged to be responsible for a number of killings—through its agents in both loyalist paramilitary groups and the Irish Republican Army (IRA)—including the murder by loyalist paramilitaries of defense lawyer Patrick Finucane in 1989. On April 24, the Ministry of Defense secured a temporary injunction against Ulster Television's *Insight* series, which was about to broadcast a program about FRU's infiltration of former soldiers into the IRA. The program alleged that members of the security forces and the public died in IRA attacks that were allowed to go ahead in order to protect those agents' cover. A permanent injunction was served on UTV on April 26 banning the station from broadcasting information about the ban.

In February 2001, the Irish government issued a public statement supporting the call for an independent international public inquiry into the March 1999 murder of human rights lawyer Rosemary Nelson. In August 1 proposals to advance the political process, the British and Irish governments called for the appointment of an international judge to investigate allegations of official collusion in several cases, including the murders of Rosemary Nelson and Patrick Finucane. The Nelson and Finucane families continued to call for independent public inquiries into the murders.

DEFENDING HUMAN RIGHTS

In July 2000 human rights activists discovered a web site listing names of persons being targeted by loyalist paramilitaries, including defense lawyers, journalists, and community activists. The police got the list off the web in December 2000. Evidence subsequently came to light that loyalists had the list and were amending it. The RUC warned hundreds of people that their names were on the list.

On September 28, journalist Martin O'Hagan, who wrote about alleged collusion between the security forces and loyalist paramilitaries, was shot dead in Lurgan.

THE ROLE OF THE INTERNATIONAL COMMUNITY

United Nations

In April, the U.N. special rapporteur on the independence of judges and lawyers and the special rapporteur on human rights defenders called for public inquiries into the murders of Rosemary Nelson and Patrick Finucane.

In November, the U.N. Human Rights Committee issued concluding observations on the United Kingdom's fifth periodic report. The committee welcomed the entry into force of the Human Rights Act 1998 and the establishment of a police ombudsman and human rights commission in Northern Ireland. It recommended that any derogation from the International Covenant on Civil and Political Righs (ICCPR) in the effort to combat terrorism comply with the requirements on derogation contained in article 4, to implement "a full, transparent, and credible accounting" of the circumstances into disputed killings in Northern Ireland, including the murders of Patrick Finucane and Rosemary Nelson, to examine the asylum system to ensure that asylum seekers' rights under the ICCPR receive full protection, and to establish a national human rights commission.

Council of Europe

In four judgments issued in May, the European Court of Human Rights held that the United Kingdom had failed to conduct effective investigations into disputed killings in Northern Ireland. The cases were brought by the families of eleven people killed by security forces and one person killed by Loyalist paramilitaries with the alleged collusion of the security forces. The court unanimously found in all four cases that the procedures for investigating the use of lethal force by police officers failed to meet the requirements of article 2 of the European Convention on Human Rights, which guarantees the right to life.

United States

On March 15, the second anniversary of Rosemary Nelson's murder, the House

Subcommittee on International Operations and Human Rights held a hearing on the review of the criminal justice system in Northern Ireland.

The U.S. State Department's *Country Reports on Human Rights Practices for 2000* adequately catalogued the concerns of human rights groups, including the lethal potential of plastic bullets, alleged collusion between security forces and loyalist paramilitaries, and the unresolved murders of lawyers Rosemary Nelson and Patrick Finucane.

Relevant Human Rights Watch Reports:

Commentary on the United Kingdom's Anti-Terrorism, Crime and Security Bill 2001, 11/01

UZBEKISTAN

HUMAN RIGHTS DEVELOPMENTS

The new U.S.-led campaign against terrorism dramatically changed Uzbekistan's international position, but its appalling human rights record remained unchanged. The government retained tight control over all media and other forms of expression, dealing harshly with dissidents and rights activists who sought to expose abuses. It did not tolerate independent political parties or social movements. State agents tortured those in custody and at least five people died in custody under highly suspicious circumstances in 2001.

The government pressed forward with a campaign of unlawful arrest, torture, and imprisonment of Muslims who practiced their faith outside state controls, and took increasing numbers of pious women into custody. Police forcibly disbanded protests by relatives of religious prisoners, and placed several under administrative arrest for demonstrating.

Seventy-three mountain villagers were convicted, after being tortured and ill-treated, on charges of abetting the Islamic Movement of Uzbekistan (IMU) insurgency in 2000 in southeastern Uzbekistan.

While authorities withheld comprehensive statistics on prisoners held on religious and political charges, conservative estimates put the total number at around 7,000. Local rights organizations estimated that in 2001 at least thirty people per week were convicted for alleged crimes related to their religious affiliation or beliefs. The majority of cases involved those accused of membership in Hizb ut-Tahrir (Party of Liberation), which espouses reestablishment of the Islamic Caliphate by peaceful means. The government of President Islam Karimov equated the group's beliefs and activities with attempted overthrow of the state, and authorities prosecuted any person in possession of the group's literature or in any way affiliated with it. They also prosecuted so-called Wahhabis, or Muslims who were not members of any organized group but who worshiped outside state controls and were subsequently branded "extremists" and "fundamentalists."

Those associated even loosely with well-known religious leaders branded as "Wahhabis" were tried in unfair proceedings on charges of conspiracy to overthrow the government, and sentenced to lengthy prison terms. On April 9, twelve men accused of taking Koran lessons and attending religious services at the mosque of Imam Abduvahid Yuldashev were sentenced to terms ranging from two-year suspended sentences to eighteen years of imprisonment. The men, who claimed that they had been engaged only in worship and study of Islamic texts, testified that police held them incommunicado and tortured them. A Tashkent court sentenced Imam Yuldashev himself to nineteen years in prison, ignoring his testimony that he was tortured and his family threatened.

Following a well-established pattern, authorities arrested or harassed the relatives of independent Muslim leaders. In at least one prominent case in 2001, police used a family member as a hostage to coerce an imam into cooperating with an investigation. On March 17, 2001, Tashkent police arrested Rahima Ahmedalieva, wife of Imam Ruhiddin Fahruddinov, whom authorities labeled a "Wahhabi" and who was believed to be in hiding, fearing arrest. Police held Akhmedalieva, conditioning her release on Fahruddinov's appearance for questioning. Police detained Akhmedalieva's nineteen-year-old daughter, Odina Maksudova, on March 20, threatened her with physical abuse, and forced her to write a statement incriminating her mother. They also threatened to send Akhmedalieva's minor children to an orphanage, "so [they] won't become 'Wahhabi,'" and tore off the religious headscarves worn by Maksudova and Akhmedalieva, ordering the younger woman not to wear religious dress again. Maksudova was released the next day.

On March 26, when Maksudova filed an appeal on behalf of her mother to the United Nations with the office of the United Nations Development Programme, police confiscated the appeal from a U.N. employee, detained Maksudova as she left the U.N. building, and forced her to disavow the appeal. On September 21, Akhmedalieva was sentenced to seven years in prison for alleged anti-state activities.

On August 23, President Karimov issued an amnesty decree for various categories of prisoners, excluding those charged with anti-state activities or sentenced to lengthy terms for alleged membership in banned religious organizations. However, an unknown number of religious prisoners sentenced earlier to relatively short terms in prison were reportedly released following the amnesty decree.

Notwithstanding the government's longstanding policy of dispersing unsanctioned public demonstrations, women in various parts of Uzbekistan protested the campaign against independent Muslims. On March 21, 2001, an estimated three hundred demonstrators, primarily women, took to the streets in Andijan to demand the release of their male relatives, imprisoned for their religious affiliations and beliefs. The participants reportedly carried signs reading, "2001: Year of the Widow and Orphan," a play on President Karimov's declaration of the year 2001 as the "Year of the Mother and Child." Police dispersed the demonstration and detained at least two female participants, carrying one off by her arms and legs.

Two days later, Andijan police reacted even more quickly to disperse a followup protest. Officers allegedly detained female demonstrators violently, fined them each 2,200 som (approximately one month's salary), and threatened to extend the prison sentences of the women's jailed relatives if they did not submit statements asking for forgiveness for their actions. After another similar demonstration, local authorities organized a public meeting to denounce the protesters.

On April 12, 2001, police violently dispersed and detained some forty women protesting outside government buildings in Tashkent, injuring at least ten. A human rights defender who witnessed the protest reported that officers fired blanks over the women's heads. Most of the women were released the same day; four were released three days later. Police allegedly beat one of the women in custody.

September 4, 2001, saw two more protests organized by female relatives of independent Muslim prisoners, to voice dissatisfaction with the August amnesty decree. Police in Karshi arrested twelve of a group of about sixty women who called for the release of their loved ones. As of this writing, their whereabouts remained unknown. In Tashkent, police arrested another ten demonstrators, including Fatima Mukadirova, the mother of two young men imprisoned for alleged membership in Hizb ut-Tahrir. Arresting officers accused Mukadirova of membership in the Islamic group and placed her under arrest on charges that she attempted the violent overthrow of the Republic of Uzbekistan. On November 5, Mukadirova was given a three-year suspended prison sentence, under which she was to report to authorities every ten days.

In 2001, the government of Uzbekistan took an important step toward transparency in the prison system with its decision to allow access for the first time ever to the International Committee of the Red Cross (ICRC) to prison facilities. However, progress proved illusory. According to prisoners' relatives, the authorities consistently ordered prisoners not to speak to the international observers and temporarily transferred political and religious prisoners from facilities prior to the visits. Conditions in Uzbekistan's prisons remained ghastly. Overcrowding forced prisoners to sleep in turns. Meals were commonly limited to one loaf of bread for four men and one cup of tea. With poor hygiene, diseases such as dysentery, eczema, kidney ailments, and tuberculosis were rampant and claimed numerous lives. Authorities routinely denied prisoners access to medicine and medical attention.

Prison guards systematically beat prisoners with wooden and rubber truncheons and exacted particularly harsh punishment on those convicted on religious charges, subjecting them to additional beatings, and forcing them to sing the national anthem and recite poems praising the president and the state. Those who attempted to observe the five daily Muslim prayers were beaten and sometimes locked in isolation cells for days on end.

Torture remained endemic in pretrial custody as well, abetted by the practices of failing to notify family members of an individual's detention and holding people incommunicado, sometimes for up to six months. Authorities systematically tortured detainees to force them into giving testimony or self-incriminating statements and used it as a form of extrajudicial punishment. At least five suspicious deaths in pre- and postconviction custody in 2001 were likely due to torture, including that of a human rights defender. In all cases officials provided implausible explanations for the cause of death.

Police detained Emin Usmon on February 11, 2001, on suspicion of "religious radicalism," and on March 1 returned his corpse to his family. Usmon, a well-known writer and commentator in Uzbekistan, had spoken out on behalf of others held on such charges. Fifty to sixty police officers surrounded Usmon's neighborhood when his corpse was returned, stopped the family from holding a viewing of the body, demanding that they bury the body immediately and preventing relatives and neighbors from attending the funeral. Initially, police told the family that Usmon had committed suicide; however, the death certificate ultimately given to the family stated that he had died of a "brain tumor." No independent medical examination was allowed. Nonetheless, one relative alleged he saw clearly an open wound on the back of Usmon's head during the procedure of preparing the body for burial.

Police also offered an implausible explanation for the death of Hazrat Kadirov, a displaced person who had spoken out about poor conditions for those displaced from Surkhandaria province. Police officers detained Kadirov for "informal questioning" on December 11, 2000; three days later, they returned his corpse. Officials claimed that Kadirov had tried to escape police custody and then had died of a heart attack. A person who viewed Kadirov's body reported seeing multiple injuries.

On October 17, 2001, Tashkent police arrested brothers Ravshan and Rasul Haidov on suspicion of membership in Hizb ut-Tahrir. Ravshan's body was returned to his family on October 18. Those who viewed the body reported that the thirty-two-year-old's neck was broken, as was one leg below the knee; that his upper back was injured; and that his body was covered with bruises. The official cause of death was "heart attack." As of this writing, twenty-five-year-old Rasul Haidov reportedly remained in intensive care in a local hospital under armed guard.

In late December 2000, Habibullah Nosirov, a Hizb ut-Tahrir member imprisoned since 1999, reportedly died from injuries sustained during beatings in prison. He was the brother of Hafizullo Nosirov, who in March 2000 was convicted for being the reputed head of Hizb ut-Tahrir in Uzbekistan.

Uzbek authorities did not respond to repeated requests for information regarding the whereabouts in custody of Bahodir Hasanov, a teacher at the Alliance Française, who was arrested in July 2000. By November 2001, he was unaccounted for.

Journalist and artist Shukhrat Bobojonov was forced to flee Uzbekistan in August 2001 under fear of arrest. State prosecutors in his hometown of Urgench had repeatedly summoned Bobojonov for questioning relating to an investigation of his membership in the Union of Artists of Uzbekistan in the early 1990's. Internews reported that Bobojonov had objected to the government's 1999 closure of his independent television station in Urgench and that he had even sued to have his broadcast license reissued.

On October 23, the National Security Service (SNB) arrested Yusup Jumaev, a well-known Uzbek poet, stating that his poetry, published in 1994 and 2000, qualified as "anti-state activities." As of this writing, Jumaev was being held in the basement of the Bukhara district SNB, where he allegedly had been tortured.

Uzbekistan executed undisclosed numbers of persons by firing squad in 2001. On October 29, the Uzbek parliament amended the criminal code to reduce from eight to four the number of crimes punishable by death.

As part of its declared aim to counter the threat of Uzbek militants based outside Uzbekistan, the government mined its borders with Kyrgyzstan and Tajikistan, with mines killing an estimated thirty civilians and injuring numerous others in 2001, according to media and government reports.

In 2001, local and international human rights organizations uncovered evidence that authorities forcibly displaced approximately 3,500 mountain villagers from their homes near the Tajik border during and after the August 2000 IMU incursions. The government had reported that the civilians had fled. The displaced persons were relocated to centers where they were cut off from interaction with the general community and deprived of means of livelihood. The military prohibited the displaced persons' return to the area even to retrieve personal belongings and razed their homes to create a *cordon sanitaire* along the border.

Obstacles to women's escape from severe domestic violence and pursuit of remedies persisted at the local and national levels. In particular, neighborhood authorities, or *mahallah* committees, thwarted women's attempts to obtain divorces and split from violent husbands by preventing them from pursuing legal remedies when they asked for assistance and encouraging their return to violent households. The authorities thereby blocked women's access to the criminal justice system. These actions were consistent with a larger government campaign to "save the family" by maintaining a low divorce rate.

Female university students expelled since 1997 for wearing *hijab*, headscarves that covered their faces, were as in the past not permitted to rematriculate unless they removed their religious garb and agreed to pay tuition. All universities in Uzbekistan were state-run, and only a small percentage of students were normally required to pay tuition.

Government officials obstructed the registration of Christian and other non-Muslim religious groups, depriving them of legal status in Uzbekistan. Proselytism remained illegal. Authorities discouraged ethnic Uzbeks in particular from converting to Christianity. In 2001 several churches reported that local officials rejected congregation lists, required for registration, which included members with Uzbek names.

DEFENDING HUMAN RIGHTS

In 2001, the Uzbek government released two human rights activists who were wrongly convicted, but it continued to harass and arrest others. One defender died in police custody, an apparent victim of extrajudicial execution. In December 2000 President Karimov ordered the release of rights defender Mahbuba Kasymova of the Independent Human Rights Organization of Uzbekistan (IHROU). A mother of five, Kasymova served one and a half years of a five-year sentence on fabricated charges brought in retaliation for her efforts to expose police abuse against independent Muslims. However, shortly after her release, authorities in Tashkent briefly detained Kasymova and threatened to arrest her again if she continued to monitor trials of those brought up on religious charges.

Seven months after Kasymova's release, on July 3, another IHROU defender, Ismail Adylov, was released from prison after serving two years of a seven-year term on wholly spurious charges that he was a member of a banned religious organization. Upon his release Adylov revealed that prison authorities had denied him medical attention and had systematically beaten him during his incarceration. The authorities attempted to deny Adylov an exit visa—official permission still necessary for travel abroad—to travel to the United States to be honored for his human rights work. Only after intense intervention by diplomatic representatives, particularly the U.S. government, did the authorities grant Adylov permission to travel.

The chairman of the IHROU, Mikhail Ardzinov, continued to be denied his passport, which was confiscated at the time of his detention in 1999. Uzbek citizens must carry their passports with them at all times; travel within the country is difficult without this form of identification and travel outside the country is impossible. Persons without passports are routinely denied their pensions or other government assistance.

Any perceptions that the Karimov government grew more tolerant of rights defenders were shattered when police apparently tortured to death Shovruk Ruzimuradov, a long-time dissident and activist in the Human Rights Society of Uzbekistan (HRSU). Officers arrested Ruzimuradov, forty-four, on June 15 in his hometown in southwestern Uzbekistan, and held him incommunicado for some twenty-two days before returning his corpse to his family on July 7.

Police blocked all entry within one kilometer of the Ruzimuradov home and turned away fellow rights defenders who traveled from Tashkent to view the body and attend the funeral services. Police threatened to arrest the activists and "tear [them] to pieces" if they investigated the case further, and expelled them from the area. A preliminary report issued by state authorities gave the cause of death as "suicide by hanging." Shortly before his death, Ruzimuradov had spoken out publicly on the arrest and conviction of seventy-three men from Surkhandaria province, on charges of collaborating with armed insurgents in 2000. He also advocated on behalf of those forcibly displaced from Surkhandaria as part of the armed forces' "mop up" operation there.

Other members of HRSU in Tashkent, Jizzakh, Khorezm, Andijan, and Kashkadaria reported being temporarily detained, subjected to intimidating interrogation and threats, and otherwise harassed in 2001.

On April 6, 2001, police detained Elena Urlaeva, a member of HRSU who worked on behalf of people dispossessed of their homes by city authorities. Authorities forcibly committed her to a state mental hospital, where staff systematically medicated Urlaeva during two months of confinement, causing her severe medical problems. Finally, on June 30, 2001, after considerable international outcry, Urlaeva was allowed to leave the hospital and return home. However, on November 6, law enforcement agents raided the office of the state human rights ombudsman, where they arrested Urlaeva. Police cleared the office, searched Urlaeva, and took her into custody. The rights defender was first held under armed guard in a hospital ward in Tashkent and then transferred to a police holding facility. She was released on November 16.

THE ROLE OF THE INTERNATIONAL COMMUNITY

United Nations

In March 2001, the U.N. Human Rights Committee considered Uzbekistan's initial report on compliance with the International Covenant on Civil and Political Rights. The committee's concluding observations were frank and highly critical of the government's report and its lack of progress implementing basic rights. The committee expressed grave concern regarding reports of torture and inhumane treatment and stated that such allegations should be investigated and persons responsible prosecuted. It also expressed concern about impediments to detainees' access to legal counsel, prison conditions, particularly deaths in prison, and forced displacement of villagers. It added that it "deplores the State party's refusal to reveal the number of persons who have been executed or condemned to death, and the grounds for their conviction . . . ."

In its February concluding observations on Uzbekistan's initial report, the U.N. Committee on the Elimination of Discrimination against Women requested that the government ". . . enact laws on violence, especially on domestic violence, including marital rape, as soon as possible and . . . ensure that violence against women and girls constitutes a crime punishable under criminal law and that women and girl victims of violence have immediate means of redress and protection." The committee also requested that the Uzbekistan government provide more information on the trafficking of women and girls.

European Union

The E.U.-Uzbekistan Cooperation Council met in January 2001 to discuss implementation of the Partnership and Cooperation Agreement (PCA), signed in July 1999. The two parties agreed to intensify cooperation in the areas of trade and investment, and to continue political dialogue. The E.U. reportedly raised human rights and rule of law issues, and future E.U. assistance to Uzbekistan for training members of the judiciary. The PCA requires that partner states guarantee basic civil and political rights. The statement following the January meeting praised the Uzbek government for granting the ICRC access to prisons.

Organization for Security and Cooperation in Europe (OSCE)

In December 2000, the Organization for Security and Cooperation in Europe (OSCE) renegotiated its presence in Uzbekistan with the government, renaming its office in Tashkent the OSCE Center. Similar centers had already been established in the other Central Asian states.

The OSCE office undertook training sessions in women's rights and continued a series of training seminars for local rights defenders. Its representatives visited Elena Urlaeva while she was forcibly confined to a mental institution.

A June visit to Central Asia by OSCE Chairman-in-office Mircea Geoana failed to include meetings in Uzbekistan. The official explanation given by the government of Uzbekistan was scheduling problems. A subsequent visit to Uzbekistan in October 2001 included meetings with President Karimov and other government officials. Scheduling problems reduced a planned meeting between the chairman-in-office and human rights defenders, a group at particular risk, to a very brief forum together with journalists; the human rights leaders had no opportunity to present issues of concern to the OSCE head.

United States

After years of relative obscurity in the U.S. foreign policy making community, Uzbekistan became an essential U.S. ally in the post-September 11 coalition against terrorism. As of this writing, it was too soon to judge whether the Bush administration's "qualitatively new relationship" with the Uzbek government would translate into enhanced pressure for human rights improvements, or whether it would be yet another squandered opportunity for leverage.

The United States' diplomatic initiatives in late 2000 succeeded in pressing the Uzbek government to allow the ICRC access to prisons. The agreement, finalized in record time, marked the first formal acceptance by the government of Uzbekistan of foreign monitors in prison and pretrial detention facilities. U.S. insistence on Uzbekistan's compliance with legislation known as the Cooperative Threat Reduction program, which states that countries receiving assistance under this program must be "committed to observing internationally recognized human rights," also resulted in the release from prison of prominent human rights activists Mahbuba Kasymova and Ismail Adylov. U.S. intervention also aided Adylov in receiving an exit visa to travel outside Uzbekistan in November 2001.

In October 2001, the U.S. government failed to designate Uzbekistan as a "country of particular concern for religious freedom" under the terms of the 1998 U.S. International Religious Freedom Act.

The United States offered security and financial assistance in exchange for use of an air base in Uzbekistan for the U.S. military operation in Afghanistan. At least 1,000 U.S. troops from the 10th Mountain Division were deployed to an Uzbek military base by mid-October. Unofficial reports also indicated that U.S. bombers had targeted the Afghanistan-based training camps of the IMU, which the United States in 2000 had placed on a list of terrorist organizations.

After meeting with U.S. Secretary of Defense Donald Rumsfeld during his November visit to the region, Uzbek Minister of Defense Qodir Guliamov stated that the military had benefited from training and joint exercises with U.S. forces and hinted that he expected other types of aid to be forthcoming. "I am confident that the kind of cooperation which is being developed now is characterized by a higher level [sic], and consequently I am positive that the forms of our cooperation with change accordingly," Guliamov said. The September 11 events also brought to light past U.S. assistance to, and joint covert operations with, Uzbekistan in efforts against Osama bin Laden.

Recognizing the potential human rights consequences of military assistance to Uzbekistan, the U.S. Congress adopted an amendment to the Foreign Operations Appropriation Act with new reporting requirements. Under the amendment, the

State Department must provide a list of U.S. security aid given to Uzbekistan, how Uzbek units used the defense articles and services, and which units engaged in violations of human rights or international humanitarian law during the reporting period.

In 2001, Uzbekistan received $63.57 million in U.S. assistance and $136 million in U.S. Export-Import Bank credits, which were granted through a certification process that included human rights conditions.

Relevant Human Rights Watch Reports:

Memorandum to the U.S. Government Regarding Religious Persecution in Uzbekistan, 8/01.
Sacrificing Women to Save the Family?: Domestic Violence in Uzbekistan, 7/01
Uzbekistan: "And it Was Hell All over Again . . .": Torture in Uzbekistan, 12/00.

FEDERAL REPUBLIC OF YUGOSLAVIA

SERBIA AND MONTENEGRO

HUMAN RIGHTS DEVELOPMENTS

The December 2000 Serbian parliamentary elections consolidated the transition from the authoritarian rule of former president Slobodan Milosevic, with the Democratic Opposition of Serbia (DOS) winning 64 percent of the vote. In Montenegro, the early elections in April 2001 served as an informal referendum about the status of the smaller of the two Yugoslav republics. Pro-independence parties only won slightly over half the votes, less than generally anticipated, but the ruling coalition continued to boycott the work of the federal institutions. The authorities in Serbia and Montenegro made little progress toward solving the federal constitutional crisis, but the real risk of armed conflict under the Milosevic government gave way to a political process.

On April 1, Serb authorities arrested Milosevic on corruption charges. Faced with mounting pressure from human rights organizations, the United States, and the European Union to surrender Milosevic for war-crimes prosecution before the International Criminal Tribunal for the former Yugoslavia (ICTY), Yugoslav President Vojislav Kostunica and other officials argued that Milosevic's transfer required adoption of a law on cooperation with the ICTY first. The Yugoslav Ministry of Justice drafted a law in June, but the Montenegrin partner in the federal coalition government, the Socialist People's Party (SNP), blocked its adoption. On June 23, the cabinet, dominated by DOS members, adopted a cooperation decree in lieu of the law. The Federal Constitutional Court, filled with appointees from the Milosevic era, stayed application of the decree while examining its constitutionality. To avoid the emerging political and legal gridlock, the government of Serbia transferred Milosevic to The Hague on June 28, invoking the Statute of the Tribunal and the Constitution of Serbia as the legal basis.

Progress on accountability for wartime abuses was otherwise disappointing. Serbian authorities arrested and surrendered to the tribunal indicted Bosnian Serb Milomir Stakic on March 23, and Bosnian Serb brothers Nenad and Pedrag Banovic on November 9. Blagoje Simic, another Bosnian Serb living in Serbia, surrendered himself to the tribunal under pressure from the Serbian government, as did retired General Pavle Strugar and former naval commander Miodrag Jokic, who both had been indicted for crimes committed in Dubrovnik in 1991. Nonetheless, at the time of this writing, at least four senior Yugoslav and Serb officials or former officials remained at liberty in Serbia who were charged with crimes against humanity committed by troops under their command in Kosovo, along with three Yugoslav Army officials indicted on charges relating to the destruction of Vukovar and two other officers indicted for crimes committed at Dubrovnik.

Public debate on crimes committed by Serb forces in Kosovo and Bosnia slowly started in 2001. Between June and September, the police exhumed five mass graves in Serbia, containing more than three hundred bodies thought to be Kosovo Albanians killed by the police and the army during the 1999 NATO bombardment. In an unprecedented move, the state-run television showed a BBC documentary about the 1995 killings of more than 7,000 Bosnian Muslims in Srebrenica.

In contrast to the Milosevic era, the political opposition in Serbia could openly express its views and operate free of government harassment. The new government initiated criminal investigations into corruption and other charges against dozens of former Milosevic cronies, with the proceedings apparently driven by the demands of the rule of law rather than by political revanchism. Only one of these cases had proceeded to trial as of October, resulting in convictions for former head of Serbian State Security Radomir Markovic and two of his closest collaborators. Their trial was closed to the public on grounds of state security, raising questions about the fairness of the proceedings.

The Serbian parliament replaced fifty-seven of two hundred presidents of municipal courts by July 2001, substantially clearing the judiciary of Milosevic appointees. Although the new government stopped short of exerting direct pressure on the judiciary, well-known judges repeatedly complained that pro-government media and some politicians obstructed judicial independence by publicly recommending criminal prosecutions and "appropriate" punishments.

An amnesty law adopted in February covered Kosovo Albanians convicted for seditious conspiracy and armed rebellion, but not those convicted on terrorism charges. When Slobodan Milosevic was ousted from power in October 2000, 850 Kosovo Albanian prisoners detained during the 1999 Kosovo war remained in Serbian prisons. By August 2001, an estimated 225 Kosovo Albanian prisoners remained, an estimated fifty of whom had been sentenced for political reasons in unfair trials.

The new Serbian government generally respected freedom of expression. Some media were closer to one or the other party in the political conflict between nationalist Yugoslav President Vojislav Kostunica and pro-Western Serbian Prime Minister Zoran Djindjic, but neither leader directly controlled the state-run media or major private outlets.

The media in Montenegro generally operated free of government intrusion. In a surprising setback, on September 3, a court in Podgorica convicted the editor of the opposition daily *Dan* on a charge of criminal libel and handed down a suspended five-month prison sentence. The newspaper had published a series of articles on cigarette smuggling, implicating a businessman associated with Montenegrin President Milo Djukanovic.

The police practice of so-called informative talks, much abused during the Milosevic era, occasionally reappeared in 2001. On May 29, State Security agents interrogated student Milos Cvorovic, an activist in a nongovernmental group in Belgrade, about his contacts with Kosovo Albanians. A reporter from Valjevo with the daily *Blic*, Predrag Radojevic, was taken to the police station on July 12 for an "informative talk" about his work as a journalist. Radojevic had written a series of articles during the previous months on the presence of the mafia in the town. *Blic*'s editor-in-chief Veselin Simonovic was also interrogated on August 14, following the publication of an article about a former State Security agent who was killed on August 3.

The authorities in Belgrade made positive steps toward reducing ethnic tensions in the Presevo valley, where ethnic Albanians were a majority of the population. As a result of months-long negotiations, armed Albanian groups there voluntarily disbanded in May, and civilian life began returning to normal. At the end of May the first multiethnic police patrols were deployed in the area, following a short training course under the auspices of the Organization for Security and Cooperation in Europe (OSCE). Two more courses were completed by mid-July. Nearly 4,000 of the estimated 15,000 local Albanians who had left their homes during and after the 1999 Kosovo conflict returned in June and July 2001.

Police brutality against Roma was a common occurrence in 2001. On September 22, two policemen broke the arm of a fourteen-year-old boy in Novi Sad after beating him and a group of other Roma children. Police in Leskovac detained Daka Zekic, a seventy-six-year-old Roma for two days in January, deprived him of food and water, and subjected him to beatings and racial insults. On March 5, four policemen beat and uttered racial insults against Miroslav Milic, a Roma teenager from Belgrade. On May 7, three police officers in Backa Topola beat up and uttered racial slurs against two Roma villagers, Stevan Brancic and Sasa Gojkov. In a positive development that may help counter these abuses, the Federal Republic of Yugoslavia acceded to the Framework Convention for the Protection of National Minorities on May 11.

According to a large-scale recount of refugees in the Federal Republic of Yugoslavia, 390,000 persons from Croatia and Bosnia were registered as refugees, a 30 percent drop from 1996 figures. The government failed to support the return of Serb refugees to their pre-war homes in Croatia and Bosnia, while facilitating Serb refugee integration in Yugoslavia. The Serbian commissioner for refugees stated that between 230,000 and 250,000 internally displaced persons from Kosovo also lived in Serbia proper.

DEFENDING HUMAN RIGHTS

With the one known exception of the police interrogation of Milos Cvorovic, human rights activists carried out their activities free of government intrusion. The positive change reflected the fact that several human rights and minority rights advocates, including federal ministers Goran Svilanovic, Momcilo Grubac, and Rasim Ljajic, assumed prominent positions in the government. The Humanitarian Law Center continued to be the leading source of reliable information on the treatment of Roma, police brutality, and violations committed by all parties in Kosovo. Among other leading human rights groups were the Helsinki Committee for Human Rights, the Belgrade Center for Human Rights, the Yugoslav Lawyers' Committee for Human Rights, and the Leskovac Council for Human Rights.

THE ROLE OF THE INTERNATIONAL COMMUNITY

United Nations

On November 1, 2000, the General Assembly approved admission of the Federal Republic of Yugoslavia to membership in the United Nations. Yugoslav efforts toward a peaceful settlement of the crisis in the Presevo valley won praise from the Security Council in December 2000 and from the U.N. Commission on Human Rights in April 2001. The commission expressed its concern at the continued detention in Serbia of Kosovo Albanian political prisoners, however, and replaced the long-standing mandate of its special rapporteur for human rights in the former Yugoslavia with a special representative to examine the situation of human rights in Yugoslavia and Bosnia and Herzegovina. The special representative, Jose Cutileiro, visited Yugoslavia at the end of August and the beginning of September. Examining the first individual petition from Yugoslavia, the Committee against Torture concluded on May 11 that Yugoslavia had violated its obligations under the Convention against Torture since its government agencies had failed to investigate promptly and effectively allegations regarding the torture of Milan Ristic, who died in February 1995 of injuries inflicted by the police.

The Federal Republic of Yugoslavia signed the Statute of the International Criminal Court on December 19, 2000, and it ratified the statute on September 6, 2001.

Organization for Security and Cooperation in Europe (OSCE)

Yugoslavia, which was suspended from the OSCE in July 1992, became a participating state following a decision by the OSCE Permanent Council on November 10, 2000. An International Election Observation Mission, including representatives of the OSCE Office for Democratic Institutions and Human Rights (ODIHR) and the OSCE Parliamentary Assembly, concluded that the December 2000 elections in Serbia were conducted in line with accepted international standards. An ODIHR mission also monitored the April 22 elections in Montenegro and found the entire electoral process transparent. On March 16, the OSCE opened a mission office in Belgrade.

Council of Europe

On November 9, 2001, Yugoslavia applied for Council of Europe membership. In January, the Parliamentary Assembly granted special guest status to the Federal Assembly of Yugoslavia and adopted conditions for membership. Among other conditions, it called on Yugoslavia to cooperate fully with the ICTY and to surrender war crimes suspects, to carry out legislative reforms including the abolition of the death penalty, and to amnesty political prisoners. On March 16, a Council of Europe office was opened in Belgrade for a renewable one-year term. The Parliamentary Assembly representatives who made up part of the International Election Observation Mission that monitored the December 23, 2000, parliamentary election in Serbia praised the way in which they were conducted. A delegation from the Parliamentary Assembly also observed and positively assessed the elections in Montenegro in April 2001.

European Union

After the fall of Slobodan Milosevic in October 2000, the European Union provided 200 million euros (U.S. $168 million) to help Serbia with electricity, heating fuel, and food payments during the winter. On February 27, 2001, European Union foreign ministers lifted all sanctions imposed on the Federal Republic of Yugoslavia since 1998, except the financial, trade, and travel restrictions on firms and individuals connected to the Milosevic regime. On April 10, the European Commission allocated the first part of a 240 million euros aid program for Yugoslavia to support energy supply, healthcare, agriculture, and medium-sized companies. Included in that sum was the allocation of 49.5 million euros for human rights projects. In mid-July, the Council of Ministers invested 300 million euros in macro financial aid for the Federal Republic of Yugoslavia, consisting of 225 million euros in loans and 75 million euros in grants.

While E.U. bodies called on the new authorities in Belgrade to cooperate with the International Criminal Tribunal for the former Yugoslavia, they failed to condition financial assistance on the country's cooperation. The European Parliament called on the Yugoslav government to release all political prisoners by presidential pardon or on the basis of an amnesty law.

In November of 2001, the European Union and a Federal Republic of Yugoslavia Consultative Task Force met in Belgrade to discuss various topics, including democracy, human rights and minority issues as well as regional cooperation and compliance with international obligations. The commissioner for external relations, Chris Patton, visited the Federal Republic of Yugoslavia in October. The two parties hoped to initiate discussions that would draw the Federal Republic of Yugoslavia closer to the European Union. Further meetings were expected in 2002.

United States

The U.S. Congress prohibited the continuation of economic aid to Belgrade past March 31, 2001, unless Yugoslavia arrested and transferred those indicted by the war crimes tribunal to its custody, cut off economic assistance to the Bosnian Serb army, and took steps in democratization and minority protection. The conditionality placed considerable pressure on Serb and Yugoslav authorities and contributed to the eleventh-hour detention of Slobodan Milosevic on April 1. On April 2, the secretary of state certified the conditions for continued aid were present but stressed that the United States' support for the holding of an international donors conference for Yugoslavia would depend on the country's continued progress toward full cooperation with the tribunal. Lack of progress and the refusal of the United States to participate led to a postponement of the conference from May 31 to the end of June. On the eve of the conference, Serbian and Yugoslav officials firmly committed themselves to cooperation, and on June 28 Slobodan Milosevic was transferred to the custody of the tribunal. The United States participated at the conference and pledged U.S.$182 million, the largest individual state pledge.

KOSOVO

HUMAN RIGHTS DEVELOPMENTS

In the third year of Kosovo's international administration the human rights situation in the province continued to be of serious concern. Violence and hostility rendered normal life impossible for Serbs, Roma, and other minorities. Participation of minorities in the November 2001 elections for the Kosovo Assembly gave, however, some hope for the prospects of ethnic coexistence in the province. The U.N. administration came under growing local and international criticism for attempting to improve the security situation by curtailing fundamental rights. And despite the efforts of the United Nations, the administration of justice continued to suffer from judicial bias, inadequate enforcement of human rights norms, and poor investigations of serious crimes.

Ibrahim Rugova's Democratic League of Kosovo (Lidhja Demokratike e Kosovës, LDK) overwhelmingly won the October 2000 municipal elections with 58 per cent of the overall vote and a majority in twenty-four out of thirty municipal assemblies. The main parties led by former KLA commanders, the Democratic Party of Kosovo (PDK), and the Alliance for the Future of Kosovo (AAK), fared less well, receiving 27.3 and 7.7 percent of the vote, respectively. Members of the more moderate LDK suffered numerous violent attacks in the months preceding the election. Moreover, the elections were marred by the collective refusal of the Kosovo Serb community to register and vote. While the United Nations Interim Administration Mission in Kosovo (UNMIK) pointed to the Belgrade authorities' influence over the Serb community's decision, the preelection environment was rife with incidents of violence and intimidation against members of the minority groups. After the elections, the special representative of the U.N. secretary-general (SRSG), who exercises ultimate legislative and executive power in Kosovo, appointed municipal assemblies in three localities with a majority Serb population. Representatives of Kosovo's Ashkalija, Bosniac, Egyptian, and Roma minority communities generally accepted appointments to the new local government bodies.

In May 2001, UNMIK promulgated a Constitutional Framework for Provisional Self-Government in Kosovo. The framework contained guarantees for the rights of the minority communities and their members, including proportional or equal representation in parliamentary committees, and safeguards against simple outvoting by the majority on matters related to the minorities' "vital interests." UNMIK retained exclusive authority in the sensitive areas of the judiciary, law enforcement, and external relations. The framework incorporated into the document a number of international human rights treaties that are directly applicable in Kosovo. Its human rights chapter suffered, however, from two serious omissions: the failure to incorporate the International Covenant on Economic, Social and Cultural Rights and the lack of any judicial review mechanisms through which individuals and groups would enforce their constitutional rights. A special constitutional chamber was established within the Supreme Court, but only governmental actors were given standing to file motions with the chamber.

Whatever promise the new Constitutional Framework held for the future of the Kosovo's minorities, their members—the Serbs and Roma in particular—continued to face severe threats to their personal safety, freedom of movement, and socioeconomic well-being. The year 2001 saw some of the worst cases since the end of the NATO campaign of organized violence targeting minorities, who make up a disproportionate 20 percent of the victims of major crimes. In late January and early February, Serb homes, churches, and cultural sites were damaged by mortar fire and other similar attacks. Some of these sites had been designated for the accommodation of potential returnees. On February 13, a convoy of Kosovo Serbs en route to Strpce, escorted by peacekeepers of the multinational Kosovo Force (KFOR), was the target of a shooting that left one person dead. Only three days later a weekly convoy of civilian buses carrying about 250 Serbs to Gracanica, with a KFOR escort of seven armored vehicles, fell victim to a brutal bomb attack killing eleven people and injuring dozens. On April 18, the head of the Federal Republic of Yugoslavia passport office in Prishtina, Aleksandar Petrovic, was killed in yet another deadly bomb attack.

Attacks on minorities appeared to be increasingly focused and sophisticated. Groups of Serbs and Roma returning from Serbia and other neighboring countries were frequent victims of armed attacks. On November 9, 2000, three Ashkalija men and a fifteen-year-old boy were shot dead, in execution style killings, a few days after they had returned to Dosevac near Prishtina. Another group of Roma that had recently gone back to Shtime was injured in a bomb attack on August 8. In August 2001 the first organized return of a group of fifty-four Serb refugees to Osojane was followed by ethnic Albanian protests in nearby Istok. These and other incidents had a devastating effect on the efforts of the international community to help refugees and internally displaced persons return to their homes. The number of returnees remained very small, and in some areas more minority residents were still leaving Kosovo than returning.

Non-Albanians were not the only victims of organized violence. In November 2000, Xhemal Mustafa, a chief aide to Rugova and head of the Kosovo Information Center, was assassinated in central Pristina. A pattern of politically motivated killings which began in the spring of 2000 continued in 2001 with several attacks against Kosovar Albanian political activists, generally LDK supporters. In April 2001, unidentified gunmen murdered Ismet Rraci, Mayor of Klina and chairman of the local LDK branch. On September 1, the houses of two LDK officials from the villages of Belobrod and Brodosavce were bombed. However, no other serious incidents took place in the run-up to the November 17 general election, and the election day itself was largely peaceful.

Twenty-six political parties and independent candidates, including representatives of five minority groups, were certified by the OSCE to contest the November election. These included a coalition of twenty Kosovo Serb parties and organizations, named Coalition Return, which decided to register at the last minute. In contrast with the 2000 municipal elections, Kosovo Serb and other minority voters registered in large numbers: 70,000 within the province and an additional 100,000 in Serbia and Montenegro. And in spite of the drawn-out hesitation both in Belgrade and among the Kosovo Serbs about their participation in the vote, about 46 percent of all eligible Kosovo Serb voters turned out to vote on November 17. In northern Kosovo, where Serbian extremists were responsible for widespread intimidation of voters into abstention, the participation of ethnic Serbs was considerably lower than the average.

Trafficking of women into Kosovo for forced prostitution continued to surge in 2001: the International Organization for Migration reported that 160 trafficked women and girls received repatriation assistance between February 2000 and May 2001. Implementation of a new UNMIK regulation providing for victim and witness assistance came slowly, and only a handful of prosecutions went forward. The United Nations disciplined four civilian police officers for alleged involvement in trafficking. According to a report issued by the OSCE Legal Systems Monitoring Section, women who brought charges for domestic violence, rape, or trafficking faced bias, discrimination, and contempt from the judicial system, and the average sentence for sexual violence cases declined from three years to one year.

DEFENDING HUMAN RIGHTS

The Humanitarian Law Center (HLC) looked into allegations of unlawful detention and monitored trials against Kosovo Serbs charged with war crimes and other serious offences. In one case it protested to UNMIK when international authorities at the Mitrovica prison denied an HLC attorney access to his clients and conducted unlawful searches of his effects. The Council for the Defense of Human Rights and Freedoms continued to monitor and report regularly on human rights violations in the province. Although the council was still more sensitive to violations of the rights of ethnic Albanians than those of non-Albanians, it condemned attacks against minority members in stronger terms than in previous years. The Ombudsperson Institution, which started work in November 2000, dealt mostly with complaints related to property rights, employment controversies, due process, and personal security. The Ombudsperson, Marek Antoni Nowicki, issued a number of public reports on human rights violations by the U.N. administration, and requested the latter to remedy them. One report concluded that a 2000 regulation on privileges and immunities granted to KFOR and UNMIK violated the property and due process rights of Kosovar individuals; another report looked into the lawfulness of cases of executive detention ordered by the SRSG and found them in violation of the defendants' rights to a fair trial.

THE ROLE OF THE INTERNATIONAL COMMUNITY

United Nations

In response to the unsatisfactory performance of the justice and law enforcement systems, UNMIK created a new justice and police component and adopted legislation to combat organized crime, weapons trafficking, and terrorism. But these measures did not result in any significant improvement in the overall security situation. Most major incidents of ethnic and political violence remained unresolved, while the SRSG ordered the prolonged detention of certain suspects. Following widespread criticism of its practices of administrative detention, in September UNMIK set up a commission of international legal experts to make final decisions on the legality of administrative detentions. A new UNMIK regulation authorized potential victims of ethnic bias in the criminal justice system to request that their case be tried by a panel with a majority of international judges. The number of international judges and prosecutors, however, fell short of what was needed to implement the regulation. UNMIK's failure to adequately consult and involve local and international organizations in drafting legislation also caused frustration.

Acting pursuant to an indictment charging Slobodan Milosevic and four other Yugoslav and Serbian officials with crimes against humanity and violations of the laws and customs of war committed in Kosovo, the Serbian authorities handed Milosevic over to the International Criminal Tribunal for the former Yugoslavia on June 28, 2001. The tribunal was also investigating allegations of crimes committed by the KLA during the 1998-1999 conflict in Kosovo; however, it had issued no public indictments at the time of writing. The U.N.'s special rapporteur on human rights in the former Yugoslavia at the time, Jiri Dienstbier, reported in January and March 2001 on the human rights situation in Kosovo. The U.N. Commission on Human Rights appointed José Cutileiro as its special representative with a one-year mandate to monitor the human rights situation in certain parts of the former Yugoslavia, including Kosovo.

Organization for Security and Cooperation in Europe (OSCE)

The OSCE Mission in Kosovo (OMIK) continued to monitor and report on the situation of Kosovo's minorities and the human rights performance of the justice system. A February OSCE report highlighted the persistence of bias in criminal proceedings, the absence of habeas corpus procedures, and the lack of effective access to defense counsel. The OSCE was particularly critical of several convictions of Kosovo Serbs and Roma charged with war crimes and genocide, which its monitors found inconsistent with the evidence presented in the courtroom. In one of the genocide cases, the OSCE called for review of the sentence by a panel of international judges. The organization of the November elections in line with international standards was a major challenge for the OSCE, which cooperated with the International Organization for Migration to open registration centers for Kosovo refugees in neighboring countries.

North Atlantic Treaty Organization (NATO)

The 40,000-strong NATO-led KFOR made greater efforts in 2001 to cooperate with the U.N. civilian police in confronting organized violence and crime. In a number of cases, however, it refused to share information with U.N. officials investigating serious crimes in which members of the Kosovo Protection Corps (KPC) were thought to be implicated. In an attempt to address a major public relations problem, KFOR offered to review Kosovar claims relating to land and properties damaged or taken by its troops without compensation. Between November 2000 and June 2001 the ombudsperson received sixty-two compensation claims against KFOR, despite making it clear that he lacked jurisdiction over the multinational force.

European Union

In January 2001 the European Union called on the Belgrade authorities to release Kosovo Albanian political prisoners detained in Serbia. E.U. officials condemned the violent attacks against Kosovo's minorities and threatened to withdraw promised economic aid if violence did not stop. The European Union nevertheless continued to be Kosovo's main donor, with 362.5 million euros pledged in 2001 for reconstruction assistance and humanitarian aid.

United States

The incoming U.S. administration avoided a blow to the stability of Kosovo and the Balkans by declaring that the United States had no intention of withdrawing troops unilaterally from the region. In July President Bush blacklisted five senior KPC officers for their support of the ethnic Albanian armed insurgency in Macedonia. The five were promptly discharged by the head of UNMIK. U.S. officials came under criticism, however, for their alleged failure to support criminal investigations involving top KPC officials, and in some cases for attempting to unduly influence the investigations.

Relevant Human Rights Watch Reports:

Under Orders: War Crimes in Kosovo, 10/01

MIDDLE EAST AND NORTH AFRICA

In Egypt, the government maintained its crackdown on human rights activists with the trial and conviction of democracy advocate Saadeddin Ibrahim and twenty-seven co-defendants.

MIDDLE EAST AND
NORTH AFRICA OVERVIEW

HUMAN RIGHTS DEVELOPMENTS

Clashes between Israelis and Palestinians that erupted in September 2000 overshadowed most other developments in the Middle East and North Africa region. Over seven hundred Palestinians and over two hundred Israelis, many of them civilians, were killed in the violence by November 2001. The conflict was marked by attacks on civilians and civilian objects by both Israeli security forces and Palestinian armed groups, suggesting that respect for fundamental human rights and humanitarian law principles counted for little among leaders of either side.

Israeli security forces were responsible for extensive abuses, including indiscriminate and excessive use of lethal force against unarmed Palestinian demonstrators; unlawful killings by Israel Defense Forces (IDF) soldiers; disproportionate IDF gunfire in response to Palestinian attacks; and inadequate IDF response to abuses by Israeli settlers against Palestinian civilians; and "closure" measures on Palestinian communities that amounted to collective punishment. They also mounted a series of killings of suspected Palestinian militants under a controversial "liquidations" policy directed against those believed responsible for orchestrating attacks against Israelis.

For its part, the Palestinian Authority (PA) did little to exercise its responsibility to take all possible measures to prevent and punish armed attacks by Palestinians against Israeli civilians, including suicide bombings. In addition, the various security forces of the Palestinian Authority carried out arbitrary arrests of alleged Palestinian "collaborators" with Israel. Many were held in prolonged detention without trial and tortured; others were sentenced to death after unfair trials and two were executed. The PA also arrested some Islamist and other militants suspected of responsibility for attacks against Israelis and held them in untried detention. Both Israeli and Palestinian authorities failed to take the necessary steps to stop the security forces under their control from committing abuses, and failed to adequately investigate and punish the perpetrators.

But even this current *intifada* dropped from international attention following the devastating September 11 attacks on New York and Washington, and in some cases governments in the region welcomed that shift of focus to justify their abusive policies. Egypt's leaders were quick to draw parallels that justified their government's harsh record. Prime Minister Atef Abeid decried human rights groups for "calling on us to give these terrorists their 'human rights,'" referring to documented reports of torture and unfair trials, and suggested that Western countries should "think of Egypt's own fight and terror as their new model." President Husni Mubarak was categorical: "those who carry out terrorist acts have no claims to human rights." In November, Egypt put ninety-four civilians, most of whom were arrested in May, on trial before a military tribunal on charges of forming a secret organization to commit terrorist acts. Three days after the September 11 attacks, Israeli Defense Minister Binyamin Ben Eliezer noted, apparently with satisfaction: "It is a fact that we have killed fourteen Palestinians in Jenin, Kabatyeh, and Tammum, with the world remaining absolutely silent," while Prime Minister Ariel Sharon repeatedly referred to Palestinian Authority President Yasir Arafat as "our Bin Laden." In October, Jordan amended its penal code and press law in order, according to Prime Minister Ali Abu Ragheb, "to cover all the needs that we are confronting now." The amendments empowered the government to close down any publications deemed to have published "false or libelous information that can undermine national unity or the country's reputation," and prescribed prison terms for publicizing in the media or on the Internet pictures "that undermine the king's dignity" or information tarnishing the reputation of the royal family.

At the same time, the fact that key al-Qaeda leaders and most of the alleged perpetrators of the September 11 attacks were nationals of Saudi Arabia and Egypt prompted unprecedented discussion in the region as well as internationally concerning the bleak rights records of those countries and of violations of human rights across the region more generally.

By contrast, several initiatives taken across the region represented tentative but important steps to investigate and hold accountable the perpetrators of gross human rights violations, including torture, summary executions, and "disappearances." While the general pattern of violations across the region remained relatively unchanged, with progress in some areas but deterioration in others, this growing effort to bring to justice those responsible for past gross violations represented a change, and one that appeared to bode well for the future. In some cases, alleged perpetrators were prosecuted in domestic courts—in Iran, unfortunately, with a frustrating outcome—while in other cases justice was sought abroad under the principle of universal jurisdiction. As local human rights groups and lawyers continued to call for an end to impunity and campaigned actively on behalf of the International Criminal Court (ICC), it became increasingly clear that the international justice movement had not bypassed the region but enjoyed growing support there.

As these disparate yet determined efforts generated publicity, inspired others to action, and put past and current human rights abusers on notice, they indicated that a culture of accountability was beginning to develop in civil society and the judiciary. Disclosures by former intelligence officials in exile also suggested that impunity had become an issue within the ranks of some governments' internal security forces. In Egypt, a local criminal court sentenced the director of the maximum security Wadi Natroun II prison to a ten-year prison term for forgery and fabricating reports in an attempt to cover up the death under torture of a criminal convict. The court also sentenced one of the prison's senior officers to a seven-year term and four sergeants to five years for beating the inmate to death. The court's judgment constituted a clear victory for Egypt's beleaguered human rights community, which has long documented and criticized the prevailing climate of impunity for torture and deaths in custody. In another case, however, an officer at Cairo's Agouza police station received only a two-year prison term for beating a detainee to death.

In Iran, a court convicted fifteen intelligence officials in January in connection with the 1998 killings of four intellectuals and political figures, and sentenced three of them to death and five to life imprisonment. The proceedings were mostly secret, however, and the trial was flawed, so information about who had ordered the murders did not emerge. An attorney for two of the defendants sought to call ten witnesses prepared to testify that former Minister of Intelligence Ghorbanali Dori Najafabadi, now a senior judicial official, who had not been indicted, had ordered the murders, but the court did not permit them to appear. Iranian investigative journalists also reported on connections between the death squads and state institutions and suggested that Dori Najafabadi and another former information minister, Ali Fallahian, were involved. In August, the Supreme Court reversed the convictions of the fifteen officials; in November, it remained unclear whether they would be retried.

In Tunisia, President Zine el-Abidine Ben Ali stated publicly more than once that his government would hold abusive members of the security forces accountable, but a climate of impunity generally prevailed and the justice system was widely perceived as an element of state repression. In July, however, a court sentenced four prison guards to four-year prison terms for torturing a criminal suspect and ordered the state to pay the victim compensation.

In Morocco, the nongovernmental Moroccan Human Rights Association (AMDH) publicly demanded that the justice minister bring charges against fourteen alleged torturers, including still-serving senior security officials and a member of parliament, but the minister did not do so. Subsequently, and perhaps as a consequence, the authorities detained thirty-six AMDH and other activists when they tried to hold a peaceful public protest in favor of accountability for past human rights abuses; they were prosecuted and initially sentenced to three months in prison, but then acquitted on appeal in November.

In Yemen too, despite a general climate of impunity, a court convicted three Criminal Investigation Department (CID) police officers in November 2000 in connection with the death of a detainee in custody, sentencing them to three-year prison terms, loss of rank and dismissal. Relatives of the victim lodged an appeal, seeking longer sentences commensurate with the offense. In November 2001, eight members of Central Security, an arm of the Interior Ministry, were awaiting trial in al-Dhali' province for the premeditated murder of a member of the opposition Yemeni Socialist Party; they were charged in July.

The search for justice also brought advocates to European courts to press their claims, an effort that was foreshadowed in late 1999 when Bahraini exiles and British human rights campaigners sought to initiate legal action in the United Kingdom against Ian Henderson, former head of Bahrain's notorious Security Intelligence Service. Tunisian torture victims pursued legal action against former Interior Minister Abdellah Kallel in Switzerland, where he was receiving medical care; after a Swiss prosecutor opened a preliminary investigation, citing Switzerland's obligations as a state party to the United Nations (U.N.) Convention against Torture, Kallel quickly left the country. And in Belgium, survivors of the September 1982 massacre by Lebanese Phalange militia of hundreds of Palestinian and other civilians at Sabra and Shatilla refugee camps in Beirut lodged a complaint against Israeli Prime Minister Ariel Sharon. He was Israel's defense minister at the time of the massacre and permitted the militia to enter the camps. Also, in late November, a Jerusalem-based organization lodged a complaint in Brussels against Palestinian Authority President Yasser Arafat, accusing him of crimes against humanity.

Activists in Morocco, aided by detailed disclosures in the country's newspapers, pressed for truth and accountability for the fierce repression practiced against dissidents during the "dirty war" of the 1960s and 1970s. One high-profile case was that of opposition leader Mehdi Ben Barka, who "disappeared" after he was picked up on a Paris street by French police and driven away in a police vehicle in October 1965. An investigating judge in France initiated an inquiry but was unable to obtain testimony from former Moroccan secret police officer Ahmed Boukhari, who alleged that Ben Barka died in France under interrogation by Moroccan agents, because Moroccan authorities imprisoned him on spurious charges. A coalition of international human rights groups urged the U.S. and French governments to declassify and release all official documents related to the case.

There were calls in Syria too for a hard look at several decades of brutal human rights abuses, but the government rounded up leading dissidents in an undisguised attempt to quash demands for reform and accountability. Human rights activist Nizar Nayouf, in France for medical treatment after nine years of imprisonment in Syria, insisted on efforts to address the horrors of his country's political past, including the summary execution of as many as 1,100 Islamist inmates at the infamous Tadmor military prison. Members of the paramilitary Defense Brigades carried out the killings over several hours on June 27, 1980, in retaliation for an assassination attempt on then President Hafez al-Asad a day earlier.

Defectors from Iraq's security apparatus continued to provide detailed information about gross human rights abuses, although a legal case against Saddam Hussein for crimes against humanity was yet to materialize. In November 2000, former Iraqi intelligence officer Captain Khalid Sajed al-Janabi alleged that a March 1998 presidential directive to "clean up Iraqi prisons" resulted in the execution of some 2,000 detainees and sentenced prisoners at Baghdad's notorious Abu Ghraib prison on April 27, 1998. A physician who worked in the prison's hospital, and fled to Jordan in July 2001, said that mass executions continued, mostly of political detainees identified by number rather than name. In some cases, according to his account, doctors were forced to inject detainees with poisons but attribute their deaths to natural causes.

The growing but still nascent efforts to press for accountability for past abuses were also reflected in the process by which governments in the region acceded to the International Criminal Court treaty of July 17, 1998. The court, which will prosecute crimes of genocide, crimes against humanity, and war crimes if national courts fail to respond, initially had a lukewarm reception from governments in the region. Only Jordan signed the treaty in 1998, and Israel and Iraq were among the seven states that voted against it. However, faced with a December 31, 2000, deadline to sign and thereby play a role in the development of the court, twelve countries in the region did so, most of them in the closing weeks of 2000. Algeria, Bahrain, Egypt, Iran, Israel, Kuwait, Oman, Morocco, Qatar, Syria, the United Arab Emirates, and Yemen thus joined 139 other states in endorsement of the court. Yet, by November 2001, no country in the region had taken the crucial step of joining forty-six other countries worldwide in ratifying the treaty. Sixty states must ratify the ICC treaty before it comes into force.

Space for independent political activity remained a scarce commodity throughout the region, with governments targeting both secularists and Islamists who sought to challenge authoritarian rule or call for reform, including by pursuing legitimate political activities such as standing for political office. The methods and scope of repression varied from country to country, although politically divergent ruling elites were united in their reluctance or refusal to open up stagnant political systems, to accommodate a diversity of opinions, and to facilitate and protect the growth of independent civil society institutions, including local media.

The impact of decades of strict constraints on peaceful opposition politics coupled with severe punitive measures for those who defied authorities was shown to carry ominous implications for stability and security. At best, it fostered a climate of intimidation and self-censorship; at worst, it led individuals and groups into clandestine, and in some cases violent opposition activities. In the aftermath of the September 11 attacks on New York and Washington, many in the region and beyond began to focus on the tough security policies of governments in the Middle East and North Africa that have contributed to radicalizing disaffected political activists, leading some of them to move their operations abroad.

Nationwide electoral democracy once again was revealed as a sham in Egypt, as authorities rounded up Islamist opposition candidates in advance of the October-November 2000 People's Assembly elections and the May-June 2001 contest for eighty-eight seats on the Consultative Council. Although these elections took place for the first time under full judicial supervision, authorities seemed determined to block peaceful Islamists, mostly members of the outlawed Muslim Brotherhood, from participating in the political system and gaining more than a token number of seats in the 444-seat lower house of parliament, still overwhelmingly controlled by President Husni Mubarak's ruling National Democratic Party. They detained hundreds of known or suspected members of the Muslim Brotherhood both before and during the elections, including candidates and their supporters. In November 2000, the military court sentenced fifteen defendants linked to the Muslim Brotherhood to prison terms of three to five years. Most were lawyers, university professors or other professionals involved in electoral politics. Similar blatant repression occurred in advance of the consultative council elections, with at least 140 Muslim Brothers arbitrarily arrested starting in mid-April, including candidates. All of them were later released without charge.

The power struggle in Iran between conservatives and reformers continued, despite the overwhelming electoral victory of President Mohamed Khatami, returned to office for a second successive term in June. The conservative clerics who controlled the judiciary and other institutions used their power to eliminate the country's independent pro-reform newspapers and other publications, and to imprison peaceful advocates of political reform, including investigative journalist Akbar Ganji, student leader Ali Afshari, and veteran politician Ezzatollah Sahhabi. In March, the Tehran Revolutionary Court ordered the closure of the Freedom Movement, a group that had long advocated constitutional Islamic rule with respect for democratic principles, and the group's leaders were among sixty political activists detained in March and April. Ayatollah Hossain Ali Montazeri remained under house arrest in Qom, despite mounting protests, though his critical analysis of Iran's political system continued to circulate widely on cassette tapes, the Internet, and through photocopied statements.

In Syria, as the government was releasing long-term political prisoners, many of them Islamists detained in the early 1980s, ten reform-minded secular activists were targeted for arrest and prosecution. The arrests followed the *de facto* closure earlier in the year of the country's independent civil forums, the lively discussion groups that emerged amid the easing of controls following the death of President Hafez al-Asad, breathing welcome life into a civil society that had been virtually moribund during decades of repression. President Bashar Asad forewarned of the clampdown when he declared in February that "the development of civil society institutions must come at a later stage and they are not therefore among our priorities." Trials of two of the reformers, parliamentarians Riad al-Seif and Mahmoud al-Homsi, were underway in a criminal court in November 2001. Eight others—including former political prisoner Riad al-Turk, prominent academic Arif Dalila, and other civil forum activists—were then behind bars, awaiting trial in the State Security Court.

In neighboring Lebanon, calls increased for the restoration of Lebanese sovereignty and full independence from Syria, including public demonstrations led by students and other anti-Syrian political activists. The redeployment of some 6,000 Syrian troops from most of metropolitan Beirut, which occurred in June, seemed only to embolden Lebanese to press more vocally for a full Syrian withdrawal. Cardinal Nasrallah Sfeir, the Maronite Catholic patriarch and a leading critic of Syrian dominance over Lebanon, commented that there was still "a long way to go before there are balanced ties." The arrest of over two hundred Christian anti-Syria activists in August, with the apparent approval of the Syrian president, generated public uproar across Lebanon's political spectrum, including charges that the state was being transformed into a military dictatorship under President Emile Lahoud, the former army commander.

The Lebanese army defended the roundups by saying it had acted in Lebanon's "high national interest," but the president of the Beirut Bar Association, Michel Lian, condemned the arrests as illegal, noting that under Lebanese law "security agencies are not part of the judicial police and therefore have no right to arrest people." Those targeted were members or supporters of the disbanded Lebanese Forces (LF) and the Free Patriotic Movement, aligned with imprisoned-for-life LF militia leader Samir Geagea and exiled Gen. Michel Aoun, respectively. Among them were ten students hastily convicted in the military court for "distributing leaflets harming the reputation of the Syrian army and of defaming the president of the Lebanese republic," and sentenced to terms of five to forty-five days in prison. Others were charged with "acts, writings and speeches not allowed by the government and which puts Lebanon in danger of aggressive acts and disturbs its relations with a sisterly state." On August 10, Lebanon's Central Security Council warned of the ongoing restrictions on freedom of assembly, stating that "any political group that does not enjoy an official license or permit is banned from staging demonstrations or organizing strikes." University students united to protest the intrusion onto the campus of St. Joseph University on November 21 of Internal Security Forces (ISF) troops, who removed photographs of plainclothes intelligence agents assaulting students and others at an earlier demonstration to protest the August arrests. The photos were part of a student display that included Lebanese flags draped in black ribbons, a reference to Syria's domination of the country. One student leader termed the ISF action "a continuation of the militarization of the regime."

The extremely poor human rights conditions in "closed" countries such as Iraq and Saudi Arabia remained beyond the detailed scrutiny of independent local or international monitors due to the utter lack of freedom of expression and association there, and the ongoing lack of access for outsiders. Critics, whether of secular or religious orientation, had no space to exercise basic rights, leaving in place distorted political enterprises beholden to an authoritarian dictator, as in the case of Iraq, or an all-powerful ruling family, as in the case of Saudi Arabia.

The year saw positive developments during the year in Bahrain. In a national referendum in February, Bahraini citizens—men and women—overwhelmingly approved a National Charter that established a two-chamber legislature. Prior to the vote, Shaikh Hamad bin Isa Al Khalifa, the country's amir, or ruler, announced an amnesty for more than four hundred persons detained or facing charges for security-related offenses, a category covering most of the country's political prisoners. More than one hundred Bahrainis who had been exiled abroad were allowed to return, and more did so later.

In the weeks following the referendum, the amir abolished the 1974 State Security Law, under which thousands of persons had been detained for years without trial, and the State Security Court, the procedures of which failed to meet international fair trial standards. In July, an amiri decree set up a general prosecuting authority under the Ministry of Justice, effectively removing prosecutorial authority from the Interior Ministry.

Other needed reforms in the penal code and laws governing publications and associations remained under study by a National Charter committee headed by the prime minister. A separate committee was charged with proposing amendments to Bahrain's 1973 constitution, whose provisions governing civil liberties had been effectively suspended by the government since 1975. Article 18 of the penal code, which prohibits political activity, remained in place. No political parties had been set up, but several political groupings—the Islamic National Reconciliation Society, the National Democratic Front, and the Association of the Arab and Islamic Center—were reportedly permitted to register as social and cultural organizations. Meetings and gatherings in clubs and professional associations continued after the referendum, although this remained technically illegal, and many Bahrainis felt that the greatest gains were made in the realm of freedom of expression, but were concerned about the lack of concrete steps to codify basic rights protections and to monitor implementation of announced reforms. These concerns were heightened in July when the official General Organization for Youth and Sports insisted that organizations secure prior approval for public meetings and adhere to guidelines promoting national unity, and in November with the publication ban against prominent columnist Hafez al-Sheikh.

With Internet use growing around the region, authorities in several countries tried to restrict its use for circulating independent information and views. Saudi authorities made no secret of their determination to continue blocking online political content that they deemed objectionable, and foreign companies all-too-eagerly bid for the contract to help the government censor what Saudis could access. Tunisian authorities continued to periodically bar Tunisians' access to web-sites of human rights organizations and foreign newspapers likely to contain criti-cal coverage of the government. Egypt, a country that had a tolerant approach to online content, carried out its first arrest of an Egyptian for something he had posted on a foreign server. Police arrested Shohdy Naguib on November 22 for hav-ing posted a provocative political poem by his late father, Naguib Surour, on his website, www.wadada.net, which was hosted in the U.S. Three days later, Naguib was released on bail and faced possible obscenity charges in connection with the poem. In Morocco, another country with a good record of tolerating online expres-sion, the government was alleged to have temporarily blocked sites maintained by al-'Adl wa'l-Ihsane, an Islamist political movement. Earlier, that movement had used the Internet in an exemplary anti-censorship fashion, electronically circulat-ing video clips that showed police beating their sympathizers during demonstra-tions—scenes that never aired on Moroccan television. In Algeria, where cybercafes were proliferating and there were no reports of website blocking, police in one city invited cybercafe owners to report on users who accessed "subversive" sites.

There was an ironic turn of the tables in October, when the U.S. government attempted to pressure the emir of Qatar, during a state visit to Washington, to rein in the region's popular al-Jazeera satellite television station, which is headquartered in Doha. The emir and other Qatari authorities publicly defended the station's right to broadcast its own programming and commentary, despite the fact that the U.S. found objectionable some of its reporting from Afghanistan and coverage of Osama bin Laden. "Because this comes from the United States, which considers itself the strongest advocate of freedom of expression, it comes as very strange and unacceptable," Jazeera's news editor Ahmed Sheikh said in an interview.

Women across the region had their rights compromised based solely on gender, suffering from severe forms of institutional and societal discrimination in nearly every aspect of their lives. Despite some positive developments, tens of millions of women continued to be denied full equality, with religion, culture, and tradition often cited to justify their continued subservience. Perpetuation of inequality was linked to unequal personal status laws—most notably in areas related to marriage, divorce, inheritance, and child custody—and the lack of effective legal redress for crimes of domestic violence. Women continued to fall victim to so-called "honor crimes," in which male family members murdered women relatives to restore fam-ily "honor"—and the perpetrators typically enjoyed impunity. See Women's Human Rights. In many states, discriminatory laws remained in effect that did not permit women to pass on their nationality to their children.

Saudi Arabia was the most extreme example, with women forced to observe an austere public dress code, denied the right to identity cards in their own names, prohibited from driving vehicles, and subject to strict segregation in education, employment, and all public venues. Moroccan and Algerian authorities took no decisive action during the year to reform the highly discriminatory codes of personal status. Women in Kuwait were still denied the right to vote and they continued to mobilize for the franchise. Saudi Arabia had no democratically elected local or national legislative institutions, and there were no women on the appointed Consultative Council.

Bahrain provided a potentially welcome departure from the prevailing scenario with the establishment of the Supreme Council for Women by a decree of the emir on August 22, and the November decision by the Shura Council to support Bahrain's accession to the United Nations Convention on the Elimination of All Forms of Discrimination against Women (CEDAW). Abdul Aziz Al Fadhel, minister of state for Shura Council Affairs, stated that the decision to sign the convention was based on article 2 of Bahrain's constitution, which states that the *Shari'a* is the main source of the country's legislation, and article 18, which stipulates that all citizens are equal and have the same rights and duties.

In another positive development, Egypt's prosecutor general rejected on May 23 complaints filed against the well-known feminist writer, Nawal al-Sa'dawi, by a lawyer who called for her to be forcibly divorced from her husband on grounds of her alleged apostasy. The case was brought following remarks she had made on religious issues during a media interview in March. The plaintiff also filed a separate case against al-Sa'dawi before the Personal Status Court, which ruled on July 30 that the case was inadmissible.

DEFENDING HUMAN RIGHTS

The human rights movement in the region maintained its vitality despite alarming prosecutions of activists in Egypt, Morocco, Syria, and Tunisia. Defenders sought to make the most of somewhat greater openness in a few countries, while well-established human rights communities elsewhere fought to defend their activities and mandates. Determined and courageous individuals pushed the boundaries of public openness in Morocco, Iran, Syria, and Tunisia, in some cases at a price. In sharp contrast, Saudi Arabia, Libya, and Iraq retained policies of absolute intolerance to any human rights related activity, and there were no human rights organizations in Qatar, Oman, and the United Arab Emirates. Some governments, including Egypt and Syria, relied on vaguely-worded laws to intimidate, stifle, or prosecute local human rights defenders and limit or totally restrict their sources of financial support from abroad.

Governments in Syria, Tunisia, Egypt, and Yemen manipulated their powers of regulation of nongovernmental organizations (NGOs) in order to harass and obstruct the activities of local human rights groups. In Egypt, the government maintained its crackdown on human rights activists with the trial and May 21 conviction of Saadeddin Ibrahim, director of the Ibn Khaldun Center for Development

Studies, and twenty-seven co-defendants. Egyptian NGOs continued their lobbying efforts despite ongoing uncertainty over the amended draft of the Law on Civil Associations and Institutions, presented to the Shura Council in April but not debated by parliament by November. A new law on associations took effect in February in Yemen, empowering the Ministry of Labor and Social Affairs to supervise NGOs and requiring the ministry's approval for all foreign-funded activities.

Hopes of greater openness in Syria were dealt a blow when President Bashar al-Asad's government arrested activists in August and September, including Habib Issa and Walid al-Bunni, who attended the July 2 founding meeting of the Independent Human Rights Society in Syria, and Kamal Labwani, a member of the administrative council of the Committees for the Defense of Human Rights. These arrests followed a period in which Syrian intellectuals and human rights activists had begun to exercise freedoms and speak out publicly in a manner impossible under the previous regime. Human rights activist Nizar Nayouf was released from prison in May after serving the majority of a ten-year prison sentence imposed in 1992, only to be informed in early September that the ruling Ba'ath party had filed a new case against him.

Despite the lack of formally-constituted human rights organizations, debate about human rights remained at the core of the power struggle in Iran between conservatives and reformers. Eight reformist parliamentarians faced charges for comments made under the cover of parliamentary immunity. In May, the International Center for Dialogue Among Civilizations and a private university in Qom hosted an unprecedented international human rights conference with a diverse group of participants in Tehran.

Civil society and political figures also challenged the status quo in Tunisia, despite heavy-handed governmental efforts to block their activities. At least four women human rights activists were assaulted by police during the year, and one, Sihem Ben Sedrine, was arrested on June 26 and detained until August 11. In Morocco, human rights groups worked to end impunity for state officials responsible for human rights abuses under the previous regime.

Bahraini human rights activists received official authorization in March to set up the Bahrain Human Rights Association, the first independent human rights monitoring group allowed in the country. In June, the association condemned attacks in two government-supported daily newspapers against Lord Avebury of the U.K., a long-time supporter of Bahraini rights groups, immediately prior to a government decision to ban a visit to the country by Avebury. In an interview in *Al-Hayat* on August 31, the association's general secretary, Sabika al-Najjar, said it was focusing on cases of persons still in exile or who lacked citizenship, and that the organization had received government permission to visit the country's prisons. In November, the association vigorously protested a government ban on publications by well-known political commentator Hafez al-Shaikh.

Violence in Algeria, Israel, and the Occupied Palestinian Territories impeded the work of human rights defenders. Israeli authorities detained at least four Palestinian field researchers from well-known human rights groups. The Palestinian Authority denied human rights lawyers access to prisons under its control, and arrested at least one Palestinian lawyer.

THE WORK OF HUMAN RIGHTS WATCH

Human Rights Watch researched and reported on a wide-range of violations across the region, with a particular focus on the use of force against civilians and restrictions on freedoms of expression, assembly, and association. We condemned efforts to gag the media or to silence dissidents and called for reforms of oppressive laws enabling such actions. We challenged governments to be accountable and permit investigations into past abuses, and we welcomed efforts to end impunity. We criticized the absence of due process in legal proceedings in civilian and military courts and sought to defend the independence of the judiciary against pressure and interference by the executive branch of government.

Throughout the year we continued to look beyond the U.S. to European governments and others for sources of influence on human rights violators in the region. In dealing with offenders we sought both to focus on gross violators but also to respond to new restrictions imposed in countries that claimed to have ended abusive practices and permitted the exercise of basic rights.

Underpinning our effectiveness were our efforts to reach a broader segment of the region's population through faster and wider dissemination of our published materials. We issued reports and communiqués in Arabic, Farsi, French, and Hebrew, as well as English, using print, radio, television, and the Internet to substantially improve their coverage in major regional and local media.

One of our highest priorities remained consultation and coordination with local and regional human rights groups in order to develop effective strategies to end abuses and address regional priorities. We also continued to defend those who were persecuted for their human rights work and to pressure governments to provide the space to enable them to conduct their work.

In February, we published on Bahrain, welcoming the release of most of the country's remaining political prisoners prior to a national referendum on proposed political reforms. We called for the abolition of State Security Courts, an end to unfair trials and to prolonged detention without trial, and urged that all Bahraini exiles be allowed to return home. Human Rights Watch also supported the need for Bahraini human rights activists to be allowed to establish independent nongovernmental groups.

In the same month, we published a critique of Yemen's referendum on constitutional amendments and local elections, held the same day, that strengthened the power of the president and the ruling General People's Congress (GPC). In particular, we drew attention to harassment of political activists, human rights defenders, and journalists in the run up to the votes.

In March, we presented a memorandum to the United Nations Human Rights Committee on Syria's compliance with the International Covenant on Civil and Political Rights. We welcomed the improvements since Bashar al-Asad replaced his father as president in July 2000—including the release of some six hundred political prisoners, the emergence of independent civic forums meeting openly and discussing agendas for political reform, and the granting of a licence to the first privately-owned newspaper since 1963—but we sounded a warning about the clampdown that threatened a return to state monopoly of all forms of public debate.

We urged the committee to give particular attention to five issues: the stripping of Syrian political exiles and their families, including children, of the right to maintain or obtain Syrian nationality; discriminatory treatment of Syria-born Kurds; discrimination against women under the personal status law and penal code; accountability for violations of the right to life and other gross human rights abuses; and violations of freedom of association.

In an eighty-two page report, *Center of the Storm: A Case Study of Human Rights Abuses in Hebron District*, published in April, Human Rights Watch documented excessive use of force and unlawful killings by Israeli forces, Palestinian targeting of Israeli civilians, and a systematic policy of Israeli blockades and curfews that amounted to collective punishment. The report also brought to light a disturbing pattern of violence committed by Israeli settlers against Palestinian civilians in and around Hebron, often committed with the knowledge of Israeli Defense Force (IDF) soldiers in the area. We urged the Israeli government and the Palestinian Authority to take immediate steps to stop abuses by the forces under their control, and called for an independent, international monitoring presence in the West Bank and Gaza Strip to monitor and report on Israeli and Palestinian abuses.

Also in April, we issued jointly with Observatory for the Protection of Human Rights Defenders a report, *A Lawsuit Against the Human Rights League, An Assault on All Rights Activists*, detailing the Tunisian authorities' actions against its human rights critics, including police actions to block meetings of human rights organizations, physical assaults on men and women activists, passport confiscations, and interruptions in phone service. We urged the French and other European Union governments to monitor the appeals court case against the Tunisian Human Rights League, which opened on April 30, and to pressure the Tunisian government to stop its harassment of human rights monitors.

In June, in the run-up to presidential elections in Iran, Human Rights Watch published *Stifling Dissent: The Human Rights Consequences of Inter-Factional Struggle in Iran*. This traced the conservative backlash that occurred after reformists won a landslide victory in parliamentary elections in February 2000, in which political and religious conservatives manipulated their control of the judiciary and the Council of Guardians, and the office of the Leader of the Islamic Republic to clamp down on pro-reformist media, political activists, intellectuals, and reform-minded government officials. The report said more than thirty-five independent newspapers and magazines had been closed down in the previous fourteen months and condemned the use of arbitrary detention, unfair trial, political violence, and restrictions on basic freedoms.

We issued a briefing on Egypt's human rights record in October that examined how more than two decades of emergency rule had been used not only against violent opponents of the government but also to stifle peaceful critics and democrats. It reported that torture remained widespread and that basic liberties such as the rights to freedom of speech and association were sharply restricted. The briefing also examined the confrontation between the state and Islamist armed political groups, including al-Jihad, some of whose key figures were reportedly associated with Osama bin Laden.

Throughout the year we also sought to defend those who were persecuted for their human rights work. In January, we wrote to Tunisian president Zine el-Abidine Ben Ali to protest various measures that stifled independent human rights activity, including the one-year prison sentence imposed on Moncef Marzouki, spokesperson of the National Council on Liberties in Tunisia, for "disseminating false news." In Egypt, we protested the May sentencing by the Supreme State Security Court of human rights defender Saadeddin Ibrahim and twenty-seven co-defendants to between one and seven year prison terms in a politically motivated unfair trial. In July, we welcomed the decision of Cairo's Administrative Court to overturn the government's refusal for unspecified "security reasons" to register the Egyptian Organization for Human Rights and called on the Egyptian government to implement the ruling without delay. In Algeria, we protested the authorities's restriction of Mohamed Smaïn, including the confiscation of his passport and national identity card, for his work on kidnappings, "disappearances," and assassinations in the western province of Relizane.

We expressed dismay at the conviction and sentencing of thirty-six Moroccan human rights activists in May on charges of holding an illegal demonstration in December 2000, organized by the Moroccan Association of Human Rights, to demand an end to impunity for the perpetrators of human rights violations. Almost a year later they were acquitted in a November 2001 appeal hearing. While welcoming the acquittal Human Rights Watch and Amnesty International jointly expressed concern in a published briefing that the right to assemble peacefully remains sharply curtailed in Morocco.

Staff and other representatives of Human Rights Watch's Middle East and North Africa division traveled during the year to Egypt, Iran, Israel and the Occupied Territories, Iraqi Kurdistan, Morocco, Tunisia, and Palestinian Authority-controlled areas. Missions involved field research, dialogue with government officials, trial observations, coordination with local and international groups and efforts at outreach, and advocacy. Human Rights Watch requests for access to Algeria, Bahrain, Saudi Arabia, and Syria were not granted and remained pending at the end of the year.

THE ROLE OF THE INTERNATIONAL COMMUNITY

European Union

The European Commission (E.C.), the executive arm of the European Union (E.U.), issued a lengthy "communication" to the Council of Ministers and the European Parliament on May 8 proposing a more coherent and consistent E.U. approach to human rights issues by "ensur[ing] that all E.C. assistance instruments are mobilized in support of human rights and democratization objectives." The document included few concrete suggestions as to how this could be achieved, however, in particular how to overcome the frequent reluctance of member states and the Council of Ministers to speak out against or take steps to end abuses in individual countries.

The most noteworthy development in the framework of the Euro-Mediterranean "Barcelona Process" was the signing, on June 25, of the Association Agreement with Egypt, after more than five years of negotiation. (See Egypt.) Previously signed agreements with Jordan and the Palestinian Authority remain to be ratified by some E.U. member states before coming into force, while negotiations continued with Algeria, Lebanon, and Syria. Tunisia's Association Agreement has been operative since March 1998, Israel's since June 2000, and Morocco's since early 2000, but there was no significant public or official discussion as to how the poor human rights records of those governments could be squared with article 2 of each agreement, which states that it is premised on "respect for human rights and democratic values." One indication of the ambiguous status of human rights was the Euro-Mediterranean conference of ministers of foreign affairs, meeting in Brussels in early November. The group's communiqué "welcomed the continuation of the political dialogue, especially with regards to human rights, by means of national and regional presentations making it possible to improve awareness and hence mutual understanding of our partners' reference systems."

A U.S. Congressional Research Service study of transfers of conventional arms, released in August, reported that almost 84 percent of the United Kingdom's arms deliveries to developing countries in the 1997-2000 period were to the Middle East. The equivalent figure for France was more than 41 percent.

United States

The Bush administration entered office on January 20 determined to have a lower profile than its predecessor in efforts to revive negotiations between Israel and the Palestinian Authority. Secretary of State Colin Powell's initial tour of the region was to solicit support for changes in the U.N. sanctions regime on Iraq, an effort that eventually failed to materialize owing to Russian resistance in the Security Council. The administration's plans to stay relatively removed from the Israeli-Palestinian conflict did not prove realistic. The administration declined to name a successor to Dennis Ross, who had served as special coordinator for the Middle East, instead naming Assistant Secretary of State for Near Eastern Affairs William Burns as U.S. chief negotiator. Secretary Powell visited the region in June in an unsuccessful effort to bring about a ceasefire. The need to forge a political and military coalition following the September 11 attacks on New York and Washington sharply increased pressure on the administration to give greater attention to the Israeli-Palestinian conflict. In November, President Bush, in a speech to the U.N. General Assembly, declared support for a Palestinian state. As the political and security situation continued to deteriorate, the president sent retired Marine Corps Gen. Anthony Zinni as a special envoy to the region. Secretary Powell said Zinni would stay there "for as long as it takes" to bring about a negotiated settlement.

Issues of human rights and democracy did not figure significantly in U.S. public diplomacy or foreign assistance programs related to the Middle East. The State Department, in its fiscal year (FY) 2002 request to Congress, budgeted U.S. $7 million—up from just under $4 million in FY 2001—under the heading of Middle East Democracy. The presentation stated that these funds would be used to support "democracy-related projects" of NGOs in Morocco, Algeria, Tunisia, Oman, and

Yemen, as well as programs for judicial reform and "protection of human and private property rights." The funds would also be used to improve the capacity and effectiveness of legislatures and elected advisory councils and to assist preparations for fair elections in Morocco and Algeria. Of the individual country presentations, human rights and democratic reform appear to be a substantial component of the program only for Morocco. Tunisia was implausibly characterized in the presentation as a "stable democratic country," and U.S. promotion of democracy in Tunisia was limited to funds for training Tunisian military officers.

Funding under the Anti-Terrorism Assistance (ATA) program, according to the State Department presentation, included working with participating countries "to increase respect for human rights among foreign police by sharing modern, humane and effective antiterrorism techniques." The presentation did not say what proportion of the $38 million requested would be for such programs, or which countries were included. Some $4.7 million of the total was earmarked for the Middle East.

The fact that the top leadership of al-Qaeda and most of the alleged perpetrators of the September 11 attacks were nationals of Saudi Arabia and Egypt focused considerable media and other attention on the authoritarian character of those states' governments, both close U.S. allies. The attacks stimulated some public reflection on U.S. neglect of democracy and human rights issues in the region. Secretary Powell, testifying before the Senate Foreign Relations Committee on October 25, acknowledged that "[in] many of these nations, leadership does not represent the street." Secretary Powell went on to say, "I have started to raise these issues and talk to some of our friends in the region and say, you know, in addition to sort of criticizing us from time to time and terrible editorials about us in your newspapers, better start taking a look in the mirror."

On October 31, Assistant Secretary of State for Democracy, Rights and Labor Lorne Craner, in a speech on "The Role of Human Rights in the administration's Foreign Policy Agenda," included a paragraph on the Middle East. After discussing China, he said: "Similarly, in the Persian Gulf, Oman is experimenting with an increasingly independent legislature and Qatar will hold local elections, with women voting, in 2003. No one, least of all me, would claim any of these countries are democracies, and it may be that the end result, many years from now, is not precisely comparable to our democratic system. The point is that the United States is now willing to assist those working to bring pluralism to their countries, even if it may only occur over the long term."

According to the Congressional Research Service's annual report on conventional arms sales, the U.S. delivered $26.4 billion in arms to the Middle East in the 1997-2000 period, or just over 62 percent of all U.S. deliveries to developing countries. Saudi Arabia ($16.2 billion), Israel ($3.9 billion), Egypt ($3.6 billion), and Kuwait ($1.5 billion) were the largest recipients.

ALGERIA

HUMAN RIGHTS DEVELOPMENTS

More than 1,500 people were killed in a tenth successive year of endemic politi-cal violence involving the security forces and armed groups claiming to be Islamist. The casualty level, although down from the mid-1990s, refuted official claims that the violence was "residual." As well as security force members and militants killed in clashes and ambushes, the casualties included hundreds of civilians who were indiscriminately attacked in their homes, at roadblocks, and in public places.

The year also saw the first mass popular protests since a state of emergency was imposed in 1992. The protests were concentrated in the Berber-majority Kabylie region. According to local nongovernmental organizations, over ninety civilians died in the unrest, most of them victims of shootings by the security forces.

In the realm of public freedoms, Algeria presented a mixed picture. Massive anti-government demonstrations were sometimes permitted, at other times for-bidden or aggressively broken up. Revisions to the penal code threatened press free-dom, yet private newspapers continued to criticize President Abdelaziz Bouteflika daily.

Sweeping impunity prevailed for the perpetrators of massive human rights vio-lations on all sides of a conflict that has claimed well over 100,000 lives.

The 1999 "Civil Harmony" law offering amnesty or leniency to surrendering militants, known as *repentis*, failed to end the political violence. There were appar-ently few new surrenders in response to President Bouteflika's suggestion in Febru-ary that the amnesty offer was still available even though the deadline specified in the law had passed. In June, the level of violence increased and spread to regions that had been relatively spared in recent years.

Much of the violence was blamed on two armed groups that had rejected the amnesty, the Armed Islamic Group (Groupe islamique armé, GIA) and the Salafist Group for Preaching and Combat. According to the often-sketchy available infor-mation, the GIA slaughtered civilians indiscriminately and systematically while the Salafist Group frequently targeted members of the security forces and government-backed militias, but also killed civilians. Attribution was often difficult because the assailants usually fled without being apprehended and rarely claimed responsibil-ity or explained their motives.

The governorates (wilayas) of Tipasa, Medea, Chlef, and Mascara were particu-larly affected, while the Mitidja south of the capital suffered a resurgence of attacks. On February 10, for example, an unidentified group of armed men gunned down four families living in a shantytown near the city of Berrouaghia. Most of the twenty-six killed were women and children. On August 12, in one of numerous attacks committed by men who had set up roadblocks on intercity roads, seventeen passengers were killed by armed men dressed in military uniforms in the wilaya of Mascara. On September 26, attackers invaded a wedding party in the city of Larbaa, killing thirteen in attendance and nine others who happened to be in their path, according to reports in Algerian private newspapers. The terror drove thousands of Algerians toward more urban areas that offered relative safety but also social and economic hardship.

A total of some 6,000 militants had applied for amnesty since the Civil Harmony law went into effect in July 1999, according to government statements made during 2001. A de jure blanket amnesty was given to members of the two armed groups that had formally agreed to disband in January 2000. Amnesty-seekers from other groups were required to disclose their past deeds to government-controlled probation committees. These bodies were charged with conducting investigations and deciding whether applicants should be exempt from prosecution or, if they were suspected of committing serious crimes, face reduced sentences.

In practice, the probation committees tended to exonerate repentis after a cursory examination, according to victims' rights groups. As a result, suspected assassins were reportedly cleared to return home without punishment, even though the Civil Harmony law states that persons who participated in killings or rape are disqualified from receiving probation or reduced sentences.

Prime Minister Ali Benflis told European Parliament member Helène Flautre in May that some four hundred surrendering militants were facing prosecution, but this figure could not be independently verified. The committees operated behind closed doors, and excluded victims, their survivors, and the public from their deliberations. Even if accurate, the figure of four hundred prosecutions would represent only 7 percent of the militants who were reported to have turned themselves in.

More than ninety Algerians were reported killed during street protests that began on April 21 and continued sporadically for months. The demonstrations were sparked by the death on April 20 of Berber high school student Guermah Massinissa, who, two days earlier, had been shot while in custody in a gendarme barracks. Local youths rejected gendarmerie claims that the shooting was accidental and alleged that the gendarmes had increasingly harassed the local population in the preceding months.

Many of the protests in the Kabylie were peaceful but in others, protesters threw stones or Molotov cocktails at gendarmes, and damaged public buildings and property, as well as private businesses. During the first and bloodiest week, gendarmes repeatedly opened fire on protesters without warning, using live ammunition. They also beat wounded persons and others not involved in the protests, according to many eyewitnesses.

The demonstrators demanded, among other things, recognition of the Berber language and cultural identity and the withdrawal of the gendarmes from the region. In June, the street rallies spread to other regions, fueled by local grievances over corruption, joblessness, and housing allocations.

On April 30, President Bouteflika announced an independent probe into the events. On May 2, he named a respected jurist, Mohand Issad, to head it. The commission's interim report, made public three months later, contrasted favorably with previous government-ordered inquiries that either were whitewashes or never came out at all. The commission found that the gendarmes had "kept the pot boiling by shooting live ammunition, ransacking, plundering, provocations of every sort, obscene language, and beatings." It concluded that self-defense claims could not justify the gendarmes' fatal shooting of fifty civilians and the wounding of another 218 by gunfire between April 22 and 28. During this period, it noted, one security force member died, by electrocution, although many were injured.

The commission's interim report did not identify gendarmes or officers responsible for the excessive use of lethal force. Issad promised to resume the inquiry in August, but further findings were unavailable as this report went to press.

Shortly after President Bouteflika's address on April 30, security forces began showing greater restraint in their use of live ammunition. Authorities also reassigned many of the troops suspected of acting harshly, and deployed riot police units who used teargas more than live bullets.

These factors helped to reduce casualties despite the larger and more widespread nature of the protests during May and June. On May 21 and 31, huge demonstrations were held, first in Tizi-Ouzou, then in Algiers. But on June 14, a Berber-dominated march of about half a million people in the capital degenerated into looting of shops and clashes involving the police, demonstrators, and local youth. Over three hundred were injured and four killed. Many of the hundreds detained by police were unaccounted for during several days; however, all were eventually released.

On June 18, President Bouteflika banned all demonstrations in Algiers "until further notice." Police were deployed massively in the city and on roads leading from the Kabylie to thwart would-be demonstrators. Pre-announced marches were blocked in this manner on July 5, August 8, and October 5.

On October 3, Prime Minister Ali Benflis met with Berber community representatives and announced that President Bouteflika had promised several initiatives. These included amending the constitution to make the Berber language, Tamazight, a national language; compensating victims of the disturbances; prosecuting those responsible for crimes and killings during the clashes; and restructuring the security forces in those areas of the Kabylie where abuses had taken place. As of October, there was no verifiable information available about prosecutions of security force members responsible for abuses during the protests, although there were unconfirmed reports of arrests.

State-controlled television and radio remained government mouthpieces, usually ignoring major demonstrations and massacres that were covered on locally available European and Arab stations. Opposition politicians received little or no television coverage except during the regularly broadcast sessions of parliament.

Private newspapers, by contrast, often criticized government actions, publishing eyewitness accounts of the gendarmerie's suppression of demonstrations, and speculating openly about President Bouteflika's future in office. However, they exercised self-censorship concerning the army's role in politics.

In June, *El-Watan* and *el-Khabar* became the first national dailies to print part of their daily circulation at a private press, loosening the indirect editorial pressure that accompanied the state's near-monopoly on printing. However, revisions to the penal code that took effect in July lengthened prison terms and increased fines for defaming or insulting the president, state institutions, or officials. The amendments were justified by officials as necessary to "preserve the dignity of the state and to protect individual and collective freedoms." As this report went to press, no journalist had yet been charged under the new amendments, which also curbed speech in mosques by lengthening to five years the maximum sentence for delivering sermons "capable of harming social cohesion."

Entry visas for foreign reporters were sometimes approved, sometimes ignored without explanation. Country specialists at the Paris dailies *Libération* and *Le Figaro* were prevented from visiting during much of the year.

Internet use continued to grow as connection fees dropped and cybercafes proliferated. There were no reports of sites being blocked, although the Internet regulations required service providers to "constantly monitor the content available to [their] subscribers to prevent access to . . . information contrary to the public order or morality." Early in 2001, police in the city of Boufarik ordered cybercafe operators regularly to submit a log of their patrons' names, and to report any activity that seemed subversive or immoral.

No progress was achieved in locating or learning the fate of the thousands of Algerians who had been forcibly "disappeared" by the security forces, primarily between 1994 and 1996. Although there were no new cases of persons who had been detained by security forces during 2001 and then remained missing for an extended period, families came forward to report additional cases dating to the 1990s. The National Association of Families of the Disappeared stated that its registry of documented cases had surpassed 7,000.

In a speech on October 9, President Bouteflika asked families of the "disappeared" to "trust the authorities" and to refrain from doing anything that "could tarnish the image of the country or of Algerians."

Government officials continued to provide statistics on cases the government claimed to have "clarified," while rarely if ever furnishing any useful information to families. For example, according to a report issued in June by European Parliament member Hélène Flautre, Justice Minister Ahmed Ouyahia told Flautre in May that out of 3,000 missing-person complaints received by the government, "a thousand had been cleared up: 833 [of the missing persons] had joined the armed groups, ninety-three had been killed, eighty-two were in detention, seventy-four had returned home, and seven had benefited from the Civil Harmony [amnesty]."

However, the authorities furnished no evidence to families that particular missing persons had joined armed groups. Few if any turned up among the thousands of armed group members who had surrendered in recent years; nor did these repentis provide information corroborating the government's claim that many of the supposedly "disappeared" had been alongside them in the mountains.

No headway was made in finding any of the several thousand Algerian civilians said to have been abducted in previous years by armed groups. Few families learned anything about relatives who had been abducted, despite the discovery in recent years of several mass grave sites believed linked to the conflict, and the surrender of thousands of militants, some of whom may have had knowledge of the abductions.

Security forces continued to torture detainees who were suspected of involvement with or knowledge of the armed groups, according to human rights lawyers. However, reports of torture declined along with the number of security-related arrests compared with previous years.

In February, ex-army officer Habib Souaïdia published in Paris *La Sale Guerre* (The Dirty War), the most detailed indictment yet of the army's conduct. Souaïdia detailed a pattern of torture and of summary executions practiced by anti-terrorist units on suspected Islamists, and other abuses that he claimed to have witnessed between 1993 and 1995. Algerian officials dismissed *La Sale Guerre* as part of a campaign to smear the government.

In another challenge to impunity, on April 25, a Paris judge opened an investigation into complaints filed against Khaled Nezzar by Algerians now living abroad who said that they, or their deceased relatives, had been tortured in the early 1990s when Nezzar was minister of defense. Nezzar, in France for the publication of his memoirs, cut short his visit and left the country that night by private plane.

In some trials, including politically sensitive ones, judges conducted the proceedings with seriousness and impartiality, but others were tainted by irregularities. In a one-day trial on April 12, Fouad Boulemia was convicted and sentenced to death for the November 1999 killing of Abdelqader Hachani, at the time the pre-eminent Front Islamique du Salut (FIS) leader who was at liberty. Boulemia told the judge he had been tortured into signing a "confession" that he now repudiated, but this claim was rejected by the court. Boulemia was questioned neither by his own lawyer nor the prosecutor. Boulemia remained in prison as of this writing.

In another case, journalist Faouzia Ababsa, managing editor of the French-language daily *l'Authentique,* was convicted of defamation on July 11 even though she had not been notified of the trial and was not present. She received a suspended six-month prison sentence and a fine.

In their indiscriminate attacks on civilians, armed groups abducted and raped girls and women, when they did not kill them on the spot. Women's rights groups decried the lack of support services for rape victims.

The more general problem of gender-based violence was dramatized by attacks on women living alone carried out by mobs of men who were apparently unaffiliated with armed groups. On the evening of July 13, more than one hundred men set upon a neighborhood of the oil-rich city of Hassi Messaoud. While other residents were spared, migrant women were pulled from their homes, beaten, clubbed, stabbed, and raped. The assault lasted well into the night, even though security forces monitor the city closely. On October 9, *El-Watan* reported that thirty-eight of the men had been charged with assault, rape, or other offenses, and of those charged twenty-nine were being held in pretrial detention. According to one version, the assailants were local residents motivated by accusations that the women practiced "loose morals." Later in the month, groups of men in the eastern city of Tebessa twice raided a neighborhood where women lived alone, assaulting three women in one instance and ransacking homes in the other. Attackers who were arrested by police claimed they were fighting "debauchery."

The highly discriminatory Family Code of 1984 remained intact. On March 8, international women's day, President Bouteflika called the code "discriminatory" and said some of its provisions ran counter to "the spirit of Islam." But neither he nor the National Assembly took any initiative to amend articles that favored men in matters of marriage, divorce, inheritance, and child custody.

On October 9, Algeria ratified the 1997 Convention on the Prohibition of the Use, Stockpiling, Production and Transfer of Anti-Personnel Mines and on Their Destruction (Mine Ban Treaty). It will enter into force for Algeria on April 1, 2002.

DEFENDING HUMAN RIGHTS

Algerian human rights and victims' rights organizations, lawyers, and certain political parties collected information and lobbied in defense of rights. The main obstacle to documenting abuses appeared to be the fear among victims and their families to testify, particularly among rural populations hard-hit by political violence.

Police generally tolerated the regular sit-ins organized by families of the "disappeared" in front of public buildings, but broke them up on occasion. An attempted march by families in the city of Relizane on September 19 was blocked on the grounds that it was unauthorized.

Mohamed Smaïn, a spokesperson of the Relizane bureau of the independent Algerian League for the Defense of Human Rights, was detained on February 23 and held for two days in connection with a defamation suit filed by Hadj Fergane, a former mayor and militia chief whom Smaïn had accused of involvement in kidnappings and extrajudicial killings. Smaïn's identification documents were seized and he was prohibited from traveling without court authorization. On October 28, with the case still pending, the gendarmerie cautioned Smaïn that the travel restriction remained in effect. The confiscated documents had not been returned. In November, however, Smaïn prevailed in another case in which a Relizane court sentenced Fergane to six months in prison for defaming Smaïn.

The National Association of Families of the Disappeared remained active even though its application for legal recognition had gone unanswered. In September, another organization of families of the "disappeared," SOS Disparus, opened a national headquarters in downtown Algiers, the first office devoted solely to this issue.

In contrast to 2000, Human Rights Watch, Amnesty International, and the International Federation for Human Rights were not permitted to conduct fieldwork in Algeria during the first ten months of 2001. However, the French freedom of expression organization Reporters sans Frontières visited in January to investigate the cases of five missing Algerian journalists.

The government continued its refusal to grant long-standing mission requests from the U.N. special rapporteurs on torture, and on extrajudicial, summary, or arbitrary executions, and the Working Group on Enforced and Involuntary Disappearances (WGEID). The International Committee of the Red Cross conducted its fourth and fifth rounds since 1999 of visits to prisons, including private interviews with inmates. Its agreement with the authorities excluded visits to facilities run by the ministries of interior or defense.

In March, authorities dissolved the nine-year-old National Human Rights Observatory, which reported to the president and was viewed as ineffective by most victims of government abuse who had sought its assistance. It was replaced in October by the National Consultative Commission for Promoting and Protecting Human Rights.

THE ROLE OF THE INTERNATIONAL COMMUNITY

European Union

E.U. countries received 20 percent of their natural gas supplies from Algeria and purchased 70 percent of Algeria's total exports.

Negotiations continued over a bilateral association agreement between the E.U. and Algeria, and the E.U. funded modest programs to support private newspapers and to train the police in forensic science and in human rights.

On June 16, the European Council, composed of the heads of government of the E.U. countries, publicly urged "all those responsible in Algeria" to "act to end the present confrontations and violence," and called on the government to "launch a political initiative to overcome the crisis by means of dialogue among all Algerians." The statement pledged the E.U.'s support for "the political, economic, and social reforms necessary for restoring peace, stability and prosperity."

Human rights received some attention at the ministerial-level "troika" meetings held in Algeria on April 24. (The troika consists of representatives of the current E.U. presidency, the commission, and the High Representative for the Common Foreign and Security Policy.) The Europeans presented a list of some thirty "disappeared" cases and requested clarification. Anna Lindh, the foreign minister of Sweden (at the time E.U. president), stated that the E.U. "takes a serious view" of "disappearances," arbitrary arrests, and torture. She also voiced concern about the proposed penal code amendments restricting press freedom.

A resolution adopted January 18 by the European Parliament condemned all forms of violence against civilians in Algeria and urged the government to cooperate with the U.N. WGEID. A resolution adopted May 17 criticized the killing of demonstrators and urged greater respect for Berber cultural and linguistic rights. In his statement before the U.N. Commission on Human Rights, the E.U. representative on March 29 urged Algeria to allow visits by U.N. human rights rapporteurs.

France

France was Algeria's leading source of imports and home to the largest Algerian community outside of Algeria. French assistance to Algeria came mainly in the form of credits for the purchase of French exports.

During the conflict that has raged in Algeria since 1992, France has been circumspect on governmental human rights abuses committed against suspected Islamists. In 2001, the French government spoke out more forcefully when the security forces killed some fifty protesters in the Kabylie during the last week of April. Kabyles (Berbers) constitute a large percentage of France's Algerian community and are politically well-organized. On May 2, Foreign Minister Hubert Vedrine warned that France could not remain silent about "the violence and repression" and urged "political dialogue." On June 19, he said the demands by the Algerian people for "real change" were "thoroughly legitimate." In an interview published in *Le Monde* of July 11, Vedrine scoffed at the accusation made by President Bouteflika and others that foreign meddling had caused the recent disturbances: "The Algerian regime knows very well that this is false, that this contestation is the result of internal problems."

On other human rights issues, France was more discreet. Vedrine, Interior Minister Daniel Vaillant, and State Secretary Michelle Demessine all visited Algiers in February and made no public statements regarding human rights at the time.

United States

Never a priority country in the region for the U.S., Algeria received greater attention during 2001. Human rights concerns were raised in bilateral meetings but remained secondary to anti-terror cooperation, U.S. private investments, and resolving the conflict over the Western Sahara.

These were among the topics discussed when President George W. Bush met with President Bouteflika on July 12 in Washington. It was the first meeting between heads of state since a military-backed coup in 1992 halted Algeria's elections. Bush reportedly urged Bouteflika to make progress on human rights, but the White House did not comment publicly on the subject.

Relations had been gradually warming prior to the summit. In February in Germany, Carlton W. Fulford, deputy commander of the American forces in Europe, received General Mohamed Lamari, chief-of-staff of the Algerian army, which is implicated in massive human rights abuses.

Following the September 11 attacks on New York and Washington, Algeria shared with Washington a list of 350 Algerians abroad with alleged links to Osama bin Laden, and a list of alleged Islamist militants inside Algeria, according to news reports. The State Department and National Security Council (NSC) declined to comment to Human Rights Watch on those reports.

U.S. interest in anti-terror cooperation was undoubtedly a factor in President Bush's receiving President Bouteflika again in Washington on November 5. The U.S. made no public comments about what they discussed. But on November 9, an NSC official told Human Rights Watch that Algeria had been asking the U.S. "to be more forthcoming" on licensing private arms sales. He added that the U.S. was maintaining its "go-slow" approach and had not changed its opposition to selling night-vision equipment, an item Algeria has long sought for counter-insurgency use.

Algeria received minimal direct aid from the U.S. However, the U.S. government-run Export-Import bank, which provides loans and guarantees to assist U.S. investment abroad, stated that its exposure in Algeria rose in the fiscal year ending September 30 to nearly U.S. $2 billion, a level matched in the Middle East and North Africa only by the bank's exposure in Saudi Arabia. Total private U.S. investment in Algeria was about U.S. $4 billion, nearly all in the energy sector.

In November 2000, Harold Koh, then-President Clinton's assistant secretary for human rights, democracy, and labor, made his first trip to Algeria. During two days he met with human rights activists and government officials. His public remarks about local rights conditions were general and brief. In the year since Koh's visit, the U.S. government made no high-level public statements on human rights except for the solid chapter on Algeria in the State Department's *Country Reports on Human Rights Practices.*

EGYPT

HUMAN RIGHTS DEVELOPMENTS

The human rights situation continued to deteriorate, marked by violations of freedom of expression, association, and assembly; widespread arrests of government opponents and prolonged detentions under state of emergency laws, in force almost continuously since 1967; and grossly unfair trials before military and state security courts.

Elections for the 454-member People's Assembly, conducted in three stages between October 18 and November 14, 2000, were the first to be held under full judicial supervision, following legislative reforms prompted by a July 2000 ruling of Egypt's Supreme Constitutional Court. The ruling National Democratic Party (NDP) won by a large majority but supporters of the Muslim Brotherhood, who could only run as independent candidates, secured seventeen seats and eleven other opposition parties shared sixteen. Despite judicial supervision, clashes between rival supporters and with the police left between nine and fifteen people dead, and scores wounded. The authorities arrested hundreds of Muslim Brotherhood-aligned and other opposition candidates and supporters in the run up to the elections and prevented others from reaching polling stations.

The authorities carried out further arrests of pro-Muslim Brotherhood candidates and supporters in advance of the May-June elections to the *Majlis al-Shura* (Consultative Council, the upper house of the parliament). These elections passed off relatively peacefully, and were also won by the NDP.

The government-controlled Political Parties Committee of the Majlis al-Shura licensed Egypt 2000, a new political party, in April, having previously rejected it in 1999 only for that decision to be overturned on April 7 by the Political Parties Tribunal. Egypt 2000 was only the second political party to be licensed since the formation of the Political Parties Committee in 1977, several other political groups having been rejected, usually on grounds that their programs did not differ significantly from those of existing registered political parties.

The Islamist opposition Labor Party, whose activities were frozen by the Political Parties Committee in May 2000, remained suspended and its publications banned. At least eleven Administrative Court rulings ordered the lifting of a ban on the party's bi-weekly newspaper, *al-Sha'ab*, as a breach of constitutionally guaranteed press freedoms. On March 20, the Administrative Court declared unlawful the government's non-compliance with its rulings and its delaying tactic of lodging appeals before courts that were clearly not competent to hear such cases. Despite this, on March 21, the Political Parties Committee confirmed the ban on *al-Sha'ab* as the Labor Party's status remained unresolved. In mid-July, a board of advisers to the Supreme Administrative Court, which has previously upheld rulings in favor of *al-Sha'ab*, supported the committee's position. The board argued that earlier Administrative Court rulings were incorrect in stating that while the committee was empowered to suspend political parties, it did not have the authority to ban publications. In the interim, *al-Sha'ab* continued to appear in an on-line version.

Magdi Hussain, *al-Sha'ab*'s imprisoned editor-in-chief, was released under a presidential pardon on December 27, 2000, as were *al-Sha'ab* journalist Salah Bdeiwi and cartoonist 'Issam Hanafi. All three were sentenced in August 1999 for defaming Minister of Agriculture Yusuf Wali. In March, Hussain was elected secretary-general of the Labor Party, but in August, party leader Ibrahim Shukri suspended him and ten others from the party's executive committee and replaced him as *al-Sha'ab*'s editor-in-chief in an effort to purge the party of Islamists and so obtain government approval to operate again.

The government continued to try civilian political suspects before military courts and in mid-October announced that 253 Islamist detainees would be tried before the Supreme Military Court. Of these, eighty-three had been arrested in May and detained for membership of an illegal organization, illegally possessing weapons, planning to overthrow the government by force, and forging official documents. They included several foreign nationals; local press speculation linking them to Osama Bin Laden's *al-Qaeda* (The Base) network was later rejected by President Husni Mubarak. The other 170 were suspected members of the banned *al-Gama'a al-Islamiyya* (Islamic Group), many of whom, according to defense lawyers, had already been held without trial for several years. All 170 reportedly faced charges of carrying out acts of political violence between 1994 and 1998. Local human rights groups condemned the decision to try more civilians in military courts, from which there is no right of appeal. Since 1992, such courts have convicted hundreds of Islamists, often after grossly unfair trials and torture during pre-trial interrogation, and handed down scores of death sentences, many of which have been carried out. On September 20, government security agents abducted publisher Farid Zahran, a leader of the Egyptian People's Committee for Solidarity with the Palestinian Uprising (EPCSPU), to forestall a demonstration on September 28 called to mark the first anniversary of the outbreak of renewed conflict between Palestinians and Israeli forces. Detained for two weeks, Zahran was accused of disseminating tendentious information aimed at disturbing public order and planning demonstrations, then released on bail on October 4.

Thousands of alleged members or supporters of banned Islamist groups contuinued to be detained without trial, but a few were released, including Hamdi Abd al-Rahman and Isma'il al-Bakl, both al-Gama'a al-Islamiyya leaders. They were released in July after serving fifteen-year prison terms for their part in the 1981 assassination of former president Anwar al-Sadat plus an additional five years when they were held illegally.

Police routinely tortured or ill-treated detainees, and there were three deaths between January and July. In two earlier deaths in custody, criminal proceedings against those accused of inflicting torture resulted in convictions. On February 7, the Shibin al-Kom criminal court sentenced the director of Wadi Natroun maximum security prison to ten years of imprisonment in connection with the death under torture of Ahmad Muhammad 'Issa, an awaiting trial prisoner, and sentenced a major to seven years and four sergeants to five year terms, dismissing all from their posts. In another case, a lieutenant at al-'Agouza police station in Cairo received a two-year prison term with labor on July 25 for beating detainee Ahmad Imam 'Abd al-Na'im to death

Egyptian courts sentenced at least sixty-nine people to death between November 2000 and November 2001 for murder, rape, and other crimes, and carried out eight executions.

The government continued to clamp down on Islamist political activists, breaching their rights to freedom of expression and association. On November 19, 2000, a military court sentenced fifteen lawyers and other professionals linked to the banned Muslim Brotherhood to prison terms of up to five years on charges including membership of an illegal organization, but acquitted five other defendants. Earlier, in October, the authorities detained hundreds of Muslim Brotherhood supporters in Cairo, Alexandria, and elsewhere in advance of the parliamentary elections, including some who were standing as independent candidates. Those held included several members of the campaigning team of Jihan al-Halafawi, the only woman candidate linked to the Muslim Brotherhood, and Labor Party members running Magdi Hussain's electoral campaign while he served his prison sentence.

This pattern was repeated in advance of the Majlis al-Shura elections. The authorities detained at least 140 Muslim Brotherhood sympathisers starting in mid-April 2001 in Asyut, Alexandria, al-Fayyum, and other centers, including some who had just registered as candidates, such as Muhammad al-Sayyid Habib, an Asyut University professor and former parliamentarian, and Abu Bakr Mitkis. All were released without charge after the elections. Twenty-five other leading members of the Muslim Brotherhood were arrested on July 15 in Imbaba for allegedly holding an illegal meeting. They included Muhammad al-Shater, a former political prisoner and reputedly a member of the Muslim Brotherhood's highest decision-making body, the *Maktab al-Irshad* (Guidance Bureau).

The government also prosecuted people on the basis of their alleged sexual orientation. In July, the authorities referred fifty-two men to the Emergency State Security Court for Misdemeanours, from which there is no right of appeal, on charges of "obscene behaviour" under the Combat of Prostitution Law (Law 10 of 1961). Two defendants were also charged with expressing "contempt for religion" under article 98(f) of the penal code, while a sixteen year old minor was sent before the Juveniles Court. Most of the defendants had been arrested on May 11 in Cairo and initially held incommunicado. During their trial, which began on July 18, the court refused to investigate allegations by some defendants that they had been tortured to make them confess and on November 14, twenty-one of them received sentences of between one and two years of imprisonment on the "obscenity" charge. The two charged with "contempt for religion" received three- and five-year terms.

The others were acquitted. The sixteen-year-old, who did have a right of appeal from the Juveniles Court, was sentenced to three years of imprisonment for "obscenity"on September 18. His appeal was due to be heard in November.

On December 6, 2001, the authorities released eighty-nine prisoners on humanitarian grounds pending a verdict by the Sohag Criminal Court. They had been among ninety-six Muslims and Coptic Christians tried in connection with communal violence at al-Kusheh village in December 1999, in which twenty Copts and one Muslim died. The Sohag Criminal Court had acquitted all the defendants except for four Muslims, who were sentenced to terms ranging between one and ten years for illegal possession of weapons, manslaughter, and damaging property, but Coptic religious leaders and families of those killed criticized the verdict and the General Prosecution quickly lodged an appeal. In July, the Court of Cassation quashed the verdict and ordered a retrial of all the defendants, which then opened in November.

In June, thousands of Copts demonstrated in Cairo over four days in protest at the publication of sexually explicit photographs of a former Coptic monk by the weekly newspaper *al-Naba'* and its sister publication *Akher Khabar,* both of whose publishing licenses the authorities withdrew on July 4. Several demonstrators were injured in clashes with the police. The authorities charged Mamdouh Mahran, editor-in-chief of *al-Naba',* with undermining public order, defaming the Coptic Church, publishing pornography, and other offences, and his trial opened on June 24 before the State Security Court for Misdemeanours. On September 16, he was convicted on all but one count and sentenced to three years of imprisonment. President Mubarak ratified the sentence on September 30, but Mahran suffered a heart attack and was then hospitalized under guard. He appealed successfully to the Administrative Court to overturn the Egypt Press Association's decision to revoke his membership, though a counter-appeal by the association to the Supreme Administrative Court was still pending by November.

In January, Sherif al-Filali, an engineer, went on trial before the Emergency Supreme State Security Court (ESSSC) charged effectively with espionage. Prosecutors alleged that he was recruited into Israel's Mossad intelligence agency by a Russian army officer, Gregory Sergevic, who was tried in his absence in the same case. During two months of pre-trial detention by the State Security Intelligence (SSI) in Cairo, al-Filali was reportedly subjected to "psychological pressure" to confess. However, while Sergevic was sentenced to life imprisonment al-Filali was acquitted. The presiding judge ruled that Egyptian law provides for acquittal if a defendant confesses before the start of a criminal investigation, as in al-Filali's case, even if the available evidence is sufficient to secure a conviction. On June 27, the state security prosecutor announced that he would seek a re-trial, permissible under emergency legislation. Verdicts of the ESSSC, which cannot be appealed, must be ratified by the president. But in September, the president's office refused to endorse the verdict. The authorities then rearrested al-Filali and his new trial opened on October 28. If convicted, he faced up to twenty-five years of imprisonment with hard labor.

The government continued to target writers for exercising their freedom of expression. In December 2000, the General Prosecution successfully appealed for

the re-trial of Salahuddin Muhsin after the State Security Court for Misdemeanours in Giza gave him a six-month suspended sentence in July 2000 for deni-
grating Islam in his writings. In January 2001, he was retried before a different
circuit of the State Security Court, convicted and sentenced to three years' imprisonment with hard labor. He had no right of appeal.

The government also continued to ban books it deemed "offensive" to society,
either because their contents were held to be sexually explicit or because they were
considered defamatory to Islam. In May, al-Azhar's Islamic Research Academy
banned two works, respectively by 'Alaa' Hamed and Ibrahim Abu Khalil on the latter ground.

Workers' rights came under attack through arbitrary measures taken against
trade union activists who were outspoken around issues such as worker safety in the
state sector. Such measures, designed to prevent them from participating in union
elections, included transfer to other companies at short notice in the run-up to
elections, and being pressurized into withdrawing their candidacy. In the run-up to
the General Federation of Trade Unions elections, which began on October 8,
scores of workers who had been disqualified from running as candidates to shop
floor committees lodged appeals before the administrative courts contesting irregularities in nomination procedures. The Center for Trade Union and Workers' Services (CTUWS), an Egyptian NGO that monitors and campaigns for workers'
rights, also came under pressure. Its director, Kamal Abbas, and Abdul Rashid Hilal,
board member and vice-chairman of the Iron and Steel Company trade union,
were both summoned before prosecution officials in Helwan in mid-September as
part of the government's attempt to stifle criticism of working conditions and of
irregularities in trade union election procedures.

In February, the Egyptian Bar Association elected a new board and chairman,
ending five years of judicial sequestration imposed by the government in 1996 for
alleged financial irregularities by board members. There was wide speculation that
the government hoped the election, held under judicial supervision, would dimin-
ish the Muslim Brotherhood's influence over the association but the outcome once
again produced a Muslim Brotherhood-dominated board, with Nasserist lawyer
Sameh 'Ashour elected as chairman.

In a landmark ruling on June 2, Egypt's Supreme Constitutional Court declared
as unconstitutional article 48 of the penal code, which punished criminal complicity to commit felonies or misdemeanours by two or more persons even if no crime
had actually been committed. The article, which provided for up to fifteen years of
imprisonment for felonies and up to three years of imprisonment for misdemeanours, was widely used against Islamists charged with security offences, and
most recently invoked in the case the Saadeddin Ibrahim. (See below.) In late July,
Prosecutor General Maher Abdel Wahed decided not to exercise his right to refer
the ruling back to the court for re-examination, and ordered the release of all prisoners convicted on the basis of article 48. In September, lawyers acting for scores of
Islamist prisoners lodged appeals with the State Security Court requesting their
release on these grounds, but by November it was unclear if any had been released.

DEFENDING HUMAN RIGHTS

An amended version of the controversial Law on Civil Associations and Institutions (Law 153 of 1999), which the Supreme Constitutional Court had overturned in June 2000, was presented to the Majlis al-Shura in April but it had not been presented to the People's Assembly by November, and the earlier Law on Private Associations and Institutions (Law 32 of 1964) remained in force. One positive amendment would allow administrative courts to hear cases arising from disputes between NGOs and the authorities, in lieu of courts of first instance, in line with the Supreme Constitutional Court ruling, but other provisions that would allow the government to control and interfere in the internal activities of NGOs, remained unchanged.

On July 1, Cairo's Administrative Court overturned the government's decision to refuse, for unspecified security reasons, to register the Egyptian Organization for Human Rights (EOHR) as a recognized NGO. Following the overturning of Law 153 of 1999, the EOHR had applied for registration under Law 32 of 1964 but was informed by the Ministry of Social Affairs in July 2000 that a decision on its application had been deferred upon a request from security officials. The EOHR took the matter to the Administrative Court in February, and the July ruling stated that since the ministry failed to process the EOHR's application within the sixty-day period specified by law, it was deemed accepted. The ruling was legally binding on the ministry and its implementation could not be deferred even if appealed before the Supreme Administrative Court, but by November the ministry had not complied.

The government maintained its crackdown on human rights activists with the trial and conviction of Saadeddin Ibrahim, director of the Ibn Khaldun Center for Development Studies, and twenty-seven co-defendants. On May 21, the Supreme State Security Court sentenced Ibrahim to seven years of imprisonment on charges of receiving funding without authorization, disseminating false information damaging to Egypt's interests, and securing funds through fraud. He and four co-defendants were acquitted on a fourth charge of conspiring to bribe public officials. The court imposed one-year suspended sentences on twenty-one defendants, and sentenced six others, including two who faced separate bribery charges, to between two and five years of imprisonment with labor.

Ten of the accused remained at large, however, having been tried in their absence. Most of the defendants were associated with two local NGOs, the Ibn Khaldun Center and the Hoda Association, five as employees and the rest as short-term contract workers. Many had been arrested in mid-2000 in connection with two projects funded by the European Union (E.U.) aimed at promoting voter education and encouraging eligible voters to register and exercise their political rights.

The seven-month trial opened on November 18, 2000. In addition to serious pre-trial irregularities, the proceedings failed to meet international standards for fair trial. Verdicts of the Supreme State Security Court, an exceptional court based on emergency legislation, could only be appealed by cassation or review, limiting the grounds for appeal to points of law and precluding the facts of the case. Defense lawyers did not have full access to prosecution documents presented to the court until four months into the trial. After sentencing, Saadeddin Ibrahim, Khaled al-Fayyad, Usama Hammad, and Mohammad Hassanein were held in Tora Mazra'at prison, and Nadia Abdel Nour and Magda al-Bey at the women's prison in Qanater. The defendants who received suspended sentences were released within days. An appeal hearing before the Court of Cassation was scheduled for December 19. The outcome of the trial was condemned by Egyptian and international human rights organizations, and both U.S. and E.U. officials voiced concern.

In June, the government shut down the offices of the Sudanese Human Rights Organization (SHRO), which had been operating in exile in Egypt since 1991. Although no official reason was given, the SHRO's president believed that the closure was the direct outcome of a report issued by the organization on the practice of slavery in Sudan.

THE ROLE OF THE INTERNATIONAL COMMUNITY

United Nations

In January, the U.N. Committee on the Rights of the Child considered Egypt's second periodic report on the implementation of the Convention on the Rights of the Child. It welcomed improvements to infant and child mortality rates, but noted that "narrow interpretations of Islamic texts by authorities, particularly in areas relating to family law, are impeding the enjoyment of some human rights under the Convention." The committee criticized continued violations of children's rights to healthcare and education, conditions for juvenile detainees, inadequate safeguards against physical or sexual abuse of children, and economic exploitation. Among other things, the committee recommended implementation of the 1996 Children's Code and the systematic involvement of "civil society, especially children's associations and advocacy groups, throughout all stages of the implementation of the Convention, including policy-making."

In January also, the U.N. Committee on the Elimination of Discrimination against Women considered Egypt's third, fourth, and fifth reports on its application of the Convention on the Elimination of All Forms of Discrimination against Women. The committee welcomed the reduction in female illiteracy rates and legislative reforms aimed at eliminating discrimination against women, particularly relating to divorce rights. However, it criticized other discriminatory laws, including the Nationality Law which bars Egyptian women married to non-Egyptians from passing on their nationality to their children, and certain provisions of the penal code. The committee recommended legislative reforms in these areas, and greater efforts by the authorities to prevent violence against women, including domestic violence, marital rape, abuses against detained women, and female genital mutilation.

In August, the U.N. Committee on the Elimination of Racial Discrimination considered Egypt's most recent reports on its implementation of the Convention on the Elimination of All Forms of Racial Discrimination. The committee noted the "significant role" of the Supreme Constitutional Court in "upholding human rights and constitutional guarantees . . . as well as the prevention and elimination of discrimination" but criticized the absence of legal provisions establishing that an ethnic or racial motivation for defamation or acts of violence be considered an aggravating factor. The committee also expressed concern about the discriminatory provisions of the Nationality Law, noting the government's promise to revise it, and recommended speedy resolution of the "difficulties relating to the registration of some non-governmental organizations dealing with the promotion and protection of human rights," particularly those working to combat racial discrimination.

The U.N. special rapporteur on torture, in his report to the Commission on Human Rights published on January 25, concluded that "torture is systematically practised by the security forces in Egypt, in particular by State Security Intelligence," and that despite government denials, the practice is "habitual, widespread and deliberate in at least a considerable part of the country." The special rapporteur cited thirty-five cases of torture and thirty-two cases of death in custody reportedly caused by torture or medical negligence that were transmitted to the government between 1997 and 1999, to which the government replied in March and October 2000. He expressed particular concern at "the persistence of the explanation of death in many of the cases as being 'a sharp drop in blood pressure,'" and stated that the government's responses reinforced rather than alleviated his concerns. The special rapporteur also criticized the government's continuing failure to permit him access to the country.

On May 25, the U.N. special representative on human rights defenders and the special rapporteur on the independence of judges and lawyers issued a joint statement of concern about the conviction of Saadeddin Ibrahim and his co-defendants following unfair trial procedures. They commented that "the conviction of these members of civil society for their human rights activities will have a chilling effect on the activities of other human rights defenders in Egypt," and called for the release of the defendants pending their appeal hearing.

European Union

On December 13, 2000, the European Commission (E.C.) issued a statement concerning the charges levelled against Saadeddin Ibrahim and some of his co-defendants that they had misused E.C. funding of two projects administered by the Ibn Khaldun Center and the Hoda Association. The projects, for which the E.C. had provided a total of 315,000 euro, involved the promotion of voter education and the exercise of political rights. The E.C. stated that "both the Ibn Khaldun and HODA projects were the subject of external mid-term audits whose reports gave no cause for concern, financial or otherwise." On May 23, a spokesman for External Affairs Commissioner Chris Patten expressed concern about the sentences passed on the defendants in the case, and said that while E.U. aid to Egypt had not been suspended, it was "encountering certain difficulties in its implementation." On June 14, the European Parliament passed a resolution expressing concern about the verdict and calling for Ibrahim "to be assured a fair trial," expressing its support for the

Ibn Khaldun Center and calling on the E.C. "to continue to support its initiatives." With reference to the case of Ibrahim and that of Nawal al-Sa'dawi, the resolution called on the E.C. "to strengthen its MEDA programme for democracy, in cooperation with the Egyptian authorities, in particular with a view to supporting freedom of expression and the independence of the media."

The Association Agreement between Egypt and the E.U., which had been under negotiation for over five years, was initialled by the two sides on January 26 and signed on June 25. The agreement, which enters into force after ratification by the parliaments of Egypt and of E.U. member states, covers economic, political, security, and social relations between the two sides. Following the signing of the agreement, Commissioner Patten stated that the "partnership is firmly based on shared political and economic interests as well as a joint commitment for the promotion of democracy and the respect of human rights." He added that the human rights provisions in the agreement would provide a framework within which human rights issues would be raised with the Egyptian authorities.

United States

The U.S. maintained the previous year's levels of foreign aid to Egypt, with the Bush administration requesting for fiscal year 2002 an estimated U.S. $1.3 billion for military assistance and U.S. $655 million for economic support funds. The administration said military assistance would "support a modern, well-trained Egyptian military that will help ensure stability in the region" and "enable Egypt to participate as a coalition partner in operations that further U.S. interests." Of the funds requested for economic assistance, an estimated 14 percent was earmarked for "programs meant to reduce the fertility rate, improve health care, support democratic institutions and increase access to schooling for girls."

Following the conviction and sentencing of Saadeddin Ibrahim and his co-defendants, a State Department spokesman said in a press briefing on May 21 that "we are deeply troubled about the outcome, and . . . we have been expressing all along our concerns about the process that resulted in this sentence." U.S. embassy staff in Cairo had observed the trial and visited Ibrahim, who held dual Egyptian-U.S. citizenship, in Mazra'at Tora prison where he was taken after sentencing.

In its *Country Reports on Human Rights Practices for 2000*, the State Department said that while the Egyptian government "generally respected the human rights of its citizens in some areas, . . . its record was poor with respect to freedom of expression and its treatment of detainees." It pointed to the government's use of emergency laws to restrict "many basic rights," including freedom of expression, assembly, and association.

A delegation from the U.S. Commission on International Religious Freedom visited Egypt from March 20-24 as part of a wider fact-finding tour of the Middle East. It met with government officials, religious leaders, academics, journalists, and NGO representatives, but several Egyptian human rights groups declined to cooperate or assist the delegates. On March 28, the commission urged President George W. Bush to raise the issue of religious freedoms with President Mubarak during the latter's U.S. visit in April. The commission's detailed findings, released on May 14 as an addendum to its annual report, concluded that "serious problems of discrimination against a number of religious groups remain widespread in Egypt," including Coptic Christians, Baha'is, and Muslims deemed by the authorities to be "fundamentalists.

President Mubarak visited Washington, D.C. in the first week of April and held talks with President Bush, political leaders, and representatives of the business community. The visit focused on continuing efforts to salvage Israeli-Palestinian peace negotiations and on economic ties between Egypt and the U.S., with Egypt calling for a free trade agreement with the U.S. There was no indication that human rights issues were discussed.

The Bush administration announced in November that an arms deal with Egypt worth an estimated U.S. $400 million had been reached, and that economic aid to Egypt would be accelerated to offset the adverse effects which the September 11 attacks on the U.S. were having on the Egyptian economy, notably the tourist industry. On November 29, a legal assistance treaty between the U.S. and Egypt came into effect, aimed at increasing cooperation in combatting transnational crimes, including drug trafficking, money laundering, and "terrorist group financing," according to the State Department.

Relevant Human Rights Watch Reports:

Egypt: Underage and Unprotected: Child Labor in Egypt's Cotton Fields, 1/01

IRAN

HUMAN RIGHTS DEVELOPMENTS

Factional conflict within Iran's clerical leadership continued to result in severe restrictions on freedom of expression, association, and political participation. Deteriorating economic conditions made worse by severe natural disasters contributed to increasing unrest and a pervasive sense of social insecurity, reflected in clashes between demonstrators and the security forces and in harsh measures against drug-traffickers and other criminals. President Mohammad Khatami won another landslide victory for those associated with the cause of political reform when he was reelected by 77 percent of voters for a second four-year term in June, but the power struggle between conservatives and reformists remained unresolved. Conservative clerics maintained a strong grip on power through the judiciary, the Council of Guardians and the office of the Leader of the Islamic Republic, Ayatollah Ali Khamenei. Promises by reformists to increase respect for basic freedoms and the rule of law remained unrealized, and severe restrictions imposed on the independent print media, the major visible gain of President Khatami's first period in office, remained in place. The judiciary, and branches of the security forces beyond the control of the elected government, resorted increasingly to intimidatory tactics, with a sharp increase in public executions and public floggings. Conservative clerics taunted critics of corporal punishment, and accused them of being opposed to Islamic rule—in some cases even calling for the shedding of the blood of such critics. Such remarks fueled an increasingly polarized political stand-off, which, coupled with governmental ineffectiveness in the face of mounting economic and social problems, contributed to a volatile situation where the threat of political violence loomed large.

The clampdown on the independent print media that had followed the sweeping reformist victory in parliamentary elections in February 2001 (see *Human Rights Watch World Report 2001*) was followed by the detention of scores of leading independent and reformist figures and activists. Many of these activists had participated in the flowering of the independent press in the late 1990s as writers, editors, and publishers. Other targeted activists included supporters of the national religious trend, a loose alliance of intellectuals and politicians advocating Islamic government with adherence to the rule of law and the constitution, who for many years had been one of the few currents of internal political opposition tolerated by the establishment.

Seventeen reformist figures, many of them prominent, were brought to trial in October 2000 in connection with their participation in an international conference on the future of Iran, held in Berlin, Germany, in April 2000. The trial before the Tehran Revolutionary Court was unfair. Many of the defendants were held in protracted incommunicado detention after returning from Berlin, during which time they were forced to make incriminating statements that formed the evidence against them at their trial. Akbar Ganji, a well-known investigative journalist who was among the accused, protested at his hearing in November 2000 that he had been beaten by his interrogators while in detention in order to pressure him to confess to crimes. Most of the trial was conducted behind closed doors.

On January 13, the court convicted seven of the defendants on vague charges of having "conspired to overthrow the system of the Islamic Republic." The severest sentences, ten years of imprisonment, were passed on Akbar Ganji and Saeed Sadr, a translator at the German embassy in Tehran. A second translator, Khalil Rostamkhani, received a nine-year sentence, even though he had not attended the conference. His wife, Roshanak Darioush, a translator of German literature into Persian, had served as a translator at the conference but did not return to Iran to face charges. The trial and the harsh sentences imposed on local employees of the German embassy appeared designed to cause maximum embarrassment to President Khatami's government in its relations with Germany, a major trade partner which he had visited in 2000, and with other European states.

The court also sentenced student leader Ali Afshari to five years in prison, and veteran politician Ezzatollah Sahhabi to four and a half years. Both were already in prison by the time the trial began in October 2000. Women's rights activists Shahla Lahidji and Mehrangiz Kar each received four-year prison sentences, but were released pending an appeal. Ezzatollah Sahhabi was also provisionally released, but he was re-arrested following public remarks he made in March and was still detained without charge in November.

An appeal court reduced Akbar Ganji's sentence to six months of imprisonment but before he could be released, the Tehran Press Court sentenced him again to a ten-year term on the same charge of conspiring to overthrow the system. He had the right of appeal but no appeal had been heard by November. In March and April, the authorities detained more than sixty political activists associated with the national religious trend, including the leadership of the formerly tolerated Freedom Movement (*Nehzat-e Azadi*). Throughout its fifty-year history the Freedom Movement had been an advocate of constitutional Islamic rule with respect for democratic principles. On March 18, the Tehran Revolutionary Court ordered the closure of the Freedom Movement, accusing it of attempting to "overthrow the Islamic regime."

These detentions further chilled the political climate in the run-up to the June presidential election as opponents of reform showed themselves determined to intimidate, silence, or punish those known to support the reformist cause. A leading conservative cleric, Ayatollah Mesbah Yazdi, stated in April: "what is being termed as reform today is in fact corruption." And other conservatives sought to discourage President Khatami, the reform movement's figurehead, from standing for a second term. When he could not be discouraged, they signaled by their actions that regardless of the outcome of the election, there would be no concession to the reformist agenda.

Another persistent challenger to the dominant orthodoxy of the conservative clerics who held power was Ayatollah Hossain Ali Montazeri, the former designated successor to Ayatollah Khomeini as Leader of the Islamic Republic. He remained under house arrest in Qom, but his criticism of the present system, especially of the institution of the *velayat-e faqih* (rule of the supreme jurist), continued to circulate by cassette tapes, photocopied statements, and through the Internet. In December 2000, the authorities detained the ayatollah's son for allegedly distributing illegal literature, but the real reason appeared to be related to the publication of Ayatollah Montazeri's memoirs on the Internet. These directly attacked the position of Supreme Leader, arguing that the concentration of power in the hands of one man was contrary to Islamic principles. Protests about the continuing restrictions on Ayatollah Montazeri's liberty mounted throughout the year. In June, the ayatollah's children (with the exception of his jailed son) circulated a letter calling for the lifting of these restrictions, and 126 out of 290 members of parliament signed a similar statement. President Khatami several times publicly criticized the stifling of dissent, including closures of newspapers and magazines, and the imprisonment of political dissidents, but he appeared unable or unwilling to remedy these problems. In February, in a speech marking the Islamic Revolution's twenty-second anniversary, he warned: "those who claim a monopoly on Islam and the revolution, those with narrow and dark views, are setting themselves against the people." He also complained repeatedly that he lacked the power to carry out his obligation as president to uphold the constitution. But even after his sweeping election victory in June, when he increased his share of the popular vote, he continued to shy away from open confrontation with his opponents and made no discernible progress in implementing his promised reforms. Increasingly, through his statements, he appeared to represent more of a safety valve for public frustration than an agent of tangible change.

A severe drought in the east and floods in the north-west exacerbated the country's economic malaise and contributed to public scapegoating of Afghan refugees and migrants, who were blamed for high unemployment and rising crime and were increasingly a target of violence. Afghans were viewed as particularly culpable for drug offenses, and thousands were detained and scores executed in an intensified official clampdown on alleged drug-traffickers. The government repatriated thousands of other Afghans under a process agreed with the United Nations High Commissioner for Refugees (UNHCR), despite insufficient safeguards to prevent those at risk of persecution being returned. At the same time, there were new influxes of refugees fleeing continuing unrest and violence in Afghanistan, although the border was officially closed by Iran. The repatriation process was halted with the onset of U.S. bombing raids in Afghanistan in October, when there were fears of a further massive influx to add to the one and a half to two million Afghan already displaced to Iran.

Law enforcement authorities made increased use of public executions and corporal punishment, often after only cursory trial proceedings. In February, five convicted drug-traffickers were publicly executed by being hanged from construction cranes in the Khak-i Sefid district of Tehran, part of an intensified clampdown on drug-traffickers, and the authorities carried out more than twenty public executions for drug-related offenses in July and August. Public floggings were also increasingly used for a wide range of social offenses, including breaches of the dress code, despite opposition from Ministry of Interior officials who questioned the effectiveness of such punishments. In July and August, clashes reportedly occurred at public floggings and executions in Tehran between police and demonstrators opposed to these punishments.

In August, the parliamentary commission charged with investigating human rights violations by public institutions, known as the Article 90 Commission, produced a report sharply critical of deteriorating prison conditions. The report itself was not made public, but members of the commission said it identified the sharp rise in the number of offenders being sent to prisons as a major cause of prison overcrowding and the high level of drug abuse among prisoners. More than two-thirds of all prison inmates were reportedly held for drug-related offenses, and AIDS and other diseases were reported to be spreading rapidly among the prison population.

The proliferation of unofficial, illegal detention centers, such as the so-called Prison 59 in Tehran, gave major cause for concern. Prison 59 was reportedly administered by the Ministry of Intelligence, the Islamic Revolutionary Guards Corps and clandestine paramilitary forces, and was entirely beyond official oversight. Political prisoners detained there or in similar facilities could be held for months at a time without their families or lawyers being informed or having any idea of their whereabouts, treatment or conditions, and being powerless to seek remedies.

The independent press, before it was closed down in mid-2000, had sought to expose the connections between certain state institutions and the clandestine underworld of death squads and enforcers. It was the investigative journalism of people such as Akbar Ganji that led to the prosecution of eighteen Intelligence Ministry officials for alleged involvement in the murder of a group of intellectuals and political leaders at the end of 1998. (See *Human Rights Watch World Report 2000*.) On January 27, fifteen of these defendants were convicted after a trial mostly held behind closed doors: three were sentenced to death, five received life imprisonment, and seven received prison terms of between two and a half and ten years. It remained unclear, however, who had ordered the murders: press investigators had pointed to senior figures, such as former information ministers Dori Najafabadi and Ali Fallahian, as possible suspects but they were not charged and no information against them emerged at the trial. On August 18, the Supreme Court reversed the convictions of the fifteen ministry officials, who may be re-tried. Lawyers representing the murder victims' families accused the judiciary of failing to ensure a thorough inquiry into the crimes.

In a similarly unrevealing trial in May, guilty verdicts were announced against the so-called Mahdaviyat group, a group linked to the authorities, who were convicted of inciting violence against Sunni Muslims and committing political killings. This trial, which involved links between state bodies and illegal political violence, was held behind closed doors. The sentences have not been publicly announced but its was reported in the press that at least one of the defendants was sentenced to death.

Earlier, on January 30, the Supreme Court rejected the appeals against conviction of ten members of the minority Jewish community in Shiraz who had been sentenced to prison terms in 2000 for allegedly maintaining contacts with Israel, considered a hostile foreign power. None of the group were released.

The conservative backlash set in motion by the sweeping reformist victory in parliamentary elections in February 2000 showed no signs of abating. By the end of November 2000, more than fifty daily and weekly newspapers had been issued with closure orders, and more than twenty leading independent and reform-minded journalists, editors, and publishers remained in prison. In January 2001, the authorities closed the philosophical and cultural monthly, *Kiyan*. The journal had published academic articles debating the philosophical underpinnings of the reform movement. The conservative faction also sought to prevent reformists being elected to the parliament. Before the June parliamentary election, held concurrently with the presidential vote, the Council of Guardians vetoed 145 out of 356 candidates nominated for the seventeen seats, a far higher proportion than in February 2000. In a further display of conservative power, in August, the parliament was forced to accept two candidates nominated by the judiciary to the Council of Guardians. The parliament initially rejected the two nominated jurists, Mohssen Ismaili and Abbas Ali Khadkhodai, claiming that they lacked adequate experience, but the head of the judiciary, an appointee of the supreme leader, refused to withdraw their names. Eventually, the Council of Expediency, another body appointed by the supreme leader headed by former president Hashemi Rafsanjani, crafted a rule change whereby the appointments were ratified without obtaining majority approval from members of parliament.

DEFENDING HUMAN RIGHTS

A few members of parliament were willing to confront what they viewed as conservative attempts to circumvent and undermine their constitutional powers as the people's elected representatives, and to speak out against violations of constitutional principles. They included outspoken parliamentarian Fatima Haqiqatjou, who protested the arrest of journalists and accused the judiciary of exceeding its constitutional functions. Her criticisms made her the target of criminal prosecution, and in August she was sentenced to twenty-two months in prison for "spreading propaganda against Islam" and insulting state officials. Haqiqatjou appealed her conviction, denying the charges and also claiming parliamentary immunity for comments made in the course of parliamentary debate. She remained at liberty pending her appeal. However, seven other reformist parliamentarians were facing charges for remarks they had made under the cover of parliamentary immunity, part of a growing struggle between conservative elements of the judiciary and reformist members of parliament.

Despite the silencing of the independent press, the debate about human rights remained at the center of the political struggle in Iran, especially within the clerical leadership. Reformist clerics repeatedly argued that there was compatibility between Islam and international human rights principles; conservative clerics, just as insistently, asserted that appeals for liberty and respect for human rights were akin to apostasy.

Hassan Youssefi Eshkevari, who was detained in August 2000 for advocating liberal interpretations of Islam supportive of international human rights principles, continued to be imprisoned. He had been convicted of apostasy in a secret trial by a Special Court for the Clergy. In September, however, he was allowed to leave prison for two days and it was unclear whether or not he remained under sentence of death.

Access to the country for independent human rights investigators remained restricted, although representatives of international human rights organizations were allowed to visit Iran to attend conferences. The U.N. special representative on Iran, Maurice Copithorne of Canada, continued to be denied access to the country, but in April he was able to meet in Geneva with Abbas Ali Alizadeh, the head of the Tehran justice department, the highest level judicial official he had been able to meet with for several years.

In May, the International Center for Dialogue Among Civilizations, headed by the reformist former minister of culture and Islamic guidance, Ataollah Mohajerani, together with a clerically-supported private university in Qom, hosted an international human rights conference in Tehran with a diverse group of participants. Iranians who attended in the conference were candid in their criticism of domestic conditions.

THE ROLE OF THE INTERNATIONAL COMMUNITY

United Nations

Iran played an active role in multilateral diplomatic efforts in the human rights field, hosting, in February, the Asian regional preparatory conference for the United Nations World Conference Against Racism, Racial Discrimination, Xenophobia and Related Intolerance (WCAR) and entering into negotiations with the Office of the United Nations High Commissioner for Human Rights over a program of technical assistance in the human rights field. In April, the United Nations Commission on Human Rights renewed the mandate of the special representative on Iran.

European Union

Relations with the E.U. continued to improve. British government minister Marjorie Mowlam visited Iran in February: she praised the government's efforts to combat drug-trafficking but criticized continuing human rights violations including the clampdown on journalists and the press. In September, Foreign Minister Kamal Kharazi met with E.U. commissioners for wide-ranging talks. Human rights concerns were again reported to be part of the agenda, but the major emphasis was on expanding trade ties.

British Foreign Secretary Jack Straw visited Iran twice following the September 11 attacks on the U.S. This first visit by a senior British minister for several years focused on the crisis in Afghanistan rather than domestic human rights issues in Iran.

United States

Contrary to some initial expectations, oil industry interests closely associated with the new Bush administration brought no discernible shift in U.S. government relations with Iran. Restrictions on freedom of expression and persecution of minority religious communities were roundly condemned in the State Department's *Country Reports on Human Rights Practices,* and the U.S. continued to voice objections to Iran's alleged efforts to obtain weapons of mass destruction, its alleged support for international terrorism, and its opposition to peace efforts between Israel and the Palestinians.

In April, the Iranian parliament convened an international conference in support of the Palestinian uprising against Israeli occupation, which was attended by representatives of numerous groups on the U.S. government's list of terrorist organizations, including Lebanese Hizbollah, and the Palestinian groups, Hamas and Islamic Jihad. At the preparatory conference for the WCAR, Iran supported the insertion of language singling out Israel and Zionism for special criticism. These high-profile forays into the Israeli-Palestinian dispute provoked U.S. ire. In April, Attorney General John Ashcroft named the government of Iran as an unindicted co-conspirator in the attack on the Khobar Towers barracks in Saudi Arabia in 1999. In May, Iran was identified as a state sponsor of terrorism in the State Department's *Patterns of Global Terrorism Report.* The Iranian government responded sharply to this accusation: "The U.S. government, which itself is one of the supporters of Israeli state-terrorism, is not in any position to judge us."

In this climate of increasing rhetorical antagonism against Iran it came as no surprise in June when the International Relations Committee of the House of Representatives voted to maintain sanctions against Iran for a further five-year term. The Bush administration had originally signaled a preference for a two-year renewal of the sanctions regime, but with opposition from Congress, the administration voiced its support for long-term enforcement of sanctions. The U.S. government continued to support policies seen as unfavorable toward Iran in disputes over control over exports of energy resources from the Caspian Basin region.

If the U.S. and Iran were clearly divided on their policies to the Israeli-Palestinian conflict, they had more in common with respect to their shared concern over the Taliban government in Afghanistan. In the aftermath of the September 11 attacks on New York and Washington, and the identification of the Afghanistan-based Osama Bin Laden as a prime suspect in these attacks, the possibility of closer cooperation between the U.S. and Iranian governments emerged as a prospect for the first time in more than twenty years.

Relevant Human Rights Watch Reports:

Iran: Stifling Dissent: The Human Rights Consequences of Inter-Factional Struggle in Iran, 6/01

IRAQ AND IRAQI KURDISTAN

HUMAN RIGHTS DEVELOPMENTS

The Iraqi government of President Saddam Hussain perpetrated widespread and gross human rights violations, including arbitrary arrests of suspected political opponents and their relatives, routine torture and ill-treatment of detainees, summary execution of military personnel and political detainees as part of a "prison cleansing" campaign, and forced expulsions of Kurds and Turkmen from Kirkuk and other regions.

The Kurdistan Democratic Party (KDP) and the Patriotic Union of Kurdistan (PUK), who controlled most of the northerly Duhok, Arbil, and Sulaimaniya provinces, sought to implement a 1998 U.S.-brokered peace settlement but did not agree to set up a unified administration for the region. There were repeated threats of military action and incursions into Kurdish-controlled areas by Iraqi government troops, and by Turkish government troops pursuing members of the opposition Kurdistan Workers' Party (PKK). Human rights abuses were committed by Kurdish opposition groups, including in the context of clashes between PUK forces and those of Islamist groups.

Economic sanctions imposed on Iraq by the United Nations Security Council in 1991 remained in force despite the continued erosion of the international consensus on the issue. The government continued to deny U.N. weapons inspectors access to Iraq. Efforts by the United States (U.S.) and the United Kingdom (U.K.) to restructure the sanctions by removing restrictions on civilian imports yet tightening controls on military goods and oil revenue failed due to other Security Council members' opposition. The Iraqi government also opposed the proposal and temporarily suspended its oil exports in protest.

HUMAN RIGHTS DEVELOPMENTS
IN GOVERNMENT-CONTROLLED IRAQ

The Iraqi authorities reportedly carried out numerous executions of military personnel suspected of involvement in alleged coup attempts. These included, in March, three air force officers, including Fawzi Hamed al-'Ubaidi and Faris Ahmad al-'Alwan, and an army major-general, Tareq al-Sa'dun. In July, the authorities executed two more air force officers in Kirkuk, including Kadhim Khairallah al-Dulaimi, and at least five Republican Guard officers, including Staff Colonel Sami Abd al-Ghaffur al-Alusi. Other executions of military personnel were carried out in August and October at Abu Ghraib prison near Baghdad; the victims included former army colonels 'Abd al-Salam Hadi al-Tikriti and Saleh Manna' Salman al-Tikriti, detained since 1995 and executed on October 8. Other senior military personnel were reportedly arrested in Baghdad in late October.

The authorities also executed numerous inmates at Abu Ghraib, al-Makasib, and other prisons, including long term untried political detainees and convicted prisoners. Some were apparently tortured first. Relatives reported that the body of 'Abd al-Wahed al-Rifa'i, hanged in March after two years in detention without trial, bore marks of torture when they collected it on March 26 from the General Security Directorate in Baghdad. Thirteen Abu Ghraib detainees, including students, were executed in August, and twenty-one prisoners convicted by special courts of killing several security agents were executed in October, including Falah Ahmad Hussain, Muhsin Yassin Kadhim, and Baqer Jassim 'Ali.

In November 2000, a former Iraqi intelligence officer who fled to Jordan in June 1999 disclosed the existence of a government "prison cleansing" campaign. Captain Khalid Sajed al-Janabi, an intelligence operative from 1979 to 1999, said a March 15, 1998 directive from the Office of the President had authorized the establishment of supervisory committees to "clean up Iraqi prisons" and that he had been appointed to the Abu Ghraib prison committee. The "cleansing" operations, he said, resulted in the execution of some 2,000 detainees and sentenced prisoners on one day, April 27, 1998. Al-Janabi also reported that at least fifty Kuwaitis detained by Iraq since the 1991 Gulf war were still being held at the General Investigative Bureau in Baghdad between April and July 1998. A doctor who worked at Abu Ghraib prison hospital before fleeing to Jordan in July also reported regular mass executions of prisoners. Maher Fakher Khashan said most of those executed were political detainees identified by serial number rather than by name, whose bodies were removed for burial in special vehicles, and that he had most recently witnessed thirty-four such executions on July 8. He reported too that prison authorities forced doctors to inject some detainees with poison and then issue death certificates attributing their deaths to natural causes.

A preliminary survey carried out in northern Iraq by the U.N. Centre for Human Settlements (Habitat) estimated the number of internally displaced persons at 805,000 by the end of October 2000, comprising 23 percent of the population. On December 4, the executive director of the U.N. Office of the Iraq Program (OIP) told the Security Council he was "greatly concerned with the increasing number of internally displaced persons," whose living conditions in some cases were "abominable." A major factor in the rising number of internally displaced persons was the government's continued expulsion of Kurds and Turkmen from their homes in Kirkuk, Tuz Khormatu, Khaniqin, and other districts as part of its "Arabization" program. Most were expelled to areas controlled by Kurdish opposition forces and a smaller number to central and southern Iraq. According to PUK officials, those expelled between January 1991 and December 2000 and resettled in areas under its control totaled 93,888, while some 25,000 others expelled during the same period were resettled in KDP-controlled areas. Scores more were reportedly expelled between January and March, particularly from the Tuz Khormatu area. In August and September, Kurdish opposition sources said the government was intensifying the rate of resettlement of Arab families in areas from which Kurds and Turkmen had been expelled, including the Lailan, Shwan, and Qara Hanjir districts of Kirkuk. The government also gave Arabs title deeds of property owned by those expelled, built new housing in villages around Altun Kopri and Tuz Khormatu to accommodate more Arab families, and substituted Arabic for Kurdish, Turkman, and Assyrian place names. On September 6, according to the government press, Iraq's Revolution Command Council issued decree 199, enabling Iraqis aged eighteen or over to change their official ethnic identity by applying to register as Arabs.

Criminal proceedings against Fowad Hussain Haidar, arrested in late June 2000 following the killing of two staff members of the U.N. Food and Agriculture Organization (FAO) in Baghdad, and the wounding of eight others, remained inconclusive. (See *Human Rights Watch World Report 2001*.) On December 5, 2000, the Security Council called on Iraq to complete its investigation into the incident, but on March 2, U.N. Secretary-General Kofi Annan said he had not been provided with the government's report into the investigation. On May 18, he informed the Security Council that on May 14, "the criminal court postponed, yet again, for the seventh time, its proceedings in the trial of the accused, to 28 May." By October, no further information was available on the case.

In his March 2 report to the Security Council on the implementation of the "oil-for-food" program, the U.N. secretary-general said that increased revenues placed the Iraqi government "in a position to reduce current malnutrition levels and improve the health status of the Iraqi people." In his May 18 report, the secretary-general expressed regret that no progress had been made on arrangements for local procurement of goods and services and the provision of a cash component, provided for under resolution 1284 (1999). He noted that an "increasing range of equipment is being imported under the program, with insufficient local resources available to undertake installation, training and maintenance." In his September 28 report, the secretary-general reiterated his concern about the increase in the "number of holds placed on applications, the total value of which was $4.05 billion as at 14 September 2001," impeding the implementation of the "oil-for-food" program. He urged the Security Council and the Sanctions Committee to further streamline approval procedures, and "allow greater latitude so that a wider variety of medicine, health supplies, foodstuffs, as well as materials and supplies for essential civilian needs can be procured and supplied most expeditiously." He also said that the program had been adversely affected by the "substantial reduction in revenues received from oil exports" decreased or totally suspended by Iraq, and well as by the "inordinate delays" and refusals in the issuance of visas by Iraq to U.N. personnel.

Concern about the overall humanitarian situation in Iraq was voiced by U.N. and other humanitarian agencies. In a December 2000 report, the International Committee of the Red Cross (ICRC) said that "despite the increased availability of food, medicines and medical equipment, following a rise in oil prices and the extension of the 'oil-for-food' programme, suffering remained widespread." Information released by the United Nations Children's Fund (UNICEF) on July 11 warned that "one in five children in the south and centre of Iraq remain so malnourished that they need special therapeutic feeding," and that child sickness rates remain "alarmingly high." The organization called for speedy implementation of the provisions of resolution 1330, which had earmarked five per cent of oil revenues for "the most vulnerable groups in Iraq."

HUMAN RIGHTS DEVELOPMENTS IN IRAQI KURDISTAN

Most of the three northerly Duhok, Arbil, and Sulaimaniya provinces remained under the control of the KDP and the PUK, which maintained separate administrative, legislative, and executive structures in areas under their control. Efforts to implement the 1998 Washington Accord began after meetings between KPD leader Mas'ud Barzani and PUK leader Jalal Talabani in January, leading to negotiations over the gradual normalization of relations between the two sides. By November, they had not agreed on a unified administration for the region; earlier, the KDP held municipal elections in areas under its control on May 26. However, the two sides eased restrictions on the free movement of people and trade between their respective areas and decreased their military presence along the ceasefire line. They also facilitated the gradual exchange of people internally displaced since the 1996 clashes, with some 1,300 families returning to their homes in Arbil, Duhok, and Sulaimaniya between June and October. The two sides also increased cooperation on security matters and prisoner exchanges. Both sides continued to grant access to their prisons to the ICRC, which reported that during 2000 it visited 792 detainees held "for security reasons or in connection with the inter-Kurdish fighting" in thirty-two places of detention.

President Hussain proposed the reopening of negotiations between the government and Kurdish political parties on July 15, but in a joint statement on July 27, the KDP and PUK set preconditions: they demanded an end to mass deportations of Kurds and Turkman, clarification of the fate of detainees in Iraqi government custody and missing persons, and acceptance by the Iraqi government of federalism as the basis of future relations between the Kurdish region and Baghdad. The government rejected these demands in August.

Iraqi troops were deployed to the northern region on several occasions, apparently with the aim of launching armed attacks on Kurdish-controlled territory. In mid-June, the government deployed tanks, armored personnel carriers, artillery and infantry units south of Arbil, coinciding with efforts by the U.K. and the U.S. to restructure the economic embargo imposed on Iraq and to impose "smart sanctions." Government troops clashed with PUK forces in the Kifri region on September 9, and in early October they reportedly entered and occupied the village of Sadawa, south-west of Arbil. The KDP said that repeated artillery bombardment of some thirty front-line villages by government troops had resulted in the displacement of their inhabitants.

There were at least eight bomb attacks in Arbil in other cities between November 2000 and October 2001. Some targeted buildings used by U.N. personnel and by local and international nongovernmental organizations (NGOs). In August, the KDP said it had arrested two men in separate incidents whose vehicles were apparently carrying explosives, and that they had confessed to working for Iraqi intelligence. Among them was a Tunisian national employed by the U.N. who was caught on July 19 while returning from Baghdad with explosives in his vehicle. He was released on July 31 and handed over to Tun Myat, U.N. humanitarian coordinator for Iraq, during his visit to Iraqi Kurdistan.

Other bomb blasts in KDP-held territory, including one in Arbil on April 23 and another in Zakho on October 15, were reportedly attributed to Islamist groups based in the region, notably *Harakat al-Tawhid al-Islami* (Islamic Unity Movement, IUM). The IUM, one of three Islamist groups which broke away at different times from the mainstream Islamic Unity Movement in Kurdistan (IUMK) and in September merged to form *Jund al-Islam* (Soldiers of God), was also held responsible by the KDP for the assassination on February 18 of Francois Hariri, governor of Arbil and member of the KDP's Central Committee. He was shot dead by unidentified assailants as he drove to work in the city. His bodyguard was also killed and his driver wounded. The KDP announced in late March that it had identified several IUM members as being responsible for the assassination, one of whom was apprehended.

Clashes between PUK forces and Jund al-Islam began in September, shortly after the group's leader, Abu 'Ubaidullah al-Shafi'i, declared *Jihad* (Holy War) against secular and other political parties in Iraqi Kurdistan deemed to have deviated from the "true path of Islam." After the September 11 attacks in the U.S., the PUK accused the group of links with Osama bin Laden's *al-Qaeda* (The Base) network and said its members included Arabs of various nationalities who had received military training in Afghanistan. The PUK also accused the group of imposing an extreme form of Islam in their strongholds of Biyara and Tawela, including barring women from employment and education, and of preventing the Naqshabandi Sufis based in the area from practicing their religious rites.

On September 22, Jund al-Islam abducted a doctor, Rebwar Sayyid 'Umar, from his surgery in Halabja and detained him for twenty days in Biyara near the border with Iran. On September 23, thirty-seven PUK fighters were killed by Jund al-Islam in the village of Kheli Hama on the Sulaimaniya-Halabja road. Several died in an ambush, but the majority was reportedly killed after surrender. Photographs of the victims made available by the PUK showed that some of the prisoners' throats had been slit and some of the dead had been beheaded or mutilated, including by having their sexual organs severed. During the ensuing clashes, an estimated one hundred PUK fighters and some forty Jund al-Islam fighters were killed. The PUK regained control of Halabja and its vicinity by September 26, arresting suspected supporters or members of Jund al-Islam, and during October the fighting extended to Sharazur, Hawraman, and elsewhere. At least thirty-eight Jund al-Islam fighters were reportedly killed in these clashes, while some twenty-four others were captured or surrendered. Other Kurdish political parties, including the KDP, offered military assistance to the PUK. On October 11, the PUK declared a ceasefire and on October 25, it issued a thirty-day amnesty for Jund al-Islam fighters. The amnesty did not cover those responsible for the assassination of Francois Hariri, or those involved in the killing of the thirty-seven PUK fighters on September 23. The PUK also said that foreign nationals among them would not be permitted to remain in Iraqi Kurdistan.

Turkish government troops launched repeated military incursions into northern Iraq in pursuit of PKK members. In December 2000, Turkey deployed several thousand troops near the Iran-Iraq border, in order, the Turkish prime minister said on January 7, 2000, to provide "technical support" to PUK forces that had been engaged in military operations against the PKK since September 2000. According to PUK officials, some 120 PKK and thirty-five PUK fighters were killed in December 2000. The PUK accused the PKK of forcibly occupying forty-six villages in areas under PUK control. Turkish troops were also deployed in PUK-held territory in July and August, and in KDP-held areas near Zakho in September. Earlier, in January 2000, the KDP and the PUK adopted a unified policy to expel the PKK from Iraqi Kurdistan.

THE ROLE OF THE INTERNATIONAL COMMUNITY

United Nations

The "oil-for-food" humanitarian relief program for Iraq was extended for a further six months on December 5, 2000, under Security Council Resolution 1330. The Sanctions Committee was requested to approve lists of supplies and equipment in the electricity and housing sectors for "fast-track" approval procedures and to expand lists in other sectors. It approved the reduction of the allocation for the U.N. Compensation Fund from 30 percent to 25 percent, transferring the additional funds to meet the costs of humanitarian supplies to vulnerable groups in central and southern Iraq. It also allowed funds of up to 600 million euros to be used for the cost of installation and maintenance of the oil industry.

Divisions within the Security Council on the sanctions policy were evident during a debate over a draft resolution proposed by the U.K. on May 22, aimed at introducing "smart sanctions" by removing most restrictions on Iraq's civilian imports while tightening controls on military goods and oil revenue. Russia, China, and France opposed the resolution, in part over the list of prohibited "dual-use" goods which would remain subject to Security Council scrutiny. Russia introduced its own counter-resolution proposing the lifting of restrictions on civilian goods once weapons inspectors were fully deployed, while Iraq suspended its oil exports on June 4 in protest at the U.K. proposal. On June 1, the "oil-for-food" program was extended for one month under resolution 1352, giving the Security Council more time to debate the issue. By July 2, however, no consensus was reached and the U.K. postponed indefinitely a vote on its draft resolution. The "oil-for-food" program was renewed for a further five months on July 3 under resolution 1360.

Weapons inspectors of the U.N. Monitoring, Verification and Inspection Commission (UNMOVIC), continued to be denied access to Iraq, with the government maintaining its rejection of resolution 1284. Talks held between Iraqi and U.N. officials in February failed to resolve the deadlock over weapons inspections, and UNMOVIC Executive Chairman Hans Blix said that documents submitted by Iraq as evidence that it no longer had weapons of mass destruction contained "very little new data."

The Iraqi government also denied Yuli Vorontsov, the secretary-general's high-level coordinator for the return of missing property and missing persons from Iraq to Kuwait, access to the country. In March, Vorontsov said Iraq was concealing information about an estimated 605 Kuwaiti and third-country nationals unaccounted for since February 1991. On July 3, Foreign Ministry officials rejected as "false facts" information submitted by Vorontsov to the Security Council on April 20, saying that his role was "partisan and less than objective." The Iraqi government declined to participate in a meeting of the Tripartite Commission scheduled for July 19 under ICRC auspices, saying its participation was conditional on the withdrawal of the U.S. and the U.K. from the Tripartite Commission. It also called on Kuwait to account for an estimated 1,142 Iraqis which it said remained unaccounted for since 1991. In August, the Security Council urged Iraq to cooperate with Vorontsov and with the ICRC to clarify the fate of those missing.

On February 14, Benon Sevan, executive director of the U.N. Office of the Iraq Program (OIP), criticized Iraq for failing to utilize increased oil revenues "to reduce current malnutrition levels and improve the health status of the Iraqi people," saying that the sums allocated for this in the government's distribution plan were not "commensurate" with the problem. In a statement to the Security Council on March 8, he expressed "grave concern over the unacceptably high level of holds placed on applications," including "some essential items required for key sectors such as electricity." He urged "all parties concerned, including the Government of Iraq, to depoliticize and facilitate the program's implementation in order to alleviate the continued suffering of the Iraqi people." In mid-April, the OIP said the Sanctions Committee had delayed some 1,685 contracts valued at U.S. $3.44 billion.

Relations with the U.N. deteriorated further when a Foreign Ministry official accused the OIP in July of financial mismanagement and impropriety, and in August requested regular audits of "oil-for-food" revenues by "independent, legal and neutral accountants." Iraq also accused the U.N. in July of deliberately delaying a visit by World Health Organization (WHO) experts, adding that Sevan was "prejudiced against Iraq." On September 5, Foreign Minister Naji Sabri al-Hadithi announced that Iraq had expelled the previous day five OIP personnel based in Baghdad, allegedly for supplying security information to "enemy states." A sixth OIP employee had been expelled on August 31, and two peacekeepers of the U.N. Iraq-Kuwait Observation Mission (UNIKOM) on August 22 for allegedly violating "standard operating procedures by . . . taking photographs." During a Security Council debate on Iraq on September 6, Iraq's U.N. ambassador Muhammad al-Douri accused the U.N. of sending "spies" to Iraq. U.N. officials denied these charges, saying that Iraq had failed to provide any supporting evidence, and that the OIP had decided to "withdraw these personnel for strictly safety reasons." Two other UNIKOM peacekeepers had left Iraq in April after government officials made similar complaints against them. On October 25, Sevan announced he had submitted documents to the Security Council providing evidence that Iraqi oil estimated at U.S. $10 million was smuggled in violation of U.N. sanctions. The government denied the charges.

Eight WHO experts visited Iraq from August 27 to 31 to finalize agreements with the government on research to be conducted on non-communicable diseases and congenital malformations in the country. In a September 5 statement, WHO announced that one major area of research agreed was a "study of environmental and other risk factors (including depleted uranium) to health." The government said that increases in cancers and birth defects among Iraqis were linked to the use of depleted uranium by allied forces during the 1991 Gulf war, and had requested the International Atomic Energy Agency (IAEA) and the U.N. Environment Programme (UNEP) to sanction a fact-finding visit.

In a December 4, 2000 resolution, the General Assembly condemned "systematic, widespread and extremely grave violations of human rights and of international humanitarian law by the Government of Iraq, resulting in an all-pervasive repression and oppression sustained by broad-based discrimination and widespread terror." These included summary and arbitrary executions, routine and systematic torture, widespread use of the death penalty, and the repression of political opponents and their families. It urged the government to abide by its international human rights and humanitarian law obligations, to cooperate with U.N. human rights mechanisms, to implement relevant Security Council resolutions, and to cooperate with the Tripartite Commission over the fate of persons unaccounted for since the withdrawal of Iraqi forces from Kuwait in 1991. The resolution also reiterated its call for the special rapporteur to be granted access to the country.

In a January 16 report to the U.N. Commission on Human Rights, the special rapporteur on Iraq Andreas Mavrommatis said he continued to receive allegations of human rights violations by the government. These included arbitrary executions, frequent arrests of Shi'a religious figures and students, torture and ill-treatment of detainees, the retroactive application of death penalty legislation, and the forcible expulsion of Kurds and others from the Kirkuk region. The rapporteur said it was "absolutely necessary" that he be allowed to visit Iraq "to verify the truthfulness of the accounts received" and urged the government to agree to this. On April 18, the commission renewed the rapporteur's mandate for another year, condemned continuing violations and urged the government to cooperate with U.N. mechanisms and grant the special rapporteur access to Iraq. In a report to the General Assembly in September, the rapporteur detailed additional information on abuses against women, religious persecution, torture and extrajudicial killings, and on the humanitarian situation in Iraq. By November, the government had still not permitted him to visit the country.

On August 16, the U.N. Subcommission on the Promotion and Protection of Human Rights decided, without a vote, to reiterate its appeal to the international community and to the Security Council for the lifting of "the embargo provisions affecting the humanitarian situation of the population of Iraq." It also urged all governments, including that of Iraq, to facilitate the delivery of food, medical supplies, and other basic needs.

European Union

In May, the European Commission announced an increased "humanitarian assistance package" for Iraq. It allocated a total of 13 million euros for the year through the European Community Humanitarian Office (ECHO), maintaining the E.U.'s position as Iraq's largest humanitarian aid donor. The program was intended to fund projects in central and southern Iraq run by U.N. specialized agencies and NGOs in the areas of health, water and sanitation, and social rehabilitation.

In a resolution adopted on November 30, 2000, on the progress achieved in the implementation of the common foreign and security policy (CFSP), the European Parliament urged "the Council and Member States to take the initiative at the United Nations to propose the formation of an ad-hoc International Tribunal on Iraq to investigate the responsibility of Saddam Hussain's regime in crimes of war, crimes against humanity and crimes of genocide."

The European Parliament debated Iraq on March 1, focusing on continued air strikes by U.S. and U.K. forces. Commissioner for External Relations Chris Patten stressed the importance of maintaining sanctions until Iraq complied with Security Council resolutions concerning weapons inspections, but noted the importance of reviewing overall policy toward Iraq and "the possibility of replacing the present sanction regime by a 'smart sanctions program' and other appropriate measures," while ensuring that Iraq did not develop weapons of mass destruction.

United States

Secretary of State Colin Powell testified before the International Relations Committee of the House of Representatives on March 7 that the Bush administration would review policy toward the economic embargo on Iraq, the "no-fly zones," and assistance to the Iraqi opposition. He said the sanctions "were starting to fall apart" and needed to be focused more clearly on preventing Iraq from developing weapons of mass destruction, while refuting claims that this represented an "easing" of pressure on the Iraqi authorities. In May, the U.S. backed a resolution introduced by the U.K. at a Security Council debate on Iraq, which aimed at removing restrictions on almost all civilian exports to Iraq while tightening controls over arms imports and over the smuggling of Iraqi oil through its neighboring countries.

The U.S. and the U.K. continued to police the "no-fly zones" over northern and southern Iraq from bases in Turkey and Saudi Arabia. In congressional testimony in March and May, Bush administration officials reaffirmed U.S. commitment to the policy, which they stated was necessary to prevent Iraq from building up its military forces and from launching air attacks on the Kurdish population in the north and the Arab Shi'a population in the south. In May, the Pentagon announced that two U.S. military commanders overseeing the "no-fly zone" operations had recommended a significant reduction in the number of sorties being flown by U.S. and U.K. pilots while maintaining the monitoring of Iraqi troop movements in these areas. The Iraqi government said three people were killed and eleven others injured after air strikes by U.S. and U.K. planes near Baghdad on February 16, and that a further twenty-three people were killed and eleven injured as a result of air strikes on June 19 over a soccer field in the city of Mosul. U.S. and U.K. government officials denied these reports, and stated that no air strikes had been launched on June 19. U.S. Defense Secretary Donald Rumsfeld said that any such incident "undoubtedly was the result of misdirected ground fire."

Members of the opposition Iraqi National Congress (INC) began training in November 2000 in the collection of evidence for use in war crimes trials as part of a wider program sanctioned under the 1998 Iraq Liberation Act. On January 10, the Clinton administration approved U.S. $12 million in aid to the INC for the distribution of food, medicine, and other humanitarian relief in government-controlled areas of Iraq. On January 30, the Bush administration authorized the INC to draw on the U.S. $4 million approved by Congress in 2000 to fund opposition activities inside Iraq, including the gathering of evidence on human rights abuses by the Iraqi government. In testimony before the International Relations Committee of the House of Representatives on March 29, the State Department said that the administration had "an active program with the Iraqi opposition … that could contribute to a change of leadership in Iraq," and that over U.S. $6.7 million had already been channeled through the INC and other groups. In mid-June, the State Department announced it was releasing an additional U.S. $6 million to the INC to fund the sending of individuals into Iraq to gather human rights and war crimes information, publications, and television broadcasting.

In its *Country Reports on Human Rights Practices for 2000*, released in February 2001, the State Department condemned Iraq's human rights record as "extremely poor." It said that "security forces committed widespread, serious, and systematic human rights abuses," and that the government continued to be responsible for disappearances, torture and summary execution of suspected political opponents, and to subject citizens to arbitrary arrest and prolonged incommunicado detention. Iraq was also one of nine countries nominated by the U.S. Commission on International Religious Freedom as being "the world's worst religious-freedom violators." In its *Annual Report on International Religious Freedom for 2001*, the State Department said that the Iraqi government's violations of religious freedoms remained severe. It noted that in addition to arbitrary arrests, prolonged detention and torture, "the regime systematically has killed senior Shi'a clerics, desecrated Shi'a mosques and holy sites, interfered with Shi'a religious education, and prevented Shi'a adherents from performing their religious rites."

ISRAEL, THE OCCUPIED WEST BANK AND GAZA STRIP, AND PALESTINIAN AUTHORITY TERRITORIES

HUMAN RIGHTS DEVELOPMENTS

Many civilians were among the over seven hundred Palestinians and over two hundred Israelis who, by November 2001, had been killed in the violence that followed the eruption of clashes between Israelis and Palestinians in September 2000. In addition, some 16,000 Palestinians and some 1,700 Israelis were injured in the violence. The conflict was marked by attacks on civilians and civilian objects by both Israeli security forces and Palestinian armed groups. Both Israeli and Palestinian authorities failed to take the necessary steps to stop the security forces under their control from committing abuses, and failed to adequately investigate and punish the perpetrators.

Israeli security forces were responsible for extensive abuses, including indiscriminate and excessive use of lethal force against unarmed Palestinian demonstrators; unlawful or suspicious killings by Israel Defense Forces (IDF) soldiers; disproportionate IDF gunfire in response to Palestinian attacks; inadequate IDF response to abuses by Israeli settlers against Palestinian civilians; and "closure" measures on Palestinian communities that amounted to collective punishment. They also mounted a series of killings of suspected Palestinian militants under a controversial "liquidations" policy directed against those they claimed to be responsible for orchestrating attacks against Israelis.

For its part, the Palestinian Authority (PA) did little to exercise its responsibility to take all possible measures to prevent and punish armed attacks by Palestinians against Israeli civilians, including suicide bombings. In addition, the various security forces of the PA carried out arbitrary arrests of alleged Palestinian "collaborators" with Israel. Many were held in prolonged detention without trial and tortured; others were sentenced to death after unfair trials and two were executed. The PA also arrested some Islamist and other militants suspected of responsibility for attacks against Israelis and held them in untried detention.

Israel and the Occupied West Bank and Gaza Strip

The Israeli-Palestinian clashes continued throughout the first ten months of 2001. In December 2000, Israeli Prime Minister Ehud Barak and his Labor Party-led coalition lost office following an early election for prime minister called by Barak. Ariel Sharon, leader of the Likud party, won a decisive victory, replacing Barak as prime minister, and fashioned a governing majority in alliance with Labor and other, mainly rightwing, parties.

The IDF resorted to excessive and indiscriminate use of lethal force, causing civilian deaths and serious injuries and damaging or destroying homes and other property. In one case directly investigated by Human Rights Watch, on December 22, 2000, IDF soldiers used live ammunition against a stone-throwing crowd of Palestinian youth in Hebron district, killing 15-year-old Arafat al-Jabarin with several shots. The soldiers, equipped with several armored cars and a tank, were located in a defensible position above and nearly 150 meters from the youths. Given the distance and the elevation, the stone throwers did not pose the "grave threat to life" that both the United Nations (U.N.) Basic Principles on the Use of Force and Firearms by Law Enforcement Officials and the IDF's own open fire regulations require before allowing the use of lethal fire. The subsequent IDF account of the incident did not allege any use of firearms by Palestinians, and said that the IDF had responded "with riot dispersal equipment." In another incident, on June 9, an IDF tank fired flechette shells in a populated area between Gaza City and the settlement of Netzarim. The shells, which spread razor-sharp darts over a wide area, killed three Palestinian women and injured three others. IDF officials initially said they fired in response to Palestinian gunfire from the area, but Prime Minister Sharon acknowledged on June 11 that the killing of the three women "should not have happened." IDF officials said that they opened an internal inquiry, but the results had not been made public as of this writing.

As the clashes continued, Palestinians fired at Israeli settlers and carried out suicide bombings against Israeli civilians while the IDF made increasing use of heavy weaponry, including F-16 fighter jets, combat helicopters, tanks, and light rockets against Palestinian targets, including PA police stations, security offices, prisons, and other installations.

Under Prime Minister Sharon, Israel maintained the "liquidations" policy initiated by the previous Barak administration, targeting individuals whom it accused of planning or carrying out attacks on Israeli security forces or civilians. The IDF used snipers, helicopter-fired missiles, tanks, and explosive devices to carry out the assassinations. When first introduced, Israeli authorities justified the policy as neessary to prevent a "clear, specific and imminent terrorist threat," but then expanded it to include those considered responsible for planning or carrying out atttacks on Israelis. In some cases, however, it appeared that those targeted were killed in circumstances where Israeli forces could have arrested them. According to Israeli and Palestinian human rights groups, at least thirty-five Palestinians were targeted under the "liquidations" policy between November 2000 and October 2001. In one case under the Barak government, on December 31, 2000, IDF snipers killed Thabet Thabet, the secretary general of Tulkarem's Fatah branch and director general of the PA's Health Ministry. Israel subsequently accused him of being the regional head of a Palestinian squad responsible for shooting at Israelis. On January 9, Thabet's widow petitioned the Israeli Supreme Court to order Prime Minister Ehud Barak to refrain from "executing people without trial." The court first accepted to hear the petition but then changed its decision when the government contended that the court had no jurisdiction in the matter.

Israeli security forces were responsible for a number of killings and shootings of Palestinian civilians under circumstances that warranted investigation and possible criminal prosecution. In January, the Israeli government publicly categorized the clashes as constituting "armed conflict" and insisted that it was therefore under no obligation to carry out investigations of wrongful deaths at the hands of its security forces. There was no investigation, for instance, of a February incident where soldiers opened fire on a minibus carrying sixteen Palestinian workers to their jobs, killing twenty-year-old Ziad Abu Swayyeh and injuring several others, one seriously. The shootings took place when the minibus, after driving around an army roadblock, followed the soldiers' orders and turned around to go back to al-Khadr, near Bethlehem.

The IDF opened investigations in only a few cases that it characterized as "criminal" and "extreme," but did not contact or interview crucial witnesses to the shootings or inform the relatives of the victims. One case the IDF military police did investigate was the wounding of Jad Allah al-Ja'bari, an elderly Palestinian municipal cleaner, after a journalist filmed most of the incident in which he was shot by an Israeli soldier near a checkpoint. The IDF said that the soldiers responsible had received a "severe reprobation" for violating open-fire instructions and that a military police investigation found that, in addition, the soldiers had failed to follow normal arrest procedures and to provide immediate medical care, interfered with the work of an accredited journalist, and provided inaccurate accounts to their superiors about the incident.

According to B'Tselem (the Israeli Information Center for Human Rights in the Occupied Territories), Israeli settlers killed at least eleven Palestinians between September 2000 and September 2001 and injured dozens more. Settlers attacked Palestinian homes, destroyed stores, automobiles and other property, uprooted trees, prevented farmers from reaching their fields, blocked major roads, stoned Palestinian cars, including ambulances, and targeted humanitarian workers, diplomats, and journalists. Following the killing by a Palestinian gunman of an Israeli settler child, one-year-old Shalhevet Pass, in Hebron on March 26, some fifty armed settlers fired on the Palestinian Abu Sneineh neighborhood, burned cars and shops, caused other damage to Palestinian property, and wounded six Israeli border police. The Israeli authorities rarely intervened to stop or prevent settler attacks against Palestinians or to investigate them. When they did, perpetrators received disproportionately light sentences if they were punished at all.

Citing security reasons, Israel imposed the most severe restrictions on West Bank and Gaza Strip Palestinians' freedom of movement since it first adopted its "closure" policy in 1993. Israeli authorities sealed off the West Bank and Gaza Strip, restricting movement of Palestinians between and within those areas as well as into Israel, effectively confining them to their towns and villages for extended periods. The IDF blocked or controlled access to towns and villages by placing cement blocks, boulders, earthen dams, and army checkpoints on roads. The IDF also imposed curfews on certain Palestinian areas in response to stone throwing or shootings to protect settlers' movement along "bypass" roads. The 30,000 Palestinian residents of the Israeli-controlled area of Hebron known as H2 were kept under a nearly continuous round-the-clock curfew, but no restrictions were placed on the five hundred Israeli settlers living in the H2 area. Palestinian drivers complained that soldiers enforcing Israel's closure policy often beat and humiliated them and their passengers, slashed tires, shot at vehicles, and confiscated keys for lengthy periods.

Curfews, closures, and blockades had a devastating impact on Palestinians' lives, obstructing access to health care, schools and universities, businesses, and places of worship. According to the World Health Organization (WHO), the closures damaged water, electricity, and sanitation services. The Palestine Red Crescent Society (PRCS) said that delays at Israeli roadblocks and checkpoints contributed to a number of deaths of Palestinians in need of medical treatment. In February, the International Committee of the Red Cross (ICRC) initiated a "Closure Relief Program" and said the policy of isolating whole villages for an extended period was "contrary to International Humanitarian Law."

The U.N. special rapporteur on the situation of human rights in the occupied Palestinian territories reported that between September 2000 and October 2001 the IDF demolished more than three hundred Palestinian homes throughout the West Bank and Gaza, for alleged security or for punitive reasons, and uprooted 385,000 fruit and olive trees. Israeli authorities also confiscated Palestinian lands in order to expand Israeli settlements and for the construction of bypass roads, as at Deir Qiddis village near Beit Sefer settlement in June. Prime Minister Sharon authorized the construction of additional settlements and settler housing units in the West Bank, in violation of international humanitarian law.

The clashes involved Palestinian Arab citizens of Israel to an extent unprecedented in earlier periods of unrest affecting the Occupied Territories. In early October 2000, Israeli police gunfire killed thirteen Arab citizens and injured hundreds during demonstrations in Arab towns and villages in northern Israel protesting Israeli policies in the West Bank and Gaza Strip. In response, the Barak government set up a Public Commission of Inquiry headed by Supreme Court Justice Theodore Or. Four special anti-terrorist police snipers later testified that they were ordered to fire at unarmed demonstrators and those wielding slingshots in Nazareth and Um al Fahm, and northern district police commander Alik Ron stated that police had not been provided with sufficient non-lethal equipment and that police snipers used live bullets.

There were new reports of torture of detainees by Israeli security forces after October 2000. The Public Committee Against Torture in Israel (PCATI), an Israeli nongovernmental organization (NGO), reported that Israeli security forces kicked detainees and beat them with rifle butts and other implements, deprived them of food and drink for long periods, exposed them to extreme heat and cold, and used other methods that Israel's High Court of Justice explicitly prohibited in a 1999 ruling, including sleep deprivation and prolonged shackling in contorted positions. In March, according to PCATI, General Security Services (GSS) interrogators forced Iyad Nasser to squat in a painful position for an extended period of time and deprived him of sleep for seven consecutive days. At the end of May, PCATI called for Attorney General Elyakim Rubinstein to intervene on behalf of over three hundred Palestinian minors arrested since October 2000 who were reported to have been doused with freezing water, beaten, deprived of sleep, and had their heads covered with sacks during interrogation. On November 23, the U.N. Committee against Torture expressed its concern that the 1999 Supreme Court decision banning certain interrogation practices did not definitely prohibit torture, and that Israel's policies of closure and house demolitions might, in some cases, constitute cruel, inhuman, or degrading treatment or punishment.

Israel continued to detain Palestinians for extended periods without charge or trial. According to statistics published by B'Tselem in October, Israel held twenty-seven Palestinians under administrative detention, including Hassan Khader Shtiyeh, held since December 1, 2000. For the first time in four years, two Palestinian Arab citizens of Israel—Ghassan Athamneh and Kamal Obeid—were detained under administrative orders. According to B'Tselem, Israeli authorities held more than 1,700 Palestinians in Israeli prisons as of October 2001. Prisoners complained of food shortages and denial of medical treatment. The ICRC reported that its family visits program to prisoners was severely hampered by Israeli closures and administrative requirements.

Discrimination in law and practice against ethnic and religious minorities and other societal groups, especially on issues of employment and social benefits remained major problems. In July, the High Court ruled unanimously when considering a petition by the Association for Civil Rights in Israel (ACRI) that Palestinian Arab citizens were entitled to fair and proportionate representation on governmental bodies. The court ruled that the principle of affirmative action should apply to the Lands Council, responsible for supervising the Israel Lands Administration (ILA) whose twenty-four members included only one Arab, first appointed in May 2000.

On April 2, 2001, the High Court rejected another petition filed by ACRI against the ILA, the Jewish Agency, and the settlement of Katzir for contempt of court. ACRI claimed these bodies had not carried out the High Court's precedent-setting Ka'adan ruling of March 2000 banning discrimination between Jews and Arabs in land allocation. The respondents argued that they retained the right to interview the Ka'adan family before reaching a decision. They were instructed to do so by the court within sixty days. In November 2001, the Katzir admissions board rejected the Arab couple's application.

Israel continued to detain Sheikh 'Abd al-Karim 'Ubayd and Hajj Mustafa al-Dirani, who were abducted by Israeli forces from Lebanon in 1989 and 1994 respectively. Israel said it was holding them as "bargaining chips" for the release of an Israeli pilot, Ron Arad, missing in Lebanon since 1986. On July 4, the Tel Aviv District Court renewed both men's detention orders until December 17, 2001, after the state contended that their release endangered national security. On August 23, a five-judge panel headed by Supreme Court Justice Aharon Barak ruled that the two detainees should be permitted visits by the ICRC; four days later, however, the court delayed implementation of this decision at the request of Arad's family and those of three soldiers abducted by Hizbullah in October 2000 pending further consideration of the case by a full bench of eleven judges. On October 31, 2001, the government stated officially that the three soldiers captured in October 2000 were dead.

In July 2001, the Israeli ministerial committee for legislation approved an application for continuity of an "Intifada Law" that would end compensation payments to Palestinians whose persons or property were harmed during the 1987-1993 intifada and preclude compensation suits by Palestinians injured during the current clashes.

Palestinian Authority

Security and military courts established by the PA continued to issue death sentences after grossly unfair trials, and the PA carried out two executions, both in January. Palestinians alleged to have collaborated with Israel faced arbitrary arrest and detention, torture and ill-treatment under interrogation, unfair trials, and the death penalty. At least five detainees died in custody; in some cases, there was evidence of torture. Some thirty Palestinians, including suspected collaborators, were victims of vigilante killings by other Palestinians; although no one was held to account for these murders. The PA also arrested and held without trial members of Islamist and other groups that claimed responsibility for attacks on Israelis. The PA released most of these detainees in October 2000, soon after the outbreak of the current intifada, despite concerns that some may have been responsible for attacks on Israeli civilians. Some of those released as well as other suspected militants were briefly detained and released periodically during the year. At the end of October 2001, following a series of attacks on Israeli civilians by Palestinian armed groups, the PA began employing administrative detention orders and detaining larger numbers of suspected militants.

In other incidents, Palestinians shot and killed Israeli drivers and passengers and fired at Israeli settlements. Israel cited the PA's failure to prevent such attacks to justify its "liquidations" policy as well as IDF attacks on PA offices and security installations .

Various PA security forces detained and tortured suspected collaborators. Khaled al-Akra, arrested in February, said that interrogators in Nablus Central Prison handcuffed him to a window and punched and beat him with sticks for six days before releasing him. In March, the British Broadcasting Corporation (BBC) reported that a letter smuggled out by inmates of a West Bank Palestinian prison warned that one of their number had been tortured for weeks to the point where his life was at risk.

Vigilante killings by Palestinians resulted in the deaths of some thirty alleged collaborators. In November 2000, Palestinian gunmen shot dead thirty-seven-year-old Kasem Khlef, suspected of collaborating with Israel in its killing of Fatah leader Hussein Abeyat. In reporting his death, Palestinian TV showed a caption that read, "He lived as a beaver and died as a dog." In February, the PA issued a statement urging Palestinians not to take the law into their own hands. Later that month, however, forty-year-old bus driver, Muhammad Musa Abd al-Rahman, was shot to death when he answered his door. The Palestinian media, citing unnamed Palestinian security officials, reported that he had collaborated with Israeli security services. The PA failed to bring to justice those responsible for those killings.

State security and military courts continued to operate despite the fact that they did not meet minimum international fair trial standards. At least thirteen persons were sentenced to death, most of them on charges of collaboration after summary trials.

The PA briefly reverted to a pattern of executions without due process. On January 13, the PA executed Allam Bani Odeh and Majdi Mikkawi after President Arafat ratified their death sentences. Both men were accused of collaboration with Israeli security services. Police firing squads carried out the executions after summary trials before Palestinian Authority security courts without access to lawyers and without the right to appeal. Bani Odeh was shot in front of a crowd of thousands in Nablus. Speaking on Israel's Channel 2 television station, Deputy Qadura Fares, chair of the Human Rights Committee at the Palestinian Legislative Council said: "In different circumstances, in the future when we have a democratic country, the defendants will receive all their rights in court, which will assure them a just trial."

As of this writing, President Arafat had not ratified eleven other death sentences, and they had not been carried out.

At least five Palestinians died in custody in 2001, bringing to twenty-eight the number of detainees known to have died in custody since the establishment of the PA in 1994. Thirty-six-year-old Salem al-Akra, arrested by Palestinian intelligence officers on February 6 on suspicion of collaborating with Israel, died in a hospital on February 27 after being transferred from Nablus central prison. A witness in Nablus who saw al-Akra's body in the hospital morgue told Human Rights Watch that it bore marks of torture: bruising on the wrists and ankles and head. An autopsy was performed but the results were not made public.

The PA failed to take adequate action against those responsible for killings of Israeli civilians. In January, three members of the Fatah organization's Tanzim militia shot dead sixteen-year-old Israeli Ofir Rahum after he was lured to Ramallah by a Palestinian woman. Six days later, masked Palestinian gunmen apparently belonging to Hamas abducted and killed two other Israelis, restaurateurs Motti Dayan and Etgar Zeitouny, as they dined in Tulkarem. The PA condemned these killings and said it would inquire into them, but no findings of any investigation had been made public by November.

Palestinian militants used firearms and bombings against Israeli settlers traveling on bypass roads and elsewhere. Children were often among the victims, as in an attack in November 2000 near the Kfar Darom settlement in Gaza which killed two adults and injured others, including five children, on a bus. On February 11, Fatah gunmen in Beit Jala shot dead Israeli settler Tsahi Sasson as he drove across a bridge near the Gush Etzion settlement, and continued firing when an ambulance arrived.

At least seventy Israelis were killed and over eight hundred injured in attacks by Palestinian suicide bombers and other militants apparently belonging to groups such as Hamas and Islamic Jihad. On June 1, a suicide bomber killed twenty-one mostly young people and injured over one hundred others outside a Tel Aviv discotheque; on August 9, another suicide bomber, apparently acting on behalf of Hamas, caused an explosion in a Jerusalem restaurant leaving eighteen, including six children, dead and many others wounded. These and other bombings and attacks that targeted or disproportionately affected civilians constituted gross violations of international humanitarian law.

The PA came under severe and repeated pressure from Israel, reinforced by military attacks on PA installations, to arrest those responsible for planning or carrying out suicide bombings and other attacks against Israelis. Under its "liquidations" policy, Israel also directly attacked and killed some of those it said were responsible. The PA took inadequate steps to identify and bring to justice those responsible for attacks on Israeli civilians but it did make some arrests. For example, in October, the PA arrested forty-five people associated with the Popular Front for the Liberation of Palestine (PFLP) after the PFLP claimed responsibility for the October 17 assassination of Israeli Tourism Minister Rehav'am Ze'evi, in retaliation for Israel's "liquidation" of PFLP Secretary General Abu Ali Mustafa a short time earlier. On

November 14, the PA released two PFLP leaders after the High Court ruled that there was no basis in law for the charge brought against them, harming the national interests of the Palestinian people. Also in October 2001, the general director of the Palestinian police issued six-month to one-year detention orders against one Hamas and six Islamic Jihad members; this was the first use of administrative detention by the PA since 1994.

PA police also clashed with Palestinian demonstrators and used excessive force. For example, on October 8, 2001, Palestinian police fired on Islamist students and other stone-throwing demonstrators in Gaza City, reportedly killing a thirteen-year-old boy and a nineteen-year-old student and injuring others.

DEFENDING HUMAN RIGHTS

Israel for the most part permitted human rights organizations to collect and disseminate information in areas under its control, but the policy of closures, blockades, and curfews restricted their freedom of movement within the West Bank and Gaza Strip areas. Palestinian lawyers were unable to visit clients held in prisons in Israel.

Israeli security forces detained several Palestinian and also Israeli human rights activists. The former included Hashem Abu Hassan, a B'Tselem field researcher, as well as Adnan al-Hajjar of the Al-Mezan Center for Human Rights, and Daoud al-Dirawi, a lawyer with the Palestinian Independent Commission for Citizens' Rights (PICCR).

Israeli authorities arrested Abed Rahman al-Ahmar, a Palestinian Human Rights Monitoring Group (PHRMG) researcher, on May 24, and detained him without trial on the basis of secret GSS evidence. His lawyers said he was beaten and shackled in custody. On November 14 , a military judge extended al-Ahmar's detention for a further six months.

On June 15, Israeli security forces arrested Sergio Yahni, director of the Alternative Information Center (AIC), during a demonstration organized by Rabbis for Human Rights and the AIC against the confiscation of Palestinian land in the Bethlehem District.

The PA continued to allow human rights organizations to operate in the territory under its jurisdiction, but continued to deny human rights workers access to prisons. On March 24, Palestinian security forces arrested lawyer Nasir al-Rifa'i at a court in Ramallah: he was reportedly held incommunicado at the Ramallah military intelligence headquarters and lawyers were denied access to him.

THE ROLE OF THE INTERNATIONAL COMMUNITY

United Nations

After visiting Israel and the Occupied Territories at the request of the October 2000 special session of the U.N. Commission on Human Rights (CHR), U.N. High

Commissioner for Human Rights Mary Robinson issued her report on November 27. She pointed to a range of abuses, including excessive use of force, restrictions on freedom of movement, and the impact of the conflict on children, and said "the bleak human rights situation in the occupied territories" warranted urgent international attention. She called too for an international monitoring presence to be deployed in the territories and for the states that are high contracting parties to the Geneva Conventions to take action "to reduce the terrible violence."

At the behest of the October 2000 special session, the U.N. established a commission of inquiry composed of three independent experts to investigate human rights and humanitarian law violations in the territories; this reported to the CHR in March. It said the "IDF, assisted by settlers on occasion" was responsible for most violations but noted that Palestinians had also committed violations, either under the authority of the PA or acting in their individual capacity. It too called for an "adequate and effective international presence" to be established "to monitor and regularly report on" continuing violations. Prior to the CHR, European Union (E.U.) ambassadors in Israel jointly confirmed that "the issues and findings" in the report "truly reflected facts on the ground" and said all its recommendations could be fully endorsed by the E.U. However, the subsequent CHR resolution 2001/7, while condemning and deploring Israeli human rights violations identified in the inquiry's report, omitted any reference to Palestinian violations; although the resolution was adopted by the CHR in April, the United States and Guatemala voted against, and twenty-two states, including the E.U. countries, abstained.

Earlier, in late 2000, the Security Council informally considered draft proposals to establish a U.N. military and police observer force in the Occupied Territories but did not proceed to a vote when the U.S indicated that it would exercise its veto. In March 2001, the U.S. did veto a draft Security Council resolution calling for the secretary-general to consult with the parties to the conflict and recommend "an appropriate mechanism to protect Palestinian civilians, including through the establishment of a U.N. observer force." Explaining the veto, chief U.S. delegate James Cunningham said the resolution prescribed a role for the secretary-general that was not realistic, given Israel's staunch opposition to a U.N. observer role, and criticized its failure to call for the protection of all civilians.

In his October 4, 2001 report to the General Assembly, the U.N. special rapporteur on the situation of human rights in the occupied Palestinian territories also raised the issue of an international monitoring presence. Noting that "International monitors or peacekeepers have been employed in many less threatening situations in the world," he questioned the failure of "the international community to persuade Israel to accept such a presence."

In November, after reviewing Israel's report on compliance with the Convention against Torture and Other Cruel, Inhuman or Degrading Treatment or Punishment, the U.N. Committee against Torture welcomed the Israeli Supreme Court's 1999 decision banning the application by interrogators of "moderate physical pressure" against persons in custody but expressed concern that the court had not expressly prohibited torture, that Israeli interrogators reportedly continued to use banned methods, and that the authorities had mounted few prosecutions of alleged perpetrators of torture or ill-treatment.

In its annual report to the General Assembly in September 2001, the U.N. Relief and Works Agency for Palestinian Refugees in the Near East (UNRWA) complained that it had encountered serious problems in providing humanitarian assistance in the July 2000 to June 2001 period due to Israeli restrictions on the freedom of movement of its staff, denial of access to UNWRA staff members who Israel detained, and threats by IDF personnel against UNRWA staff members, including Commissioner General Peter Hansen.

On October 25, 2001, the Security Council issued a Presidential Statement that reproduced and "supported all elements" of a statement that representatives of the U.S., E.U., Russia, and the U.N. issued earlier in the day in Gaza. This urged the PA to ensure "strict implementation of the ceasefire" and called on Israel to halt extra-judicial killings, ensure greater restraint by the IDF, fully respect the ceasefire, and "move swiftly to ease the closures."

European Union

The E.U. continued to be the major donor to the Palestinian Authority. Total project support by the European Commission for the year 2000 amounted to U.S. $119 million; $80 million represented a "special cash facility" for the PA's Ministry of Finance. The E.U. increased its support to compensate in part for the PA's loss of $226 million—approximately 60 percent of its public revenue—in customs and tax revenues withheld by Israel following the outbreak of the intifada. European Commission funding to the PA amounted to U.S. $106 million from January to October 2001, but this was conditioned on the PA's adoption of an austerity budget, a freeze in public sector employment, and consolidation of all PA public revenues into a single Ministry of Finance account. The E.U. also conditioned its assistance for the judiciary on the PA's implementation of a judicial reform draft law enacted by the Palestine Legislative Council but still awaiting President Arafat's approval. Other large donors to the PA judiciary, notably Japan via the U.N. Development Program and Saudi Arabia via the World Bank, did not insist on similar conditions.

Israel was not eligible for direct E.U. financial aid. According to press reports in December, France declined to sell Israel tear-gas launchers and grenades that it had requested.

The E.U. strongly criticized the PA's execution of two alleged collaborators with Israel in early 2001 and called for an end to such executions. Subsequently, the State Security Court imposed further death sentences but they were not ratified by President Arafat and the PA had carried out no further executions as of November.

The Swedish government, then holding the presidency, delivered the E.U.'s most comprehensive statement on human rights violations by Israel and the PA at the CHR in April. In this, the E.U. reaffirmed the applicability of the Fourth Geneva Convention to the Occupied Territories as "binding international humanitarian law," praised the balanced nature of the high commissioner's November 2000 report, and regretted Israel's refusal to cooperate with the special rapporteur. The statement criticized and called for an end to abuses by both sides. With regard to Israel, the E.U. specifically criticized disproportionate and indiscriminate use of force, extrajudicial executions, closures as a form of collective punishment, and the retention of laws that discriminate against Palestinian Arab citizens of Israel. With regard to the PA, the E.U. criticized torture, deaths in detention, use of the death penalty, and restrictions on freedom of expression. During the CHR session, the E.U. abstained on a resolution that condemned Israeli human rights and humanitarian law violations in the Occupied Territories but sponsored another that expressed "grave concern" at continuing Israeli settlement activities "since all these actions are illegal, constitute a violation of the Geneva Convention relative to the Protection of Civilian Persons in Time of War, and are a major obstacle to peace."

In a May 17 resolution, the European Parliament expressed its "deep consternation" at the number of civilian victims of the clashes, condemned excessive use of force by Israel, Palestinian attacks against Israeli civilians, called for the U.N. Security Council to authorize the dispatch of an observer mission, and regretted the decision of some states not to support the CHR resolution condemning human rights violations in the Occupied Territories. The parliamentary resolution also urged the European Commission and E.U. member states to "avoid any indirect complicity in illegal settlements" by strictly applying rules-of-origin regulations to E.U. duty-free imports from Israel.

On November 24, a spokesman for the European Commission stated that the E.U.'s executive arm had decided to advise the customs authorities of member states to require Israeli exporters to deposit funds to cover duties that might be imposed retroactively on imports that are determined to originate from illegal settlements. Some member states, however, reportedly remained reluctant to implement this decision on the grounds that it would impede E.U. efforts to persuade Israel to resume peace negotiations with the PA.

On June 18, lawyers representing twenty-eight survivors of the 1982 Sabra and Shatila massacres in Lebanon in 1982 filed a complaint against Prime Minister Sharon, who was Israel's defense minister at the time, accusing him of war crimes, crimes against humanity, and genocide. The suit was filed in Belgium under legislation allowing prosecution of such crimes in Belgian courts even if they were committed elsewhere and neither the perpetrators nor the victims were Belgian nationals. A court heard opening arguments from the Belgian prosecutor and Sharon's attorney on November 27 on the issue of whether a Belgian magistrate could continue his investigation into the charges and start legal proceedings in Belgium. Belgian officials expected a decision in late January.

On the day before the November 27 hearing, lawyers representing some thirty Israelis filed a complaint in a Brussels court accusing President Arafat and other Palestinian officials and leaders of "murder, crimes against humanity, and genocide." The complaint named Arafat as the "principal conspirator" in a number of attacks on civilians carried out by Palestinians since 1966 in both Israel and other countries.

In Denmark, there were protests after Israel named Carmi Gillon, former head of the General Security Services, or Shabak, as its ambassador beginning in August. On July 9, Gillon was reported in Denmark's *Jyllands Posten* newspaper to have acknowledged his direct involvement in a hundred interrogations of Palestinian security detainees using techniques widely held to amounting to torture or ill-treatment. In a statement, the Danish Foreign Ministry, which had recently accepted Gillon's accreditation, said the government "strongly oppos[ed] all forms and acts of torture" but that it was a foreign government's "own responsibility" to decide who represented it in Denmark.

United States

Israel, the largest recipient of U.S. military and economic assistance, received an estimated $1,980 million in military assistance and $840 million in Economic Support Funds for fiscal year (FY) 2001, ending in September. The administration requested $2,040 million in military aid and $720 million in support funds for FY 2002, beginning in October. According to the State Department, these funds "will enable the Israeli government to meet cash flow requirements associated with the procurement of U.S. origin systems such as F-16 fighter aircraft, the Apache Longbow attack helicopter, field vehicles, and advanced armaments."

The U.S. provided an estimated $85 million to the West Bank and Gaza in FY 2001; $75 million was budgeted for FY 2002. This assistance was channeled through U.S. private voluntary organizations and Palestinian NGOs, and was not provided directly to the Palestinian Authority.

The Clinton administration continued its efforts to broker peace talks between Israel and the PA even in its final weeks. On December 23, 2000, President Clinton orally presented "a series of options" to Palestinian and Israeli negotiators in Washington, D.C. These proposals reportedly called for Palestinian refugees to be able to return to their homeland, defined as a "viable and contiguous" Palestinian state comprising approximately 95 percent of the West Bank and Gaza, while land annexed by Israel would include 80 percent of the settler population. Further Israeli-Palestinian talks in Taba, however, failed to reach agreement before President Clinton (and Prime Minister Barak) left office.

The Bush administration conspicuously declined to replicate the same level of involvement in trying to bring the two sides together and confined itself to promoting the recommendations of the Sharm al-Sheikh Fact-Finding Committee, whose report was issued on April 30. The committee, a five-member international body set up at the Sharm al-Sheikh summit in October 2000 and headed by former U.S. senator George Mitchell, proposed sequential steps towards a resumption of peace talks, starting with a ceasefire and "cooling-off" period. The committee, in its introduction to the report, wrote that a resolution to the conflict required that "agreed commitments be implemented, international law respected, and human rights protected." Although its recommendations were not framed in terms of human rights and humanitarian law, many were broadly consistent with those principles, such as adopting non-lethal IDF responses to unarmed demonstrators, conducting impartial investigations into alleged unlawful deaths, and effective PA steps to halt armed attacks against Israeli civilians.

Following the attacks of September 11, the Bush administration intensified its efforts to secure a ceasefire and to restart political negotiations. On November 19, in a major foreign policy speech, Secretary of State Colin Powell called on the PA to "arrest, prosecute and punish the perpetrators of terrorist acts," criticized Israeli settlements, and said that "the occupation must end." He announced that retired Marine Corps Gen. Anthony Zinni would travel to the region as his special advisor to "get that ceasefire in place." Powell later said that Zinni would remain in the region "as long as it takes." As of late November, however, the first steps toward a ceasefire remained elusive.

The State Department's *Country Reports on Human Rights Practices for 2000* was comprehensive in its treatment of Israeli and PA human rights violations. However, generally, the State Department's criticism in response to specific violations was couched in language that labeled them "provocative" or "unhelpful," rather than as violations of international human rights or humanitarian law. Former assistant secretary of state Edward Walker, speaking about Israeli use of U.S. helicopter gunships in residential areas, told the *Baltimore Sun* on May 27, shortly after he left office, "It was a clear administration position that this was an excessive use of force." The public comments of the press spokesperson, however, were typically limited to expressions of "concern," although a press briefing given by State Department spokesman Philip Reeker on October 23, 2001, was a notable exception, Reeker stating: "We deeply regret and deplore Israeli Defense Force actions that have killed numerous Palestinian civilians over the weekend. The deaths of these innocent civilians under the circumstances reported in recent days are unacceptable, and we call upon Israel to ensure that its armed forces exercise greater discipline and restraint."

Israeli use of U.S.-supplied weapons in the clashes, and in particular the use of helicopter gunships in targeted killings of individual Palestinian militants, raised questions among several members of Congress and in the public as to whether such use violated the Arms Export Control Act (AECA). In a September press briefing, State Department spokesman Richard Boucher said, "We've made it quite clear that we are opposed to the use of heavy weaponry and in these circumstances, particularly in populated areas where the risk of innocent casualties is very high," but he did not comment on this as a possible violation of the AECA on the grounds that he wished to avoid "pushing this into a legalistic discussion."

On September 9, the State Department released an August 17 response of Secretary of State Colin Powell to U.S. Representative John Conyers, who had raised the question of possible AECA violations in a public letter to Powell. "Based on our assessment of the totality of the underlying facts and circumstances," Powell wrote, "we believe that a report [to Congress] under section 3c of the AECA is not required." The administration "has been monitoring Israeli actions carefully and will continue to do so," Powell added.

Relevant Human Rights Watch Reports:

Israel: Second Class: Discrimination Against Palestinian Arab Children in Israel's Schools, 12/01

Israel, the Occupied West Bank and Gaza Strip, and Palestinian Authority Territories: Justice Undermined: Balancing Security and Human Rights in the Palestinian Justice System, 11/01

Israel, the Occupied West Bank and Gaza Strip, and Palestinian Authority Territories: Center of the Storm: A Case Study of Human Rights Abuses in Hebron District, 4/01

MOROCCO

HUMAN RIGHTS DEVELOPMENTS

Selective acts of repression limited the liberalization process started by the late King Hassan II and continued by his son, King Mohamed VI. Compared with previous years, there was freer public discussion of Berber rights, the Western Sahara conflict, and past human rights abuses. But with the occasional move to ban a newspaper, forbid a rally, beat up protesters, or jail whistle-blowers, the government remained the arbiter of how and when Moroccans could exercise their rights.

Speaking July 30 on the second anniversary of his accession to the throne, Mohamed VI called for "a modern democratic state, founded on public liberties and human rights." But neither he nor Prime Minister Abderrahmane Youssoufi— a former victim of repression and longtime human rights activist—proved forceful advocates of human rights in the face of repeated violations.

The authorities frequently barred or broke up meetings or protests, using powers provided by the Law on Public Assemblies to prevent gatherings deemed capable of "disturbing public order," even when they were peaceful. On January 12, the Interior Ministry banned a demonstration called by human rights organizations in front of Dar al-Mokri, a former secret detention center in Rabat. In June and July, the ministry prevented Berber rights groups from holding a meeting and a conference. It also banned a demonstration called for October 21 in Rabat against the U.S. air strikes in Afghanistan. At other times, police sometimes tolerated, sometimes broke up, sit-ins and rallies by workers and by groups representing the unemployed.

Trials of over 160 demonstrators arrested when police violently dispersed rallies on December 9 and 10, 2000 continued throughout much of the year. In the first instance, human rights activists had planned a peaceful sit-in near the parliament building in Rabat to demand accountability for past abusers, but police intercepted, beat up, and arrested participants before they could reach the venue. They were jailed overnight and on May 16 thirty-six of them were convicted and sentenced to three months in prison and fined for holding an "unauthorized demonstration." The defendants, mostly members of the Moroccan Human Rights Association (Association Marocaine des droits de l'Homme, AMDH) and the Forum for Justice and Truth, remained free on appeal and on November 21 were acquitted. However, none of the police who beat them without provocation were charged. Many observers believed that the harsh suppression of the demonstration was prompted by the AMDH's public naming of fourteen alleged torturers, including still-serving senior security officials and a member of parliament, and its demanding that the justice minister bring charges against them.

On December 10, 2000, police in Rabat and at least six other cities forcibly dispersed demonstrations staged by Islamists. Some 130 persons were arrested and eventually charged in connection with the rallies. Some received terms of up to one year in prison, but as of this writing they were all free either because appeals courts had reduced their sentences or had yet to issue a verdict.

Morocco's private print media enjoyed considerable freedom, but mostly avoided criticism of the military, as well as direct criticism of the king, his predecessors, and the monarchy. For much of the year, newspapers were filled with revelations about the "dirty war" carried out against dissidents during the 1960s and 1970s. Former inmates of the secret Tazmamart prison described the horrendous conditions that led to the death of half of its inmates. Victims of torture and relatives of the "disappeared" also told their stories in the pages of newspapers. While torturers were accused by name, a taboo remained against implicating King Hassan II in the repression of those years. In addition, the memoir of Malika Oufkir, *Stolen Lives: Twenty Years in a Desert Jail*, was banned in Morocco. The book, a best-seller in the United States, described how her entire family was jailed for nearly two decades in reprisal for a failed coup attempt by her father, Interior Minister Mohamed Oufkir, in 1972.

Delving into sensitive past dossiers proved costly to the French-language *Le Journal*, its Arabic sister publication *as-Sahifa*, and *Demain*. In December 2000, Prime Minister Youssoufi of the Socialist Party banned the three weeklies, exercising a power granted his office by article 77 of the press code. *Le Journal* and *as-Sahifa* had just printed, and *Demain* commented on, a previously unpublished letter dating from 1974, in which a Socialist Party leader of the time implicated party leaders (including, from the letter's context, Youssoufi himself) in an unsuccessful coup attempt against Hassan II. Minister of Culture and Communication Mohamed Achaari said the newspapers had "launched campaigns using false reports against the political stability of Morocco and its democratic experience."

After re-launching *Le Journal* under a slightly different name (*Le Journal Hebdomadaire*), publication director Aboubakr Jamaï and general director Ali Amar were sentenced on March 1 respectively to three months and two months in prison and ordered to pay large fines. The verdict came in a defamation suit filed by Foreign Minister Mohamed Benaïssa, citing articles published in 2000 that charged him with squandering public monies in real estate transactions while serving as ambassador to the United States. Amar and Jamaï remained free pending their appeal, which got under way in November. On November 21, Ali Mrabet, editor of *Demain* magazine, received a four-month prison sentence and a fine for "disseminating false information likely to disturb the public order." The charge related to an article about the possible sale of a royal palace. Mrabet remained free as of this writing.

The Council of Ministers on September 6 approved amendments to the press code that retained the penalty of imprisonment for defamation. The bill, which still required approval by parliament as this report went to press, also preserved the executive branch's power to seize or suspend publications. On several occasions, authorities prevented, without explanation, the sale of issues of foreign publications when they contained sensitive coverage of Morocco. They seized, for example, the May 17 issue of the French weekly *Courrier International*, which carried a feature on Berbers in Morocco and a caricature of Mohamed VI.

Morocco had more than 2,150 cybercafes and between 300,000 and 400,000

Internet users, according to a September 13 letter from the Moroccan embassy in Washington to Human Rights Watch. The letter also claimed that the government did not censor or block any web content. However, the Islamist association al-'Adl wa'l-Ihsan (Justice and Charity), which is tolerated but not legally authorized, reported that authorities blocked its websites in April, including that of its organ *Risalat al-Futouwa* (www.el-fotowa.com). The embassy declined Human Rights Watch's repeated requests for comment. Al-'Adl wa'l-Ihsan also claimed that the paper edition of *Risalat al-Futouwa* was seized on occasion and that printers were pressured by authorities not to print it.

The number of political prisoners, much diminished by a series of releases and pardons in recent years, was further reduced with the freeing of fifty-six prisoners on November 7. These included Mohamed Daddach, a Sahraoui who was arrested in 1979 and was serving a life sentence for having deserted from the Moroccan security forces. However, King Mohamed VI's assertion, in an interview published in the London-based daily *ash-Sharq al-Awsat* on July 24, that "there is today not a single political prisoner in Morocco," was misleading as there remained a small number of prisoners, including Islamists and supporters of independence for the disputed Western Sahara, who were being held for nonviolent expression.

One political prisoner, army captain Mustapha Adib, had been convicted in 2000 in a military court of disobeying orders and insulting the army, charges that were clearly formulated to punish him for denouncing corrupt officers and then speaking out about the retaliatory harassment he had suffered. He was arrested in December 1999, one day after his complaints were quoted by the French daily *Le Monde*. On February 21, 2001, the Supreme Court confirmed Adib's sentence of two and a half years in prison and a discharge from the army. He was due to be released in June 2002.

In public forums, Moroccans made great strides in exposing the acts of repression committed during the reign of Hassan II. On the government side, steps were taken to acknowledge past wrongs and compensate some victims. Those official steps, though modest, were unparalleled in the Middle East and North Africa.

An arbitration commission, created in 1999 at King Mohamed VI's request within the official Human Rights Advisory Board (Conseil Consultatif des droits de l'Homme, CCDH), determined the amount to be paid to victims of prolonged illegal detention and to the relatives of "disappeared" persons who had applied for compensation. The CCDH announced in June that the arbitration commission had since its creation paid out compensation to 712 persons in 376 cases.

Yet critics pointed out that the process of compensating victims was neither transparent nor accompanied by any larger truth-seeking project. Some relatives of persons who "disappeared" said they would accept no money so long as the fate of their loved ones was not revealed. Other victims said they wanted the abusers either identified or held accountable before they would seek compensation.

Critics also faulted the process for making "disappearances" and illegal detention eligible for compensation while arbitrarily ignoring other types of abuse, including torture and imprisonment on political charges. Another flaw to the process was that the CCDH had recognized only 112 cases of "disappearance" and said it had no information about other cases. Local human rights organizations have documented some two hundred unresolved "disappearances" in Morocco and the Western Sahara and believe the number could be as high as six hundred. The families of "disappeared" persons whose cases were not recognized by the CCDH were left without any standing before the compensation commission or any other government agency. In July, a delegation representing the families of twelve "disappeared" Sahraouis visited Rabat in order to follow up on the dossiers they had submitted to officials more than a year earlier. They were sent from ministry to ministry but, as with their earlier initiative, received not a shred of information.

The year's most sensational revelations about the past came from Ahmed Boukhari, the first secret police officer to reveal the inner workings of King Hassan II's repression of dissidents in the 1960s and 1970s. In an exposé published June 29-30 in *Le Journal Hebdomadaire* and the French daily *Le Monde*, Boukhari also purported to answer one of the great mysteries of Moroccan political history: the fate of Mehdi Ben Barka, the exiled opposition leader who was abducted in Paris in 1965 and never seen again. According to Boukhari, Ben Barka died in France while under interrogation by Moroccan agents, who arranged secretly to fly his body back to Morocco. There, police dissolved it in acid.

Instead of opening a judicial inquiry into the credible allegations of murder and "disappearances" proffered by Boukhari, authorities instead jailed him on charges of writing bad checks. His imprisonment on August 13 prevented him from complying with a subpoena to testify in Paris before a French judge investigating Ben Barka's disappearance. The timing of Boukhari's arrest and his pre-trial detention left little doubt that he was being jailed to punish him for speaking out, and to intimidate other would-be whistle-blowers. On August 27, Boukhari was convicted and given a year in prison, a sentence that was reduced on appeal to three months.

The trials of Boukhari and Mustapha Adib illustrated the judiciary's lack of independence, despite pledges of reform from Minister of Justice Omar Azzimane. In July, King Mohamed VI promoted Mohamed Mechbal, the military prosecutor who had prosecuted Adib in 2000, to the rank of brigadier-general.

Travel restrictions, once commonly imposed on ex-prisoners and human rights activists, were used sparingly. Some dissidents were allowed to travel abroad for the first time in years. On January 17, Ahmed Marzouki was given his first passport since his release from Tazmamart prison in 1991, enabling him to go to Europe to publicize his new book, *Tazmamart, Cell 10*. In July, Lahcène Moutiq, a Rabat-based Sahraoui member of the Forum for Truth and Justice, got his first passport in years to attend a human rights course in France. However, Sahraoui human rights activists Brahim Noumri and Mahmoud el-Hamed were turned back at the Casablanca airport on March 24, as they were about to fly to Geneva to attend the U.N. Commission on Human Rights. Authorities detained them at the airport for several hours and confiscated documents containing data and testimonies about abuses against Sahraouis. The documents had not been returned as of mid-October.

In March, King Mohamed VI formed yet another commission to examine reforming Morocco's personal status code. On November 23, he publicly urged the new commission to work both on proposals to improve the application of existing laws and on a longer-term "substantial reform" of the code. Women's rights activists, who have long sought to amend the code's sexually discriminatory provisions (see Women's Human Rights), criticized the commission for taking too long to make recommendations.

Minister of Islamic Affairs Abdelkebir M'daghri Alaoui tacitly condoned verbal attacks by state-administered mosque preachers against Hakima Chaoui, a poet and member of the AMDH. The trouble began when the Islamist newspaper *at-Tajdid* accused her of insulting the Prophet Muhammad in a poem in favor of women's rights that she had written and recited on March 8, International Women's Day. She subsequently received phone threats and in August was shouted down at a public meeting. Minister Alaoui commented on the attacks on Chaoui, "While the reputation and dignity of individuals are to be protected and respected, protecting the person of the Prophet does take priority, as does upholding sacred, religious and national principles."

Prisoners in Morocco suffered from severe overcrowding, inadequate medical care, unhygienic conditions, contagious diseases, and mixing of minors and adults. These conditions were described in the first major report issued by the Moroccan Prisons Observatory, an independent monitoring organization formed in 1999. The group conducted several inspection visits during 2000 and said its access to facilities and prisoners was unrestricted.

As of June, 1,479 Moroccan soldiers remained prisoners of the Polisario Front in Tindouf, Algeria, according to the International Committee of the Red Cross (ICRC), which visited them regularly. Of these, 840 had been held by the Polisario Front for over twenty years, bargaining chips in the long-festering conflict. King Mohamed VI softened the late Hassan II's stance of rejecting anything short of a single repatriation of all Moroccan prisoners of war held by the Polisario, enabling two batches of some two hundred imprisoned soldiers each to return to Morocco during 2000.

During 2001, the ICRC urged the immediate repatriation of all prisoners of war. Morocco was not believed to be holding any, although it held in prison a small number of Sahraouis civilians convicted of pro-independence activities, and continued to provide no information on the whereabouts of Sahraoui civilians who had been forcibly "disappeared" during the years of conflict.

DEFENDING HUMAN RIGHTS

Morocco's human rights movement generally enjoyed considerable freedom to meet, collect information, and convey its perspectives in the print press. However, this freedom was tempered by the brutal arrest and prosecution of activists who demonstrated on December 9, 2000, the jailing of whistle-blower ex-policeman Ahmed Boukhari, and the constant pressure facing rights defenders in the Western Sahara.

In January, the International Federation of Human Rights held its world congress in Morocco, the first time a major international rights group has done so in the Arab world.

THE ROLE OF THE INTERNATIONAL COMMUNITY

European Union

Relations between the European Union (E.U.) and Morocco focused on economic and social issues following the Association Agreement that came into force in early 2000. Respect for human rights and democratic principles was an essential element of the legally binding agreement, but the E.U. did not publicly raise any human rights concerns at the time of the October 9 E.U.-Morocco Association Council meeting. European Union policy continued to be guided by a desire to curb migration, legal and illegal, from Morocco to member countries such as France, Spain, and Belgium. However, the E.U. provided 1.2 million euros for projects on freedom of expression, migration, promotion of women's rights in Morocco, as well as human rights education and prison reform.

United Nations

United Nations Secretary-General Kofi Annan, in his April 24 report on the Western Sahara conflict, urged the "parties to arrange the early repatriation of all prisoners." Security Council Resolution 1359 of June 29 asked the parties "to solve the fate of people unaccounted for" and to "abide by their obligations under international humanitarian law to release without further delay all those held since the start of the conflict."

SAUDI ARABIA

HUMAN RIGHTS DEVELOPMENTS

Saudi Arabia's human rights record remained poor and there were no discernible improvements in 2001. The government took no steps to ease restrictions in the key areas of freedom of association and expression, women's rights, and religious freedom, or move toward a more open and tolerant society. The continued absence of institutions independent of the government, such as political parties and nongovernmental organizations (NGOs), allowed the ruling royal family to maintain its historic franchise on power, beyond public reproach and accountability. A May 24 royal decree increased the members of the all-male Consultative Council from ninety to 120, although the appointed body remained toothless with respect to any substantive oversight of the executive branch of government. Workers, including millions of foreigners, were not permitted to form trade unions, strike, or engage in collective bargaining, and household servants—numbering an estimated one million foreigners—continued to be excluded from protection under the labor law. The kingdom also remained off-limits to international human rights organizations, and no one inside the country dared to break the long-standing taboo on openly scrutinizing and reporting human rights abuses.

On October 1, the Council of Ministers approved a 225-article penal code, scheduled to come into force ninety days after its publication in the official gazette. The government said that the code prohibited "coercion, or infliction of physical or moral harm on those arrested," granted criminal suspects "the right to receive legal assistance from a lawyer," and prohibited "detention or imprisonment except in jails or special secure units, and then only on the issuance of a court order." The law also set a five-day limit on detention by criminal investigators, specifying that detainees "shall be released if there is no justification or if there is not enough evidence," although in cases of "serious crimes" the interior minister also had the right to detain suspects. The council also approved on October 1 a forty-three-article law regulating the legal profession.

The practical effect of these new laws, once in force, remained to be seen. Cases during the year involving detained foreign nationals continued to illustrate fundamental flaws in the Saudi judicial system that facilitate human rights violations, including prolonged incommunicado detention, inadequate safeguards against torture and ill treatment of prisoners during interrogation, denial of access to lawyers, and the lack of transparency of legal proceedings. Several foreign governments complained that Saudi authorities had not provided timely notification of the arrest of their nationals and in some cases had denied consular officials access to detainees for long periods. Twice during the year authorities used televised "confessions" to brand suspects guilty of violent activities before they were charged or tried, a practice at odds with the government's affirmation in 2000 that "in the Islamic *shariah*, presumption of innocence is the fundamental principle in criminal proceedings."

One person was killed and others injured in a series of bombing attacks in Riyadh and Khobar between November 2000 and March 2001, which the authorities said were a consequence of turf wars among expatriates involved in the illegal but highly lucrative alcohol trade. (See below.) Two other attacks followed in Khobar: on May 2, a U.S. citizen was seriously injured, and on October 6, a U.S. citizen and another victim who was not identified were killed and four foreigners wounded. Authorities announced on November 14 that the second person killed was a Palestinian dentist who worked in Riyadh, whom they alleged was the perpetrator of the bombing.

Three foreign residents of Saudi Arabia—Alexander Mitchell, British; William Sampson, Canadian; and Raaf Schifer, Belgian—appeared on Saudi state television on February 4, "confessing" to two separate car bombings in Riyadh that killed one Briton and injured others in November 2000. The videotaped statements were made after the detainees had been held incommunicado for over a month without their respective consulates being informed and were aired before completion of the criminal investigation or formal charging. According to the Canadian government, the Saudi interior minister confirmed on February 13 that Sampson had not been permitted to consult with a lawyer during the investigation stage of the proceedings. By November, the three men continued to be held in solitary confinement and a trial was several months away, according to one of their lawyers.

The videotaped "confessions" of three British citizens, who admitted involvement in three bombings between December 2000 and March 2001, were shown on Saudi television on August 13. James Lee, James Cottle, and Les Walker said they had "received orders" to carry out attacks in Riyadh on January 10 and March 15, and in Khobar on December 15. The Khobar bombing injured one person; the March explosion injured two. As was the case during the February "confessions," the suspects did not disclose any motives for their actions, nor who had ordered the violence. The British government said it was informed by Saudi authorities about the "confessions" the day before the broadcast but was not told of the charges or a trial date. These men were also held in solitary confinement, and as of early November a trial was not expected for several months.

Two accused Chechen airplane hijackers, one of them a minor, were reportedly brought to trial in September but denied legal representation. On September 5, *Okaz* newspaper quoted Judge Sheikh Saleh bin Muhamed al-Luhaidan, chairman of the Supreme Judicial Council and a member of the Senior Council of Ulema (religious scholars), as saying: "A case such as this requires no defense lawyer because the hijacking occurred and the hijackers are known and have confessed their crimes." The same day the Russian Foreign Ministry said that it had not received "official confirmation" of the trial nor a response from Saudi authorities to its request for the extradition of the two Chechens, named as Deni Magomerzayev, nineteen, and Eriskhan Arsayev, sixteen. The teenagers were apprehended following the abortive hijacking of a Russian passenger plane flying from Moscow to Istanbul on March 16. The aircraft was forced to land in Medina; three people were killed, including the third alleged hijacker, when Saudi forces stormed the plane to release the passengers and crew.

Trials continued to be conducted behind closed doors. A Riyadh court on May 26 sentenced four British citizens to flogging and prison terms for illegal alcohol trading, but British authorities said they were not notified until May 31. The court sentenced Kelvin Hawkins to two and a half years of imprisonment and five hundred lashes, while Paul Moss, David Mornin, and Ken Hartley received lesser terms and punishment of three hundred to five hundred lashes each.

Relations between the government and the minority Ismaili Shiite community remained tense in the wake of violent clashes with security forces that erupted in Najran province in April 2000 and resulted in scores of arrests. In April 2001, twelve Ismailis signed a petition to Crown Prince Abdullah, complaining about official discrimination, unfair trials, and prolonged imprisonment, and an Ismaili delegation delivered the petition and other documents to the palace in Jeddah on April 29. The next day, a security official arrived in a special bus, which the delegation understood to mean that the governor wished to see them. Instead, at least six members of the delegation were taken to security headquarters in Jeddah and imprisoned there; as of this writing, in November, it was unclear whether they were still being held.

Death sentences by beheading were carried out throughout the year, mostly for murder, rape, or drug-trafficking. By mid-November, at least seventy-five Saudis and foreigners had been executed, according to Reuters. Foreign governments rarely raised fair-trial concerns publicly when their nationals were sentenced to execution. However, a sharp rise in the number of Indians beheaded on drug-related offenses (from one in 1998 to twenty-four in 2000, according to the Indian ambassador to Saudi Arabia) prompted some Indian officials to press for an Indian government investigation of the duping of Indian migrant workers, mainly from the state of Kerala, by drug dealers posing as job recruiters.

The government's highly publicized ratification in 2000 of the Convention on the Elimination of All Forms of Discrimination against Women prompted no initiatives to give Saudi women equal rights with men. Women were not permitted identity cards in their own name, only "family cards" in the name of their husband or father, did not enjoy freedom of movement, were not permitted to drive, and lacked equal rights with men with respect to the nationality of their children, among other discriminatory practices. On April 26, Prince Nayef stated that the government would not lift the ban on women driving: "It is not possible, and there are no studies on the subject at all."

The Saudi public gained access to the Internet in 1999 and the number of users reached an estimated 500,000 in 2001. The government continued to block what official censors viewed as objectionable web sites, ranging from pornography to politics. Ibrahim al-Fareeh, Internet supervisor at King Abdul Aziz Center for Science and Technology (KACST), which controlled access to the Internet, told the Associated Press in April that KACST was about to launch a new campaign, with advanced equipment, to block a further 200,000 sites, raising to 400,000 the number of sites off-limits to Saudi users

Some seven million foreigners worked in the kingdom, many of them from India, Egypt, Indonesia, Pakistan, the Philippines, and Bangladesh. Conditions were particularly difficult for the estimated one million women who were employed as domestic workers, a job category not covered by the labor law. Over 19,000 women domestics fled from their employers in 2000, a Labor Ministry official acknowledged in April, citing mistreatment, nonpayment of wages, and other grievances. The Philippines ambassador told his government that many Filipino workers in Saudi Arabia were "subjected to poor living conditions, salary underpayment, insufficient food, inhuman working conditions, and long hours of work without rest or day off," *Business World* (Manila) reported on March 2. He said Saudi employers illegally "sold" Filipino workers to new sponsors for 2,000 riyals (U.S. $533) when employment contracts expired or the workers were no longer needed, although Saudi authorities had banned such transfers of sponsorship.

Some 370,000 Indonesians were employed in the kingdom, most of them reportedly women domestic workers. In July, the Indonesian government temporarily suspended sending workers to Saudi Arabia pending a formal memorandum of understanding (MoU) under which Saudi authorities agreed to afford greater legal protection to Indonesian migrant workers. Under the MoU, signed in September, the Saudi embassy in Jakarta was to provide the Indonesian Labor Ministry "a weekly list of laborers granted visas and the names of Indonesian recruitment offices handling the process." Also, all visa applications were to be processed through certified labor recruitment offices in both countries, and efforts made to prevent labor recruiters "from manipulating costs, official papers, medical reports and sending unqualified manpower."

The uncertain future of the remaining 5,200 Iraqi refugees in the Rafha desert camp near the Saudi-Iraq border received publicity when dozens of refugees began a hunger strike on June 23 to press demands for resettlement in third countries. Those at Rafha were the last of some 33,000 Iraqi refugees who had been held at the camp since the end of the Gulf war in 1991, of whom 25,000 were resettled in Europe, North America, and Australia, while some 3,000 voluntarily returned to Iraq. The suspension of resettlement programs for these refugees in 1997 left those who remained at the camp no option other than repatriation to Iraq, but the majority of them did not want to return there, according to the United Nations High Commissioner for Refugees (UNHCR). The government reportedly more than tripled the grant it provided to returnees to 10,000 riyals (U.S. $2,666), but apparently without effect. In July, the government said the Iraqi refugees were "treated well," and denied "allegations of rioting, detention of refugees, or incidents of beating, insults or torture." It added that although the Defense Ministry supervised the camp, it was "UNHCR, not the Kingdom, that [was] in charge of resettlement demands by the remaining 5,000 refugees."

DEFENDING HUMAN RIGHTS

Saudi Arabia remained one of the region's embarrassing wastelands with respect to an openly functioning network of independent human rights lawyers, other activists, and institutions. As a result, victims of abuse and their supporters were left isolated and vulnerable, and the timely documentation of rights violations was exceedingly difficult. International human rights organizations were not granted access during the year, and foreign journalists based in the country rarely investigated and reported allegations of abuse.

In March, a seven-member delegation from the U.S. Commission on International Religious Freedom (see below) visited Saudi Arabia and interviewed senior government officials who, it reported, "expressed a desire to continue dialogue with the U.S. government on religious freedom issues."

THE ROLE OF THE INTERNATIONAL COMMUNITY

United Nations

In January, the U.N. Committee on the Rights of the Child examined the kingdom's initial report on compliance with the Convention on the Rights of the Child. In its concluding observations, the committee criticized the Saudi authorities' "narrow interpretations of Islamic texts," asserting that this "imped[ed] the enjoyment of many human rights protected under the convention." It cited in particular provisions of domestic law that discriminated against females and non-Muslims, and allowed flogging as a judicial punishment.

The committee found "direct and indirect discrimination against girls and children born out of wedlock, including in areas relating to civil status (e.g. lack of identity cards for females) and personal status (e.g. inheritance, custody, and guardianship)," and expressed concern that the nationality law did not "grant equal citizenship status to children of Saudi women married to non-nationals." The committee noted that the age of majority was not defined under Saudi law and commented that as a result the death penalty could be imposed for offenses committed when suspects were under eighteen years old, a violation of the convention. It further commented that persons under eighteen "may be sentenced to a variety of methods of cruel, inhuman or degrading treatment or punishment such as flogging, stoning and amputation, which are systematically imposed by judicial authorities." The committee urged the government to "end the imposition" of such practices on "persons who may have committed crimes while under eighteen."

The U.N. special rapporteur on the independence of judges and lawyers was scheduled to conduct a fact-finding visit to the kingdom from October 11-19, pursuant to an invitation that the government extended in 2000. The visit was postponed because of security concerns; as of November 5 it had not been rescheduled.

In 1997, Saudi Arabia became a state party to the Convention against Torture and Other Cruel, Inhuman or Degrading Treatment or Punishment. The kingdom's initial report to the U.N. Committee against Torture, submitted in February, was scheduled to be examined by the committee at its November 12-23 session in Geneva but the government asked for a postponement shortly before the session.

United States

Ties between the U.S. and Saudi Arabia were cemented by long-standing mutual military and economic interests. The U.S. remained the world's leading supplier of defense equipment and services to the kingdom, with military exports in 2000 totaling almost U.S. $2 billion, according to the U.S. Department of Commerce. The department also reported that Saudi Arabia was the twenty-fourth-largest export market for U.S. companies, with merchandise exports of $6.2 billion in 2000, and that U.S. investment in the kingdom climbed to $4.8 billion in the same year. Saudi exports to the U.S. were $14.2 billion in 2000 as oil prices increased.

Five U.S.-based multinationals were among the eight international energy companies selected in May for three major natural gas exploration and development projects and related water, power, and petrochemical facilities, with initial foreign investment estimated at $20 billion. ExxonMobil, the kingdom's leading foreign investor, was chosen to lead two of the ventures: the largest in South Ghawar, with Royal Dutch/Shell, BP, and Phillips Petroleum, and the Red Sea project, with the participation of Enron and Occidental. Participants in the third project, in the Rub al-Khali near Shaybah, were Royal Dutch/Shell, TotalFina Elf, and Conoco. The government signed preparatory agreements with the companies on June 3, with the Houston-based Marathon Oil Company replacing Enron, which withdrew on June 1.

In addition to the State Department's annual country report, which once again bluntly described the broad pattern of rights abuses in Saudi Arabia, other reports contributed additional information and analysis. For example, the U.S. Commission on International Religious Freedom recommended to the State Department on August 16 the designation of Saudi Arabia as one of nine "countries of particular concern." In its accompanying report, the commission charged that Saudi Arabia "suppresses religious views of both Saudi and non-Saudi Muslims that do not conform to official positions," including the minority Shiite and Ismaili communities. The commission dismissed the government's claim that non-Muslims were permitted private worship. It said that the definition of the term was "vague," and that individuals engaged in such activity have been "arrested, imprisoned, deported and harassed by the authorities." The commission noted that "diplomatic personnel from Western countries face difficulties in their religious practice" and that the problems were "compounded for foreign guest workers who have no diplomatic standing and little or no access to private religious services conducted at diplomatic facilities." The State Department's 2001 international religious freedom report, published on October 26, found that freedom of religion "does not exist" in Saudi Arabia, but, as in 2000, the kingdom was not designated one of the countries of particular concern.

The State Department's *Trafficking in Persons Report*, published in July, identified Saudi Arabia as one of the world's destination countries for trafficked persons, and noted that workers from India, the Philippines, Indonesia, Thailand, Bangladesh, and the Horn of Africa "have reported being forced into domestic servitude and sexual exploitation." The report said that the Saudi government did not acknowledge trafficking as a problem and authorities had not crafted legislation or undertaken other "significant efforts" to combat it.

In its annual patterns of global terrorism report, released in April, the State Department raised concerns that Saudi authorities were not enforcing consistently their requirement that NGOs and private voluntary agencies obtain government authorization "before soliciting contributions for domestic or international causes," and over allegations that "some international terrorist organization representatives solicited and collected funds from private citizens in Saudi Arabia."

Prior to the September 11 attacks on New York and Washington, there were clear strains in the U.S.-Saudi relationship over the Saudi government's dissatisfaction with what it considered the pro-Israel stance of the Bush administration. A White House invitation to Crown Prince Abdullah to visit Washington in 2001 was rejected twice, in May and in July. The Saudi government also postponed indefinitely the Washington annual meeting of the joint Saudi-U.S. military committee, scheduled for August.

Another source of bilateral tension was the June 21 U.S. federal grand jury indictment of thirteen Saudis and one unnamed Lebanese for planning and carrying out the June 1996 bombing of the Khobar Towers military housing complex in Dhahran, which killed nineteen U.S. servicemen and injured another 372 Americans. The defendants included Hani al-Sayegh, who was arrested in Canada in March 1997, transferred to the U.S. in June 1997 on a pledge that he would cooperate with U.S. investigators, and then deported to Saudi Arabia in October 1999 after he allegedly reneged on his promise and was denied political asylum in the U.S. The indictment named the Saudi defendants as members of the Saudi Hizballah organization and identified most of them as Shi'a Muslims from Qatif. On June 21, U.S. Attorney General John Ashcroft said the suspects had received support from unnamed Iranian officials. The indictment, he said, "explains that elements of the Iranian government inspired, supported, and supervised members of the Saudi Hizballah . . . .[T]he charged defendants reported their surveillance activities to Iranian officials and were supported and directed in those activities by Iranian officials." Despite these serious allegations, no Iranian was named as a defendant in the indictment.

The indictment apparently caught the Saudi government by surprise and senior officials expressed irritation. Interior Minister Prince Nayef bin Abdel Aziz confirmed that eleven of the suspects were imprisoned in Saudi Arabia and would be tried in a Saudi court, but in an interview with the daily *al-Riyadh*, published on June 23, he said: "The Americans never informed us or coordinated with us on this issue." He also disputed the existence of the Saudi Hizballah group mentioned in the indictment, saying there was no such group, although some individuals might be "linked to the Lebanese Hizbollah." Prince Nayef said on June 30 that the suspects in Saudi custody would never be sent to the U.S. for trial, adding: "We have nothing whatsoever to do with the U.S. court, and we are not concerned with what has been said or what is going to be decided by the U.S."

Following the September 11 attacks on the U.S., Saudi officials announced "full support" for international anti-terrorist initiatives, and pledged to keep stable oil prices and supplies. But there were signs of further strain in U.S.-Saudi relations. In September, the government withdrew its diplomatic recognition of Afghanistan's Taliban government for "defaming Islam by harboring and supporting terrorists," but senior officials said they would not permit the U.S. to use its military facilities in Saudi Arabia to carry out offensive operations against Arab or Muslim states.

U.S. Defense Secretary Donald Rumsfeld visited the kingdom on October 4 and met King Fahd, Crown Prince Abdullah, and Minister of Defense Prince Sultan but he said nothing publicly about the Bush administration's specific requests for Saudi government assistance in its global anti-terror campaign. After meeting Rumsfeld, Prince Sultan suggested that the U.S. had made no requests, and said that the question of Saudi support "was not a point of discussion." Rumsfeld, however, stated that "there are any number of countries that are doing things that are public, there are any number of countries that are doing things that are exactly the same privately," and said the U.S. appreciated the "public support" of Saudi Arabia and "the things they are doing to assist us."

But tensions were evident, particularly following the FBI's September 27 press release that described seven of the nineteen men suspected of the September 11 hijackings as "possible" Saudi nationals. In addition, the FBI list of twenty-two "Most Wanted Terrorists," issued on October 10, included Osama bin Laden, who was stripped of his Saudi citizenship in 1994, and four other Saudi nationals implicated in the 1996 Khobar Towers bombing.

By mid-October, Saudi officials began to voice complaints publicly. Prince Nayef, quoted on October 15, said that the U.S. had provided no "material evidence" that Saudi nationals were among the hijackers. He similarly criticized allegations about private Saudi financing of terrorist groups and U.S. requests to freeze assets, saying it was "unacceptable to take any action without providing the evidence that there are some [suspicious] accounts in the kingdom." He added that the government had previously "requested the United States, Britain and some European countries to cooperate with us in this field, but found no [positive] response."

The *New York Times* reported on October 25 that unnamed U.S. federal authorities were "now sure" that fifteen of the nineteen hijackers were Saudi citizens, based on "weeks of investigation" in the U.S. and Saudi Arabia, and that Saudi authorities "assisted" the U.S. in confirming their identities. On October 31, the *Washington Post* reported that eleven of the alleged Saudi hijackers had been issued U.S. visas in Jeddah and four others received visas in Riyadh, citing U.S. State Department documents made available to the newspaper.

SYRIA

HUMAN RIGHTS DEVELOPMENTS

President Bashar al-Asad's government launched a crackdown on peaceful but outspoken advocates of reform in August, sending a clear message that it would tolerate a political opening only on its own terms and according to its own timetable. Authorities arrested leading critics and others active in the freewheeling discussion groups, or civil society forums, that emerged as Syrians sought to claim freedoms that had been denied them during the thirty-year rule of former president Hafez al-Asad. The arrests reversed a trend toward greater openness in a country long dominated by the ruling Arab Ba'th Socialist Party and institutions it controls, and followed earlier positive developments. These included the release of some six hundred political prisoners under a presidential amnesty in November 2000, a January 2001 announcement that the emergency law in force since 1963 was "frozen" and "not applied," and the release in May 2001 of Nizar Nayouf, then the last remaining imprisoned human rights activist. In addition, the government initially relaxed some controls on the press, but in September introduced a tough new decree that regulated the press and other publications as part of a wider strategy to control critical expression.

The crackdown began with the arrest of Mamoun al-Homsi, an independent member of parliament, on August 9. Previously, the authorities did not acknowledge or give reasons for detentions, but in this case the Interior Ministry confirmed al-Homsi's arrest on August 10, charging that a list of political demands that he had issued publicly on August 7, when commencing a hunger strike at his office, constituted "an attempt to change the constitution by illegal means, trying to stop the authorities from carrying out their duties mentioned in the law, trying to harm national unity, defaming the state and insulting the legislative, executive and judicial authorities." The ministry also alleged that al-Homsi owed almost U.S. $1 million in back taxes and had issued his call for political changes, ranging from the lifting of the emergency law to stronger anti-corruption measures, in order to portray himself "as a political victim whereas in fact he is someone accused of a crime."

Al-Homsi's trial began in Damascus criminal court on October 30, and continued as of mid-November.

On September 1, the authorities arrested seventy-one-year-old Riad al-Turk, head of the unauthorized Communist Party Political Bureau and possibly Syria's best known former political prisoner. Official sources said he had been detained "in accordance with Syrian criminal and penal procedure law." The government's *al-Thawrah* newspaper reported on September 5 that he had "expressed views that encroach upon the constitution, violate the general law, and defame the state." By mid-November, al-Turk was still being held, reportedly awaiting trial in the State Security Court, whose procedures do not satisfy international fair trial standards, including the right of appeal to a higher tribunal.

The authorities next detained Riad al-Seif, another member of parliament and a vocal champion of political reform, on September 6. He was later charged, according to his lawyer, with "seeking to change the constitution through illegal means," "inciting inter-religious division," "forming a secret society," and "organizing subversive meetings" and "gatherings aimed at causing disorder." The day before al-Seif's arrest, hundreds of people had attended the National Dialogue Forum, a weekly political gathering that he hosted at his home. Al-Seif suspended the forum in March and opened it in September only after he was unable to obtain an official permit. He had also planned to launch a new political party, the Movement for Social Peace, with a platform that included ending the Ba'th party's grip on political power. In February, a prosecutor had questioned al-Seif about the proposed party's aims, and reportedly accused him of threatening the constitution and "attempting to create a sectarian rift." Al-Seif's trial commenced in the Damascus criminal court on October 31 and continued as of mid-November.

Seven more activists were arrested and imprisoned between September 9-12. These included prominent economist Arif Dalila, founding member of the nongovernmental Committees for the Revival of Civil Society, and others involved in the civil forum movement: lawyer Habib Issa, engineer Fawaz Tello, Hassan Saadoun, and Habib Saleh. Two of those arrested, Issa and physician Walid al-Bunni, were at the July 2 founding meeting of the independent Human Rights Society in Syria, and physician Kamal Labwani was a member of the administrative council of the Committees for the Defense of Human Rights. Issa was also a member of the defense team for the detained parliamentarians and before his arrest had spoken about the cases on the pan-Arab al-Jazeera television station. As of mid-November, all seven were awaiting trail before the State Security Court.

In the months preceding the clampdown, senior officials signaled the government's increasing unease with the opening up of public debate. On January 29, Information Minister Adnan Omran warned publicly that discussions about reform "must be responsible," and disparaged the term "civil society," describing it as "an American expression." President Asad also took up this theme in an interview published on February 8 in the pan-Arabic daily *al-Sharq al-Awsat*, stating that civic organizations should complement and be "based on" state institutions, "not built on their ruins," and that in Syria "the development of civil society institutions must come at a later stage and they are not therefore among our priorities."

In mid-February, the government imposed controls on the independent civic forums, compromising the unprecedented freedom of assembly that Syrian activists and their supporters had been enjoying. Meetings reportedly could no longer be held without prior government approval, a list of participants, and a copy of the speakers' lectures. In March, President Asad warned further that there were "principles in Syria which nobody should break," citing "the Ba'th party, the armed forces, and the policies of president Hafez al-Asad." He added: "Challenging these fundamentals amounts to harming the national interest . . . and serving the nation's enemies." An internal Ba'th party memorandum, publicized in March, echoed the president's remarks. It charged ominously that groups which sought to "weaken the state and dwarf its role" were, "intentionally or not, serving the enemies of the homeland."

Another human rights setback occurred on September 22, when President Asad issued a restrictive decree governing newspapers and other periodical publications as well as anything else printed in Syria, from books to pamphlets and posters. Decree no. 50/2001 granted the executive, specifically, the prime minister and the minister of information, powers to regulate publishers, printers, distributors, and bookstores, and provided harsh criminal penalties for violations of the decree, including substantial fines and imprisonment for up to three years.

Article 29 of the decree listed banned topics, including "details of secret trials," "articles and reports about national security, national unity, details of the security and safety of the army, its movements, weapons, supplies, equipment and camps," and material "affecting the right to privacy." Article 51a criminalized the publication of "falsehoods" and "fabricated reports," with imprisonment of one to three years for violators and/or hefty fines. The article added, in sweepingly vague language, that the maximum penalties "shall be imposed if such acts have been committed by reason of ill-will, or caused public unrest, or harm to international relations, offense to state dignity, national unity, the morale of the army and the armed forces, or caused some damage to the national economy and the currency." Violators of articles 29 and 51a were further penalized with suspension of their publications for periods of one week to six months.

The decree also prohibited "propaganda publications" financed "directly or indirectly" by foreign countries, companies or foundations, raising concern that it could be used to target independent civil society groups that receive funding from abroad. Breaches of this provision brought fines and prison terms of six months to one year.

The decree also required that all periodicals, including those of "legally established political parties," obtain in advance a license to publish from the prime minister, who was empowered to deny licenses "for reasons he deems to be related to public interest." Nongovernmental organizations (NGOs), professional associations, and unions, however, were exempted from this licensing requirement, but it remained to be seen if NGOs without official legal status would be permitted to publish magazines or other periodicals.

Other provisions of the decree, set out in article 16, limited the ownership of periodical publications to Syrian Arabs, suggesting that members of the Kurdish minority and stateless Kurds born in Syria were excluded as well as foreigners. The same article also barred ownership to anyone convicted of a criminal offense, stripped of civil or political rights, or "dismissed from employment," penalties that had been imposed on many peaceful critics of the government who were previously imprisoned on criminal charges after State Security Court trials. The decree also required all periodical publications to obtain Information Ministry approval before they changed their owner, director, or chief editor, and distributors and sellers of foreign periodicals to submit advance copies to the same ministry, which can ban their entry or circulation if they "infringe upon national sovereignty and security or offend public morality."

The issue of Lebanese in secret Syrian custody, including those who were apprehended on Lebanese soil by Lebanese or Syrian security forces and then "disappeared," remained unresolved, despite official Syrian government acknowledgment that it had been holding scores of prisoners. On December 11, 2000, Syrian authorities transferred fifty-four prisoners to Lebanon; forty-six of them were Lebanese and eight were Palestinians. One of the Lebanese, Khaled Tawfiq, said he had been held for thirteen years. Several days later, Lebanon's prosecutor general released a list of another ninety-five Lebanese who remained jailed in Syria for alleged criminal offenses committed on Syrian territory. Despite Syrian government assertions that the file was now closed, Lebanese human rights organizations insisted that there were additional Lebanese held in unacknowledged detention in Syria, including some whose relatives had managed to visit them over the years. Other "disappeared" included twenty-six Lebanese soldiers who were last seen alive on October 13, 1990, the day Syrian troops began fighting against forces loyal to Gen. Michel Aoun.

DEFENDING HUMAN RIGHTS

Human rights organizations lacked official legal status and could be denied authorization in arbitrary fashion under the broadly worded 1958 private associations law, article 2, which states: "Any association which is established for an illicit reason or purpose, or which contravenes the law or the moral code, or the purpose of which is to prejudice the integrity or form of the republican government shall be null and void." The government also reported to the U.N. Human Rights Committee (HRC) that the law placed "restrictions" on the establishment of private associations "in order to protect public safety, national security, public order, public health and morals and rights of others."

One recently organized human rights group that elected its board of directors in July told Human Rights Watch that it would seek authorization from the government but planned to carry out activities during this process. One of the group's leaders said he was under surveillance by several security agencies, and that family members had been questioned about his activities as a form of intimidation and pressure. Another activist and former political prisoner reported that security forces monitored his telephone and mail and that he was "not feeling safe."

Despite such pressures and in contrast to earlier years, intellectuals and human rights activists in Syria openly issued regular communiqués and statements, proposing sweepings reforms and criticizing government actions. In January, over

1,000 intellectuals and others signed the Basic Document, a petition circulated by the Committees for the Revival of Civil Society. This called for political reform, including free elections, press freedom, the lifting of emergency law, and an end to the Ba'th party's political domination. The document noted "the consequences of undermining democracy in the name of socialism," and said that in Syria the rule of law had been "replaced by patronage, rights by favors, and the general interest by personal interest."

Following the arrest of member of parliament Mamoun al-Homsi in August, the Committees for the Defense of Human Rights issued a statement that called for his release and urged the government to "stop using the judiciary as an instrument of pressure or terror against political activists." In a separate document, thirty-five intellectuals and human rights activists also condemned the arrest and advocated al-Homsi's release.

Human rights activist Nizar Nayouf was released from prison in May after serving in solitary confinement most of the ten-year prison sentence that the State Security Court imposed in 1992. Following international publicity, he was provided a passport and finally allowed to leave Syria in July to seek medical treatment in France. Following his release, Nayouf campaigned for accountability for past abuses, including torture, deaths in detention, and extrajudicial executions. He told Human Rights Watch that while still in Syria he had formed the National Council for Truth, Justice and Reconciliation to document abuses, press for the perpetrators to be brought to justice, and assist former political prisoners who were stripped of their civil and political rights and denied reemployment in their former jobs.

On September 3, Nayouf's lawyer Anwar al-Bunni reported that lawyers from the Ba'th party had filed a case against Nayouf, accusing him of seeking to change the constitution by illegal means, creating sectarian strife, and publishing abroad reports harmful to the state. Nayouf, who was still in France, was ordered to appear before an investigating judge for questioning.

Syria remained largely closed to international human rights organizations, although authorities permitted a representative of the New York-based Committee to Protect Journalists to visit the country in April and May; the mission took place without government interference.

THE ROLE OF THE INTERNATIONAL COMMUNITY

United Nations

In March, the U.N. Human Rights Committee considered Syria's second periodic report on compliance with the International Covenant on Civil and Political Rights (ICCPR), due since 1984. The committee criticized the long delay and the lack of factual information in the report, expressed concern about the "quasi-permanent state of emergency" in force since 1963, and called for lifting of the emergency law "as soon as possible." The committee also expressed concern about extrajudicial executions, torture, inhumane prison conditions, and "disappearances," including those of Lebanese nationals taken into custody in Lebanon and transferred to Syria.

The HRC also criticized restrictions on freedom of assembly and association, noting that "only political parties wishing to participate in the political activities of the National Progressive Front, led by the Ba'th party, are allowed," and the denial of passports to many Syrian exiles and their children, urging the government to "facilitate the return to the country of all Syrian citizens wishing to do so." The committee also urged the authorities to urgently "find a solution to the statelessness of numerous Kurds in Syria and to allow Kurdish children born in Syria to acquire Syrian nationality."

With regard to the death penalty, the HRC called for a reduction in the number of offenses punishable by death and asked the government to provide within one year the number of death sentences passed since 1990, the names of those condemned and the grounds on which they were sentenced, and the dates of executions.

European Union

Commercial ties between Syria and the European Union (E.U.) remained strong but these links did not yield any sustained advocacy on the long-overdue need for human rights improvements, including basic rights such as freedom of expression and association. The E.U. was Syria's main trading partner, with the trade balance in favor of Damascus. Some 60 percent of Syrian exports, primarily petroleum products and cotton, were destined for E.U. states, with Italy, Germany, and France leading the importers. Thirty-one percent of Syria's imports were from the E.U., with Italy, Germany , and France also the major suppliers.

The government made clear that it sought substantial European financial aid to upgrade the manufacturing sector and increase its competitiveness. On April 4, Dr. Muhamed Tawfiq Simaq, who heads Syria's Industry Committee, said the country required some $5.6 billion for a ten-year industrial development plan and "we expect the E.U. to provide generous assistance."

Syria and the European Union continued to negotiate a Euro-Mediterranean Association Agreement, an economic pact designed to result in a free trade zone. Five rounds of talks took place between May 1998 and December 2000, and the negotiations continued in 2001. Prior to the launch of two days of negotiations in Damascus in April, a senior government official voiced dissatisfaction at what was apparently perceived as E.U. pressure over political and economic issues. "We believe that the development of democracy should be based on the national development [of the country] and not result from foreign diktats, and that is where one of the problems in the negotiations lies," Issam Zaim, Syria's state planning minister of state, was quoted as saying. The head of the E.U. delegation in Syria, Marc Pierini, responded that "there was nothing in the substance of the project for an [association] accord, nor in the character or style of the negotiations which could lead one to think of a diktat." Association agreements included standard language specifying that the agreements were premised on "respect for human rights and democratic values."

Apparent tensions with respect to the pace of economic reform led the E.U. to publish a statement noting that "Syria has decided itself that it needed to reform its economy," and that the E.U. was "not trying to impose any kind of formula on it."

The E.U. position, the statement said, was that "a sustained rhythm of reforms" was "an essential signal to the outside world" needed to attract investment.

United States

The U.S. offered little in the way of public criticism of Syria's human rights practices, which the State Department once again assessed as "poor." The Bush administration seemed more concerned to use any leverage it did have to press the government to adhere to U.N. supervision of the Iraq sanctions regime as bilateral relations warmed considerably between Syria and Iraq, and to keep a close watch on the volatile Lebanon-Israel border, where Hizballah guerrillas continued to attack Israeli military forces in support of Syrian and Lebanese government claims that the disputed Shebaa Farms area, in the foothills of the Israeli-annexed Golan Heights, was Lebanese, not Syrian, territory occupied by Israel.

On January 23, State Department spokesman Richard Boucher said that U.S. officials had discussions with the Syrian government about the reopening in November 2000 of the oil pipeline from Iraq to the Syrian Mediterranean port of Banias. Boucher said that the U.S. would support a Syrian request to have the pipeline named as an official route for Iraq's oil exports, under the supervision of the U.N.'s oil for food program.

Edward Walker, assistant secretary of state in the State Department's Bureau of Near Eastern Affairs, discussed Syria in testimony on March 29 before the subcommittee on the Middle East and South Asia of the House of Representatives Committee on International Relations. He cited as positive developments the government's pledge to the U.S. to submit to U.N. supervision of its oil trade with Iraq, and said that economic reform initiatives, particularly in the banking sector, represented "the beginning of movement in the right direction." Secretary Walker made no comments about political reform or human rights, although he criticized President Asad as being "intractable on the question of Israel," called his statement at the March 27 Arab League summit meeting in Amman "unacceptable," and said that the "jury is still out on Mr. Bashar." In his speech, President Asad termed Israel "a racist society and more racist than Nazism."

Syria remained one of the seven countries on the U.S. list of state sponsors of international terrorism. The State Department's patterns of global terrorism report, released in April 2000, said that Syria "appeared to maintain its longstanding ban on attacks launched from Syrian territory or against Western targets," and "generally upheld its agreement with [Turkey] not to support the Kurdish PKK." But the report also charged that Syria "continued to provide safe haven and support to several terrorist groups, some of which maintained training camps or other facilities on Syrian territory." The report noted that the Popular Front for the Liberation of Palestine-General Command (PFLP-GC), the Palestine Islamic Jihad (PIJ), Fatah-the-Intifada, and the Popular Front for the Liberation of Palestine (PFLP) "maintained their headquarters in Damascus," and that Hamas was permitted "to open a new main office in Damascus in March, although the arrangement may be temporary while Hamas continues to seek permission to reestablish its headquarters in Jordan." The State Department said that Syria "granted a variety of terrorist groups—including Hamas, the PFLP-GC, and the PIJ—basing privileges or refuge in areas of Lebanon's Bekaa Valley under Syrian control." It also said that Syria "did not act to stop Hizballah and Palestinian rejectionist groups from carrying out anti-Israeli attacks," and that "Damascus also served as the primary transit point for terrorist operatives traveling to Lebanon and for the resupply of weapons to Hizballah."

In the wake of the September 11 attacks in New York and Washington, which Syria condemned, newly appointed U.S. Ambassador to Syria Theodore Kattouf met in Damascus with Foreign Minister Farouq al-Shara'. According to a Syrian official quoted by Reuters, the topics of discussion at the September 15 meeting included "bilateral cooperation," among other issues. The Syrian government publicly insisted on a distinction between terrorism, which it said it opposed, and resistance to foreign occupation, presumably by the Palestinian and Lebanese groups that it supported. On October 11, U.S. Deputy Secretary of State Richard Armitage was asked about the consequences for countries such as Syria that did not satisfy U.S. requests for cooperation in the global anti-terrorism effort. "The consequences might be whatever the coalition finds worthy and it runs the gamut from isolation to financial investigation, all the way up through possibly military action." At a press conference later that day, President Bush appeared to soften Armitage's remarks: "The Syrians have talked to us about how they can help in the war against terrorism . . . [W]e take that seriously and we'll give them an opportunity to do so." The next day, Syria's Foreign Ministry reportedly summoned Ambassador Kattouf and protested Armitage's statement.

TUNISIA

HUMAN RIGHTS DEVELOPMENTS

Government critics and human rights activists were arrested or harassed and hundreds of political prisoners were confined under harsh conditions. Mainstream media allowed almost no criticism of the government, and genuine opposition parties were either banned or actively impeded.

Nevertheless, civil society organizations, political prisoners, former prisoners, and previously silent political figures increasingly challenged the status quo.

The most disturbing new trend was the resort to physical force by plainclothes police against human rights defenders and critics of the government. But suspected members of the banned Islamist movement, an-Nahda, remained the chief target for repression. They comprised most of the country's political prisoners, estimated to number 1,000. The vast majority had been convicted on such charges as membership in "unauthorized" organizations or holding "unauthorized" meetings, and had not been linked to any act of violence.

Although the renewed activism within civil society did not lead to mass rallies or demonstrations—which remained banned by the authorities—it took new forms. First, many spoke out against the candidature of President Zine el-Abidine Ben Ali for a fourth term in 2004, which would require a constitutional amendment. Second, rights activists focused as never before on the plight of persecuted Islamists, eroding the government's effort to portray them as violent extremists. Third, in cooperation with allies overseas, Tunisian rights activists cited alleged torturers by name and campaigned to hold them accountable.

Tunis Civil Court Judge Mokhtar Yahiaoui shattered the reserve of his profession by denouncing the lack of judicial independence in an open letter, dated July 6, to President Ben Ali. Yahiaoui decried that judges "render verdicts dictated to them by political authorities and enjoy no discretion to exercise any objectivity or critical scrutiny." Yahiaoui was suspended without pay, but reinstated two weeks later after wide protests.

The judge affirmed what human rights organizations had long contended: that the justice system was a pillar of state repression. Judges routinely curtailed political defendants' right to fair trial, vetoing defense requests to subpoena witnesses and preventing lawyers from questioning defendants on the stand, on the grounds that the defendants' statements to the police or the judge sufficed. Lawyers often faced obstacles that prevented their obtaining timely access to their detained clients and to case documents before the start of proceedings.

On November 24, 2000, Judge Tahar al-Yefreni insisted on proceeding with a trial of eight men accused of belonging to an "unauthorized" Islamist organization, even though defendants Abdellatif Bouhjila and Yassine Benzarti were semi-conscious from a hunger strike and unable to respond to questions, and their lawyers had walked out in protest. The judge sentenced the two men to seventeen and eleven years in prison respectively, sentences that were confirmed on appeal in March.

In separate cases, three Tunisians who lived abroad were arrested upon their arrival in Tunisia, informed that they had previously been convicted in their absence on political charges, then re-tried and imprisoned. Mehdi Zougah, a French-Tunisian dual national, was arrested in August 2000 and told he had been convicted for conducting Nahda activities ten years earlier while living in France. (Tunisian law permits the prosecution of Tunisians for "illegal" political activities abroad even when they are legal in the host country.) The charges, which Zougah denied, were based on the testimony of an accuser who had reportedly retracted his accusations but who was not brought to testify before the court. Zougah was convicted again on February 22 and sentenced to two years in prison, one of them suspended. He was freed March 30 and allowed to return to France, after French President Jacques Chirac raised his case with President Ben Ali.

Law student Haroun Mbarek was arrested shortly after Canada deported him to Tunisia on January 6. In a case much like Zougah's, Mbarek was convicted and sentenced to three years in prison in March. But on May 26, Mbarek was conditionally released. In September, he returned to Canada, and on October 4, an appeals court reduced his sentence.

Lotfi Farhat fared worse than Zougah, who had French nationality, and Mbarek, who benefited from the solicitude of embarrassed Canadian officials. Visiting from France in August 2000, Farhat was seized and held incommunicado in a cell at the

Ministry of Interior headquarters. There, Farhat later told his lawyers, police beat him, confined him in contorted positions, and suspended him by his feet while lowering his head into a bucket filled with dirty water. Allegedly under these conditions, he signed a confession that was the sole evidence against him when a military court convicted him on January 31 to seven years in prison for plotting against the government as a member of a terrorist organization operating abroad. The military court, whose verdict was not subject to appeal, accepted Farhat's "confession," ruling that his torture claim was "not proven."

Tunisia's media remained tightly controlled, despite repeated public prompting by officials for more boldness. In an interview published in Tunisian papers on May 11, President Ben Ali exhorted journalists to "write on any subject you choose; there are no taboos except what is prohibited by law and press ethics." The parliament adopted revisions to the press code that eliminated the offense of "defaming the public order" and reduced the number of press offenses punishable by prison terms.

Despite these welcome steps, cautious critical coverage could be found only in a few low-circulation magazines. Privately-owned daily newspapers were indistinguishable from the governmental ones, except for attacking even more scurrilously the government's critics.

Bolder publications were either banned or confiscated. Issues of *Al-Maoukif* (The Platform), organ of the small, legal Progressive Socialist Rally, were seized at the printers. Authorities refused to grant the necessary license to leftist journalist Jalal Zoughlami to launch *Kaws el-Karama* (The Arc of Dignity). After Zoughlami published the journal anyway he was assaulted on February 3 in downtown Tunis by men wielding iron bars who were believed to be police agents. Then on February 6, men in plainclothes attacked Zoughlami and several supporters outside his Tunis home, breaking bones and bloodying faces. On February 21, when staff members of the French freedom-of-expression group Reporters sans Frontières (RSF) handed out *Kaws el-Karama* in the streets of Tunis, plainclothes police seized their copies and expelled two of the RSF workers to France. As of November 1, Zoughlami was still denied a passport.

Issues of foreign newspapers that contained critical coverage of Tunisia were banned from circulation. These included the April 6 issue of the Paris daily *Le Monde*, which featured an interview with the new human rights minister, Slaheddine Maâoui, vowing a new spirit of openness and reform.

Tunisian radio and television, which were state-run, shunned negative coverage of government policies, other than tame criticism heard on some talk shows. In a refreshing exception, government television aired a debate on democracy on July 17 in which opposition politician Ismaïl Boulahia urged greater judicial independence.

Hamma Hammami, the leader of the banned Tunisian Communist Workers Party, entered his fourth year in hiding in February. In 1999, he had been sentenced in his absence to nine years in prison for "maintenance of an association that incites hatred," along with other charges that were frequently used to stifle nonviolent political dissent. Two of his convicted co-defendants also remained in hiding during 2001.

Mohamed Mouada, the former leader of the legal, once-strong Socialist Democratic Movement, was re-imprisoned on June 19. Mouada had been conditionally released from prison in 1996 after serving one year of an eleven-year sentence on trumped-up charges. His re-arrest came after he signed a joint manifesto on March 20 with exiled Nahda leader Rachid Ghannouchi, in favor of public freedoms and against a fourth term for President Ben Ali. Mouada went on to broadcast his views on al-Mustakillah television, a London-based satellite station that has given a regular platform to Tunisian dissidents. The pretext for the re-arrest of Mouada, who is in his sixties, was unspecified violations of the terms of his conditional release.

Political prisoners and ex-prisoners staged individual and collective hunger strikes to protest harsh conditions, lack of medical care, and the harassment of their relatives. Among the worst-treated prisoners were Nahda leaders such as Ali Laaridh and Sadok Chorou, who have served more than ten years in isolation from other prisoners and were often deprived of reading and writing materials. Generally, prisoners were confined in overcrowded and unhygienic group cells, and political prisoners were constantly shuffled among facilities without regard to the proximity of their families.

In April, parliament adopted a prison reform law that, among other things, required the separation of pre-trial and convicted prisoners and restricted the use of force by guards. As of October, it was too early to tell whether the new laws had improved conditions. No independent organization was authorized to inspect prisons. However, liberal access was granted to the state-appointed Higher Committee of Human Rights and Fundamental Liberties. The committee did not publicize its findings but claimed, in a letter to Human Rights Watch dated August 30, that its confidential reports to President Ben Ali contributed to improvements in conditions.

Suspected Islamists who were released from prison faced arbitrary measures such as passport denials, onerous and disruptive requirements for signing in with the police, and pressures on employers to refrain from hiring them. To protest his ordeal as an ex-prisoner, Ali Sghaïer took some of his seven children to the market in Douz in August 2000 and held up a sign that read, "I am prevented from working and cannot feed my children, would anyone like to buy them?" Sghaïer was promptly arrested and put back in prison for six months for refusing to obey an extrajudicial order that he sign in regularly with the police. He was released in February 2001.

Since independence, Tunisian women have made considerable advances toward equality with men—including in the way that their political and civil rights were curtailed. At least four women human rights activists were assaulted by police during the year and one was jailed. Police harassed the wives of suspected Islamists in jail or in exile. The leading independent women's rights group, the Tunisian Association of Democratic Women, was occasionally prevented from convening public meetings.

In February, a torture victim filed a complaint in the Geneva canton of Switzerland against ex-interior minister Abdellah Kallel when he traveled there for a heart operation. The complaint accused Kallel of ordering and supervising the torture of the plaintiff in the Ministry of Interior headquarters in Tunis. The local prosecutor, citing Switzerland's ratification of the U.N. Convention against Torture, deemed the complaint sufficiently well-founded to open a preliminary investigation. Kallel hastily departed the country.

In August, some human rights groups protested the designation of Habib Ammar as head of the organizing committee of the Mediterranean Games that were held in Tunis in September. They alleged that Ammar was implicated in torture as an official of the Interior Ministry in the 1980s.

President Ben Ali stated publicly more than once that abusers in the security forces would be held accountable. But the fact that plainclothes police repeatedly brutalized human rights lawyers and activists in public places, even when victims filed formal complaints and eyewitnesses were abundant, reflected the climate of impunity. In an encouraging exception, four prison guards were given four-year prison sentences in July for torturing a common-law suspect, and the state was ordered to pay compensation.

DEFENDING HUMAN RIGHTS

While authorities stopped short of stamping out human rights activity, they sought to contain it through intimidation and harassment. Two outspoken activists were jailed and a state-encouraged lawsuit kept the dynamic leadership of the Tunisian Human Rights League (Ligue Tunisienne des droits de l'Homme, LTDH) in legal limbo much of the year.

The suit against the LTDH was filed by four of its members, after the chief of the ruling Constitutional Democratic Rally condemned the outcome of the LTDH's internal election in October 2000. The suit asked the court to nullify the elections on the grounds of procedural irregularities.

In November 2000, a Tunis court issued an interim order suspending the newly elected executive committee and evicting it from the LTDH's offices. The committee defiantly persisted in issuing communiqués critical of rights violations and in meeting in private homes and offices. The police responded by preventing a number of LTDH gatherings. The LTDH's president and a vice-president were summoned to court on charges of disobeying a court order.

On February 12, the court nullified the League's election. But that ruling was softened by a logically baffling decision issued by the appeals court on June 21. The higher court upheld the nullification but assigned the task of ordering a new vote to the executive committee whose election had been nullified. The league leadership continued its activities, although it faced legal uncertainty and its meetings were sometimes prevented by police actions.

The other key human rights organization was the National Council on Liberties in Tunisia (Conseil National pour les Libertés en Tunisie, CNLT), which has been denied legal recognition since its formation in 1998. CNLT co-founder Nejib Hosni was jailed in December 2000 to serve the remainder of an eight-year sentence on trumped-up charges of fraud. The pretext of Hosni's re-arrest was that he had violated the terms of his earlier release by resuming his law practice. In this instance, as before, it appeared Hosni was jailed to punish his vigorous defense of political defendants, including Islamists. Supported by the Tunisian Bar Association and an international campaign, Hosni was freed by presidential pardon on May 12.

Sihem Ben Sedrine, the CNLT's spokesperson and editor of the online journal *Kalima*, was arrested on June 26 upon her return from London, where she had condemned judicial corruption in an interview on al-Mustakilla television. Questioned by the court for disseminating "false" news and defaming a judge, Ben Sedrine remained in prison until August 11. On September 6, she was arbitrarily prevented from traveling abroad. As this report went to press, no trial date had been set.

Moncef Marzouki, former CNLT spokesperson, was convicted on December 30, 2000 of involvement in an "unauthorized" association (the CNLT) and of spreading "false" information in connection with criticism of a public charity's lack of transparency. When Marzouki refused to appeal his conviction and one-year prison sentence, citing the lack of judicial independence, the prosecution appealed the sentence as too lenient. Although provisionally at liberty, Marzouki, who had been fired in 2000 for political reasons from his post as professor of medicine, suffered constant harassment. His phone service was cut off most of the time. Police kept him under surveillance and sometimes questioned visitors to his home in Sousse. Barred from leaving the country, he could not take up a university post offered to him in France. The travel ban continued even after an appeals court on September 29 converted his one-year prison sentence to a suspended one and maintained in place the deprivation of his civil liberties.

Other members of the CNLT, such as Sadri Khiari and Nejib Hosni, were among the many Tunisians arbitrarily deprived of passports for all or part of the year. CNLT member Omar Mestiri was twice—on December 15, 2000 and September 6, 2001—picked up by police as they were breaking up human rights gatherings, forced into an unmarked car, and then dropped later in the day at a distant location.

Plainclothes police stationed outside the office of the CNLT in downtown Tunis often turned away and sometimes assaulted persons attempting to reach it. CNLT member Khedija Cherif was among several members punched and turned away on March 1. On March 10, men in plainclothes again assaulted Cherif near a courthouse and seized documents regarding the complaint she had filed about the earlier assault. Human Rights Minister Maâoui claimed in *Le Monde* on April 6 that a police agent had been sanctioned for the "intolerable" assault on Cherif. But Cherif was never informed of any follow-up. Later in April, another woman activist, LTDH vice president Souhayr Belhassen, was slapped and called a "traitor" by men in plainclothes at Tunis airport, after customs officers had confiscated papers she was bringing into the country.

President Ben Ali set the tone for branding human rights activists as "traitors." In an interview with Tunisian dailies published on May 11, he denounced "the use of human rights as a pretext, particularly to feed malicious smear campaigns . . . by . . . some who have mortgaged their conscience to serve certain quarters outside their country."

On September 29, police in Tunis assaulted two delegates from Amnesty International who were on an official visit, and confiscated their research materials. Jerome Bellion-Jourdan and Philip Luther were stopped by traffic police, then forced into a car without license plates by plainclothesmen who forcibly seized their belongings. Bellion's and Luther's equipment was later returned to them, but not their documents and film. As of early November, Tunisian authorities had not responded to Amnesty International's formal complaint about the incident.

Trials were generally open, and diplomats and foreign observers were free to attend. However, French lawyer Eric Plouvier, sent by the Observatory for the Protection of Human Rights Defenders to observe the LTDH trial, was refused entry to the country on January 28. Also, Tunisia did not lift the *de facto* ban on visits by Amnesty International researcher Donatella Rovera and International Federation for Human Rights ex-president Patrick Baudoin.

THE ROLE OF THE INTERNATIONAL COMMUNITY

European Union

The European Union (E.U.) expressed concern about human rights violations to the Tunisian government, but did not suggest that those violations could jeopardize the three-year-old Association Agreement with Tunisia, the first such bilateral pact to take effect between the E.U. and a Mediterranean country.

Romano Prodi, the first president of the European Commission to visit North Africa, met in Tunis with Tunisian officials on January 12. In a public statement that day, Prodi indicated that his talks focused on trade and cooperation. Rather than use his public remarks to signal human rights concerns, Prodi praised Tunisia's economic reforms and declared, "The European Union respects Tunisia's decision-making autonomy and does not want to involve itself in the country's internal affairs." Human rights were reportedly higher on the agenda of European Commissioner Chris Patten when he met in Tunis with President Ben Ali and Prime Minister Mohamed Ghannouchi on June 19.

The European Parliament adopted on December 14, 2000, a resolution urging E.U. institutions to "use all the means provided by the Association Agreement" to promote human rights, regretting that the pact's "promotion of human rights as a key element" had "not sufficed to encourage the Tunisian authorities to advance along the path of democracy and human rights."

France

France is Tunisia's leading trade partner. Its U.S. $100 million in loans and grants to Tunisia surpasses, on a per capita basis, the aid it gives to any other country.

Human rights issues began to strain the close alliance in 2000, as the French government emerged from its public reserve. Pressure on Paris came partly from a more assertive human rights community in Tunisia and its sympathizers in France. In addition, France's National Consultative Commission on Human Rights on January 25, 2001, urged the government to intervene more in response to the "degradation of the state of public liberties and human rights in Tunisia." The national bureau of France's Socialist Party—the party of Prime Minister Lionel Jospin—

issued in April 2001, a statement saying it "could no longer maintain normal relations" with Tunisia's ruling party as long as "democratic and human rights organizations were effectively being silenced."

In January and February alone, French authorities publicly criticized the conviction of Moncef Marzouki, the pressures against the LTDH, the refusal to allow French trial observer Eric Plouvier to enter Tunisia, the beating by "unknown" men of Jalal Zoughlami, and "the growing resort to violence by Tunisian security forces toward human rights defenders." The French embassy also sent observers more frequently to political trials.

Le Parisien of April 1, quoted Foreign Minister Hubert Vedrine as saying that "democratic frustration was growing in Tunisia" and that the country's economic "success" should enable the country "to advance more in terms of democratization."

In a trip that was delayed over human rights disputes, French Minister of Cooperation Charles Josselin became on May 31 the first French minister to visit Tunisia in over a year. According to a report in *Le Monde* of April 5, Tunisian authorities had threatened to curtail Josselin's high-level meetings if he met also with a group of human rights activists that included representatives of the CNLT, which lacked legal "authorization." (See above.) Josselin ended up meeting a smaller group of human rights activists and was granted access to President Ben Ali and other top officials, with whom human rights was reportedly discussed.

United States

Although Tunisia was not a focus of its foreign policy, the U.S. viewed it as an ally in a turbulent region, pursuing market reforms and supporting U.S. initiatives. The U.S. conducted several joint military exercises with Tunisia, but provided it with minimal foreign assistance. There were few high-level bilateral meetings during the year, and no public statements from Washington regarding human rights.

The main U.S. contributions to rights promotion were the frank chapter in the State Department's *Country Reports on Human Rights Practices* and a U.S. embassy staff that actively monitored conditions on the ground. United States diplomats met regularly with human rights activists and attended many political trials, including those of human rights defenders and Islamists.

The embassy did not voice U.S. concerns through public statements, although the embassy told Human Rights Watch it "uses many opportunities to discuss human rights with the Tunisian government."

Relevant Human Rights Watch Reports:

Tunisia: A Lawsuit Against the Human Rights League: An Assault on all Rights Activists, 4/01

YEMEN

HUMAN RIGHTS DEVELOPMENTS

The security forces continued to exercise wide powers and to commit abuses, including arbitrary arrest, torture, and killings of civilians with virtual impunity. The press came under increasing pressure and the number of executions increased. Early in the year, unknown persons set off a series of bomb explosions in Aden and al-Dhali' province in the south, and kidnapping of both Yemenis and foreigners remained a major security issue.

A nationwide referendum in February 2001, approved constitutional amendments that strengthened the position of President Ali Abdallah Salih and his ruling General People's Congress (GPC). The parliamentary term was increased from four to six years and the president's right to decree laws when parliament was in recess was abolished but the amendments lengthened the presidential term from five to seven years, and authorized the president to appoint a 111-member Consultative Council. Opposition activists expressed concern that this body would allow the president to offset the role of the elected parliament, thus augmenting indirect executive control over legislation.

Local council elections held at the same time as the referendum, were marred by violence and opposition charges that voter registration lists had been rigged. Unofficial sources reported that some forty persons died and more than a hundred were injured in clashes with security forces and among supporters of different parties on election day and in its aftermath; the government said eleven persons were killed and twenty-three were injured. In one incident reported in the *Yemen Times*, security and military forces responded to a vote-counting dispute between the GPC and the *Islah* party representatives by opening fire indiscriminately, using heavy and medium-caliber weapons, in villages in Ibb governorate. Local people returned fire, which continued for more than three hours. Six persons died, seven were wounded and thirty-five arrested. Due to disputes over irregularities in at least twenty percent of the poll centers, final results were never officially announced. The General People's Congress claimed a comfortable majority in the councils, but opposition leaders charged that the authorities had tampered with the results of both the referendum and the local council elections.

Security forces attached to Central Security, under control of the Ministry of Interior, and the Political Security Office (PSO) which reports directly to President Salih, committed abuses with virtual impunity. In July, Abdallah Salih al-Maitami, an unsuccessful independent candidate in the Ibb local council elections, was summoned by Central Security, beaten, shackled, and had his head forcibly shaved. Two days after his arrest, on July 7, government forces entered the old city of Ibb, detained thirty-five persons apparently at random, searched nine houses without warrants, and demolished the Maitami family's house. At least fourteen of those detained were later released, eleven were held without charges as of this writing. In

August, al-Maitami and two others were brought to trial on charges of assault against security officials. They were on trial in November 2001 and incarcerated at Ibb central prison, where they were kept together with convicted criminals; al-Maitami was subject to further mistreatment.

In October, the PSO detained Abd al-Salam Nur ad-Din Hamad and Ahmad Saif, two visiting academics affiliated to the Centre for Red Sea Studies at Exeter University in the United Kingdom. During the two-day detention, they were blind-folded and beaten while being interrogated about "spying for foreign powers, and maintaining a relationship with Osama bin Laden, Israel and the separatists," the latter referring to the 1994 southern Yemeni effort to declare an independent state. Yemeni officials denied that they were ill-treated and justified the detentions as one of their "preventive measures" following the September 11 attacks in the U.S.

Police and security forces detained suspected members of radical Islamist groups throughout the year; thirty-five were arrested in December, another thir-teen in January, and fifteen in June. Further arrests were carried out in the after-math of the September 11 attacks on New York and Washington, and by late October, the *Yemen Times* reported, several hundred "Afghan Arabs" (Islamists who had returned after spending time in Afghanistan) had been picked up for ques-tioning in Sana'a, Taizz, and Aden. Many were reportedly released within days, however. At least eight suspects in the October 2000 attack on the USS Cole were still held without charge in November, most of whom had been held well beyond the maximum six-month period permitted under the criminal code of procedure.

Despite the general climate of impunity, three police officers of the Criminal Investigation Department, Aqil al-Maqtari, Yahya al-Rub', and Husain Ghanima, were convicted in November 2000 in connection with the death in custody of Sulaiman Salih in al-Hudaida. They received three-year prison terms and were stripped of their rank and dismissed; relatives of the deceased lodged an appeal seeking to have the sentences increased. In July, eight members of the Central Secu-rity in al-Dhali' province were charged with the premeditated murder of Hamdi Salih Husain of the opposition Yemeni Socialist Party (YSP); the trial was pending at this writing.

The press came under increased government pressure as the authorities harassed journalists and embroiled opposition and independent newspapers in court battles. In April, the Ministry of Information confiscated the first issue of *Huquq al-Insan* (Human Rights), the monthly publication of "The Activists" (*al-nushata'*) human rights group ostensibly because the group had filed registration documents one week prior to publication rather than the ten days required by the press law. *Yemen Times* journalist Hasan al-Za'idi was detained by the PSO in both June and September, each time for about fourteen days, reportedly for being a dis-tant relative of Al Za'idi tribesmen who had been involved in the kidnapping of two foreigners. No charges were filed against him.

In June 2001, the prosecution office implemented parts of a 1997 judgment passed against the opposition weekly *al-Shura* and its former editors, and sus-pended the paper for six months. The paper continued publication under a new license and name, but another defamation case was pending at this writing.

Defamation, which is loosely defined under Yemeni press law, was the most fre-quent charge levied against independent and opposition papers, both by the government and by private citizens; by November, cases were pending against *al-Ayyam, Sawt al-Shura, al-Umma, al-Ra'i al-'Amm, al-Wahdawi, al-Shumu'* and *as-Sahwa*. The press also came under attack for "inaccurate reporting." In September, the editor of Aden-based *al-Haqiqa*, Faris al-Yafi'i, was sentenced to a three-month jail term and a fine of YR 5000 (U.S. $30) for "insulting an official" after he incorrectly reported that the governor of Aden was about to resign.

The government took action against members of the opposition Yemeni Socialist Party in al-Dhali' province, arresting members of YSP-affiliated "popular committees" after they mounted a peaceful demonstration against police and military abuses in October 2000, but did not implement its threat, made in 2000, to dissolve the party. Some YSP-affiliated journalists and military who had lived in exile since 1994 returned to the country and President Salih reportedly ordered the YSP headquarters in Ma'alla in the city of Aden to be returned to the party. Those detained in al-Dhali' by Central Security and the PSO included YSP member Fadl al-Ja'adi and journalists Ahmad Harmal and Muhammad Ali Muhsin: all three were detained in November 2000, the first two for more than three weeks on incitement charges. Authorities prevented access to lawyers during interrogation and denied family visits.

A new law of associations took effect in February 2001, empowering the Ministry of Labor and Social Affairs to supervise nongovernmental organizations (NGOs). Registration was considered valid by default if the ministry failed to process an application within one month. NGOs were allowed to receive foreign funds upon notification of the ministry, and foreign-funded activities needed explicit approval. A minimum of forty-one members was required to establish an association. Penalties for violating any of the law's provisions entailed prison sentences of up to one year and penalties up to YR 100,000 (U.S. $600).

The government restricted access to the Internet indirectly by monopolizing service and keeping prices prohibitively high. As in previous years, mobile phones and pagers were rendered inoperable before major occasions like national holidays.

The media reported seventy-three executions for premeditated murder between March 2001 and mid-October 2001, compared to fifty-two from mid-1998 to early 2001. A large number of other offenses carried the death penalty, among them armed banditry, apostasy, rape, and treason.

Women continued to face discrimination in personal status law. Only a male guardian could contract marriage for women who had no way to give meaningful consent. In October 2001, the cabinet referred to the parliament an amendment to the personal status law proposed by the governmental Women's National Committee to introduce a minimum age—eighteen years—for marriage. However, by November the proposal, which lacked effective safeguards to protect women from underage, forced, and polygamous marriage, had not been passed by the parliament.

DEFENDING HUMAN RIGHTS

Local human rights groups conducted training and awareness raising workshops and lobbied successfully to remove some of the restrictions in the draft law on associations. Local chapters of Amnesty International operated in the major cities. The government did not respond to reports of human rights violations monitored by local groups.

The Women's Affairs Support Center, a women's rights group, ran workshops on violence against women, media training, and other issues, and helped train local rights activists. The Human Rights Information and Training Center and the Arabic Sisters Forum also addressed issues related to the treatment of women by police and in prison.

Four governmental human rights bodies—the Ministry for Human Rights, the Supreme National Committee for Human Rights, and the human rights committees of the Consultative Council and parliament—continued to operate. In early October 2001, the parliamentary body, the Committee for General Liberties, published a report criticizing the use of pre-trial detention by the CID and prison overcrowding.

THE ROLE OF THE INTERNATIONAL COMMUNITY

United States

Relations between Yemen and the United States remained strained in the aftermath of the October 2000 attack on the USS Cole in Aden harbor. The U.S. Federal Bureau of Investigation (FBI) reportedly wished to interview certain high-ranking Yemenis but President Salih told the Qatar-based *al-Jazeera* satellite television station on September 5 that "Yemen will not permit the Americans to interrogate any Yemeni citizens, whatever his capacity." The trial of eight persons arrested in connection with the USS Cole attack continued to be postponed, reportedly at Washington's request.

Following the September 11, 2001, attacks in New York and Washington, however, U.S. law enforcement sources reported that Yemen's cooperation with U.S. investigations had improved.

U.S. economic assistance to Yemen increased from none in fiscal year (FY) 2000 to almost U.S. $4 million in FY 2001 and $5 million in FY 2002. Expenditures on training programs for Yemeni military officers in the U.S. doubled to $250,000 in FY 2002. In its presentation to Congress requesting these funds, the State Department characterized Yemen as "at the forefront of the Arab world in both democratic and economic reform" and said the country had "taken significant strides toward opening its multiparty political system to full public participation, including women." The State Department's annual human rights country reports for 2000 stated that Yemen's human rights record "continued to improve" but that problems such as torture and arbitrary detention remained. "There are significant limitations on citizens' ability to change their government," the report said.

UNITED STATES

A guard walks through a cell block in a United States prison. © 2000 AURORA PHOTOS

UNITED STATES

During the first eight months of George W. Bush's presidency, the promotion of human rights occupied a low priority in the administration's domestic political agenda. The president and Attorney General John Ashcroft were criticized for insufficient concern about violations of individual rights and liberties, particularly in the criminal justice context. Questions about the government's commitment to protect basic rights increased markedly as it developed anti-terrorist measures after the September 11 attacks on New York and Washington. New laws permitting the indefinite detention of non-citizens, special military commissions to try suspected terrorists, the detention of over 1,000 people, and the abrogation of the confidentiality of attorney-client communications for certain detainees, demonstrated the administration's troubling disregard for well established human rights safeguards as it sought to protect national security. Indeed, in taking steps to defend the U.S. from terrorists, the government adopted measures that eroded key values and principles it said it sought to protect, including the rule of law.

Human rights violations prevalent during previous years continued under the new president. They were most apparent in the criminal justice system—including police brutality, unjustified racial disparities in incarceration, abusive conditions of confinement, and use of the death penalty, including the execution of mentally handicapped and juvenile offenders. But extensively documented violations also included violations of immigrants' rights, workers' rights (including those of migrant workers), harassment of gay, lesbian, bisexual, and transgender youth in schools, and of gay and lesbian members of the armed forces.

ANTI-TERRORISM MEASURES IN THE UNITED STATES

By November, over 1,100 people, mostly Arab or Muslim men, had been detained in connection with the government's investigation into the September 11 attacks and its efforts to preempt further acts of terrorism. The government stopped updating the tally of those detained so firm figures were unavailable. After refusing to make any information about the detainees public, including their names, location of detention, or the nature of charges against them, Attorney General Ashcroft finally announced on November 27 that 548 detainees were being held on immigration charges and that federal criminal charges had been filed against 104 people. Senior law enforcement officials acknowledged that only a small number of those in custody were believed to have links to terrorism. The immigration charges were primarily for routine immigration violations, such as overstaying a visa, and the criminal charges also were primarily for crimes that seemed unrelated to terrorism, ranging from credit card fraud to theft. Another two dozen or so people were being detained as material witnesses. An unknown number of individuals were held in local and state facilities in relation to the investigation of the September 11 attacks.

The government's refusal to reveal all the locations where the detainees were being confined and its failure to grant access to known places of detention to independent monitoring groups left many questions unanswered about the detainees' treatment. Individual detainees reported problems with obtaining prompt access to legal counsel, harsh conditions of confinement, and verbal and physical mistreatment—especially in local jails used by the federal government to house detainees with criminal inmates—but by the end of November it was still too early to determine if there was any pattern of mistreatment.

The apparent refusal of some detainees to answer questions about possible links with the al-Qaeda network led to a debate in the media about the possible need for torture, "truth serums," or sending the detainees to countries where harsher interrogation tactics were common. The Federal Bureau of Investigation (FBI) denied press reports that it had discussed such possibilities. Former military officials, various political and criminal justice analysts, and others publicly argued that "extraordinary times require extraordinary measures." As of late November there were no reports of abusive interrogation measures used against the detainees, but the public debate over such measures underscored the need for greater transparency regarding the location and treatment of the detainees.

The administration successfully secured from Congress a new anti-terrorism law, the U.S. Patriot Act of 2001, that gave the attorney general unprecedented powers to detain non-citizens on national security grounds. Under the law, the attorney general could certify and detain non-citizens if he had "reasonable grounds to believe" they had engaged in any of a broad range of terrorist acts or otherwise threatened national security. After seven days, such individuals had to be charged with a crime or an immigration violation or else be released. Certified aliens who could not be deported could be held in custody indefinitely until the attorney general determined that the person in question no longer presented a threat to national security. The government released no information about the number of people certified under this law.

The possibility of indefinite administrative detention of non-citizens was also raised by the terms of a new interim Immigration and Naturalization Service (INS) rule issued on September 17. This increased from twenty-four to forty-eight hours the period a non-citizen could be detained by the INS before it had to make a determination whether the detainee should remain in custody or be released on bond or recognizance and whether to issue a notice to appear and warrant of arrest. But "in situations involving an emergency or other extraordinary circumstances," the new measure stated, the forty-eight hour rule is suspended and the determinations must simply be made "within a reasonable period of time." The language triggering the exception was signally vague, the time limit for the exception was open ended, and there was no provision for judicial review of the detention—raising the possibility that non-U.S. citizens could be subjected to arbitrary and prolonged indefinite detention without charges or recourse.

On October 31, the Justice Department issued a new rule that permitted the federal government to monitor communications between inmates in federal custody and their attorneys. Inmates were defined to include not only persons convicted of a crime but anyone held as "witnesses, detainees or otherwise." Under the rule, communications could be monitored when the attorney general had "reasonable suspicion" that the inmate would use communications with counsel to "further or facilitate" acts of terrorism. In abrogating the confidentiality of attorney-client communications and subjecting those communications to government surveillance, the rule directly infringed on the right to counsel. Nevertheless, the administration contended the right to counsel was protected because the inmate would be notified before the monitoring began and a court order would be required before any non-privileged information could be used by investigators or prosecutors.

On November 13, President Bush issued a highly controversial military order authorizing the use of special military commissions to try non-citizens accused of supporting or engaging in terrorist acts. Citing the danger to national safety posed by international terrorism, the president claimed it was "not practicable" to try terrorists under "the principles of law and the rules of evidence" that apply in the U.S.'s domestic criminal justice system. Military commissions—ad hoc tribunals not subject to the rules governing regular military courts-martial and their due process safeguards—could function swiftly and secretly. There need be no presumption of innocence, nor protection against forced confessions. Under the president's order, persons convicted by such commissions would have no right of appeal to a higher court, a key fair trial requirement under international law, and they could be sentenced to death by a two-thirds majority of the presiding officers. The language of the order suggested the president may also have sought to preclude habeas corpus petitions. The precise rules under which the commissions would function had not been publicly issued by the end of November.

The order authorized military detention and trial for violations of the laws of war or other "applicable laws" of anyone who is not a U.S. citizen if the president should determine that "there is reason to believe" such an individual is or was a member of al-Qaeda; had engaged in, aided or conspired to commit acts of international terrorism; or had harbored terrorists. Terrorism, however, was not defined in the president's order. The order permitted military jurisdiction over non-citizen civilians in the U.S. who otherwise would be subject to regular criminal trials with the full panoply of due process safeguards that accompany such proceedings. Unlike the other domestic anti-terrorism measures, the order provoked strong protests from across the political spectrum. Some members of Congress urged the administration to rescind the order, and Judiciary Committee hearings were scheduled for the end of November and December to assess the order as well as other administration actions following the September 11 attacks.

OVERINCARCERATION, DRUGS, AND RACE

In 2000, the number of adults under the supervision of the criminal justice system—behind bars, on parole or on probation—reached a record 6.47 million, or one in every thirty-two adults. The rate and absolute number of confined persons continued to grow, although less than in previous years, but the number of inmates in state prisons fell slightly in the second half of 2000. The rate of incarceration in prison and jail was 699 inmates per 100,000, making the U.S. the world leader in incarceration, surpassing Russia's rate of 644 per 100,000, and giving the U.S. an incarceration rate that was five to eight times higher than those of European countries. Including inmates locked in prison, jails, juvenile detention and immigration facilities, the number of persons behind bars topped two million. One in every 143 Americans was incarcerated, with racial minorities disproportionately affected. Blacks and Hispanics accounted for 62.6 percent of all state or federal prisoners even though they represent only 24 percent of total U.S. residents. Almost 10 percent of black non-Hispanic men aged from twenty-five to twenty-nine were in prison in 2000, compared to 1.1 percent of white men in the same age group.

The continued growth in the prison population, despite years of falling crime rates, reflected the impact of public policies that lengthened sentences, imposed mandatory prison terms even for minor, nonviolent drug crimes, and restricted opportunities for early release. Also to blame was the high number of parolees returned to prison, many for technical parole violations. Fifty two percent of the state prison population had been convicted of nonviolent crimes, including 21 percent for drug crimes (nearly a quarter of a million persons). Slightly more than 1.5 million state and local arrests were made in 1999 (the most recent year for which data is available) for drug abuse violations, 46 percent of which involved marijuana. Four out of every five drug arrests were for possession of an illegal substance. Some 460,000 persons were behind bars for drug offenses, a tenfold increase over 1980. Blacks constituted 57.6 percent of all drug offenders in state prison, Hispanics 20.7 percent, and whites 20.2 percent.

Confronted with bulging prison populations, soaring costs, and a high percentage of low level nonviolent offenders among inmates, some states began to move away from punitive mandatory sentences for nonviolent offenders. For example, Mississippi enacted a law allowing nonviolent first offenders to seek parole after serving 25 percent of their sentence instead of 85 percent. Louisiana, almost half of whose state prison population was convicted on drug-related charges, ended mandatory prison time for certain nonviolent criminals, including persons convicted of simple possession of small drug amounts, and shortened the length of mandatory sentences for drug sellers. In Indiana, lawmakers repealed mandatory twenty-year sentences for many drug offenders, restoring sentencing discretion to judges. In New York, legislators debated but did not pass reforms of the state's draconian drug laws that would reduce mandate sentences, increase judicial discretion, and expand opportunities for alternatives to prison. In November 2000, Californians approved a ballot initiative mandating treatment instead of incarceration for those guilty of drug possession or use.

PRISON CONDITIONS

Although over 40 billion dollars a year is spent on incarceration, the burgeoning prison population overwhelmed the ability of corrections authorities to provide safe, humane, and productive conditions of confinement. Politicians, who had been eager to enact sentencing laws sending more people guilty of marginal crimes to prison for longer sentences, were less eager to pay for the costs of operating high quality facilities. Corrections officials lacked the funds to recruit, properly train and retain adequate numbers of staff, to provide work, training or educational programs that would keep inmates occupied and help them learn new skills, or to provide substance abuse treatment or other rehabilitative activities. Most prisons were overcrowded, impoverished facilities; many were rife with violence and gangs. Growing recognition of the importance of preparing inmates for reentry to their communities—about 600,000 are released from prison annually—prompted more public attention to the need for rehabilitation programs, but little new funding was made available.

Inmate violence in prisons caused injury and death. There were more than 31,000 inmate upon inmate assaults, a quarter of which resulted in injuries requiring medical attention in 1999 (the most recent year for which data was available). According to the Department of Justice, 10 percent of state inmates reported they had been injured in a fight while in prison.

Rape was a common as well as a psychologically and physically devastating form of violence among inmates. Certain prisoners were targeted for sexual exploitation upon entering a penal facility, particularly those who were young, small, physically weak, white, gay, first offenders or convicted of a sexual offense against a minor. In extreme cases, some prisoners became "slaves" of their rapists. Although no conclusive national data existed regarding the prevalence of prisoner-on-prisoner rape, the most recent statistical survey showed that 21 percent of inmates in seven prisons had experienced at least one episode of pressured or forced sex since entering prison. Some rapes were brutal, leaving victims beaten, injured and, in the most extreme cases, dead. Staff generally ignored or even reacted hostilely to inmates' complaints of rape. Indeed, in many cases, they took actions that made sexual victimization likely. Most correctional authorities denied that prisoner on prisoner rape was a serious problem and failed to implement reasonable prevention and punishment measures.

The use of electric stun and restraint devices against prison and jail inmates caused injury and even death. In Florida, an inmate died after being kept for a day in a restraining chair that immobilized him. Autopsy results were not available. In Virginia, prison officials suspended the use of the Ultron II stun gun, which delivers 50,000 volts of electricity, after an autopsy implicated the weapon in the death in 2000 of Lawrence Frazier, an inmate at Wallens Ridge State Prison. Frazier, an insulin dependent inmate, began struggling with corrections officers during a period when his blood sugar was dangerously low. The officers discharged the stun device three times at him and then placed him in restraints. Frazier lapsed into a coma and died several days later. In February, criminal charges were filed against six correctional officers in Arkansas who beat handcuffed prisoners and shocked them with a stun gun and a cattle prod on their buttocks and testicles.

Inmates in Virginia's supermaximum and high security prisons were placed in five point restraints—limbs tied to the four corners of a bed frame with an additional strap across the chest, leaving them fixed in a spread-eagled position unable to move or tend to normal bodily functions. Although U.S. law prohibits corporal punishment and five point restraints should only be used in emergency situations, officers subjected inmates to restraints in response to minor nonviolent offenses, including publicly masturbating, kicking the doors, and swearing at officers. Some were kept restrained on their backs for as long as two or three days and forced to urinate on themselves. The Department of Corrections implicitly acknowledged the improper practice, settled a lawsuit challenging the use of restraints in one of the prisons, and instituted a changed restraints policy. The Federal Bureau of Prisons agreed to pay nearly $100,000 dollars to settle a lawsuit filed by an inmate who was tied to a bed for five days, forced to urinate and defecate on himself.

Plaintiff inmates in class action lawsuits claimed abusive conditions in supermaximum security prisons in Illinois, Ohio, Wisconsin, and Virginia. A lawsuit filed on behalf of Connecticut inmates housed at Virginia's Wallens Ridge State Prison alleged that excessive force was endemic. According to the inmates' lawyer, prison records revealed that guards shocked the Connecticut prisoners with stun weapons thirty-three times, and placed them in five point restraints seventy-nine times over a nineteen month period. In a one-year period, thirty-seven Connecticut inmates were hit when guards fired rubber rounds. In Wisconsin, inmates filed a suit challenging conditions in that state's two-year-old ultra-high security prison in Boscobel—including round the clock confinement for all but a few hours a week in small windowless cells, exercise limited to solitary activity in tiny, unheated rooms without exercise equipment, and twenty-four-hour video surveillance that allowed female guards to watch male inmates shower and urinate. In the most restrictive level of the prison, personal possessions for inmates were limited to one religious text, one box of legal materials, and twenty-five personal letters. Inmates were not permitted to possess clocks, radios, watches, cassette players, or televisions, were subject to extreme seasonal temperature fluctuations, and had to conduct visits other than with lawyers through video screens. They had little natural light and no access to the outdoors. Those confined at the Boscobel prison included eight inmates aged under eighteen. Plaintiffs claimed that the conditions of social isolation, idleness, and limited sensory stimulus aggravated the symptoms of mentally ill inmates. In October, a federal judge ordered the Wisconsin Department of Corrections to remove five seriously mentally ill inmates from the prison, to arrange for an independent psychiatric examination of all inmates with certain characteristics suggesting mental illness, and to remove from the prison any inmate revealed to be seriously mentally ill. The Department of Corrections said that it would not appeal this order.

Mental health claims were also part of a lawsuit filed by inmates at Ohio's supermax prison, a facility that confines only 1 percent of the state's inmate population but which in a two year period had three suicides, accounting for 15 percent of all suicides in the state's prison system.

In recent years, many states enacted laws criminalizing custodial sexual misconduct and corrections departments adopted programs to address this abuse. But the problem remained widespread, and investigation and prosecution of such cases was frequently hampered by lack of commitment or resources. In Alaska, a jury awarded nearly $1.4 million to five women in a civil action arising from their being sexually assaulted by a guard. In Indiana, a woman who cooperated with the authorities after serving her sentence, was subsequently prosecuted for prostitution because she acknowledged during her testimony that a corrections official had given her cigarettes even as he engaged in custodial sexual misconduct. Such response violated the spirit of the law on custodial sexual misconduct that explicitly excluded consent as a defense and was likely to deter women from reporting sexual misconduct.

POLICE BRUTALITY

There were thousands of allegations of police abuse, including excessive use of force, such as unjustified shootings, beatings, fatal chokings, and rough treatment, but overwhelming barriers to accountability remained, enabling officers responsible for human rights violations to escape due punishment. Victims seeking redress faced obstacles that ranged from overt intimidation to the reluctance of local and federal prosecutors to take on police brutality cases. During fiscal year 2000, approximately 12,000 civil rights complaints, most alleging police abuse, were submitted to the U.S. Department of Justice, but over the same period just fifty-four officers were either convicted or pled guilty to crimes under the civil rights statute stemming from complaints during 2000 and previous years.

In April, a white police officer, Stephen Roach, shot dead an unarmed black man wanted on misdemeanor warrants in Cincinnati, Ohio. The response to the shooting of Timothy Thomas revealed deep distrust of the police among some in Cincinnati, leading to protests and rioting. Police made hundreds of arrests and dozens of people were injured in three days of violence and property damage.

In September, Roach was acquitted by the county judge, in a non-jury trial that he requested, on misdemeanor charges in relation to the Thomas shooting. In another case, after a jury deadlocked, county prosecutors in Ohio simply dropped charges of involuntary manslaughter against another police officer arising from the asphyxiation death of suspect Roger Owensby, while another officer was acquitted of assault charges in the same case. Prosecutors announced they would not pursue charges against Cincinnati officers who fired beanbag projectiles against persons attending the Thomas funeral.

In October, the Justice Department issued a preliminary findings letter stemming from its inquiry into police policies and practices in Cincinnati. It called for sweeping changes to the police department's policies on the use of force, training of officers in appropriate use of force, and in its record-keeping and mechanisms for investigating allegations of police abuse.

In November 2000, the Los Angeles City Council approved the consent decree negotiated between the Justice Department and city officials following the Justice

Department's inquiry into police policies and practices in the city. In June 2001, a federal judge approved the agreement, making Los Angeles's police department only the third city force to be required to operate under a federal consent decree following Justice Department "pattern or practice" civil rights inquiries. (Police forces in Steubenville, Ohio and Pittsburgh, Pennsylvania operated under similar consent decrees, as did the New Jersey State Police.) The decree established an outside monitor to ensure that the department collects data on the race of people subjected to vehicle and pedestrian stops and implements a computerized system for tracking complaints, disciplinary actions, and other data regarding officers' performance, among other reform requirements.

In New York City, however, it was reported in May 2001 that a Justice Department "pattern or practice" inquiry into the use of excessive force that began after the August 1997 assault on Abner Louima was dropped by the Justice Department, while a separate inquiry into alleged racial profiling by the department's force stalled. Information about progress in approximately fifteen other pending inquiries into other police departments' policies and practices was not made public. In the District of Columbia, city officials and the Justice Department came to an agreement to make reforms in the city's police department after the police chief requested the Justice Department's assistance in dealing with officers' use of excessive force and the department's poor accountability systems.

RACIAL DISCRIMINATION

In August, the U.N. Committee on the Elimination of Racial Discrimination issued its first report reviewing U.S. compliance with the Convention on the Elimination of All Forms of Racial Discrimination (CERD). The committee commended the "detailed, frank and comprehensive" U.S. compliance report despite its being submitted five years late, and noted U.S. progress in some areas in addressing racial discrimination and the extensive constitutional and legislative framework for the protection of civil rights.

The committee also expressed many concerns about continuing racial discrimination and the U.S. failure to live up to key provisions of CERD, noting that the U.S. had failed to implement the treaty and had too limited an understanding of the scope of the treaty's protections. In particular, the committee pointed to the obligation on the U.S. to prohibit racial discrimination in all its forms, including practices and legislation that, while not discriminatory by intent, may be so in effect. The committee recommended that the U.S. review existing laws and policies to ensure effective protection against discrimination and the elimination of any unjustifiable disparate impact, as required by CERD.

Other areas of concern highlighted by the committee included police brutality, notably against minority groups and foreigners; disproportionately high incarceration rates of African-Americans and Hispanics and the need to ensure equal treatment in the criminal justice system; racial disparities in the application in the death penalty; felony disenfranchisement, particularly affecting minorities after they have served criminal sentences; treatment of indigenous peoples; and racial discrimination and disparities in housing, employment, education, and health care. The committee also noted that officials at the federal, state, and local level failed to collect statistics necessary to determine the extent of discrimination and official response to it.

Responding to questions put by the committee, U.S. officials failed to accept the scope and obligations of CERD: they repeated the contention that intentional discrimination is prohibited by U.S. law, while ignoring the disparate impact provisions of CERD. For example, the written response of the U.S. to the committee's questions, dismissed concerns about disparate incarceration rates by pointing to various causes for those disparities but without offering any clear plan to comply with the treaty's provisions regarding disparate impact.

The U.S. response also stated that there was no need to enact legislation to implement CERD domestically, arguing that U.S. law was already in compliance with its provisions. It acknowledged that the U.S. had no centralized data system for recording complaints of racial discrimination at the local, state, or federal levels, and at the same time insisted that there was no pervasive discrimination problem without providing any data to support this contention.

In September, the U.S. abruptly and publicly withdrew its delegation from the United Nations World Conference Against Racism, Racial Discrimination, Xenophobia and Related Intolerance (WCAR) in Durban, South Africa, citing concern about references to Zionism in draft documents before the conference. However, it was clear that the Bush administration also felt serious unease about calls made within the WCAR context for reparations for slavery and other forms of severe racial discrimination in the United States. The administration had already signaled its lack of support for the conference through its failure to contribute significant funding or to identify goals it hoped to achieve other than preventing examination of past practices in the U.S. By not participating, the administration missed an important opportunity to review both the positive and negative aspects of its record on racial discrimination and plans to address continuing shortcomings. Many U.S. nongovernmental civil rights groups attended the WCAR, however, and contributed to its declaration and program of action to intensify the struggle against racial, ethnic, and other forms of discrimination.

HATE CRIMES

Following the September 11 attacks on New York and Washington, private individuals committed xenophobic acts of harassment and aggression against Muslims, Sikhs, and people of Middle Eastern and South Asian descent. By November, monitoring groups around the country had received almost 1,000 complaints alleging crimes apparently motivated by bias and hate, including four murders. Violent assaults, death threats, shootings, and vandalism at mosques and Sikh temples were reported; at several U.S. universities foreign students from the Middle East and South Asia were attacked; and members of the affected communities feared to leave their homes, go to work, or wear traditional clothing in public for fear of attack. Investigations into, and prosecutions of, those responsible for various attacks against members of the affected minority groups were pending in November.

The initial response of key political leaders was commendable. President Bush,

Attorney General Ashcroft, New York City Mayor Rudolph Giuliani, and other officials urged the public to reject national or religious stereotyping that would blame whole communities for the acts of terrorism committed by a few, simply because they shared the same religious, ethnic, or national identity.

IMMIGRANTS' RIGHTS

The anti-immigration sentiment that led to the enactment of the stringent 1996 Illegal Immigration Reform and Immigrant Responsibility Act seemed to have weakened prior to the September 11 attacks. Many public figures commented favorably on the contribution of immigrants to U.S. economic and cultural life, and President Bush announced that he would seek to regularize the status of the more than three million undocumented Mexican workers residing in the U.S.

Immigrants' activists gained ground not only in the political arena but also before the U.S. Supreme Court. In June, the country's highest court ruled that the government could not continue to imprison deportable immigrants whose home countries either would not accept them or no longer existed: the decision most immediately affected more than 3,400 non-citizens then subject to indefinite detention by the Immigration and Naturalization Service (INS). Supreme Court Justice Stephen Breyer, for the majority, wrote: "Freedom from imprisonment—from government custody, detention, or other forms of physical restraint—lies at the heart of the liberty that [the constitution] protects. The serious constitutional problem arising out of a statute that, in these circumstances, permits an indefinite, perhaps permanent, deprivation of human liberty without any such protection is obvious."

In June, the Supreme Court also issued a ruling that affirmed the right of legal immigrants to have their cases reviewed by a court before facing deportation. The court also ruled that immigration laws passed in 1996—making deportation automatic for an expanded group of immigrants—could not be applied retroactively.

Detention practices following the September 11 attacks were especially troubling. As noted, law enforcement officials detained at least 1,100 people in connection with the investigation into the September attack. In late November, the government announced that 104 were being held on federal criminal charges and 548 were being held on immigration charges. While it released the names of persons charged with federal crimes, it continued its refusal to release the names, places of detention, or specific violations of those held on immigration charges. Human Rights Watch and other U.S.-based civil and human rights group filed a Freedom of Information Act request in October to seek information about the detainees. Human Rights Watch also sought direct access to detainees in custody in relation to the investigation of the September 11 attacks. By late November, INS officials had denied the Human Rights Watch request to visit one New Jersey jail holding INS detainees and authorities had failed to respond to other, similar requests for access at other facilities.

Some attorneys representing detainees reported difficulty in locating and advising their clients; others said that the authorities did not properly advise their clients of their rights. It took days for some families to find out where their detained relatives were being held.

In recent years, the number of people in INS detention has grown dramatically to an average nationally of 22,000 per day, compared to 6,700 per day in 1995. This increasing population continued to seriously impact the capacity of the INS to provide humane and safe detention conditions, and a lack of adequate space in federal facilities caused the INS to disperse some detainees to local jails. In 2001, more than half of all INS detainees were held in prisons or local jails intended for criminal inmates, exposing them to treatment and conditions inappropriate to their administrative detainee status and hampering their access to legal assistance. Asylum-seekers, who by conservative estimates made up at least 5 percent of the detainee population, continued to be detained as the rule, not the exception, in breach of international standards relating to the treatment of asylum-seekers. In its own facilities, the INS implemented some standards regarding treatment and conditions, but INS detainees assigned to jails were under the direct control of jail officials and INS monitoring of such jails was minimal.

The INS continued to detain unaccompanied children for lengthy periods before releasing them to family members or appropriate guardians, and acknowledged that it held about 5,000 children in its custody annually. Rights groups criticized the INS for denying full access to independent monitors and lawyers who represented the detained children in a successful class-action lawsuit challenging the conditions of confinement for youth in INS custody. In a positive development, Senator Dianne Feinstein proposed legislation that would correct these and other abusive conditions for unaccompanied children in the United States.

The 1996 Illegal Immigration Reform and Immigration Responsibility Act's expedited removal proceedings, intended to process and deport individuals who enter the United States without valid documents with minimum delay, imperiled genuine asylum seekers and resulted in immigrants being detained in increasing numbers. Asylum seekers with questionable documents were sent to "secondary inspection" where they had to convey their fears regarding return to their country of origin. The expedited process was characterized by excessive secrecy, making it virtually impossible to monitor the fairness of INS officials' decisions at each stage of the initial review.

The September 11 attacks sparked several legislative proposals to tighten control of U.S. borders by employing more Border Patrol agents, whose number had already increased rapidly to over 9,000, more than double the 1993 total. This rapid increase raised concern that serious oversight deficiencies that have affected the Border Patrol, particularly its capacity to investigate complaints of abuse by Border Patrol agents, would become more acute. As in previous years, in 2001, Border Patrol agents shot a number of border-crossers in questionable circumstances, in some cases fatally wounding them. Agents, who were not required to wear protective gear although this would reduce their risk of injury, said they shot migrants who they feared were about to throw rocks at them.

Migrants who sought to enter the U.S. illegally by crossing the border with Mexico continued to die of exposure or drowning in high numbers. In the first half of 2001, 188 perished; in 2000, 499 died. In 1996, the first year for which there was comprehensive data, there were eighty-seven deaths. As a result of the current INS strategy of concentrating border control in urban centers, many migrants opted to cross the border at remote locations that required them to traverse particularly hazardous desert terrain and to depend on smugglers. Many also crossed through private ranches, to which local ranchers responded by carrying out armed patrols along the border, in some cases beyond their own property, and organizing volunteer-based "missions" to hold border crossers. This resulted in the death or injury of several migrants at the hands of ranchers, and an inadequate response by the authorities to abuses committed against migrants by ranchers. In August, a rancher charged in connection with the death of a Mexican border crosser who had entered his property a year before to ask for water, but whom he shot dead, was convicted on a misdemeanor deadly conduct charge, given a 180-day suspended sentence and fined $4,000.

DEATH PENALTY

By November, the U.S. had carried out sixty-two executions since the beginning of 2001 (compared to a total of eighty-five in the whole of 2000) and 3,717 men and women were on death row. In Texas, the authorities carried out fifteen executions compared to forty in 2000, and Virginia executed two prisoners compared to eight in the same period of 2000. Against this trend, Oklahoma executed sixteen inmates, a record number for the state.

Public confidence in the fairness and reliability of the death penalty continued to erode, despite strong support for the June 11 execution of Timothy McVeigh, convicted of the 1995 bombing of the Oklahoma City federal center that killed 168 people. Polls showed support for the death penalty fell to its lowest point in years— 63 percent—and dropped even further to 46 percent—when life in prison was offered as an option. Flaws in the death penalty process were highlighted by the revelation, five days before McVeigh was originally scheduled to be executed, that in one of the most prominent cases of the decade, the FBI had failed to turn over thousands of pages of documents to McVeigh's lawyers, forcing the U.S. Department of Justice to delay his execution for a month.

The mishandling of the McVeigh case, the first federal execution since 1963, exemplified the fallibility of the capital punishment process that continued to be documented in reports from around the country of judicial error, false testimony, incompetent defense lawyers, and poor laboratory work in capital cases. In May, following an Oklahoma City Police Department report on multiple errors by local police chemist Joyce Gilchrist, the Oklahoma State Bureau of Investigation launched an investigation into all the cases—including twenty-three capital cases—in which she had been involved. Oklahoma death row inmate Alfred Brian Mitchell's death sentence was overturned because of what the court called Gilchrist's "untrue" testimony.

Supreme Court Justice Sandra Day O'Connor, long considered a supporter of the death penalty, publicly expressed her concern that "the system may well be allowing some innocent defendants to be executed. " She cited statistics showing that defendants in Texas who were represented by court-appointed counsel, were far more likely to be convicted and to receive a death sentence than those who retained their own attorneys. By September, five men had been exonerated and released in 2001 after years on death row, bringing the total of innocent persons released from death row since 1973 to ninety-eight.

The fairness of the federal death penalty system, particularly in relation to racial and geographic disparities, was also called into question. A September 2000 report issued by the Justice Department documented stark racial and geographic disparities in the prosecution of federal capital cases, leading President Bill Clinton to issue a temporary reprieve for Juan Raul Garza, who faced execution in December 2000.

In June 2001, the Justice Department issued a supplemental report concluding that there was no evidence that minority defendants were subjected to bias in federal capital cases. That conclusion was not supported by the data in the report, which acknowledged the impossibility of acquiring the necessary data during the review period allowed. The June report, however, did put forward several explanations for the disproportionate number of minorities on death row, though none of these appeared adequate when closely examined by Human Rights Watch and others. Acknowledging the shortcomings of the June report, the Justice Department stated that it would undertake a comprehensive study of racial and geographic disparities in the application of the federal death penalty, but by November the report had not been released.

The June report concluded that there was no racial inequity in the administration of the federal death penalty because there was no evidence of discriminatory intent or actual bias on the part of prosecutors. Under the CERD, however, the U.S. is obligated to prohibit practices that have either the purpose or effect of discriminating on the basis of race. Commenting in its August report on the U.S., the U.N. committee observed: "there is a disturbing correlation between race, both of the victim and the defendant, and the imposition of the death penalty."

The continued use of the death penalty by U.S. federal and state authorities was strongly criticized by European countries, notably European Union (E.U.) states, as inconsistent with human rights principles. In April, as in previous years, the U.N. Commission on Human Rights adopted a resolution sponsored by the E.U. that urged the U.S. to move toward abolition of the death penalty, and called particularly for the U.S. to cease executing juvenile offenders and prisoners with any form of mental disorder. In June, the Council of Europe voted to remove the observer status of the U.S. and Japan if they did not end their use of the death penalty by January 1, 2003. Prominent former U.S. diplomats also spoke out on the issue in the press and in a court brief, stating that the U.S. executions of prisoners with mental retardation hampered U.S. diplomatic relations and damaged the country's reputation as a leader in human rights and its foreign policy interests.

In June, the World Court ruled that the U.S. had violated the Vienna Convention on Consular Relations in the case of two German nationals executed by the state of Arizona in 1999. Karl and Walter LaGrand had not been informed of their right under the Vienna Convention to seek assistance from the German consulate; Amnesty International reported that fifteen other foreign nationals executed in the U.S. since 1993 had also not been informed of their consular rights. In June, Oklahoma Governor Frank Keating granted a thirty-day reprieve to a Mexican national, Gerardo Valdez, who had not been told of his right to contact his consulate. In September, the state's highest court granted Valdez an indefinite stay of execution. As of November 2001, 119 foreign nationals remained on death row.

In March, Human Rights Watch reported that at least thirty-five men with mental retardation had been executed in the U.S. since 1976, even though their mental impairment limited their moral culpability and harmed their ability to protect their legal rights. Mounting domestic and international criticism of executing the mentally retarded spurred five states to enact legislation this year prohibiting such executions. In Texas, where at least six prisoners with mental retardation have been executed, and where others remained on death row, the legislature passed a similar bill, only for Governor Rick Perry to veto it. The Supreme Court agreed to hear the appeal of North Carolina death row inmate Ernest McCarver, who sought to obtain a ruling that the U.S. constitution prohibited the execution of prisoners with mental retardation as "cruel and unusual" punishment, and then agreed to substitute the case of Daryl Atkins, a Virginia death row inmate, when McCarver benefited from North Carolina's enactment of legislation barring the execution of prisoners with mental retardation. Previously, in 1989 the Supreme Court ruled that the U.S. constitution did not bar the execution of prisoners with mental retardation, noting the absence of a national consensus against such executions. At that time, only two states prohibited such executions, but that number had increased by November 2001 to eighteen states, as well as the federal government, while a further twelve permitted no executions at all. The Atkins case was awaiting consideration by the Supreme Court in November 2001. In June, the Supreme Court overturned the death sentence of Johnny Paul Penry, because the sentencing instructions that the trial court gave to the jury did not permit it to give due consideration to his mental abilities.

Prompted by a request from Human Rights Watch, the McAlester Regional Health Center decided to cease providing the Oklahoma Department of Corrections with the drugs used in lethal injections. The health center agreed that assisting the state in the implementation of the death penalty was inconsistent with its mission as a hospital.

The United States was virtually alone in imposing sentences of death on those who were children at the time of the crimes for which they were convicted. Eighty-five juvenile offenders were on death rows in fifteen U.S. states as of July 1, 2001. With thirty-one juvenile offenders on its death row, Texas accounted for over one-third of the national total. In all, twenty-three U.S. states continued to allow the death penalty to be imposed for crimes committed by those below the age of eighteen.

Two juvenile offenders received last-minute stays of execution after their attorneys presented new evidence or raised constitutional issues on appeal. On August 15, Napoleon Beazley, convicted in Texas for a murder he committed at age seventeen, came within hours of execution when the Texas Court of Criminal Appeals issued a stay to enable it to consider whether his first appellate attorney provided ineffective assistance. Earlier, in March, Missouri death row inmate Antonio Richardson received a stay from the U.S. Supreme Court. Sixteen at the time of his crime, Richardson may have mental retardation; his case was on hold pending the Supreme Court ruling on the constitutionality of imposing the death sentence on persons with mental retardation.

LABOR RIGHTS

There were continuing labor rights violations affecting workers in many sectors. One particularly vulnerable group was the more than 4,000 migrant domestic workers with special temporary visas. These special visas, termed A-3, G-5, and B-1, allowed migrant domestic workers, most of whom were women, to work for U.S.-based foreign diplomats and officials of international organizations, as well as for other foreigners temporarily in the United States and U.S. citizens who resided abroad but were temporarily in the United States. In a report published in June 2001, Human Rights Watch detailed how these special visa programs were conducive to and facilitated violations of the workers' human rights.

In the worst cases, domestic workers were victims of trafficking—deceived about the conditions of their employment, brought to the United States, and held in servitude or performing forced labor. They worked excessive hours for wages significantly below the statutory minimum, were rarely allowed to leave their employers' premises, and were subject to psychological, physical, and sometimes sexual abuse. As their visas were employer-based, however, workers who left their employer even to escape abuse lost their legal immigration status in the U.S. If, alternatively, a worker lodged a legal complaint, it was unlikely that her rights would be protected as none of the relevant authorities—the Department of State, the INS and the Department of Labor-monitored employer treatment of these workers or kept effective records on them and their employers. Also, there was no guarantee that the INS would allow a complainant to remain in the U.S. to seek legal redress or that her rights would be protected under U.S. law, as live-in domestic workers were excluded from important U.S. labor legislation. This included the overtime provisions of the Fair Labor Standard Act, the National Labor Relations Act, the Occupational Safety and Health Act, and, in practice, Title VII protections against sexual harassment in the workplace.

GAY AND LESBIAN RIGHTS

Lesbian, gay, bisexual, and transgender youth in many U.S. schools were another vulnerable group whose rights were violated. They were harassed and targeted for violence by their peers, including physical attack, mock rape, unwelcome sexual advances, taunts, obscene notes or graffiti, and the destruction of personal property. Adding to the problem, as Human Rights Watch showed in a report based on research in seven states that it published in May, school officials and teachers often failed to intervene to stop the harassment or to hold the abusive students accountable, and, in the worst cases, participated in acts of harassment. Teachers who were lesbian, gay, bisexual, or transgender were themselves reluctant to openly acknowledge their sexual orientation at school for fear of losing their jobs. The problem was further exacerbated by the failure of federal, state, and local authorities to enact laws expressly protecting students from discrimination on the basis of sexual orientation or gender. The discrimination, harassment, and violence inflicted on students interfered with their right to obtain an education. The emotional impact may have been a factor contributing to the disproportionately high incidence of alcohol abuse and drug addiction as well as suicide attempts among lesbian, gay, bisexual, and transgender youth.

Anti-gay harassment was also pervasive in the military. Seven years after the "Don't Ask, Don't Tell" policy was codified as law and implemented, the military's own surveys and investigations found that training on how to implement the law was deficient and that anti-gay harassment remained widespread. Many military personnel who faced verbal or physical harassment and feared for their safety made statements declaring that they were gay, knowing that it would mean the end of their careers but also that if they complained officially about anti-gay harassment they would probably face an intrusive inquiry and discharge. Harassers, however, were rarely punished.

Although the "Don't Ask, Don't Tell" policy was ostensibly intended to allow gay, lesbian, and bisexual service members to remain in the military, discharges increased significantly after the policy's adoption. From 1994 to 2000, more than 6,500 servicemembers were discharged under the policy, with a record number of 1,231 separations during 2000. Women were discharged at a disproportionately high rate, while the policy provided an additional means for men to harass women servicemembers by threatening to "out" those who refused their advances or threatened to report them, thus ending their careers.

The U.S. was increasingly out of step internationally in maintaining restrictions on homosexuals serving in the military. Most of its North Atlantic Treaty Organization (NATO) and other allies either allowed homosexuals to serve openly or had no policy on the issue. In September 1999, the European Court of Human Rights rejected a United Kingdom ban on homosexuals serving in the military—the ban's justifications were nearly identical to those used to support the "Don't Ask, Don't Tell" policy.

Relevant Human Rights Watch Reports:

Hidden in the Home: Abuse of Domestic Workers with Special Visas in the United States, 6/01

Hatred in the Hallways: Violence and Discrimination Against Lesbian, Gay, Bisexual, and Transgender Students in U.S. Schools, 5/01

No Escape: Male Rape in U.S. Prisons, 4/01

Beyond Reason: The Death Penalty and Offenders with Mental Retardation, 3/01

ARMS

Victims of landmines in Afghanistan.

The arrival of the Bush administration in the White House in January ushered in an approach to U.S. foreign policy that could only be described as a reflexive unilateralism. It seemed there was not a single multilateral treaty that the new government was willing to join or retain. Treaty negotiations soon ran up against freshly drawn "red lines," that is, baseline positions that, it was made clear, were essentially nonnegotiable. As a result, these negotiations were either scuttled or resulted in watered-down documents that reflected a common denominator heavily colored by what the United States presented as its vital national interests.

This was true especially for negotiations involving issues of international arms control. In 2001, these included talks on the 1972 bilateral Anti-Ballistic Missile Systems (ABM) treaty, the 1972 Biological Weapons Convention (BWC), and small arms and light weapons (at a U.N. conference in July). The review of the 1980 Conventional Weapons Convention (CCW) was scheduled for December; negotiations at preparatory committee meetings ("prepcoms") took place in April and September. In mid-September, States Parties to the 1997 Mine Ban Treaty met to review that treaty, as they had every year since 1997; as a non-signatory, the U.S. was not involved in this review.

After the September 11 attacks on New York and Washington, D.C., the U.S. government no longer could hew to a strict unilateralist line. It suddenly was faced with the need to build a broad international coalition to respond to the attacks. However, in the middle of November it remained unclear whether this would bring a renewed U.S. commitment to multilateral treaties. Moreover, one victim of the new U.S. preoccupation with its self-proclaimed fight against terrorism was the effort to curb the proliferation of small arms and small weapons. While this remained an issue of pressing concern for those who suffered directly from the impact of the spread of small arms, especially those living in zones of armed conflict in Africa and elsewhere, the fear was that supplier countries would turn their attention away from the urgent need to impose stricter export controls.

Consistent with its emphasis on small arms and light weapons, in 2001, Human Rights Watch was engaged primarily in the U.N. conference on small arms, and in the review of the Mine Ban Treaty.

ANTIPERSONNEL LANDMINES

Important strides were made in 2001 in the effort to eradicate antipersonnel landmines, despite the reality that antipersonnel mines continued to be laid and to take far too many victims. It was evident that the 1997 Mine Ban Treaty, and the ban movement more generally, were making a significant difference. A growing number of governments joined the Mine Ban Treaty and there was a decreased use of antipersonnel mines, a dramatic drop in production, an almost complete halt to trade, and progress in the rapid destruction of stockpiled mines. There were also fewer mine victims in key affected countries and more land was demined.

Between November 2000 and November 12, 2001, the number of States Parties to the 1997 Convention on the Prohibition of the Use, Stockpiling, Production, and Transfer of Anti-Personnel Mines and On Their Destruction (Mine Ban Treaty) grew to 122. Among the new adherents were Romania and Chile, both major producers and exporters in the past, and Eritrea, which was using antipersonnel mines in combat as recently as June 2000. An additional twenty countries had signed but not yet ratified the Mine Ban Treaty. The foreign ministers of Greece, Turkey, and Yugoslavia pledged to ratify or accede to the treaty shortly.

Fifty-two countries had not yet joined the treaty. This included most of the Middle East, most of the former Soviet republics, and many Asian nations. Major producers such as the United States, Russia, China, India, and Pakistan were not part of the treaty. Yet virtually all of the nonsignatories had endorsed the notion of a comprehensive ban on antipersonnel mines at some point in time, and many had already at least partially embraced the Mine Ban Treaty. United Nations General Assembly Resolution 55/33v calling for universalization of the Mine Ban Treaty was adopted in November 2000 by a vote of 143 in favor, none opposed, and twenty-two abstentions. Nineteen nonsignatories voted for the resolution.

The Mine Ban Treaty intersessional work program, with week-long meetings in Geneva in December 2000 and May 2001, successfully fulfilled its intended purpose in helping to maintain a focus on the landmines crisis, in becoming a meeting place for all key mine action players, and in stimulating momentum to fully implement the Mine Ban Treaty. The four intersessional Standing Committees on Victim Assistance, Mine Clearance, Stockpile Destruction, and General Status and Operation of the Convention helped to provide a global picture of priorities, as well as to consolidate and concentrate global mine action efforts. Compliance with all key articles of the convention became an overall focus of the second intersessional year. A Universalization Contact Group was formed, coordinated by Canada, with participation by a number of States Parties, the International Campaign to Ban Landmines (ICBL) and International Committee of the Red Cross (ICRC). In addition to many bilateral efforts to promote adherence to the Mine Ban Treaty, there were important regional conferences aimed at universalization, notably in Bamako, Mali in February.

The Third Meeting of States Parties to the Mine Ban Treaty was held in Managua, Nicaragua in September. States Parties, in close cooperation with the ICBL, developed an action plan for the year and issued a strong final declaration.

Just prior to the Managua meeting, the ICBL released the 1,175-page *Landmine Monitor Report 2001*, its third annual report looking at the landmine situation in every country of the world. The report, the product of a network of 122 researchers from ninety-five countries, cited many positive developments, including more than 185 million square meters of land cleared of mines in 2000; a revised estimate of new mine casualties of 15,000–20,000 per year, compared to previous estimates of 26,000 per year; destruction of another five million stockpiled antipersonnel mines, bringing the total to 27 million in recent years; no known significant exports of antipersonnel mines; and a reduction in the number of producers from fifty-five to fourteen (with Turkey and Yugoslavia being removed from the list in the past year). However, the Landmine Monitor also identified use of antipersonnel mines in twenty-three conflicts by fifteen governments and more than thirty rebel groups in this reporting period (May 2000 to mid-2001). It reported a "strong possibility" of use by Mine Ban Treaty state party Uganda in June 2000 in the Democratic Republic of Congo, and called on states parties to seek clarification urgently.

The Second Annual Conference of States Parties to Amended Protocol II (Landmines) of the Convention on Conventional Weapons (CCW) was held in Geneva in December 2000, and there were preparatory meetings in December 2000, April 2001, and September 2001 for the Second CCW Review Conference, to be held in December 2001. Proposals presented and discussed at these meetings included: extension of the treaty's scope, compliance issues, antivehicle mines, wound ballistics, and the explosive remnants of war.

In the United States there were indications in late 2000 that the Clinton administration would announce several significant steps toward a ban on antipersonnel mines prior to departing office, but this did not materialize. Decisions were left to the incoming administration on controversial issues such as procurement of RADAM (a new "mixed" system combining existing antitank and antipersonnel mines) and a "man-in-the-loop" munition developed as an alternative to antipersonnel mines but which contains a feature to revert the munition to mine status. The Bush administration had not made a formal policy statement on antipersonnel mines by mid-November, and key developments were on hold pending completion of a comprehensive review of landmine policy and actions that began in June. The U.S. continued to be the leader in contributions to global mine clearance, devoting nearly U.S. $100 million in both FY 2000 and FY 2001.

SMALL ARMS AND LIGHT WEAPONS

The United Nations Conference on the Illicit Trade in Small Arms and Light Weapons in All Its Aspects, mandated in December 1999 by the General Assembly, was held in July 2001 in New York. Flawed both in concept and in execution, it was considered a near-total failure by the human rights and humanitarian communities. While participating states did manage to produce a conference document (the program of action) despite a long list of contentious issues, the document was weak. The program of action ascribed primary responsibility for dealing with the black-market trade in small arms to states, yet did not allude to, much less prescribe, any measures to curb the flow of weapons to abusive actors through the irresponsible arms trade practices of governments themselves. The document did not codify any standards for the arms trade based on international humanitarian law or human rights, and made only a few vague references to the humanitarian urgency of the unchecked proliferation of small arms. It did not establish a transparent universal system for marking and tracing weapons, or record-keeping and reporting mechanisms (such as an international public register of small arms transfers). Finally, the program of action was not legally binding, nor did it mandate the negotiation of other legally binding documents, such as a treaty on measures to regulate the activities of independent brokers.

Confusion over the conference mandate hampered progress from the beginning, and the scope of the conference was still being debated by the third and final prepcom in March. The conference title referred specifically to the "illicit" trade in small arms, but by adding the phrase "in all its aspects," the door was left open for states to tackle a critical facet of the problem: the legal, government-sponsored trade. However, while many states were adamant that battling the illicit trade in small arms was the responsibility of governments (as opposed to nongovernmental organizations, which were marginalized throughout the process), the same states insisted that the conference should not address government responsibility for creating the problem. Ignoring the fact that virtually every illicitly traded weapon was first traded legally, and that weapons were routinely traded "legally" to abusive forces, the conference rejected demands from civil society and some government delegations to develop stronger export controls and international standards governing the arms trade practices of states.

From the beginning, it was expected that major arms exporters, including most of the Permament Five members of the U.N. Security Council, would try to water down any program of action. The surprise was the emergence of the United States, rather than Russia or China, in this respect. The U.S. had itself boasted relatively decent arms trade control mechanisms, including curbs on exports to human rights abusers and measures to ensure transparency. Yet with the change in administration following immediately after the second prepcom in January, the U.S. delegation began taking a blatantly obstructionist approach. An uncompromising U.S. position was articulated in an opening statement to the conference which shocked most observers and reflected the Bush administration's disdain for multilateral arms control and multilateralism in general. The statement set down several positions which were said to be nonnegotiable, rejecting a mandatory Review Conference, the participation of nongovernmental organizations, and all "measures that would constrain legal trade and legal manufacturing of small arms." It was clear throughout the conference that the domestic gun lobby wielded heavy influence in the U.S. delegation, imposing on the conference a belief that talk of international arms trade control would lead to the demise of the putative constitutional right of U.S. citizens to own guns. Other states antagonistic to the conference's objectives were all too willing to let the U.S. dismantle the conference.

Other factors also hampered progress at the conference. Lack of interest in the process in general, and in the humanitarian dimension in particular, was evident in the make-up of most delegations. Many states refused to send senior Foreign Ministry representatives to the conference, and most delegations were staffed primarily by arms control experts (where staffed with any expertise at all) who were unfamiliar with human rights and international humanitarian law. Further distracting states from turning their focus to the humanitarian and human rights implications of small arms, where it belonged, were debates over peripheral issues, such as non-state actors, self-determination, and self-defense, as well as myriad disputes over definitions.

Civil society was effectively excluded from participating in the conference. Limitations on NGO access were not officially agreed until the beginning of the conference itself, where it was decided that NGOs would be allowed to watch plenary proceedings from the gallery but could be sent out at any point if delegates opted for a closed session. (NGOs were also allowed one three-hour session to address delegates at each prepcom and during the conference.) States also debated whether or not to include language calling for civil society participation in the program of action. The U.S. in its opening statement opposed this, claiming that such participation was not "consistent with democratic principles," and other delegations insisted that implementation of the program of action was the exclusive realm of states. The document did, however, contain language on civil society cooperation in some areas.

In addition, negotiating the program of action was a consensus-driven process that allowed rejectionist states such as the U.S. to hijack the outcome by simply refusing to compromise on key issues, resulting in a document based on the lowest common denominator that was predictably weak, even on those issues that were not cut from the final draft. One positive outcome was the commitment to a review conference after five years, making this the only red-line position on which the U.S. delegation was eventually willing to back down. The conference also served to raise the profile of small arms proliferation internationally, and allowed civil society organizations to rally around a specific event and develop momentum and focus for future work.

Relevant Human Rights Watch Reports:

Landmine Monitor Report 2001: Toward a Mine-Free World, 9/01
Crisis of Impunity: The Role of Pakistan, Russia, and Iran in Fueling the Civil War in Afghanistan, 07/01

CHILDREN'S RIGHTS

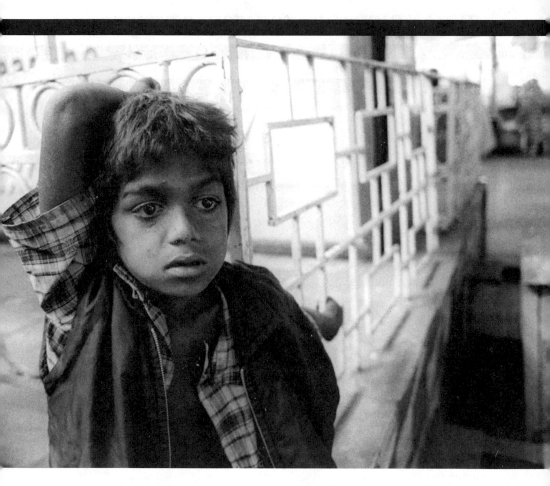

A street child in Bombay, India.

CHILDREN'S RIGHTS

Violations of children's rights were all too common in 2001. Children were beaten and tortured by police, forced to work long hours under hazardous conditions, or warehoused in detention centers and orphanages. Millions crossed international borders in search of safety or were displaced within their own countries. Hundreds of thousands served as soldiers in armed conflicts.

In documenting human rights abuses, Human Rights Watch has traditionally focused its efforts on monitoring state compliance with civil and political rights. But the denial of economic and social rights, such as the right to education, health, or shelter, often bars individuals from the effective enjoyment of their civil and political rights.

Children are especially vulnerable to this dynamic. They frequently do not benefit from the progressive realization of economic and social rights—to the contrary, they often suffer discrimination in basic education, health care, and other services. In particular, girls are often subjected to intentionally discriminatory treatment or disproportionately affected by abuses. The deprivation of these fundamental rights prevents children from realizing their full potential later in life. With limited capacity to participate as equals in civil society, they are ill-equipped as adults to defend their rights and to secure these rights for their own children.

In recognition of these facts, Human Rights Watch examined children's access to education, focusing on violence and discriminatory treatment in schools—often at the hands of other students with official acquiescence or encouragement, in extreme cases perpetrated by teachers and other staff members. We also began to examine the devastating effect of the human immunodeficiency virus/acquired immune deficiency syndrome (HIV/AIDS) pandemic on children around the world. At the same time, we continued to monitor the human rights abuses suffered by child soldiers, children in conflict with the law, children who were refugees, migrants, stateless, or deprived of the benefits of citizenship, and children who labored under hazardous conditions.

Effective remedies for these children must include a reaffirmation of their civil and political rights. No girl or boy should be made a child soldier or a bonded laborer. No child should be excluded from school because of her caste, color, religion, or gender. At the same time, real protection from such abuses requires measures to ensure that children enjoy access to education and health services and protection for their other economic and social rights.

VIOLATIONS OF THE RIGHT TO EDUCATION

"Children do not lose their human rights by virtue of passing through the school gates."

United Nations Committee on the Rights of the Child,
General Comment No. 1, The Aims of Education, April 2001

The Convention on the Rights of the Child establishes that children enjoy the right to an education. Article 29 of the convention specifies five goals of education, including "the development of the child's personality, talents and mental and physical abilities to their fullest potential," "the development of respect for the child's parents, his or her own cultural identity, language and values, for the national values of the country in which the child is living, the country from which he or she may originate, and for civilizations different from his or her own," and "the preparation of the child for responsible life in a free society, in the spirit of understanding, peace, tolerance, equality of sexes, and friendships among all peoples, ethnic, national and religious groups and persons of indigenous origin."

Children have the right to freedom from discrimination in education. This right flows from the nondiscrimination provisions of the Convention on the Rights of the Child, the International Covenant on Civil and Political Rights, the International Covenant on Economic, Social and Cultural Rights, the Convention on the Elimination of All Forms of Discrimination Against Women, and the International Convention on the Elimination of All Forms of Racial Discrimination. It is explicitly guaranteed in the Convention against Discrimination in Education, which had ninety states party as of July 2001.

As with other economic, social, and cultural rights, the right to education may be achieved progressively. A state party to the International Covenant on Economic, Social and Cultural Rights agrees "to take steps . . . to the maximum of its available resources" to realize the right to education. But the prohibition on discrimination in education is not progressive. As the Committee on Economic, Social and Cultural Rights has observed, the right to freedom from discrimination in education "is subject to neither progressive realization nor the availability of resources; it applies fully and immediately to all aspects of education and encompasses all internationally prohibited grounds of discrimination."

Instead of facilitating the healthy development of children and providing them with equal opportunities for education, schools were too often sites of intolerance and discrimination. In some cases, school officials failed to protect students from harassment or attacks by classmates. In others, they themselves participated in harassment or violence against particular youth because of their gender, race, ethnicity, religion, nationality, sexual orientation, social group, or other status.

In many parts of the world, children from minorities and other socially disadvantaged groups were denied education or segregated in inferior educational programs that limited their opportunities for growth and restricted their access to higher education and employment.

A 2001 Human Rights Watch investigation found pervasive and systematic discrimination against nearly one-fourth of Israel's 1.6 million schoolchildren—Palestinian Arab citizens—who were educated in a public school system that was wholly separate from the schools of the Jewish majority. The Israeli government spent less per Palestinian Arab child than per Jewish child, and Arab schools were inferior to Jewish schools in virtually every respect. Arab schools offered fewer facilities and educational opportunities than were offered other Israeli children, and some lacked basic learning facilities like libraries, computers, science laboratories, and recreation space. Palestinian Arab children attended schools with larger classes and fewer teachers than those in the Jewish school system, with some children having to travel long distances to reach the nearest school. Palestinian Arab children with disabilities were particularly marginalized. Many Palestinian Arab communities lacked kindergartens for three- and four-year-old students, despite legislation making such schools—and attendance—obligatory. Jewish three-year-olds attended kindergarten at four times the rate of their Palestinian Arab counterparts; Jewish four-year-olds at three times the rate.

Palestinian Arab students studied from a government-prescribed Arabic curriculum that was derived from the Hebrew curriculum: common subjects were developed with little or no Palestinian Arab participation, and they were translated years after the Hebrew language material was published. The government devoted inadequate resources to developing the subjects unique to Arab education, and Palestinian Arab teachers had significantly less choice in textbooks and teaching materials than did Jewish teachers. The curricula's content often alienated students and teachers alike, particularly the study of Jewish religious texts, which was required in secondary-level Hebrew language classes.

Palestinian Arab students dropped out of school at three times the rate of Jewish students and were less likely to pass the national exams common to the two systems for a high school diploma. Only a handful made it to university. Among Palestinian Arabs, the Negev Bedouin and children in villages not recognized as legal by the Israeli government fared the worst in every respect. In its 2001 report to the Committee on the Rights of the Child, Israel acknowledged the gaps between Arab and Jewish education, but as of October 2001 it had failed to take necessary steps to equalize the two systems.

In countries throughout Europe, Romani children, sometimes known as Gypsies, received substandard education when they attended schools at all. In November 2000 the parents association of Greece's Halastra Public School closed the school to prevent enrollment of thirty-two Romani children. The Romani children were split up and sent to different schools, often quite far from their homes. Segregation also took the form of educational tracking, in which Romani children were arbitrarily sent to "special schools" for children with cognitive deficits or behavioral problems. According to the European Roma Rights Center, Romani children in the Czech Republic were fifteen times more likely to be placed in remedial education, placement that greatly restricted their secondary school opportunities. When Romani children did attend integrated schools, they often faced harassment by other students and lowered expectations from teachers, factors that contributed to their high dropout rates.

In many countries in Asia and Africa, including Nepal, Sri Lanka, and Japan, children whose parents belonged to lower-caste or other shunned descent-based social groups faced widespread discrimination in access to education and had markedly lower literacy rates and school attendance rates than the general population. In India, Dalit children, also called "untouchables," were largely segregated from others and restricted to the worst government schools, deficient in basic infrastructure, classrooms, teachers, and teaching aids, where they faced abusive, discriminatory treatment at the hands of their teachers and fellow students. Half of all Dalit children did not complete primary school, and less than one-quarter completed secondary school, despite state assistance in primary education and constitutional provisions guaranteeing free, compulsory primary education for all children up to age fourteen. Those children who did stay in school were typically enrolled in vernacular schools, whose graduates suffered serious disadvantages in a job market that favored English-language school graduates.

Children in detention were frequently denied their right to an education on equal terms with their peers. We found that, with the exception of the few juvenile institutions, Pakistan's prisons did not provide education to children in juvenile wards. Religious foundations provided religious instruction; secular subjects were rarely available and when they were, were taught by adult prisoners not necessarily trained as teachers. Children in the three detention facilities specifically designed for youth receive education through the eighth grade, but educational facilities were understaffed and provided with few or no teaching aids. In Kenya, we found that some juvenile detention centers provided secondary school instruction only to boys, while other facilities offered no secondary education at all. Palestinian children detained in Israel's Telmond Prison continued to be denied an education equivalent to that of detained Jewish children. In the United States, Human Rights Watch's investigation of detention facilities in the states of Louisiana and Maryland found that the education offered was in many cases seriously deficient; some facilities offered no classes whatsoever for some or all of their juvenile detainees. Detention officials implemented changes only after the release of our reports, pressure by local groups, and investigations by the U.S. Department of Justice or the U.S. Department of Education.

Noncitizen children were often denied any education at all when states set impossibly high barriers to education for refugee, asylum seeker, immigrant, and stateless children. Many countries required schools to report on students' or parents' legal status, knowing that undocumented migrants' fear of deportation would lead them to keep their children at home. In February 2001, the Greek parliament considered draft legislation that would have required migrant children to provide documentation showing their legal status in Greece in order to enroll in public schools. The requirement of such documentation would have effectively barred school attendance for children of undocumented or irregular migrants. The provisions were dropped from the final bill following protests by Greek nongovernmental organizations, migrants groups, and Human Rights Watch (see Greece).

A 2000 Human Rights Watch report found that Kuwaiti government officials frequently denied children of Bidun residents the birth certificates and other official documents needed to attend public and private schools, claiming they were "illegal residents" even when their families had lived in Kuwait for decades, or even generations. Human Rights Watch's 2000 report on Rohingya refugees from Burma found that Malaysian officials frequently expelled Rohingya children from primary schools when they could not prove legal residency, despite a provision in Malaysia's constitution that granted citizenship to children born on its territory who, like these refugees, would otherwise be stateless.

Children born in the Dominican Republic to Haitian parents were routinely denied identity documents even though the Dominican constitution conferred citizenship on all persons born within the country. Lacking legal documentation, children of Haitian descent were frequently denied access to Dominican schools. Although primary schools tended to be flexible with regard to the admission of undocumented children, policies varied from district to district. Undocumented children were generally denied high school diplomas, and, in many cases, were not allowed to take the mandatory national examinations that were a prerequisite for entry into secondary school. In July 2001, the Dominican vice president announced that public schools would be instructed to admit all children, regardless of documentation, but as of this writing it was not clear that this decision was being implemented.

Children in conflict zones braved tremendous dangers to reach those schools still in operation. Following the September 29, 2000 renewal of violent clashes in the Israeli-occupied West Bank and Gaza Strip (see Israel, the Occupied West Bank and Gaza Strip, and Palestinian Authority Territories), Palestinian children were frequently blocked from attending school by widespread road closures, curfews, and attacks by armed Israeli soldiers and settlers. Those who did reach school did not always find safety. In dozens of reported incidences, schools have been tear gassed, hit by live ammunition, or damaged by artillery shell fragments. Some Jewish Israeli children living in illegal but government-sponsored settlements in the West Bank and Gaza Strip faced difficulties in reaching schools as armed Palestinians increasingly targeted for attacks Israelis traveling or living in these areas. For example, on November 20, 2000, five Israeli children from the Kafr Darom settlement in the Gaza Strip were injured, three seriously, when Palestinian militants detonated a roadside bomb as a caravan of military and civilian vehicles passed. The children were on their way to a school in a nearby settlement. A teacher and a school worker traveling with them were killed.

Human Rights Watch investigations during the clashes found that in the Israeli-controlled H-2 section of Hebron, Palestinian schools serving some 12,000 children were closed for almost five months during almost continuous curfews imposed on Palestinians. Israel announced in January 2001 that schools in the area would be allowed to operate during curfews, but Israeli soldiers continued to prevent some teachers and students from reaching these schools, and three major schools serving 1,845 students remained closed because Israel had turned their grounds into military bases. Children living in the H-2 area who transferred to schools in Palestinian-controlled areas were still subject to the curfew, and Israeli soldiers often prevented them from returning home at night if a curfew was reimposed. Palestinian primary school students in Hebron told Human Rights Watch that they were frequently cursed, stoned, or beaten by armed settlers while on their way to or from school. Israeli soldiers or police rarely intervened, they said, except to beat or arrest Palestinian children who struck back.

In Northern Ireland, parents and politicians complained that police failed to adequately protect Catholic minority school children from attacks in September

2001 by Loyalist protesters. (Some Unionists—those who want to maintain the union between Northern Ireland and the United Kingdom—call themselves "Loyalists," some of whom support the use of violence for political ends.) The protesters sought to keep the children from reaching the Holy Cross Primary School, a Catholic school located near a Protestant-dominated enclave in the Ardoyne section of Belfast. Loyalist protesters spit, cursed, and threw bottles and stones at the children and their parents. A Loyalist paramilitary organization took responsibility for a petrol bomb explosion outside the school while children and parents were approaching. Loyalist paramilitaries warned parents to keep their children away from the school and police informed some parents that death threats had been issued against them.

In eastern Democratic Republic of Congo, a December 2000 investigation by Human Rights Watch found that schools were a common site of child recruitment by rebel groups backed by Rwanda. Frequent targeting of schools for such recruitment caused some parents to keep their children from attending school and some schools to be shut down. Because soldiers are known to abduct children from school, the mere appearance of soldiers in the vicinity of a school can cause the children to panic. In December 2000, soldiers approached a secondary school near Goma one morning while classes were underway; the students scattered and ran. The school suspended classes for some time afterward as parents and pupils were not prepared to risk further raids by soldiers bent on seizing students to serve as child soldiers.

Elsewhere in the region, a Burundi rebel group abducted more than 150 students from two schools in November 2001 and burned several classrooms.

Worldwide, children of many social groups were all too often subject to violence and harassment that undermined their opportunities to learn, caused them to drop out of school, or resulted in psychological trauma, physical injury, and even death.

Lesbian, gay, bisexual, and transgender youth in many U.S. schools were subjected to unrelenting harassment from their peers. A 2001 Human Rights Watch report found that harassment and violence against lesbian, gay, bisexual, and transgender youth took many forms, including brutal physical attacks, mock rapes, unwelcome sexual advances and other acts of sexual harassment, taunts, obscene notes or graffiti, and the destruction of personal property.

Over time, verbal harassment often escalated into physical violence. These abuses were compounded by the failure of federal, state, and local governments to enact laws that would provide students with express protection from discrimination based on their actual or perceived sexual orientation or gender identity.

Such abuses were not limited to the United States. Researchers studying lesbian, gay, bisexual, and transgender youth in Australia, Canada, France, New Zealand, and the United Kingdom, among other countries, reached similar conclusions about the pervasiveness of antigay violence in schools. The Europe Region of the International Lesbian and Gay Association concluded that teachers and other adults were "more likely to reject than support" gay and lesbian youth. Amnesty International reported that gay youth elsewhere in the world suffered torture and ill-treatment because of their sexual orientation or gender identity.

Discrimination, harassment, and violence hampered students' ability to get an education and took a tremendous toll on their emotional well-being. Perhaps because so many lesbian, gay, bisexual, and transgender youth experienced abuses on a daily basis, these youth were more likely than their heterosexual peers to use alcohol or other drugs, engage in risky sexual behaviors, or run away from home. A disproportionate number of lesbian, gay, bisexual, and transgender youth attempted or considered suicide—youth who report attractions to or relationships with persons of the same sex were more than twice as likely as their heterosexual counterparts to attempt suicide, a 1998 study found.

The abuse of lesbian, gay, bisexual, and transgender youth was frequently predicated on the belief that girls and boys must adhere strictly to rigid rules of conduct, dress, and appearances based on their sex. That is, homophobia was linked to stereotypical gender roles. Boys were expected to be athletic, strong, stoic, and dominant relative to girls. Girls were expected to be attentive to boys and to accept a subordinate status to them. Regardless of their sexual orientation or gender identity, youth who violated these rules ran the risk of punishment at the hands of their peers and at times by adults. Transgender youth were the most vulnerable to violence by peers and harassment by adults.

Discussions of antigay violence in schools often focused on the youthful perpetrators of these acts and failed to consider the responsibility of teachers and other school officials to maintain a safe learning environment for all youth.

Despite the pervasiveness of the abuse, few school officials intervened to stop the harassment or to hold the abusive students accountable. The most common response to harassment, according to the students we interviewed, was no response at all. More disturbing, some teachers and administrators actually took part in acts of harassment.

In addition, teachers and administrators were themselves subjected to harassment, often with few legal recourses. In every one of the seven U.S. states that Human Rights Watch visited—California, Georgia, Kansas, Massachusetts, New York, Texas, and Utah—teachers were reluctant to be open about their sexual orientation at school because they feared losing their jobs. Of the states we visited, only California and Massachusetts prohibit discrimination in private employment on the basis of sexual orientation. Nationwide, only eleven state and the District of Columbia offer protection against sexual orientation-based discrimination in private employment; eighteen states and the District of Columbia prohibit such discrimination in private employment.

Corporal punishment was permitted as a method of school discipline in at least sixty-five countries, according to EPOCH (End Physical Punishment of Children) Worldwide. Children were spanked, slapped, caned, strapped, or beaten by teachers as a result of misbehavior, poor academic performance, or sometimes for no reason at all.

Human Rights Watch investigated the use of corporal punishment in Kenyan schools in 1999, visiting twenty schools and interviewing more than 200 children. We found that schoolchildren were routinely subjected to caning, slapping, and whipping by their teachers, sometimes on a daily basis. Such school "discipline" regularly resulted in bruises, cuts, and humiliation and in some cases serious injury or death.

Corporal punishment was used against Kenyan students for a wide range of disciplinary infractions, some of which were serious and others extraordinarily minor. For example, children were physically punished for coming to school late, missing school without permission (even for illness), or having a dirty or torn school uniform. They were also punished for unsatisfactory performance or for not being able to afford school fees.

In a welcome development in April 2001, Kenya's minister of education formally banned corporal punishment in the schools as a matter of policy and proposed to Parliament the elimination of the sections of the Education Act of 1968 that provided for such punishment. However, the official notice did not establish penalties for teachers who continued to carry out acts of corporal punishment or provide for training in alternative methods of discipline. Many teachers expressed dissatisfaction with the ban, asserting that they would be unable to maintain order in the classroom without resorting to corporal punishment.

Girls constituted nearly two-thirds of the 130 million children out of school in the developing world, according to 1998 estimates by the United Nations Children's Fund. In part, this disparity reflected the serious obstacles girls faced at school. Gender-based violence—rape, sexual assault, sexual abuse, and sexual harassment—was chief among these obstacles.

In 2000, Human Rights Watch investigated gender-based violence in South Africa's schools, Based on interviews with dozens of students, teachers, and government officials, we found that South African schoolgirls of every race and economic group encountered sexual violence and harassment on a daily basis. Girls reported that they were raped in school bathrooms, in empty classrooms and hallways, and in hostels and dormitories. Girls were also fondled, subjected to aggressive sexual advances, and verbally degraded at school. They suffered such abuses at the hands of both teachers and other students.

Too often, school authorities concealed sexual violence and delayed disciplinary action against those who committed such acts. Some school officials failed to respond adequately because they simply did not know what to do; some responded with hostility and indifference toward girls who complained of sexual violence and harassment. Others were afraid to assist their students. In many instances, schools actively discouraged the victims of school-based sexual violence from alerting anyone outside the school.

The South African government has recognized publicly the problems faced in prosecuting cases of violence against women and girls in its criminal justice system. Human Rights Watch's research confirmed that coordination in such cases between the education and justice systems was often ineffective, ill-conceived, or nonexistent. School officials, police, and prosecutors were often confused about their responsibility for resolving such cases, and the tendency of all actors to shift responsibility meant that cases of violence against girls were regularly ignored.

In some countries, school officials used the threat of denial of education to intimidate or punish students whose behavior or religious belief was seen to challenge mainstream norms or dominant political trends. Girls were frequent targets of such policies. For example, beginning in 1994, and increasingly after 1997, female Muslim students of all ages in Uzbekistan faced harassment and even expulsion for wearing hijab, a religious head covering, to government schools. Turkey prevented girls from attending most government schools if they chose to wear hijab, and after 1997 enforced this policy increasingly energetically. Girls who continued to wear religious attire to school could be charged with "interrupting education," a criminal offence punished by incarceration for up to two years. Turkish law also allowed schools to expel girls deemed to be "unchaste," an accusation officials often made against girls who challenged conservative social norms. A 1995 Ministry of Education circular provided for high school students' "expulsion from the formal education system" based on "proof of unchastity," and in July 2001 Minister of Health Osman Durmus decreed that "virginity tests" could be performed on medical high school students "known to be having sex or engaging in prostitution." Banned since 1999, such gynecological exams involved intimidation and pain and violated girls' right to bodily integrity. Prior to the ban, some girls attempted suicide rather than submit to this abusive examination. The minister of health indicated that the implementation of such examinations was not planned, but the circular remains in force.

Girls in Taliban-controlled areas of Afghanistan were often banned from receiving all but elementary levels of education. Some girls were able to attend home-based schools secretly, but these schools were forcibly closed upon discovery. A teacher told Human Rights Watch that she and her students, girls in grades one through seven, were beaten in June 2001 by members of the Taliban's Religious Police. "The Taliban have paralyzed half of society—half of society is dead in Afghanistan because the women are prevented from working or studying," another woman explained to Human Rights Watch in September 2001 (see Afghanistan and Women's Rights).

The rapid spread of HIV/AIDS posed a particular and complex threat to children's realization of their right to education, especially in sub-Saharan Africa where the epidemic has been most destructive. In December 2000 UNICEF made its first global call for free and compulsory primary education at the African Development Forum on leadership and HIV/AIDS.

Reaching children with appropriate information on HIV transmission and care for those with AIDS is arguably the most effective means of combating the epidemic over the long term, yet schools in Africa were called upon to be part of the solution to AIDS at a time when the epidemic itself had left them weaker than ever. In many countries in eastern and southern Africa, teachers died of AIDS at rates much higher than those of the general population. The government of Zambia, for example, began reporting in 1998 that teachers in government primary and secondary schools were dying faster than they could be replaced. In many countries rural and marginal areas were particularly affected by teacher shortages when teachers ill with AIDS chose to be near the larger and better equipped hospitals in urban areas. In Botswana, the country with the highest HIV prevalence rate in the world, some government schools closed for lack of qualified staff.

Education too often became unaffordable for children in AIDS-affected families when the illness caused the incapacitation and death of breadwinners as well as expenditure of scarce household resources on medical services. As ill or dying parents became unable to pay school fees, children were called upon to leave their studies and earn income or become heads of household. A study in a heavily AIDS-affected region of Zimbabwe in 2000 found that 48 percent of primary school-age orphans had dropped out, and none orphaned by AIDS in secondary school were unable to continue their studies. In many countries, government statistics confirmed that, particularly among primary school-aged children, girls in AIDS-affected families were more likely than boys to be withdrawn from school when parents were short of resources or needed help caring for the family.

The belief that schools themselves were a locus for HIV transmission served as a barrier to children's exercising their right to education. A 1999 Oxfam study in Mozambique reported that parents cited the fear that their daughters would contract HIV at school as the principal reason for keeping their daughters out of school. Children themselves, including many of those interviewed by Human Rights Watch in Kenya in 2001, described stigmatization and ostracism of AIDS-affected children or orphans in school.

HIV/AIDS AND CHILDREN'S RIGHTS

HIV/AIDS continued to pose an acute threat to children's human rights in general. Unlike many virulent epidemics in history that have killed mainly young children and the elderly, AIDS for the most part infects and kills adults aged eighteen to forty years, in or near the most productive years of their lives. Globally, most persons in this age group are parents. Thus, for children, the epidemic too often represents both the loss of a parent or parents and exposure to the stigma and discrimination that go hand in hand with AIDS throughout the world.

In heavily affected countries, for each child who had lost a parent to AIDS, one or two school-age children were likely to be caring for an ill parent, acting as breadwinners for the household, or otherwise unable to attend school because of AIDS. Children who were not orphaned were also affected when orphans were brought into their homes or when they themselves were infected with HIV. Thus, AIDS-affected children comprised a much larger population than just orphans.

In sub-Saharan Africa—the most heavily AIDS-affected region of the world—AIDS orphaned children at a rate unprecedented in history. The United Nations conservatively estimated that by December 2000, about 13 million children under age fifteen in sub-Saharan Africa had lost their mother or both parents to AIDS. In July 2000, the United States Bureau of the Census, which keeps data on AIDS independent of the United Nations, estimated that there were about 15 million children under age fifteen who had lost at least one parent to AIDS in Africa and that by 2010 this number would be at least 28 million, including over 30 percent of all children under age fifteen in five countries of eastern and southern Africa. The percentage of the child population represented by orphans will remain very high in some African countries for decades, according to the Census Bureau.

AIDS's impact on children was felt far beyond Africa as the epidemic's devastation spread to other regions of the world. In Thailand, the estimated 300,000 deaths from AIDS since the beginning of the epidemic have resulted in many orphans, of which a large percentage are thought to be in the care of a grandparent or other relative. The most rapid spread of HIV/AIDS was experienced in Eastern Europe and the former Soviet states, where widespread use of injected drugs drove the epidemic. Children were affected both as they were drawn into drug use at a young age and as they lost their parents. Globally, access to services such as syringe exchange or simple materials for syringe sterilization, which would reduce the likelihood of HIV transmission, was limited, partly due to the stigmatization of drug users and their families. Numbers of children orphaned and otherwise made vulnerable by AIDS also grew rapidly in the heavily affected countries of the Caribbean basin.

But African children saw the worst of it. The United Nations estimated in December 2000 that 92 percent of children orphaned by AIDS were in sub-Saharan Africa, where AIDS ate away at communities already wracked by poverty, war, and corruption. In the African countries hardest hit by HIV/AIDS, the extended family was traditionally the source of support and care for orphans and other children needing special protection. In the face of enormous numbers of children without parental care, the extended family became increasingly overextended, if not completely unraveled, and unable to provide its traditional level of protection and support. The pattern was all too commonly seen: a parent became ill, the loss of his or her labor in the household or income generated outside the household and increased medical expenses impoverished the family, and school fees became unaffordable. Children were withdrawn from school and required to care for sick household members and young children, engaged in income-generating activities, or some combination of these.

Unskilled children who had to become the family breadwinners were particularly vulnerable to exploitation and being forced into the worst forms of child labor, a situation greatly exacerbated by the stigma of AIDS. The United Nations Children's Fund (UNICEF) reported in July 2001 that AIDS was pushing large numbers of children into hazardous labor in Kenya, Uganda, Mozambique, Ethiopia, Lesotho, and South Africa. An investigation of the experience of one hundred children orphaned by AIDS in South Africa, summarized in a June 2001 report by the Nelson Mandela Children's Fund, found widespread hunger and other deprivation among these children and a number of girls as young as eight being forced to engage in prostitution to survive. Other research in Africa in 2000 and 2001 attributed the large rise in the number of street children in countries such as Zambia and Kenya to HIV/AIDS.

Loss of inheritance rights was another common problem of children orphaned by AIDS, as documented by Human Rights Watch's investigation of the problem in Kenya in a report released in June 2001. AIDS orphaned over a million children in Kenya by the end of 2000 and affected many more in other ways. A large percentage of the children interviewed by Human Rights Watch experienced the unlawful appropriation of property, usually by distant relatives, that the children were entitled to inherit. NGO reports suggested that thousands of children in the country have had this experience. Property-grabbing from children on a large scale is a relatively recent phenomenon in the country, related again both to AIDS and to the deterioration of the extended family. Human Rights Watch concluded that the existing institutions of the judicial system in Kenya did not allow for adequate consideration of property cases of children and recommended that the government establish a streamlined, user-friendly mechanism for civil court hearings of these cases.

One of the most frequent AIDS-related rights violations suffered by children worldwide was that of their right to information on HIV/AIDS, a matter of life and death for children where the epidemic has a foothold. While most government HIV/AIDS programs in Africa have focused on information in some form, a number of reports released in 2001 showed young people to have poor access to appropriate information across Africa. This problem was compounded by the effect of AIDS on school enrollment, but even for children able to stay in school, appropriate AIDS information—particularly in the later primary school years, where it was arguably most needed—is absent from too many government curricula. In Kenya, for example, resistance by Roman Catholic leaders to education on sex and reproductive health impeded the development of an AIDS curriculum for primary and secondary schools until 2000 and continued to handicap its full implementation in 2001.

The U.N. General Assembly Special Session on HIV/AIDS in June agreed that all countries should work toward implementation by 2005 of comprehensive national programs to protect and support children affected by AIDS, including "providing appropriate counseling and psychosocial support, ensuring their enrolment in school and access to shelter . . . and protect[ing] orphans and vulnerable children from all forms of abuse, violence, exploitation, discrimination, trafficking and loss of inheritance." The emergency already faced by children affected by AIDS urgently demanded a comprehensive response.

CHILD SOLDIERS

Support continued to grow for an international treaty prohibiting the use of children in armed conflict. The optional protocol to the Convention on the Rights of the Child, adopted by the U.N. General Assembly in May 2000, established eighteen as the minimum age for direct participation in armed conflict, for forced or compulsory recruitment, and for any recruitment or use by nongovernmental armed groups. From November 2000 to mid-November 2001 the number of nations that signed the protocol grew from seventy to eighty-seven, and the number of ratifications increased from three (Canada, Bangladesh, and Sri Lanka) to ten, with the addition of Andorra, Morocco, Panama, Iceland, Vietnam, Holy See, the Democratic Republic of Congo and New Zealand. Having reached the ten ratifications needed, the protocol will enter into force on February 12, 2002.

Demobilizations of child soldiers took place in several countries. In late February, the United Nations Children's Fund (UNICEF) coordinated the demobilization of over 2,500 children between the ages of eight and eighteen from the Sudan People's Liberation Army (SPLA) in Southern Sudan, airlifting them to transition camps. By September 2001 the last of the group had been reunited with their families. UNICEF indicated that the process of demobilization would continue in 2002 until all SPLA child soldiers—an estimated 10,000 before the February initiative—were demobilized. From May through November over 2,903 children, including 1,506 from the rebel Revolutionary United Front and 1,303 from government-allied militias were released and/or disarmed in Sierra Leone. In mid-May, the government of the Democratic Republic of Congo (DRC) decreed the demobilization of child soldiers serving in its army who, according to conservative estimates, numbered in the thousands. In June, President Joseph Kabila announced that the DRC would no longer recruit child soldiers, and ordered an education campaign for military commanders to facilitate the demobilization of children. By July, teams of government and civil society workers were touring military barracks to identify child soldiers and prepare for family reunification and their reintegration into society.

However, the recruitment and use of children remained a global problem. The Coalition to Stop the Use of Child Soldiers released its first global survey in June, finding that more than half a million children were subject to recruitment into national armed forces, paramilitaries, or non-state armed groups in a total of eighty-seven countries, and at least 300,000 of these children were actively participating in armed conflicts in forty-one countries.

In the eastern Democratic Republic of Congo, rebel groupings backed by the governments of Uganda and Rwanda coerced and forced children to join their ranks. Instructors from the two occupying armies trained the recruits for their respective local surrogates, and in certain cases Congolese children were taken to Uganda and Rwanda for further training. A December 2000 U.N. report estimated that between 15 and 30 percent of all newly recruited combatants in the DRC were children under eighteen years of age, and a substantial number were under age twelve. The Rwandan-backed Congolese Rally for Democracy-Goma (Rassemblement Congolais pour la Démocratie-Goma, RCD-Goma) conducted an intensive recruitment drive in late 2000 and abducted children from schools, roadsides, markets, and their homes. In some communities, schools were closed and children and young men began sleeping outdoors, away from their homes, to avoid recruitment.

A Rutshuru resident reported that RCD-Goma and Rwandan Patriotic Army (RPA) soldiers abducted boys and girls from his community in November 2000, targeting children and youth between the ages of thirteen and twenty. In other cases, Human Rights Watch received reports of children aged twelve and even younger being recruited and sent to camps for military training.

International criticism prompted the RCD-Goma to pledge in early April 2001 to end the recruitment of child soldiers and demobilize those in their ranks. But just a few days later at a ceremony marking the end of a training program at the Mushaki military camp, nearly 1800 of the 3000 graduates were observed to be children aged twelve to seventeen. By mid-year, it became apparent that the RCD recruitment plan had continued unabated in rural areas.

The opposition Army for the Liberation of Rwanda (Armeé pour la Libération du Rwanda, ALIR) abducted children as young as ten in the eastern Democratic Republic of Congo. Children recruited by ALIR were given weapons training and used to fetch water, do other domestic chores, and transport supplies. Children were also used by ALIR to shout or bang on pots to create diversions during battle. Some older children, aged sixteen and seventeen, were used to participate directly in combat. At least one fifteen-year-old also served in the ranks of the Local Defense Force, a Rwandan auxiliary force, which engaged in combat against ALIR.

At least several dozen ALIR children were killed in combat between May and

September; the actual number may have been far higher. In early August, 280 children from ALIR were in Rwandan government custody after having been captured or surrendered. Over fifty of these children were Congolese and were handed over to RCD rebel authorities in eastern Congo, while the Rwandan children were sent to a rehabilitation center south of Kigali.

In Burundi, military and civilian authorities recruited hundreds of children as paramilitaries known as "Guardians of the Peace." One source estimated that between 750 and 900 children aged seven to twelve years of age were recruited and trained in one year in Burundi. Recent recruitment spared very young children, but recruitment of those fourteen and older continued. Recruits were subjected to harsh conditions, and frequently beaten by soldiers. In one training program, three young recruits—aged twelve, fifteen, and seventeen years—died as a result of beatings suffered during their training. Many others died in combat after being sent into battle ahead of regular soldiers.

A Burundian rebel group, the Forces for the Defense of Democracy (Forces pour la Défense de la Démocratie, FDD), abducted thirty students in grades four to six from Kirambi primary school in the eastern province of Ruyigi on November 6, 2001. Three days later, other FDD rebels abducted more than one hundred students from Musema high school in Kayanza province and burned the school to the ground. The rebels forced the students to transport good stolen from nearby homes and shops and beat those who faltered en route. Rebels reportedly told the students that they would turn them into soldiers to help in their war against the government, now in its eighth year. As of November 15, the FDD had released the students from Musema high school, but twenty-three Kirambi primary school boys between the ages of twelve and sixteen were still in the hands of the rebel group.

In Liberia children fleeing the fighting in the north of the country were forcibly recruited and later trained by government forces to help fight insurgents. Credible sources reported to Human Rights Watch that from January through April 2001 scores of children as young as nine were taken off of buses as they fled the fighting, at military checkpoints, or from camps for the internally displaced. They were reportedly later trained for military service by government forces. Other aid agencies reported that Liberian insurgents from the Liberians United for Reconciliation and Democracy (LURD), based in Guinea, abducted numerous children during raids on villages in northern Liberia.

In Colombia, the government estimated that up to 10,000 members of the armed groups operating there, including guerrillas and army-backed paramilitaries, were under eighteen. In late 2000, independent observers reported to Human Rights Watch that dozens of children were among the supposed guerrillas registered as killed or captured after an encounter between government troops and the FARC-EP (Fuerzas Armadas Revolucionarias de Colombia-Ejército del Pueblo, FARC-EP). The Colombian Army announced that thirty-two of those captured were aged seventeen or under, including several younger than fourteen, and a third were females. Of those killed, twenty were said by the army to be children.

Colombian paramilitaries linked to the army also continued to recruit and use children. In July, paramilitaries reportedly seized a youth detention center and abducted ten children in an apparent recruitment drive.

In July, UNICEF criticized the rebel Liberation Tigers of Tamil Eelam in Sri Lanka for recruiting and using child soldiers as young as age twelve. The United Nations reported increased recruitment activity by the Tigers in or near schools, despite assurances given in 1998 to the special representative to the U.N. secretary-general on children and armed conflict, Olara Otunnu, to end the recruitment of children under the age of seventeen.

CHILDREN IN THE JUSTICE SYSTEM

The treatment of children in the justice system continued to raise concerns in 2001. Abuses often began with the first contact with law enforcement officials, during which children were at risk of ill-treatment, torture, and even death. Asma Jahangir, the United Nations special rapporteur on extrajudicial executions, highlighted an extreme example in September, charging that up to 800 children and young adults had been murdered in Honduras since 1998, many at the hands of police.

In June, the Inter-American Court of Human Rights ordered Guatemala to pay nearly U.S. $500,000 in a case brought on behalf of five street children killed by police. The court also directed Guatemala to name a youth educational center for the children, establish a memorial to them, and provide other nonmonetary reparations. The case was the first in which the Inter-American Court had ordered reparations, including monetary damages, in a case involving violations of children's rights.

Once arrested and charged, children were often held in poor conditions of confinement, sometimes together with adults. A former child soldier under sentence of death died on September 26 after contracting tuberculosis in Kinshasa's central prison, a local group reported. In Paraguay, Amnesty International and Defence for Children International-Paraguay Section reported that children were warehoused in overcrowded prisons for adults, where they were subjected to constant ill-treatment and daily isolation. Palestinian children held in Israel's Telmond Prison reported that they were subjected to attacks by adult inmates and severe beatings by guards. Yemen reported to the Committee on the Rights of the Child in 1999 that its reformatories and penal institutions housing children lacked educational and social services, provided poor quality and insufficient food, and frequently used corporal punishment and torture. In Saudi Arabia, the 1977 Detention and Imprisonment Regulations permitted flogging and other corporal punishment as disciplinary measures for children in detention.

Because of the low numbers of girls typically in detention, they were at particular risk of being housed with adults. For example, Yemen, which lacked separate facilities for girls awaiting trial or after sentencing, housed girls with adult prisoners in penal facilities. Saudi Arabia's 1975 Statutes of the Welfare Institutions for Young Women also allowed girls to be held with adult detainees.

Sentencing practices also raised serious human rights concerns. Countries around the world continued to detain children for "status offenses," acts that would not be crimes if committed by an adult. In Yemen, for example, the vast majority of children in custodial institutions were "potential delinquents," a category that included children found begging, orphans, and children whose fathers were absent or whose parents were divorced or separated, according to its 1999 report to the Committee on the Rights of the Child.

In Egypt, a boy between the ages of fifteen and seventeen was sentenced to three years of imprisonment for "indecency and debauchery" by a juvenile court in September. One of at least fifty-five men arrested during the year in a crackdown against homosexuality, the boy was convicted on the basis of a confession that he said had been extracted under torture. Police made most of the arrests in a May 11 raid on a Cairo discotheque popular with gay men. Egypt does not criminalize consensual sexual relations between members of the same sex; the adult men, who also claimed that they were subject to beatings and other abuses while detained, were charged with "obscene behavior" and "contempt of religion" (see Egypt chapter).

Many countries continued to impose corporal punishment on children as part of their sentence. The Committee on the Rights of the Child found that in Saudi Arabia, judicial authorities regularly sentenced people who were children at the time of their offenses to flogging, stoning, and amputation. In Nigeria's Kebbi State, a fifteen-year-old boy was reportedly sentenced to the amputation of one of his hands after he was convicted of stealing 32,000 Naira (approximately U.S. $285). It was not known if the sentence had been carried out at the time of writing.

Following a trend that began in the early 1990s, the United States continued to try children as adults for a large number of offenses that had traditionally been handled in the juvenile justice system.

The United States was also virtually alone in imposing sentences of death on those who were children at the time of the crimes for which they were convicted. On October 22, 2001, the state executed Gerald Lee Mitchell, who became the eighteenth juvenile offender executed in the U.S. and the tenth in Texas since 1976. Eighty-three juvenile offenders were on death rows in fifteen U.S. states as of October 1. With twenty-nine juvenile offenders on its death row, Texas accounted for over one-third of the national total. In all, twenty-three U.S. states continued to allow the death penalty to be imposed for crimes committed by those below the age of eighteen.

Two juvenile offenders received last-minute stays of execution after their attorneys presented new evidence or raised constitutional issues on appeal. On August 15, Napoleon Beazley, convicted in Texas for a murder he committed at age seventeen, came within hours of execution when the Texas Court of Criminal Appeals issued a stay to enable it to consider whether his first appellate attorney provided ineffective assistance. Missouri death row inmate Antonio Richardson received a stay from the U.S. Supreme Court in March. Sixteen at the time of his crime, Richardson may be mentally retarded; his case was on hold while the Supreme Court resolved another case that questioned the constitutionality of imposing the death sentence on persons with mental retardation.

In Pakistan, where a July 2000 ordinance raised the minimum age for capital punishment to eighteen, forty-nine people remained on death row for crimes they committed as children, the *Dawn* reported in July 2001.

The Democratic Republic of Congo and Iran had mixed records on capital punishment during the year. Following a meeting with Human Rights Watch in May 2001, the Democratic Republic of Congo agreed to spare the lives of four child soldiers. The four were arrested and sentenced to death by the Court of Military Order when they were between fourteen and sixteen years of age. President Joseph Kabila subsequently commuted the sentences of these children, along with that of a fifth former child soldier, to five years' imprisonment. At least one additional former child soldier remained under sentence of death, according to the World Organization Against Torture (Organisation mondiale contre la torture, OMCT). In Iran, the death sentence of a thirteen-year-old boy was commuted to life imprisonment, Amnesty International reported; the reduced sentence may still violate international standards, which prohibited the imposition of capital punishment or life imprisonment without possibility of release for offenses committed by persons below the age of eighteen.

REFUGEE AND MIGRANT CHILDREN

Refugee and migrant children, among the world's most vulnerable populations, were at particular risk of abuse when they were separated from their parents and other caregivers.

In July, local authorities in the Spanish autonomous enclaves of Ceuta and Melilla stepped up summary expulsions of unaccompanied Moroccan children living there. The children, including some as young as eleven, were reportedly beaten and threatened by both Spanish and Moroccan police and did not receive individualized review of their cases before Spanish authorities dumped them on the Moroccan side of the border.

In Greece, unaccompanied children were largely excluded from participation in the June 5 to August 2 program that gave legal status to undocumented immigrants who could prove they had arrived in Greece before June 2, 2000. Under the terms of the program, undocumented migrants who could not provide extensive documentation of their presence—including proof of identity, wage receipts, utility payment receipts, and other documents unaccompanied children could not be expected to have—were subject to forced deportation if they did not leave the country voluntarily.

In the United States, the Immigration and Naturalization Service (INS) continued to detain a substantial proportion of the unaccompanied children in its custody in jail-like settings, sometimes holding them in cells with juvenile offenders. The agency was criticized for denying full access to independent monitors, including the Women's Commission for Refugee Women and Children and the lawyers who represented detained children in a successful class-action lawsuit challenging the conditions of confinement for youth in INS custody. In a positive development, Senator Dianne Feinstein proposed legislation that would correct these and other abusive conditions for unaccompanied children in the United States.

CHILD LABOR

With the addition of Estonia at the end of September, one hundred countries had ratified the International Labor Organization's Convention concerning the Prohibition and Immediate Action for the Elimination of the Worst Forms of Child Labor (ILO Convention 182), which prohibits debt bondage, forced or compulsory labor (including forced recruitment into military service), prostitution and the production of pornography, and other work likely to "harm the health, safety or morals of children." Nevertheless, far too many children around the world worked under conditions that were hazardous to their health and safety. In Ecuador, a 2001 Human Rights Watch investigation found that children were routinely employed in the banana industry, where they were exposed to pesticides and required to perform hazardous labor. In addition, two girls interviewed by Human Rights Watch reported that they were often subjected to sexual harassment by their supervisors.

In a tragic development, Carlos Alberto Santos de Oliveira, president of the Sergipe Citrus Fruit Workers' Union and known for his advocacy in opposition to child labor, was killed on September 23 by two gunmen who shot him eight times at point-blank range in the Brazilian town of Pedrinhas, in Sergipe state.

THE ROLE OF THE INTERNATIONAL COMMUNITY

Eighty heads of state and over 1,000 nongovernmental organizations were expected to attend a U.N. General Assembly Special Session for Children in New York from September 19-21. The session was intended to evaluate progress made in meeting the goals of the 1990 World Summit on Children and to adopt a declaration and plan of action for the future. The draft plan of action identified four priority areas: health, education, HIV/AIDS, and protection from violence, abuse, neglect, and exploitation. Following the September 11 attacks on New York and Washington, the session was postponed until 2002.

Hundreds of nongovernmental organizations from around the world participated in two preparatory committee sessions held during the year. A Child Rights Caucus led by Human Rights Watch and Save the Children won the support of governments for the inclusion of key issues in the draft plan of action, notably concerning protection for children from violence, abuse and exploitation.

The draft declaration and plan of action did not break significant new ground, however, as many governments were unwilling to move beyond previously agreed commitments to children. The United States, one of only two states that have failed to ratify the Convention on the Rights of the Child, opposed a rights-oriented plan of action and sought to minimize references to the convention. Joined by the Holy See and a grouping of primarily Islamic countries, the United States also sought to roll back international agreements regarding the access of adolescents to sexual and reproductive health care, information, and services. Issues related to child labor, armed conflict, and mobilization of resources were also contentious.

The Committee on the Rights of the Child continued a focus on violence against children by holding a second general day of discussion on the topic, focused on violence against children in the home and in schools. A similar discussion day had been held in 2001 on violence against children in state-run institutions and in the context of "law and public order." Among its final recommendations, the committee urged the General Assembly to initiate an in-depth study of violence against children, comparable to the ground-breaking U.N. study led by Graça Machel on the impact of armed conflict on children. In late November, the U.N.'s Third Committee passed a resolution requesting the secretary-general to "conduct an in-depth study on the issue of violence against children . . . and to put forward recommendations, for consideration by member states, for appropriate action, including effective remedies and preventive and rehabilitation measures."

Relevant Human Rights Watch Reports

To Protect the People: The Government-Sponsored "Self-Defense" Program in Burundi, 12/01.

Israel: Second Class: Discrimination Against Palestinian Arab Children in Israel's Schools, 12/01

Humanity Denied: Systematic Violations of Women's Rights in Afghanistan, 10/01

Caste Discrimination: A Global Concern, 9/01

Easy Targets: Violence Against Children Worldwide, 9/01

Kenya: In the Shadow of Death: HIV/AIDS and Children's Rights in Kenya, 6/01

Democratic Republic of Congo: Reluctant Recruits: Children and Adults Forcibly Recruited for Military Service in North Kivu, 5/01

United States: Hatred in the Hallways: Violence and Discrimination Against Lesbian, Gay, Bisexual, and Transgender Students in U.S. Schools, 5/01.

Israel, the Occupied West Bank and Gaza Strip, and the Palestinian Authority Territories: Center of the Storm: A Case Study of Human Rights Abuses in Hebron District, 4/01

South Africa: Scared at School: Sexual Violence Against Girls in South African Schools, 3/01

Egypt: Underage and Underprotected: Child Labor in Egypt's Cotton Fields, 1/01

WOMEN'S HUMAN RIGHTS

An Afghan widow living in a refugee camp in Pakistan in April 2001.

WOMEN'S HUMAN RIGHTS

O ne of the greatest challenges of governments in 2001 was to make respect for women's rights a more permanent and central part of the international human rights agenda. Women's rights activists made notable progress on several fronts—leading governments to condemn sexual violence against women in armed conflict, holding governments accountable for failing to protect women from domestic violence, and forcing governments to acknowledge and treat trafficking as a human rights crisis. However, governments' reluctance to promote respect for women's rights systematically and thoroughly undercut these gains every day. Many governments' commitment to women's human rights remained at best tenuous and at worst nonexistent. The international women's rights community moved forward, pressing to protect women's bodily integrity and right to sexual autonomy, to examine the ways that race or ethnicity and gender intersect to deny women human rights, and to protect women from gender-specific violations of the laws of war.

The September 11 attacks on the U.S. triggered an international debate about the motivation of the attackers and a just response. The subsequent U.S.-led military action against the Taliban in Afghanistan focused international attention on the plight of Afghans generally, and in particular on Afghan women. Governments in the U.S.-led coalition and those outside it argued that the Taliban's behavior toward women—including banning women from most types of work, forcing women to wear a head-to-toe enveloping garment, and banning women from education beyond primary school—was unparalleled in severity and constituted a systematic attack on women's human rights and dignity. Yet, while the international community recoiled at these abuses, the women's human rights record of other governments with similar practices, such as Saudi Arabia, received minimal criticism.

Critics of the Taliban virtually ignored Saudi Arabia, where women faced systematic discrimination in all aspects of their lives: they were denied equality of opportunity in access to work, forced to comply with a restrictive dress code, and segregated in public life. Religious police punished infractions of the dress code with public beatings. Kuwait's record on women's rights was also dismal: the Kuwaiti government denied women the right to vote, segregated them, and required them to veil in public.

The international community's lack of complaint about the women's human rights records in these countries underscored a reality that women's rights activists grappled with everywhere: women's rights must still be negotiated, and violations of women's rights often generate only fleeting interest. Many governments, through overt discrimination, attacked women's rights in ways that essentially stripped women of their legal personhood. For example, the governments of Nigeria, Kenya, Zambia, and other African states denied women equal inheritance and property rights. The Thai government denied women who married non-nationals the right to buy and own property in their own names. Egypt discriminated against women who married non-nationals by refusing to allow them to transfer their nationality to their children. Syria conditioned a woman's choice in marriage on the consent of a male family member. Although having no such restriction for men, Venezuela prevented women from marrying until ten months after a divorce or annulment.

Governments that condemned some types of violence and discrimination against women often failed to prosecute others. Thus, Jordan and Pakistan condemned domestic violence but still offered reduced sentences to males who committed "honor" crimes against female family members. South Africa condemned sexual violence broadly, but failed to take adequate steps to protect girls in school from widespread sexual violence at the hands of teachers and students. Guatemala passed sophisticated domestic violence legislation but was content to let stand discriminatory labor law provisions that denied tens of thousands of female domestic workers equality under the labor code. Nigeria deplored the treatment of trafficked Nigerians abroad, but did little at home to stop domestic trafficking of Nigerians.

The international women's human rights movement functioned as the antidote to government complacency and lack of commitment. In every arena, women's rights activists challenged governments' cursory commitment to women's human rights. Toward the end of 2000, in part as a result of an ongoing campaign by women's rights and peace activists to highlight the particular insecurity of women in times of armed conflict, both the U.N. Security Council and the European Parliament adopted resolutions on women and peace- building, that explicitly called on governments to ensure that women participate both in peace negotiations and post-conflict reconstruction planning. Women's rights activists in Peru caused the government to modify its domestic violence law in January 2001 so that conciliation sessions between abusers and victims were no longer mandatory. At the United Nations World Conference Against Racism, Racial Discrimination, Xenophobia and Related Intolerance (WCAR), women's rights activists successfully worked to have the final document reflect how sex and race intersected to render women vulnerable to sexual violence in armed conflict and to trafficking, and reinforced women's right to transfer their nationality, on an equal basis with men, to their children. In mid-October 2001, activists rallied to press the Ethiopian government to lift a ban on the only women's rights organization advocating for women's rights in Ethiopia.

As governments responded to the September 11 attacks in the U.S., there was danger that a pattern of political expediency in governments' concern for women's rights would continue.

The following section describes key developments in women's human rights spanning a dozen countries in 2001. Our monitoring showed that violence and discrimination remained pervasive components of many women's lives. Governments both actively violated women's human rights and failed to prevent abuses by private actors.

HUMAN RIGHTS DEVELOPMENTS

As states and nongovernmental organizations (NGOs) throughout the world prepared for the WCAR, women's human rights activists explored the intersection between race, ethnicity, or religion and gender and the impact of this intersection on women's ability to enjoy human rights and fundamental freedoms. As some of the cases below illustrate, women often experienced violations of their rights based on their race or nationality as well as on their sex, gender, or sexual orientation. Women experienced racism and sexism not as separate events but as violations that were mutually reinforcing. For example, soldiers and noncombatants subjected women to sexual violence in armed conflict not just because they were women but also because they were women of a particular race, nationality, ethnicity, or religion. Indeed, armed factions often portrayed acts of sexual violence against women in conflict zones as attacks on the entire community, a community typically identified by a shared race, religion or ethnicity. Likewise, women were vulnerable to trafficking into forced labor, not just because they were poor and uneducated, but also because in many countries their poverty and illiteracy was a function of discrimination against women of a particular race, ethnicity, or religion. But the impact of this convergence of racism and sexism did not end with women experiencing trafficking-related human rights violations; it also affected how government officials, such as police and prosecutors, in both sending and receiving countries perceived them. Governments treated trafficked women as illegal immigrants at best, criminals at worst. As a result, governments denied many trafficked women any meaningful access to justice or financial redress.

Women experienced widespread violations of labor rights because of their race and gender. In some cases, states created such varied categories of workers that some women were unable to prove discrimination compared to women of different races. They were also unable to prove discrimination compared to men of the same race. For example, in the U.S. manufacturing sector, white women may be employed in the front offices as secretaries and receptionists while black men may be employed in the factory, making it impossible for black women to prove discrimination because the employer hires women and hires blacks. But states did not just violate women's rights in the public sphere; they also persisted in enforcing laws and condoning practices that discriminated against women in the private sphere. Governments defended these discriminatory laws and practices as essential to maintaining the integrity of religion and culture. Numerous governments, as in Morocco and Peru, continued to uphold laws that gave women inferior legal status within the family and that violated women's rights to change or retain their nationality. Some countries, such as Syria and Malaysia, violated women's right to enter into marriage with their free and full consent as well as their right to dissolve a marriage on an equal basis with men. The motivation behind these discriminatory laws appeared to be to keep women from marrying men of a different nationality, ethnicity, or religion.

WOMEN'S STATUS IN THE FAMILY

Laws and practices governing women's personal status—their legal capacity and role in the family—continued to deny women rights. While the type of discrimination varied from region to region, women throughout the world found that their relationship to a male relative or husband determined their rights.

Sub-Saharan African countries continued to use statutory and customary law to discriminate against women with regard to property ownership and inheritance. The explosive increase in numbers of young widows with children as a result of the Human Immunodeficiency Virus/Acquired Immunodeficiency Syndrome (HIV/AIDS) pandemic and wars in the region starkly exposed the critical link between denial of women's rights and extreme poverty. Zambia provided an example of a country devastated by HIV/AIDS and extreme poverty where the majority of women continued to live under customary law that denied them the right to inherit property from deceased male relatives. Although Zambia ratified the Convention on the Elimination of All Forms of Discrimination against Women (CEDAW) in the mid-1980s, and its constitution outlawed sex discrimination, the constitution itself gave primacy to customary law in matters of inheritance. War widows in Sierra Leone faced similar prohibitions in customary law. In Nigeria, Ghana, Kenya, Uganda, and Zimbabwe, statutory law reforms over the past twenty years gave women equal rights to inheritance but judges in these countries continued to apply customary law.

Personal status laws in Syria and Morocco, among other countries, continued to curtail women's rights entering into marriage, during marriage, and at the dissolution of marriage. In Syria, the minimum age for marriage was eighteen for boys and seventeen for girls. If a woman over the age of seventeen married without the consent of a male guardian, the guardian could demand the annulment of the marriage if the husband was not of the same social standing as the wife, and as long as the wife was not pregnant. Further, a Muslim Syrian woman could not marry a non-Muslim, while a Muslim man had absolute freedom to choose a spouse. Syrian law also assigned different rights and responsibilities for women and men during marriage. A wife's "disobedience" could lead to forfeiture of her husband's responsibility to provide support. A man could legally have up to four wives simultaneously, while a woman could have only one husband. Women did not have the same rights as men to end marriage: while the personal status law provided for the unilateral and unconditional right of a husband to effect divorce by repudiation (the repetition, before the wife and a witness, of "I divorce you" three times), a woman seeking divorce was required to go to court and prove that her husband had neglected his marital duties.

Women's rights activists in Morocco continued their long standing campaign to eliminate discriminatory provisions in the personal status code under which Moroccan women continued to be discriminated against with respect to legal standing, marriage, divorce, child custody, and inheritance. It appeared that, as was the case with the reform of the personal status code in 1993, the king would be the final arbiter on women's rights. On March 5, 2001, the King Mohammed VI formed a royal commission comprising religious scholars, judges, sociologists, and doctors to consider amending the code. In a speech on April 27, 2001, he reiterated his commitment to improving the status of Moroccan women and eliminating discrimination against them according to the Islamic *sharia* and the values of justice and equality. An advisory committee appointed by Prime Minister El-Yousoufi had failed to act on the issue during 2000.

Women's rights activists welcomed a long-overdue development in Brazil: in August 2001, the Brazilian Congress adopted a law that, after twenty-six years of protest and debate, removed the most discriminatory provisions of the 1916 civil code. Most significant, the new code gave both women and men equal authority in the family, abolishing paternal power, the legal concept that men had total control over decision-making in the family. Elsewhere in Latin America, however, laws governing women's roles in the family reflected entrenched beliefs within society that women are subordinate to men. The Chilean civil code continued to grant husbands control over household decisions and their wives' property. In countries such as Argentina, Mexico, and Colombia, the civil codes established lower marriage ages for girls (sixteen, fourteen, and twelve, respectively) than for boys, while women in Venezuela could not remarry until ten months after divorce or annulment, unless they proved they were not pregnant.

A serious consequence of limitations on women's equality in their private lives, such as whom to marry, was loss of citizenship for themselves and/or their children. Nationality laws in such disparate countries as Egypt, Sri Lanka, and Bangladesh denied women the right to transfer citizenship to their children. These laws, designed in part to curtail immigration and thus maintain the purity, loyalty, and cohesion of the nation, demonstrated the way in which discrimination on the bases of national origin and gender intersected to further entrench women's subordinate status in the family and in society. Despite years of protest and lawsuits by women's human rights groups, in May 2001 the State Consultative Council of Egypt dismissed the recent parliamentary plea to amend the 1975 Nationality Law. Under this law, which contradicted the constitution, an Egyptian man could automatically transfer his nationality to his children while an Egyptian woman could do so only under limited circumstances: when the child was born in Egypt to a stateless father or to a father of unknown nationality, or when the child's relationship to his or her father could not be legally established. The Egyptian Center for Women's Rights estimated that thousands of women married to foreigners and as many as one million children continued to suffer discrimination under this law.

LABOR RIGHTS

Governments continued to fail to protect women's labor rights through enacting and enforcing laws outlawing discrimination. In many countries, women faced severe discrimination in employment practices and violence in the workplace, including sexual harassment, with little or no protection. Afghanistan, Guatemala, and South Africa, among many countries, provided examples involving work and working conditions for women in factories, homes, and on farms.

In Taliban-controlled Afghanistan, women were not permitted to work outside the home, unless they were healthcare professionals, or widows. The latter, estimated to number 40,000 in Kabul alone, were mostly unable to obtain paid employment and were reduced to begging to support their families and faced constant harassment and violence at the hands of the religious police.

In Guatemala, where domestic workers number tens of thousands and domestic labor is one of the principal forms of employment for poor, especially indigenous women, the adoption of specific legislation to protect domestic workers remained a low priority for the government. Under threat of losing its beneficiary status under the U.S. Generalized System of Preferences (GSP) trade act, Guatemala reformed its labor code with respect to freedom of association during 2001, to bring it more in line with International Labor Organization conventions. However, the government missed an opportunity to remedy the unequal treatment of domestic workers who, under the current labor code, suffered discrimination as a group: the code denied domestic workers the right to the eight-hour workday and the minimum wage, limited their right to national holidays and rest, and based access to healthcare on employer largesse. The author of the Guatemalan labor code candidly acknowledged to Human Rights Watch that gender stereotypes and perceptions about the role of domestic workers in the family, as well as racist attitudes toward indigenous women, influenced the low priority attached to their rights when drafting Guatemala's labor legislation. In its export-processing sector (maquiladoras, assembly plants for export goods), Guatemala also systematically denied women workers the enjoyment of full labor rights, continuing to discriminate against women on the grounds of reproductive status. Some factories required job seekers to state whether they were pregnant, and denied full benefits to employees who became pregnant post-hire. Though aware of the problem, the government took no significant action to combating such sex discrimination in the maquiladora sector.

In the United States, live-in domestic workers remained explicitly excluded from protection under the National Labor Relations Act, the Occupational Safety and Health Act, and the overtime provisions of the Fair Labor Standards Act. The exclusion of domestic workers from basic U.S. labor rights and protections was based on gender stereotypes and perceptions about the role of domestic workers in the family, and had a disproportionate impact on women, thus constituting disparate impact sex discrimination.

Around the world, women perform farm work. In post-apartheid South Africa, the government made efforts to overcome the legacy of apartheid in commercial farming areas: new laws provided full labor rights for farmworkers, including women. Yet, in practice, racist and sexist attitudes remained pervasive on farms: women farmworkers were the lowest paid, had the fewest benefits, were often forced to become squatters, and were targets of harassment and violence by farmers and farmworkers alike. In 2001, Human Rights Watch found that the situation of women on South African farms was precarious: personal relationships were divided on racial and patriarchal lines, with women subjected to discrimination, violence, and abuse. Women farmworkers were more likely to be seasonal or temporary workers than men, and usually did more menial, less remunerative work, such as planting or harvesting. Employers viewed women's labor as a supplement to men's labor even in situations in which women did the same types of jobs and worked as long hours as men. Women's dependence on men for access to housing rendered them vulnerable to abuse within the workplace and home, and employers denied many women farmworkers statutory maternity benefits.

TRAFFICKING

Corrupt officials, complicit state authorities, xenophobia, and a profound lack of political will coalesced to guarantee impunity for traffickers and to exacerbate the suffering of their victims worldwide. Traffickers moved their human victims around the globe, held them in debt bondage, seized their passports, and threatened them or their families with harm if they resisted. Ever-tightening border controls and the lack of legal opportunities to migrate often forced women to turn to traffickers, increasing their vulnerability to abuse. Sold as chattel and forced to work for little or no pay, trafficked persons feared local law enforcement authorities, perceiving, in many cases correctly, that an appeal to police would end in prosecution and deportation, rather than protection. Trafficking victims from ethnic minority communities faced an even more daunting situation, including at its worst xenophobic violence, racism, and, in the case of trafficked hilltribe women and girls in Thailand, statelessness. States continued to fail to combat trafficking. The token prosecutions of traffickers merely proved the rule.

One positive development brightened the picture slightly in 2001. The opening for signature of the Protocol to Prevent, Suppress, and Punish Trafficking in Persons, Especially Women and Children, Supplementing the United Nations Convention against Transnational Organized Crime, marked a small step forward in the battle against trafficking. By late November, one hundred countries had signed the protocol, committing their governments to punish traffickers and protect the human rights of trafficking victims, but only three had ratified it (forty ratifications are needed for it to come into force).

Lackluster anti-trafficking efforts in Nigeria, Bosnia and Herzegovina, Colombia, Japan, and Israel illustrated the disheartening trends, however. Even countries that ratified the protocol, such as Nigeria, failed to adhere to those commitments. Women's organizations protested that Nigeria fell far short in the effective investigation and prosecution of individuals engaged in trafficking of women and children. The 2001 U.S. State Department report on trafficking in persons cited widespread corruption among law enforcement officials as a major stumbling block to combating trafficking in Nigeria. Trafficking victims alleged that some Nigerian immigration officials colluded with traffickers, assisting them in forging documents and bringing persons across borders, and accused others of actively engaging in trafficking. Nigerian citizens, mostly women and children, facing stark conditions and oppressive poverty, chose to migrate but found themselves preyed upon by traffickers who transported them to Lagos and other cities and forced them into domestic servitude or prostitution. Traffickers seized all wages to pay off the trafficking victims' debt. In addition to trafficking within Nigeria, traffickers also sent Nigerian citizens to other West African countries to work on farm plantations or as domestic workers.

Other signatories to the protocol showed little progress in combating trafficking in women. Bosnia and Herzegovina failed signally to confront endemic corruption and state complicity in trafficking. Traffickers and employers held women trafficked from Ukraine, Moldova, and Romania in debt bondage in brothels throughout Bosnia and Herzegovina. Trafficked women reported to the United Nations (U.N.) that their employers sometimes forced them to provide free sexual services to local police officers. In a handful of cases, Bosnian police actively participated in trafficking, either as part owners or employees of the clubs, or by procuring false documents for traffickers. Trafficking victims, terrified of retaliation by traffickers, feared reporting the abuse to law enforcement authorities. Eager to fan that fear, employers routinely claimed that they counted police officers among their friends.

The U.N. also stood accused of complicity in trafficking when allegations emerged that International Police Task Force (IPTF) officers—United Nations police charged with monitoring local Bosnian police—had gone to brothels as clients and, in a small number of cases, purchased women for personal use. In December 2000, the U.N. repatriated an American IPTF officer after learning that he had purchased a Moldovan woman from a Sarajevo brothel for 6,000 Deutschmarks (U.S. $2,777). In June 2001, Jacques Klein, special representative of the U.N. secretary-general for the United Nations mission in Bosnia and Herzegovina, defended the anti-trafficking measures implemented by the mission, declaring that the U.N. mission had a zero-tolerance policy for sexual or other serious misconduct.

The justice system within Bosnia and Herzegovina rarely delivered convictions of traffickers in the cases brought to court. U.N. officials and NGO leaders blamed inadequate laws and a lack of political will on the part of the Bosnian government for the failure to gain convictions of traffickers. Most often, trafficking victims, not traffickers, faced prosecution, detention, and fines for illegal entry into the state, document fraud, and failure to procure a work permit—all administrative violations that directly arose from their status as trafficking victims. In March 1999, the U.N. stepped in to facilitate voluntary repatriation of trafficking victims through an International Organization for Migration (IOM) program, but some trafficked women fell through the cracks of the screening process, serving thirty-day sentences in Bosnian prisons before facing deportation. By October 2001, the IOM had completed over three hundred voluntary repatriations of victims ranging in age from thirteen to thirty-six years old.

Government authorities in Colombia, another signatory to the protocol, estimated that between two and ten women were trafficked from Colombia each day, the vast majority of them to Europe. In July 2001, new anti-trafficking legislation went into effect; however, the legislation only treated trafficking victims as those who had been trafficked outside of Colombia for forced prostitution, failing to protect persons trafficked into other forms of forced labor. In addition, NGOs lamented that the law established prison sentences of just four to six years for traffickers. In mid-2001, the Colombian Congress began debating an anti-trafficking bill that would enhance the definition of trafficking, the range of victims protected, and the severity of the penalties for the crime. Experts warned that passage of the bill could take up to a year and a half. Colombia also failed to implement a witness protection system to ensure the safety of victims who agreed to cooperate in the prosecution of traffickers.

In Japan, women trafficked into the sex industry accounted for a significant proportion of the estimated 260,000 undocumented migrants. Yet, the government, a non-signatory to the protocol, took no concrete steps to prevent trafficking and continued to treat trafficked women as illegal immigrants, detaining them and failing to provide them human rights protections. The minority of trafficked women who managed to escape from their employers with the help of NGOs or their embassies found themselves placed in detention and then deported as illegal aliens, unable to seek redress or sue for compensation.

Thailand continued to be a major country of origin for women trafficked into the Japan's so-called snack bars. Discrimination against minority groups in Thailand heightened some women's vulnerability to trafficking. Hilltribe women, denied citizenship and rights by the Thai government, suffered from extremely limited educational and employment opportunities. Since births among the hilltribe communities were often not registered, and because hilltribe people did not possess official Thai citizenship, hilltribe people were left effectively stateless. The Thai government frequently refused to allow hilltribe women trafficked to Japan to return to Thailand, denying that they qualified as Thai citizens.

Israel, meanwhile, failed to provide even minimal human rights protections for persons trafficked into its territory for domestic servitude, agricultural labor, forced prostitution, and construction work despite the passage of an anti-trafficking law in 2000. Trafficking victims feared cooperating with law enforcement officials and had no incentive to do so, absent witness protection, shelter, and relief from deportation, or legal assistance. State complicity and corruption also played a role in trafficking into Israel. In March 2001, the Hotline for Migrant Workers, an Israeli NGO working with trafficking victims, reported to the United Nations Human Rights Commission that six trafficking cases involved policemen: in one case a policeman stood accused of managing a brothel; in four cases police officers tipped brothel owners off on upcoming raids; and in another case a policeman faced charges of selling a trafficked woman to another brothel owner after arresting her. Israeli authorities continued to treat trafficked women as criminals rather than victims, and failed to prosecute those responsible for trafficking. The U.S. State Department report on trafficking in persons ranked Israel in the lowest tier of countries for failing to combat trafficking.

WOMEN IN CONFLICT AND REFUGEES

Women continued to face abuses associated with armed conflict and civil unrest. Rape and sexual assault, in particular, were employed to achieve specific military or political objectives. When women sought refuge in other countries, they continued to experience sexual and other forms of physical violence in and around refugee camps. While acts of sexual violence in the context of armed conflict were recognized internationally as a war crime and a crime against humanity, perpetrators were rarely brought to justice. Moreover, in armed conflicts, women suffered from a broad array of abuses not limited to violence by combatants.

In the former Yugoslavia, Indonesia, the Democratic Republic of Congo, Guinea, and Tanzania among other states, women continuously suffered conflict-related abuse or its sequelae, and waited in vain for justice.

As of November 2001, the International Criminal Tribunal for the former Yugoslavia (ICTY) had failed to bring even a single indictment on rape as a war crime in Kosovo. Women's access to justice also suffered with regard to post-conflict violence, which continued unabated. In October 2000, the Organization for Security and Cooperation in Europe (OSCE) released a scathing report detailing how women victims of sexual violence in Kosovo confronted discrimination, intimidation, and bias in the criminal justice system. A follow-up report issued by the OSCE in early 2001 indicated that the Kosovo judicial system had failed to remedy those ongoing problems and continued to handle sexual assault cases "superficially . . . illustrating disregard for the serious nature of such cases for both the alleged victim and the defendant." The OSCE reported that the majority of rape and sexual assault cases involved juvenile victims.

In Indonesia, despite substantial evidence of the frequent occurrence of sexual violence in the conflict in Aceh between Indonesian security forces and the armed insurgent Free Aceh Movement (GAM), very few cases were reported to the authorities—and one particularly notorious case showed why. The case involved five women from South Aceh district who reported being sexually abused by members of the Indonesian paramilitary police, Brimob, in February 2001. Human rights NGOs brought the women to Banda Aceh, the provincial capital, where the case and their identities were widely publicized. Taken into police custody for questioning, the women publicly recanted their stories, instead saying it was members of the armed insurgency, GAM, who had abducted them and forced them to say that Brimob had assaulted them. The lack of protection for victims of sexual violence and NGOs' inexperience in handling such a case in a highly politicized context made the women into pawns of the police. The end result was that the relevant human rights violations remained uninvestigated and unpunished.

In an ongoing conflict largely ignored by the international community, the Congolese Rally for Democracy (RCD) and its Rwandan allies, along with Hutu rebels and Mai Mai forces, continued to abduct women and commit sexual violence against them in eastern Congo. In 2001, Human Rights Watch and other organizations found that these groups had raped thousands of women and girls of all ethnic groups. In many cases, Mai Mai and Rwandan Hutu rebels raped women, often in front of their husbands, families, or community as a public humiliation and demonstration of power, when families fled an area under control by a certain group, and moved into what was perceived as the "enemy's" territory. Mai Mai and Rwandan Hutu rebels took women and girls hostage and kept them as "wives" for several weeks or months, releasing them after capturing other women. The health consequences of such sexual violence were enormous. Many women died as a result of the rapes, and unknown numbers contracted HIV/AIDS, all aggravated by the lack of accessible medical and counseling services.

Even after fleeing conflict in search of sanctuary from violence, women refugees frequently found that there was no meaningful refuge—they simply escaped violence in conflict to be confronted by different types of violence in refugee camps or en route to refugee camps. Guinean security personnel and civilians, during the relocation of some 60,000 Liberian and Sierra Leonese refugees from the border to the interior of the country, regularly harassed refugees. Checkpoints along the roads were particularly dangerous places, where Guinean security forces often subjected refugees to arbitrary strip searches, beatings, sexual assault, and extortion—while allegedly screening refugees for the presence of rebel marks.

Refugee camps in Tanzania continued to showcase some of the dangers facing women in flight, especially refugees from Burundi. Local Tanzanians and other refugees physically and sexually assaulted women refugees with impunity, both inside and outside refugee camps. The United Nations High Commissioner for Refugees (UNHCR) and aid agencies working with the camps sought to raise awareness among refugees about sexual and gender-based violence, and provided counseling to victims, but UNHCR reported a continuing high evidence of domestic violence, recording some 1,739 cases in Tanzania's Burundian refugee camps between April and December 2000. UNHCR said some Tanzanian authorities were prosecuting some rape cases. Generally, however, the Tanzanian justice system failed to provide an effective remedy for victims of sexual and domestic violence in the camps, such cases often being seen by the authorities as "private" domestic matters beyond the scope of state intervention.

VIOLENCE AGAINST WOMEN

Violence and the threat of violence were ever-present in women's public and private lives. In situations of political upheaval, state custody, domestic contexts, and other situations involving private actors and NGOs, women's physical and sexual integrity was at risk in all regions. Zimbabwe, the United States, Uzbekistan, Turkey, and Jordan provided stark examples.

Since it came to power in 1980, the Zimbabwe government had promised to enact land reform measures to redistribute to black Zimbabweans lands taken under white ownership during colonial rule, though without making significant progress before the end of 2000. In 2001, however, groups of ruling party supporters and reputed veterans of the war against colonial rule seized control of many white-owned farms by force in what the government described as a "spontaneous and popular uprising." Many black farmworkers, as well as white farmworkers and their families, were assaulted in the process. Some were killed. Many women on farms and in rural areas were raped or sexually assaulted with impunity. Victims reported to Human Rights Watch that they could obtain no redress from the police who declined to intervene in rape cases they saw occurring within a political context.

In the U.S., the California State Legislature held hearings in January 2001 to address reports of continuing mental, physical, and sexual abuse, as well as medical neglect in the state's women's prisons. The hearings were prompted by the deaths of nine women at the Central California Women's Facility within a two-month period at the end of 2000. Initially, the California Department of Corrections attributed some of the deaths to prisoners taking tainted drugs, but autopsies discounted that. The state authorities said they would investigate the deaths, but the findings were not available at this writing.

Legislators also expressed concern over reports that some women inmates who requested medical attention prior to their deaths did not receive immediate attention. In one case, the cellmates of a deceased prisoner alleged that corrections officers had mocked the dying woman's pleas for assistance shortly before she died. There was particular concern that medical technical assistants (MTAs), prison guards with minimal medical training, were responsible for determining whether women inmates should see medical staff. After the State Legislature hearings, a new bill was introduced to remove MTAs from decision-making on women inmate's health care access to clinicians; it was still under consideration in November.

In Uzbekistan, instead of protecting women from domestic violence, the state enforced a policy of "reconciliation" aimed at limiting the number of divorces. Local officials and community leaders coerced women into remaining with abusive partners, often thwarting their efforts to escape the violence by leaving their marriages. In some cases, local authorities refused to provide documents to women attempting to file for divorce. More frequently, officials and medical doctors sought to convince the women to return to violent spouses in order to "save the family," and be "better wives." Local law enforcement only rarely completed police reports of women's complaints or investigated cases of domestic violence, more often placing families on a list for periodic police visits that did little to protect women from ongoing abuse. Under article 103 of the Criminal Code for "driving a person to suicide," authorities pursued charges against perpetrators of violence against women only if the woman committed suicide. NGOs in Uzbekistan attempted to provide hotlines and services to victims of domestic violence, but their resources were limited, and their services rarely reached beyond urban areas.

In Turkey, in both urban and rural areas, family members murder an estimated two hundred girls and women in the name of honor each year. In 2001, judges trying "honor" killing cases often reduced the penalties for perpetrators, holding that the victim had "provoked" the murder by transgressing codes of conduct imposed on women by society. Older relatives sometimes arranged for underage boys in the family to commit "honor" murders because penalties for minors were lower, in some cases as little as two years in prison. Domestic violence was also pervasive in Turkey; women's human rights activists condemned the authorities' lack of response to domestic violence and called for increased government funding to establish shelters and provide legal services. The government, however, appeared intent to reinstate virginity tests for women students wishing to become nurses and medical technicians. In July, Minister of Health Osman Durmus issued a directive to circumvent a 1999 ban on virginity tests and permit girls to be examined with parental permission and a judge's order if the nursing school suspected them of "immoral behavior." Local women's rights groups condemned the directive, saying schools would use it to expel girls that they wanted to dismiss for other reasons. Amid the outcry provoked by the decree, Durmus denied that he had authorized the reinstatement of the exams but the directive was not rescinded.

In Jordan, despite an extensive grassroots public awareness and signature campaign since 1999 run by the Jordanian National Committee to Eliminate the So-called Crimes of Honor, the government failed to repeal the law that allowed for a reduced sentence for the perpetrators of "honor crimes." In 2001, at least nineteen women were reported killed in the name of honor by November, and the government had still to make good on its promise to open a shelter for women whose families threatened their lives on grounds of "honor," and continued to hold threatened women in corrections facilities.

THE ROLE OF THE INTERNATIONAL COMMUNITY

The war in Afghanistan mobilized international attention to women's human rights in that country, with the U.S. government and its allies giving women's rights a prominent place in the propaganda war against the Taliban. In 2001, however, there seemed to be a disconnect between the U.S. and the international community's rhetorical commitment to equality and a willingness to adopt and implement policies that fully integrated attention to women's human rights. In 2001, U.N.-sponsored meetings addressed critical issues such as the gender dimensions of racism, gender-based persecution as grounds for asylum, and an international protocol on the collection of forensic evidence in cases of sexual violence. At the same time, the U.S. and the European Union took steps on trafficking, international treaty ratification, funding for women's health, and trade that marginalized or ignored women's human rights. Women's rights activists found that many of these steps were tentative and inconsistent, and hoped that the international community's concern for women's rights in Afghanistan would be long-lasting and would result in stepped-up efforts to recognize women's human rights violations and curtail them also in other parts of the world.

United Nations

The WCAR, held in Durban, South Africa, from August 31 through September 8, 2001, survived a lengthy preparatory process that was dominated by strong disagreements with governments over issues such as reparations for slavery, the Israel/Palestine question, caste and racism, and the inclusion of gender-related issues.

As part of the WCAR preparatory process, the U.N. Division for the Advancement of Women (DAW) convened a meeting in November 2000, in Zagreb, Croatia, at which women's rights experts analyzed the intersectionality of gender and race. However, the document produced at this meeting, because it was not the result of an official regional preparatory meeting, was then left out of the compilation documents the conference secretariat prepared.

Successfully, women's rights groups advocated for the inclusion of clear references in the WCAR's official declaration and plan of action to the impact of racism and related intolerance on women belonging to racial and other minority communities and to the need for governments to address gender-specific concerns such as protecting women from sexual violence in ethnic-based armed conflicts.

Women's rights activists also successfully lobbied for the inclusion of a call to governments to allow women to confer nationality on their children and spouses, on the same basis as men.

The actual value of the WCAR, and the extent to which governments will honor the commitments they made there, remained to be seen. The U.N. had an important follow-up role to play and it was hoped that the of Committee on the Elimination of All Forms of Discrimination against Women (CEDAW Committee) would develop a basis for governments to report regularly on their efforts to address the confluence of racism and sexism.

The role of the CEDAW Committee expanded in 2001, as the Optional Protocol to the Convention on the Elimination of All Forms of Discrimination against Women came into force on December 22, 2000, enabling the committee to receive and consider complaints from individuals or groups within its jurisdiction. As of November 2001, the committee had yet to explore any complaints initiated under the protocol.

Despite the WCAR's explicit acknowledgement that women are targeted for sexual violence in armed conflicts on the basis of their ethnic or related identities, the ad hoc international criminal tribunals for the former Yugoslavia (ICTY) and Rwanda (ICTR) continued to compile a mixed record on investigations and prosecutions of crimes of sexual violence that occurred in the to which they relate.

On February 22, 2001, the ICTY issued a landmark verdict for rape, torture, and sexual enslavement, holding that rape and enslavement rose to the level of crimes against humanity in the Bosnian town of Foca. Sixteen victims of rape testified during the trial, describing months of sexual slavery and multiple gang rapes. The case marked the first time that an international tribunal charged defendants solely for crimes of sexual violence against women and girls and the first time that the ICTY convicted a defendant for rape as a crime against humanity. Women's human rights experts hailed the decision, while expressing concern for the safety and well-being of the witnesses who testified in the trial, as three of those accused in the case had not been apprehended.

In January 2001, Biljana Plavsic, a former member of the Presidency of the Serbian republic whose indictment was sealed, surrendered to the ICTY. The ICTY immediately unsealed the indictment revealing that Plavsic would face charges of command responsibility for war crimes and crimes against humanity, including acts of sexual violence. With the former Bosnian Serb leaders Radovan Karadzic and Ratko Mladic still at large, Plavsic became the highest-ranking Serbian official in the dock on charges that included sexual violence.

In June 2001, the former Serbian President, Slobodan Milosevic, was arrested and extradited to The Hague to face trial before the ICTY for crimes committed during the conflicts in Bosnia-Herzegovina, Croatia, and Kosovo. Milosevic was charged with responsibility for crimes of genocide, deportation, and persecution, either by giving direct orders or through omission as effective commander of Serbian police, army and paramilitary groups. He was also indicted in relation to sexual assaults inflicted by Serbian forces on Kosovo Albanian women, although initially the indictment failed to include these gender-specific crimes.

The Rwanda tribunal's ineffective record of prosecuting rape and other sexual violence continued in 2001. This failure to address effectively sexual violence was a result of, among other things, lack of staff awareness about sexual violence, poor training on investigating and prosecuting crimes of sexual violence, and a general attitude of according low priority to sexual violence offences.

Since the landmark Akayesu verdict in 1998, the first and only case as yet in which rape was found to be an act of genocide, the ICTR has brought several more indictments for rape. In some, however, the rape count was only added belatedly, typically when witnesses alluded to rape and sexual violence while testifying in court, raising serious questions about the quality of investigations and decision-making on drafting indictments. In February, the tribunal's judges rejected a belated prosecution attempt to add sexual violence charges against the three defendants facing genocide and crimes against humanity charges in the Cyangugu case. Prosecutors did not ask to amend the indictment but nevertheless to bring in rape testimony, arguing that the Akayesu precedent holding that rape was a part of genocide should suffice.

Women fleeing conflict may have a stronger claim to asylum if they also have a well-founded fear of gender-based persecution. Consequently, as part of the Global Consultations marking the fiftieth anniversary of the 1951 Convention Relating to the Status of Refugees, UNHCR convened a roundtable of experts to examine the issue of gender-based persecution and made recommendations on the interpretation of the refugee convention.

Meanwhile, the World Health Organization convened a group of forensic experts to begin drafting a standard protocol for the collection of evidence in cases of sexual violence. The meeting, held in June in Geneva, ended with a plan for the drafting and field-testing of the protocol in the next year. If successful, the protocol will be a tool for documenting sexual violence in countries in which such evidence is limited to the examiner's evaluations of the victim's virginity.

Unites States

Nearly a year into the presidency of George W. Bush, the U.S. program on women's human rights remained ill-defined, notwithstanding high level public condemnation of the Taliban for their abuse of women's rights in Afghanistan. The issue of women's rights did not feature visibly in any of Secretary of State Colin L. Powell's foreign visits but, to its credit, the Bush administration retained the position of senior coordinator for international women's issues, an office that in the past had played a critical role in the coordination and spearheading of women's human rights issues at the State Department. At this writing, although no appointment had been announced to head the office, U.S. women's rights activists remained hopeful that the office would be headed by an individual with broad, demonstrable expertise in the women's human rights movement.

President Bush initiated his term with an assault on freedom of expression in the context of global women's health. One of his first acts as president was to reinstate a U.S. government policy, known variously as the "Mexico City Policy" and the "global gag rule," which required international women's health advocates to sacrifice their right to free expression in exchange for U.S. funding. The restriction, first adopted by President Reagan in 1984, prohibited international family planning NGOs from receiving U.S. funds if, with their own separate funds, they engaged in legal abortion-related activities. The Bush administration's argument that U.S. taxpayers' money should not be used to pay for abortion was disingenuous, given that since 1973, U.S. law had banned the use of U.S. funds for abortions in foreign countries.

The Bush administration featured trafficking as an important component of its women's human rights program. In July 2000, under the terms of the Victims of Trafficking and Violence Protection Act of 2000, the U.S. State Department released its first annual trafficking report, evaluating the performance of eighty-two countries, putting each in one of three categories depending on how its domestic efforts met the legislation's minimum standards for the elimination of trafficking. The report was notable for its candid criticism of a number of allies. Unfortunately, it focused primarily on trafficking for prostitution, to the exclusion of trafficking into other forms of forced labor; paid scant attention to the role of state complicity in trafficking; failed to criticize instances in which countries summarily arrested or deported trafficking victims; and failed to note and evaluate in-country services for trafficking victims. In October, the State Department named a head for the Office to Monitor and Combat Trafficking, whose establishment was called for by the 2000 legislation.

While the Bush administration seemed to acknowledge the connection between women's limited economic opportunities and their vulnerability to trafficking, it nevertheless failed to make use of international mechanisms that strengthen respect for women workers' rights, such as the labor rights side agreement to the North American Free Trade Agreement (NAFTA). In July 1997, the U.S. National Administrative Office (U.S. NAO), the office charged with hearing complaints against Mexico and Canada under NAFTA, accepted for review a case co-sponsored by Human Rights Watch against Mexico that alleged Mexican government failure to enforce its labor code to curtail widespread pregnancy-based discrimination in export-processing factories (maquiladoras) along the U.S.-Mexico border. In January 1998, the U.S. NAO found, among other things, that the Mexican constitution and labor code prohibited discrimination based on sex and that there were contradictory interpretations of Mexico's law regarding the illegality of pregnancy testing. In October 1998, various programs, conferences, and meetings were held as part of a ministerial consultation agreement that Mexico, the United States, and Canada had signed, but these had little effect. In November 2001, however the final U.S. NAO report was more than two years overdue, underscoring the inadequacy of the mechanism for addressing women's labor rights violations.

The U.S. Congress also appeared in November about to squander an opportunity to support women's labor rights, in connection with renewal of the Generalized System of Preferences (GSP), a trade regime that allows over one hundred beneficiary countries to export certain goods to the U.S. paying little or no tariffs. Since 1984, this has conditioned eligibility on respect for what the U.S. has termed "internationally recognized worker rights," including freedom of association; the right to organize and bargain collectively; the prohibition on the use of forced or compulsory labor; a minimum age for employment of children; and acceptable conditions of work with respect to minimum wages, hours of work, and occupational safety and health—but not freedom from discrimination. The renewal of GSP by the House of Representatives offered a real but missed opportunity to address this significant omission, though at the time of this writing it was hoped that the Senate, under pressure from women's and labor rights activists, would include in the law language prohibiting sex discrimination.

The year ended with the U.S. Senate having failed to ratify CEDAW. Advocates of the convention urged the new chair of the Senate Foreign Relations Committee, Senator Joseph Biden, to schedule a hearing and vote on the treaty, but it appeared unlikely at the time of this writing that he would do so.

European Union

In Europe, racism and xenophobia led to increased hostility and violence against asylum seekers, refugees, trafficking victims and migrants, male and female alike. Women seeking to migrate to Europe, particularly women from developing countries, were denied virtually any legal means of doing so and as a result became easy prey for traffickers. The "fortress Europe" approach to immigration led some women migrants into the hands of traffickers, trapping them in debt bondage, forced labor, and abuse. Trafficking for forced prostitution received disproportionate attention in rhetoric and policy in Europe, while trafficking into other forms of forced labor, including domestic servitude, flourished in near obscurity. According to a report by a coalition of German NGOs known as KOK that combats trafficking in human beings, increasing numbers of women from countries in Africa, Asia, Latin America, and Eastern Europe worked in Germany as nannies, domestic servants, cleaners, maids, and nurses. Some migrants ended up in debt bondage, physical and sexual violence, and, in some cases, slavery-like conditions.

Meanwhile, the European Union funded anti-trafficking grants programs that plowed money into conferences, research, and meetings, neglecting desperately needed programs to support victims of trafficking and to train police in human rights related to trafficking. In addition, much of the funding allocated in 2001 under the Stop anti-trafficking program, a funding program designed to finance anti-trafficking efforts, flowed to government ministries and universities: of the eighteen programs funded, only four grants involved NGOs. In addition, almost all of the programs funded focused on women and children trafficked from the former Soviet Union and Eastern Europe, largely ignoring the plight of victims from the global south.

The European Commission allocated 20 million euros (U.S. $17.2 million) over three years through the Daphne Programme for grants to NGOs and public institutions working to prevent violence against women, children, and young people in Europe, countries hoping to gain admission to the European Union, and members of the European Free Trade Association.

On the policy side of the trafficking debate, the European Union acknowledged the growing phenomenon of trafficking into the European Union. The Commission outlined "a comprehensive European strategy" on trafficking in women, including prevention programs, efforts to criminalize trafficking in all of the member states, support for victims, and cooperation with countries of origin. Unfortunately, much of the policy flowing from Brussels continued to center around a law enforcement approach to trafficking, rather than integrating the human rights of victims. States were fining airlines that transported migrants and asylum seekers and implementing increasingly restrictive visa regimes. The obstacles to travel translated into higher debts for trafficked persons in countries of destination and higher profits for traffickers, who simply increased the fees demanded of migrants. In December 2000, the Commission proposed a Council Framework decision, an agreement among the countries of the European Union to harmonize their legislation, on combating trafficking in human beings that focused almost entirely on harmonization of criminal penalties, criminalization of trafficking, and adoption of a common definition of the crime. Recommendations made by the European Parliament and a coalition of NGOs to remedy the lack of human rights protections in the document went unheeded.

Council of Europe

The Council of Europe, under the auspices of the "Police and Human Rights— Beyond 2000" program, published a series of pamphlets and training manuals on human rights, including one, the "VIP Guide," on violence against women. The guide, launched on the web and in book form at a conference in December 2000, included training modules on trafficking, domestic violence, rape, stalking, "honor killings," and sexual harassment. While the guide provided excellent basic information on these violations of women's human rights, the other pamphlets and training modules prepared under the program failed to integrate women's human rights concerns adequately. For example, almost all of the documents mentioned domestic violence at least in passing but failed to include other forms of violence against women.

Organization for Security and Cooperation in Europe (OSCE)

In February 2001, the Office for Democratic Institutions and Human Rights (ODIHR), which is charged with implementing and funding human rights programs of the OSCE, announced the establishment of an anti-trafficking project fund financed by the United Kingdom. The OSCE continued its leadership role within the Stability Pact for South Eastern Europe, pressing participating countries to adopt national plans of action and to take concrete steps to combat trafficking. But many NGOs in the region remained skeptical about the political will of governments to implement the elaborately crafted action plans, fearing another onslaught of rhetoric without action.

Relevant Human Rights Watch Reports:

Afghanistan: Humanity Denied: Systematic Violation of Women's Rights in Afghanistan, 10/01

South Africa: Unequal Protection: The State Response to Violent Crime on South African Farms, 8/01

SPECIAL ISSUES AND CAMPAIGNS

Internally displaced family in Sierra Leone.

ACADEMIC FREEDOM

Extremism thrived in countries where assaults on academic freedom fostered a climate of ignorance and intolerance. In Afghanistan, the ruling Taliban's first actions were to shut down most higher education and ban women and girls from attending school. But in less extreme forms, governments around the world justified violations of human rights by casting all critical thought as an attack on public morality, national security, or cultural purity. In the wake of the attacks on New York City and Washington, several academics in the United States and Canada came under official or public pressure for questioning various aspects of their governments' past or projected policies. With another international conflict simmering, violations of academic freedom were likely to increase around the globe.

Even before September 11, 2001, academic groups were growing increasingly aware of the importance of international cooperation and coordination in support of their colleagues' freedom. The international Network on Education and Academic Rights (NEAR) was created in June 2001 to serve as a repository and clearinghouse for information about academic freedom cases. With initial funding from UNESCO, the network promised to expand on the existing contact and cooperation between academics and academic groups. As the network's name indicated, NEAR's understanding of academic freedom embraced not just the civil and political rights of scholars and their students, but also the social, economic, and cultural rights associated with the fundamental human right to education.

The right to education and academic freedom suffered numerous violations around the globe. Oppressive governments punished academics for exercising their right and responsibility to question and criticize their societies. In a troubling development, several armed opposition groups also resorted to this method of silencing their critics. Ideological controls over the nature and content of academic material were apparent around the world, and students who in many countries served as leaders in social development were targeted and persecuted. Many governments also blocked the access of vulnerable and disenfranchised segments of their population to education through their acts or omissions.

REPRESSION OF ACADEMICS

The Chinese government's detention of several academics was the year's most publicized example of an assault on academic freedom and the subject of an international campaign by Human Rights Watch. The arrest, conviction, and eventual release of several of the detained scholars, and the broad international support on their behalf, demonstrated both the importance of concerted action in defending academic freedom and the fragility of this right. An undetermined number of scholars were detained during this crackdown; while some were released after a few days, others remained in detention for over a year. Those released all said that they had been warned by the Chinese government against publicizing the details of their incarceration.

Xu Zerong, a political scientist at the Guangdong Academy of Social Sciences as well as at Zhongshan University, was detained on June 24, 2000, and formally arrested a month later. Others seized were Li Shaomin, a business professor at the City University of Hong Kong detained on February 11, 2001, and Gao Zhan, a sociologist pursuing her research at the American University in Washington, D.C., detained on February 11, 2001. Several of the detainees studied at universities in the United States or the United Kingdom and resided outside China for significant lengths of time. Li, a naturalized U.S. citizen, studied at Harvard and Princeton Universities, in the U.S.; Gao, a resident of the U.S., studied at Syracuse University and worked at American University, both also in the U.S., and Xu studied at Oxford University in the U.K.

The detention of these scholars prompted a worldwide campaign on their behalf by Human Rights Watch and academic groups in the U.S. and abroad. Because of their personal links to the United States, Gao and Li's cases received significant international attention. Some of the greatest media scrutiny focused on an unprecedented petition signed by over four hundred China scholars from some fifteen countries asking the Chinese government either to release the detained scholars or to immediately address the charges against them in a court in accord with international standards of due process. Partly in response to this pressure, and partly in an effort to improve its relations with the United States, China eventually expelled these scholars from the country after summarily convicting them of "espionage." The trials were widely criticized for falling short of international and domestic standards; each lasted only a few hours, and the defendants did not have any meaningful time to prepare for their defense.

While the release of some of the detained scholars showed the effectiveness of a well-coordinated international response from the academic community, Xu, along with an unknown number of other scholars, remained in detention. Furthermore, many China scholars publicly stated that they curtailed their research activity to avoid subjects potentially offensive to the Chinese government.

The same pattern of persecuting academics in order to curb their intellectual activity recurred around the world. In Iran, a number of prominent academics were arrested in March and April as part of a broader campaign of stifling dissent apparently aimed at countering the widespread support for reform of Iran's political system. In the weeks immediately preceding Iran's presidential elections, authorities arrested at least ten scholars among a group of forty-two figures associated with the liberal Iran Freedom Movement, a banned but previously tolerated political party. Among the scholars arrested were Gholam-Abbas Tavassoli, a sociologist at Tehran University and formerly chancellor of Isfahan University, Hadi Hadizadeh, a prominent physicist, Ghaffar Farzadi, Mohammad Mehdi-Jafari, Habibollah Peyman, Reza Raisdoosti, and Mohammad Maleki. Tavassoli was released two days after his arrest, but several other academics remained in jail.

In response, more than one hundred faculty members from Iran's universities signed an appeal to the government requesting the release of their colleagues. Widespread student protests in support of the detained academics also occurred at universities in Tehran and other cities, and were met by heavy handed police reaction.

These attacks on academic freedom formed the backdrop to a critical rise in the "brain drain" phenomenon among Iran's academics and university graduates. According to a report issued by the Iranian government in May 2001, tens of thousands of academics and professionals left Iran for Western countries in the preceding twelve months. Commenting on this report, chancellors from several Iranian universities blamed the mass exodus of educated Iranians on the "continual psychological insecurity on the campuses."

In Egypt, Saad Eddin Ibrahim, a prominent sociologist and a critic of the government, went on trial on charges of impugning Egypt's international reputation (having reported on Egypt's flawed October 2000 parliamentary elections), accepting foreign funds without authorization (based on a grant from the European Union), and "embezzlement." On May 21, 2001, Ibrahim and twenty-seven colleagues from his think tank, the Ibn Khaldun Center for Development Studies, were convicted in a trial criticized by observers from Human Rights Watch as having predetermined its ruling. Twenty-one defendants (nine of whom were tried in absentia) received one-year suspended sentences and six others (one tried in absentia) received sentences ranging between two and five years' imprisonment with labor. The six serving custodial sentences at the time of writing were: Saadeddin Ibrahim, Khaled Ahmed Mohamed al-Fayyad, Usama Hashem Mohamed 'Ali and Mohamed Hassanein 'Amara (held at Tora Mazra'at Prison), and Nadia Mohamed Abdel Nour and Magda Ibrahim al-Bey (held at the Women's Prison in Qanater. Ibrahim was sentenced to seven years in prison.

A flawed trial surrounded the death sentence handed down in the case of Dr. Yunas Shaikh, a physiologist who taught at Nishtar Medical College in Pakistan. Dr. Shaikh was accused of "blasphemy" by students affiliated with the Majlis Tahaffuz Khatm-i-Nabuwat (The Committee for the Protection of the Finality of Prophethood), a fundamentalist religious organization, based on his remarks during class that the Prophet Mohammad may not have followed Islamic hygienic precepts before he received the revelation that called him to prophethood. According to eyewitnesses, dozens of members of the Majlis Tahaffuz appeared at his trial in an effort to intimidate the court during the proceedings. Dr. Shaikh's conviction came under a law that allows any citizen to initiate a prosecution for blasphemy, although this law has been widely criticized by political and religious leaders. Dr. Shaikh appealed the verdict.

In Tunisia, Human Rights Watch issued a joint statement with several academic groups to protest the escalating attacks on academics advocating democratic reforms and the rule of law. The statement of March 2001 noted two attacks against Khedija Cherif, a sociologist at the University of Tunis and a prominent advocate of women's right. On March 1, Cherif was beaten, sexually harassed, and verbally abused as she was attempting to attend a meeting of the National Council on Liberties in Tunisia (Conseil National des Libertes en Tunisie, CNLT). In the same incident, the unidentified assailants also attacked Abdel Kader Ben Khemis, a professor at the University of Sousse. The Tunisian government also continued its harassment of Dr. Moncef Marzouki, the CNLT's former spokesperson. In December 2000, he received a one-year sentence, later suspended on appeal, on trumped-up charges of "belonging to an illegal organization" and "disseminating false information," stemming from his former activity with the CNLT. Marzouki had already been improperly dismissed from his position teaching public health at the University of Sousse and barred from any other type of employment, which resulted in extreme economic hardship. He is under constant surveillance and is only allowed intermittent telephone contact. At this writing it is unclear whether he will be allowed to leave the country to assume a teaching position abroad; an attempt in March 2001 to leave for a two-year faculty post in France was thwarted at the airport despite assurances from judicial authorities that he could leave.

Dayan Dawood, rector of Syiah Kuala University in Banda Aceh, capital of the restive Aceh province of Indonesia, was killed on September 5 by unidentified men. He was the second Acehnese rector to be killed in as many years. Aceh has witnessed increased violence in recent years as pro-independence guerrillas battle counterinsurgency forces of the Indonesian military and police. Both groups have been responsible for political assassinations and both sides have accused the other in Dawood's murder. Dawood met with Human Rights Watch in December 2000 and discussed his hope that the university could play a role in forming a nonviolent resolution to the conflict in Aceh.

Attacks by army-linked paramilitaries on academics were rampant in Colombia, where over two dozen scholars and students were killed over the last eighteen months. Most of the attacks were carried out by paramilitary groups contesting what critics described as the left-wing academic environment of Colombia's thirty-two public universities. As set out in a 2001 report by Human Rights Watch, these groups enjoyed tacit, and at times explicit, support from certain Colombian military units. In May, Miguel Angel Vargas, the president of a regional university teachers union, was assassinated by gunmen in the northeastern Colombian city of Valledupar, the home of the Universidad Popular de Valledupar. His brother Lisandro Vargas, also a professor, was gunned down two months ago in Barranquilla, the capital of Atlantico province. The University of Atlántico witnessed the greatest number of attacks: In October 2000, forty-six-year-old Alfredo Castro, a critic of corruption at the university, was shot by unidentified assassins in front of his family. On August 26, 2000, Luis Meza, also from the university, was killed by gunmen.

Similar tactics were used by the militant Basque separatist movement, Euzkadi Ta Askatasuna (ETA). The group took taken credit for several attacks on universities and academics in the Basque region of Spain after the beginning of the 2000 academic year. ETA admitted that it had left a parcel bomb in an elevator in Lejona Campus of the University of the Basque Country on December 18, 2000. The bomb misfired, narrowly missing Edurne Uriarte, an outspoken critic of ETA's tactics. She subsequently stopped teaching out of fear of further assassination attempts. Mikel María Azurmendi and José María Portillo also stopped teaching at universities in the Basque region and moved abroad after attempts on their lives.

CENSORSHIP AND IDEOLOGICAL CONTROLS

In many countries where academics were not physically assaulted or barred from carrying out their responsibilities, governments attempted to muzzle scholars through restrictive regulations on the substance of their work. Censorship and pre-publication previews of scholarly work is still the norm in China, North Korea, Iran, and, to varying degrees, in much of the Arab world from Iraq to Morocco.

In May and June, a Human Rights Watch investigation in Turkey found that universities there were subject to a strict system of centralized control established by the military after the 1980 coup d'etat. This system was administered by a central body known by its Turkish acronym, YOK, which controlled every aspect of higher education in Turkey, including budgets and academic placement at every level. The organization had fostered a climate of fear and self-censorship in Turkey's universities by accusing any critical academics of harboring leftist, religious, or separatist tendencies—and sometimes all at the same time.

Human Rights Watch interviewed some forty academics from more than a dozen universities around Turkey who had been punished under YOK's ideological controls. Aside from being subject to criminal sanctions, academics could be banned from teaching for life, or internally exiled to any academic institution in the country. While it was academics with religious tendencies who at this time faced the brunt of the repression, YOK targeted any academic work that contained "leftist" ideas or that acknowledged the existence of problems for ethnic minorities in Turkey. In one particularly egregious example last year, YOK attempted to shut down a private university, Fatih University, because of allegations that it was sympathetic to religious political groups. This claim was rejected by the judicial system, but YOK continued to harass Fatih University.

Ideological controls returned, or increased, in several states of the former Soviet Union. In Belarus, Yury Bandazhevsky was convicted in June 2001 of "accepting bribes" from students and was sentenced to eight years of imprisonment. He was a leading researcher into the health effects of radiation fallout from the Chernobyl disaster, a subject that was highly politicized in Belarus. Amnesty International named Bandazhevsky a prisoner of conscience in August 2001.

In Central Asia, the government of Turkmenistan continued its campaign against academic freedom and intellectual activity. In January, the country's largest library shut its doors; the library had served as a haven for academics and was the country's last window to foreign scholarship. By June, the last operating Islamic school was also closed.

Russian scholars and their colleagues elsewhere expressed alarm about a new set of regulations issued by the Russian Academy of Sciences governing all contact and cooperation between the country's 53,000 scientific researchers and outside institutions. These regulations required greater monitoring, and possible restriction of, such contact. While some academics feared that this signaled a return to Soviet-era policies, it was not clear how broadly these regulations would be implemented. Anecdotal reports suggested that scientists working in areas of "hard" science—physics, biotechnology, chemistry—had decreased cooperation with foreign counterparts due to the new requirements that they inform their superiors of any contact with foreign scholars or institutions and that all research proposals must be vetted by the Russian Academy of Sciences.

India also instituted regulations governing attendance of foreigners at international academic meetings held in India. The Indian Home Ministry issued a circular ordering security clearance before holding such gatherings, singling out participants from Afghanistan, Bangladesh, China, Pakistan, and Sri Lanka. Similarly, the ministry issued an edict requiring prior approval for all international academic meetings.

India's governing Hindu nationalist Bharatiya Janata Party continued its policy of "Hinduizing" education at all levels. India's University Grants Commission earmarked funds for university courses in astrology, a move that sparked strong opposition from India's academic community. A lawsuit brought by a group of academics contesting the new university program was before the Supreme Court of India.

SUPPRESSION OF STUDENT ACTIVISM

University students, typically among the most politically active groups of civil society, were frequent targets of government repression. Some of the worst abuses occurred in the Horn of Africa, where the governments of Ethiopia and Eritrea both cracked down on student. With the end of the ruinous border war between these two countries, students were among the first groups to register public dissatisfaction with their governments' conduct.

Ethiopian security forces used excessive force in dealing with student protests in April 2001, and used the protests as an excuse for attacking civil society. Students at the university were at the forefront at a nation-wide movement for greater political freedom. Students at Addis Ababa University were engaged in ongoing negotiations with Minister of Education Genet Zewde over their request to resume publication of a banned campus magazine and the removal of security troops currently stationed on campuses. A number of attacks by security forces culminated in an effort on April 17 to force the students to end their protests.

Heavily armed members of the Special Forces branch of the security forces raided the Addis Ababa University campus, confronting students and civilians as protesters disaffected with government policies joined the clashes in support of the students. At least forty people were killed by security forces in the ensuing disturbances, and eyewitnesses testified that security forces fired live ammunition at protesters and beat unresisting bystanders, including children. More that two thousand students were detained during the raids; while most were released within a few days, an undetermined remained in jail. Some one hundred students escaped the government crackdown by going to Kenya, and seventy escaped to neighboring Djibouti. These students were being held at internment camps under harsh conditions.

Across the border, in Eritrea, students also expressed their disillusionment with government policies after the war with Ethiopia. A broad clampdown on civil society and critical political voices was apparently triggered by an increasingly tense standoff between the government and university students demanding greater academic freedom and social liberties. The focus of student protest at the University of Asmara, the country's only university, was a mandatory summer work program during which students performed public service around the country during their holidays. In 2001, the students protested the appalling conditions of previous camps. On July 31, the police arrested the president of the Asmara University student council, Semere Kesete, and he remained in jail without charge.

On August 10, four hundred students protesting Kesete's arrest were rounded up and sent to a work camp in Wia, a desert site near the Red Sea where daytime temperatures hovered at about 38 degrees Celsius (100 degrees Fahrenheit). Eventually some 1,700 other students were taken to the camps. The government acknowledged that at least two students died of heatstroke. Parents of students who were protesting the treatment of their children were also arrested. The students were ultimately allowed to return to the university, but at this writing at least twenty members of the student union remained in detention.

In Papua, Indonesia's easternmost province, students played an important part in the broad civilian independence movement that emerged alongside a decades-old armed insurgency. In a spiraling cycle of violence, police killed three students and beat up and tortured dozens of others following a December 2000 rebel attack on a police post in Abepura, near the provincial capital Jayapura.

ACCESS TO EDUCATION

As pointed out by the U.N. Committee on Economic, Social and Cultural Rights, academic freedom was rooted in the fundamental human right to education. Another key component of this right was that governments must educate their citizens without discrimination through their acts or their omissions.

A groundbreaking report by Human Rights Watch based on its research in South Africa demonstrated that the high incidence of rape and sexual assault against girls in schools constituted a serious obstacle to the education of girls in that country. Irrespective of their race or social class, thousands of girls suffered gender-based violence at the hands of their teachers and classmates. The report found that the government of South Africa, which had one of the highest rates of rape in the world, has been remiss in addressing this violence: school officials were often unaware of or unwilling to enforce disciplinary procedures against violators, and many girls were discouraged by their schools or families from pursuing criminal sanctions.

The release of Human Rights Watch's report, *Scared at School*, in March 2001 prompted a widespread and heated national debate. South African authorities pledged to take concrete steps to coordinate appropriate responses between educational and judicial authorities and to develop a national plan to protect South African girls and provide them with an adequate education.

In a letter to Iran's Guardian Council, the body dominated by religious clergy that must approve all new laws, Human Rights Watch denounced the decision to block a parliamentary bill that would have extended to Iranian women the same rights as men to study at universities abroad. Women could study abroad—but only with permission from a male guardian, and only men could receive financial assistance for studying overseas. In January 2001, the Guardian Council overturned the decision of Iran's parliament, which voted by a two-to-one margin to amend a law that prohibited women from studying abroad without the permission of a male guardian. While the percentage of girls and women participating at all levels of education rose over the past two decades since Islamic rule began in Iran, women still faced significant legal discrimination in personal status matters, in the ability to travel freely, and in choosing freely how to pursue higher education. As a result of the massive public outcry, the law eventually passed with some slight amendments.

Discrimination based on race, ethnicity, and sexual orientation too often kept students from receiving an adequate education. A 2001 Human Rights Watch investigation found that Israel provided its Palestinian Arab citizens with a markedly inferior education when compared with their Jewish peers. Discrimination based on caste status was also a concern, as evident in the widespread cases of discrimination against members of India's Dalit community, which belong to the lowest rung of the traditional caste hierarchy. (See Children's Rights.)

Human Rights Watch also criticized Israel for interfering with the ability of university students in the Palestinian-governed areas of the West Bank to pursue their education. Since September 2000, Bir Zeit University, located outside Ramallah, has faced a military blockade that often prevented students from attending classes and at times shut down the university completely. On March 7, 2001, a few hours after Prime Minister Ariel Sharon took office, the Israeli Defense Forces cut the only road connecting Bir Zeit University to Ramallah, located about five miles away. An IDF checkpoint, frequently supported by an armored personnel carrier, had since then stopped traffic on the road, obstructing access to the university.

Relevant Human Rights Watch Reports:

Israel: Second Class: Discrimination Against Palestinian Arab Children in Israel's Schools, 12/01
Indonesia: Violence and Political Impasse in Papua, 7/01
Hatred in the Hallways: Violence and Discrimination Against Lesbian, Gay, Bisexual, and Transgender Students in U.S. Schools, 5/01
Scared at School: Sexual Violence Against Girls in South African Schools, 3/01

BUSINESS AND HUMAN RIGHTS

INTRODUCTION

Voluntary standard-setting, enforcement, legal actions, and other efforts characterized efforts to ensure corporate responsibility in relation to human rights in 2001. In previous years, the debate focused on whether corporations and business generally should have any responsibility for human rights. In 2001, significant

progress was made toward defining the appropriate roles of business and corporations. The debate also expanded into assessing the appropriate roles of government,
and the range of actors expanded significantly. Discussion of the relationship
between business and human rights was no longer limited to just corporations and
nongovernmental organizations (NGOs), as multilateral financial institutions, the
United Nations, and governments began to address these issues more consistently.
However, much more remained to be done, including to ensure the application of
existing standards and to develop binding standards of corporate responsibility. As
in previous years, the apparel and footwear and extractive industries were the main
focus of scrutiny.

THE APPAREL AND FOOTWEAR INDUSTRY

Three key monitoring initiatives being undertaken by the Fair Labor Association, Social Accountability International, and the Workers' Rights Consortium
continued to make progress toward developing viable monitoring programs.

Fair Labor Association (FLA)

The FLA, a voluntary monitoring initiative developed by NGOs and apparel
companies, began to accredit independent external monitors and monitor factories
in 2001. By October, the FLA had ten member companies: Adidas-Salomon AG,
GEAR For Sports, Levi Strauss & Co, Liz Claiborne, Nike, Patagonia, Polo Ralph
Lauren, Reebok, Eddie Bauer, and Phillips-Van Heusen; as well as approximately
160 affiliated colleges and universities. At the same time, nine independent monitoring firms: Cal Safety Corporation, COVERCO, Global Standards, Intertek Testing Services, the Kenan Institute, LIFT-Standards, Merchandise Testing Labs,
Phulki, and Verite were accredited by the FLA to conduct external monitoring in
member company factories. In August, external monitoring began at member factories in Bangladesh, China, Guatemala, Indonesia, the Philippines, Thailand, and
the United States. The FLA expected that around one hundred external inspections
of factories would be carried out in 2001, most of them in Asia.

Social Accountability International (SAI)

SAI, an organization that oversees the implementation of its SA-8000 workplace
standard, continued to certify factories in 2001. By October, SAI had certified eighty
factories in twenty-one countries and had eight agencies that were accredited to
monitor factories' compliance with the standard. The organization also managed a
"Signatory Membership" program for companies that allows companies to join SAI
after committing to progressively implement the SA-8000 standards in some of its
facilities. By October, eight companies and one U.N. agency had joined the signatory membership program: Amana, Avon Products, Cutter&Buck, Dole Food,
Eileen Fisher, Otto Versand, Toys R Us, Vogele, and the United Nations' Office for
Project Services (UNOPS).

Workers Rights Consortium (WRC)

The WRC monitors compliance with the apparel manufacturing codes of conduct of approximately eighty-eight colleges and universities and undertook two investigations in 2001, one in Mexico and the other in the U.S.

In January, WRC representatives investigated conditions at the Kukdong International Mexico S.A. de C.V. factory in Atlixco, Mexico, which manufactures college and university sweatshirts for Nike and Reebok. The factory management had been accused of labor rights violations including unlawful employment of children, physical and verbal abuse of workers, failure to provide maternity leave and benefits, firing workers engaged in union activities, refusing to reinstate workers who participated in a work stoppage earlier in January, and a failure to honor the terms of a binding agreement between Kukdong management and its workers. The WRC concluded that many of the allegations were well-founded and launched a campaign to seek redress for the workers. As a result, and due to pressure from Nike and Reebok, in late September, Kukdong (now renamed Mexmode International) agreed to a new collective bargaining agreement with workers and to make improvements in working conditions.

In July, the WRC investigated conditions at the New Era Cap Company's factory in Derby, New York state following allegations by workers that the company was not in compliance with various college and university codes of conduct. Specifically, workers complained that the company had violated health and safety provisions, engaged in age discrimination, and had breached workers' rights of freedom of association and collective bargaining, including by firing or transferring union activists. The investigation was still in progress in October.

THE ENERGY INDUSTRY

There was a continuing focus on the energy industry. In some cases, standard-setting efforts (see below) brought improvements in companies' practices, but in several others those seeking to remedy companies' behavior did so through resorting to lawsuits. The management of revenues by oil producing governments and the consequences of the Bush Administration's renewed focus on energy security were also serious areas of concern, particularly after the September 11 attack on the U.S. when the Bush Administration appeared to be willing to overlook the poor human rights records of oil-rich, but abusive and undemocratic governments as it sought to find allies in its war against terrorism.

Angola

On April 3, 2000, as part of a larger agreement on economic reform, the International Monetary Fund (IMF) and the Angolan government reached an agreement to monitor oil revenues. Known as the "Oil Diagnostic," it would be supervised by the World Bank and implemented by KPMG, an international accounting firm that also had the Angolan central bank as a client. It was an effort by the IMF and World Bank to assess the percentage of government oil revenues being deposited in the central bank. The Angolan budget had previously been opaque, raising concerns among multilateral financial institutions, NGOs, companies, and foreign governments that oil revenues were being used secretly to finance arms purchases and that future oil production was mortgaged against immediate oil-backed loans. Some oil revenues bypassed the Ministry of Finance and the central bank and went directly to the state-owned Sociedade Nacional de Combustiveis de Angola (Sonangol) company, or to the Presidency to procure weapons. The Oil Diagnostic continued to progress, but the government of Angola encountered serious problems with the IMF over its non-compliance with the terms of the IMF's overall program and its continuing lack of transparency. (See below.)

The government was also embarrassed by an arms-for-oil scandal. In December 2000, French authorities arrested Pierre Falcone, a Franco Brazilian businessman whose company, Falcon Oil, held an equity stake in Angolan deepwater oil block thirty-one. He was accused of tax fraud and other offences in connection with his alleged involvement in brokering an arms-for-oil deal with the Angolan government in the early 1990s. Charges were also brought against Jean Claude Mitterrand, the son of former French President Francois Mitterrand. Charges against both men were dropped in June 2001 though a new investigation was opened against Mitterrand in October.

According to the *Washington Post*, another Falcone company, Brenco International, had brokered arms deals involving the sale of surplus Russian military equipment to the Angolan government. The first deal, the newspaper reported, was worth approximately U.S. $47 million and took place on November 7, 1993, while a second deal, worth some U.S. $563 million, took place in 1994. In both cases, the weapons purchases were said to have been paid for with Angolan proceeds from oil sales—with Sonangol, for example, paying some of the money for the 1994 transaction to French bank accounts controlled by a Czech firm, ZTS OSOS, that provided some of the weapons.

In February, Angolan President José Eduardo dos Santos acknowledged that the arms deals between ZTS OSOS, Falcone, and the government had taken place, but said that the deals were legitimate. Dos Santos went further, praising Falcone for his efforts which, he said, had helped to preserve "democracy and the rule of law" in Angola. He described Falcone's actions as a "gesture of confidence and friendship on the part of the French State" toward the Angolan government that had helped facilitate the "spectacular growth in cooperation with France in the petroleum sector" and in other economic activities. Dos Santos also questioned why the French authorities were investigating and had arrested Falcone since the arms were not bought from French companies or in France, but from companies in Eastern Europe.

Although the government has committed itself to improving human rights, it remained hostile to public inquiry or criticism of its use of oil revenues. For example, on January 24, 2001, police beat and arrested eight members of the opposition Party for Democracy and Progress in Angola (PADPA) who staged a peaceful hunger strike outside the Luanda residence of President dos Santos, calling for him to resign on grounds of economic mismanagement and corruption. The protestors also called for disclosure of the details of the French arms-for-oil deal, and criticized the government's discontinuation of peace negotiations with the rebel National Union for the Total Independence of Angola (UNITA). Following this incident, the state Rádio Nacional de Angola broadcast an official statement warning people not to demonstrate against the government. Two of the eight demonstrators were quickly released. The six others were charged with holding an "illegal protest," but the charges were dismissed when they appeared in court on January 29.

The Bush Energy Strategy

President Bush released the report of the National Energy Policy Development Group, a White House panel led by Vice-President Richard Cheney, on May 17. The report was intended to "develop a national energy policy designed to help the private sector, and, as necessary and appropriate, State and local governments, promote dependable, affordable and environmentally sound production and distribution of energy for the future." Remarkably, the report's 170 pages and 105 recommendations did not once acknowledge the impact energy development may have on human rights. Instead, the report suggested making energy security an even greater priority in U.S. relations with some of the worst violators of human rights around the world, while proposing no strategy to keep necessary oil investment from perpetuating dictatorships or fueling conflicts, as it had in countries such as Angola, Nigeria, Sudan, and Iraq.

The report recognized the need for "more transparent, accountable, and responsible use of oil resources" in Africa. However, it only addressed this issue regarding energy development in Africa, and only in the context of enhancing "the security and stability of investment." The report did not address the misuse of oil revenues in other parts of the world, and ignored the detrimental impact this has had on human rights and democratic development in countries such as Azerbaijan and Kazakhstan. The report omitted any reference to the need for U.S. energy corporations to adopt the highest human rights standards when operating in other countries. By October, it was still not clear how forcefully the Administration would pursue the strategy proposed in the aftermath of the September 11 attacks on the U.S

ExxonMobil

On June 11, 2001 the International Labor Rights Fund (ILRF), a U.S. NGO, filed a lawsuit on behalf of seven anonymous plaintiffs against ExxonMobil in a U.S. Federal Court in the District of Columbia. The suit alleged that the Indonesian military provided "security services" for the company's joint-venture operation in Indonesia's conflict-ridden Aceh province, and that the Indonesian military had committed "genocide, murder, torture, crimes against humanity, sexual violence, and kidnapping" while providing security for the company from 1999 to 2001. The plaintiffs alleged that these activities violated the U.S. Alien Tort Claims Act, the Torture Victims Protection Act, international human rights law, and the statutory and common law of the District of Colombia. The suit held that ExxonMobil was liable for the alleged abuses because it provided "logistical and material" support to the military, and because the company was aware of widespread abuses committed by the military but had failed to take any action to prevent those abuses. Exxon-Mobil vigorously denied the allegations and said the lawsuit "recently filed by the International Labor Rights Fund (ILRF) containing these allegations is without merit and designed to bring publicity to their organization."

Unocal

In October, the court case filed in the U.S. against the Unocal Corporation because of its operations in Burma was still under appeal to the Ninth Circuit Federal Court of Appeals. Plaintiffs in the case alleged that Unocal was complicit in human rights violations committed by Burmese military forces who had been assigned to guard the company's Yadana gas pipeline. U.S. Federal District Judge Ronald Lew dismissed the case on August 31, 2000. He ruled that there was insufficient evidence to show that Unocal had actively participated in or conspired with the Burmese military to commit human rights violations and that Unocal, as part of a joint-venture arrangement (along with TotalFina-Elf, the Myanma Oil and Gas Enterprise, and the Petroleum Authority of Thailand), was not a state-actor and so could not be liable for human rights violations by the Burmese military. The plaintiffs filed a parallel case in the California Superior Court, however, as Unocal is based in California, and there, Superior Court Judge Victoria Gerrard Chaney ruled on August 20 that the case could proceed.

THE ROLE OF MULTILATERAL INSTITUTIONS

Multilateral institutions, particularly the IMF, and to a lesser extent, the World Bank and the United Nations sought to ensure that both companies and governments act in a responsible manner. Despite the different degrees of progress, these institutions all made clear that issues related to business and human rights were critical components of their activities.

International Monetary Fund (IMF)

The IMF took strong measures to ensure that governments manage crucial resources such as oil in a transparent and accountable manner, indicating that if it were to act consistently throughout the world, it could help significantly to improve governance standards among opaque and unaccountable governments. The IMF demonstrated this particularly in its relations with the Republic of Congo (Congo-Brazzaville), the Democratic Republic of Congo, and Angola.

Republic of Congo (Congo-Brazzaville)

In April 2001, the IMF sharply and repeatedly criticized the government of Congo-Brazzaville, warning that there would be no further IMF lending as long as "the petroleum sector lacks transparency." Despite IMF requests, the government had yet to audit the state-owned Congolese National Petroleum Company or the petroleum sector as a whole. The IMF again criticized the government in June for excessive spending, massive customs fraud, and the slow pace of reforms, and declared that the country would not qualify for debt relief until the government began to seriously address these problems.

Democratic Republic of Congo (DRC)

A Staff Monitored Program (SMP) began to monitor reforms by the government, which assured the IMF in June in a memorandum of intent that it would ensure good governance and complete transparency in the mining and diamond sector. The government also committed to eliminate "abuses of authority by individuals and nontax administrations involving intimidation, arbitrary arrests and dishonest profit seeking . . . ." The agreement, scheduled to run until March 2002, appeared to provide a good basis for reform of the DRC's precarious economy and public administration.

Angola

The IMF allowed the SMP that it had agreed with the government to expire in June 2001. The government had committed to make ten major reforms but had only implemented two. It had also failed to publish the quarterly Oil Diagnostic studies that began at the start of 2001 and were intended to ascertain whether all oil revenue were being deposited in the central bank, rather than siphoned off for secret arms purchases or alleged corruption. On August 14, the IMF stated publicly that it would not cooperate further with the government until the latter complied with the requirement of the conditions of the previously agreed SMP and significantly increased transparency by publishing data on oil and other government revenues and expenditures, and conducting an audit of the central bank. Despite the SMP's expiry, the Oil Diagnostic as a contractual arrangement whose completion was a requirement of further IMF cooperation would continue. The government, however, did little to increase transparency.

World Bank

The World Bank began a process to assess its impact on human rights in the oil, gas, and mining industries. In July, it appointed Dr. Emil Salim, Indonesia's former state minister for population and environment, as the "Eminent Person" who would lead the bank's extractive industries review and "discuss its future role in the extractive industries with concerned stakeholders." This review had been announced by World Bank President James Wolfensohn at the September 2000 annual meetings of the World Bank and IMF held in Prague in response to repeated NGO criticism of the bank's lending policies and the negative human rights and environmental impacts of the oil, gas, and mining industries. The review represented a compromise between the bank and NGOs opposed to its lending to these industries and was due to be completed within some twelve months, during which regional and international consultations would be held to assess the bank's performance in the extractive industry. A parallel process to review the bank's performance in these industries by the bank's own Operations Evaluations Department and Operations Evaluations Group was also announced.

A final report, drawing in both reviews and making recommendations to the World Bank's board of directors is due to be submitted by November 2002. In October 2001, it was too early to tell whether the assessment would lead to human rights considerations playing a larger part in the bank's lending policies in the extractive industries.

United Nations

The U.N. took a two-track approach toward corporate responsibility in 2001. The highly publicized Global Compact (G.C.) had a disappointing impact in 2001 but the Sub-Commission for the Promotion and Protection of Human Rights made some progress towards developing a set of U.N. principles on the conduct of corporations.

The G.C., a voluntary initiative to encourage corporations to adopt nine key principles on human rights, labor rights, and the environment, was launched by U.N. Secretary-General Kofi Annan in July 2000. Its impact was limited in 2001, however, by two key shortcomings: the lack of any system for monitoring corporate compliance and the failure of the U.N. to apply these same standards to its own agencies and their procurement. Instead of addressing these problems, the G.C. preferred to convene meetings between corporations, trades unions, and NGOs to discuss issues such as the role of companies in conflict zones. The G.C. also developed a "Learning Forum" to discuss best practices.

In August, the Sub-Commission for the Protection and Promotion of Human Rights agreed to extend until 2004 the mandate of its working group on the impact of transnational corporations on human rights. Established in 1999, the group had already developed draft principles on the conduct of corporations which, once refined, could lead to the adoption of a new U.N. standard or global guidelines for the conduct of corporations and provide a basis for assessing their performance.

LAWSUITS UNDER THE ALIEN TORTS CLAIMS ACT (ATCA)

New lawsuits were brought to compel improvements in corporate behavior. In addition to those against ExxonMobil, suits under the ATCA were brought against several U.S. corporations on account of their alleged complicity in human rights violations and several earlier lawsuits continued to wind their way through U.S. courts.

A lawsuit alleging that local Colombian bottlers for the Coca Cola company maintained "open relations" with Colombian paramilitaries as "part of a program to intimidate trade union leaders" was filed on July 21 in the U.S. District Court for the Southern District in Miami, Florida. The suit also alleged that a manager at one of the bottling plants "ordered" the murder of trade unionist Isidora Segundo Gil after he had allegedly threatened to kill trade unionists because of their union activities, and that five members of SINALTRAINAL, the Colombian union representing Coca Cola workers, had been "subjected to torture, kidnapping, and/or unlawful detention in order to encourage them to cease their trade union activities" by the paramilitaries. These events allegedly occurred between 1995 and 2000. The case was filed by the International Labor Rights Fund (ILRF), the United Steelworkers Union, SINALTRAINAL, the estate of Isidro Segundo Gil, and the five trade unionists who were allegedly subjected to human rights abuses. Coca Cola and the other defendants strongly denied the allegations, Coca Cola also noting that "[w]hile we continue to conduct a detailed review of these allegations, we have no reason to believe and no information that demonstrates either bottler named in the suit has in anyway instigated, condoned or encouraged the criminal activities alleged . . . [t]he information we have gathered has reinforced our belief that the claims in this suit are either totally inaccurate, based on distortions of actual events or omit information that, when provided, clarifies that the bottlers had no involvement in the actions attributed to them." In October, Coca Cola filed a motion to dismiss the suit in the Florida courts.

In September, the ILRF and the Massachusetts-based law firm of Cristobal Bonifaz filed a suit in a District of Columbia court against Dyncorp, a Virginia-based company, on behalf of eight Ecuadoran plaintiffs. The plaintiffs alleged that they had suffered adverse health effects after a Dyncorp plane sprayed pesticides over their land when it crossed the Ecuadoran border as it was engaged in cocoa eradication in Colombia, and accused Dyncorp of violating both U.S. and international laws including the ATCA, the Torture Victims Protection Act, and the International Covenant on Civil and Political Rights. The company did not make any public statements about the case other then to state that it was company policy not to comment on issues of active litigation.

THE ROLE OF GOVERNMENTS

Several governments and multilateral bodies became more actively involved in corporate social responsibility issues, primarily promoting voluntary initiatives by corporations and NGOs to adhere to high standards. Such increased governmental involvement was a necessary precursor to developing binding standards on corporations that governments could adopt, but some governments took steps that would limit possibilities for holding corporations accountable.

European Union (E.U.)

The European Commission presented a "green paper"—a nonbonding document to stimulate public comment—titled "Promoting a European Framework for Corporate Social Responsibility" in July. It urged companies to voluntarily pursue social responsibility in their operations around the world and throughout their supply chains, called for increased voluntary social auditing, the development of ethical labeling, and the promotion of socially responsible investment. However, it did not envision any binding regulatory role for the E.U. that would ensure companies act responsibly.

In June, the European Commission proposed new regulations for its Generalized System of Preferences (GSP) that included a more expansive definition of labor rights violations that could be actionable under the GSP enforcement mechanisms. Currently, the E.U. can penalize countries by withdrawing their GSP trade benefits only in cases of forced labor or exports made with prison labor. Under the new proposal, trade preferences could be withdrawn due to a "serious and systematic violation" of freedom of association, the right to collective bargaining, of prohibitions on child labor, discrimination in employment, or forced or compulsory labor (including prison labor exports). At the same time, the commission proposed to restrict the labor rights compliance mechanism that triggers investigations of violations of the GSP labor provisions by eliminating the standing of nongovernmental bodies to submit a complaint. Currently, complaints can be submitted to the commission by any interested party, defined as "a Member State, or any natural or legal person, or association not endowed with legal personality, which can show an interest in such withdrawal." Although the complaints mechanism has been used only twice, both times by the International Confederation of Free Trade Unions (ICFTU) to submit complaints against Burma and Pakistan in 1995, the new proposal omitted the language that defined who could submit a complaint, effectively limiting this only to E.U. member states. An E.U. official told HRW that the E.U. "want[ed] to avoid to address the issue of standing, on purpose."

United States and United Kingdom

On December 20, 2001, the governments of the United States and United Kingdom launched the Voluntary Principles on Security and Human Rights. Beginning in February 2000, the principles were formulated as a result of discussions between the U.S. Department of State, the U.K. Foreign and Commonwealth Office, transnational oil and mining companies, human rights organizations, unions, and business organizations. The companies involved in the process included BP, Royal Dutch/Shell, Chevron, Texaco, Rio Tinto Zinc, and Freeport McMoRan. Human Rights Watch, Amnesty International, the Lawyers' Committee for Human Rights, and International Alert were among the human rights organizations involved in the process. The International Federation of Chemical, Energy, Mine, and General Workers' Unions was the representative for trade unions. The Prince of Wales' Business Leaders Forum and Business for Social Responsibility were the participating business organizations. The drafting of the principles formed part of a limited, but positive ongoing effort to ensure that corporate security arrangements fully respect human rights. Several meetings were held in 2001 to discuss the implementation of the principles and to encourage other governments and companies to adopt them. In October, it was still too early to assess whether the principles would have a lasting and positive effect on human rights.

CHILD SOLDIERS CAMPAIGN

G lobal efforts to end the use of child soldiers continued to advance during the year. Following the United Nations' adoption in May 2000 of a new treaty to end the participation of children under the age of eighteen in armed conflict (an optional protocol to the Convention on the Rights of the Child), the number of countries signing the treaty grew to eighty-seven, and the number of ratifications increased to ten. Having achieved the ten ratifications needed, the protocol will enter into force on February 12, 2002.

The Coalition to Stop the Use of Child Soldiers continued its campaigning efforts to achieve broad ratification and implementation of the protocol. Coalition members, including national campaigns in many countries, lobbied governments to sign and/or ratify the protocol in advance of the session. Campaign activities in Australia, Bangladesh, Belgium, Colombia, Germany, Indonesia, Israel, Italy, Japan, Nepal, Pakistan, Paraguay, Peru, Philippines, Russia, Sierra Leone, the United Kingdom, and the United States included public education, exhibitions, media campaigns, petition drives, symposia, street theater, children's demonstrations, marches, meetings with governments, and parliamentary initiatives.

In several countries campaign efforts resulted in changes of laws regulating recruitment. In Italy, sustained campaigning saw the adoption of new legislation raising the minimum age of recruitment to eighteen. In Israel, after persistent NGO efforts, the Israeli Defence Forces announced that it would end the deployment of under-eighteens and stop accepting conscripts before their eighteenth birthday. In East Timor, the National Council adopted military legislation setting eighteen as the minimum age for military recruitment. In Greece, after petitioning by coalition members, a new law was adopted in 2001 that annulled previous legislation that allowed the conscription of under-eighteens. Legislation to prohibit the voluntary recruitment of under-eighteens was also under discussion in the Greek Parliament. In the Netherlands, coalition members worked with members of parliament to introduce a draft bill that would raise the minimum age for recruitment into the Dutch Armed Forces to eighteen.

Support for the efforts to end the use of child soldiers also came from Pope John Paul II, who devoted February 2001 to prayer for an end to the exploitation of children in armed conflict under the theme "Never Again Child Soldiers," and from the World Veterans Federation, which adopted a resolution in December 2000 calling for universal ratification of the protocol.

The Amman Conference on the Use of Child Soldiers was held in Amman, Jordan from April 8-10, 2001 under the patronage of Her Majesty Queen Rania Al-Abdallah. This was the fifth in a series of regional conferences organized by the coalition in order to highlight the worldwide exploitation of children as soldiers and build momentum and effective strategies for a global ban on such abuse.

The conference was attended by representatives of the governments of Algeria, Bahrain, Egypt, Jordan, Morocco, Qatar, Saudi Arabia, Sudan, Syria, Tunisia, and

Turkey. Participants also included representatives from the Palestinian Authority and more than seventy representatives of local and international NGOs from across the region, national human rights and children's rights institutions, international agencies, and U.N. bodies. At the conclusion of the conference, participants adopted the Amman Declaration on the Use of Children as Soldiers, which strongly condemned the military recruitment and use of children by governments and armed groups across the region, called for prompt ratification and implementation of the new Optional Protocol to the Convention on the Rights of the Child on the involvement of children in armed conflict and other international standards, and included a large number of concrete recommendations for follow up in the region.

Prior to and following the Amman conference, the coalition held consultations in Israel with the deputy minister of defense, representatives of the Israeli Defence Forces, Ministry of Foreign Affairs officials, members of the Knesset and with non-governmental organizations to discuss military recruitment policy and issues related to the use of children as soldiers in the Middle East.

In June 2001, the Coalition to Stop the Use of Child Soldiers published the first-ever global survey of child soldiers, documenting military recruitment by government armed forces, civil militia, paramilitaries, and non-state armed groups in 180 countries. It found that more than half a million children were recruited into government forces and armed groups in more than eighty-seven countries, and that at least 300,000 of these children were actively fighting in forty-one countries.

The coalition released the report at press conferences in Johannesburg and in New York, where it was also presented to NGO and government delegates to the final preparatory meeting for the U.N. Special Session on Children. National coalitions also released the report from various locations around the world, including Bangkok, Karachi, and Kathmandu; Amman and Beirut; London, Paris, Rome, and Stockholm; and Asuncion and Bogotá.

During the year, the coalition also developed several country programs to strengthen national and regional initiatives by nongovernmental organizations to address the participation of children in armed conflict. In Colombia, national coalition members held a series of successful workshops in conflict zones of the countries, the first series focusing on recruitment prevention with key local actors and the second focusing on indigenous and Afro-Colombian children at risk of recruitment. In Southeast Asia, regional and national NGOs organized a national workshop for the Philippines in Mindanao, bringing together nearly forty NGOs and local government agencies. The workshop assessed trends in the New People's Army, and in Mindanao's separatist and indigenous people's conflicts; prepared a strategic plan for influencing the evolving peace process between the government and armed groups in the country; and created a loose NGO coalition for follow-up. Additional workshops were scheduled to take place before the end of the year in other countries of South and Southeast Asia.

Through its international, regional and national partners, the Coalition also launched a number of targeted campaigning actions during the year, including on the use of child soldiers during the conflict between Ethiopia and Eritrea; deaths of underage military conscripts in Paraguay; the establishment of a Special Court to try war crimes (including child recruitment) in Sierra Leone; recruitment policy and practice by the United Kingdom; and child recruitment by government forces and armed groups in the Democratic Republic of Congo and neighboring countries that are party to the conflict.

HIV/AIDS AND HUMAN RIGHTS

In July, Human Rights Watch established its own program dedicated to addressing the problem of HIV/AIDS and human rights. The program will document violations related to HIV/AIDS and advocate for legal and policy protections. The program will work in partnership with NGOs around the world to produce original research on AIDS-related human rights abuses, including in the areas of women's rights, children's rights, rights of migrants and refugees, discrimination on the basis of HIV status, and rights of prisoners.

The prominence of the human immunodeficiency virus/acquired immune deficiency syndrome (HIV/AIDS) pandemic on the global policy and aid agendas reached a peak in 2001, but the world's appreciation of AIDS as a human rights crisis still had a long way to go. Human rights abuses that aggravate the HIV/AIDS epidemic were highly prevalent across the globe in 2001, as they have been since the early days of the disease. Addressing AIDS-related human rights abuses remained an undersupported part of national HIV/AIDS programs, compromising the overall effectiveness of national programs. By December 2000, HIV/AIDS had claimed 22 million lives globally, and 36 million persons were infected with the disease, over 70 percent of them in sub-Saharan Africa.

HIV/AIDS is fueled by discrimination and repression in many ways. The subordinate status of women and girls in many settings makes them unable to refuse unsafe or coercive sex. They frequently have less access than their male counterparts to appropriate and accurate information about HIV transmission and the care of persons with AIDS. They also face a variety of legal and cultural impediments to treatment of sexually transmitted disease other than AIDS, which in turn increases their biological vulnerability to HIV transmission. The United Nations Fund for Women (UNIFEM) concluded in a 2001 statement that the HIV/AIDS epidemic would never have attained its catastrophic proportions, especially in Africa, without discrimination against and subordination of women.

Discrimination against gay men, injecting drug users, and sex workers in many countries has marginalized these groups from the preventive services (condoms, clean syringes for drug users, HIV testing and counseling, for example) and treatment they need. Laws and policies favoring obligatory HIV testing and identification of sex partners among some socially marginalized groups have served to drive underground those who most need services. Drug users attempting to reduce their risk of acquiring HIV by participating in needle exchange programs have faced repression and violence in some countries. Prisoners in many parts of the world are subject to sexual violence and are denied services that would help protect them from HIV transmission through drug use.

HIV/AIDS has had particular impact in depriving children of their rights. AIDS preferentially claims the lives of sexually active adults in the prime of their productive lives, many of whom are parents. In Africa alone, over 13 million children under age fifteen have lost a mother or both parents to AIDS, according to the United Nations. This social crisis also has severe human rights consequences as children orphaned by AIDS and those with ill parents are often forced to leave school and become breadwinners, sometimes in hazardous jobs, and frequently face abandonment, disinheritance and abuse as AIDS also ravages the extended family members who would otherwise support them.

The course of the AIDS epidemic continues to be determined by people's ability to realize their right to treatment and preventive services. AIDS is no longer a leading cause of death for young adults in North America and Western Europe, largely because of access to costly antiretroviral drugs in these regions. The same treatment remains largely out of reach in developing countries.

KEY GLOBAL DEVELOPMENTS

Following the historic U.N. Security Council session in January 2000 on HIV/AIDS as a security threat, the General Assembly committed itself to holding a special session on HIV/AIDS in 2001. The special session in June 2001 was an occasion for highlighting the human rights dimension of the AIDS crisis, to which the conference's final declaration referred in general terms. The process of composing the declaration, however, graphically illustrated human rights challenges that remain. In the deliberations over the wording of the declaration, a number of countries, principally Middle Eastern countries and the United States, objected to the naming of men who have sex with men, injecting drug users, and sex workers as high-risk groups with respect to HIV/AIDS. In spite of support from many other countries for explicit inclusion of these groups to highlight the need for programs to reach them, in the end they were not named in the final document. The declaration, therefore, became an unwitting example of the stigmatization that persons in these groups face every day and that impedes their access to services and support.

The year 2001 saw a dramatic strengthening of the global civil society movement in favor of the right to treatment for HIV/AIDS. Pressure from non-governmental organizations (NGOs) across the world was credited with contributing to the withdrawal in April of a lawsuit brought against the government of South Africa by thirty-nine multinational pharmaceutical companies. The drug companies had challenged the implementation of a 1997 South African law that would have facilitated the country's production and importation of cheaper generic antiretroviral drugs. While the dropping of the suit did not stir the government of South Africa to increase AIDS drug access, legislative action followed quickly in Kenya and was pending in several other countries, to enable a greater flow of cheaper drugs to persons with AIDS.

The government of Brazil was in the global spotlight in 2001 as its national program on AIDS continued to make locally produced antiretroviral drugs widely available in the country. AIDS activists in Brazil pointed out that flaws remained in the program, but the dramatic reduction in deaths from AIDS in the country and the more widespread use of preventive services because people knew that treatment was available were testimony to the effectiveness of the government's approach. The legal foundation of Brazil's AIDS program is a national law by which patents are not honored in the country if the holder of the patent does not begin manufacturing the product in Brazil within three years of the awarding of the patent. In May 2000, the United States initiated an action against Brazil in the World Trade Organization (WTO), asking the WTO to review Brazil's patent laws. Under considerable public pressure, just two months after the withdrawal of the pharmaceutical industry's law suit in South Africa, the office of the U.S. Trade Representative announced in June 2001 that it would drop its action against Brazil if Brazil agreed to notify U.S.-based patent holders when it planned to manufacture generic versions of their drugs.

Brazil presented a resolution to the U.N. Commission on Human Rights in March, asserting the human right of all persons with HIV/AIDS to treatment that includes antiretroviral drugs. The resolution passed unanimously over the abstention of the U.S. The WTO ministerial meeting in Qatar in November resulted in a consensus of member states that the WTO agreement on global patent rules "does not and should not prevent members from taking measures to protect public health." Although developing countries had sought a statement of even stronger support for putting public health before patents, treatment access advocates praised the Qatar consensus as a step forward and said they would work in 2002 for more concrete language on patents and public health emergencies.

In April and May, United Nations Secretary-General Kofi Annan spearheaded an effort to establish a global fund to which public and private donors could contribute as part of a strengthened multilateral response to HIV/AIDS. Some treatment access advocates had been pushing for an international funding mechanism to draw in new resources to improve AIDS drug access for the poor. It was unclear whether the new global fund would serve this purpose as its mandate will include HIV/AIDS, tuberculosis and malaria, and the United States, among others, has expressed its preference that the AIDS focus of the fund be mainly prevention. Many questions remained about how the fund would be administered, how the interests of persons with AIDS would be represented in its decision-making, and especially whether the fund would ever have the U.S. $7 to $10 billion per year in resources envisioned by Kofi Annan. The Bush Administration's pledge of U.S. $200 million to the fund was widely criticized as inadequate. Pledges to the fund totaled about U.S. $1.4 billion in October 2001.

CHALLENGES BY REGION

Africa

Sub-Saharan Africa is the epicenter of HIV/AIDS. The disease constitutes a humanitarian emergency, having killed about 18 million persons since the mid-1980s, more than all of Africa's wars over that period. With historically unimaginable numbers of deaths of adults in their productive years, health and education services and economic productivity overall have deteriorated as a result of AIDS, along with the erosion of the extended family and community-based institutions. Silence and denial have characterized the response of many African leaders to this catastrophe. Although more African leaders are beginning to speak out about HIV/AIDS, including those who gathered for an African summit on AIDS in Abuja, Nigeria in April 2001, programs, policies and resources remain inadequate to the task of stemming the crisis.

Africa is the only region where women and girls outnumber men and boys among persons living with AIDS. In nearly all of the heavily affected countries of eastern and southern Africa, the rate of HIV infection among girls aged fifteen to nineteen years is four to seven times higher than that of boys. In most countries, girls are also more likely than boys to be pulled out of school when a parent becomes ill, and they frequently have to become the breadwinners of the family. AIDS-affected children, including large numbers of girls, continued to swell the numbers of street children in certain countries, with NGOs reporting that girls orphaned by AIDS increasingly find themselves having to engage in prostitution to survive, putting them at high risk of HIV transmission. The subordinate status of women and girls in the region had clearly facilitated the epidemic's rapid spread and destructive impact.

Lack of access to treatment has been a defining feature of the African AIDS crisis. In August, Nigeria and Cameroon both contracted with Cipla, an India-based generic drug manufacturer, to supply large-scale treatment programs for persons with AIDS. The humanitarian NGO Médecins Sans Frontières (MSF) also launched large pilot treatment programs in seven African countries. These initiatives will be examined closely for lessons on good practices to ensure wider-scale treatment access on the continent.

Eastern Europe

The fastest growing AIDS epidemic in the last few years has been in eastern Europe and the former Soviet states. It is fueled largely by the widespread use of injected drugs, a phenomenon that has grown with poverty, high unemployment and other aspects of the economic transition in the region as well as the easy availability of narcotic drugs. Access to services such as needle exchange and treatment for opportunistic infections remains very limited in many parts of the region. According to the Open Society Institute, which has been a leader in establishing AIDS-related services in the region, injecting drug use is highly prevalent among sex workers, homeless youth, and prisoners——groups likely to face stigmatization, marginalization and even abuse by the authorities in some settings.

Asia

It is feared that the numbers of persons infected and living with AIDS in Asia will surpass even the huge totals in Africa in the coming years. The epidemic in India, already well established in some states, is facilitated by subordination of women and discrimination against gay men and sex workers. Extremely high rates of infection among injecting drug users and sex workers in parts of Southeast Asia are driving a rapidly accelerating epidemic. Steep rises in infection rates in some parts of China, in some cases apparently fueled by the use of unsterilized needles in health facilities or blood sales centers, came to light in 2001. Public alarm over local media accounts of AIDS "outbreaks" reportedly led to incarceration of HIV-positive persons by local authorities and other drastic measures.

Caribbean and Latin America

The Caribbean basin contains several countries that have the highest rates of HIV infection outside sub-Saharan Africa. Policies and legal protections against AIDS-related discrimination have not caught up with the pace of the epidemic in a number of Latin American countries. Discrimination against HIV-positive gay men and sex workers and many instances of forced HIV testing of these groups and others have been reported in the media. In addition, with a fairly well developed capacity for generic drug production in some countries, the right to AIDS drugs has become a focus of civil society action. The national AIDS program in Brazil set a high standard in making locally produced generic drugs widely available to persons with AIDS. The proposed Free Trade Agreement for the Americas discussed at the regional summit in Quebec, Canada in May would afford even greater protection to patent-holding drug companies than they already enjoy under the terms of the WTO's intellectual property rules.

WIDENING RANGE OF ABUSES

Even as some aspects of the fight against AIDS have become better established, the range of human rights abuses linked to all stages of HIV/AIDS epidemics around the world has widened. In eastern and southern Africa, where HIV infection is so prevalent that it is no longer meaningful to stigmatize minority or "high-risk" groups, stigmatization of persons seeking AIDS-related care, especially women and girls, continues to drive the epidemic. Women have reported to health workers in several countries that they are aware of the risk of transmitting HIV to their infants through breastfeeding, but feel they have to take that risk because not breastfeeding will highlight their HIV-positive status and subject them to hostile and even violent reprisals from their husbands or partners. Denial of AIDS as a cause of death remains the rule rather than the exception even in the highest-prevalence countries, contributing to the stigmatization of those courageous enough to speak openly about their illness.

Children have a right to, and a life-and-death need for, access to good information on HIV transmission and care for persons with AIDS. Formal education, especially at the primary level, is an ideal vehicle for meeting this need. In many countries, however, AIDS education in school has been strongly opposed by religious groups and others who have alleged that sex education in schools encourages promiscuity. In Africa, this denial of children's and young people's right to information is compounded by the inability of many AIDS-affected children to stay in school. When a parent or other adult in the household is ill with AIDS, children are withdrawn from school to provide care, to earn income for the family, or because a family encumbered by the cost of treating a sick person can no longer afford to keep a child in school. A Human Rights Watch investigation in Kenya in February and March showed that children are further disadvantaged and entrenched in poverty by a lack of protection of their inheritance rights. Kenya is not the only country in Africa in which the state authorities have failed to institute legal to protect the rights of the hundreds of thousands of children who now find themselves without relatives to help protect their property.

Human rights protections continue to be the weakest part of generally feeble responses to AIDS on the part of many African governments. Kenya again illustrates an alarming pattern. The head of state did not even mention HIV/AIDS in public until late 1999, by which time about 14 percent of the adult population was already infected. In July 2001 he announced that he would urge parliament to institute capital punishment for persons who transmit HIV intentionally and portrayed this measure as an effective means of protecting women from AIDS. While intentional transmission of HIV, where it can be demonstrated, should be punishable by law, Kenya is one of many countries where an estimated 90 to 95 percent of HIV-positive persons do not even know their HIV status. It is unlikely, therefore, that focusing on "intentional" transmission would do much to curtail the epidemic. Meanwhile, policies and programs that could go a long way to improving access of women and girls to information and services remain non-existent or grossly underfunded.

HIV/AIDS in war was the object of international attention during the year. Soldiers in many armed conflicts were thought or in some cases known to have very high rates of HIV infection. To the extent that sexual coercion and sexual violence directed toward the civilian population are instruments of war, HIV/AIDS renders them more lethal. In January, as part of a Security Council session on HIV/AIDS, the United Nations Joint Programme on HIV/AIDS (UNAIDS) and the U.N.'s Department of Peacekeeping Operations undertook a joint project to reduce the likelihood that U.N. peacekeepers would contract or transmit HIV as part of their operations. The declaration of the U.N. special session on HIV/AIDS called on governments to improve HIV/AIDS awareness and prevention activities targeted at their armed forces.

Relevant Human Rights Watch Reports:

In the Shadow of Death: HIV/AIDS and Children's Rights in Kenya, 6/01
No Escape: Male Rape in U.S. Prisons, 4/01
Scared at School: Sexual Violence Against Girls in South African Schools, 3/01

HUMAN RIGHTS WATCH
INTERNATIONAL FILM FESTIVAL

The Human Rights Watch International Film Festival was created in 1988 to advance public education on human rights issues and concerns using the unique mediums of film and video. Each year, the festival exhibits the finest films and videos with human rights themes in theaters throughout the United States and several other countries, a reflection of both the scope of the festival and its increasingly global appeal. The 2001 festival featured thirty-eight provocative films (twenty-one of which were premieres), from fifteen countries. The festival included feature-length fiction films, documentaries, and animation. In 2001, selected films from the festival showcased in twenty-eight cities throughout the U.S.

In selecting films for the festival, Human Rights Watch concentrates equally on artistic merit and human rights content. The festival encourages filmmakers around the world to address human rights subject matter in their work and presents films and videos from both new and established international filmmakers. Each year, the festival's programming committee screens more than five hundred films and videos to create a program that represents a range of countries and issues. Once a film is nominated for a place in the program, staff of the relevant divisions of Human Rights Watch also view the work to confirm its accuracy in the portrayal of human rights concerns. Though the festival rules out films that contain unacceptable inaccuracies of fact, we do not bar any films on the basis of a particular point of view.

The 2001 festival was presented over a two-week period in New York as a collaborative venture with the Film Society of Lincoln Center. The festival reached out to a broader audience by co-presenting selected films with four important New York festivals: the African Film Festival, Margaret Mead Film and Video Festival, New York Latino Film Festival, and the New Festival/New York Lesbian and Gay Film Festival, as well as several independent media organizations: the Association of Independent Video and Filmmakers, DoubleTake, the Educational Video Center, MediaRights.org, Pixelpress.org, and POV/The American Documentary. A majority of the screenings were followed by discussions with the filmmakers, media activists and Human Rights Watch staff on the issues represented in each work.

The festival's presence on-line expanded greatly this year. In collaboration with MediaRights.org, a community web site created by media activists, we co-presented our first on line festival, "Media That Matters Online Film Festival." This series featured twelve short films and videos on U.S. (domestic) human rights issues for the entire month of June. Audiences from around the world were able to view these short works via the Internet and to then take immediate action by engaging in several campaigns made available on-line.

In association with Pixelpress.org, the film festival sponsored the multimedia presentation *Juvenile Justice*-a photograph and web site project which explores the lives of five adolescents and their struggle with the California criminal justice system. Award winning photographer Joseph Rodriguez drew on his own personal history as an incarcerated youth and contrasts this with the lives and stories of his subjects in Northern California. Many of these youth are being judged in court as adults. *Juvenile Justice* has encouraged on-line dialogue about several current human concerns and issues and the power of art (as an agent for change), between teens, parents, teachers, human rights activist, and artists.

The 2001 opening night celebration presented the U.S. premiere of the re-release of Hector Babenco's, *Kiss of a Spider Woman*, the first independent film to win an Academy Award for Best Actor and to be honored with four top Academy nominations, including Best Picture. After a critically acclaimed, yet limited release in 1986, the film virtually disappeared and was not again available to audiences until June 2001. Babenco's groundbreaking film set in a Latin American metropolis in the mid-1970's, explores the unlikely relationship that develops between two prisoners: one political revolutionary, the other a flamboyant homosexual convicted and imprisoned on "morality" charges. The film's emotional drama remains as strong today as fifteen years ago.

As part of the opening night program, the festival annually awards a prize in the name of cinematographer and director Nestor Almendros, who was also a cherished friend of the festival and Human Rights Watch. The award, which includes a cash prize of U.S.$5,000, goes to a deserving and courageous filmmaker in recognition of his or her contributions to human rights through film. The 2001 festival awarded the Nestor Almendros Prize to the three Italian filmmakers of the documentary *Jung(War): In the Land of the Mujaheddin*: Fabrizio Lazzaretti, Giuseppe Pettito, and Alberto Vendemmiati. These filmmakers demonstrated enormous courage filming in northern Afghanistan during war time, and their compassion for the people of Afghanistan is strikingly evident in this intimate, accomplished film.

Responding to the tragedy on September 11, the festival began to distribute *Jung (War): In the land of the Mujaheddin* on VHS format, free of charge, for community organization and festival screenings. To date the festival has responded to over one hundred requests with thirty screenings confirmed across the U.S. and Canada, including a theatrical run at the Cinema Village in New York City which began at the end of November.

In 1995, in honor of Irene Diamond, a longtime board member and supporter of Human Rights Watch, the festival launched the Irene Diamond Lifetime Achievement Award, presented annually to a director whose life's work demonstrates an outstanding commitment to human rights and film. Previous recipients have included Costa Gavras, Ousmane Sembene, Barbara Kopple, and Alan J. Pakula. This year, the award was presented to Haitian filmmaker Raoul Peck. Peck's exceptional body of documentary and fiction films focuses on the human rights situation in Haiti over the past forty years. His newest work, *Lumumba*, a dramatic portrait of legendary African leader Patrice Lumumba (and the first prime minister of the Congo following its independence) premiered at this year's New York festival and continues to screen theatrically throughout the U.S. to sold out audiences.

Highlights of the 2001 festival included the world premiere of Stephanie Black's *Life and Debt*, an extraordinary documentary exploring the complexities and dangers of economic globalization for Jamaica and developing countries around the world. Musician Ziggy Marley gave a special musical introduction for our audiences before the film screenings. Other highlights included; *Promises*, a moving insight into the Middle East conflict as seen through the eyes of seven children, both

Palestinian and Israeli, growing up in Jerusalem today. The festival hosted its first day of all youth programming-media by and for youth- about human rights issues. *Trembling Before G-d*, Sandi Simcha Dubowski's landmark documentary film about Hasidic and Orthodox Jews who "come out" as gays and lesbians, closed this year's festival.

Each year the festival holds a series of special film screenings for high school students and their teachers in an effort to encourage dialogue about human rights in the classroom. Daytime screenings are followed by discussions among the students, their teachers, visiting filmmakers, and Human Rights Watch staff. In 2001, in conjunction with our newly launched San Francisco festival, we hosted a special screening for public high school students of the documentary, *Public Enemy*, which focuses on four key members of the Black Panthers. Bobby Seale, a protagonist in the film and a co-founder of the Black Panthers, spent two hours in lively, heated, and passionate post-screening discussion with the youth audience.

In 1996 the festival expanded to London. The 2001 London festival produced with the Ritzy Theater in Brixton showcased the United Kingdom's premiere of Julian Schnabel's magnificent and lush *Before Night Falls*. The film chronicles the life of Cuban writer Reinaldo Arenas, one of the major artists to emerged from the Latin American literary boom of the 1960s. Running afoul of the Castro regime as both a political dissident and openly gay man, Arenas was harassed, imprisoned, and physically abused-all the more so because he managed to smuggle out and publish his works abroad. Schnabel capture's Arenas's extraordinary life with remarkable honesty.

The London festival featured the timely screening of *Caravan of Death*, journalist Isabel Hilton's documentary on Judge Juan Guzman's attempts to put former Chilean military ruler General Augusto Pinochet on trial for crimes he committed twenty-seven years ago. The festival also featured a special United Kingdom premiere of *Bamboozled*, Spike Lee's latest film, a blistering satire of network television's pitfalls and prejudices.

In a further effort to expand the festival's scope, a selected package of traveling films from the festival was created in 1994. The Traveling Festival is presented annually in a growing number of sites and cities. As of November 2001, the showcase had been presented in Salt Lake City, Utah; Portland, Oregon; Denver, Colorado; Seattle, Washington; Chicago, Illinois; and Riverside, California. In an effort to expand its capacity to raise awareness about human rights issues in the United States and abroad, the film festival created a web site with numerous support materials and links to Human Rights Watch's work on a variety of topics. We have facilitated filmmaker appearances at a number of traveling festival sites, which further enhances the audience's ability to discuss the films screened and analyze the issues they raise. In addition, we produced full-scale film festivals in both Boston and the San Francisco Bay Area for the first time where came together and discussed human rights issues in a community-based setting. These two festivals were unique in their geographical scope: the Boston festival was hosted at the Museum of Fine Arts in midtown, the Coolidge Corner theater in Brookline and the International Institute in downtown Boston. The Bay Area festival venues were equally broad: playing at The Pacific Film Archive in Berkeley, the Yerba Buena Center in downtown San Francisco, and the Rafael Film Center in Rafael, California.

INTERNATIONAL CAMPAIGN
TO BAN LANDMINES

The International Campaign to Ban Landmines (ICBL), launched in 1992 by Human Rights Watch and five other nongovernmental organizations, brought together over 1,400 human rights, humanitarian, children's, peace, disability, veterans, medical, humanitarian mine action, development, arms control, religious, environmental, and women's groups in over ninety countries who worked locally, nationally, regionally, and internationally to ban antipersonnel landmines. The ICBL was coordinated by international committee of thirteen organizations, including Human Rights Watch, which remained one of the most active campaign members. The ICBL and Jody Williams (a member of the Advisory Committee of the Human Rights Watch Arms Division) were jointly awarded the 1997 Nobel Peace Prize.

Progress toward the complete eradication of antipersonnel mines continued at an impressive pace, and the ICBL continued its intense global activity. Perhaps most notable were the further development of the ICBL's groundbreaking Landmine Monitor system, and the ICBL's extensive involvement in the "intersessional" work program of the 1997 Mine Ban Treaty. The ICBL engaged in numerous major events, including Ban Landmines Week and the ICBL General Meeting in Washington D.C. in March, the meetings of the Intersessional Standing Committees of the Mine Ban Treaty in December 2000 and May 2001, as well as a series of ten regional ICBL and Landmine Monitor meetings. In addition, the ICBL participated in several other regional and thematic meetings; undertook ICBL advocacy missions; sent a variety of letters to decision-makers; issued numerous Action Alerts; published activity reports; and issued quarterly Landmine Updates. Much of this information was disseminated via the ICBL website.

Campaign priorities were universalization of the Mine Ban Treaty—convincing recalcitrant nations to accede to the treaty—and ensuring effective implementation of the treaty. Particular targets were states of the former Soviet Union and the Middle East/North Africa, as well as the United States. Key issues of concern included: how to respond to violations of the ban treaty; antivehicle mines with antihandling devices which were prohibited by the treaty; joint military operations between States Parties and nonsignatories using mines; and continued stockpiling and transit of mines by nonsignatories in the territory of States Parties. Other priorities included: promoting increased funding for sustainable and appropriate mine action programs; promoting increased funding for comprehensive victim assistance programs and greater involvement of mine victims and mine-affected communities in the planning and implementation of such programs; and exploring ways to encourage non-state actors to commit to the banning of antipersonnel mines.

Four permanent working groups and one ad hoc working group of the ICBL led these efforts to address the various aspects of the humanitarian landmines crisis. They were the Treaty Working Group (chaired by Human Rights Watch), the Working Group on Victim Assistance, the Mine Action Working Group, and the Non-State Actors Working Group, as well as the ad-hoc Ethics and Justice Working Group.

The Third General Meeting of the ICBL, a biennial meeting of representatives of its national campaigns and member organizations, met in Washington D.C., on March 6-7, 2001. Some 160 participants from eighty country campaigns of the ICBL and representatives of international organizations attended the General Meeting, as well as twenty NGO observers from an additional ten countries. The meeting adopted an "ICBL 2004 Action Plan" that laid out a detailed universalization and implementation strategy for its members. It could be followed by country, by region, by year and/or by mine-related issue (i.e., mine action, survivor assistance, etc).

The General Meeting was held during Ban Landmines Week in Washington D.C. Two hundred mine survivors, deminers, and campaigners from ninety countries came together in Washington, D.C., marking the first time that the ICBL converged in the U.S. Simultaneously, two hundred activists from forty-six of the fifty states, including members of Students Against Landmines from schools nationwide, met in Washington for a U.S. Campaign to Ban Landmines national conference and four days of activities including over three hundred meetings with their Congressional representatives. Also during this week was the global meeting of Landmine Monitor researchers for review and submission of their draft reports for *Landmine Monitor Report 2001*.

The campaign committed to significant ICBL participation in the intersessional work program established in May 1999 at the First Meeting of States Parties. ICBL Working Groups took the lead in liaising with the four Standing Committees. The intersessional work program was aimed at consolidating and concentrating global mine action efforts, and highlighting the role of the Mine Ban Treaty as a comprehensive framework for mine action. The Standing Committees served to facilitate the implementation of provisions of the Mine Ban Treaty, with extensive input, recommendations, and action points from the ICBL. The four Standing Committees on Victim Assistance; Mine Clearance; Stockpile Destruction; and General Status and Operation of the Convention met during week-long sessions in Geneva in December 2000 and May 2001. The intersessional work proved to be an important mechanism to both spur and measure progress made in the full implementation of the Mine Ban Treaty. In September 2001 the Third Meeting of States Parties was held in Managua, Nicaragua, resulting in an extensive action program for the coming year.

Just prior to the Managua meeting, the ICBL released the 1,175-page *Landmine Monitor Report 2001*, the third annual report to emerge from the Landmine Monitor system. The Landmine Monitor network grew to 122 researchers in ninety-five countries, and the system and the annual report were widely recognized as a crucial element in addressing the landmine crisis.

The ICBL held day-long campaign seminars in conjunction with a new series of Landmine Monitor regional researcher meetings. At each ICBL session, campaigners strategized on work in the region, discussing campaign priorities, sharpening advocacy and media skills, as well as conducting events to raise public awareness.

These meetings also provided an opportunity for regional campaigners to discuss and contribute to the ICBL 2004 Action Plan. The series of meetings began in October 2000 in Yalta for campaigners from Former Soviet Union/Central Asia. In November, a regional meeting in the Americas was held in Buenos Aires before the Second Hemispheric Conference on Banning Landmines. In Buenos Aires, the ICBL also challenged the region's signatories of the Mine Ban Treaty to complete ratification, and challenged States Parties to complete destruction of stockpiles and submit outstanding article 7 transparency reports by the Third Meeting of States Parties. At the conclusion of the seminar, the government co-chairs from Argentina and Canada issued these calls as the "Managua Challenge." In Djibouti a meeting was held, also in November, in conjunction with a Regional Conference on Landmines for the Horn of Africa and Gulf of Aden. Tokyo was the venue for another regional meeting of campaigners in November, held to coincide with stockpile destruction and a fundraising marathon run to generate funds for demining in Cambodia. Another regional meeting was held from November 28-30 in Lomé, Togo, for Francophone African campaigners. European campaigners met in Geneva during the Intersessional Standing Committee meetings, and they also held a regional campaign meeting in Geneva in May 2001 to further strategize and coordinate advocacy plans for the region. Campaigners from the Middle East and North Africa met in Beirut in January 2001, where activities included an advocacy session, and a public event where Lebanese mine action organizations showcased their work. Campaigners from Southern Africa met in Johannesburg in January while those from Southeast Asia met in Bangkok. There they participated in a stockpile destruction ceremony and held a roundtable to present their research to diplomatic representatives in Bangkok. Their neighbors from South Asia met in Kathmandu in Nepal, where they also held roundtables, an advocacy seminar, and a media briefing.

The ICBL also participated in numerous workshops, seminars, and conferences. Among them was the Seminar on Universalization and Implementation of the Ottawa Convention in Africa, held in Bamako, Mali from February 15-16, 2001. The Bamako meeting, co-hosted by the governments of Mali, Canada, and France, marked the first time since May 1997 that countries from all of Africa came together to discuss the landmine ban. Members of the ICBL, including landmine survivors, deminers, and campaigners from throughout the continent, participated in this conference. The ICBL participated in the Seminar on the Destruction of the PFM1 mine which was held in Budapest from February 1-2, 2001, and in March 2001, the ICBL participated in the U.N. Asia Pacific Regional Disarmament Conference in Wellington, New Zealand, and also in a symposium on the Impact of Landmines in Sri Lanka.

National seminars or workshops were held in countries including Afghanistan, Angola, Australia, Colombia, Georgia, Germany, India, Japan, Lebanon, Nepal, Nigeria, Pakistan, Peru, South Africa, Yemen, and the U.S. New campaigners began activities in Ecuador, Egypt, Ethiopia, Mongolia, Nagorno-Karabakh, Peru, and Turkey.

Additionally, ICBL Ambassadors, staff, and members undertook a number of advocacy and awareness-building missions, including to Australia, Canada, Fiji,

France, Guatemala, Greece, India, Japan, South Africa, Spain, Taiwan and Belgium (for the European Council and Parliament). The ICBL sent letters to heads of state, issued media releases, and engaged in other advocacy activities on the occasions of international events such as the Asia-Europe Summit, the U.N. General Assembly in New York, government summits such as of the European Union, the Francophonie, the Organization of American States, the Organization of African Unity, the Assembly of African Francophone Parliamentarians, the Rio Group, MERCOSUR, Association of Southeast Asian Nations, and the Inter-Parliamentary Union. Letters to heads of state and media releases were also issued on the occasions of bilateral visits of heads of state. Letters to heads of state were also sent to mark Mine Ban Treaty anniversaries of December 3 and March 1 urging governments to accede to or ratify the treaty. Letters were also sent congratulating new ratifications, and urging all signatories to ratify before the Third Meeting of States Parties in September 2001. Letters were also sent prior to the two meetings of the Standing Committee on the General Status and Operation of the Convention highlighting issues of concern to the ICBL in preparation for the meetings.

As in previous years, the third anniversary of the opening for signature of the Mine Ban Treaty galvanized campaigners into action worldwide. On December 3, 2000, which coincided with the International Day for Disabled Persons, activities were held around the globe, from exhibits, to concerts, film screenings and hockey on prosthetics matches. Similarly the first anniversary of the entry into force of the treaty on March 1, 2001 further spurred action worldwide. A concerted campaign effort in anticipation of Ban Landmines Week targeted the United States, urging the newly-elected President Bush to join the treaty. The ICBL also issued regular Action Alerts, including several Ratification Campaign Action Alerts, prior to March 1, 2001 and again in May 2001, in anticipation of the Third Meeting of States Parties to be held in September.

INTERNATIONAL JUSTICE

INTRODUCTION

The components of the emerging system of international justice took further shape in 2001. The apprehension of Slobodan Milosevic by the International Criminal Tribunal for the former Yugoslavia (ICTY) and the rapidly growing number of states parties to the International Criminal Court treaty demonstrated the effectiveness of and growing commitment to international justice. International prosecutions helped to open national court systems that had previously been inaccessible to victims in Chile, Argentina, and Chad. The attacks in the United States on September 11 underscored for many states the need to strengthen mechanisms of international justice.

While new trends for greater accountability developed, progress was uneven and in some instances there were setbacks. The establishment of the mixed national-international courts for Sierra Leone and Cambodia, originally seen as a possible alternative to Security Council-created ad hoc tribunals, stalled. International prosecutions suffered a setback when Senegal's Cour de Cassation dismissed charges against Hissene Habre and challenges confronted Belgium's progressive law on universal jurisdiction.

INTERNATIONAL COURTS

International Criminal Tribunal for the Former Yugoslavia (ICTY)

During 2001, as the International Criminal Tribunal for the former Yugoslavia secured custody of senior officials, including former Bosnian Serb President Biljana Plavsic and Yugoslav President Slobodan Milosevic, it continued to contribute to the jurisprudence of international criminal law.

In its developing case law, the tribunal issued a highly significant ruling in the Foca case, convicting three men for rape, torture, and enslavement as crimes against humanity. The Foca case was the first indictment by an international tribunal solely for crimes of sexual violence against women as crimes against humanity and resulted in the first conviction by the ICTY for rape and enslavement as crimes against humanity. The tribunal ruled that the defendants had enslaved women and that enslavement did not necessarily require the buying or selling of a human being as had been traditionally required.

On October 23, the Appeals Chamber overturned the Trial Chamber's convictions in Prosecutor v. Zoran Krupeskic and Others. The Appeals Chamber found that the lower chamber, which had convicted all of the defendants, failed to do so with sufficient evidence for every count. This decision sent a clear message that the interests of the accused to a fair trial were paramount.

Slobodan Milosevic

Indicted in May 1999 for crimes against humanity and war crimes in Kosovo, Yugoslavia's handing over of Slobodan Milosevic to the tribunal was an historic milestone for international justice. U.S. law had imposed an April 1 deadline for Yugoslavia's cooperation with the tribunal in order to continue the flow of U.S. economic aid. While Milosevic's arrest was linked to U.S. government economic support for Yugoslavia, it was carried out by Serbian officials who were increasingly open to confronting the past. Milosevic's apprehension on corruption charges was a first step toward justice for the victims of the Balkan wars. Given the severity of the crimes charged in the ICTY indictment, Human Rights Watch insisted that Milosevic be surrendered to The Hague.

Even more importantly for Belgrade than the bilateral U.S. economic aid was the prospect of more than $1 billion in assistance that an international donors' conference would pledge for Yugoslavia. After Milosevic's arrest on April 1, U.S. Secretary of State Colin Powell certified that the required threshold of cooperation had been met, but announced that U.S. support for the international donors' conference would depend on "continued progress" by Yugoslavia. Human Rights Watch urged that specific benchmarks in this regard include the transfer of Milosevic and other indictees to the tribunal.

With Milosevic in custody, some argued that rather than turning him over to the ICTY, he should have been tried in Yugoslavia on corruption charges or possibly for war crimes. In Belgrade splits emerged between Republic of Serbia officials, Yugoslav President Kostunica, and Yugoslav Cabinet members over cooperation with the tribunal. President Kostunica repeatedly denigrated the tribunal and stated that he would never surrender Milosevic, a former head of state, to it. Increasingly, Kostunica sought to deflect international pressure by insisting that Yugoslavia could not surrender any ICTY indictee until it first adopted an enabling law. This stance patently ignored Yugoslavia's overriding international law obligation, mandated by numerous Security Council resolutions, to cooperate.

The opposition of pro-Milosevic deputies in the Yugoslav Parliament made it politically impossible to enact a cooperation law. After several unsuccessful attempts to pass legislation, on June 23 the Yugoslav Cabinet adopted a decree authorizing transfer of Yugoslav nationals. Milosevic filed a challenge before the Constitutional Court of Yugoslavia contesting the lawfulness of that decree. The court, composed of Milosevic appointees, unanimously suspended the decree. Serbian Prime Minister Zoran Djindic, citing the primacy of international law obligations, stated that Milosevic's transfer would go ahead even if the Constitutional Court struck down the decree. On June 28, one day prior to the international donors' conference and before the Constitutional Court had issued its ruling, the Serbian authorities surrendered Milosevic to The Hague.

Slobodan Milosevic's transfer to the United Nations war crimes tribunal was a victory for the victims of the Balkan wars and a transformative moment for international justice. The prosecution of a former head of state, indicted when he was a sitting president by an international tribunal was a groundbreaking precedent. More than a crude "payoff" for international economic support, Milosevic's surrender strengthened those authorities in Belgrade who sought to confront the crimes committed in the name of the Serbian people. After Milosevic's arrest in Belgrade and his surrender to The Hague, police began to uncover gravesites in Serbia containing the bodies of ethnic Albanians murdered in Kosovo and reburied in Serbia to avoid detection.

Many senior ICTY indictees, including former Bosnian Serb military commander General Ratko Mladic and Radovan Karadzic, formerly president of the Bosnian Serb Republic, remained at large. These two were charged with genocide in connection with the massacre of 7,000 Bosnian men at Srebrenica in July 1995. It was believed that at least eleven other indictees were living in Yugoslavia, however, Yugoslav officials had continued to stonewall all of the tribunal's requests for cooperation.

Foreshadowing some of the difficulties in prosecuting former heads of state in international fora, Slobodan Milosevic's initial court appearances in The Hague underscored the realities of a lengthy and difficult trial. Choosing to represent himself, Milosevic had denounced the tribunal's legitimacy and had not presented, as of mid-November, a legal defense. While it was necessary for the proceedings to move in an efficient and orderly way, it was vitally important that Milosevic's right to conduct his defense be scrupulously respected. At an August 30 status conference, Judge Richard May announced the appointment of three amici curiae to "assist the court" in the trial. These lawyers were not Milosevic's attorneys and it was crucial that they did not interfere with his right to a defense.

On October 9, the Prosecutor submitted a new indictment against Milosevic for events in Croatia in 1991-1992. It contained thirty-two counts of crimes against humanity, violations of the laws or customs of war, and war crimes. On November 23, the tribunal announced an indictment stemming from the 1992-1995 war in Bosnia that charged Milosevic with twenty-nine counts, including crimes against humanity and genocide.

MIXED NATIONAL-INTERNATIONAL COURTS

Sierra Leone

Despite the urgent need for accountability in Sierra Leone, progress in establishing the Special Court for Sierra Leone stalled in 2001. In 2000, the United Nations and the Government of Sierra Leone agreed to create a court that combined national and international components to try those individuals most responsible for serious crimes. This hybrid model was seen as an alternative to another Security Council-created ad hoc tribunal. The court would be based in Freetown, Sierra Leone, and would have both international and Sierra Leonean judges, prosecutors and staff.

The delay was due largely to the months-long impasse over the court's budget. There were several factors at work, including, dissatisfaction with the Security Council's decision to fund the court through voluntary, as opposed to assessed, contributions; a lack of confidence and commitment to this particular kind of hybrid court among some states; and disagreement between potential donor states and the United Nations Secretariat.

A group of "interested states" supporting the Special Court's early establishment were critical of the Secretariat's initial budget proposal, which totaled $114 million for three years of operations. These delegates regarded the U.N. Secretariat's estimates as excessive and sought to economize on the court's operations without affecting the quality of justice. As a result of a series of meetings between the Secretariat, the "interested states," and the Security Council, the Secretariat issued a revised budget on June 14. Under this budget, $16.8 million was required for the first year and $40 million for the next two years.

In mid-July Secretary-General Kofi Annan announced his decision to go forward with the Special Court's establishment despite a shortfall in pledges. As of mid-November, the small number of states that had pledged contributions included Canada, the Czech Republic, Denmark, Germany, Mauritius, the Netherlands, Lesotho, Finland, Norway, Sweden, the United Kingdom, and the United States.

There was further delay when the government of Sierra Leone proposed in late August to extend the court's temporal jurisdiction back in time to 1991, a position Human Rights Watch had long supported. This proposal was opposed by the United Nations Secretariat, the United States, and the United Kingdom. Human

Rights Watch sent a letter to the Security Council stressing the importance of a 1991 start date as well as the urgent need to get the court going. At this writing, the issue had not been resolved.

In early November, the court's Management Committee, mandated to oversee administrative and budgetary matters, held its first meeting in New York with the U.N. Secretariat and scheduled a planning mission to Freetown for January 2002. The mission was tasked to inspect conditions and prepare a detailed blueprint on the court's establishment for the secretary-general.

Cambodia

There was little progress in establishing the mixed national-international tribunal for Cambodia. While the authorities in Phnom Penh approved the statute, they failed to address serious concerns raised by the U.N. (See Cambodia.)

East Timor

As part of creating an East Timorese court system after the devastation of September 1999, the United Nations Transitional Administration in East Timor (UNTAET) decided to establish an international panel of the Dili district court to investigate international crimes that had occurred during 1999. In January 2001, the court handed down its first conviction, sentencing a pro-Indonesia militia member to twelve years in prison. Many low-ranking militia members had been detained, some for more than a year. It was a source of great frustration inside East Timor that justice proceeded so slowly. Inadequate training of investigators, changes in administrative structure, and a profound lack of resources and personnel plagued the court's investigative process.

INTERNATIONAL CRIMINAL COURT (ICC)

On July 17, 1998, when the Rome Statute of the International Criminal Court was adopted, only the most optimistic people imagined that it might take less than five years to garner the required sixty ratifications necessary for its entry into force. In the first half of 2001 it became a near certainty that this would happen as early as the first half of 2002. And the commitment to bringing the court into being as quickly as possible came from every region of the world.

At the General Assembly General Debate of the 56th Session of the United Nations in November 2001, many heads of state and foreign ministers made special mention of the ICC in their interventions, demonstrating the growing worldwide support for the ICC. Among those who highlighted the significance of the court were Argentina, Brazil, Canada, Chile, Czech Republic, France, Germany, Ireland, and Mexico.

From October 2000 to November 2001 twenty-six countries ratified the Rome Statute, bringing the total to forty-six. There were ten ratifications from the Americas, ten from Africa, five from the Asia/Pacific region and twenty-one from Europe. Many other countries are poised to ratify in the coming months.

A small number of states adopted domestic legislation to implement the Rome Statute. These include the Canada, New Zealand and the United Kingdom. As of the end of October 2001, a number of other countries, including Argentina, Australia, Germany, and South Africa had advanced in the process of drafting such law. Importantly, an increasing number of other states were recognizing the importance of comprehensive implementing law and were beginning the process of preparing it. Human Rights Watch saw the adoption of good implementing law as key to the effective functioning of the ICC and, in the past year, we made formal and informal submissions on draft implementing law in a number of countries, including Argentina, Australia, South Africa, and the United Kingdom.

The breadth of support for the ICC became evident in the final months of the year 2000 when states rushed to sign the Rome Statute before the December 31, 2000 deadline. Nineteen states signed during the last three weeks of December, bringing the total number of signatories to one hundred and thirty-nine countries. Iran, Israel, and the U.S. all signed on the very last day.

International Criminal Court Campaign Developments

The worldwide campaign for the ratification of the Rome Statute was assisted by many regional, subregional and national meetings. These meetings brought government, civil society, and legal experts together to discuss the complex task of preparing for ratification and developing national law implementing the Rome Statute. For example, in June, the government of Argentina, Human Rights Watch, and the Coalition of NGO's for the ICC co-convened an Iberoamerican conference in Buenos Aires for more than seventy governmental and nongovernmental actors working on the ICC.

In addition, national level conferences and workshops were held in many countries around the world, including Bangladesh, Brazil, Cambodia, Ecuador, Mexico, Paraguay, and the Philippines. Subregional meetings were held in Namibia for Southern Africa, in Hong Kong for East Asia, in Bangkok for South East Asia, in Ghana for West Africa, and in Peru for the Andean States. These meetings were crucial to raising awareness about the ICC and helped to develop the expertise necessary for ratification and implementation into national law of the Rome Statute. Human Rights Watch actively participated in many such meetings. We also continued to visit target countries around the world to advocate directly with governments for ratification and implementation of the Rome Statute.

As happened last year, regional organizations, such as the Organization of American States (OAS), Economic Community of West African States (ECOWAS), the Rio Group, the Southern African Development Cooperation (SADC) organization, the European Union (E.U.), and the Council of Europe, took the opportunity of their annual assemblies and other meetings to reaffirm their commitment to the ICC and to call on their member states to ratify without delay. For example, in June 2001, in a move long anticipated by Human Rights Watch, the E.U. adopted a Common Position on the ICC. The Common Position, which binds the member states, was unequivocal in its support for the ICC and lists the means by which the E.U. and its member states would work for the early establishment of the ICC.

Americas

The number of ratifications in the Americas more than doubled over the year with the ratifications of Antigua and Barbuda, Argentina, Costa Rica, Dominica, Paraguay, and Peru. Important advances toward ratification were made in key states in the region including Brazil and Mexico, both of which will require a constitutional amendment as part of the ratification process. Argentina established an inter-ministerial commission to prepare comprehensive draft legislation to implement the Rome Statute into domestic law. Many other states in the region expressed the political will to be among the first sixty countries to ratify the Rome Statute.

Europe

Twenty European states ratified the Rome Statute, including twelve members of the European Union. The United Kingdom adopted comprehensive legislation implementing the Rome Statute, but it unfortunately did not include provision for the exercise of universal jurisdiction over the ICC crimes it incorporated into its domestic law.

In addition to adopting the Common Position, the European Union also sent a demarche to the U.S. government in June calling on the U.S. to be a partner in the establishment of the ICC rather than opposing it.

Croatia and the Federal Republic of Yugoslavia, both subject to the jurisdiction of the International Criminal Tribunal for the former Yugoslavia, ratified this year. Poland became the third Eastern European state to ratify. However, in many Eastern European states the question of compatibility of the Rome Statute with national constitutions continued to loom large, delaying ratification in a number of countries, including the Czech Republic and Slovenia.

Africa

Following South Africa's ratification in November 2000, the momentum for ratification and implementation continued to grow among African countries in 2001. Both Nigeria and the Central African Republic ratified in September/October and others states, such as Angola, Benin, Congo/Brazzaville, and Cote d'Ivoire were making good progress towards ratification. There was more awareness of the issues involved in ratifying and implementing the Statute, particularly constitutional issues, and some states that ratified last year, including Botswana, Lesotho, Mali, Namibia, and South Africa, began work on implementation.

Middle East/North Africa

Countries in this region were slow to ratify: no state had ratified at the time of writing. However, eight states in the region signed the Rome Statute in the last year, bringing the total number of signatories from the region to eleven.

Asia/Pacific

Countries in the Asia/Pacific region continue to be the most wary of the ICC and this was reflected in the low numbers of ratifications in the region. Tajikistan was the only Asian state to have ratified. However, several began to examine the implications of ratification, including the Philippines and Thailand. In addition, the

Cambodian prime minister publicly stated his support for the ICC and sent the ratification bill to the National Assembly for its approval. A number of states in this region signed the treaty in the last year, including Iran and the Philippines.

In the Pacific, New Zealand, Nauru, and the Marshall Islands joined Fiji as states parties. New Zealand adopted comprehensive implementing legislation covering its obligation to cooperate with the ICC and incorporating the ICC crimes into national law so that national courts could prosecute them. Importantly, New Zealand also provided for the exercise of universal jurisdiction over the ICC crimes. Australia had completed its draft implementing legislation and invited public comment on it. It was expected to ratify in 2002. Human Rights Watch testified before an Australian Parliamentary Committee inquiry into the ICC in February 2001.

United States

In a very welcome move, President Clinton authorized signature on December 31, 2000, the last possible day for signing the Rome Statute. In his accompanying statement, he referred to continued concern about key elements of the Statute. He asserted the United States' commitment to bringing perpetrators of genocide, war crimes, and crimes against humanity to justice, but he firmly maintained that the signature did not signal U.S. approval of all aspects of the Rome Statute. Nonetheless, he explained that signature was essential for the U.S. to continue to work with other states to influence the evolution of the ICC.

Upon taking office, the Bush Administration announced that it would undertake a review of U.S. policy toward the ICC, which, at the time of writing had not been finalized. It was clear that the Bush administration did not support the ICC and would not refer the Rome Statute to Congress for ratification.

The United States Congress had expressed its hostility to the court more directly with the passage by the House of Representatives of the misnamed "American Servicemembers Protection Act" (ASPA). This legislation would prohibit any U.S. cooperation with the Court and would attempt to penalize countries that ratify the treaty. It had been characterized as "The Hague Invasion Act" because it also authorized the U.S. to use all means necessary to liberate any U.S. or allied persons detained on behalf of the proposed ICC.

The American Citizen's Protection and War Criminal Prosecutions Act of 2001 was presented by Senator Dodd to the Senate Foreign Relations Committee. Dodd planned to introduce this more reasonable bill to the Senate as an alternative to the ASPA.

The Bush administration expressed its support for the ASPA amendment in a State Department letter to Senator Helms on September 25, 2001. The administration's hostility to the ICC contrasted with its efforts to create a coalition to combat terrorism in the wake of the September 11 attacks. Almost all major U.S. allies were among the strongest supporters of the ICC and some had responded with alarm to the administration's support for Helms' legislation.

Throughout the year, Human Rights Watch continued to make known our opposition to the attitude of the U.S. towards the court. In particular, we met with, and wrote to, administration officials and legislators.

Preparatory Commissions

The Preparatory Commission for the ICC met twice in the past year. Meetings were held at U.N. headquarters in New York. The seventh session in March 2001 included discussion on a number of supplementary instruments included in the mandate of the commission. At the eighth session of the Preparatory Commission (September 24 - October 6, 2001) four of these instruments were adopted. They were the Relationship Agreement between the U.N. and the ICC, Rules for the Assembly of States Parties, the Financial Rules and Regulations for the ICC, and the Agreement on Privileges and Immunities. Negotiations are expected to continue in early 2002 on the Headquarters Agreement between the Host State and the ICC, the First Year Budget for the ICC, and the elaboration of the crime of aggression. Importantly, the commission also adopted a "road map," which detailed a timetable for the completion of a number of practical matters essential for the establishment of the ICC and which must be undertaken in advance of the entry into force of the Rome Statute. These included establishment of an interlocutor between the host state, the Netherlands, and the ICC and preparing documents for the first Assembly of States Parties.

The Preparatory Commission would stay in existence until the end of the first meeting of the Assembly of States Parties. This was expected to take place soon after the sixtieth ratification and entry into force of the Rome Statute. In expectation of the Rome Statute's entry into force by the middle of 2002, the General Assembly's Sixth Committee session in November 2001 approved two Preparatory Commissions for 2002, to take place in April and July, as well as authorizing the First Assembly of States Parties.

UNIVERSAL JURISDICTION

Habré Case

In February 2000, a Senegalese court indicted Chad's exiled former dictator, Hissène Habré, on charges of torture and crimes against humanity, and placed him under house arrest. It was the first time that an African had been charged with atrocities by the court of another African country. In March 2001, however, Senegal's Court of Final Appeals ruled that he could not be tried in Senegal for crimes allegedly committed in Chad. Habré's victims then sought his extradition to Belgium. The United Nations Committee against Torture and high U.N. officials subsequently requested Senegal not to let Habré leave the country except via extradition, and Senegal had agreed to hold him. In the meantime, the case opened new possibilities for justice in Chad itself.

Habré ruled Chad from 1982 until he was deposed in 1990 by current president Idriss Déby and fled to Senegal. Habré's one-party regime, supported by the United States and France, was marked by widespread abuse and campaigns against the ethnic Sara (1984), the Hadjerai (1987), and the Zaghawa (1989). In 1992, a truth commission accused Habré's government of 40,000 murders and systematic torture.

Chadian victims had sought to bring Habré to justice since his fall. With many ranking officials of the Déby government, including Déby himself, involved in Habré's crimes, however, the new government did not pursue Habré's extradition from Senegal.

In 1999, with the Pinochet precedent in mind, the Chadian Association for the Promotion and Defense of Human Rights requested Human Rights Watch's assistance in bringing Habré to justice in Senegal. The Chadian Association of Victims of Political Repression and Crime (AVCRP) representing hundreds of Habré's victims, helped prepare the evidence. Meanwhile, a coalition of Chadian, Senegalese, and international NGOs was quietly organized to support the complaint.

In a criminal complaint filed in Dakar on January 26, 2000, the plaintiffs accused Habré of torture and crimes against humanity, providing details of ninety-seven political killings, one hundred and forty-two cases of torture, one hundred "disappearances," and seven hundred thirty-six arbitrary arrests, most carried out by Habré's dreaded DDS (Documentation and Security Directorate). A 1992 report by a French medical team on torture under Habré was also submitted to the court. After a number of victims gave closed-door testimony before the Investigating Judge, the judge called in Habré on February 3, 2000 and indicted him on charges of crimes against humanity and torture and placed him under house arrest.

After Abdoulaye Wade was elected president of Senegal in March 2000, the state prosecutor supported Habré's motion to dismiss the case. President Wade also headed a panel that removed the Investigating Judge. Habré reportedly spent lavishly to influence the outcome of the case.

On July 4, 2000, an appeals court dismissed the charges against Habré, ruling that Senegal had not enacted legislation to implement the Convention against Torture and therefore had no jurisdiction to pursue crimes that were not committed in Senegal. The United Nations special rapporteurs on the independence of judges and lawyers and on torture made a rare joint and public expression of their concern to the government of Senegal over the dismissal and the surrounding circumstances. The victims appealed the dismissal to the Cour de Cassation, Senegal's Court of Final Appeals.

On March 20, 2001, following repeated declarations by Senegal's president that Habré would never be tried in Senegal, Senegal's Cour de Cassation affirmed the appeals court decision. The effort to prosecute Habré continued, however.

In November 2000, Chadian victims had already filed a criminal complaint against Habré in Belgium, which has expansive jurisdictional laws, to create the possibility of extradition to stand trial there. That case was being actively investigated. The Belgian judge was seeking to visit Chad and it was hoped that in due course he would issue an international arrest warrant against Habré.

In addition, the victims filed a complaint against Senegal before the United Nations Committee against Torture (CAT) for violation of Senegal's obligations under the Torture Convention to prosecute or extradite Habré, asking the committee to recommend that Senegal amend its laws and either reinitiate the investigation against Habré or directly compensate the victims for their loss.

In April 2001, President Wade abruptly announced that he had asked Habré to leave Senegal. While this represented an important acknowledgement of the victims' efforts, they feared that Habré would move to a country out of reach of an extradition request or a final U.N. ruling and asked the CAT to issue an interim ruling to preserve their ability to bring him to justice. The CAT responded by asking Senegal "not to expel Mr. Hissène Habré and to take all necessary measures to prevent Mr. Hissène Habré from leaving Senegalese territory except pursuant to an extradition." After the same request was made by high U.N. officials including, according to Wade, Kofi Annan, Wade announced that he would hold Habré. Habré's supporters had since then made clear that he was looking to escape.

The victims and their supporters continued to wage an international campaign to deny Habré a safe haven, even if he were able to leave Senegal. Madagascar, Mauritania, and Pakistan, countries reportedly contacted by Habré, stated publicly that they would not grant refuge to Habré after NGOs brought the issue to public attention.

In the meantime, the case opened up new avenues for justice in Chad itself. Just as Pinochet's arrest in Britain broke the spell of Pinochet's impunity in Chile, the Habré indictment in Senegal had an immediate impact back in Chad. The victims who had initiated the case gained a new stature in Chadian society, having accomplished something no one had thought possible, and announced their intention to file criminal charges in Chadian courts against their direct torturers. President Idriss Déby met with the Association of Victims' leadership to tell them that "the time for justice has come" and that he would support their cases. Déby also promised to clean up the administration by removing all former DDS agents, Habré's political police, and to grant full access to the files of the Truth Commission to the International Committee.

On October 26, 2000, seventeen victims lodged criminal complaints for torture, murder, and "disappearance" against named members of the DDS. The case was initially thrown out by the Investigating Judge who ruled that Chadian civil courts had no jurisdiction to hear complaints against the DDS because a 1993 statute had provided for a special criminal court to try "Habré and his accomplices," though that court never existed. The victims appealed and the appeals court turned to the Constitutional Court for advice, which ruled that the 1993 statute was unconstitutional. In May 2001, after the cases were reinstated, a new investigating judge began to hear witnesses. More than twenty victims filed new cases.

The victims' actions were a direct challenge to the continuing power of Habré's accomplices, who began to respond violently. The victims' Chadian lawyer, Jacqueline Moudeina, had a grenade thrown at her by security forces commanded by one of the ex-DDS defendants and was evacuated to a hospital in France, her leg full of shrapnel.

Belgian Law

Belgium's law providing Belgian courts with universal jurisdiction authority over genocide, crimes against humanity and war crimes is a model. The law had provided important opportunities in the struggle against impunity.

Rwandan Genocide Trials

In April, the Cour d'Assises in Brussels began a trial of four Rwandans accused of involvement in the 1994 Rwandan genocide. None of the four were government officials at the time of the genocide. Two of the defendants were nuns. Most unusually and importantly, a jury of Belgian citizens heard the case, and in June, found all four of the accused guilty. The jury trial validated the involvement of citizens in the pursuit of international justice. In the course of the proceedings, more than fifty witnesses traveled from Rwanda to appear in the courtroom. The trial and the conviction were covered extensively by radio in Rwanda.

Ariel Sharon

Controversy mounted in Europe in 2001 over Israeli Prime Minister Ariel Sharon's responsibility for the 1982 killings in the Palestinian refugee camps of Sabra and Shatila. The Israeli Government's Kahan Commission that had investigated the massacre in 1983 concluded that the then minister of defense, Sharon, bore "personal responsibility" and that he should "draw the appropriate personal conclusions arising out of the defects revealed with regard to the manner in which he discharged the duties of his office." The findings of the Kahan Commission, however authoritative in terms of investigation and documentation, could not substitute for proceedings in a criminal court in Israel or elsewhere that would bring to justice those responsible for the deliberate killing of hundreds of innocent civilians. In June, after the airing of a BBC documentary on the massacre, survivors lodged a complaint against Ariel Sharon in a Belgian court.

When Prime Minister Sharon visited the United States in July, Human Rights Watch urged that a criminal investigation be launched into his role in the massacre and asked that the U.S. government encourage Sharon to cooperate with any investigation. As prime minister, Sharon could invoke immunity from prosecution. However, this should not preclude an active criminal investigation either in Israel or elsewhere.

Democratic Republic of Congo v. Belgium at the International Court of Justice

In a potentially serious challenge to universal jurisdiction, the Democratic Republic of Congo (DRC) filed a case on April 11, 2000 with the International Court of Justice (ICJ) contesting the lawfulness of a Belgian arrest warrant issued against the DRC's then acting foreign minister, Abdoulaye Yerodia Ndombasi. A Belgian investigating judge had charged Yerodia with genocide, war crimes, and crimes against humanity. The accusations were based on public calls Yerodia had made for the Congolese population to kill members of the Tutsi ethnic group at the start of the rebellion against Congolese President Laurent Kabila in August 1998. The arrest warrant was based on a 1999 Belgian law giving Belgian courts the authority to prosecute individuals accused of atrocities regardless of the crimes' connection to Belgium or the accused's presence on Belgian soil. The Democratic Republic of the Congo contended that the law violated its territorial integrity and that the international arrest warrant was invalid as its acting foreign minister enjoyed diplomatic immunity.

The DRC sought provisional remedies from the court to have the arrest warrant invalidated. After several days of oral arguments in November 2000, the court denied the DRC's request for provisional measures. On October 15, 2001, the ICJ heard arguments on the substantive claims. The DRC dropped the challenge to the fundamental lawfulness of universal jurisdiction in its pleading to the ICJ.

Internal Challenges

An increasing number of cases were filed in Belgian courts under its universal jurisdiction law. Many of these charged current and former heads of state with serious crimes, including Fidel Castro, Ange Felix Patasse, Yasir Arafat, and Hashemi Rafsanjani. Because of the provisions of Belgian law, these cases were initiated even when the accused was not present on Belgian territory. This proliferation of cases prompted some in the Belgian government to reconsider its universal jurisdiction law. In July, when Belgium assumed the rotating presidency of the European Union, the Belgian cabinet considered amending the law in Parliament, but was unable to reach agreement. Belgium's Chambre d'Accusation was to determine the admissibility of several cases filed against current heads of state, including, the case of Ariel Sharon and the Ivory Coast's Laurent Gbagbo. Through these cases the court was to decide whether to reinterpret the law to require the defendant's presence on Belgian soil before a case could move forward. In late November 2001, the International Commission of Jurists, the International Federation of Human Rights Leagues (FIDH), and Human Rights Watch issued a joint press release expressing support for the Belgian law. Shortly thereafter the court announced that it would likely issue its decision in January 2002. Whatever the decision, it would be appealed to Belgium's highest court, the Cour de Cassation.

Dutch Courts and Colonel Desi Bouterese

Of course, Belgium was not the only state with universal jurisdiction legislation. Over several years trials of low and mid-level accused had taken place in Switzerland, Denmark, and Germany on the basis of universal jurisdiction, but efforts to invoke universal jurisdiction were not always successful.

In March 2001, an Amsterdam Appeals Court issued an important ruling allowing Dutch prosecutors to investigate the "possible involvement" of former Suriname dictator Desi Bouterse in serious human rights crimes in 1982. The Appeals Court authorized the retrospective application of Dutch legislation implementing the Convention Against Torture. The judges found that because the acts had been prohibited by preemptory norms of international law, it was permissible to apply the 1988 Dutch enabling legislation to acts that had occurred six years prior to the law's enactment. In September, however, the Dutch Supreme Court reversed the Appeals Court decision.

INCREASED ACCESS TO NATIONAL COURTS

Despite the failure to hold Augusto Pinochet to account in Chilean courts, the synergy between justice at the international level and increased access to national courts continued most clearly in the Americas. Most of the results were positive.

Ricardo Miguel Cavallo

In August 2000, Mexican authorities arrested Ricardo Miguel Cavallo, a former Argentine navy lieutenant, at the request of Spanish investigating judge Baltasar Garzon. In February 2001, Mexican Foreign Minister Jorge G. Castaneda authorized Cavallo's extradition to face charges in Spain for human rights violations in Argentina during that country's "Dirty War." Cavallo's lawyers filed an amparo petition (recurso de amparo) before a federal court (the Juzgado Primero "B" de Distrito en Materia de Amparo) challenging the constitutionality of the foreign minister's decision. A decision from the court was still pending. Should it reject Cavallo's petition, he would have the option of filing a judicial appeal, which would ultimately be considered by the Mexican Supreme Court.

Argentine Amnesty Law

On March 6, Argentine Federal Judge Gabriel Cavallo struck down as unconstitutional two laws that had barred prosecution of those responsible for human rights crimes: the "Full Stop" and "Due Obedience" laws. This ruling would clear the way for trials of military officials accused of human rights crimes during the "Dirty War." The ruling was issued in a 1978 murder-kidnapping case and was an important step in ending more than two decades of impunity. In November, the Buenos Aires Federal Court upheld Judge Cavallo's decision by rejecting the defendant's appeal. Argentina's Supreme Court would review the case.

Alfredo Astiz

On July 1, former Argentinean naval officer Alfredo Astiz surrendered to Interpol in Buenos Aires. He was arrested on orders of Argentine Federal Judge María Servini de Cubría, who received a formal request for his extradition from an Italian court. Captain Astiz, notorious for human rights abuses committed during Argentina's military dictatorship (1976-1983), was charged in Italy with the kidnapping and torture of three Italian-Argentines. Human Rights Watch had called on President Fernando De la Rúa of Argentina to extradite Astiz to Italy. In a setback for international justice, the Argentine Foreign Ministry decided to release him on August 21.

Relevant Human Rights Watch Reports:

Making the International Criminal Court Work: A Handbook for Implementing the Rome Statute, 9/01

LESBIAN, GAY, BISEXUAL, AND TRANSGENDER RIGHTS

Although the visibility of lesbian, gay, bisexual, and transgender people throughout the world continued to rise in 2001, their increased visibility was accompanied by attacks based on sexual orientation and gender identity. Human rights activists who sought to use the human rights framework to call to account states that participated in these rights abuses or condoned them also came under attack. In virtually every country in the world people suffered from de jure and de facto discrimination based on their actual or perceived sexual orientation. In some countries, sexual minorities lived with the very real threat of being deprived of their right to life and security of person. A small number of countries continued to impose the death penalty for private sexual acts between consenting adults. In several others, sexual minorities were targeted for extrajudicial executions. In many countries, police or other members of the security forces actively participated in the persecution of lesbians, gay, bisexual, and transgender people, including their arbitrary detention and torture. Pervasive bias within the criminal justice system in many countries effectively precluded members of sexual minorities from seeking redress.

These attacks on human rights and fundamental freedoms also occurred in international fora where states were gathered to promote, not attack, human rights. For example, in New York in June at the U.N. General Assembly Special Session on HIV/AIDS, delegates attempted to ban nongovernmental representative Karyn Kaplan from the International Gay and Lesbian Human Rights Commission (IGLHRC) from speaking at an official roundtable. Delegates from Sudan, Syria, Pakistan, Libya, Malaysia, Egypt, Iran, Saudi Arabia, and Morocco criticized in their verbal statements any recognition of sexual minorities. Although the U.N. General Assembly eventually voted in a closed plenary session to allow Kaplan to speak at the roundtable, the final document did not include any explicit reference to lesbian, gay, bisexual, and transgender people despite the fact that sexual minorities were at increased risk of HIV infection in many countries.

The rights of sexual minorities also came under attack at the U.N. Commission on Human Rights where delegates objected to the inclusion of cases of extrajudicial executions of sexual minorities in the report of the U.N. special rapporteur on extrajudicial, summary, and arbitrary executions. Delegates argued that the special rapporteur overstepped her mandate by addressing these crimes. The resolution renewing her mandate was stripped of language explicitly recognizing that sexual minorities were vulnerable to extrajudicial executions.

Other intergovernmental bodies played a strong role in upholding the rights of lesbian, gay, bisexual, and transgender people. Under article 13 of the Treaty of Amsterdam, which entered into force in 1999, the European Union could adopt measures to combat discrimination based on sexual orientation, among other grounds. In addition, the Charter of Fundamental Rights of the European Union, adopted in December 2000, included sexual orientation among the prohibited grounds of discrimination. However, the European Union's governing bodies could only act to implement these provisions within their area of competence, which generally excluded criminal law, family law, and education. In a directive that entered into force in December 2000, the European Council called upon member states to take steps within three years to ban sexual orientation discrimination in employment.

The European Union was also required to assess the respect for human rights, including the principle of equality, in the twelve countries with which it had opened negotiations for accession to membership. The twelve countries were Bulgaria, Cyprus, the Czech Republic, Estonia, Hungary, Latvia, Lithuania, Malta, Romania, Poland, Slovakia, and Slovenia. (In addition, Turkey was a candidate for membership in the European Union but was not currently in negotiations.) Five of the thirteen countries that had applied for membership—Bulgaria, Cyprus, Estonia, Hungary, and Lithuania—maintained discriminatory provisions in their criminal laws, according to the European branch of the International Lesbian and Gay Association. In July, the Romanian government adopted a decree decriminalizing gay relationships between consenting adults, effectively nullifying a law that allowed sentences of up to five years imprisonment for homosexual relationships "occurring in public or which provoke a public scandal."

After a European Parliament intergroup on gay and lesbian rights held a hearing in June 2001, E.U. Enlargement Commissioner Guenter Verheugen confirmed that "full attention" would be given in the accession review process to issues related to discrimination based on sexual orientation. The European Parliament, which must approve applications for membership in the European Union, stated in 1998 that it would not give its consent to the accession of a country that violated the rights of lesbians and gay men.

PERSECUTION

Lesbian, gay, bisexual, and transgender people were vilified by officials of several countries. They were denied equal enjoyment and protection before the law in a significant number of countries. They were arrested and tried, sometimes under national security laws, for private consensual acts. In Namibia, President Samuel Nujoma continued to vilify gay men and lesbians, stating, "The Republic of Namibia does not allow homosexuality, lesbianism here. Police are ordered to arrest you, and deport you, and imprison you too." The nationally televised speech came just two weeks after the Namibian Supreme Court overturned a lower court ruling recognizing the right of one member of a same sex couple to confer permanent residency on the other. Soon after the speech, the Rainbow Project, a nongovernmental human rights organization working with sexual minorities, started receiving reports of harassment and beatings by the Special Field Forces, a security unit reporting directly to the president. Nujoma later clarified his statement, "Traditional leaders, governors, see to it that there are no criminals, gays and lesbians in your villages and regions. We . . . have not fought for an independent Namibia that gives rights to botsotsos [criminals], gays and lesbians to do their bad things here."

In November, Malaysian Prime Minister Mahathir Mohamad also verbally attacked gays, announcing that he would expel any gay British government minister if he came to Malaysia with a partner. Mahathir explained in an interview with BBC radio, "the British people accept homosexual ministers. But if they ever come here bringing their boyfriend along, we will throw them out. We will not accept them."

In February, confusion reigned about the fate of two women who were reportedly sentenced to death for "unnatural behavior" in the city of Boosaaso in the self-declared autonomous region of Puntland, northeast Somalia. The news of the sentence was first published in a local weekly and was subsequently picked up by the national and international press in Mogadishu. When the reports of the case generated significant international attention on Puntland, the authorities denied the reports and instead accused journalists of inventing the story to discredit the government. The authorities also accused the editor of the weekly paper of making false assertions and published statements. Lost amid all the debate about the politics of the government's relationship with the press was any clarification regarding the two women named in the report.

Lesbian, gay, bisexual, and transgender people faced arrest for consensual sexual activities and many of those arrested reported being tortured by the police. In Egypt, a sixteen-year-old boy was convicted of "debauchery" on September 18 for allegedly engaging in sexual relations with men. The boy received a sentence of three years' imprisonment with labor followed by three years of probation. His sentence was on appeal at this writing. The youth said that police extracted a confession from him after subjecting him to painful beating on the soles of the feet. He did not have access to a lawyer during his interrogation, and he was not allowed to contact his family during the first two weeks of his detention. Press and spectators were allowed to attend and report on the September and October hearings, and the boy's name, photo, and accounts of the charges and sentence have appeared in Egypt's semi-official press.

The boy was one of fifty-three people detained and charged with similar offenses after a crackdown in May against men presumed to be gay. The others, all adults, were arrested and subjected to violations of standard arrest procedures according to their defense attorneys. There were reports that the men were beaten and subjected to forensic examinations in order to ascertain if they had engaged in anal sex. They were prosecuted before an Emergency State Security Court, which reached a verdict on November 14. Twenty-three were sentenced to between one and five years of hard labor; twenty-nine were acquitted. Because the trial took place before an Emergency State Security Court, those convicted could not appeal their sentences.

Despite urgent appeals from the U.N. special rapporteurs on the independence of judges and lawyers, and torture and the Working Group on Arbitrary Detention, the Egyptian authorities not only went through with the prosecutions of the men, but a day after the sentencing in the first case, police arrested and charged four more men on the same grounds. They too were reportedly tortured. As Egypt did not expressly outlaw homosexual acts, the charges included "habitual practice of debauchery" and "contempt of religion."

In March, two men in Lebanon were convicted by a military court of defaming the Vice Squad (Police des Moeurs) and fined U.S. $200. In July, on appeal to the Military Court of Cassation, the conviction of one of the men was overturned. The case began in April 2000 when two plainclothes police officers from the Vice Squad entered the office of Destinations, an internet service provider (IPS), seeking the identities of the person who had financed and installed a website with gay related content, including the need for legal reform within Lebanon. Ziad Mugraby, the manager of the IPS refused to cooperate with the warrantless search. He was subsequently order to appear the next day for questioning. After repeated threats and interrogations, Mugraby turned to Multi-Initiative on Rights, Search, Assist and Defend (MIRSAD), a human rights nongovernmental organization in Lebanon for support. In July, director of MIRSAD Kamal el Batal was also questioned by the police. The two men were subsequently tried in a military court for defamation based on their publicizing the circumstances of the case. Batal's conviction was overturned.

On July 7, police raided the offices of the Bharosa Trust and the Naz Foundation International in Lucknow, organizations that worked on HIV/AIDS prevention, arresting several staff members. Although subsequently released on bail, the staff members were charged under article 377 of the Indian Penal Code, a provision that prohibited "carnal intercourse against the order of nature." Article 377 had been used repeatedly to justify discrimination and police brutality against gay, lesbian, and bisexual individuals.

Members of sexual minorities also faced detention in psychiatric hospitals in several countries. In April, the National Human Rights Commission of India missed a significant opportunity to address this violation when it announced that it did "not want to take cognizance" of a case brought before the commission objecting to involuntary aversion therapy and other forms of psychiatric abuse aimed at "converting" homosexuals. The commission explained its decision by stating, "sexual minority rights did not fall under the purview of human rights."

More than a year after the murder of transgender activist Dayana (Jose Luis Nieves), transgender people living in Venezuela continued to face unrelenting police harassment. The Commander of Police in the state of Carabobo announced, "homosexuals and prostitutes are to be ruled by the police code. They cannot move freely in the streets." Activists reported that this attitude by the police had led to an atmosphere of fear and intimidation within the transgender community.

Another transgender activist, Diane Sacayan in Argentina, who had publicly denounced police harassment and abuse of transvestites, was arrested in the city of Don Bosco in February and charged with robbery. As of this writing, she was still in detention and had not had the evidence against her presented at a preliminary hearing. Sacayan reported being tortured by the police and alleged that that she was arrested not for robbery but for refusing to pay a bribe to the local police. Stigmatization of transgender people made them particularly vulnerable to abuse by the authorities. Transvestites in Argentina were arrested under a law prohibiting the wearing of the clothes of the opposite sex, a prima facie violation of freedom of expression.

The persecution of transgender people in Argentina led to a historic meeting of activists with U.N. Special Rapporteur on Freedom of Expression Dr. Abid Hussain. The meeting followed the issuing of a joint statement by six U.N. experts urging lesbian, gay, bisexual, and transgender activists to send them information regarding human rights violations based on sexual orientation or gender identity.

DISCRIMINATION

Although lesbian, gay, bisexual, and transgender people continued to experience de jure and de facto discrimination in virtually every country in the world, several significant changes occurred in 2001. Netherlands became the first state to allow same sex couples to marry. Just three years after implementing a domestic partnership law, the legislature, by a significant majority, passed a law to end discrimination in marriage. The law went into effect on April 1. The law required that at least one partner be a Dutch citizen or resident, as required for heterosexual couples who marry.

In another groundbreaking decision, Colombia's Supreme Court issued a decision on October granting conjugal visits to a lesbian in prison and her partner. The decision in the Montoya case not only ended the practice of gender and sexual orientation based discrimination regarding conjugal visits for prisoners. The ruling could also could resolve the ongoing case of Marta Alverez, who faced similar discrimination and brought the first sexual orientation-related case ever presented to the Inter-American Commission on Human Rights. The case was heard by the commission in October 1999. After the hearing, the parties entered into settlement negotiations. The law, prior to this decision, granted conjugal visits to heterosexual male inmates but limited conjugal visits to the spouses of heterosexual female inmates. The government admitted that its practice was discriminatory but argued that the restrictions on conjugal visits promoted security, discipline, and morality in the prisons. The government also argued that Latin American cultures did not tolerate homosexuality.

In September, Judge Kathleen Satchwell, a judge in South Africa, won the right for her female partner to enjoy the same benefits as those previously reserved for "spouses" of married heterosexual judges. Although South Africa continued to take the lead on human rights protections for gays and lesbians, Minister of Justice Penuell Maduna fought the Satchwell case to the bitter end, revealing deep-seated reservations about the constitution's equality clause. Also in September, a South African Court ruled that gay and lesbian couples could adopt children. The judgment was appealed to the Constitutional Court.

The issue of bias remained a serious concern for sexual minorities worldwide. A report released in February by the Judicial Council of California, revealed that anti-gay bias was a major problem in the court system statewide in California. Over half of all gay men and lesbians interviewed regarding their court experiences reported hearing anti-gay comments or experiencing anti-gay actions when sexual orientation became an issue. Nearly a third of all court employees believed that it was unsafe for them to be openly identified as gay or lesbian in the workplace. This bias remained even though California was one of the United States' most progressive states regarding lesbian and gay equality.

In Finland, a new law allowed gays and lesbians to register as couples and obtain some of the same benefits previously reserved for married couples or relatives, such as the right to inherit property and to visit if one partner was hospitalized. However, unlike in South Africa, gay and lesbian couples were still banned from adopting children or taking a common surname.

Seven years after the military's "Don't Ask, Don't Tell" policy was codified as law and implemented, the United States military's own surveys and investigations found that training on how to implement the law was deficient and that anti-gay harassment remained pervasive in the military. Many military personnel who faced verbal or physical harassment and feared for their safety made statements acknowledging they were gay, knowing that it would mean the end of their careers, but also aware that if they complained officially about anti-gay harassment they would probably themselves face an intrusive inquiry and discharge. They also knew that harassers were rarely punished.

Although the "Don't Ask, Don't Tell" policy was ostensibly intended to allow gay, lesbian, and bisexual service members to remain in the military, discharges increased significantly after the policy's adoption. From 1994 to 2000, more than 6,500 servicemembers were discharged under the policy, with a record number of 1,231 separations during 2000. Women were discharged at a disproportionately high rate, while the policy provided an additional means for men to harass women service members by threatening to "out" those who refused their advances or threatened to report them, thus ending their careers.

The U.S. was increasingly out of step internationally in maintaining restrictions on homosexuals serving in the military. Most of its NATO and other allies either allowed homosexuals to serve openly or had no policy on the issue. In September 1999, the European Court of Human Rights rejected a United Kingdom ban on homosexuals serving in the military; the justification for that ban had been similar to that used to defend the U.S. military's "Don't Ask, Don't Tell" policy.

Each day was a test of survival for many lesbian, gay, bisexual, and transgender students in U.S. public schools. Our 2001 report, based on interviews in rural and urban areas of seven U.S. states, documented rampant discrimination against those who failed to conform to rigid rules of how boys and girls should behave. We found that harassment often began at an early stage and escalated rapidly in middle and high school. Teachers, administrators, and counselors not only neglected to defend students from harassment but in some cases participated in discriminatory behavior themselves.

As a result, many lesbian, gay, bisexual, and transgender students remained closeted, unable to express a fundamental aspect of their identity. Students who were more vocal about their sexual orientation or gender identity were targeted for physical and psychological violence. Girls in general and lesbians in particular were especially vulnerable to the compounded effects of sexism and homophobia, which they frequently suffered in silence, ignored by school authorities. The physical and psychological toll of unaddressed verbal and physical abuse was often profoundly dehabilitating, affecting students' schoolwork and their mental well-being; some students dropped out of school, sank into depression, or even attempted suicide.

In response to increasing evidence of harassment of lesbian, gay, bisexual, and transgender students in U.S. schools, Senator Paul Wellstone introduced legislation to conduct a federal study of the level of sexual harassment against sexual minority students by peers and school officials. The study would include analysis of the effectiveness of guidelines issue by the Office of Civil Rights at the U.S. Department of Education in 1997 that specifically addressed the safety of gay and lesbian students. As of this writing, the bill was in committee.

Relevant Human Rights Watch Reports:

United States: Hatred in the Hallways: Violence and Discrimination Against Lesbian, Gay, Bisexual, and Transgender Students in U.S. Schools, 5/01

PRISONS

Prisoner numbers continued to rise in countries all over the world, resulting in severe overcrowding of prisons and other detention facilities. Even where legislation permitted alternatives to incarceration as a criminal sanction, authorities in most countries neglected them in preference to confinement.

While conditions of detention varied greatly from country to country and facility to facility, standards in most countries were shockingly low, and in some case horrific. Prisons and jails in even the richest and most developed countries were plagued by massive overcrowding, decaying physical infrastructure, inadequate sanitation, lack of medical care, guard abuse and corruption, and prisoner-on-prisoner violence. In many countries abysmal prison conditions were life threatening, leading to inmate deaths from disease, malnutrition, and physical abuse. With few exceptions, neither the public nor political leaders were willing to commit the financial resources needed to improve prison conditions. By barring human rights groups, journalists, and other outside observers access to their penal facilities, prison officials in many countries sought to shield substandard conditions from scrutiny.

ABUSIVE TREATMENT OF PRISONERS

Violence was rife in many prisons. In some countries, including Brazil, Kenya, Venezuela, and Panama, prison homicides were so frequent as to seem routine. Inmates were usually killed by other inmates rather than by guards, but inmate-on-inmate violence was often the predictable result of official negligence. By neglecting to supervise and control the inmates within their facilities, by failing to respond adequately or at all to incidents of violence, by corruptly allowing the entry of weapons and drugs into the prisons, and by generally abetting the tyranny of the strongest prisoners over the weakest, prison authorities were directly complicit in the violence against their charges. In some countries, for example Mexico, inmates were able to control fellow inmates with little interference from prison authorities, and to engage in violence, sexual abuse, drugs and arms trafficking, coercion, and influence peddling.

Incidents of collective violence, particularly in South America, also led to inmate deaths and injuries. In May, clashes between rival inmate gangs at two prisons in Venezuela, El Rodeo and Tocuyito, left twelve inmates dead and at least thirty-three wounded. During 2000, 276 Venezuelan prisoners were killed during gang fights or riots. In a February uprising coordinated by a prison gang, 20,000 prisoners took some 7,000 hostages, including at least twenty-seven guards, in over two dozen prisons in Sao Paulo state in Brazil. During the seventeen-hour revolt, sixteen prisoners were killed and seventy-seven wounded; four police agents were also wounded. It was unclear how many of the prisoners were killed by the police, but they apparently shot at least three prisoners in the back. Three other prisoners suffocated to death after guards left them locked in a sweltering van. The Sao Paulo prison system is notorious for under-staffing, extreme overcrowding, deaths in custody, use of torture, and lack of medical and sanitation facilities. More uprisings followed in other Brazilian states in March. In a juvenile detention center in Alagoas, four inmates died after other prisoners set them on fire. In Colombia, ten prisoners died and twenty-three were wounded in a July gun battle among inmates in Bogota's Modelo prison. After quelling the violence, authorities found small arms, grenades, machine guns, and ammunition inside the prison. The Procuracy opened an investigation against various prison officials for failing to maintain security and prevent the violence.

Physical abuse of prisoners by guards remained another chronic problem. The U.N. special rapporteur against torture reported in April that torture and ill-treatment were widespread in Brazil's prisons and detention centers. There and elsewhere, unwarranted beatings were so common as to be an integral part of prison life in many prison systems, including Angola, Armenia, Brazil, the Democratic Republic of Congo, Egypt, Iran, Iraq, Malaysia, Mexico, South Africa, Thailand, and Vietnam, among other countries. In Indonesia, officers punished inmates with electric shock batons and by stapling their ears, nose and lips. In the United States, electronic stun devices were used to control inmates. Some countries continued to permit corporal punishment and the routine use of leg irons, fetters, shackles, and chains. The heavy bar fetters used in Pakistani prisons, for example, turned simple movements such as walking into painful ordeals. Some prisoners contracted gangrene and required amputations. In Iraq, some prisoners in two prisons were reportedly locked in metal boxes the size of coffins that were opened for only thirty minutes each day.

Women prisoners were vulnerable to custodial sexual abuse. The problem was widespread in the United States, where male guards outnumbered women guards in many women's prisons. In some countries, Haiti being a conspicuous example, female prisoners were even held together with male inmates, a situation that exposed them to rampant sexual abuse and violence.

In contravention of international standards, juvenile inmates were often held together with adults. Many of Pakistan's jails and police lockups mixed juvenile and adult prisoners, as did certain detention facilities in Nicaragua, Kenya, South Africa, Sudan, Turkey, the United States, and Zambia, among other countries.

Male inmate on inmate rape was common in many prison systems. In the United

States, rape was a widespread problem facilitated by staff indifference and even, in some instances, complicity, as well as by a lack of effective prevention and punishment systems. In South Africa, the Office of the Inspecting Judge reported that fellow prisoners sodomized an estimated 70 to 80 percent of arrested suspects.

Corruption and extortion accompanied the low salaries generally paid to guards and their inadequate training and supervision. In exchange for contraband or special treatment, inmates in many countries supplemented guards' salaries with bribes. Powerful inmates in Colombian, Indian, and Mexican prisons, among others, enjoyed cellular phones, rich diets, and comfortable lodgings, while other inmates were held in squalor. Prisoners in many countries complained that they must buy their food, medicine and other necessities from guards or bribe guards to allow goods to be brought into the facility.

Increasing levels of overcrowding—prevalent in most countries for which information was available—compounded substandard conditions. Inadequate living space, poor or nonexistent ventilation, limited sanitation facilities, low levels of cleanliness and hygiene, and inadequate food and medical supplies made prisons life-threatening in many countries, including Armenia, Burma, Kenya, Mozambique, Nigeria, Peru, Russia, Sudan, Tanzania, Zambia. In the central prison in Karachi, Pakistan, there were four times as many prisoners as the prison was designed to hold, and only two toilets available per hundred prisoners. In Uzbekistan, ten to fifteen inmates were reportedly confined in cells designed for four. In Peru's Lurigancho men's prison, 6,000 inmates were held in a facility built to accommodate 1,500. The La Loma prison in Mexico, built to hold two hundred prisoners, housed nearly 1,200. In Bolivia, cells were "sold" to incoming prisoners by previous occupants or other prisoners; in the poorest areas, cells measured three by four by six feet and lacked ventilation, lighting, or beds. The crowding in some prisons is so bad that prisoners must sleep sitting up. In Angola, whose prison population is five times larger than the prison system's capacity, many prisons lacked financial support from the government.

In many countries, prison authorities failed to provide basic necessities to prisoners, who were obligated to depend on families, friends or international relief organizations for food, blankets, mattresses, toiletries, and even toilet paper. Insufficient food or poor diet leading to many cases of malnutrition, semi-starvation and even death, was a serious problem in countries such as Angola, Armenia, Azerbaijan, Burundi, Cambodia, Colombia, Cuba, Ethiopia, Haiti, Mexico, Mozambique, Pakistan, Peru, Russia, Tajikistan, Tanzania, Turkmenistan, Uganda, and Uzbekistan.

Another common problem was governments' continued reliance on antiquated and physically decaying prison facilities. Nineteenth-century prisons needing constant upkeep remained in use in Italy, Mexico, Russia, the United Kingdom, and the United States, among other counties, and more modern facilities were often in severe disrepair due to lack of maintenance. Many prisons lacked adequate sanitation facilities, a problem compounded by overcrowding. Some cells lacked toilets or latrines, requiring prisoners to "slop out," that is, defecate in buckets that they periodically emptied. In the United Kingdom, for example, there were still five prisons in Scotland where inmates still had to slop out although the Committee for the Prevention of Torture condemned the practice as "inhuman" more than a decade ago. Inmates at Makala prison in the Democratic Republic of Congo had no toilets and had to urinate and defecate on the floor.

Detained migrants awaiting deportation were also frequently confined in appalling conditions. In Greece, for example, migrants held at the Alexandras Avenue police station in Athens were confined for long periods in grossly over-crowded conditions. The detainees had little access to medical care, exercise, and fresh air. They lacked adequate food and sleeping conditions, and were kept in a dirty and roach infested environment.

A different set of concerns was raised by the spread of ultra-modern "super-maximum" security prisons. Originally prevalent in the United States, where politicians and state corrections authorities promoted them as part of a politically popular quest for more "austere" prison conditions, the supermax model was increasingly followed in other countries. Prisoners confined in such facilities spent an average of twenty-three hours a day in their cells, enduring extreme social isolation, enforced idleness, and extraordinarily limited recreational and educa-tional opportunities. While prison authorities defended the use of super-maxi-mum security facilities by asserting that they held only the most dangerous, disruptive, or escape-prone inmates, few safeguards existed to prevent other pris-oners from being arbitrarily or discriminatorily transferred to such facilities. In Australia, the inspector of custodial services found that some prisoners were being held indefinitely in special high security units without knowing why or when their isolation would end.

Beginning in December 2000, the Turkish government opened six "F-type" pris-ons for prisoners held for offenses tried in the state security courts. Concerned about conditions in the new prisons, where they were to be held in cells rather than communal wards, hundreds of prisoners began a hunger strike in October 2000. By November, thirty-eight prisoners or former prisoners and four prisoners' relatives had died in the hunger strike, and at least 399 prisoners had been released because of poor health. Twenty-eight prisoners were killed on December 19, 2000 when the government sent soldiers into twenty prisons to break the protest and transfer inmates to the new facilities. Some prisoners deliberately burned themselves to death. Inmates in the F-type prisons were initially held in small group isolation, locked in shared cells and deprived of opportunities for exercise, work, education or other social activities. However, new legislation was passed in May to enable out-of-cell activities, in which some prisoners were permitted to engage. Prisoners reported being subjected to "disciplinary" beatings.

Fiscal constraints and competing budget priorities were to blame for prison deficiencies in some countries, but as the supermax example suggests, harsh prison conditions were sometimes purposefully imposed. In Peru, notably, a punitive motive was evident in the decision to hold top-security prisoners in the high-alti-tude Challapalca and Yanamayo prisons, whose remote locations and miserable conditions led the Inter-American Commission on Human Rights to declare in 2000 that they were "unfit" to serve as places of detention. The European Court of Human Rights ruled in April that conditions in the segregation unit of Koridallos prison in Greece constituted treatment in violation of article 3 of the European Convention on Human Rights. The inmate who brought the case for several months had been practically confined continuously to his bed in a small cell shared with another inmate; the cell had no ventilation, no windows and no privacy for the in-cell toilet.

With few means to draw public attention to violations of their rights or to secure improved conditions, prisoners around the world resorted to riots, hunger strikes, self-mutilation, and other forms of protest. In Guatemala, over 1,000 prisoners temporarily took control of the country's main detention facility in Guatemala City, to demand improved conditions. In Venezuela, inmates at El Rodeo prison in June held 250 visitors and guards hostage for three days until officials agreed to study prison conditions and ways to address agonizingly slow pace of legal cases.

In Bolivia, nearly 3,000 prisoners went on strike to demand inclusion in a new amnesty law. Three women prisoners had themselves tied to slabs of wood with cord and sheets and raised to the highest point at the prison so that they could be seen, as if crucified, by the public. Four other women had their lips sewn together in an effort to obtain amnesty. About 950 male inmates of an Argentine prison in Buenos Aires began a mass hunger strike in January, demanding the shortening of their sentences. Protests and violent mutinies, in which guards and visitors are often taken hostage, have become commonplace in Argentina's crowded, filthy and violent prisons. In Nepal, jail inmates demanding better conditions started attacking the guards, who opened fire, killing one and injuring about a dozen more.

UNSENTENCED PRISONERS

Although comprehensive figures were impossible to obtain, the available statistics showed that a large proportion of the world's prisoners had not been convicted of any crime, but were instead being detained pending trial. In countries as varied as Bangladesh, Burundi, Chad, the Dominican Republic, Ecuador, El Salvador, Guatemala, Haiti, India, Mali, Nigeria, Pakistan, Peru, Rwanda, Uganda, and Venezuela, unsentenced prisoners made up the majority of the prison population. In South Africa, 64,000 people—more than one third of the country's prisoners—were incarcerated awaiting trial. Fifty-nine percent of the inmates in Central American prisons were unsentenced, with Honduras having the highest percentage: 87 percent. Worse, such detainees were in many instances held for years before eventually being acquitted of the crime with which they were charged. Prisoners also continued to be held after the expiration of their sentences in some countries. In many countries, prisoners awaiting trial were confined together with sentenced prisoners.

HEALTH

Health care in most prisons was poor to non-existent. Even in developed countries, medical services for prisoners were often seriously inadequate. In April, the British Medical Association warned that limited medical resources, medical staff shortages and poor prison management were contributing to a prison health care crisis in England and Wales.

The spread of communicable diseases in numerous prison systems was the predictable result of overcrowding, malnutrition, poor ventilation, lack of potable water, inadequate sanitation, and lack of medical care. Tuberculosis (TB) continued to ravage prison populations around the world, including those of Armenia, Azerbaijan, Belarus, Brazil, Cuba, India, Peru, Russia, Turkmenistan, Uzbekistan, and Venezuela. Twelve percent of the prison population in Kazakhstan had tuberculosis.

Penal facilities around the world reported grossly disproportionate rates of HIV infection and of confirmed AIDS cases. A November 2000 government study estimated that the HIV infection rate among prisoners in Canada was at least fifteen times higher than in the general population. The corresponding figure in the United States was about six times higher, and similar disparities were evident elsewhere. While overcrowding and a lack of appropriate services facilitated the spread of many infectious diseases in prison, HIV/AIDS resulted particularly from the failure of prison authorities both to protect inmates from sexual violence and to offer even simple and cheap services such as access to condoms. Segregation of HIV-positive prisoners, in some cases causing their marginalization from basic services, remained common in several countries and was practiced in three U.S. states (Alabama, Mississippi and South Carolina). Regular access to services such as needle sterilization or needle exchange in prisons was a distant dream in most countries outside of Western Europe.

Access to antiretroviral drugs contributed to lower death rates from AIDS among prisoners in Western Europe, North America and some Latin American countries, but they were unavailable elsewhere, including in Eastern Europe, which has the fastest growing AIDS epidemic in the world. The Centers for Disease Control of the U.S. government reported late in 2000, however, that U.S. prisoners have a higher rate of drug-resistant strains of HIV than the general population due to irregular supplies of drugs and because inmates have medicines taken away from them when they are processed in and out of the prison system.

In 2001, there was increasing awareness that hepatitis C had joined HIV/AIDS and tuberculosis as a major scourge of prisoners. The hepatitis C virus (HCV), like HIV, can cause liver failure and death and is transmitted through needle sharing, tattooing with used needles, and sharing of shaving equipment. Canada estimated that HCV was fifty times more prevalent among its prisoners than in the general population. In 2001, inmates brought legal actions against several U.S. states for failure to provide adequate HCV treatment.

DEFENDING PRISONERS' HUMAN RIGHTS

Struggling against governmental tendencies toward secrecy and silence on prison abuses, numerous local human rights groups around the world sought to obtain access to prisons, monitor prison conditions, and publicize the abuses they found.. In some countries, government human rights ombudspersons, parliamentary commissions, and other official monitors also helped call attention to abuses. In the United Kingdom, notably, the chief inspector of prisons continued his vigorous investigation and forthright criticism of conditions in the country's penal facilities. In many countries, however, authorities permitted no outside scrutiny of penal conditions.

At the regional level, prison monitoring mechanisms were active. The European Committee for the Prevention of Torture (CPT) continued its important work, inspecting penal institutions in Georgia, Greece, Malta, Moldova, the Russian Federation (Chechen Republic), Slovenia, Spain, Switzerland, Turkey, and the United Kingdom and publishing reports on penal conditions in Austria, Croatia, France, Greece, Hungary, Lithuania, the former Yugoslav Republic of Macedonia, Northern Ireland, Portugal, and Turkey.

In Africa, the special rapporteur on prisons and conditions of detention, an adjunct to the African Commission on Human and Peoples' Rights, visited prisons in Malawi, Namibia and Mozambique. The General Assembly of the Organization of American States adopted a resolution endorsing efforts to draft an Inter-American Declaration on Persons Deprived of Liberty.

UNITED NATIONS MONITORING EFFORTS

The vast scale and chronic nature of human rights violations in the world's prisons have long been of concern to the United Nations, as demonstrated by the 1955 promulgation of the U.N. Standard Minimum Rules for the Treatment of Prisoners. Indeed, the international community's failure to adopt these standards in practice, even while it has embraced them in theory, has inspired the United Nations' most recent prisons effort.

For nearly a decade, a U.N. working group has been hammering out a draft treaty that would establish a U.N. subcommittee authorized to make regular and ad hoc visits to places of detention in states party to the treaty, including prisons, jails, and police lockups. As described in the draft treaty—conceived as an optional protocol to the Convention against Torture—the primary goal of the subcommittee would be to prevent torture and other ill-treatment. Based on the information obtained during its periodic and ad hoc visits, the subcommittee would make detailed recommendations to state authorities regarding necessary improvements to their detention facilities.

The working group's most recent session, in October 2000, ended without any progress being made toward the completion of a draft treaty. The session revealed the wide gap that remains between countries on such fundamental issues as which places should be subject to visits, whether prior consent must be obtained, whether reservations to the optional protocol should be allowed, and the impact of national legislation on the nature and scope of visits.

Other U.N. bodies pressed countries to improve their prison conditions. The U.N. Special Rapporteur on torture, whose mandate was renewed for another three years by the U.N. Commission on Human Rights, reported findings of widespread torture in Brazil and Azerbaijan, based on his visits to those countries in 2000.

Relevant Human Rights Watch Reports:

No Escape: Male Rape in U.S. Prisons, 4/01
Beyond Reason: The Death Penalty and Offenders with Mental Retardation, 3/01

RACIAL DISCRIMINATION
AND RELATED INTOLERANCE

HUMAN RIGHTS DEVELOPMENTS

Ethnicity, often combined with religion, fueled and shaped conflict and systemic human rights abuse in many countries around the globe in the year of the third United Nations World Conference Against Racism, Racial Discrimination, Xenophobia and Related Intolerance (WCAR). Caste discrimination—based on descent—held an estimated 250 million people locked in conditions of oppression and intolerance. National and local leaders propagated hate and intolerance, seeking political advantage in the discriminatory animus of racist movements. Across the world, racism and related intolerance skewed the administration of justice and denied or limited minorities and other marginalized groups' access to education and employment, to health care and housing—and to protection against exploitation.

The widespread fear generated by the attacks on the United States (U.S.) on September 11—and aspects of the global antiterrorism campaign that followed—added a new dimension to xenophobia and intolerance in many parts of the world. New antiterrorism measures introduced in the United States and under consideration in many other countries reduced safeguards against arbitrary arrest on discriminatory grounds and posed particular challenges to the rights of asylum seekers and migrants.

In Africa, ethnicity remained a potent engine of conflict in years-long wars of secession, inter-communal violence, and in partisan struggles for power as political leaders played the ethnic card to mobilize supporters and to demonize their rivals. Inter-ethnic clashes remained a pervasive feature of conflicts in the Great Lakes region and other parts of Africa. In the Democratic Republic of Congo's (DRC) eastern provinces, spiralling conflicts involved both troops of the regular armies of Uganda and Rwanda and militias sponsored by both regional powers. In Rwanda and Burundi longstanding internal conflicts continued; those leading Rwanda's rebel forces included former leaders of the 1994 genocide. Sudan's long internal war was fueled not only by the ethnic and religious divide between north and south but also by ethnic divisions between the southern rebels. Renewed conflict in Liberia also followed largely ethnic lines; government forces perceived ethnic Mandingo citizens indiscriminately as opposition supporters, and subjected them to violent attacks because of their ethnicity. Clashes spurred by ethnicity and religion in Nigeria cost thousands of lives. (See Africa Overview.)

Determining who should be considered a national and who a foreigner also generated xenophobia and violence in some African countries. In Côte D'Ivoire, as Human Rights Watch detailed in a report it published in August, officials incited xenophobic violence around elections in October and December 2000. They promoted intolerance based on ethnic and religious differences that led gendarmes and civilian supporters to attack Ivorians from the largely Muslim north of the country—and others held to be "foreigners." The report documented more than two hundred killings, as well as torture, rape, and arbitrary detentions, committed with impunity.

In Brazil, indigenous people were moved off their land, threatened, and killed in land disputes in circumstances that suggested the acquiescence of public authorities. Indigenous leader Francisco de Assis Santana was murdered on August 23 in Pesqueira, Pernambuco, apparently in connection with his struggles for Xucuru land rights in the territory. Members of the Guarani community were reportedly fired on in November 2000 by police allegedly hired by a rancher who had taken over their land. In February, several cases were reported of alleged sexual abuse by army soldiers against Yanomami women in the Surucucus region of the Amazon. (See Brazil.)

In Asia, the full complexity of the inter-ethnic and sectarian struggles in Afghanistan burst belatedly upon the international consciousness only after the attacks of September 11 and the launching of the U.S.-led military campaign against the Taliban. Earlier, Human Rights Watch documented a series of incidents in which largely ethnic Pashtun Taliban forces committed gross abuses, including summary executions and the destruction of homes against civilians belonging to minorities it associated with its rivals—Aymaqs, Hazaras, and Uzbeks, suspected of supporting forces linked to the anti-Taliban Northern Alliance. (See Afghanistan.)

In Burma (Myanmar), government troops burned villages and forcibly displaced tens of thousands of villagers in areas affected by ethnic-based insurgencies. Hundreds of thousands were internally displaced in the ethnic minority states while others fled to Thailand. (See Burma.)

In Indonesia, ethnicity and religion were factors shaping regional conflicts—sometimes accentuating divisions between internal migrants and indigenous populations. The conflict in Aceh and communal violence in West Kalimantan resulted in many civilian casualties, while little progress was shown in the resolution of conflicts in the Moluccas, Central Sulawesi, and Papua. Well over one million people were reported displaced, half of them from the Moluccas.

Sri Lanka's civil war, too, continued to claim a steady toll of civilian deaths. Both the government and Tamil secessionist forces were responsible for serious abuses and internal displacement created enormous hardship. (See Sri Lanka.)

In Europe, the question of who belongs in the nation state continued to impact harshly upon displaced populations in the former Yugoslavia and many parts of the former Soviet Union, as well as migrants and refugees seeking a better life in an increasingly hostile Western Europe. Across the region, Roma were victimized by discrimination in every aspect of their lives.

In Bulgaria, discrimination against Roma persisted in virtually every aspect of public life. Roma were beaten by police and private individuals beat and shot at Roma on numerous occasions with impunity. An Open Society Institute study released in September detailed discrimination against Roma in the provision of housing, social services and health care. (See Bulgaria.)

In the Czech Republic, de facto discrimination against Roma affected access to justice, education, housing, employment, and public services. Racist attacks on Roma continued, but police and prosecutors frequently failed to adequately investigate and prosecute Roma complaints. (See Czech Republic.)

The Greek government took steps to address discrimination with an action plan for Roma, designed to address health, education and housing needs. The resettlement of a Roma community under the plan was marred, however, by discrimination against the community's children, whose attendance at local schools was opposed by other residents. One school closed in November 2000 rather than admit thirty-two Roma children. (See Greece.)

In Hungary, Roma faced continuing discrimination in employment, education, and the criminal justice system, as well as physical attacks and the firebombing of their homes. The French government granted asylum to fifteen Hungarian Roma who were part of a group who fled from the Hungarian village of Zamoly to Strasbourg during 2000 to escape threats, physical attacks and the destruction of their homes. Anti-Semitic programming continued on state radio and anti-Jewish statements by the vice-president of the parliamentary Hungarian Truth and Life Party were widely disseminated. (See Hungary.)

In Serbia and Montenegro, too, police brutality against Roma was common, although the Federal Republic of Yugoslavia acceded to the Council of Europe's 1994 Framework Convention for the Protection of National Minorities on May 11.

Roma, Serbs, and other minorities faced continued violence in post-war Kosovo. Organized violence targeting minorities, including attacks on Serb homes, churches, and cultural sites, persisted, while convoys escorted by peacekeepers of the multinational Kosovo Force (KFOR) were attacked by gunmen: eleven people were killed and dozens injured in the most serious attack. United Nations (U.N.) police had at the time of writing failed to bring the perpetrators to justice. (See Federal Republic of Yugoslavia.)

Ethnically-motivated violence also continued to shake Bosnia and Herzegovina. In Republika Srpska and, less frequently, in the Croat parts of the Federation, attackers shot at returnees because of their ethnic identity and destroyed houses reconstructed for them. (See Bosnia and Herzegovina.)

Although European Union (E.U.) states vigorously demanded that Eastern European countries take measures to combat discrimination against Roma, the steps they took themselves to restrict immigration and bar access to their territories and asylum determination procedures for asylum seekers were often discriminatory. The deployment of British immigration officials to Prague's Ruzyne Airport in July followed a wave of asylum claims by mostly-Roma Czech citizens. British officials there barred 120 travellers—the majority of them Roma—before protests at their targeting of Roma led to the temporary suspension of the pre-flight screenings. (See Czech Republic.)

In Greece, following the September 11 attacks in the U.S., authorities fearing a large influx of Afghan refugees refused to allow many asylum seekers even to apply for refugee status, issuing expedited expulsion orders instead. (See Greece.) In Spain, officials equated the global campaign against international terrorism with the fight against illegal immigration.

Some states' concepts of nationality also resulted in severe restrictions of minority rights, even to the extent of denying minorities official recognition or restricting the use of their language. In February, Sotiris Blatsas of the Society for Aromanian (Vlach) Culture was tried in Greece and convicted of "disseminating false information" because he had published a list of minority languages spoken in Greece. He had distributed a publication of the E.U.'s European Bureau for Lesser Used Languages (EBLUL) at an Aromanian festival in July 1995. He was sentenced to fifteen months in prison.

In Turkey, state policies that denied recognition of the Kurdish minority were enforced through censorship and imprisonment. Controls on freedom of expression continued to prevent broadcasting and education in Kurdish. Local governors prohibited the use of Kurdish street names and banned plays, cassettes, and films in Kurdish on the grounds that they were "separatist." Those that challenged or tested state policies on ethnicity in their statements or writings—Kurds and non-Kurds alike—faced prosecution and imprisonment.

In Morocco, there was freer discussion of the rights of the Berber minority, but authorities twice barred the holding of meetings to address the issues. Authorities seized an issue of the French weekly *Courrier International* which carried a feature on Berbers in Morocco. (See Morocco.)

The United Kingdom's (U.K.'s) response to the September 11 attacks on the United States included proposed emergency measures that threatened to undermine civil liberties and the rights of refugees and migrants. Draft anti-terrorism legislation provided for the indefinite detention of foreigners with limited judicial review and restricted the rights of suspects to seek asylum. September 11 was also followed by a dramatic rise in attacks on Muslims living in the U.K. The attacks were condemned by the government—with measures to toughen enforcement of hate crimes legislation—but new government calls for anti-terrorist measures, more restrictive immigration and asylum controls, and for halting the flow of Afghan refugees into Europe contributed to an increasingly hostile climate toward refugees and migrants in the U.K.

In the United States, longstanding patterns of discrimination in the criminal justice system persisted, with the U.N. Committee on the Elimination of Racial Discrimination highlighting police brutality, notably against minority groups and foreigners; disproportionately high incarceration rates of black and Hispanic Americans; racial disparities in the application of the death penalty; and the effect of felony disenfranchisement on minorities. Measures introduced in the aftermath of the September 11 attacks raised concerns that minorities and foreigners distinguished by their ethnicity would be subject to new forms of abusive discriminatory treatment. New laws and other measures permitted the indefinite detention of noncitizens and over 1,000 people were detained, mostly Arab or Muslim men.

The September 11 attacks were followed in the United States by a wave of racist attacks against Muslims, Sikhs, and people of Middle Eastern and South Asian descent—with almost 1,000 reported by November. President Bush and other officials condemned the violence and urged the public to reject national or religious stereotyping that would blame whole communities for the acts of terrorism committed by a few, simply because they shared the same religious, ethnic, or national identity. (See United States.)

WHO BELONGS?

In an era of "ethnic cleansing," ethnic and religious pogroms, genocide, and massive displacement across borders, the question "who belongs?" in a community or in a nation came to assume life and death proportions. In some cases the designated outsiders faced oppression and exploitation at home—for example India's Dalits or Europe's Roma—locked in a subordinate status and vulnerable to violence by private citizens and authorities alike. In others, as in parts of Indonesia, Africa's Great Lakes region, and West Africa (and in the 1990s, the former Yugoslavia), minorities became outsiders overnight, caught up in political movements of terror and exclusion whose leaders were bent upon the physical destruction or expulsion of those not of the dominant ethnicity or religion.

Although "who belongs?" was often defined in terms of citizenship, this too became an increasingly mutable concept as new independent states emerged and multiethnic states broke down. The denial or deprivation of citizenship could turn solely on the basis of ethnicity or national origin—particularly in conflict situations and periods of political transition. In some cases, however, whole communities of "nationals without nationality" had long been denied citizenship on discriminatory grounds.

States that defined citizenship in terms of racial or national Apurity@ often discriminated both on grounds of ethnicity and national origin and on the basis of gender. As citizenship was restricted to the children of male nationals, female citizens were discouraged from marrying men of another nationality because their children would be denied citizenship. Naturalization policies, too, were often wholly or largely founded on discriminatory grounds, while shielded from criticism as a sovereign prerogative of states.

Racial and gender discrimination intersected where citizenship was restricted to the children of male nationals, the norm in many countries of the Middle East, North Africa, and parts of Sub-Saharan Africa. Ethnic Kurdish women who were classified as stateless "foreigners" in Syria could marry Syrian citizens with prior authorization from the interior ministry, but ethnic Kurdish men with this status were not permitted to marry female Syrian citizens. If they did so, the marriages were not legally recognized and both spouses were described as unmarried on their identity cards. "[I]n the case that a Syrian female should have the audacity to marry any foreigner . . . that marriage is considered illegal," the government stated in 1996. "As a result, neither it nor the children that ensue will be registered in the civil registers."

In Kuwait, authorities continued to deny citizenship to some 120,000 of the minority Bidun, many of whose families had lived in Kuwait for generations and had no claim to citizenship of another country.

Denial of citizenship affected minority populations that were indigenous to a country or had been present for generations—as well as majorities. The end of the apartheid regime in South Africa spelled an end to denationalization taken to an extreme: a "homelands" policy whose advocates aimed to make black South Africans citizens of "bantustans"—and no longer citizens of South Africa. Moves to strip the citizenship of more than a million Zairean nationals of the Banyarwanda ethnic group after 1991 spurred domestic and interstate conflict there. Ethiopia summarily denationalized and expelled some 70,000 Ethiopian citizens of Eritrean origin after war broke out with Eritrea in May 1998—while Eritrea carried out summary expulsions to Ethiopia on a lesser scale. Progress in post-war negotiations offered hope of a review of the administrative measures by which Ethiopians of Eritrean origin were summarily stripped of their citizenship.

The military junta ruling Burma excluded hundreds of thousands of members of Burma's minorities from citizenship with a 1982 citizenship law. In the 1990s more than 250,000 Rohingya Muslims fled to neighboring Bangladesh. In 2001, most Rohingya remained without full citizenship rights.

In Southeast Asia, the government of Thailand had issued special identity documents to some 300,000 members of the country's ethnic minority hill tribes, but these indigenous people were denied a nationality or full citizenship rights. Hundreds of thousands of other hill tribe villagers were unregistered and officially considered illegal immigrants. This particularly affected hill tribe women who were victims of trafficking to Japan and who, once free of their traffickers, could not gain readmission to Thailand.

In South Asia, the government of Bhutan stripped of citizenship and expelled more than 100,000 Bhutanese of ethnic Nepali origin in the early 1990s, the majority of whom were still refugees. Bhutanese refugees spent a tenth year in exile in camps in southeast Nepal, deprived of their right to return home. Despite the start in early 2001 of a joint Nepal-Bhutan verification program to determine the status of these refugees, no refugees had returned as of late November.

In the Americas, racial discrimination and related intolerance colored the treatment of migrants as well as the implementation of laws concerning nationality. Over half a million Haitians and Dominicans of Haitian descent lived in the Dominican Republic, where certain government policies reflected racial discrimination and xenophobia. Because the Dominican government made it difficult for Haitians to obtain legal residency documents, the vast majority were undocumented. In violation of the Dominican constitution, Haitians' Dominican-born children were frequently denied Dominican citizenship. Haitians' precarious legal status left them vulnerable to economic exploitation, arbitrary expulsion, and violations of basic rights.

In Europe, the disintegration of the Soviet Union led to discriminatory norms for citizenship in several newly independent countries. In the breakup of the former Yugoslavia, the terrorizing and physical expulsion of minorities coincided with measures to deny citizenship to members of ethnic minorities residing there or seeking to return to their homes. Elsewhere in Europe, citizenship laws enacted by

Slovakia and the Czech Republic after the division of Czechoslovakia served directly to exclude Roma citizens from citizenship in the new republics: international pressure led to reforms of the relevant laws, although obstacles remained, and Roma continued to suffer discrimination.

UNITED NATIONS WORLD CONFERENCE AGAINST RACISM

The third United Nations World Conference Against Racism, Racial Discrimination, Xenophobia and Related Intolerance was held in Durban, South Africa from August 31 to September 8, 2001. The first such conference since the end of apartheid, this WCAR provided governments with an opportunity to combat both the overt and more subtle forms of racial discrimination that existed abroad and at home—a potential, sadly, that was largely unrealized. A great failing of the conference was the inability of participants—governments and nongovernmental organizations alike—to forge a common front to combat racism and related intolerance in the spirit and within the framework of the International Convention on the Elimination of All Forms of Racial Discrimination.

The WCAR was plagued by a series of acrimonious disputes over the Israel/Palestine question; the issue of reparations for slavery and colonialism; and other issues. Both the United States and Israel withdrew at an early stage, citing anti-Israel sentiment, and there was divisiveness and intolerance within the NGO community itself on this and other issues. Yet in some respects, including on questions such as the protection of migrants and refugees, repairing the legacy of slavery, and equal nationality rights for women, significant progress was made.

The WCAR process led to an unprecedented mobilization of victims of racism from communities around the world, which served to reinforce and reinvigorate many community, national, and regional anti-racism movements. Groups seeking to break the bonds of discrimination forged new alliances across continents with hitherto unknown partners—not least as the United States civil rights movement and black Latin Americans found common cause with South Asia's Dalit movement. The heightened international profile given to caste discrimination—despite India's successful efforts to prevent the WCAR from addressing the issue head on—was a significant outcome.

U.S. government participation in the WCAR process was marked with scarcely veiled hostility—although hundreds of U.S. NGOs participated actively and enthusiastically in the preparatory meetings and NGO forum. The administration warned NGOs and governments that the conference should not lead to any new programs to combat racism, any new legal standards, any additional money to fund anti-racism efforts, or any follow-up. It warned the conference not to call for reparations for slavery and the trans-Atlantic slave trade or to adopt language specifically criticizing Israel.

In the end, attending governments did reach compromise language on the Middle East, which included specific reference to "the plight of Palestinian people under foreign occupation," but no specific reference to Israel's or any other government's human rights practices. Compromise language was also reached on reparations, calling for governments to take "appropriate and effective measures to halt and reverse the lasting consequences of [racism, racial discrimination, xenophobia and related intolerance]."

The U.S. government's decision to withdraw from the conference meant that the administration lost a paramount opportunity for the administration to join and shape the collective voice of the international community in moving forward together in the struggle against racism. The U.S. lost a chance to lead by example, while appearing to duck the international spotlight thrown on its own problems of racial discrimination—to the dismay of the large NGO delegation attending from the United States.

The summit called for far-reaching programs to address intolerance and discrimination against the 150 million migrants in the world, including education campaigns and prevention of workplace bias. It asked countries to combat intolerance against refugees, and included a reference reminding governments of the standards agreed in the 1951 U.N. Refugee Convention. It called on states to protect the more than 30 million people displaced in their own countries, referring to the U.N. guidelines on the internally displaced. It asked countries to monitor and ensure accountability for police misconduct and to eliminate "racial profiling." The conference called on countries to fund anti-racism efforts and public awareness campaigns in schools and the media and to promote tolerance and openness to diversity. It urged governments to collect data disaggregated by race, as a first means of identifying and then addressing discrimination in access to health care and the provision of government services.

The conference acknowledged that slavery and the slave trade "are a crime against humanity and should always have been so," and said that states had a "moral obligation" to "take appropriate and effective measures to halt and reverse the lasting consequences of those practices." This was an historic recognition of the criminality of slavery and the moral obligation to repair its lasting damage.

In a significant step pressed by its women's caucus, the conference urged countries to allow women the right, on an equal basis with men, to pass on their nationality to their children and spouses, a right denied in many countries. The conference program of action also acknowledged the multiple and unique ways in which racism and sexism interact to deny women their human rights.

Discrimination by reason of caste was a constant theme of the conference, not least through public demonstrations and effective lobbying by the International Dalit Solidarity Network (IDSN) and by India's National Campaign on Dalit Human Rights (NCDHR). Caste or "work and descent" discrimination was referred to in many plenary speeches by government delegates. Reflecting the emphasis on caste in the WCAR's preparatory process, the Sub-Commission on the Promotion and Protection of Human Rights in August 2001 passed by consensus a decision to continue a study on work and descent-based discrimination.

India's actions to keep caste out of the final conference documents served effectively to stimulate international press coverage of the issue and to heighten pressure for scrutiny through the international machinery of human rights. The conference did not formally extend the desired recognition that caste-based discrimination blighted the lives of hundreds of millions—but the attendant awareness generated by the conference sent a clear message that international programs were required to remedy its consequences and to establish practical measures to facilitate its abolition.

Despite the conference's failings and lost opportunities, South African Foreign Affairs Minister Nkosazana Dlamini-Zuma described the final agreements as "a new road-map for the fight against racism." But the conference was only a first step; the real test is whether governments will deliver on what they agreed. Human Rights Watch, for its part, will be working to ensure that they do.

THE WORK OF HUMAN RIGHTS WATCH

The fight against racism, racial discrimination, and related intolerance was an integral part of Human Rights Watch's regional and thematic research and advocacy program. In the context of the WCAR, the organization focused especially on caste discrimination; the protection of migrants and refugees; discrimination in the denial of citizenship rights; on racial discrimination in criminal justice and in the administration of state institutions, services, and resources; and the link between racial or ethnic and gender discrimination. In the run-up to the conference, Human Rights Watch also pressed for the WCAR to adopt a policy on reparations for past abuses to address the most pressing needs arising from slavery, the slave trade, certain especially racist aspects of colonialism, and other extreme official racist practices. Our program of action included the publication of a series of short reports, campaign action with partner nongovernmental organizations (NGOs), and participation in official and informal preparatory meetings and the conference itself.

Caste Discrimination

In much of Asia, parts of Africa, and in the South Asian diaspora caste was coterminous with race in the definition and exclusion of groups distinguished by their descent Over 250 million people worldwide suffered under a hidden apartheid of segregation, modern-day slavery, and other extreme forms of discrimination because they were born into a marginalized, subordinate caste. Although India was home to the largest affected community—some 160 million people—caste-based abuse was also rampant in Nepal, Sri Lanka, Bangladesh, Pakistan, Japan, and parts of West Africa—and in the South Asian diaspora.

Caste discrimination was within the scope of the International Convention on the Elimination of All Forms of Racial Discrimination, which defined racial discrimination to include discrimination by reason of "race, colour, *descent*, or national or ethnic origin ..." (emphasis added). The Committee on the Elimination of Racial Discrimination affirmed that caste discrimination was founded on descent—and constituted racial discrimination in the terms of the convention. It did so most expressly in a 1996 comment on India's report on compliance with the convention—India had denied that caste discrimination was a form of racial discrimination that it must address to meet its treaty obligations.

Human Rights Watch helped ensure that the WCAR brought caste discrimination to international attention and to overcome the efforts to exclude its discussion by the very governments which displayed complacency about caste discrimination at home. India's government argued that efforts to raise the caste issue were part of an "external agenda"—echoing what South Africa's former white minority government long contended when the international community spoke out against apartheid.

In *Caste Discrimination: A Global Concern,* Human Rights Watch challenged the efforts of certain governments to keep caste discrimination a shameful secret— excluded even from the World Conference. The report, which documented the global scope of caste discrimination, cited the language of international law and intergovernmental human rights bodies that brought caste discrimination—a form of discrimination by reason of descent—squarely within the current of the international fight against racism.

Refugees and Migrants

Xenophobia toward migrants, refugees, and asylum seekers became a global trend over the past decade, while a barrage of new, restrictive policies in industrialized countries emerged even before the events of September 2001. But the antiterrorism measures instituted in many countries after the September attacks promised to further restrict access to asylum determination procedures and to curtail the civil liberties of migrants. New measures under the antiterrorism rubric threatened further grave consequences for migrants and refugees—compounded by the strains of the burgeoning world economic crisis.

In its work to combat discrimination against refugees and migrants, Human Rights Watch pressed for countries to ratify and implement the International Convention on the Protection of the Rights of All Migrant Workers and Members of Their Families, identify measures to reinforce the international refugee protection regime, and develop an international monitoring system by which to better detect and remedy discriminatory treatment of migrants and refugees. (See Refugees, Asylum Seekers, Migrants, and Internally Displaced Persons.)

Citizenship Rights

We sought to win recognition of the problem of denial or deprivation of citizenship on racial and related grounds, and the intersection of race and gender in discriminatory citizenship laws and practices. To this end, we encouraged U.N. committees created by the treaties on women's rights and on children's rights to put this issue on their agendas, and for the U.N. High Commissioner on Human Rights to set in motion a study of potentially discriminatory norms by which states determined who was a citizen or naturalized citizen. We said international measures of conflict resolution and early warning should address questions of citizenship and denationalization founded on discriminatory grounds. These issues should be recognized as major factors in the generation of massive human rights abuse, including genocide, and armed conflict, and the generation of refugee flows.

In some countries with large populations of "citizens without citizenship," where particular ethnic groups were singled out as less than citizens, although they were not mere aliens, a remedy to this discriminatory practice was within ready reach even under existing law. Members of Syria's native Kurdish population who were denied official Syrian nationality were not permitted to own land, housing, or a business, or to register a motor vehicle—and their children faced major obstacles to formal education. Yet the Syrian government's 2000 report to the U.N. Human Rights Committee made clear that the nationality law specifically provided for the granting of citizenship to all Kurdish children born in Syria, irrespective of the legal status of their parents, if the Syrian government should choose to invoke it. An important first step against discrimination in citizenship rights was to implement international norms to combat statelessness.

As an immediate bulwark against the discriminatory denial of nationality, we encouraged the WCAR to promote the ratification of international agreements on statelessness, and for children's rights activists to demand the implementation of the Convention on the Rights of the Child's strong safeguards against statelessness. We urged the Committee on the Rights of the Child to call on states to describe their safeguards against racial, ethnic, and gender discrimination in citizenship laws and practices in their regular reports to the committee. Populations with longstanding claims to nationality in their country of residence whose children remained stateless required particularly urgent attention. Similarly, we encouraged the Committee for the Elimination of Racial Discrimination and the Committee on the Elimination of Discrimination against Women to consider the discriminatory manner in which race, ethnicity, and national origin intersected with gender in citizenship and naturalization policies, and request states to address these issues when reporting to these committees.

Discrimination in Criminal Justice and Public Administration

Discrimination in the administration of justice—whether in policing, criminal prosecutions, trials, sentencing, or imprisonment—caused extraordinary harm to individuals and societies alike. Members of racial, ethnic, and other minorities or vulnerable groups often faced harassment, arbitrary detention, and abusive treatment by the law enforcement apparatus and disparate treatment by prosecutors and the courts.

Police disproportionately targeted members of marginalized groups for arrest in many countries. Members of these groups also faced disproportionate prosecutions, unfair trials, and disproportionately severe sentences on criminal charges. Humiliating treatment, beatings, sexual abuse, and shooting deaths of members of marginalized groups often contrasted starkly with treatment accorded to others and members of these groups often had little recourse to legal remedies to abuse.

Ostensibly race- or descent-neutral laws could have a disparate impact on vulnerable minorities—or even majorities—as a consequence of prosecutorial discretion or sentencing policies or the nature of the law itself. The resulting impact on particular descent-based groups could be vastly disproportionate to the actual involvement of members of these groups in the overall pattern of criminal activity.

For example, although there were more white drug offenders than black in the United States, blacks constituted 57.6 percent of all drug offenders sent to state prison. In racial profiling, stop and search provisions were abused to target suspects on discriminatory grounds: A 1998 study of police stop and search patterns in England and Wales by the British Home Office found that blacks were 7.5 times more likely to be stopped and searched than whites. A 1997 Australian study, in turn, found that Aboriginal people in Australia were 9.2 times more likely to be arrested, 23.7 times more likely to be imprisoned as an adult, and 48 times more likely to be imprisoned as juveniles than non-Aborigines.

Criminal penalties that were accompanied by temporary or permanent disenfranchisement further excluded members of groups already facing discriminatory treatment from participation in political life and accentuated and perpetuated their economic, social, and political marginalization. In 1998 it was reported that an estimated 3.9 million U.S. citizens were disenfranchised, including over one million who had fully completed their sentences. This hit black men in particular, with 13 percent—1.4 million—disenfranchised.

The discriminatory effect of public policy and administrative practice often prevented the enjoyment of fundamental human rights even in the absence of overt discriminatory intent. This was often most evident in the administration of social services, education, and public housing to exclude or marginalize members of particular groups.

The denial of equal access by minorities to education was a major concern in several regions. In certain countries in Asia, including Nepal, Sri Lanka, and Japan, children whose parents belonged to lower-caste or shunned, descent-based social groups faced widespread discrimination in access to education and had markedly lower literacy rates and school attendance rates than the general population. In India, children of Dalits who attended school were largely restricted to the worst government schools, where they faced discriminatory and abusive treatment at the hands of their teachers and fellow students.

In August, the U.N. Committee on the Elimination of Racial Discrimination issued "concluding observations" following review of China's report on its implementation of the convention. The committee expressed concern about discrimination in education, particularly in Tibet.

In Europe, Romani children suffered extreme discrimination in their access to education, through relegation to segregated schools, routine assignment to "special" facilities intended for children with learning disabilities, or no schooling at all. In schools that were not segregated, Romani children faced harassment from students—and sometimes by teachers—as well as racial slurs and lowered expectations, contributing to a high dropout rate.

In Bosnia and Herzegovina, a Human Rights Watch investigation identified concern at discrimination in schools—including a discriminatory grade-school curriculum—as a major impediment to the return of minority displaced families to their pre-war homes.

A 2001 Human Rights Watch investigation found pervasive and systematic discrimination against nearly one-fourth of Israel's 1.6 million schoolchildren—Palestinian Arab citizens—who were educated in a public school system that was wholly separate from the Jewish majority. The Israeli government spent less per

Palestinian Arab child than per Jewish child, and Arab schools were inferior to Jewish schools in virtually every respect. Among Palestinian Arabs, the Negev Bedouin and children in villages denied legal status by the Israeli government fared worst in every respect. In its 2001 report to the Committee on the Rights of the Child, Israel acknowledged the gap between Arab and Jewish education, but despite a commitment to closing the gap it had failed to take necessary steps to equalize the two systems. (See Children's Rights.)

Human Rights Watch encouraged the WCAR to give a new impetus for states to systematically collect and report data on law enforcement and the administration of justice, with a view to identifying and remedying any discriminatory purpose or effect; and to monitor the administration of public affairs in such areas as education, health care, housing, and the enforcement of labor rights, with a view to identifying and remedying any discriminatory purpose or effect in public policy and programs.

Reparations

In advance of the World Conference, Human Rights Watch called for governments to make reparations to counter the most severe continuing effects of slavery, segregation, racist aspects of colonialism, and other extreme forms of racism in the past. We said efforts should focus first on groups that continue to suffer the most severe hardships, with long-term commitments to correct the damage done to the groups left most seriously disadvantaged. We encouraged the WCAR to adopt proposals in favor of providing reparations to the descendants of past victims. To this end we pressed for priority to be given measures to address the social and economic foundations of today's victims' continuing marginalization—through means such as investment in education, housing, health care, or job training.

Human Rights Watch argued that the descendants of a victim of human rights abuse should be able to pursue claims of reparations—that the right to reparations was not extinguished with the death of the victim. Reparations would consist of compensation, acknowledgment of past abuses, an end to ongoing abuses, and, as much as possible, restoration of the state of affairs that would have prevailed had there been no abuses. To establish priorities for reparations, Human Rights Watch proposed the establishment of national panels as well as one or more international panels to look at the effect of the slave trade and other international forms of systemic abuse. These panels would focus on tracing these effects not for particular individuals but for groups. The panels would serve as a form of truth commission aiming to determine how a government's past racist practices had contributed to contemporary deprivation domestically and across world regions. They would educate the public, acknowledge responsibility, and propose methods of redress and making amends.

Relevant Human Rights Watch Reports:

Israel: Second Class: Discrimination Against Palestinian Arab Children in Israel's Schools, 12/01
Under Orders: War Crimes in Kosovo, 10/01

Crimes Against Civilians: Abuses by Macedonian Forces in Ljuboten, August 10-12, 2001, 9/01

Caste Discrimination: A Global Concern, 8/01

The New Racism: The Political Manipulation of Ethnicity in Cote D'Ivoire, 8/01

Unequal Protection: The State Response to Violence Crime on south African Farms, 08/01

The War in Aceh, 8/01

Violence and Political Impasse in Papua, 7/01

Hidden in The Home: Abuse of Domestic Workers with Special Visas, 6/01

No Escape: Male Rape in U.S. Prisons, 4/01

The "Dirty War" in Chechnya: Forced Disappearances, Torture, and Summary Executions, 3/01

Uganda in Eastern DRC: Fueling Political and Ethnic Strife, 3/01

Massacres of Hazaras in Afghanistan, 2/01

REFUGEES, ASYLUM SEEKERS, MIGRANTS, AND INTERNALLY DISPLACED PERSONS

INTRODUCTION: THE YEAR IN PROFILE

Fiftieth Anniversary of the 1951 Refugee Convention

2001 was a critical year for refugee protection. The year marked the fiftieth anniversary of the 1951 Convention Relating to the Status of Refugees (Refugee Convention)—the foundation of the international refugee protection regime. A series of global consultations on international refugee protection organized by the office of the United Nations High Commissioner for Refugees (UNHCR) was due to culminate in December 2001 at the first ever meeting of state parties to the Refugee Convention to reaffirm their commitment to the treaty. The Inter Parliamentary Union, the Council of Europe, the Organization of American States, and the Organization of African Unity all adopted resolutions and recommendations reaffirming their commitment to the convention in 2001.

Nevertheless, the Refugee Convention came under relentless attack—not least by the same industrialized states that were responsible for its formulation. Many states failed to accede to the 1951 Refugee Convention and its 1967 Protocol. Asian countries, including Bangladesh, Bhutan, Burma, India, Indonesia, Malaysia, Nepal, Pakistan, Singapore, Sri Lanka, Thailand, and Vietnam, were particularly remiss in this regard.

United Nations World Conference Against Racism

In August and September 2001, governments met in Durban, South Africa for the third U.N. World Conference Against Racism, Racial Discrimination, Xenophobia and Related Intolerance (WCAR). Although the protection of refugees and migrants featured prominently on the agenda, discussions regarding refugee protection were contentious and some governments argued for the removal of references to the Refugee Convention from the conference documents.

Fiftieth Anniversary of UNHCR
and New High Commissioner, Ruud Lubbers

The year 2000 also marked the fiftieth anniversary of UNHCR—the international agency mandated to protect and assist refugees. At the end of 2000 Sadako Ogata stood down after serving for ten years as high commissioner for refugees. Ogata was replaced by former Dutch Prime Minister Ruud Lubbers who took up his new position in January 2001. Lubbers' principle challenge as the new high commissioner was to revitalize UNHCR's core protection mandate and to take a strong stance with governments, particularly in Western Europe, that were undermining fundamental international refugee protection standards and seeking to erode the 1951 Refugee Convention.

Within the first months of taking office, Lubbers was tested with two of the most chronic and complex refugee crises in the world, Guinea and Afghanistan. Lubbers' first mission was to the West Africa sub-region in February 2001 where the conflicts in Liberia and Sierra Leone spilled over both countries' borders and threatened to destabilize Guinea, displacing thousands of refugees and Guineans and killing hundreds. In April and May, Lubbers visited Afghanistan, Iran, and Pakistan to assess the world's second largest refugee emergency.

In both cases he was criticized for his handling of the situation and made controversial proposals about possible solutions. Human rights and humanitarian groups criticized Lubbers' proposal to establish "safe passages" to enable refugees fleeing the turmoil in Guinea to return to Sierra Leone through rebel-controlled territory, citing widespread abuse by Revolutionary United Front (RUF) rebels in these areas. NGOs also criticized Lubbers for placing too much attention on the repatriation of Afghan refugees during his visits to the region, and argued that conditions inside Afghanistan were not conducive to return.

Impact of September 11 on Refugees and Migrants

Having sorely neglected the Afghan refugee crisis for years, the September 11 attacks on the United States focused international attention on the dire humanitarian crisis in Afghanistan and the chronic refugee situation across its borders in Pakistan and Iran. At the same time, anti-immigration measures were the centerpiece of many governments' efforts to combat terrorism in the aftermath of September 11. Many countries, including the U.S. and the United Kingdom, rushed to push through emergency anti-terrorism legislation that curtailed the rights of refugees, asylum seekers, and migrants. Human Rights Watch argued that states must balance legitimate security concerns with respect for the rights of refugees, asylum seekers, and migrants, and should not use counter-terrorism measures as a guise to roll-back well-established refugee and human rights protection standards.

REFUGEE PROTECTION POST SEPTEMBER 11

Protecting Afghan Refugees

Humanitarian crisis in Afghanistan

Before U.S.-led attacks began in October 2001, Afghanistan had already suffered over twenty years of foreign invasion and civil war, political turmoil, human rights abuses, coupled with a devastating three year drought. More than five million of Afghanistan's estimated 27 million people were displaced—four million as refugees and one million internally displaced. The severe drought brought many parts of the country to the verge of famine, while Taliban restrictions on relief agencies severely hampered the delivery of assistance and civilian access to basic services. Some five million people inside Afghanistan were entirely dependent on international aid, according to the World Food Programme (WFP).

The U.S. led bombing campaign, fears of forced conscription by the Taliban, fears of reprisals by and conflict between both the Taliban and Northern Alliance forces, general insecurity, the rapidly deteriorating humanitarian situation, and the onset of winter caused hundreds of thousands more Afghans to flee their homes in the weeks after September 11.

Conditions inside Afghanistan further deteriorated after September 11 when international relief staff were forced to withdraw after the Taliban declared that it could no longer guarantee their security. As the U.S. led attacks on Afghanistan progressed, aid agencies warned of an impending humanitarian disaster. The U.N. reported that the Taliban had confiscated food supplies from the U.N. and relief agencies. In addition, several relief agencies, including the warehouses of the International Committee of the Red Cross (ICRC) and the compound of a U.N.-affiliated demining agency Afghan Technical Consultants (ATC), were hit during the U.S. bombing offensive, killing and injuring staff.

By mid-November, significant advances by Northern Alliance troops and the withdrawal of the Taliban from major cities, including Kabul, had enabled aid agencies to resume some of their assistance operations and allowed some international staff to return to Afghanistan. Nevertheless, security remained precarious and there continued to be reports of looting by both Taliban and Northern Alliance forces. Aid agencies warned that time was running out to get aid through to the millions of starving Afghans if they were to survive the winter.

Treatment of Refugees in Neighboring Countries

Most Afghan refugees during the past two decades have fled to the country's immediate neighbors—over two million to Pakistan, and between one and a half and two million to Iran. Faced with such numbers and receiving little help from the international community, both these countries tightened their policies and officially closed their borders to Afghan refugees in 2000. Tajikistan also closed its borders to Afghan refugees in September 2000.

After September 11, Afghanistan's three other neighbors, Turkmenistan, Uzbekistan, and China, also closed their borders to Afghan refugees citing security concerns as well as their inability to absorb more refugees.

These governments' actions directly undermined core refugee protection standards, in particular the right to seek and enjoy asylum, set out in article 14 of the 1948 Universal Declaration of Human Rights (UDHR), and the principle of *non-refoulement*—the right of refugees not to be returned to a country where their lives or freedom could be threatened, as stipulated under article 33 of the Refugee Convention. Iran, China, Tajikistan, and Turkmenistan are all parties to and so bound by the 1951 Refugee Convention and its 1967 Protocol. Although Pakistan and Uzbekistan are not parties to the convention, the obligation of non-refoulement now constitutes a generally accepted principle of customary international law, and is binding on these states also.

Iran and Pakistan: Camps Inside Afghanistan Risk Safety of Refugees

Instead of allowing refugees to enter their territories, both Pakistan and Iran called instead for the establishment of camps on the Afghan side of their borders, in violation of their international obligations. These camps posed serious risks for the security of the refugees and aid workers who were in danger of being caught between warring factions in Afghanistan. Access to the camps by relief agencies was extremely limited.

The Iranian Red Crescent Society assisted with the establishment of two camps in northwestern Afghanistan close to the Iranian border. Mile-46, with a population of some 1,000 displaced persons, was established in an area under the control of the Northern Alliance forces, while Makaki camp with a population of 6,000 was, until Northern Alliance advances in mid-November, in a Taliban controlled area. Close to the Pakistan border, the Spin Boldak camp, with a population of over 3,000 displaced Afghans, was established in an area under strong Taliban control.

On November 12, UNHCR reported that Makaki camp was caught between Taliban troops, who still controlled the camp and advancing Northern Alliance troops pushing to take control of the area, forcing aid workers to withdraw and endangering civilians inside the camp. On November 14, the area fell to the Northern Alliance.

The lack of security in the camps made it difficult for aid agencies to operate safely, and by early November there were reports that several thousand Afghans were camped in the open around Makaki camp which was already filled beyond capacity. Aid agencies expressed concern about the health of displaced people in and around Makaki camp as winter approached.

Despite this, Iran continued to keep its borders shut to fleeing Afghans. The interior minister, Abdolvahed Musavi-Lari, stated that "it is better and more efficient to provide the refugees with assistance within their homes for humanitarian reasons," an assertion belied by conditions on the ground inside Makaki camp and elsewhere in Afghanistan.

Border Closures Endangers Refugees Lives

Despite the official closure of Pakistan's 1,560 mile border, UNHCR estimated that at least 150,000 Afghan refugees crossed unofficially into the country between September 11 and mid-November 2001. Many refugees traversed through dangerous mountain passes and were forced to pay exorbitant fees to smugglers or large bribes to border control guards in order to enter Pakistan. In mid-October, Pakistan agreed that particularly "vulnerable" refugees, including the elderly, sick, and some women and children would be allowed to enter, but most refugees fleeing Afghanistan were not admitted. Many who could not afford to pay the high smuggler fees and bribes to border guards were trapped on the Afghanistan side of the border.

Lack of Security Inside Pakistan

With an existing population of over two million Afghan refugees, Pakistan had tightened its refugee policies throughout the previous year. In November 2000 the government instituted a policy to detain and deport newly arrived Afghans in the North West Frontier Province (NWFP) and all Afghans who were already residing in Pakistan without official documentation. Between October 2000 and May 2001, according to the government, it forcibly returned some 7,633 Afghans, mostly men and boys. Other new arrivals were placed at Jalozai refugee camp but the government did not permit UNHCR to register them in order to determine whether or not they were in need of refugee protection. In August, however, the government and UNHCR agreed to jointly screen all the refugees at Jalozai camp and at the longer established Nasirbagh camp in order to determine which refugees could stay in Pakistan and which would be returned to Afghanistan, but the screening was suspended following the September 11 attacks.

Despite maintaining an official position of closed borders, the Pakistan authorities announced shortly after September 11 that they would set up new refugee camps in the event of a mass influx from Afghanistan. The sites were located in the Federally Administered Tribal Areas close to the Afghanistan border in the NWFP, that were unstable and insecure, difficult to reach, and lacked an adequate water supply and infrastructure. The location of refugee camps so close to the Afghanistan border was contrary to international standards which stipulate that camps must be located at a "safe distance" from international frontiers to protect against cross border attacks or military incursions.

Fifteen camps were established by mid-November but they were mostly empty as refugees who entered Pakistan unofficially feared to report to camp authorities and risk deportation, and preferred to stay with family or friends in Peshawar, Quetta, and other urban areas. Many of these so-called "invisible refugees" were Hazaras, Uzbek, or Tajik ethnic minorities. They lived in a state of legal limbo, undocumented and unassisted, and constantly at risk of being picked up by the police, detained, and returned to Afghanistan.

In early November, UNHCR and the Pakistan government agreed to move refugees from Killi Faizo, an insecure and overcrowded temporary staging camp near the Chaman border crossing in Baluchistan province, to Roghani camp, sixteen kilometers away. Under the same agreement, UNHCR began the transfer of refugees from the new Jalozai camp in Peshawar to Kotkai camp in Bajaur agency.

The new camp was located in a strongly pro-Taliban area only five kilometers from the Afghan border, raising fears for the security of the refugees, many of whom were from ethnic minorities and of forced recruitment by the Taliban. However, as the Pakistan authorities said that they would close new Jalozai camp, many refugees, especially those most dependent on relief assistance including women who were heads of household and widows, felt obliged to move to the camps despite their fears.

Eroding Refugee Protection in Iran

Iran steadfastly kept its 560 mile border with Afghanistan closed, and also deported thousands of Afghan refugees. On November 9, UNHCR reported that Iranian authorities had deported at least 350 refugees in a matter of days.

Iran's tough policies toward Afghan refugees pre-dated September 11. Out of the one and a half to two million Afghans living in Iran, the government estimated that as many as half a million were undocumented. Very few Afghans in Iran lived in camps. Most eked out a miserable existence in the cities where their lack of documentation and the government's increasingly tough policies towards them meant they were excluded from the formal labor market and had little or no access to education, health care, or other benefits.

In 1999, the U.S. Committee for Refugees estimated that Iran had forcibly returned some 100,000 Afghan refugees. In an attempt to prevent further forced deportations, UNHCR and the government of Iran agreed to a joint repatriation program in April 2000. Under this program Afghans could either receive a repatriation package from UNHCR and return to Afghanistan, or present their claims for continued protection in Iran at a screening center. UNHCR also set up repatriation centers to facilitate the repatriation of documented and undocumented Afghans wishing to return to their homes. Many NGOs charged that it was premature for refugees to return to drought and conflict-ridden Afghanistan. Despite the screening program, the U.S. Committee for Refugees estimated that as many as 50,000 returns were involuntary in 2000.

In mid-November 2001, UNHCR and Iran agreed to resume the screening program in order to repatriate Afghans without refugee status, a move that UNHCR hoped would stem summary deportations. Some NGOs cautioned that a flawed process could result in the forced return of hundreds of thousands of refugees.

At the same time, UNHCR reported a rise in spontaneous returns of refugees, particularly ethnic Uzbeks, Tajiks, and Hazaras, to areas of Afghanistan captured by the Northern Alliance.

Refugees Stranded on Tajikistan Border

Tajikistan closed its frontier with Afghanistan in September 2000 and thousands of Russian Federal border guards controlled the border. By September 11, there were already over 10,000 internally displaced Afghans on small islands in the Pyanj River, which divides the two countries, waiting for an opportunity to cross into Tajikistan, who were subject at times to crossfire between Northern Alliance and Taliban forces. Their numbers steadily increased prior to and during the U.S.-led military offensive in Afghanistan. Some were receiving assistance from aid agencies. On September 20, President Emomali Rakhmonov stated that Tajikistan would not allow any Afghan refugees to enter for fear of infiltration by Islamic militants and for economic reasons.

The Need for International Assistance and Action

By refusing to allow refugees entry into their territory and calling for the establishment of camps instead within Afghanistan, deporting refugees, and setting up refugee camps in dangerous and insecure areas, neighboring countries breached their international obligations toward Afghan refugees and threatened their safety and security. At the same time, the wider international community had an obligation to assist these countries to cope with large refugee influxes through financial and logistical support, as well as helping to find long-term solutions, including through third country resettlement. There was an urgent need for donor states and international agencies, such as UNHCR, to call on neighboring countries to keep their borders open, provide full and safe protection to refugees, and cease summary deportations. NGOs criticized UNHCR and donor states for not being sufficiently proactive in pushing neighboring countries to abide by their international obligations.

A Global Backlash Against Refugees and Migrants

Security concerns in the wake of the September 11 attacks prompted governments around the world to introduce emergency legislation and tighter immigration controls. In many countries, such measures were introduced in an existing climate of growing hostility and restrictions on the rights of refugees, asylum seekers, and migrants. Several governments introduced measures that seriously eroded their obligations under the 1951 Refugee Convention and undermined the fundamental right to seek and enjoy asylum, as stipulated in the UDHR. It was ironic that in the year marking the fiftieth anniversary of the Refugee Convention, the very same governments responsible for its establishment sought to depart from their obligations under this treaty.

Not only did doors close to Afghan refugees in neighboring countries, but also further afield. According to UNHCR, Afghan refugees arrived in countries as distant and geographically dispersed as Australia, Cambodia, Cuba, and Iceland in 2000. In 1999 and 2000, the number of Afghans who sought asylum in Europe nearly doubled, with Germany, the Netherlands, and the United Kingdom receiving the largest numbers of applications. Fears of a mass influx of Afghan refugees after September 11, prompted several countries to introduce harsh policies.

United States

The United States was one of the first countries to respond to the events of September 11 with emergency anti-terrorism legislation that severely curtailed the rights of non-citizens and permitted their indefinite detention. Despite vigorous protest by human rights, civil liberties, and immigrants' rights organizations, the "USA Patriot Act" was passed on October 26. The procedures leading to the passage of the anti-terrorism bill were flawed and rushed. Congress was unable to meet and fully consider the legislation as it was amended, meaning that problematic provisions of the legislation were never fully considered and debated by members of Congress.

The legislation granted unprecedented broad powers to the attorney general to "certify" and then detain any non-citizen, including an asylum-seeker, legal permanent resident, or a refugee, who he had "reasonable grounds to believe" was engaged in terrorist activities or other activities that endangered national security. A certified immigrant who had been charged with an immigration violation but who could not be deported would remain in custody until the attorney general determined that he or she no longer met the criteria for certification. While judicial review of the detention would be permitted, there were no meaningful, prompt, or periodic reviews to ensure the detention was warranted.

The overly broad and vague criteria for subjecting a non-citizen to detention could allow the attorney general to certify and detain any non-citizen in the U.S. who had any connection, however tenuous or distant in time, with any group that had ever unlawfully used a weapon to endanger a person. Given the focus of the law enforcement efforts in the wake of September 11, there were concerns that such language created the risk of arbitrary application and could disproportionately impact individuals from certain countries or religious groups, including asylum seekers and refugees. The legislation contravened the prohibition against prolonged, arbitrary, or unlawful detention in international human rights law and UNHCR's guidelines on the detention of asylum seekers.

In October, the U.S. government also announced that for national security reasons it had suspended all resettlement of refugees to the U.S., including Afghan refugees who were waiting to leave Pakistan. In 2000, the U.S. took 90 percent of the 4,000 Afghan refugees resettled out of Pakistan. The moratorium affected some 20,000 refugees from countries across the world who had been cleared by the Immigration and Naturalization Service (INS) for resettlement to the U.S. Refugee organizations criticized the moratorium, arguing that it was unnecessary and only increased the suffering of refugees from war-torn countries like Iraq, Sierra Leone, and Somalia, many of whom had spent years in desperate refugee camps waiting to be resettled.

Western Europe

In a worrying trend throughout Europe, governments linked anti-terrorism measures with the fight against illegal immigration and introduced measures that severely curtailed the rights of refugees and migrants. Spain's foreign minister, for example, voiced concerns that international terrorists could be smuggled into Spain and said that "[t]he strengthening of the fight against illegal immigration is also a strengthening of the anti-terrorist fight."

In Hungary, all Afghan asylum seekers were transferred from open reception centers to facilities with heightened security measures. In Greece, Afghan refugees who arrived after the September 11 attacks received a hostile reception as the government refused to allow them to apply for asylum, violating its obligations under the Refugee Convention. In the wake of vociferous international pressure, the government subsequently permitted some refugees to apply for asylum.

In Germany, advocacy groups reported that efforts to include adequate human rights safeguards for refugees in proposed asylum legislation suffered a serious setback in the aftermath of the September 11 attacks with many viewing the new legislation as a necessary measure to strengthen national security. More positively, however, the German government announced in November that it would introduce legislation to reverse its practice of excluding victims of persecution by non-state agents from refugee protection, such as asylum seekers from Somalia, Algeria, and Afghanistan.

European Union

After September 11, there were concerns that E.U. efforts to safeguard internal security could result in the exclusion or expulsion of refugees and migrants from member states without adequate safeguards.

United Kingdom

Following September 11, the British Home Secretary David Blunkett proposed far-reaching measures to restrict entry into the U.K. and strengthen national security. Outlined in a new Anti-Terrorism, Crime and Security Bill, these proposals were before parliament at the time of writing.

Civil liberties, refugee advocacy, and human rights NGOs were concerned that the bill would permit the unlawful indefinite detention of foreigners suspected of terrorism-related activity without access to effective appeal procedures and deny some asylum seekers individual determination of their asylum claims without recourse. The bill's broad and overly inclusive definition of terrorism would include any person with "links" to an international terrorist group, suggesting that this could lead to "guilt by association" and the targeting of individuals based on their political, national, ethnic, or religious affiliation. The bill's provisions seriously undermined the fundamental right to seek asylum and the purpose and intent of the Refugee Convention, and represented a departure from well-established refugee protection standards.

Racist attacks against Afghans and other Muslims living in the U.K. increased dramatically after September 11. These included damage to property, bomb threats against mosques, physical and verbal abuse of Muslim women wearing headscarves, and gang assaults targeting Arab and South Asian men. In one attack an Afghan taxi driver was beaten so severely he was paralyzed from the neck down. Both Prime Minister Tony Blair and Home Secretary David Blunkett condemned the attacks and called for tolerance.

Australia

Australia faced a barrage of international criticism for its excessively harsh and restrictive immigration and asylum policies. In August, the government turned back a boatload of mainly Afghan asylum seekers who had been rescued at sea by a Norwegian freighter, the *Tampa*, from a sinking Indonesian ferry, and refused to let them land on Australian territory. Most of the 438 asylum seekers were eventually sent to the Pacific island state of Nauru; others were sent to New Zealand. Following the September 11 attacks, Defense Minister Peter Reith justified Australia's actions, arguing that it should reserve the right to refuse entry on security grounds to "unauthorized arrivals".

Following the Tampa incident and the September 11 attacks on the U.S., the government adopted new and unprecedented immigration legislation in an expedited manner on September 26. Under the legislation, it "excised" various Australian territories, such as Christmas Island, Ashmore and Cartier Islands, and the Cocos Islands, from its "migration zone" and refused to consider asylum applications from anyone arriving at those places. Instead, the asylum seekers were transported to other non-Australian Pacific island states while their refugee claims were assessed, or simply sent back to sea. Human rights, refugee, and advocacy organizations charged that by forcing boats of asylum seekers back into international waters, Australia was endangering the lives of asylum seekers, undermining the right to seek asylum, and potentially violating non-refoulement obligations.

The new legislation also required the detention of asylum seekers arriving at an "excised offshore place" without any right to judicial review. Australia's policy of mandatory detention for all unauthorized arrivals continued to be widely condemned.

Between August and November, Australia turned back several boatloads of asylum seekers from Afghanistan, Iraq, and other countries in the Middle East and South Asia, and returned them to international waters. Many of the boats arrived in Australia via Indonesia, which was not a party to the 1951 Refugee Convention and lacked laws and procedures for determining refugee status.

THE CRISIS IN GUINEA

Host to one of Africa's largest and most unstable refugee populations in 2000—an estimated half a million Sierra Leonean and Liberian refugees—Guinea was faced with a national security crisis as the violence from its conflict-ridden neighbors spilled over and threatened to destabilize the country. Blaming the refugees for much of the insecurity, Guinea repeatedly closed its borders to Sierra Leonean and Liberian refugees between August 2000 and mid-2001, in violation of its international obligations not to return refugees to a country where their lives or freedom could be threatened. While acknowledging the serious security problems facing Guinea, Human Rights Watch called on the government not to violate its international obligations to refugees and urged donors to provide the necessary support and assistance to help Guinea cope with the crisis.

Between August and mid-2001, a combination of Sierra Leonean Revolutionary United Front (RUF) rebels and armed Liberian forces repeatedly attacked and burned refugee camps and Guinean villages along the border, killing, injuring, abducting, and forcing their residents to flee. The Liberian government also launched cross-border attacks, accusing Guinea of providing support and hosting a Liberian rebel group, the Liberians United for Reconciliation and Democracy (LURD).

Tens of thousands of refugees and local Guineans living in the border regions were forcibly displaced by the conflict and hundreds were killed. Faced with a no-win situation, some refugees fled back into RUF-controlled parts of Sierra Leone to escape the violence and suffered similar abuses at the hands of RUF rebels to those that originally caused their flight, including rape, murder, forced recruitment, and abduction for forced labor. Others fled inland into Guinea where they also faced abuses, including beatings, strip searches, extortion, sexual assault, arbitrary arrest and detention, and widespread intimidation, at the hands of the Guinean authorities and local militia groups.

Security was not only volatile for the refugees, but also for relief agencies and aid workers. In September 2000, the head of the UNHCR office in the town of Macenta on the Liberian border, was murdered by unidentified attackers, and in December the UNHCR office in Gueckedou was destroyed in fighting between government troops and rebels, during which hundreds of civilians were reportedly killed and led thousands of refugees and local people to flee. By December, assistance to the Parrot's Beak region, bordering RUF-held areas of Sierra Leone, was largely cut off due to the deteriorating security situation, leaving hundreds of thousands of refugees without access to food or protection.

After six months of violence, UNHCR and the Guinean government agreed in February to relocate the border refugee camps further inland and to assist Sierra Leonean refugees who wanted to return home to do so by boat from Conakry, but continuing violence in the border region delayed the relocation until April. By May, some 60,000 refugees had moved inland and an estimated 35,000 refugees had returned to Sierra Leone. However, tens of thousands of refugees in the border region remained unaccounted for. By mid-2001, the situation in Guinea seemed significantly calmer.

The problems in Guinea were exacerbated by the failure of the international community to provide sufficient funding and support for the refugees. Aware that the refugee camps were located dangerously close to the borders with Sierra Leone and Liberia, UNHCR sought funding to move the camps further inland in 1999. However, little or no funds were forthcoming due in part to the international attention then on Kosovo, and thus the camps in the border region remained vulnerable to attack and military incursions. If funds had been provided earlier to move the camps, some of the problems faced by the refugees in 2000 and 2001 could have been averted.

COMBATING RACISM AND XENOPHOBIA AGAINST REFUGEES AND MIGRANTS

United Nations World Conference Against Racism

After two years of regional and expert preparatory meetings, the third U.N. World Conference Against Racism, Racial Discrimination, Xenophobia and Related Intolerance (WCAR), was held in Durban, South Africa, from August 31 to September 8, 2001. Lobbying on refugee and migrants rights was organized through an effective NGO caucus of immigrant and refugee advocacy groups.

Despite efforts by some governments to exclude any reference to the 1951 Refugee Convention, the WCAR affirmed the convention's importance and states' obligation to comply with it; recognized racism and ethnic intolerance as among the root causes of refugee flows; called for greater efforts to combat racism and xenophobia against migrants, asylum seekers, and refugees; urged states to seek durable solutions to refugee crises, including voluntary return to countries of origin, third country resettlement, and where appropriate and feasible, local integration; upheld the right of return for refugees; and called for a more equitable international response to refugee crises.

The conference also called on states to promote and make use of the U.N. Guiding Principles on Internal Displacement, though otherwise the WCAR gave little consideration to the problems of internally displaced persons.

While not legally binding, the WCAR Declaration and Program of Action was an important affirmation of international standards and principles relating to refugees, migrants, and asylum seekers and a useful vehicle for coalition building among NGOs concerned with the rights of migrants and refugees.

Racism and Refugees: The Interface

Throughout 2001, refugees, asylum seekers, and migrants were victims of repeated racial discrimination, racist attacks, xenophobia, and ethnic intolerance. Racism was both a cause and a product of forced displacement, and an obstacle to its solution. Refugees fled countries such as Afghanistan, Burma, Burundi, Macedonia, Sri Lanka, and Turkey to escape racism and ethnic intolerance, but often then encountered further discrimination, xenophobia, or racist attacks in their host countries. At the same time, millions of refugees were unable to return to their own countries because of racial and ethnic discrimination.

Industrialized states continued to introduce a barrage of restrictive policies and practices targeting asylum seekers, refugees, and migrants. Negative and inaccurate portrayals of these groups in the media and inflammatory, xenophobic rhetoric by politicians and public officials in many Western countries contributed to a climate of hostility. There was also an alarming rise in racist and xenophobic violence against asylum seekers, refugees, and migrants in many industrialized countries, as well as in traditionally generous host countries in the developing world.

Xenophobic Rhetoric: The Case of Australia

Many governments manipulated and incited xenophobic fears for short-term political gain. In Australia, for example, Minister for Immigration and Multicultural Affairs Phillip Ruddock made a series of inflammatory and xenophobic statements about immigration and asylum between November 1999 and August 2001, suggesting that mandatory detention policies protected the Australian public against communicable diseases brought in by illegals and that whole villages of Iraqis and others were preparing to travel to Australia. The refusal by Australia to allow boatloads of mostly Afghan and Iraqi refugees and migrants entry to its territory came in the run-up to a general election campaign, in which the government sought to demonstrate a tough stance on asylum and immigration and fuelled xenophobic fears among the public with inflammatory accounts of "floods" of refugees on the move to Australia. The rhetoric and tough policies paid off, as John Howard's government won a third term in office at the mid-November elections.

Racist Attacks in Europe

There was a high incidence of racially motivated attacks and violence against refugees, asylum seekers, and migrants in European countries. In the U.K., the dispersal of asylum seekers to remote or deprived areas resulted in increased attacks. In August, Firsat Dag, a Kurdish asylum seeker, was stabbed to death in an unprovoked racial attack in Glasgow. Days later an Iranian asylum seeker was also stabbed, and a Kurdish asylum seeker in Hull had his throat slashed. NGOs, UNHCR, and the inter-governmental European Commission against Racism and Intolerance, amongst others, linked the attacks to the negative portrayal of asylum seekers by politicians and the media, particularly during the May general election campaign.

In Russia, there were attacks on African students in Moscow, including many refugees, by mobs of youth, often wielding weapons or bottles. Most victims feared to report such attacks to the police; those that did generally found the police unwilling to investigate.

Racism as a Barrier to Safe Return: The Case of Bhutan

Racism and ethnic discrimination prevented the safe return of millions of refugees. Despite the commencement of a joint verification process by the Bhutanese and Nepalese governments in early 2001 to ascertain the status of 100,000 Bhutanese refugees in camps in Nepal, by November no refugees had returned to Bhutan.

The refugees, mostly ethnic Nepalese, were expelled from southern Bhutan in the early 1990s. Many were arbitrarily stripped of their nationality prior to their expulsion after Bhutan amended its nationality laws in the late 1980s to deny nationality rights to most southern Bhutanese.

After nine rounds of ministerial talks between Bhutan and Nepal, the Bhutanese government still refused to accept the refugees back, claiming that they were not bona fide Bhutanese citizens. At the tenth round of talks in December 2000, following concerted pressure by the U.S., the E.U., and the U.N., the two governments finally agreed to start a joint verification of the refugees. This would determine the refugees' nationality status, with a view to their ultimate repatriation to Bhutan.

However, international NGOs were concerned about the Bhutanese government's refusal to allow UNHCR to monitor the verification process, the lack of independent scrutiny, and the excruciatingly slow progress of the process that continued to deny thousands of refugees the right to return to their own country.

CONCLUSION: THE CHALLENGES AHEAD

As the year ended, core refugee protection principles were under serious threat across the globe and the future for millions of refugees, asylum seekers, and migrants was uncertain. In the aftermath of September 11, governments faced a critical challenge to address legitimate national security concerns without undermining long-enshrined refugee protection and human rights standards and further eroding the rights of refugees, asylum seekers, and migrants. Governments hosting large, long-term refugee populations faced the challenge of continuing to provide protection and keep their borders open, while the international community had a heightened responsibility to provide sufficient funding and support and to seek effective solutions to chronic refugee crises. The fiftieth anniversary of the Refugee Convention provided states with an opportunity to ratify and accede to the convention and its 1967 Protocol, to fully and unequivocally reaffirm their commitment to the convention as the centerpiece of refugee protection, and to repeal legislation, policies, and practices that undermined the spirit and letter of the convention. Finally, the conclusion of the third WCAR challenged states to put into practice the directives outlined in its final declaration and program of action. In particular, governments were challenged to address racism and discrimination as root causes of refugee flows; reverse policies and practices that discriminate against migrants, asylum seekers, and refugees; avoid inflammatory and xenophobic portrayals of asylum seekers, refugees, and migrants; take vigorous action to investigate and bring to justice perpetrators of racist violence against migrants and refugees; and seek long-term solutions to refugee situations, particularly where refugees are blocked from returning to their home country or integrating into a host country because of discrimination and racism.

Relevant Human Rights Watch Reports:

Guinea: Refugees Still at Risk: Continuing Refugee Protection Concerns in Guinea,
     7/01
Uprooting the Rural Poor in Rwanda, 5/01
UNHCR at 50: What Future for Refugee Protection? 12/00

APPENDIX

AWARDS

HELLMAN/HAMMETT GRANTS

The Hellman/Hammett grants are given annually by Human Rights Watch to recognize the courage of writers around the world who have been targets of political persecution and are in financial need. Twenty-seven writers from twenty countries received grants in 2001. Some recipients were in prison; many were forced to flee their homelands; all have been harassed, assaulted, or threatened. Each case is different, but all were persecuted for expressing opinions, reporting stories, or disseminating ideas that offended their governments.

In many countries, governments use a variety of tactics—from military and presidential decrees, criminal libel and sedition laws to intimidatory criminal violence to silence critics. Writers and journalists are often thrown in jail merely for providing information from nongovernmental sources. As a result, in addition to those who are directly targeted, many others are silenced by threats and self-censorship.

The Hellman/Hammett grant program began in 1989 when the estates of American authors Lillian Hellman and Dashiell Hammett asked Human Rights Watch to design a program for writers in financial need as a result of expressing their views. By publicizing the persecution that the grant recipients endure, Human Rights Watch focuses attention on censorship and suppression of free speech. In some cases, the publicity is a protection against further abuse. In other cases, the writers request anonymity because of the dangerous circumstances in which they and their families are living.

Following are short biographies of the recipients in 2001 whose names can be safely released:

Aung Pwint (Burma), an imprisoned poet whose work expresses the feelings of ordinary people about the social and economic crisis in their country, has been repeatedly targeted by the military government because of his contacts with the rebellious student movement. He was arrested in 1967 and detained for a year, and arrested again in 1978 and held for seventeen months. During the 1988 pro-democracy movement, he served as joint secretary of the People's Peaceful Demonstration Committee in the Delta region. Subsequently, he joined a fledgling media group, which produced videos and calendars. In 1996, the military government banned his videos because they were considered to show too negative a picture of Burmese society and living standards. In 1999, he was arrested and sentenced to an eight-year prison term.

Mikel Azurmendi (Spain), who writes poetry, children's tales, political commentary, and essays on Basque history, is a professor of social anthropology at the University of Bilbao. His major contribution has been to deconstruct the theory of "ethnic exclusionism" that radical nationalists use to define the Basque historical experience. In the 1960s, Azurmendi was a member of the armed separatist group ETA. After its violent attacks on the Franco regime, he left to join the Basque pro-democracy movement. He is a founder of the Foro Ermua, one of the most prestigious groups promoting peace and democracy in the Basque region. Meanwhile, ETA has systematically subjected him to threats, painting "Azurmendi to the firing wall" on his office, and distributing pamphlets urging that he be killed. After a bomb attack in August 2000, he fled to the United States.

Bei Ling (China), poet and essayist, came to the United States in 1988 on an exchange with a Chinese-language newspaper. After the Tiananmen Square protest, he stayed and founded *Tendency Quarterly*, a scholarly literary magazine. By 1998, Bei Ling began to travel to China, Hong Kong, and Taiwan, researching, writing, and editing *Tendency*. In 2000, he rented an apartment and opened editorial offices in Beijing. After printing the summer issue of *Tendency* in Beijing, he was detained for two weeks in August 2000 and charged with "illegal publication." Beijing security forces interrogated him and threatened a ten-year prison term. They offered leni-ency if he provided information about the identity of Chinese citizens who had helped to produce *Tendency*. Bei Ling refused. After an international protest, Chinese authorities levied a $24,000 fine and permitted him to return to the United States.

Daniel Bekoutou (Chad) is an investigative journalist whose problems started when he uncovered financial scandals in health and environmental programs in Senegal, where he lived in exile. In November 1999, he was attacked and badly beaten by operatives who accused him of writing overly critical articles on Chad's president Idress Deby. Then Bekoutou began covering the case of Hissène Habré, Chad's exiled former dictator who was indicted in Senegal on torture charges. Bekoutou wrote numerous articles exposing political killings, torture, and "disappearances" during the Habré regime. He played a key role in keeping newspapers from prematurely leaking news of the Habré indictment, which would have given Habré time to flee. The day after Habré's indictment, Bekoutou began receiving death threats. Fearing for his life, he fled to Paris.

Bui Ngoc Tan (Vietnam) started a career in journalism in 1954, writing in accord with the Vietnamese Communist Party (VCP) line. Gradually, he became critical of the VCP perspective. He was arrested as a "revisionist and antiparty element" in 1968 and imprisoned without trial until 1973. After his release, he wrote stories and novels but, banned from publishing, earned his living as a laborer. In 1995, he was permitted to publish again. *Nhung Nguoi Rach Viec* (These People with Nothing to Do), published in 1995, and *Mot Ngay Dai Dang Dang* (A Very Long and Boring Day), published in 1999, were mildly critical of the ruling regime. In 2000, he published *Chuyen Ke Nam 2000* (Story Told in Year 2000), a denunciation of the government's detention policy. Too much for the censors, the book was recalled and burned. The Hai Phong police have subjected him to numerous interrogations and keep him under heavy surveillance.

Chan Mony (Cambodia), journalist, has written mostly on social issues and public safety—law enforcement, robberies, mob violence, and street demonstrations. At the time of writing, he worked for the *Evening News* in Phnom Penh, an English language newspaper generally regarded as leaning toward the ruling Cambodian People's Party. In March 1997, while he was covering a peaceful demonstration in front of the National Assembly, someone threw grenades into the crowd killing at least sixteen people and injuring hundreds of others. Mony's right leg was broken and shrapnel pierced his left eye. Members of a bodyguard unit of Prime Minister Hun Sen were implicated in the attack, but no one has ever been arrested. Mony's eye injury continued to cause pain.

Mridula Garg (India) has been a prolific writer in many genres, including fiction, plays, essays, and journalism. In 1979, she was charged under the penal code with writing pornographic literature, and a warrant was issued for her arrest based on two pages from one novel. Many in the government said that the indictment had no basis and would be withdrawn, but it was not, and police returned to her house "almost every month" for the next two years to harass her. The literary magazine, *Sarika,* conducted a campaign against her, publishing vulgar letters about her in more than a dozen issues over the period of more than one year. *Aniya,* a political and historical epic novel published in 1980, was condemned unread. Garg did not give up or compromise her writing. In the next twenty years, she published fifteen books, of which only four were novels, but the label "shock value fiction" stuck, and her work has been denied serious literary assessment.

Carmen Gurruchaga (Spain), journalist, has covered nationalism, Basque politics, and terrorism-related issues in print and on radio and television since 1989. In December 1997, a bomb was found by the front door of the apartment where she lived with her two sons. She had written a front-page story about a fugitive Basque youth who was acquitted by a jury in a controversial trial even though he had admitted killing two policemen. The article said that he had been discovered in Cuba and might be receiving support from militant Basque separatists in exile there. The bombing caused Gurruchaga to move from her lifelong home in San Sebastian to Madrid. Her name is often found on "black lists," and Molotov cocktails have been thrown at her office.

Kong Bun Chhoeun (Cambodia), novelist and songwriter, has been writing prolifically since the 1950s, but was forced to became a farmer while the Khmer Rouge were in power. It is likely he would have been killed had he revealed his identity. With the collapse of the Khmer Rouge, he resumed writing. The plot of his last novel, *The Destiny of Marina,* or *Acid-Laced Vengeance,* published in 2000, bore many similarities to the 1999 scandal of a karaoke singer who was attacked with acid by the jealous wife of a government official. The book addressed the problem of official impunity in Cambodia. After publication, Kong Bun Chhoeun received death threats from the husband of the woman who had mutilated the singer. In November 2000, Kong Bun Chhoen fled to Thailand.

Moncef Marzouki (Tunisia) is a medical doctor and leading human rights activist whose writing is banned in Tunisia. Some of his work has been published in Arabic in Egypt; some in French has been published in Europe. Dr. Marzouki was jailed for four months in 1994 after announcing his candidacy in the presidential election. The government also closed the community medical clinic that he founded. Threats to him and his family caused his wife and daughters to move to Europe. In June 1999, he was abducted by security officials and held incommunicado for several days. He has been denied a passport, preventing him from travel abroad for professional reasons or to visit his family. He has faced repeated judicial investigations on spurious charges. In December 2000, he was sentenced to one year in prison for "defaming the authorities" and "spreading false information."

Gemechu Melka Tufa (Ethiopia), pen name Motii Biya, journalist and author of several books on Oromo society and history, was arrested in 1997. His arrest is thought to be connected to newspaper columns he wrote and his membership in the Ethiopian Human Rights League. He was held without charge or trial for more than two years and then released on bail. After a period of liberty in Addis Ababa, the capital, he fled the country in fear of persecution. He was granted refugee status and received political asylum in Canada.

Dunya Mikhail (Iraq) is a widely published poet and journalist whose allegorical book, *Diary of a Wave Outside the Sea,* was banned in Iraq. She wrote anti-war poems that could not be published in Iraq because they were deemed "subversive." Warned that her "life is at risk" if she does not "stop anti-government writings" she sought asylum and fled to the United States.

Octovanius Mote (Indonesia), bureau chief in the capital of Irian Jaya (West Papua) for Indonesia's biggest and best-known newspaper, *Kompas,* served as rapporteur for a "national dialogue" on Irian Jaya between President Habibie and one hundred community leaders. Habibie's participation was conditioned on the participants' acceptance of a ban on discussion of independence. This not withstanding, the leaders presented Habibie with a petition demanding independence when they came to Jakarta for the dialogue. A few months later, Mote and four intellectuals who had been involved in the dialogue were the object of fabricated charges that they had been buying arms. Although not detained, the charges resulted in their blacklisting to keep them from leaving the country. The same day the travel restrictions were imposed, Mote boarded a plane for the United States as part of a U.S. Information Agency Visitors Program. In August 2000, as he was preparing to go back home, the crackdown on Irian Jaya's independence movement took a sharp turn for the worse prompting Mote to postpone his return. The Open Society Institute gave him a grant to stay at Cornell University for a year.

Hasan Mujtaba (Pakistan), journalist, has written extensively on political corruption, the role of senior politicians and their aides in the drug trade, trafficking Bangladeshi women into Pakistan with the help of Pakistani border forces, recruitment of teenage students from Islamic seminaries to fight with the Taliban in Afghanistan, urban decay, and male homosexuality. He is also a published poet in his native language, Sindhi. Mujtaba's life has been threatened repeatedly, most recently prompted by his research into treatment of Pakistan's Hindu minority. In April 1999, he came to the United States to receive an award from the Johns Hopkins School of Advanced International Studies and stayed to seek asylum.

Grigory Pasko (Russia), journalist and naval officer, was arrested in 1997 and charged with state treason (article 275 of the criminal code) in retaliation for his writing about the dumping of radioactive waste in the Sea of Japan. Russian authorities claimed that he intended to pass state secrets to a foreign power. After spending twenty months in prison, he was acquitted of the treason charges—a verdict that was appealed—and found guilty of a lesser charge, abuse of office, for which he was sentenced to three years and amnestied. Pasko rejected the amnesty. In November 2000, the Military Board of the Russian Supreme Court accepted the prosecution's appeal of the acquittal of treason charges. That trial opened in July 2001 at the Pacific Fleet Military Courthouse in Vladivostok and was continuing. If convicted, Pasko faced a prison sentence of twelve to twenty years.

Marta Petreu (Romania), poet, philosopher, and university professor in Cluj, founded and edits the magazine *Apostrof,* an important voice of reason and integrity in Romania today. She has written critically about Romanian extreme right ideology, provoking repressive reactions from many antidemocratic political groups, gradually isolating herself and *Apostrof.* She received threats and was attacked by a mob at a public reading.

Pham Que Duong (Vietnam) started his career in the People's Liberation Army in 1945 at age fourteen. Over the next forty years he rose to the rank of colonel. In 1982, he became editor in chief of *Tap Chi Lich Su Quan Su* (Military History Review) and devoted all of his time to writing. In 1986, he was fired because he refused to obey orders not to report about the careers of dismissed officers. In 1990, he was investigated and accused of supporting Tran Xuan Bach, secretary general of the Vietnamese Communist Party (VCP), for the seventh Congress, who was expelled for advocating pluralism. In 1999, Pham Que Duong quit the VCP in solidarity with a prominent outspoken dissident and became a democracy activist. His house has been searched several times, his telephone tapped, his e-mail suppressed, and he was often summoned to police headquarters for questioning.

Esmat Qaney (Afghanistan), novelist and short story writer, fled from Afghanistan's Zabol province in 1980, and subsequently settled in the Pakistani city of Quetta. Following the mujahideen takeover of Kabul in 1992, the government of President Burhanuddin Rabbani judged his novel *The Fifth Marriage* hostile to Islamic teachings and burned copies of it. In the summer of 2000, after publication of a collection of stories, *Zeera Ra Wastawai Khair Yusai* (Send Charity, God Bless

You), Taliban authorities ruling Afghanistan found the book was an "insult to religious leaders" and issued a decree branding Qaney and his publisher, Mustafa Sahar, "apostates." Taliban supporters in Quetta seized all copies of the book and burned them outside a mosque. Fearing for his safety, Qaney left his family and went into hiding.

San San Nweh (Burma), novelist and poet, has spent long periods in prison for her political activities. She has been serving her current ten-year sentence since October 1994 for "fomenting trouble" by producing anti-government reports and sending them to foreign journalists. She has been offered freedom if she renounces all political activity, but she has regularly refused to do so, despite being forced to sit cross-legged in a cramped cell with three other political convicts and barred from speaking for more than fifteen minutes a day. She was plagued with poor health—kidney infections, high blood pressure, and eye problems.

Wang Yiliang (China), poet and essayist, has been involved in underground literary activity since the early 1980s. State security authorities have kept him under close surveillance, have regularly summoned him for interrogation and detention, and banned publication of his work. In January 2000, Wang Yi Liang was arrested for "disrupting social order" and sentenced to two years of "reeducation through labor."

Sanar Yurdatapan (Turkey), songwriter and composer, has also written fiction and was a regular columnist for the Kurdish daily newspaper, *Ozgur Gundem*. Following the military coup in 1980, he lived in exile in Germany for eleven years. On his return in 1991, he threw himself into human rights work. He has developed an original method for attacking repression of free expression. When someone was convicted for expressing a nonviolent opinion, he found a prominent person to republish the statement and accompanied the republication with a disclaimer defending the person's right to express his views, not the views themselves. The republications were cheap photocopies, but this was enough to trigger prosecution under Turkish law. When prosecutors were reluctant to lodge charges against prominent people, Yurdatapan forced them to prosecute by threatening prosecution for not carrying out their duties. He has published forty-three Freedom for Freedom of Expression booklets. The first one caused ninety defendants to be charged. The last one had 70,000 publishers who are all now subject to state prosecution. The prosecutors usually found ways to avoid concluding the cases, but in attempts to stop Yurdatapan they have lodged trumped-up charges against him and imprisoned him three times.

MISSIONS

AFRICA DIVISION

Angola: Research on internally displaced persons (May).

Belgium: Advocacy (March, June); monitoring Rwanda genocide trial (June); advocacy (September–October).

Burundi: Research on war crimes (February); workshop with local NGOs on human rights monitoring (March, July); research on progress toward a peace agreement and reduction in civilian killings (June); research on government-sponsored paramilitary forces and advocacy regarding issues of justice and im-punity (September).

Canada: Annual meeting of the Coalition on Women in Conflict on advocacy on prosecution of gender-based crimes at the International Criminal Tribunal for Rwanda (November).

Côte d'Ivoire: Investigation of election-related violence and massacres (February-March).

Democratic Republic of Congo (DRC): Investigation of Ugandan-occupied areas (December 2000); work with local NGOs (March, July); advocacy and research on child soldiers and armed groups (July); investigation of sexual violence and related workshops (October-November).

France: Advocacy (March, June).

Gambia: African Commission on Human and Peoples' Rights (October).

Guinea: Investigation of abuses against Sierra Leonean and Liberian refugees (May); investigation of human rights conditions in refugee camps (July).

Italy: Advocacy related to the DRC (July).

Kenya: Conference presentation on human rights and oil in Sudan (May); workshop on the DRC and research (November).

Nigeria: Observer at "Shell stakeholders consultation workshop" in Warri, Delta

State, and research on current situation in the delta (March); presented paper on corporate social responsibility at Britain-Nigeria Law Week, Abuja (April); investigation of vigilantism (June); investigation of intercommunal killings in Jos and vigilantism in southeast (September-October).

Rwanda: Research on local elections (February); work with local NGOs (March, July); research and advocacy (June); investigation of popular justice, advocacy (September).

South Africa: Research on violence in commercial farming areas (February); advocacy and workshop with NGOs (August); presentation to government conference on rural safety (October).

Sudan: Conference of the Wunlit Peace Council (April).

Switzerland: Advocacy at U.N. Human Rights Commissions meeting on the issue of national human rights commission in Africa (April).

Tanzania: Investigation of election-related massacres and human rights violations on the semi-autonomous islands of Zanzibar and Pemba (July-August); meetings with ICTR trial teams (September-October).

Togo: Third regional meeting of African national human rights institutions (March).

Uganda: Investigation of pre-election human rights environment (February-March); work with local NGOs (March, August).

Zambia: Work with southern African human rights network (August).

Zimbabwe: Research on human rights abuses related to land seizures (July-August).

AMERICAS DIVISION

Argentina: Research on the progress of court investigations into human rights violations under the military dictatorship (April, July).

Chile: Advocacy launch of *Progress Stalled: Setbacks in Freedom of Expression Reform in Chile* (March); Liberty and Ethics seminar, University of Chile (November).

Colombia: Research on military-paramilitary ties (January); meetings with Colombian officials and public release of *The Sixth Division* (October).

Dominican Republic: Research on the treatment of Haitian migrants and Dominico-Haitians (June).

Ecuador: Research on child labor and obstacles to freedom of association in the banana sector (May).

Haiti: Interviews with Haitians deported from the Dominican Republic, as well as human rights monitors who work with recent deportees (June).

Mexico: Assessment of impact of the change in government on human rights conditions (December 2000); research on military abuses in Guerrero, and failure to properly investigate and prosecute such abuses (March/April, June); research on violence against and harassment of lesbians, gays, bisexuals, and transgender persons (September).

Peru: Research on progress of rule of law and accountability issues under the new government of Alejandro Toledo (September).

Uruguay: Participation in Human Rights Conference sponsored by U.S. Southern Command in Montevideo (October).

Venezuela: Investigation into the implementation of Venezuela's new constitution and violations of labor rights and free expression (January).

ASIA DIVISION

Cambodia: Attend trial in Kampot, concerning murder of a Commune Council Candidate (March); attended indigenous land rights trial in Ratanakiri, (March); researched ethnic minority asylum seekers from Vietnam and advocacy in regard to Cambodian government and UNHCR policies towards them (March, September); trial observation of Cambodian Freedom Fighters in Phnom Penh (June).

East Timor: Research on justice system (December 2000).

Hong Kong: Advocacy on human rights concerns (April).

India: Attended the National Campaign for Dalit Human Rights' Global Conference Against Caste Discrimination in New Delhi (March); researched allegations of caste and religious discrimination in the distribution of earthquake relief in Gujarat (March).

Indonesia: Research in Aceh (December 2000); research in Papua (February-March); research in Aceh and training of Acehnese NGOs in Jakarta (May); further training of Acehnese NGOs in Jakarta and research in Aceh (August).

Japan: Advocacy focusing on Japanese foreign policy and domestic trafficking (April).

Malaysia: Attendance at an Asia-Pacific intergovernmental workshop, facilitated by the Office of the High Commissioner on Human Rights on the impact of globalization; meetings with key human rights defenders and the families of activists detained under the Internal Security Act (May).

Pakistan: Research to interview refugees forcibly displaced by the Taliban in Afghanistan's Bamiyan and Balkh provinces, and refugee protection issues in Pakistan (August).

Sri Lanka: Subregional NGO workshop on South Asia; research on internally displaced people in Sri Lanka (February); research on abuses against civilians by all parties to the conflict (October-November).

Thailand: Research in northern Thailand on displacement of ethnic Shan villagers from Burma and of Shan refugees in Thailand (February); attendance at the Ninth Asia-Pacific Workshop on Regional Cooperation for the Promotion and Protection of Human Rights, (February-March); NGO training on the Thai-Burmese border (August); participation in the Asia-wide consultation in Bangkok between NGOs and Hina Jilani, special representative of the U.N. secretary-general on human rights defenders (November).

United Kingdom: Advocacy and development meetings with British government officials on British policy in Asia (November 2000); attendance at a meeting of the International Dalit Solidarity Network (October).

United Nations World Conference Against Racism: Attendance at the Asian regional preparatory meeting (Tehran, Iran, February); attendance at the second regional preparatory meeting (Geneva, Switzerland, May); attendance at the third regional preparatory meeting (Geneva, August); attendance at the WCAR (South Africa, August-September).

EUROPE AND CENTRAL ASIA DIVISION

Albania: Research on freedom of expression issues, including civil and criminal defamation lawsuits brought against journalists and threats to their personal security and ability to work free of fear (November).

Armenia: Attended and addressed strategy session of Caucasus region Soros Foundations (June).

Austria: Meetings at the OSCE to advocate for the OSCE Assistance Group's redeployment to Chechnya, Vienna (March); meetings at the OSCE to discuss mission activities in Chechnya, Macedonia (June, July, October).

Belgium: Responded to release of E.U. Accession Partnership for Turkey, Brussels (November 2000); responded to E.U. internal security measures after September

11, Brussels (October); advocacy on the prison situation in Turkey as well as Turkey's E.U. membership, Brussels (April, May).

Bosnia and Herzegovina: Follow-up research for a report on the return of refugees who were displaced from their homes during the 1992-1995 conflict (September).

Croatia: Research on the return of Croatian Serbs since January 2000 obstruction of return (August-September).

Czech Republic: Advocacy on Chechnya at the UNCHR, Prague (March).

France: Joint advocacy to lobby Council of Europe regarding the prison crisis in Turkey (March); advocacy at Parliamentary Assembly sessions regarding Russian abuses in Chechnya (January, April); migrants coalition work at European preparation meeting for WCAR (May).

Georgia: On-going research and advocacy from Tblisi office, including on religious freedom.

Greece: Research on migrants' human rights (November 2000).

Macedonia: Three research missions to investigate abuses by the Macedonian government and the National Liberation Army (NLA) (May-August); meetings with government officials, Skopje (October).

Netherlands: Meetings on Chechnya at the Dutch Foreign Ministry, Amsterdam (October).

Norway: Advocacy effort to gain support for a resolution on Chechnya at the UNCHR, Oslo (March).

Poland: Advocacy effort to gain support for a resolution on Chechnya at the UNCHR, Warsaw (March).

Romania: Advocacy at the IHF Executive Committee quarterly meeting, a conference on minority rights in the region, and with the Romanian Foreign Ministry (February).

Russian Federation: Research on continuing abuses, mass graves, forced disappearances, and sweep operations, Ingushetia (November-December 2000, February-March, June-July); attended the opening of the trial of Col. Yuri Budanov, Rostov-on-Don (February).

Spain: Research on child migrants' human rights (July-August); research on admission, detention, and expulsion of adult migrants (October-November).

Sweden: Advocacy effort to gain support for a resolution on Chechnya at the UNCHR, Stockholm (March).

Switzerland: Advocacy on Chechnya at the UNCHR, Bern (March) and at the U.N. Commission on Human Rights, Geneva (April); advocacy on migrants, Geneva (May).

Tajikistan: Monitored human rights abuses in northeast Afghanistan and assessed the human rights situation in Tajikistan (October-November).

Turkey: Participated in Initiative for Freedom of Expression event, Istanbul and Ankara (November 2000); joint research and advocacy on December prison massacre (January); research on government's village return program, southeast Turkey (June-July).

United Kingdom: Advocacy on Chechnya, London (February, October); annual meeting of the European Bank for Reconstruction and Development, London (April); advocacy on U.K. anti-terror and immigration restrictions after September 11, London (October).

Uzbekistan: Research on humanitarian law violations (May-June); attended the trial of seventy-three men on charges of collaboration with IMU fighters (May-June).

Federal Republic of Yugoslavia: Researched the transition following the defeat of Slobodan Milosevic in the October 2000 presidential election (November 2000); released report on abuses committed during the 1999 war in Kosovo, Pristina, Djakovica, and Belgrade (October).

MIDDLE EAST AND NORTH AFRICA DIVISION

Egypt: Research on political arrests and freedom of expression issues; advocacy for report, *Underage and Unprotected: Child Labor in Egypt's Cotton Fields* (January-February); research on deaths in custody and government accountability mechanisms; meetings with government officials and attendance at regional NGO conference for the World Conference Against Racism (July); trial observations (January, April, August, October-November).

Iran: Sought meetings with government officials and attended regional U.N. conference for the World Conference Against Racism (February).

Iraq and Iraqi Kurdistan: Research on internally displaced persons (March).

Israel, the Occupied West Bank and Gaza Strip, and Palestinian Authority Territories: Research on human rights and humanitarian law abuses related to the Intifada (October 2000, November 2000, February, June-August); advocacy for report, *Center of the Storm: Human Rights Abuses in Hebron* (April); advocacy (May-June); research on the administration of justice by the Palestinian Authority (August-September).

Morocco: Observation of the trial of thirty-six human rights activists in Rabat (February); attendance of the appeals hearing of the same case (September); attendance of the appeals hearing in the case of Ahmed Boukhari (September).

Tunisia: Research (February).

ARMS DIVISION

Argentina: Participation in regional Landmine Monitor researchers meeting and International Campaign to Ban Landmines (ICBL) advocacy events (November 2000).

Armenia: Participation in regional Landmine Monitor researchers meeting and ICBL advocacy events (November).

Belgium: Participation in regional Landmine Monitor Core Group meeting (October); participation in meeting of Facilitation Committee of the International Action Network on Small Arms (October).

Canada: Participation in Mine Ban Treaty Implementation Seminar (April); participation in United Nations Mine Action Strategy Seminar (June).

Czech Republic: Research on arms trade policy and practices (June-July).

Djibouti: Participation in regional Landmine Monitor researchers meeting and a regional government conference on landmines (November 2000).

Ethiopia: Participation in small arms conference hosted by the Bonn International Center for Conversion, advocacy (April).

Japan: Participation in regional Landmine Monitor researchers meeting and ICBL advocacy events (November 2000).

Republic of Korea: Participation in regional Landmine Monitor researchers meeting and ICBL advocacy events (October).

Lebanon: Participation in regional Landmine Monitor researchers meeting and ICBL advocacy events (January).

Mali: Participation in diplomatic All-Africa Regional Landmine Conference (February).

New Zealand: Participation in U.N. Asia-Pacific Regional Disarmament Conference (March).

Nepal: Participation in regional Landmine Monitor researchers meeting and ICBL advocacy events (January).

Nicaragua: Participation in the Third Meeting of States Parties to the Mine Ban Treaty and Global Landmine Monitor researchers meeting (September).

Poland: Research on arms trade policy and practices (June).

Romania: Advocacy and research, meetings on arms export practices in Central/Eastern Europe (April).

Slovakia: Research on arms trade policy and practices (July).

South Africa: Participation in regional Landmine Monitor researchers meeting (January).

Switzerland: Participation in intersessional Standing Committee meetings on the Mine Ban Treaty (December 2000); regional Landmine Monitor researchers meeting (December 2000); Second Annual Conference of States parties to Protocol II to the Convention on Conventional Weapons (CCW) (December 2000); meeting of Landmine Monitor Research Coordinators (December 2000, May); International Committee of the Red Cross, Experts Seminar on Antivehicle Mines and Antihandling Devices (March); participation in Prepcom for the CCW Review (April); intersessional Standing Committee meetings on the Mine Ban Treaty, ICBL Coordination Committee meeting and Landmine Monitor Core Group and Coordination Team meetings (May); CCW Prepcoms (August, September).

United States: Participation in "Ban Landmines Week" in Washington, D.C., including Global Landmine Monitor researchers meeting, International Campaign to Ban Landmines General Meeting and U.S. Campaign to Ban Landmines events (March); meeting of the Facilitation Committee on the International Action Network on Small Arms (November 2000); advocacy on U.N. Conference on the Illicit Trade in Small Arms and Light Weapons and Prepcoms (January, March, July); advocacy meetings with United States government and United Nations officials on report on military assistance to parties to Afghanistan's civil war (August-September).

CHILDREN'S RIGHTS DIVISION

Belgium: Participation in European Parliament hearing on lesbians and gay men in the E.U. accession countries (June).

Ecuador: Research on child labor in Ecuador (May).

Israel, the Occupied West Bank and Gaza Strip, and Palestinian Authority Territories: Research on discrimination against Palestinian Arab children in Israeli schools (November-December 2000); consultations with government and NGO representative regarding the Optional Protocol to the Convention on the Rights of the Child on the involvement of children in armed conflict (April).

Kenya: Research on the impact of HIV/AIDS on the rights of children in Kenya (February-March).

Japan: Participation in symposium on the rehabilitation of child soldiers (November 2000).

Jordan: Participation in the Amman Conference on the Use of Children as Soldiers (April).

Spain and Morocco: Research on unaccompanied migrant children in Spain (October-November).

Switzerland: Advocacy at U.N. Commission on Human Rights (April); advocacy to release report on violence against children; participation in Committee on the Rights of the Child theme day on violence against children (June).

United States: Testimony before Maryland House Judiciary Committee on juvenile justice issues (February); participation in preparatory sessions for the U.N. Special Session on Children (January-February, June); testimony before Texas House Criminal Jurisprudence Committee on the death penalty and juvenile offenders (April); advocacy and release of report on violence and discrimination against gay, lesbian, bisexual and transgender students, California (May, August).

WOMEN'S RIGHTS DIVISION

Bosnia and Hercegovina: Research trafficking of women from former Soviet Union and Eastern Europe for forced prostitution (March-April).

Egypt: Research of torture (March-April).

Greece: Advocacy on trafficking of persons (November 2000).

Jordan: Research on "honor" crimes (October).

Pakistan: Research on newly arrived Afghan women refugees to ascertain conditions for women inside Afghanistan (August).

South Africa and Namibia: Research on state-sponsored discrimination and violence against lesbians, gays, bisexuals, and transgender persons in southern Africa (July).

Tanzania: Research on prosecution of gender-based crimes at the International Criminal Tribunal of Rwanda (July).

INTERNATIONAL JUSTICE

International Criminal Court (ICC) Advocacy

Africa: Gambia, Senegal, Mali, and Burkina Faso, (October/November); Democratic Republic of Congo, (June/July); Namibia, SADC Meeting for the ICC (May); Tanzania and Zambia, including meetings with government officials, parliamentarians, and media (May); Namibia, Malawi, and South Africa, including meetings with parliamentarians (October 2000).

Americas: Peru, ICC ratification and implementation conference for the Andes region (October); Paraguay, Workshop on Implementation of the Rome Statute of the International Criminal Court into domestic law (August); Mexico (July); Argentina, Regional Seminar For the Ratification and Implementation of the Statute Of the International Criminal Court (June); Bolivia (June); Jamaica, CARICOM Conference on the International Criminal Court, promoting the ratification and establishment of the ICC in the Caribbean (May); Ecuador and Peru (February).

Asia and South Pacific Region: Australia and Thailand (September); Australia and the Cook Islands (October 2000).

Europe: Hungary (October); Hungary, Poland, and Slovenia (April); The Hague, Netherlands (January).

Prosecutions

Belgium: Meetings with lawyers and Belgian authorities on case against Hissène Habré (June, July, October, November).

Chad: Research into crimes by Hissène Habré (March-April), joint mission with FIDH to document Habré's crimes (July-November).

Netherlands: Observation of trial of Slobodan Milosovic at The Hague (October 2000, August, July).

Senegal: Court hearings on case against Hissène Habré (May), consultations on extradition of Habré (October).

Other

Costa Rica: OAS/ICRC International Humanitarian Law Regional Meeting (March).

2001 HUMAN RIGHTS WATCH PUBLICATIONS

Afghanistan
Humanity Denied: Systematic Denial of Women's Rights, 10/01, 27pp.
Crisis of Impunity: The Role of Pakistan, Russia, and Iran in Fueling the Civil War, 07/01, 58pp.
Massacres of Hazaras in Afghanistan, 02/01, 12pp.

Africa
Protectors or Pretenders? Government Human Rights Commissions in Africa, 01/01, 428pp.

Canada, Mexico, and the United States
Trading Away Rights: The Unfulfilled Promise of NAFTA's Labor Side Agreement, 04/01, 65pp.

Chile
Progress Stalled: Setbacks in Freedom of Expression Reform, 03/01, 46pp.

Colombia
Beyond Negotiation: International Humanitarian Law and Its Application to the Conduct of the FARC-EP, 08/01, 22pp.
Colombia: The "Sixth Division": Military-Paramilitary Ties and U.S. Policy in Colombia, 09/01, 138pp.

Cote D'Ivoire
The New Racism: The Political Manipulation of Ethnicity in Cote D'Ivoire, 08/01, 68pp.

Democratic Republic of Congo (DRC)
Reluctant Recruits: Children & Adults Forcibly Recruited for Military Service in North Kivu, 05/01, 19pp.
Uganda in Eastern DRC: Fueling Political and Ethnic Strife, 03/01, 46pp.

Egypt
Underage And Unprotected: Child Labor in Egypt's Cotton Fields, 01/01, 20pp.

General
September 11 Attacks: Crimes Against Humanity: The Aftermath, A Compilation of Human Rights Documents, Volume II: November 6, 2001, 114pp.

September 11 Attacks: Crimes Against Humanity: The Aftermath, A Compilation of Human Rights Documents, Volume I: October 15, 2001, 114pp.

International Criminal Court: Making The International Criminal Court Work: A Handbook for Implementing the Rome Statute, 09/01, 32pp.

Caste Discrimination: A Global Concern, 08/01, 60pp.

Landmine Monitor Report 2001: Toward a Mine-Free World, 08/01, 1216pp.

Human Rights Watch World Report 2001, 12/00, 540pp.

Guinea

Refugees Still At Risk: Continuing Refugee Protection Concerns in Guinea, 07/01, 21pp.

Indonesia

The War in Aceh, 08/01, 41pp.

Violence and Political Impasse in Papua, 07/01, 27pp.

Iran

Stifling Dissent: The Human Rights Consequences of Inter-Factional Struggle, 05/01, 20pp.

Israel, the Occupied West Bank and Gaza Strip, and Palestinian Authority Territories

Second Class: Discrimination Against Palestinian Arab Children in Israel's Schools, 12/01, 200pp.

Justice Undermined: Balancing Security and Human Rights in the Palestian Justice System, 11/01, 51pp.

Center of The Storm: A Case Study of Human Rights Abuses in Hebron District, 04/01, 156pp.

Kenya

In The Shadow of Death: HIV/AIDS and Children's Rights in Kenya, 06/01, 35pp.

Macedonia

Crimes Against Civilians: Abuses by Macedonian Forces in Ljuboten, August 10-12, 2001, 09/01.

Mexico

Military Injustice: Mexico's Failure to Punish Army Abuses, 12/01, 23pp.

Rwanda

Uprooting The Rural Poor, 05/01, 102pp.

Russia

Burying The Evidence: The Botched Investigation into a Mass Grave in Chechnya, 05/01, 26pp.

The "Dirty War" in Chechnya: Forced Disappearances, Torture, and Summary Executions, 03/01, 42pp.

South Africa

Unequal Protection: The State Response to Violence Crime on South African Farms, 08/01.

Scared At School: Sexual Violence Against Girls in the South African Schools, 03/01.

Tunisia

A Lawsuit Against the Human Rights League, An Assault on All Rights Activists, 04/01, 28pp.

Turkey

Small Group Isolation in F-Type Prisons and Violent Transfers of Prisoners to Sincan, Kandira, and Edirne Prisons on December 19, 2000, 04/01, 23pp.

Uganda

Not A Level Playing Field: Government Violations in the Lead-Up to the Election, 02/01, 12pp.

United States

Hidden in The Home: Abuse of Domestic Workers with Special Visas, 6/01, 56pp.

Beyond Reason: The Death Penalty and Offenders with Mental Retardation, 03/01, 50pp.

Hatred in The Hallways: Violence and Discrimination Against Lesbian, Gay, Bisexual, and Transgender Students in U.S. Schools, 05/01, 220pp.

No Escape: Male Rape in U.S. Prisons, 04/01, 396pp.

Uzbekistan

Sacrificing Women To Save The Family: Domestic Violence in Uzbekistan, 07/01, 54pp.

Uzbekistan: "And it was Hell All Over Again. . .": Torture in Uzbekistan, 12/00, 62pp.

Federal Republic of Yugoslavia

Under Orders: War Crimes in Kosovo, 10/01, 623pp.

STAFF AND COMMITTEES

HUMAN RIGHTS WATCH STAFF

Executive
Kenneth Roth, executive director; Jennifer Gaboury, executive assistant.

Advocacy
Reed Brody, advocacy director; Lotte Leicht, Brussels office director; Tom Malinowski, Washington advocacy director; Joanna Weschler, U.N. representative; Loubna Freih, associate U.N. representative; John Emerson, web advocate; Leon Peijnenburg, E.U. advocacy coordinator; Jacqueline Brandner (through 6/01), Maura Dundon, Natalie Rainer, associates; Olivier Bercault, Alexia Lastchenko, consultants.

Communications
Carroll Bogert, communications director; Jean-Paul Marthoz, European press director; Minky Worden, electronic media director; Jagdish Parikh, on-line communications content coordinator; Urmi Shah, press and information officer (London); Vanessa Saenen, press coordinator (Brussels); Evan Weinberger, associate; Kelly Tisdale, consultant.

Development and Outreach
Michele Alexander, development and outreach director; Michael Cooper, deputy development and outreach director (New York Committee) (through 10/01); Rachel Weintraub, international special events director; Rona Peligal, foundation relations director; Randy Chamberlain, foundation relations associate director; Ruty Ambalo, major gifts and planned giving director; Pam Bruns, California Committee (South) director; Emma Cherniavsky, California Committee (South) associate director; Clint Dalton, California Committee (North) director; Marie Janson, European Council director; Veronica Matushaj, creative services manager/photo editor; Michelle Leisure, international special events manager; Vanessa Estella, Adam Greenfield (through 4/01), office administrators (Los Angeles); Zoe Gottlieb, Thomas Yeh, associates; Raymond P. Happy (Community Counselling Services), Jane Ivey, Rafael Jimenez, Marie-Ange Kalenga, Corinne Servily (EuroAmerican Communications), consultants.

Finance and Administration
Barbara Guglielmo, finance and administration director; Suzanna Davidson, con-

troller; Anderson Allen, office manager (Washington, D.C.); Christian Peña, office manager (New York); Rachael Noronha, office administrator (London); Vanessa Saenen, office administrator (Brussels); Mei Tang, accountant; Abdou Seye, accounting assistant; Anna Angvall, Gil Colon, Sparkle Pierre, receptionists (New York); Assie Koroma, receptionist (Washington, D.C.).

Human Resources
Maria Pignataro Nielsen, human resources director; Arelis Baird, personnel manager; Anna Angvall, human resources assistant; Ernest Ulrich, consultant; Josephine Mescallado, assistant.

Information Technology
Walid Ayoub, information technology director; Amin Khair, network administrator; Bruce Robinson, office/help desk associate (Washington, D.C.); Edward Valentini, consultant.

International Film Festival
Bruni Burres, international film festival director; John Anderson, international film festival associate director; Andrea Holley, traveling festival manager.

International Justice
Richard Dicker, international justice director; Pascal Kambale, Indira Rosenthal, Brigitte Suhr, counsel; Leah Snyder, associate; Michael Cottier, consultant.

Legal Office
Wilder Tayler, legal and policy director; Dinah PoKempner, general counsel (on leave); James Ross, senior legal advisor; Andrew Ayers, special assistant/associate.

Operations
John T. Green, operations director; Allyson Collins, Washington office associate director; Rebecca Hart, special assistant/board liaison; Patrick Minges, publicatons director; Sobeira Genao, publications manager; Fitzroy Hepkins, mail manager; Gil Colon, Jose Martinez, associates.

Program
Malcolm Smart, program director; Michael McClintock, deputy program director; Joanne Csete, HIV/AIDS and human rights director; Arvind Ganesan, business and human rights director; Rachael Reilly, refugee policy director; Saman Zia-Zarifi, academic freedom director; Peter Bouckaert, senior emergencies researcher; Allyson Collins, senior researcher (United States); Jamie Fellner, associate counsel (United States); Jacqueline Brandner (through 6/01), Sam David (through 7/01), Maura Dundon, Jonathan Horowitz, Alison Hughes, Natalie Rainer, associates; Marcia Allina, Cynthia Brown, Aimee Comrie, Gail Cooper, Erika George, Tasha Gill, Joel Harding, John Sifton, Sophia Stamatopoulou-Robbins, consultants.

2000-2001 Fellowship Recipients

Darlene Miller, Michael Bloomberg Fellow; Michael Lerner, Leonard H. Sandler Fellow; Daniel Wilkinson, Orville Schell Fellow; Anna Wuerth, Alan R., Finberg Fellow; Jacqueline Asiimwe, Georgetown Women's Law and Public Policy Fellow.

AFRICA DIVISION

Staff

Peter Takirambudde, executive director; Bronwen Manby, deputy director; Suliman Ali Baldo, senior researcher; Corinne Dufka, researcher; Janet Fleischman, Washington director; Juliane Kippenberg, NGO liaison; Binaifer Nowrojee, senior researcher; Sara Rakita, researcher; Jemera Rone, counsel; Tony Tate, researcher; Alex Vines, senior researcher; Maria Burnett, research assistant; Ethel Higonnet (through 6/01), Tamar Satnet (through 5/01), T. Jeffrey Scott, associates; Alison DesForges, Andrea Lari, Rena-Marie Strand, consultants; Ryan Hahn, Chiwoniso Kaitano, assistants.

Advisory Committee

Vincent A. Mai, chair; Carole Artigiani, Robert L. Bernstein, William Carmichael, Michael Chege, Roberta Cohen, Carol Corillon, Cheryl "Imani" Countess, Alison L. DesForges, R. Harcourt Dodds, Stephen Ellmann, Aaron Etra, Gail M. Gerhart, Nadine Hack, Arthur C. Helton, Alice H. Henkin, Robert Joffe, Edward Kannyo, Thomas Karis, Wendy Keys, Dan Martin, Samuel K. Murumba, Muna Ndulo, James C. N. Paul, Dorothy Q. Thomas, Dirk van Zyl Smit, R. Keith Walton, Claude E. Welch, Jr., Maureen White, Aristide R. Zolberg.

AMERICAS DIVISION

Staff

José Miguel Vivanco, executive director; Joanne Mariner, deputy director; Sebastian Brett, researcher; Robin Kirk, researcher; Carol Pier, researcher; Jonathan Balcom, Marijke Conklin, Tzeitel Cruz-Donat (through 6/01), associates; Charles Call, Anne Fuller, Anne Manuel, consultants.

Advisory Committee

Stephen L. Kass, chair; Marina Pinto Kaufman, vice-chair; David Nachman, vice chair; Roland Algrant, Peter D. Bell, Marcelo Bronstein, Paul Chevigny, Roberto Cuellar, Dorothy Cullman, Tom J. Farer, Alejandro Garro, Peter Hakim, Ronald G. Hellman, Bianca Jagger, Mark Kaplan, Margaret A. Lang, Kenneth Maxwell, Jocelyn McCalla, Bruce Rabb, Michael Shifter, George Soros, Julien Studley, Rose Styron, Javier Timerman, Horacio Verbitsky, and José Zalaquett.

ASIA DIVISION

Staff
Sidney Jones, executive director; Joe Saunders, deputy director; Sara Colm, researcher; Jeannine Guthrie, NGO liaison; Mike Jendrzejczyk, Washington director; Smita Narula, senior researcher; Vikram Parekh, researcher; Gary Risser, researcher; Jan van der Made, researcher; Adam Bassine (through 6/01), Liz Weiss, Wen-Hua Yang, associates; Tae-Ung Baik, Nicolas Becquelin, Cynthia Brown, Eva Galabru, Patricia Gossman, Sikeena Karmali, John Sifton, Mickey Spiegel, consultants.

Advisory Committee
Maureen Aung-Thwin, Edward J. Baker, Harry Barnes, Robert L. Bernstein, Jagdish Bhagwati, Greg Carr, Jerome Cohen, Clarence Dias, John Despres, Dolores A. Donovan, Frances Fitzgerald, Adrienne Germain, Merle Goldman, Paul Hoffman, Sharon Hom, Rounaq Jahan, Virginia Leary, Joanne Leedom-Ackerman, Daniel Lev, Perry Link, Bishop Paul Moore, Andrew Nathan, Yuri Orlov, Victoria Riskin, Sheila Rothman, Barnett R. Rubin, Orville Schell, James Scott, Frances Seymour, Steven R. Shapiro, Eric Stover, Kathleen Peratis, and Bruce Rabb.

EUROPE AND CENTRAL ASIA DIVISION

Staff
Holly Cartner (through 7/01), Elizabeth Andersen, executive directors; Rachel Denber, deputy director; Alexander Anderson, researcher; Matilda Bogner, researcher; Cassandra Cavanaugh, senior researcher; Julie Chadbourne, researcher; Julia Hall, senior researcher; Bogdan Ivanisevic, researcher; Diederik Lohman, Moscow office director; Alexander Petrov, Moscow office deputy director; Anna Neistat, researcher; Acacia Shields, researcher; Jonathan Sugden, researcher; Liudmila Belova, Rachel Bien, Elizabeth Eagen, Georgi Gogia, Ani Mason, Maria Pulzetti, associates; Johanna Bjorken, Casey Reckman, Marie Struthers, Ben Ward, consultants.

Advisory Steering Committee
Peter Osnos, chair; Alice Henkin, vice-chair; Mort Abramowitz, Henri Barkey, Barbara Finberg, Felice Gaer, Michael Gellert, Paul Goble, Stanley Hoffmann, Robert James, Jeri Laber, Walter Link, Kati Marton, Prema Mathai-Davis, Karl Meyer, Joel Motley, Herbert Okun, Jane Olson, Hannah Pakula, Kathleen Peratis, Barnett Rubin, Colette Shulman, Leon Sigal, Malcolm Smith, George Soros, Marc Stoffel, Donald Sutherland, Ruti Teitel, Mark von Hagen, Mark Walton, William Zabel, Ambassador Warren Zimmermann.

MIDDLE EAST AND NORTH AFRICA DIVISION

Staff
Hanny Megally, executive director; Eric Goldstein, associate director; Hania Mufti, London office director; Elahé Sharifpour-Hicks, researcher; Virginia Sherry, associate director; Miranda Sissons, researcher; Joe Stork, advocacy director; James Darrow, Tobie Barton (through 7/01), Dalia Haj-Omar, Erin Sawaya (through 8/01), associates; Firass Abi-Younes, Juliette Abu'l 'Uyyun, Abdul Hussein Aziz, Haizam Amirah-Fernandez, Chris Cobb, Gamal Eid, Nicholas Howen, Mahmud Qandil, Donatella Rovera, consultants.

Advisory Committee
Lisa Anderson, co-chair; Gary Sick, co-chair; Bruce Rabb, vice-chair; Khaled Abou El-Fadl, Shaul Bakhash, M. Cherif Bassiouni, Martin Blumenthal, Paul Chevigny, Helena Cobban, Edith Everett, Mansour Farhang, Christopher E. George, Rita E. Hauser, Ulrich Haynes, Rev. J. Bryan Hehir, Edy Kaufman, Marina Pinto Kaufman, Samir Khalaf, Judith Kipper, Ann M. Lesch, Stephen P. Marks, Rolando Matalon, Phillip Mattar, Sheila Nemazee, Jane Schaller, Jean-Francois Seznec, Charles Shamas, Sanford Solender, Shibley Telhami, Andrew Whitley, Napoleon B. Williams, Jr., James J. Zogby.

ARMS DIVISION

Staff
Joost R. Hiltermann, executive director; Stephen D. Goose, program director; Reuben Brigety II, researcher; Mark Hiznay, senior researcher; Lisa Misol, researcher; Alex Vines, senior researcher (on leave); Mary Wareham, senior advocate (Landmines); Hannah Novak, Charli Wyatt, associates; William Arkin, Robin Bhatty, Robin Fallas, Lora Lumpe, consultants.

Advisory Committee
Torsten N. Wiesel, chair; Nicole Ball, vice-chair; David Brown, vice-chair; Vincent McGee, vice-chair; Ken Anderson, Ahmed H. Esa, Alastair Hay, Lao Mong Hay, Patricia L. Irvin, Michael Klare, Frederick J. Knecht, Edward Laurance, Graça Machel, Laurie Nathan, Janne E. Nolan, Josephine Odera, Ambassador Ahmedou Ould-Abdallah, Julian Perry Robinson, Andrew J. Pierre, Eugénia Piza-Lopez, David Rieff, Kumar Rupesinghe, John Ryle, Mohamed M. Sahnoun, Archbishop Emeritus Desmond Tutu, R. Keith Walton, Jody Williams, and Thomas Winship.

CHILDREN'S RIGHTS DIVISION

Staff
Lois Whitman, executive director; Jo Becker, advocacy director; Clarisa Bencomo,

researcher; Michael Bochenek, researcher; Zama Coursen-Neff, researcher; Shalu Rozario (through 6/01), Dana Sommers, associates.

Advisory Committee

Jane Green Schaller, chair; Roland Algrant, vice-chair; Goldie Alfasi-Siffert, Michelle India Baird, Phyllis W. Beck, James Bell, Albina du Boisrouvray, Rachel Brett, Bernardine Dohrn, Fr. Robert Drinan, Rosa Ehrenreich, Barbara Finberg, Gail Furman, Lisa Hedley, Anita Howe-Waxman, Kathleen Hunt, Eugene Isenberg, Sheila B. Kamerman, Rhoda Karpatkin, Kela Leon, Alan Levine, Miriam Lyons, Hadassah Brooks Morgan, Joy Moser, Prexy Nesbitt, Elena Nightingale, Martha J. Olson, Marta Santos Pais, Susan Rappaport, Jack Rendler, Robert G. Schwartz, Mark I. Soler, Lisa Sullivan, William Taggart, William L. Taylor, Yodon Thonden, Geraldine Van Bueren, Peter Volmink, James D. Weill, and Derrick Wong.

WOMEN'S RIGHTS DIVISION

Staff

Regan Ralph (through 4/01), LaShawn Jefferson, executive directors; Farhat Bokhari, researcher; Widney Brown, advocacy director; Chirumbidzo Mabuwa, researcher; Isis Nusair, researcher; Jude Sunderland, researcher; Martina Vandenberg, researcher; Tejal Jesrani, Smita Varia, associates; Roya Boroumand, consultant.

Advisory Committee

Katherine Peratis, chair; Lisa Crooms, vice-chair; Mahnaz Afkhami, Roland Algrant, Helen Bernstein, Cynthia Brown, Beverlee Bruce, Charlotte Bunch, Holly Burkhalter, Gina H. Despres, Julie Dorf, Joan Dunlop, Claire Flom, Adrienne Germain, Zhu Hong, Marina Pinto Kaufman, Asma Khader, Gara LaMarche, Joyce Mends-Cole, Yolanda Moses, Marysa Navarro-Aranguren, Susan Osnos, Susan J. Petersen-Kennedy, Marina Pisklakova, Catherine Powell, Geeta Rao Gupta, Celina Romany, Margaret Schuler, and Domna C. Stanton.

HUMAN RIGHTS WATCH COUNCIL

California Committee South

Mike Farrell, co-chair; Vicki Riskin, co-chair; Zazi Pope, vice-chair.

International Board Representatives
Jane Olson and Sid Sheinberg.

Elaine Attias, Rev. Ed Bacon, Joan Willens Beerman, Rabbi Leonard Beerman, Terree Bowers, Tammy Boyer, Joan Burns, Justin Connolly, Geoffrey Cowan, Nancy Cushing-Jones, Peggy Davis, Stephen Davis, Phyllis de Picciotto, Mary Estrin, Jonathan Feldman, Rob Force, Gregory H. Fox, Eric Garcetti, Danny Glover,